AF714427

New Criminal Laws Past And Present Bharatiya Nyaya Sanhita, 2023 With IPC 1860

OrangeBooks Publication

1st Floor, Rajhans Arcade, Mall Road, Kohka, Bhilai, Chhattisgarh 490020

Website:**www.orangebooks.in**

© Copyright, 2024, Author

All rights reserved. No part of this book may be reproduced, stored in a retrieval system, or transmitted, in any form by any means, electronic, mechanical, magnetic, optical, chemical, manual, photocopying, recording or otherwise, without the prior written consent of its writer.

First Edition, 2024

ISBN: 978-93-6554-584-5

NEW CRIMINAL LAWS

PAST AND PRESENT

BHARATIYA NYAYA SANHITA, 2023 WITH IPC 1860.

EDITED BY
MONISHA BISWAL

OrangeBooks Publication
www.orangebooks.in

Dedication

This book is dedicated with deepest gratitude to my uncle, Shri. Ranjan Kumar Biswal, Retired Secretary to RDC Southern Range, Government of Odisha, whose wisdom and leadership have been a guiding light in my life. And my parents, whose unwavering love and support have been my greatest strength—my father, Dr. Shyamghan Biswal, Retired Director of Public Health, Government of Odisha, whose lifelong dedication to public service has instilled in me the values of compassion, integrity, and perseverance, and my mother, Mrs Sumati Biswal, a passionate politician and social activist, whose unwavering commitment to justice and equality has always inspired me to strive for a better world. Their combined influence has shaped my path, and it is to them that I owe everything I have achieved.

Preface

The legal landscape of our country is continually evolving, and with it, the need for comprehensive and accessible legal texts becomes ever more critical. This book is my humble attempt to contribute to the growing body of literature that seeks to demystify and elucidate the intricacies of our legal system.

In writing this book, I aimed to provide a clear and structured analysis of the key legal principles, ensuring that it is both informative for seasoned professionals and accessible to students and those new to the field. Each chapter has been meticulously crafted to offer in-depth insights into the relevant legal doctrines, supported by historical context and practical examples.

The journey of creating this book has been both challenging and rewarding. It has allowed me to refine my understanding of the subject matter and present it in a manner that I hope will be beneficial to a wide audience. I am deeply aware that the law is not static, and as such, this book is intended to be a living document, one that will hopefully inspire further discussion and exploration.

I am excited to share this work with you and invite you to engage with the material critically and thoughtfully. May this book serve as a valuable tool in your legal journey, whether you are a student, a practitioner, or simply someone with a passion for justice.

~ Monisha Biswal

Content

Introduction

The Bharatiya Nyaya Sanhita1 (BNS) 2023

It a significant legislative reform in India, aimed at modernizing and overhauling the country's criminal laws. Here are some key highlights:

Comprehensive Overhaul: The BNS 2023 replaces the Indian Penal Code (IPC) of 1860, [2]which had remained largely unchanged since the colonial era.

Modernization: It aims to update and consolidate criminal laws to reflect contemporary societal values and norms.

Gender-Neutral Provisions: One notable change is the introduction of gender-neutral provisions, including those related to adultery.

Enhanced Penalties: The new code includes stricter penalties for various offenses to deter criminal activities more effectively.

Streamlined Procedures: It also seeks to streamline criminal procedures to ensure faster and more efficient justice delivery.

The **Bharatiya Nyaya Sanhita (BNS)**, which replaced the Indian Penal Code, comprises **20 chapters and 358 sections**. This new code aims to modernize India's criminal law framework, introducing several new offences and updating penalties for existing ones.

The **Bharatiya Nyaya Sanhita (BNS)**[3], also known as the Indian Justice Code, is a significant legislative reform in India's criminal justice system.

---

[1] www.taxmann.com

[2] lipidworld.biomedcentral.com

[3] lhsscollective.in

Here's a brief timeline of its development:

August 11, 2023: Amit Shah, the Minister of Home Affairs, introduced the Bharatiya Nyaya Sanhita Bill, 2023 in the Lok Sabha.

December 12, 2023: The original bill was withdrawn, and the Bharatiya Nyaya (Second) Sanhita Bill, 2023 was introduced in the Lok Sabha.

December 20, 2023: The [4]bill was passed by the Lok Sabha.

December 21, 2023: The bill was passed by the Rajya Sabha.

December 25, 2023: The bill received the assent of the President of India.

July 1, 2024: The Bharatiya Nyaya Sanhita came into effect, replacing the Indian Penal Code.

The Indian Penal Code (IPC) has a rich history.

Timeline of its key milestones: -

1834: The first Law Commission was established under the Charter Act of 1833, with Lord Macaulay as its chairman. This commission was tasked with drafting a comprehensive penal code for India.

1860: The IPC was drafted and presented to the Governor-General of India in Council. It was passed into law on October 6, 1860, and came into force on January 1, 1862.

Post-Independence (1947): After India gained independence, the IPC continued to be the primary criminal code, with various amendments made over the years to address new types of crimes and changing societal norms. - 2023: The IPC was repealed and replaced by the Bharatiya Nyaya Sanhita (BNS) in December 2023.

The new code came into effect on July 1, 2024. The BNS introduces several new offences, increases punishments for existing ones, and incorporates modern legal concepts to better address contemporary issues. The Bharatiya Nyaya Sanhita (BNS), which translates to the Indian Justice

---

[4] pdfcookie.com

Code, is a significant overhaul of India's criminal law system, replacing the Indian Penal Code (IPC) of1860.

The BNS was introduced to modernize and address contemporary legal challenges such as cybercrime, environmental law, and human rights.

Key points about the making and implementation of the BNS:

Legislative Process: The BNS was introduced in the Lok Sabha on August 11, 2023, by Home Minister Amit Shah.

It was passed by both houses of Parliament in December 2023 and received the President's assent on December 25, 2023.

Modernization: The BNS includes clearer definitions of crimes, simpler procedures, and tougher penalties for crimes against women and children. It also covers new areas such as cyber offenses and organized crime, and incorporates international human rights standards.

Educational Impact: The introduction of the BNS requires significant changes in law school curricula. Courses need to be updated, and teachers retrained to reflect the new legal rules and principles.

This shift emphasizes practical training and internships to help students navigate the new legal landscape.

New Offenses and Penalties: The BNS adds 20 new offenses and drops 19 provisions from the IPC. It increases imprisonment terms for 33 offenses and fines for 83 offenses. It also introduces mandatory minimum punishments for 23 offenses and community service sentences for six offenses.

The BNS aims to create a more efficient and just legal system in India, reflecting the country's evolving legal needs and societal values.

Criticisms

The Bharatiya Nyaya Sanhita (BNS): 2023 has faced several criticisms since its introduction. Here are some key points of criticism: Gender-Specific Application: Critics argue that certain sections of the BNS are gender-specific and do not adequately address the needs of marginalized groups, such as the LGBTQ+ community.

Lack of Inclusivity: There are concerns that the BNS does not sufficiently protect the rights of marginalized communities and fails to be inclusive in its approach. Colonial Legacy: While the BNS aims to replace outdated colonial laws, some critics believe that it still retains elements of the colonial legal framework and does not fully reflect the modern aspirations of Indian society.

Implementation Challenges: The success of the BNS depends on its vigilant enforcement, judicial scrutiny, and ongoing evaluation. Critics worry that without proper implementation, the intended benefits of the new laws may not be realized. Shift from Punitive to Restorative Justice: Although the BNS aims to shift from a punitive approach to a more restorative one, some critics argue that this shift may not be sufficient to address the complexities of modern criminal justice.

Public Perception: The introduction of the BNS has sparked significant controversy and debate, with some sections of society expressing scepticism about the new laws and their potential impact. Despite these criticisms, the BNS represents a significant step towards modernizing India's criminal justice system and addressing the evolving needs of society. It remains to be seen how these criticisms will be addressed and how the BNS will be implemented in practice.

Chapter - I Priliminary

BNS Section 1 (1)

Definition: Short Title, Commencement, and Application.

Bharatiya Nyaya Sanhita (BNS) Section 1(1) outlines the basic framework for the Act:

Short Title: This Act is called the [5]Bharatiya Nyaya Sanhita, 2023.

Commencement: It has come into force on a date appointed by the Central Government through a notification in the Official Gazette, i.e. 01 July 2024.

Application: The Act applies to every person within India and to certain acts committed outside India by Indian citizens or on Indian-registered ships or aircraft.

Illustration: If an Indian citizen commits a crime abroad, such as murder, they [6]can be tried and convicted in India as if the crime had been committed within India.

Examples:

Example 1: An Indian citizen commits theft on an Indian ship in international waters. They can be prosecuted under BNS.

Example 2: A cybercrime targeting an Indian computer resource from outside India can be prosecuted under BNS.

Comment: BNS Section 1(1) ensures that the law has a broad application, covering acts committed both within and outside India, provided they involve Indian citizens or interests. This helps in maintaining legal

---

[5] www.taxmann.com

[6] pdfcookie.com

accountability and justice for crimes affecting India and its citizens globally.

Comparison: With IPC Section 1 Indian Penal Code (IPC) Section 1 is similar in structure but has some differences:

Short Title: This Act is called the Indian Penal Code.

Commencement: It came into force on January 1, 1862.

Application: It applies to the whole of India except the State of Jammu and Kashmir (now applicable to the entire country post the abrogation of Article 370).

Key Differences Date of Commencement: IPC has a fixed commencement date, whereas BNS allows for different dates for different provisions.

Geographical Scope: IPC originally excluded Jammu and Kashmir, while BNS applies uniformly across India.

Modernization: BNS includes provisions for modern crimes like cybercrimes, reflecting contemporary legal needs.

BNS Section 1 (2)

Definition: Commencement

Bhartiya [7]Nyaya Sanhita (BNS) Section 1(2) is a new section, and outlines the commencement details of the Act:

Commencement: This section states that the Act shall come into force on such date as the Central Government may, by notification in the Official Gazette, appoint. Different dates may be appointed for different provisions of this Sanhita.

Illustration: Imagine the government decides that the provisions related to cybercrimes will come into effect on January 1, 2024, while the provisions related to traditional crimes like theft and assault will come into effect on March 1, 2024. This staggered approach allows for a phased

[7] www.taxmann.com

implementation of the law. But this has come in to force from 01 July 2024.

Examples:

Example 1: The Central Government issues a notification stating that the sections of the BNS dealing with financial crimes will commence on April 1, [8]2024. This means that any financial crime committed after this date will be prosecuted under the BNS.

Example 2: If the government decides that the provisions related to environmental crimes will commence on June 1, 2024, then any environmental crime committed after this date will be subject to the new regulations under the BNS.

Comment: The flexibility provided by Section 1(2) allows the government to implement the BNS in a controlled and systematic manner. This is particularly useful for ensuring that all necessary administrative and judicial mechanisms are in place before the law is fully operational. It also allows for adjustments based on the readiness of different sectors to comply with the new legal framework.

BNS Section 1(3)

Definition: [9]Punishment of Offences Committed Within India

Bharatiya Nyaya Sanhita (BNS) Section 1(3) states: **Punishment of Offences Committed Within India**: Every person shall be liable to punishment under this [10]Sanhita and not otherwise for every act or omission contrary to the provisions thereof, of which he shall be guilty within India.

Illustration: If a person commits theft in Delhi, they will be [11]prosecuted and punished under the provisions of the BNS.

---

[8] moam.info

[9] pdfcookie.com

[10] www.taxmann.com

[11] ir.nbu.ac.in

Examples:

Example 1: A person commits fraud in Mumbai. They will be tried and punished according to the relevant sections of the BNS.

Example 2: An individual is found guilty of assault in Chennai. The punishment will be determined based on the BNS guidelines.

Comment: This section ensures that any act or omission that violates the provisions of the BNS within the [12]territory of India will be subject to [13]punishment under this law. It establishes the jurisdiction and applicability of the BNS for offences committed within India, ensuring legal accountability and uniformity in the enforcement of criminal laws.

Comparison: Indian Penal Code (IPC) Section 2 is similar in its scope and intent: [14]**Punishment of Offences Committed Within India**: Every person shall be liable to punishment under this Code and not otherwise for every act or omission contrary to the provisions thereof, of [15]which he shall be guilty within India.

BNS Section 1(4)

[16]Definition: Punishment of Offences Committed Beyond, [17]Which by Law May Be Tried Within India

Bharatiya Nyaya Sanhita (BNS) Section 1(4) states: Punishment of Offences Committed Beyond, Which by Law May Be Tried Within India: Any person liable, by any law for the time being in [18]force in India, to be tried for an offence committed beyond India shall be dealt with according

---

[12] www.bareactslive.com

[13] pdfcookie.com

[14] pdfcookie.com

[15] ir.nbu.ac.in

[16] www.bareactslive.com

[17] pdfcookie.com

[18] www.taxmann.com

to the provisions of this Sanhita for any act committed beyond India in the same manner as if such act had been committed within India.

Illustration: If an Indian citizen commits a cybercrime while residing in another country, they can be prosecuted under the BNS as if the crime [19]had been committed within India.

Examples

Example 1: An Indian national commits a financial fraud while working in the UK. They can be tried and punished under the BNS upon their return to India.

Example 2: A person on an Indian-registered aircraft commits [20]an act of terrorism while the aircraft is in international airspace. They can be prosecuted under the BNS.

Comment: This section ensures that Indian law can be applied to offences committed by Indian citizens or on Indian-registered entities (like ships or aircraft) outside the territorial boundaries of India. It extends the reach of Indian criminal law to ensure that offenders cannot escape justice by committing crimes abroad.

Comparison: Indian Penal Code (IPC) Section 3 is similar in its scope and intent: [21]Punishment of Offences Committed Beyond, But Which by Law May Be Tried Within India: [22]Any person liable, by any [23]Indian law, to be tried for an offence committed beyond India shall be dealt with according to the provisions of this Code for any act committed beyond India in the same manner as if such act had been committed within India.

---

[19] pdfcookie.com

[20] www.bareactslive.com

[21] www.bareactslive.com

[22] pdfcookie.com

[23] www.bareactslive.com

BNS Section 1(5)

Definition: [24]Short title, Commencement and Application - [25]Extension of Code to Extra-Territorial Offences.

This section specifies that the BNS applies to: **Indian citizens committing crimes abroad. Crimes committed on Indian-registered ships or aircraft. Crimes targeting computer systems located in India**, regardless of where the act took place.

Illustration: If an Indian citizen commits a crime in a foreign country, they can be prosecuted under the BNS as if the crime [26]had been committed in India.

Examples:

Example 1: An Indian citizen commits fraud while on a business trip to another country. They can be tried under the BNS upon their return to India.

Example 2: A cyber-attack is launched from a foreign country targeting servers located in India. The perpetrator can be prosecuted under the BNS.

Comment: The BNS aims to modernize and simplify the legal framework by consolidating and updating the provisions of the IPC. The inclusion of extra-territorial offences ensures that Indian law can address crimes committed by its citizens or against its interests, even beyond its borders.

Comparison: Indian Penal Code (IPC) Section 4 also deals with the extension of the code to extra-territorial offences. It states that the IPC applies to: **Any offence committed by an Indian citizen anywhere. Any offence committed [27]on any ship or aircraft registered in India. [28]Any**

---

[24] www.taxmann.com

[25] pdfcookie.com

[26] www.bareactslive.com

[27] pdfcookie.com

[28] www.bareactslive.com

offence committed by any person [29]targeting a computer resource located in India.

BNS Section 1(6)

Definition: Short title, Commencement and Application- "Certain Laws Not to Be Affected by This Act".

Bharatiya Nyaya Sanhita (BNS) Section 1(6) ensures [30]that the provisions of the BNS do not override or affect any special or local laws. This is a saving clause that maintains the integrity and applicability of other specific legislations. Text of BNS Section 1(6)[31]"Nothing in this Sanhita shall affect the provisions of any Act for punishing mutiny and desertion of officers, soldiers, sailors or airmen in the service of the Government of India or the provisions of any special or local law."

Illustration: If there is a special law dealing with the punishment of mutiny in the armed forces, the provisions of the BNS will not interfere with or override that special law.

Examples:

Example 1: The Armed Forces (Special Powers) Act (AFSPA) has specific provisions for dealing with certain offences. These provisions will remain unaffected by the BNS.

Example 2: A local law in a particular state addressing a unique issue, such as a state-specific environmental regulation, will continue to operate independently of the BNS.

Comment: The inclusion of this saving clause in both the BNS and IPC ensures that the general provisions of these codes do not interfere with the operation of other specific laws. This is crucial for maintaining the legal framework's coherence and ensuring that specialized laws continue to function effectively without being overridden by more general provisions.

---

[29] www.taxmann.com

[30] www.bareactslive.com

[31] www.taxmann.com

Comparison: With IPC Section 5Indian Penal Code (IPC) Section 5 also contains a similar saving clause. It states: "Nothing in this Act shall affect the provisions of any Act for punishing mutiny and desertion of officers, soldiers, sailors or airmen in the service of the Government of India, or the provisions of any special or local law."

BNS Section 2

Definitions: Definitions

Definitions included in this section: Act: Includes both a [32]series of acts and a single act. Animal: Any living creature other than a human being. Counterfeit: Causing one thing to resemble another with the intent to deceive. Court: A judge or a body of judges empowered to act judicially. Death: Refers to the death of a human being. Dishonestly: Doing an [33]act with the intention of causing wrongful gain or loss. Document: [34]Any matter expressed or described upon any substance by means of letters, figures, or marks intended to be used as evidence. Fraudulently: Doing something with the intent to defraud. Classification of Offence and Punishment the BNS classifies offences and prescribes punishments based on the severity and nature of the crime.

For example: Bailable Offences: Less serious crimes where bail is granted as a matter of right.

Non-Bailable Offences: More severe crimes where bail is granted at the court's discretion.

Illustrations: Document: A writing expressing the terms of a contract, a cheque, a power-of-attorney, or a map intended to be used as evidence. Counterfeit: When a person causes one thing to resemble another, intending to deceive, it is presumed that the person intended to practice deception.

---

[32] pdfcookie.com

[33] www.wipo.int

[34] pdfcookie.com

Examples:

Examples 1: In a recent judgment, the clear definitions provided by Section 2 helped streamline the judicial process, leading to a quicker resolution of the case.

Comment: Section 2 of the BNS is crucial as it lays down the foundational definitions that guide the interpretation and application of the entire legal code. These definitions ensure clarity and consistency in legal proceedings.

Comparison: With IPC The BNS 2023 aims to modernize and streamline India's legal framework, changing sections and replacing the Indian Penal Code (IPC) of 1860.

BNS Section 2(1)

Definition: Section 2(1) of the [35]Bharatiya Nyaya Sanhita (BNS) 2023 defines various terms used within the Sanhita. For instance, it defines "act" as including both a [36]series of acts and a single act.

Example: Example of "Document": A cheque upon a banker is considered a document as it is a matter expressed upon a substance by means of letters, figures, or marks intended to be used as evidence.

Comment: The definitions provided in Section 2(1) are crucial for the interpretation and application of the BNS. They ensure clarity and consistency in understanding the terms used in various sections of the Sanhita.

Comparison: IPC Section 33 defines the term "act" to include both a series of acts and a single act, and the term "omission" to include a [37]series of omissions as well as a single omission. Summary of Comparison: Both BNS Section 2(1) and IPC Section 33 provide definitions that are essential for the interpretation of their respective codes. The definitions in both

---

[35] www.taxmann.com

[36] pdfcookie.com

[37] www.bareactslive.com

sections are similar, particularly in how they define "act" to include both a series of acts and a single act. The BNS, however, includes more detailed definitions and illustrations for various terms compared to the IPC.

BNS Section 2(2)

Definition: Section 2(2) of the [38]Bharatiya Nyaya Sanhita (BNS) 2023 defines "animal" [39]as any living creature other than a human being.

Example: Example: If a law within the BNS refers to the protection of animals, Section 2(2) clarifies that this protection does not extend to humans but includes all other living creatures.

Comment: The definition of "animal" in Section 2(2) is crucial for interpreting various provisions in the BNS that involve animals, ensuring that there is no ambiguity in legal proceedings.

Comparison: IPC Section 47 defines "animal" as any living creature, other than a human being. Summary of Comparison: Both BNS Section 2(2) and IPC Section 47 provide the same definition for "animal," ensuring consistency in legal interpretation across both codes. The definitions are identical, highlighting the continuity in legal terminology between the IPC and the newer BNS.

BNS Section 2(3)

Definition: Section 2(3) of the Bharatiya Nyaya Sanhita (BNS) 2023, which is a new section, and defines "child" as any person below the age of 18 years.

Example: If a law within the BNS refers to [40]the protection of children from exploitation, Section 2(3) [41]clarifies that this protection applies to all individuals under 18 years of age.

---

[38] www.taxmann.com

[39] pdfcookie.com

[40] Submitted to University of Kashmir, Srinagar on 2024-09-12 11-01

[41] refubium.fu-berlin.de

Comment: The definition of "child" in Section 2(3) is crucial for the application of laws related to minors. It ensures that any legal provisions referring to children are clearly understood to apply to individuals under 18 years of age.

Comparison: The Indian Penal Code (IPC) does not have a specific section that defines "child" [42]in the same manner as BNS Section 2(3). Various sections of the IPC refer to minors or children, but the age definition can vary depending on the context. Summary of Comparison: BNS Section 2(3) provides a clear and uniform definition of "child" as any person below 18 years, which is a new provision compared to the IPC. This uniform definition helps in the consistent application of laws related to children across different legal contexts within the BNS.

BNS Section 2 (4)

Definition: Defines "counterfeit" as causing one thing to resemble another with the intention of practicing deception, or knowing it is likely that deception will be practiced.

Illustrations:

Example 1: Producing fake currency notes that closely resemble real ones to trick people into accepting them as genuine.

Example 2: Forging a signature on a legal document to make it appear as if it was signed by someone else. This definition is crucial for addressing crimes involving forgery and fraud. It covers a wide range of deceptive practices, ensuring that acts intended to mislead are thoroughly addressed under the law.

Comment: The definition of "Court" in BNS Section 2(4) is crucial for understanding the jurisdiction and authority of judicial bodies under the new legal framework. It ensures clarity in legal proceedings by specifying who or what can be considered a judicial authority.

---

[42] indiankanoon.org

Comparison: BNS 2(4) and IPC 28 – "Counterfeit" BNS 2(4) Definition: Defines "counterfeit" as causing [43]one thing to resemble another with the intention of practicing deception or knowing it is likely that deception will be practiced. IPC 28 – Definition: Defines "counterfeit" similarly, as causing one thing to resemble another with the intent to deceive or knowing it likely that deception will be practiced.

BNS Section 2(5)

Definition: Section 2(5) of the Bharatiya Nyaya Sanhita, 2023, defines "Court" as follows: "Court" means a [44]Judge who is empowered by law to act judicially alone, or a body of Judges, which is empowered by law to act judicially as a body, when such Judge or body of Judges is acting judicially

Illustration: If a single Judge in a district court is hearing a case, that Judge is considered a "Court" under BNS Section 2(5). Similarly, if a bench of three Judges in a High Court is hearing an appeal, that bench is also considered a "Court".

Example: Single Judge: A Magistrate hearing a criminal case. Body of Judges: A Division Bench of the High Court hearing a writ petition. Comparison with IPC Section 20IPC Section 20 defines "Court of Justice" as: "The words 'Court of Justice' denote a Judge who is empowered by law to act judicially alone, or a body of Judges which is empowered by law to act judicially as a body, when such Judge or body of Judges is acting judicially."

Comment: The definition of "Court" in BNS Section 2(5) is similar to IPC Section 20 but uses the term "Court" instead of "Court of Justice". This change simplifies the terminology while maintaining the same legal concept.

Comparison: BNS Section 2(5) - "Court" and IPC Section 20 - "Court of Justice"

---

[43] indiankanoon.org

[44] indiankanoon.org

BNS Section 2(5) - "Court": Defines "court" as a judge or body of judges empowered by law to act judicially. This includes individual judges and judicial panels functioning within their legal authority.

IPC Section 20 - "Court of Justice": Defines "Court of Justice" [45]as a judge or a body of judges who are empowered by law to act judicially alone or as a body, specifically when they are acting judicially.

BNS Section 2(6)

Definition: BNS, Section 2(6) defines "death" [46]as the death of a human being unless the context indicates otherwise. IPC Section 46 Definition: Similarly, IPC Section 46 defines "death" as the death of a human being unless the context indicates otherwise. IPC: The IPC, being an older code, does not include these modern definitions and provisions. It spreads definitions across multiple sections rather than consolidating them.

Examples:

Example 1: A person who has suffered severe trauma and shows no signs of heartbeat, breathing, or brain activity is considered deceased under this definition.

Example 2: In a medical context, a doctor might declare a patient dead when all attempts to revive them have failed, confirming the absence of vital functions.

Comment: Understanding and defining "death" is critical in both legal and medical contexts. This clear definition ensures uniformity in handling matters like inheritance, insurance claims, and criminal cases. It also helps medical professionals in making critical decisions regarding end-of-life care and organ donation. By including specific criteria (heartbeat, respiration, brain activity), the law provides a clear and practical guideline

---

[45] indiankanoon.org

[46] indiankanoon.org

for determining death, which is essential for legal clarity and ethical medical practice.

Comparison: Both BNS Section 2(6) and IPC Section 46 define "death" in the same way, but the BNS provides a more modern and consolidated approach to legal definitions and punishments, reflecting contemporary issues and advancements.

BNS Section 2(7)

Definition: BNS Section 2(7) defines "dishonestly" as doing anything with the intention of causing wrongful gain to one person or wrongful loss to another person. IPC Section 24 Definition: IPC Section 24 defines "dishonestly" as doing anything with the intention of causing wrongful gain to one person or wrongful loss to another person.

Comment: Both BNS Section 2(7) and IPC Section 24 define "dishonestly" in the same way, but the BNS provides a more modern and consolidated approach to legal definitions and punishments, reflecting contemporary issues and advancements.

BNS Section 2(8)

Definition: BNS Section 2(8) defines [47]"document" as any matter expressed or described upon any substance by means of letters, figures, or marks, or by more than one of those means, intended to be used, or which may be used, for the purpose of recording that matter. This definition includes electronic and digital records.

Comment: Both BNS Section 2(8) and IPC Sections 29 and 29A define "document" in a similar way, but the BNS "changes" and provides a more modern and consolidated approach, reflecting contemporary issues and advancements.

[47] indiankanoon.org

Comparison: IPC Section 29: Defines "document" similarly as [48]any matter expressed or described upon any substance by means of letters, figures, or marks, or by more than one of those means, intended to be used, or which may be used, for the purpose of recording that matter.

Section 29A: Specifically includes electronic records within the definition of "document". BNS: The BNS aims to modernize and simplify the legal language and structure, making it more accessible and relevant to current societal norms and technological advancements. IPC: The IPC, while comprehensive, is seen as outdated in some respects, necessitating the updates provided by the BNS.

BNS Section 2(9)

Definition: [49]"BNS Section 2 (9) states fraudulently A person is said to do a thing fraudulently if they do it with intent to defraud but not otherwise.

Comment: Both the BNS and IPC provide a clear and concise definition of "fraudulently," which is crucial for understanding and applying the law in cases involving fraud. The primary difference lies in the organizational structure of the definitions within the respective codes.

Comparison: Both BNS Section 2 (9) states fraudulently and IPC Section 25 Define **"fraudulently"** in nearly identical terms, focusing on the intent to defraud. Difference: The BNS consolidates definitions in a single section for easier reference, whereas the IPC spreads definitions across multiple sections.

BNS Section 2(10)

Definition: BNS section 2 (10) defines "gender" to include male, female, and transgender. This is a significant update and changes the

---

[48] indiankanoon.org

[49] indiankanoon.org

Indian Penal Code (IPC) Section 8, which only recognizes male and female genders.

Illustration: If a law refers to "any person," under BNS, it explicitly includes males, females, and transgender individuals. For example, in a case of harassment, the victim could be of any gender, including transgender.

Example: A transgender person facing discrimination at work can seek legal recourse under the BNS, which explicitly recognizes their gender.

Comment: The inclusion of "transgender" in BNS Section 2(10) reflects a progressive step towards gender inclusivity and recognition of diverse gender identities. This change aligns with contemporary understandings of gender and aims to provide better protection and rights to transgender individuals.

Comparison: IPC Section 8 Defines gender as male and female only. BNS Section 2(10): Expands the definition to include transgender individuals, thereby broadening the scope of legal protections and rights. This update in the BNS is a crucial move towards ensuring equality and non-discrimination for all genders in the legal framework of India.

BNS Section 2(11)

Definition: Defines "good faith" as an act done with due care and attention. This definition remains consistent with Indian Penal Code (IPC) Section 52, which also emphasizes that an act is not considered [50]done in good faith if it is done without due care and attention.

Illustration: If a person donates money to a charity believing it to be legitimate, but it turns out to be a scam, the donation was made in good faith if the person took reasonable steps to verify the charity's legitimacy.

Example: A doctor performing emergency surgery on a patient without the patient's consent, believing it to be necessary to save the patient's life,

[50] indiankanoon.org

acts in good faith if the doctor [51]has taken all reasonable steps to ensure the surgery is essential.

Comment: [52]The concept of "good faith" is crucial in legal contexts as it provides a defence against liability when actions are taken with honest intentions and reasonable care. [53]It ensures that individuals are not unfairly penalized for actions taken with genuine belief and due diligence.

Comparison: IPC Section 52 Defines good faith as actions done with due care and attention. BNS Section 2(11): Retains the same definition, ensuring continuity and clarity in legal interpretations. This consistency between the BNS and IPC helps maintain a stable legal framework while ensuring that actions taken with honest intentions and reasonable care are protected under the law.

BNS Section 2(12)

Definition: Defines "Government" as any authority or body of persons or institution established by the Constitution or by any law made by the Parliament or by the State Legislature.

Illustration: If a person commits an offense against a public servant, such as a police officer, while they are performing their official duties, it is considered an offense against the government.

Example: Bribing a government official to obtain a license or permit is an offense against the government.

Comment: This definition is crucial as it clarifies that any act against a public servant or institution established by law is considered an act against the government. This broad definition ensures that all entities performing public duties are protected under the law.

Comparison: Indian Penal Code (IPC) Section 17 also defines "Government" but in a slightly different context. It includes the Central

---

[51] repositorio.uchile.cl

[52] libguides.usc.edu

[53] www.linkedin.com

Government, the State Government, and any local authority. Similarity: Both definitions aim to protect public servants and institutions from offenses. Difference: The IPC specifically mentions local authorities, whereas the BNS focuses on authorities established by the Constitution or law. Conclusion Both sections aim to safeguard the integrity of public institutions and officials, ensuring that any offense against them is treated with the seriousness it deserves. The BNS provides a more modern and comprehensive approach, aligning with contemporary legal standards.

BNS Section 2(13)

Definition: Defines "Harbour" as providing [54]a person with shelter, food, drink, money, clothes, arms, ammunition, [55]or means of conveyance, or assisting a person by any means to evade apprehension.

Illustration: If someone hides a fugitive in their home and provides them with food and money to help them avoid capture by the police, they are harbouring the fugitive.

Example: A person who gives shelter and financial support to a criminal on the run from law enforcement is guilty of harbouring.

Comment: This definition is comprehensive, [56]covering various forms of assistance that can help a person evade arrest. It ensures that anyone aiding a fugitive, regardless of the type of support provided, can be held accountable under the law.

Comparison: [57]Indian Penal Code (IPC) Section 52A also defines "Harbour" but includes specific exceptions. It states that harbouring does not include cases where the harbour is given by the wife or husband of the person harboured, except in certain sections like 157 and 130.Similarity: Both definitions aim to prevent individuals from aiding fugitives and

---

[54] indiankanoon.org

[55] www.bareactslive.com

[56] indiankanoon.org

[57] indiankanoon.org

obstructing justice. Difference: The IPC provides specific exceptions for spouses, which are not mentioned in the BNS definition. Conclusion Both sections aim to deter people from assisting fugitives, but the BNS offers a broader definition without exceptions for spouses. This modern approach ensures that all forms of assistance to evade apprehension are covered under the law.

BNS Section 2(14)

Definition: Defines "Injury" as any harm illegally [58]caused to a person in body, mind, reputation, or property.

Illustration: If someone physically assaults another person, causing bodily harm, it is considered an injury under this section.

Example: Defamation, where false statements are made about someone, damaging their reputation, is also classified as an injury.

Comment: This definition is comprehensive, covering physical, mental, reputational, and property-related harm. It ensures that all forms of illegal harm are recognized and can be addressed legally.

Comparison: Indian Penal Code (IPC) Section 44 defines "Injury" similarly as any harm illegally [59]caused to a person in body, mind, reputation, or property. Similarity: Both definitions cover the same types of harm, ensuring a broad scope of protection. Difference: There is no significant difference in the definitions provided by BNS and IPC, indicating consistency in legal terminology across these codes. Both BNS and IPC provide a robust framework for addressing various forms of harm, ensuring [60]that individuals are protected from illegal actions that affect their physical, mental, reputational, or property well-being.

---

[58] indiankanoon.org

[59] indiankanoon.org

[60] www.linkedin.com

BNS Section 2(15)

Definition: Defines "Illegal" and "Legally Bound to Do" as follows: Illegal: This term applies to anything that constitutes an offense, [61]is prohibited by law, or provides grounds for a civil action. Legally Bound to Do: A person [62]is said to be legally bound to do something if it is illegal for them to omit it.

Illustration: If a law requires a person to file their taxes by a certain date, failing to do so would be illegal, and thus, they are legally bound to file their taxes.

Example: A business owner is legally bound to ensure their establishment meets safety regulations. If they fail to do so, it is considered illegal.

Comment: This definition is crucial as it clarifies the obligations imposed by law. It ensures that individuals and entities understand their legal duties and the consequences of failing to fulfil them.

Comparison: with IPC Section 43 Indian Penal Code (IPC) Section 43 defines "Illegal" similarly, encompassing everything that is an offense, prohibited by law, or provides grounds for a civil action. It also states [63]that a person is legally bound to do whatever it is illegal for them to omit. Similarity: Both definitions cover the same aspects, ensuring consistency in legal obligations and prohibitions.

BNS Section 2(16)

Definition: Definition: Section 2(16) of the Bharatiya Nyaya Sanhita (BNS) defines a "Judge" as not only individuals officially designated as judges but also those who have the authority to render definitive judgments in any legal proceeding, whether civil or criminal. This

---

[61] pdfcookie.com

[62] indiankanoon.org

[63] indiankanoon.org

includes individuals whose judgments, [64]if not appealed against, would be considered final.

Illustration: Imagine a scenario where a tribunal member, who is not officially designated as a judge, makes a ruling in a civil dispute. According to BNS Section 2(16), this tribunal member would be considered a "Judge" because their decision is authoritative and final unless appealed.

Examples: Civil Court Judge: A judge in a civil court who decides on matters such as property disputes or contract issues. Criminal Court Judge: A judge in a criminal court who presides over cases involving criminal offenses. Tribunal Member: A member of a tribunal who makes binding decisions in specialized areas like labor disputes or tax issues.

Comment: The definition in BNS is broad and inclusive, ensuring that all individuals with the authority to make binding legal decisions are recognized as judges. This helps in maintaining the integrity and consistency of the legal system by acknowledging the roles of various judicial authorities.

Comparison: IPC Section 19 – "Judge": The Indian Penal Code (IPC) Section 19 defines a "Judge" as any person who is officially designated as a judge or who is empowered by law to [65]give a definitive judgment in any legal proceeding, civil or criminal. This includes individuals who can make decisions that, if not appealed against, would be considered. While both BNS and IPC recognize individuals with the authority to make final judgments as judges, BNS uses a more inclusive approach by explicitly stating that it includes those not officially designated as judges. Scope: BNS consolidates definitions in a single section for easier reference, whereas IPC spreads definitions across various sections. Both BNS Section 2(16) and IPC Section 19 aim to define the term "Judge" comprehensively. However, BNS provides a more streamlined and inclusive definition, reflecting modern legal practices and ensuring clarity in the judicial process.

---

[64] indiankanoon.org

[65] indiankanoon.org

BNS Section 2(17)

Definition: Section 2(17) of the Bharatiya Nyaya Sanhita (BNS) defines "Life" as the state of being alive, encompassing the physical and biological functions that sustain a [66]human being.

Illustration: Consider a patient in a hospital who is on life support. Despite being unconscious, the patient's heart is still beating, and they are breathing with the help of machines. According to BNS Section 2(17), this patient is considered to have "life" because their biological functions are active.

Examples: Medical Scenario: A person in a vegetative state with functioning vital organs is considered to have "life." Legal Context: In a case involving the right to life, the court would assess whether the individual's biological functions are active to determine if they are alive.

Comment: The definition in BNS is clear and focuses on the biological aspect of life. This clarity is crucial in legal contexts, especially in cases involving medical decisions, end-of-life care, and the right to life. It ensures that there is a consistent understanding of what constitutes "life" in various legal scenarios.

Comparison: IPC Section 45 – "Life": The Indian Penal Code (IPC) Section 45 defines "Life" similarly as the state of being alive, including the physical and biological functions that sustain a human being. Both BNS and IPC use similar terminology to define "life," focusing on the biological functions that indicate a person is alive. Scope: The definitions are largely consistent, with no significant differences in their interpretation or application. Both BNS Section 2(17) and IPC Section 45 provide a clear and consistent definition of "life," emphasizing the importance of biological functions. This consistency helps ensure that legal interpretations and applications remain uniform across different legal contexts.

---

[66] indiankanoon.org

BNS Section 2(18)

Definition: Section 2(18) of the Bharatiya Nyaya Sanhita (BNS) defines "Local Law" as a law that is [67]applicable only to a particular part of India.

Illustration: Imagine a state in India that has its own specific regulations regarding the sale of alcohol. These regulations are only applicable within that state and not in other parts of the country. According to BNS Section 2(18), these regulations would be considered "Local Law."

Examples: State-Specific Traffic Rules: Some states may have unique traffic regulations that differ from national laws. Regional Environmental Laws: Certain regions might have specific environmental protection laws tailored to their local ecosystems. Municipal Ordinances: Local government bodies may pass ordinances that apply only within their jurisdiction, such as noise control regulations.

Comment: The definition in BNS emphasizes the regional applicability of certain laws, recognizing that different parts of India may have unique legal needs and contexts. This allows for flexibility and specificity in legal governance, ensuring that local issues can be addressed effectively.

Comparison: IPC Section 42 – "Local Law": The Indian Penal Code (IPC) Section 42 defines "Local Law" similarly as a law that is [68]applicable only to a particular part of India. Both BNS and IPC use the same terminology to define "Local Law," focusing on the regional applicability of such laws. Scope: The definitions are consistent across both BNS and IPC, with no significant differences in their interpretation or application Both BNS Section 2(18) and IPC Section 42 provide a clear and consistent definition of "Local Law," highlighting the importance of regional legal frameworks. This consistency helps ensure that legal interpretations and applications remain uniform across different legal contexts.

---

[67] indiankanoon.org

[68] indiankanoon.org

BNS Section 2(19)

Definition: [69]Defines "Man" as a male human being of any age. This definition is straightforward and aligns with common understanding.

Illustration: If a law mentions that a "man" is responsible for a certain action, it refers to any male human being, regardless of his age.

Example: In a case where a "man" is accused of theft, this term would apply to any male individual, whether he is a minor or an adult.

Comment: The BNS consolidates definitions into a single section for easier reference, which can be more user-friendly compared to the IPC's scattered approach.

Comparison: IPC Section 10 defines "man" as a male human being of any age, similar to BNS 2(19)2. However, the IPC does not consolidate definitions in a single section but spreads them across various sections.

BNS Section 2(20)

Definition: "Month and Year" in the Bharatiya Nyaya Sanhita (BNS) 2023 specifies that the terms "month" and "year" are to be understood [70]according to the Gregorian calendar.

Illustration: If a law states that a contract is valid for one "year," it means a period of 12 months as per the Gregorian calendar.

Example: A lease agreement starting on January 1, 2024, and ending on December 31, 2024, is considered to be for one "year."

Comment: This change in BNS reflects a modernization effort, aligning legal definitions with contemporary standards and practices. Comparison with IPC Section 49: IPC Section 49 also defines "month" and "year" but refers to the British calendar. The BNS updates this to the Gregorian calendar, which is more universally recognized and used today.

---

[69] indiankanoon.org

[70] blog.ipleaders.in

BNS Section 2(21)

Definition: Defines **"movable property"** as property of every description, except land and things attached to the earth or permanently fastened to anything which is attached to the earth.

Examples:

Example 1: A car is considered movable property because it can be moved from one place to another.

Example 2: A piece of furniture, such as a table or chair, is also movable property as it is not attached to the earth.

Comment: This definition is broad and includes all types of property that are not immovable. It simplifies the understanding by excluding only land and items permanently attached to it. This can include tangible items like vehicles and furniture, as well as intangible items like stocks and bonds, The broader definition in BNS allows for a more comprehensive understanding of movable property, accommodating modern forms of property like [71]digital assets, which are not explicitly covered under the IPC's definition.

Comparison: [72]The Indian Penal Code (IPC) Section 22 defines "movable property" as corporeal property of every description, except land and things attached to the earth or permanently fastened to anything which is attached to the earth The IPC specifically mentions "corporeal property," which means tangible physical property. In contrast, the BNS definition does not limit itself to corporeal property, thereby including both tangible and intangible properties. Inclusivity BNS's definition is more inclusive as it covers all types of property except immovable ones, whereas IPC's definition is restricted to tangible items.

---

[71] slate.com

[72] blog.ipleaders.in

BNS Section 2(22)

Definition: Number BNS Section 2(22) states that [73]unless the context otherwise requires, words importing the singular number include the plural number, and words importing the plural number include the singular number.

Examples:

Example 1: If a law mentions "a vehicle," it can be interpreted to include "vehicles" as well.

Example 2: If a regulation refers to "employees," it can also mean "an employee."

Comment: This provision ensures flexibility in legal interpretation, preventing unnecessary complications due to singular or plural usage. It allows for a broader application of laws and regulations, making them more adaptable to various situations.

Comparison: 9IPC Section 9: The Indian Penal Code (IPC) Section 9 similarly states that unless there is something repugnant in the subject or context, words importing the singular number include the plural number, and words importing the plural number include the singular number. Both sections essentially convey the same rule, ensuring that singular and plural terms are interchangeable unless the context dictates otherwise. The principle is applied uniformly in both the BNS and IPC, ensuring consistency in legal interpretation across different legal texts. Both BNS Section 2(22) and IPC Section 9 aim to simplify legal language and interpretation, ensuring that laws are not rendered ineffective due to the strict singular or plural usage. This approach promotes clarity and flexibility in legal proceedings.

---

[73] www.indiacode.nic.in

BNS Section 2(23)

Definition: BNS Section 2(23) defines "Oath" as including a solemn affirmation substituted by law for an oath, and any declaration required or authorized by law to be made before a public servant or to be used for the purpose of proof, whether in a court or not.

Examples:

Example 1: A witness in a court case may take an oath or make a solemn affirmation to tell the truth.

Example 2: A public official might be required to make a declaration of assets before assuming office.

Comment: This definition ensures that both traditional oaths and legally recognized affirmations or declarations are treated with the same level of seriousness and legal validity. It broadens the scope to include various forms of declarations used for legal purposes, ensuring flexibility and inclusivity in legal proceedings.

Comparison: IPC Section 51: The Indian Penal Code (IPC) Section 51 defines "oath" as including a solemn affirmation substituted by law for an oath, and any declaration required or authorized by law to be made before a public servant or to be used for the purpose of proof. Both sections are nearly identical in their wording and scope, ensuring that oaths, affirmations, and declarations are legally binding and recognized. IPC Both BNS Section 2(23) and IPC Section 51 aim to provide a comprehensive definition of "oath" that includes various forms of legally recognized declarations. [74]This ensures that all such declarations are treated with the same seriousness and legal standing, promoting consistency and reliability in legal processes.

[74] www.writinglaw.com

BNS Section 2(24)

Definition: Defines "offence" as any act or omission made punishable by this Sanhita, except in the chapters and sections mentioned in sub-clauses (a) and (b). Specifically: Sub-clause (a): In Chapter III and certain sections, the term "offence" includes acts punishable under this Sanhita or any special or local law. Sub-clause (b): In specified sections, the term "offence" includes acts punishable under special or local laws with imprisonment for six months or more, with or without fine.

Examples:

Example 1: Theft, as defined and punishable under the BNS, is an offence.

Example 2: Violating a local environmental regulation that carries a penalty of imprisonment for six months or more is also considered an offence under this definition.

Comment: This definition is comprehensive, covering a wide range [75]of acts and omissions that are punishable under various laws. It ensures that both general and specific legal provisions are included, providing clarity and consistency in the application of the law.

Comparison: IPC Section 40: The Indian Penal Code (IPC) Section 40 defines "offence" as any act or omission made punishable by this Code. It also includes acts punishable under any special or local law, provided the context requires. Both definitions are similar in that they include acts punishable under the respective codes and other laws. However, the BNS explicitly lists specific chapters and sections where the definition applies differently. Specificity: The BNS provides more detailed sub-clauses to clarify the application of the term "offence" in different contexts, whereas the IPC offers a more general definition. Examples: BNS Example: An act of fraud punishable under a special financial regulation is considered an offence under BNS if it meets the criteria specified in sub-clause (b). IPC

[75] antimoneylaunderinglaw.com

Example: An act of bribery [76]punishable under the Prevention of Corruption Act is considered an offence under IPC when the context requires. Comment: Both BNS Section 2(24) and IPC Section 40 aim to provide a clear and inclusive definition of "offence" to ensure that all punishable acts and omissions are covered. The BNS's detailed sub-clauses offer additional clarity, making it easier to understand the application of the term in various legal contexts.

BNS Section 2(25)

Definition: "Omission" defines an omission as the failure to perform an act that is legally required. This is distinct from an act, which involves a positive action.

Illustration: If a person is legally required to file their income tax returns by a certain date and fails to do so, this failure is considered an omission.

Example: A lifeguard who fails to save a drowning person, despite being on duty and capable of doing so, commits an omission.

Comment: The concept of omission is crucial in legal contexts because it establishes liability not just for actions taken, but also for actions not taken when there is a legal duty to act. This ensures that individuals and entities cannot escape responsibility simply by inaction.

Comparison: with IPC Section 33: IPC Section 33 defines both "act" and "omission" together, stating that the word "act" denotes as well a series of acts as a single act, and the word "omission" denotes as well a series of omissions as a single omission. BNS separates the definitions of "act" and "omission" into distinct subsections (2(1) for "act" and 2(25) for "omission"), providing clearer and more focused definitions. Consolidation in IPC: IPC combines both definitions in a single section, which might be less clear but provides a holistic view of actions and inactions together0lql.By separating these definitions, the BNS aims to provide more clarity and specificity, which can help in better understanding and applying the law.

---

[76] www.indiacode.nic.in

BNS Section 2(26)

Definition: "Person" Bharatiya Nyaya Sanhita (BNS) Section 2(26) defines the term **"person"** to include any company, association, or body of persons, whether incorporated or not.

Illustration: If a company commits an offence, it can be prosecuted under the BNS as a "person."

Example 1: A corporation involved in environmental pollution can be held liable under the BNS.

Example 2: An unregistered association of individuals engaging in fraudulent activities can be prosecuted as a "person" under the BNS.

Comparison: Indian Penal Code (IPC) Section 11 similarly defines "person" to include any company or association or body of persons, whether incorporated or not. Both the BNS and IPC use similar language to define "person," ensuring consistency in legal interpretation. Consolidation: The BNS consolidates definitions into a single section for easier reference, whereas the IPC spreads definitions across multiple sections. The definition of "person" in both the BNS and IPC is broad and inclusive, ensuring that legal accountability extends to various entities beyond just individuals. This is crucial for addressing offences committed by corporate bodies and associations, thereby reinforcing the legal framework's comprehensiveness.

BNS Section 2(27)

Definition: "Public" Bharatiya Nyaya Sanhita (BNS) Section 2(27) Defines "public" to include any class of the public or any community.

Illustration: If a law refers to actions affecting the "public," it includes any group or community within the general population.

Examples:

Example 1: A regulation aimed at preventing public nuisance would apply to actions that disturb any community or class of people.

Example 2: A law protecting public health would cover measures affecting any segment of the population, such as a vaccination campaign targeting a specific community.

Comparison: Indian Penal Code (IPC) Section 12 similarly defines "public" to include any class of the public or any community. Both the BNS and IPC use similar language to define "public," ensuring consistency in legal interpretation. Consolidation: The BNS consolidates definitions into a single section for easier reference, whereas the IPC spreads definitions across multiple sections. Comment The definition of "public" in both the BNS and IPC is broad and inclusive, ensuring that laws can be applied to various groups within the population. This is crucial for addressing issues that affect different communities and ensuring comprehensive legal coverage.

BNS Section 2(28)

Definition: Defines a **"public servant"** as a person falling under any of the following descriptions: Every commissioned officer in the Army, Navy, or Air Force. Every judge or person empowered by law to discharge [77]adjudicatory functions. Every officer of a court of justice, including those who investigate, report, or authenticate documents. Every juryman, assessor, or member of a panchayat assisting a court of justice or public servant. Every arbitrator or person to whom any cause or matter has been referred for decision by a court of justice. Every person holding an office by virtue of which they can place or keep any person in confinement. Every officer of the government whose duty it is to prevent offenses, bring offenders to justice, or protect public health, safety, or convenience. Every officer responsible for managing government property or executing revenue processes. Every officer responsible for public elections or maintaining electoral rolls.

Illustration: A police officer who enforces the law and maintains public order is considered a public servant under BNS Section 2(28).

[77] www.indiacode.nic.in

Example: A judge presiding over a court case. A government health inspector ensuring compliance with health regulations. An election officer overseeing the conduct of elections.

Comment: Both BNS Section 2(28) and IPC Section 21 aim to define the scope of individuals considered public servants, ensuring accountability and legal clarity. The BNS consolidates definitions for easier reference, while the IPC provides a detailed list of roles and responsibilities.

Comparison: IPC Section 21 also defines "public servant" but includes a broader range of descriptions: Commissioned officers in the Military, Naval, or Air Forces of India. Judges and those empowered to discharge adjudicatory functions. Officers of a court of justice involved in various judicial processes. Jurymen, assessors, or panchayat members assisting a court of justice. Arbitrators or persons referred by a court for decision-making. Persons holding offices that empower them to confine individuals. Government officers tasked with preventing offenses and protecting public welfare. Officers managing government property or executing revenue processes. Officers responsible for public elections and maintaining electoral rolls.

BNS Section 2(29)

Definition: "reason to believe" as [78]a situation where a person has sufficient cause to believe something, but not otherwise.

Illustration: If a person finds a letter indicating that a certain property is stolen, they have "reason to believe" that the property is stolen.

Examples: A bank manager receives a report showing unusual transactions in an account. The manager has "reason to believe" that the account is being used for money laundering. A customs officer finds a hidden compartment in a suitcase during an inspection. The officer has "reason to believe" that the suitcase contains contraband.

Comment: Both BNS Section 2(29) and IPC Section 26 aim to establish a clear standard for what constitutes "reason to believe," ensuring that

---

[78] study.com

actions based on this belief are grounded in sufficient cause. The BNS consolidates definitions for easier reference, while the IPC provides a detailed list of roles and responsibilities.

Comparison: IPC Section 26 also defines "reason to believe" similarly, stating that a [79]person is said to have "reason to believe" something if they have sufficient cause to believe it, but not otherwise. This section emphasizes a higher threshold than mere suspicion, requiring concrete reasons or evidence to form such a belief.

BNS Section 2(30)

Definition: Defines **"Special law"** as any law that is not part of the general law but is enacted for specific purposes or to address particular issues. This section consolidates definitions that were previously scattered across various sections in the Indian Penal Code (IPC).

Example: A special law could be the Prevention of Corruption Act, which specifically addresses corruption-related offenses, unlike the general provisions in the IPC. Another example is the Protection of Children from Sexual Offences (POCSO) Act, which deals exclusively with sexual offenses against children.

Comment: The consolidation of definitions in BNS makes it easier to reference and understand specific terms without having to navigate through multiple sections. This approach enhances clarity and accessibility for legal practitioners and the general public.

Comparison: IPC Section 41 defines "Special law" similarly, as a law that is not part of the general law but is enacted for specific purposes. The primary difference lies in the organization and presentation. In the IPC, definitions are spread across various sections, whereas BNS consolidates them into a single section for ease of reference.

---

[79] www.indiacode.nic.in

BNS Section 2(31)

Definition: Defines **"Valuable security"** as a document that is, or purports to be, a legal right or obligation, or which is evidence of such a right or obligation. This definition is crucial for understanding various offenses related to fraud, forgery, and property.

Example: An example of a valuable security could be a promissory note, which is a written promise to pay a specified sum of money to a certain person or the bearer of the note. Another example is a share certificate, which represents ownership in a company and entitles the holder to a share of the profits.

Comment: The definition of valuable security in BNS is designed to cover a wide range of documents [80]that can be used to establish or transfer rights and obligations. This broad definition helps in addressing various forms of financial and property-related crimes more effectively.

Comparison: Section 30 also defines "Valuable security" in a similar manner, as a document that creates, extends, transfers, extinguishes, or releases any legal right or obligation. The primary difference between the two sections lies in their consolidation and presentation. BNS aims to streamline and modernize the legal definitions, making them more accessible and easier to reference.

BNS Section 2(32)

Definition: Defines **"Vessel"** as any ship, boat, or any other description of vessel used in navigation. This definition is crucial for understanding various offenses related to maritime activities and navigation.

Examples: Example of a vessel could be a cargo ship used for transporting goods across seas. Another example is a fishing boat used by fishermen to catch fish in rivers or oceans.

Comment: The definition of "vessel" in BNS is broad and inclusive, covering all types of watercrafts used in navigation. This comprehensive

---

[80] blog.ipleaders.in

definition helps in addressing various legal issues related to maritime law, ensuring that all types of vessels are covered under the law.

Comparison: IPC Section 48 also defines "Vessel" in a similar manner, as any ship or boat, or any other description of vessel used in navigation. The primary difference between the two sections lies in their consolidation and presentation. BNS aims to streamline and modernize the legal definitions, making them more accessible and easier to reference.

BNS Section 2(33)

Definition: Defines **"Voluntarily"** as an act done with free will and without any coercion or undue influence. This definition is crucial for determining the intent behind various actions, especially in criminal law.

Example: An example of acting voluntarily could be a person donating money to charity out of their own free will, without any pressure or obligation. Another example is a person confessing to a crime without any coercion from law enforcement.

Comment: The definition of "voluntarily" in BNS emphasizes the importance of free will and [81]the absence of coercion. This is essential in legal contexts to ensure that actions and confessions are genuine and not influenced by external pressures.

Comparison: IPC Section 39 also defines "Voluntarily" in a similar manner, stating that a person is said to cause an effect "voluntarily" when they cause it by means of their own free will. The primary difference between the two sections lies in their consolidation and presentation. BNS aims to streamline and modernize the legal definitions, making them more accessible and easier to reference.

---

[81] www.indiacode.nic.in

BNS Section 2(34)

Definition: Defines a **"will"** as a testamentary document, which is a legal declaration by a person (the testator) about how their property should be distributed after their death.

Illustration: Imagine a person named Raj, who writes a will stating that his house should go to his daughter, his car to his son, and his savings to a charity. This document, signed and witnessed, is Raj's will.

Example: Simple Will: A document where a person specifies the distribution of their assets. Joint Will: A single will made by two people, usually spouses, [82]that comes into effect after both have passed away. Living Will: A document that outlines a person's wishes regarding medical treatment in [83]situations where they are unable to communicate their decisions.

Comment: The definition of a will in BNS Section 2(34) is crucial as it ensures that the testator's wishes are legally recognized and followed after their death. It provides a clear framework for the distribution of assets, reducing potential disputes among heirs. IPC Section 31 – "A Will" Definition: IPC Section 31 also defines "a will" as any testamentary document. This section ensures that the term "will" is uniformly understood and applied across various legal contexts.

Comparison: Both BNS Section 2(34) and IPC Section 31 define a will as a testamentary document, ensuring clarity and uniformity in legal proceedings. While the definitions are similar, the BNS is a more recent codification, reflecting contemporary legal needs and societal changes. The IPC, being older, has been the foundation of criminal law in India but may not address modern complexities as comprehensively as the BNS. Both sections play a vital role in the legal system by providing a clear definition of a will, ensuring that the testator's wishes are respected and legally binding. The BNS, being a newer code, aims to address modern

---

[82] austlii.edu.au

[83] study.com

legal challenges more effectively while maintaining the foundational principles established by the IPC.

BNS Section 2(35)

Definition: Defines a **"Woman"** as a female human being of any age.

Illustration: Consider a scenario where a woman named Priya is involved in a legal case. Under BNS Section 2(35), Priya is recognized as a woman regardless of her age, ensuring that all legal protections and considerations applicable to women are extended to her.

Example: Criminal Cases: In cases of assault or harassment, the definition ensures that any female, whether a minor or an adult, is protected under the law. Inheritance Laws: When dealing with inheritance, a female heir is recognized as a woman, ensuring her rights are protected. Employment Laws: In workplace discrimination cases, the definition ensures that female employees of any age are covered.

Comment: The definition in BNS Section 2(35) is crucial for ensuring that all females, regardless of age, are afforded the same legal rights and protections. This inclusive definition helps in addressing various legal issues comprehensively, ensuring that no female is excluded from legal protections due to age. IPC Section 10 – "Woman" Definition: IPC Section 10 defines a "woman" as a female human being of any age.

Comparison: Both BNS Section 2(35) and IPC Section 10 define a woman as a [84]female human being of any age, ensuring consistency in legal interpretation. The primary difference lies in the context and application. The BNS is a more recent codification, reflecting contemporary legal needs and societal changes, while the IPC, being older, has served as the foundation of criminal law in India for many years. Both sections play a vital role in the legal system by providing a clear and inclusive definition of a woman, ensuring that females of all ages are protected under the law. The BNS, being a newer code, aims to address

---

[84] pdfcookie.com

modern legal challenges more effectively while maintaining the foundational principles established by the IPC.

BNS Section 2(36)

Definition: "**Wrongful Gain**" BNS Section 2(36) defines "wrongful gain" as [85]the gain by unlawful means of property to which the person [86]gaining is not legally entitled.

Illustration: Imagine a person named Ravi who finds a wallet on the street and decides to keep it, knowing it belongs to someone else. By keeping the wallet, Ravi gains wrongfully because he is not legally entitled to the wallet or its contents.

Example: Theft: If someone steals a bicycle and sells it, the money obtained from the sale is a wrongful gain. Fraud: If a person deceives another into transferring money to them under false pretences, the money received is a wrongful gain. Embezzlement: If an employee diverts company funds for personal use, the diverted funds represent a wrongful gain.

Comment: The definition of wrongful gain in BNS Section 2(36) is essential for identifying and addressing acts where individuals unlawfully benefit at the expense of others. It helps in ensuring that justice is served by penalizing those who gain through illegal means. IPC Section 23 Clause 1 – "Wrongful Gain" Definition: IPC Section 23 defines "wrongful gain" as gain by unlawful means of property to which the person gaining is not legally entitled.

Comparison: Both BNS Section 2(36) and IPC Section 23 define wrongful gain in the same way, emphasizing the unlawful acquisition of property to which the person is not entitled. Difference: The primary difference lies in the codification and context. The BNS is a more recent legal framework designed to address contemporary issues, while the IPC has been the cornerstone of criminal law in India since 1860. The BNS

---

[85] www.bareactslive.com

[86] pdfcookie.com

may incorporate more modern legal interpretations and applications. Conclusion Both sections play a crucial role in the legal system by providing a clear definition of wrongful gain, ensuring that individuals who unlawfully benefit at the expense of others are held accountable. The BNS, being a newer code, aims to address modern legal challenges more effectively while maintaining the foundational principles established by the IPC.

BNS Section 2(37)

Definition: BNS Section 2(37) defines **"wrongful loss"** as the [87]loss by unlawful means of property to which the person losing it is legally entitled. Illustration: Consider a scenario where a person named Anil owns a piece of land. If someone forges documents and illegally sells Anil's land to another person, Anil suffers a wrongful loss because he is unlawfully deprived of his property.

Examples: Theft: If someone's mobile phone is stolen, the owner suffers a wrongful loss as they are unlawfully deprived of their property. Fraud: If a person is tricked into transferring money to a scammer, the victim experiences a wrongful loss of their funds. Vandalism: If someone's car is deliberately damaged, the owner incurs a wrongful loss due to the unlawful destruction of their property.

Comment: The definition of wrongful loss in BNS Section 2(37) is crucial for identifying and addressing situations where individuals are unlawfully deprived of their property. It ensures that victims of such acts can seek legal redress and that perpetrators are held accountable. IPC Section 23 Clause 2 – "Wrongful Loss" Definition: IPC Section 23 Clause 2 defines "wrongful loss" as the loss by unlawful means of property to which the person losing it is legally entitled. It further explains that a person is said to lose wrongfully when they are wrongfully kept out of any [88]property, as well as when they are wrongfully deprived of property.

---

[87] pdfcookie.com

[88] www.bareactslive.com

Comparison: Both BNS Section 2(37) and IPC Section 23 Clause 2 define wrongful loss in a similar manner, emphasizing the unlawful deprivation of property to which the person is legally entitled. The BNS, being a more recent codification, may incorporate modern legal interpretations and applications, while the IPC has been the foundational criminal law in India since 1860. The BNS aims to address contemporary legal challenges more effectively. Both sections play a vital role in the legal system by providing a clear definition of wrongful loss, ensuring that individuals who are unlawfully deprived of their property can seek justice. The BNS, being a newer code, aims to address modern legal challenges more effectively while maintaining the foundational principles established by the IPC.

BNS Section 2(38)

Definition: "Gaining Wrongfully, Losing Wrongfully" [89]A person is said to gain wrongfully when they acquire or retain property by unlawful means. Losing Wrongfully: A person is said to lose wrongfully when they are wrongfully kept out of any property or wrongfully deprived of property. Illustration: Gaining Wrongfully: If Person A finds a wallet and decides to keep it instead of returning it to the rightful owner, Person A gains wrongfully. Losing Wrongfully: If Person B is evicted from their home without legal justification, Person B loses wrongfully.

Examples:

Gaining Wrongfully: A shopkeeper sells goods at a higher price than legally allowed, thereby gaining wrongfully. Losing Wrongfully: A tenant is forcefully removed from their rented apartment without following due legal process, resulting in wrongful loss.

Comment: This section emphasizes the importance of lawful possession and the legal consequences of acquiring or retaining property through unlawful means. It aims to protect individuals from being wrongfully deprived of their property and ensures that any gain or loss of property is justified by law. Comparison with IPC Section 23 Clause 3IPC Section 23: Wrongful Gain: Gain by unlawful means of property to which the

[89] pdfcookie.com

person gaining is not legally entitled. Wrongful Loss: Loss by unlawful means of property to which the person losing it is legally entitled.

Comparison: Both BNS Section 2(38) and IPC Section 23 define wrongful gain and wrongful loss similarly, focusing on the unlawful acquisition or deprivation [90]of property. The key difference lies in the terminology and structure. BNS consolidates definitions in a single section for easier reference, while IPC spreads them across multiple sections. BNS aims to modernize and simplify the legal language, making it more accessible and aligned with contemporary legal standards.

BNS Section 2(39)

Definition: "Words and Expressions Used, but Not Defined" This section addresses [91]words and expressions that are used in the Bharatiya Nyaya Sanhita (BNS) but are not explicitly defined within it. For such terms, their [92]meanings are derived from other relevant laws, such as the Information Technology Act, 2000, and the Bharatiya Nagarik Suraksha Sanhita, 2023 (BNSS).

Illustration: [93]If the term "digital signature" is used in the BNS but not defined, its meaning would be taken from the Information Technology Act, 2000.

Examples: Digital Signature: If BNS mentions "digital signature" without defining it, the definition from the Information Technology Act, 2000, would apply. Public Servant: If the term "public servant" is used but not defined in BNS, the definition from the BNSS would be used.

Comment: This provision ensures consistency and clarity by referring to established definitions in other relevant laws. It avoids redundancy and ensures that the legal terminology remains up-to-date with current standards and practices. Comparison with IPC Section 29AIPC Section

---

[90] pdfcookie.com

[91] prsindia.org

[92] Ethics and Halakhah in Levinas by Michae-2009

[93] www.bareactslive.com

29A: This section of the Indian [94]Penal Code (IPC) states that words and expressions not defined in the IPC but defined in other laws shall have the meanings assigned to them in those laws.

Comparison: Both BNS Section 2(39) and IPC Section 29A serve the same purpose: to provide clarity on terms not defined within the respective codes by referring to definitions in other relevant laws. The BNS broadens the scope by explicitly mentioning specific acts like the Information Technology Act, 2000, and the BNSS, [95]ensuring a more comprehensive and modern approach.

BNS Section 3(1)

Definition: "General Explanations" This section states that throughout the Bharatiya Nyaya Sanhita (BNS), every definition of an offence, every penal provision, and every illustration of such definitions or provisions shall be understood subject to the exceptions contained in the chapter entitled "General Exceptions," even [96]if those exceptions are not repeated in the definitions, provisions, or illustrations.

Examples:

Example 1: The BNS defines theft but does not explicitly state [97]that a child under seven years cannot commit theft. However, this definition is understood to be subject to the general exception that nothing is an offence if done by a child under seven years of age.

Example 2: A police officer, without a warrant, apprehends a person who has committed murder. The officer is not guilty of wrongful confinement because the act falls under the general exception that exempts actions performed by a person bound by law to do so.

---

[94] pdfcookie.com

[95] docplayer.net

[96] www.bareactslive.com

[97] pdfcookie.com

Examples 3: Self-Defence: If a person causes harm to another in self-defence, this act is not considered an offence due to the general exception of self-defence. Insanity: An individual committing an act while legally insane is not held criminally responsible, as per the general exceptions.

Comment: This section ensures that all definitions and provisions within the BNS are interpreted with the general exceptions in mind, promoting a comprehensive understanding of the law. It prevents redundancy by not repeating exceptions in every definition or provision, thus streamlining the legal text.

Comparison: with IPC Section 6IPC Section 6: Similar to BNS Section 3(1), IPC Section 6 states that throughout the Indian Penal Code (IPC), every definition of an offence, every penal provision, and every illustration of such definitions or provisions shall be understood subject to the exceptions contained in the chapter entitled "General Exceptions," even if those [98]exceptions are not repeated in the definitions, provisions, or illustrations.

Both sections serve the same purpose: ensuring that the general exceptions apply universally to all definitions and provisions within their respective codes. The BNS aims to modernize and simplify the language and structure, making it more accessible and aligned with contemporary legal standards, while the IPC retains its traditional format.

BNS Section 3(2)

Definition: "General Explanations – Sense of Expression Once Explained"

This section states that every expression [99]explained in any part of the Bharatiya Nyaya Sanhita (BNS) is used consistently throughout the entire Sanhita in accordance with that explanation.

[98] www.bareactslive.com

[99] pdfcookie.com

Illustration: If the term "public servant" is defined in one part of the BNS, it will carry the same meaning wherever it appears in the BNS, unless a different meaning is explicitly stated.

Examples: Public Servant: If "public servant" is defined in Chapter 1, it will have the same meaning in Chapter 5, ensuring consistency Property: If "property" is defined to include both movable and immovable assets in one section, this definition will apply throughout the BNS.

Comment: This provision ensures uniformity and clarity in the interpretation of terms used in the BNS. It prevents confusion and ambiguity by maintaining consistent definitions across all sections, making the legal text more coherent and easier to understand. Comparison with IPC Section 7IPC Section 7: This section of the Indian Penal Code (IPC) states that every expression which is explained in any part of the IPC is used in every part of the IPC in conformity with the explanation.

Comparison: Both BNS Section 3(2) and IPC Section 7 serve the same purpose: ensuring that terms defined in one part of the code are used consistently throughout the entire code. The BNS aims to modernize and simplify the language and structure, making it more accessible and aligned with contemporary legal standards, while the IPC retains its traditional format.

BNS Section 3(3)

Definition: General Explanations – Property in Possession of Wife, Clerk, or Servant. Text of Section 3(3): "When property is in the possession of a person's spouse, clerk, or servant, on account of that person, it is in that person's possession within the meaning of this Sanhita. Explanation: A person employed temporarily or on a particular occasion in the capacity of a clerk or servant, is a clerk or servant within the meaning of this sub-section."

Illustration: Imagine a scenario where Mr. A owns a valuable painting. He asks his wife, Mrs. A, to keep it safe at home. According to BNS Section 3(3), the painting is considered to be in Mr. A's possession, even though it is physically with Mrs. A.

Example: Clerk: Mr. B, a businessman, gives important documents to his clerk, Mr. C, for safekeeping. Legally, these documents are still in Mr. B's possession. Servant: Mrs. D hands over her jewellery to her household servant, Ms. E, for cleaning. The jewellery remains in Mrs. D's possession under the law.

Comment: This section clarifies that possession is not merely about physical control but also about legal control. It ensures that property held by close associates (spouse, clerk, servant) on behalf of the owner is legally considered to be in the owner's possession. This provision helps in legal proceedings where the actual physical holder of the property might not be the rightful owner.

Comparison: IPC Section 27: "When property is in the possession of a person's wife, clerk, or servant, on account of that person, it is in that person's possession within the meaning of this Code." Both sections use similar language, but BNS Section 3(3) includes an explicit explanation about temporary or occasional employment, which is not explicitly mentioned in IPC Section 27. Context: BNS Section 3(3) [100]is part of the Bharatiya Nyaya Sanhita, a newer legal framework, while IPC Section 27 is part of the older Indian Penal Code. The BNS aims to modernize and clarify legal provisions. Both sections serve the same purpose of defining possession in legal terms, ensuring that property held by close associates is legally considered to be in the owner's possession. The BNS section provides a bit more clarity by explicitly including temporary or occasional employees.

BNS Section 3(4)

Definition: General Explanations – [101]Words Referring to Acts Include Illegal Omissions Text of Section 3(4): "In every Part of this Sanhita, except where a contrary intention appears from the context, words which refer to acts done extend also to illegal omissions."

---

[100] prsindia.org

[101] pdfcookie.com

Illustration: Consider a scenario where Mr. X is legally required to provide food to his dependent, Mr. Y. If Mr. X intentionally fails to do so, resulting in harm to Mr. Y, this omission is treated as an act under BNS Section 3(4).

Examples: Parental Duty: A parent, Ms. A, is required by law to ensure her child, B, attends school. If Ms. A deliberately prevents B from attending school, this omission is considered an act. Employer Responsibility: An employer, Mr. C, must ensure safe working conditions for his employees. If Mr. C neglects this duty, leading to an accident, his omission is treated as an act.

Comment: This section emphasizes that the law considers [102]not only actions but also failures to act (illegal omissions) as significant. It ensures that individuals cannot escape liability simply by failing to perform a required duty. This provision is crucial for maintaining accountability in various legal contexts.

Comparison: IPC Section 32: "In every Part of this Code, except where a contrary intention appears from the context, words which refer to acts done extend also to illegal omissions." and Both sections use almost identical language, reflecting their shared purpose. However, BNS Section 3(4) is part of the [103]Bharatiya Nyaya Sanhita, a modern legal framework, while IPC Section 32 belongs to the older Indian Penal Code. Modernization: The BNS aims to update and clarify legal provisions, potentially offering more detailed explanations and contemporary relevance. Both sections serve to ensure that illegal omissions are treated as acts under the law, promoting accountability and justice. The BNS section aligns closely with the IPC section but is part of a broader effort to modernize and streamline legal interpretations

[102] The right and the good by J-1992

[103] prsindia.org

BNS Section 3(5)

Definition: General Explanations – Act [104]Done by Several Persons in Furtherance of Common Intention. Text of Section 3(5): "When a criminal act is done by several persons in furtherance of the common intention of all, each of such persons is liable for that act in the same manner as if it were done by him alone."

Illustration: Imagine Mr. A and Mr. B plan to rob a bank together. During the robbery, Mr. A holds the staff at gunpoint while Mr. B collects the money. Even if Mr. B did not directly threaten anyone, both Mr. A and Mr. B are equally liable for the robbery because they acted with a common intention.

Examples: Group Assault: If a group of people, including Mr. X, Mr. Y, and Mr. Z, attack another person with the shared intention of causing harm, each member of the group is equally responsible for the assault, regardless of who delivered the final blow. Theft: Ms. A and Ms. B agree to steal a car. Ms. A disables the alarm system while Ms. B drives the car away. Both are equally liable for the theft.

Comment: This section establishes the principle of joint liability, ensuring that all participants in a criminal act are held accountable, regardless of their individual roles. It underscores the importance of shared intention in determining liability, promoting justice by preventing individuals from escaping responsibility by claiming a minor role.

Comparison: IPC Section 34: "When a criminal act is done by several persons in furtherance of the common intention of all, each of such persons is liable for that act in the same manner as if it were done by him alone." Both sections use identical language, reflecting their shared purpose. However, BNS Section 3(5) is part of the Bharatiya Nyaya Sanhita, a modern legal framework, while IPC Section 34 belongs to the older Indian Penal Code. Modernization: The BNS aims to update and clarify legal provisions, potentially offering more detailed explanations and contemporary. Both sections serve to ensure that individuals acting with a

---

[104] pdfcookie.com

common intention in committing a crime are equally liable, promoting accountability and justice. The BNS section aligns closely with the IPC section but is part of a broader effort to modernize and streamline legal interpretations.

BNS Section 3(6)

Definition: General Explanations – [105]When Such an Act is Criminal by Reason of Its Being Done with a Criminal Knowledge or Intention. "Whenever an act, which is criminal only by reason of its being done with a criminal knowledge or intention, is done by several persons, each of such persons who joins in the act with such knowledge or intention is liable for the act in the same manner as if the act were done by him alone with that knowledge or intention."

Illustration: Imagine Mr. A and Mr. B both know that setting a fire in a forest is illegal and dangerous. They decide to do it anyway, intending to cause harm. Even if Mr. A only provides the matches and Mr. B lights the fire, [106]both are equally liable for the criminal act because they shared the criminal knowledge and intention.

Examples: Fraud: Ms. X and Mr. Y conspire to defraud a company. Ms. X provides insider information, and Mr. Y executes the fraudulent transactions. Both are equally liable because they acted with shared criminal knowledge and intention. Burglary: Mr. C and Mr. D plan a burglary. Mr. C disables the security system, and Mr. D enters the house to steal valuables. [107]Both are equally responsible for the burglary due to their shared criminal intent.

Comment: This section ensures that all participants in a [108]criminal act are held accountable if they share the criminal knowledge or intention. It prevents individuals from escaping liability by claiming a minor role in

---

[105] pdfcookie.com

[106] advocatetanmoy.com

[107] en.nsd.pku.edu.cn

[108] pdfcookie.com

the act. This principle is crucial for maintaining justice and accountability in criminal law.

Comparison: with IPC Section 35: IPC Section 35: "Whenever an act, which is criminal only by reason of its being done with a criminal knowledge or intention, is done by several persons, each of such persons who joins in the act with such knowledge or intention is liable for the act in the same manner as if the act were done by him alone with that knowledge or intention." Both sections use identical language, reflecting their shared purpose. However, BNS Section 3(6) is part of the Bharatiya Nyaya Sanhita, a modern legal framework, while IPC Section 35 belongs to the older Indian Penal Code. Modernization: The BNS aims to update and clarify legal provisions, potentially offering more detailed explanations and contemporary relevance. Both sections ensure that individuals acting with criminal knowledge or intention are [109]equally liable for the criminal act, promoting accountability and justice. The BNS section aligns closely with the IPC section but is part of a broader effort to modernize and streamline legal interpretations.

BNS Section 3(7)

Definition: General Explanations – [110]Effect Caused Partly by Act and Partly by Omission "Wherever the causing of a certain effect, or an attempt to cause that effect, by an act or by an omission, is an offence, it is to be understood that the causing of that effect partly by an act and partly by an omission is the same offence". Illustration: Imagine a scenario where a person is responsible for maintaining a dam. If they negligently fail to close a gate (an omission) and simultaneously release water from another gate (an act), causing flooding downstream, the combined effect of the act and omission would be considered the same offence under this section.

Examples: Medical Negligence: A doctor prescribes the wrong medication (act) and fails to monitor the patient's condition (omission),

---

[109] advocatetanmoy.com

[110] pdfcookie.com

leading to the patient's harm. Traffic Accident: A driver speeds (act) and fails to apply brakes in time (omission), causing an accident.

Comment: This section emphasizes that the [111]law does not differentiate between the effects caused solely by an act, solely by an omission, or a combination of both. The focus is on the resultant effect and the culpability of the individual for causing that effect, regardless of whether it was through action, inaction, or both.

Comparison: With IPC Section 36: IPC Section 36 states: "Wherever the causing of a certain effect, or an attempt to cause that effect, by an act or by an omission, is an offence, it is to be understood that the causing of that effect partly by an act and partly by an omission is the same offence." Both sections are essentially identical in wording and intent. They clarify that the law treats the combined effect of actions and omissions as a single offence. This ensures that individuals cannot escape liability by arguing that the harmful [112]effect was not solely due to their actions or omissions but a combination of both.

BNS Section 3(8)

Definition: General Explanations - [113]Cooperation by Doing One of Several Acts Constituting an Offence Section 3(8) [114]of the Bharatiya Nyaya Sanhita (BNS) 2023 provides a general explanation regarding the cooperation in the commission of an offense [115]by doing one of several acts constituting that offense.

Illustration: If A and B agree to murder Z by administering small doses of poison at different times, and A administers one of those doses, A has committed the offense of murder by cooperating in the commission of the offense.

---

[111] journals.openedition.org

[112] Properties of auditory stream formation by Moore-2012

[113] www.bareactslive.com

[114] prsindia.org

[115] pdfcookie.com

Example: Suppose A and B conspire to rob a bank. A agrees to disable the security system while B enters the bank to steal the money. Even if A only disables the security system without directly taking any money, A is still considered to have committed the offense of robbery by cooperating in the commission of the offense.

Comment: This section clarifies that when an offense is committed through several acts, anyone who intentionally cooperates in the commission of that offense by performing any one of those acts, either alone or jointly with another person, is considered to have committed the offense. It emphasizes the principle of joint liability in criminal law.

Comparison: Section 37 of the Indian Penal Code (IPC) also addresses the same concept: IPC Section 37: States that when an offense is committed by means of several acts, whoever intentionally cooperates in the commission of that offense by doing any one of those acts, either singly or jointly with any other person, commits that offense. BNS 3(8): Reflects updated legal terminology and provisions in the new Bharatiya Nyaya Sanhita. IPC 37: [116]Part of the older Indian Penal Code framework, now replaced by BNS 3(8).

BNS Section 3(9)

Definition: General Explanations - Persons Concerned in Criminal Act May Be Guilty of Different Offences Section 3(9) of the [117]Bharatiya Nyaya Sanhita (BNS) 2023 states that when several persons are engaged or concerned in the commission of a criminal act, they may be guilty of different offenses by means of that act.

Illustration: If A and B conspire to commit a robbery, and A actually commits the robbery while B acts as a lookout, both A and B can be held guilty of different offenses. A can be charged with the offense of robbery,

---

[116] hyderabadpolice.gov.in

[117] bprd.nic.in

while B [118]can be charged with the offense of aiding and abetting the robbery.

Example: Suppose A and B plan to steal a car. A breaks into the car and drives it away, while B keeps watch to alert A of any approaching people. A can be charged with theft and unauthorized use of a vehicle, while B can be charged with aiding and abetting the theft.

Comment: This section clarifies that individuals involved in a criminal act can be held accountable for different offenses based on their specific roles and actions. It ensures that each person's level of involvement and responsibility is appropriately addressed in the legal system.

Comparison: With IPC Section 38Section 38 [119]of the Indian Penal Code (IPC) also addresses the same concept: IPC Section 38: [120]States that where several persons are engaged or concerned in the commission of a criminal act, they may be guilty of different offenses by means of that act. BNS 3(9): Reflects updated legal terminology and provisions in the new Bharatiya Nyaya Sanhita. IPC 38: Part of the older Indian Penal Code framework, now replaced by BNS 3(9).

[118] www.ijlmh.com

[119] core.ac.uk

[120] bprd.nic.in

CHAPTER -II; OF PUNISHMENTS

BNS Section 4

Definition: Punishments Section 4 of the Bharatiya Nyaya Sanhita (BNS) 2023 outlines the types of punishments that offenders are liable to under the provisions of this Sanhita. Types of Punishments Death: Reserved for the most heinous crimes. Imprisonment for Life: Imprisonment for the remainder of a person's natural life3.Imprisonment: This is of two descriptions: Rigorous: Imprisonment with hard labor. Simple: Imprisonment without hard labor. Forfeiture of Property: Confiscation of property related to the crime. Fine: Monetary penalty. Community Service: Offenders may be required to perform community service as part of their punishment.

Illustration: [121]If a person is convicted of a serious crime like murder, [122]they may be sentenced to death or life imprisonment.

Example: A person found guilty of embezzling a large sum of money might face rigorous imprisonment and a substantial fine.

Comment: This section provides a comprehensive framework for the types of punishments that can be imposed, ensuring that the punishment fits the severity of the crime. It aims to balance justice and rehabilitation, offering a range of options from capital punishment to community service.

Comparison: Section 53 of the Indian Penal Code (IPC) also enumerates the types of punishments [123]that can be imposed on offenders. The punishments listed under IPC Section 53 are similar to those in BNS 4,

---

[121] scholar.uwindsor.ca

[122] core.ac.uk

[123] indiankanoon.org

including death, imprisonment for life, rigorous and simple imprisonment, forfeiture of property, and fine. BNS 4: Reflects updated legal terminology and provisions in the new Bharatiya Nyaya Sanhita. IPC 53: Part of the older Indian Penal Code framework, now replaced by BNS 4.

BNS Section 5

Definition: Commutation of Sentence Section 5 of the Bharatiya Nyaya Sanhita (BNS) 2023 deals with the commutation of sentences, specifically for death sentences and life imprisonment. Commutation of Sentence Death Sentence: The appropriate government may commute a death sentence to [124]any other punishment provided by this Sanhita [125]without the consent of the offender. Life Imprisonment: The appropriate government may commute a life imprisonment sentence to imprisonment of either description for a term not exceeding fourteen years without the consent of the offender.

Illustration: If a person is sentenced to death for a serious crime, the government has the authority to change [126]the sentence to life imprisonment or a lesser term.

Example: A person convicted of murder and sentenced to death may have their sentence commuted to life imprisonment, meaning they will spend the rest of their life in prison instead of facing execution.

Comment: This section ensures that the power to commute sentences lies with the appropriate government, providing a mechanism for mercy and leniency in the justice system. It allows for the possibility of reducing the severity of a sentence, particularly in cases where there may be mitigating circumstances or a change in societal views on punishment.

---

[124] devgan.in

[125] bprd.nic.in

[126] indiankanoon.org

Comparison: With IPC Sections 54 & 55 Section 54 [127]of the Indian Penal Code (IPC) [128]states that in every case where a sentence of death has been [129]passed, the appropriate government may commute the punishment to any other punishment provided by the Code [130]without the consent of the offender. Section 55 of the IPC states that in every case where a sentence of life imprisonment has [131]been passed, the appropriate government may commute the punishment for imprisonment of either description for a term not exceeding fourteen years[132] without the consent of the offender. Reflects updated legal terminology and provisions in the new Bharatiya Nyaya Sanhita. IPC Sections 54 & 55: Part of the older Indian Penal Code framework, now replaced by BNS 5.

Explanation to Section 5:

Definition: Commutation of Sentence Explanation to Section 5 of the Bharatiya Nyaya Sanhita (BNS) 2023 clarifies the term "appropriate Government" for the purposes of commutation of sentences. Explanation Appropriate Government: For the purposes of this section, the expression "appropriate Gover innment" means: Central Government: In cases where the sentence is a sentence of death or is for an offense against any law relating to a matter to which the executive power of the Union extends. State Government: In cases where the sentence (whether of death or not) is for an offense against any law relating to a matter to which the executive power of the State extends.

Illustration: If a person is sentenced to death for a crime that falls under Union law, the Central Government has the authority to commute the sentence. If the crime falls under State law, the State Government has the authority to commute the sentence.

---

[127] core.ac.uk

[128] indiankanoon.org

[129]devgan.in

[130] bprd.nic.in

[131]devgan.in

[132]bprd.nic.in

Example: Suppose a person is sentenced to death for a federal offense like terrorism. The Central Government can commute the death sentence to life imprisonment. If the offense is a state-level crime like robbery, the State Government can commute the sentence.

Comment: This explanation ensures clarity on which level of government has the authority to commute sentences, [133]depending on the nature of the offense. It helps streamline the process and ensures that the appropriate authority is [134]involved in the decision-making.

Comparison: With IPC Section 55ASection 55A of the Indian Penal Code (IPC) also defines the term "appropriate Government" in a similar manner: IPC Section 55A: States that in sections 54 and 55, the expression "appropriate Government" means: Central Government: [135]In cases where the sentence is a sentence of death or is for an offense against any law relating to a matter to which the executive power of the Union extends. State Government: In cases where the sentence (whether of death or not) is for an offense against any law relating to a matter to which the executive power of the State extends. BNS Explanation to Section 5: Reflects updated legal terminology and provisions in the new Bharatiya Nyaya Sanhita. IPC Section 55A: Part of the older Indian Penal Code framework, now replaced by the explanation in BNS.

BNS Section 6

Definition: Fractions of Terms of Punishment Section 6 of the Bharatiya Nyaya Sanhita (BNS) 2023 provides guidelines for calculating fractions of terms of punishment, particularly when imprisonment for life is involved. Explanation Imprisonment for Life: In calculating fractions of terms of punishment, imprisonment for life is reckoned as equivalent to imprisonment for twenty years unless otherwise provided.

---

[133]www.ijlmh.com

[134]indiankanoon.org

[135]bprd.nic.in

Illustration: If a person is sentenced to imprisonment for life and the court decides to reduce the sentence by half, the reduced term would be ten years (half of twenty years).

Example: Suppose a person is sentenced to imprisonment for life (equivalent to twenty years) for a crime. [136]If the court decides to reduce the sentence by one-third, the reduced term would be approximately 6.67 years (one-third of twenty years).

Comment: This section ensures a standardized approach to [137]calculating fractions of terms of punishment, particularly for life imprisonment. It helps maintain consistency and fairness in sentencing, ensuring that reductions in sentences are applied uniformly.

Comparison: Section 57 [138]of the Indian Penal Code (IPC) also addresses the calculation of [139]fractions of terms of punishment: IPC Section 57: States that in calculating fractions of terms of punishment, imprisonment for life shall be reckoned as equivalent to imprisonment for twenty years. BNS 6: Reflects updated legal terminology and provisions in the new Bharatiya Nyaya Sanhita. IPC 57: Part of the older Indian Penal Code framework, now replaced by BNS 6.

BNS Section 7

Definition: Sentence May Be (in Certain Cases of Imprisonment) Wholly or Partly Rigorous or Simple Section 7 of the Bharatiya Nyaya Sanhita (BNS) 2023 states that in every case where an offender is punishable with imprisonment that may be of either description (rigorous or simple), it is within the court's discretion to direct that such imprisonment shall be wholly rigorous, wholly simple, or partly rigorous and partly simple.

---

[136]core.ac.uk

[137]bprd.nic.in

[138]core.ac.uk

[139]bprd.nic.in

Illustration: [140]If a person is sentenced to imprisonment for a crime, the court may decide that the first half of the sentence will be rigorous (with hard labor) and the second half simple (without hard labor).

Example: Suppose a person is sentenced to 10 years of imprisonment for theft. The court may order that the first 5 years be rigorous imprisonment and the remaining 5 years be simple imprisonment.

Comment: This section provides flexibility to the courts in determining the nature of imprisonment based on the circumstances of the case and the offender's condition. It allows for a more tailored approach to sentencing, ensuring that the punishment is appropriate and just.

Comparison: Section 60 of the Indian Penal Code (IPC) also addresses the same concept:IPC Section 60: States that [141]in every case where an offender is punishable with imprisonment which may be of either description, it shall be competent to the Court which sentences such offender to direct in the sentence that such imprisonment shall be wholly rigorous, or that such imprisonment shall be wholly simple, or that any part of such imprisonment shall be rigorous and the rest simple. Reflects updated legal terminology and provisions in the new Bharatiya Nyaya Sanhita. IPC 60: Part of the older Indian Penal Code framework, now replaced by BNS.

BNS Section 8(1)

Definition: Amount of Fine, Liability in Default of Payment of Fine, etc. Section 8 (1) of the Bharatiya Nyaya Sanhita (BNS) 2023 states that where no sum is expressed to which a fine may extend, the amount of fine to which the offender is liable is unlimited, but shall not be excessive.

Illustration: If a law specifies a fine for an offense but does not set a maximum limit, the court can impose any amount as a fine, provided it is not excessive.

---

[140]jajharkhand.in

[141]bprd.nic.in

Example: Suppose [142]a person is convicted of a minor offense that carries a fine but no specific limit is mentioned. [143]The court can impose a fine of ₹10,000, but it must ensure that the amount is reasonable and not excessive.

Comment: This section provides flexibility to the courts in determining the amount of fine, ensuring that fines are proportionate to the offense while preventing arbitrary or excessive penalties. It balances the need for punishment with fairness and justice.

Comparison: Section 63 of the Indian Penal Code (IPC) also addresses the amount of fine: IPC Section 63: States that where no sum is expressed to which a fine may extend, the amount of fine to which the offender is liable is unlimited, but shall not be excessive. BNS 8(1): Reflects updated legal terminology and provisions in the new Bharatiya Nyaya Sanhita. IPC 63: Part of the older [144]Indian Penal Code framework, now replaced by BNS 8(1).

BNS Section 8 (2)

Definition: Sentence of Imprisonment for Non-Payment of Fine Section 8 (2) of the Bharatiya Nyaya Sanhita (BNS) 2023 states that in cases [145]where an offender is sentenced to a fine, whether with or without imprisonment, the court may direct [146]that, in default of payment of the fine, the offender shall suffer imprisonment for a certain term1.

Illustration: If a person is fined ₹10,000 for a minor offense and fails to pay the fine, the court may order that the person be imprisoned for an additional term, say 3 months, until the fine is paid.

---

[142]scholar.uwindsor.ca

[143]core.ac.uk

[144]devgan.in

[145]www.ilo.org

[146]bprd.nic.in

Example: Suppose a person is sentenced to [147]6 months of imprisonment and a fine of ₹5,000 for a traffic violation. If the person does not pay the fine, the court may direct that the person serves an additional 2 months of imprisonment in default of payment.

Comment: This section ensures that there is a consequence for failing to pay a fine, which helps enforce court orders and maintain the integrity of the judicial system. It provides a clear mechanism for dealing with non-compliance with financial penalties.

Comparison: Section 64 of the Indian Penal Code (IPC) addresses the consequences faced by individuals who fail to pay a fine imposed as part of their sentence: IPC Section 64: States that [148]in every case of an offense punishable with imprisonment as well as fine, in which the offender is sentenced to a fine, whether with or without [149]imprisonment, and in every case of an offense punishable with imprisonment or fine, or with fine only, in which the offender is sentenced to a fine, it shall be competent to the Court which sentences such offender to direct by the sentence that, in default of payment of the fine, the offender shall suffer imprisonment for a certain term2. BNS 8(2): Reflects updated legal terminology and provisions in the new Bharatiya Nyaya Sanhita. IPC 64: Part of the older Indian Penal Code framework, now replaced by BNS 8(2).

BNS Section 8(3)

Definition: Limit to Imprisonment for Non-Payment of Fine, when imprisonment and fine awardable Section 8(3) [150]of the Bharatiya Nyaya Sanhita (BNS) 2023 states that the term for which the court directs the offender to be imprisoned in default of payment of a fine shall not exceed one-fourth of the term of imprisonment which is the

[147]core.ac.uk

[148]bprd.nic.in

[149]devgan.in

[150]bprd.nic.in

maximum fixed for the offense, if the offense is punishable with imprisonment as well as fine1.

Illustration: If the [151]maximum term of imprisonment for an offense is 4 years, and the offender is fined but fails to pay, the additional imprisonment for non-payment of the fine should not exceed 1 year (one-fourth of 4 years).

Example: Suppose a [152]person is convicted of a crime that carries a maximum imprisonment of 2 years and a fine. If the person does not pay the fine, the court can impose an additional imprisonment of up to 6 months (one-fourth of 2 years).

Comment: This section ensures that the additional punishment for non-payment of a fine is proportionate to the severity of the original offense. It prevents excessively long imprisonment terms for defaulting on fines, maintaining a balance between enforcing court orders and avoiding disproportionate penalties.

Comparison: Section 65 [153]of the Indian Penal Code (IPC) also addresses the same concept: IPC Section 65: States that the term for which the court directs the offender to be imprisoned in default of payment of a fine shall not exceed one-fourth of the term of imprisonment which is the maximum fixed for the offense, if the offense is punishable with imprisonment as well as fine. BNS 8(3): Reflects updated legal terminology and provisions in the new Bharatiya Nyaya Sanhita. IPC 65: Part of the older Indian Penal Code framework, now replaced by BNS 8(3).

BNS Section 8(4)

Definition: Description of Imprisonment for Non-Payment of Fine Section 8(4) of the Bharatiya Nyaya Sanhita (BNS) 2023 specifies that the imprisonment for non-payment of a fine shall be simple imprisonment.

---

[151]core.ac.uk

[152] core.ac.uk

[153]scholar.uwindsor.ca

Illustration: If a person is fined ₹10,000 for a minor offense and fails to pay the fine, the court may order that the person serve simple [154]imprisonment for a certain term, say 2 months, until the fine is paid.

Example: Suppose a [155]person is fined ₹5,000 for a traffic violation and does not pay the fine. The court may direct that the person serves simple imprisonment for up to 2 months until the fine is paid.

Comment: This section ensures that the additional punishment for non-payment of a fine is not overly harsh and is proportionate to the offense. Simple imprisonment is less severe than rigorous imprisonment, making it a fairer consequence for failing to [156]pay a fine.

Comparison: Section 66 [157]of the Indian Penal Code (IPC) also addresses the consequences of non-payment of a fine: IPC Section 66: States that in cases where an offender is sentenced to a fine, whether with or without imprisonment, and in cases where the offender is sentenced to imprisonment or fine, or with fine only, it shall be competent to the Court which sentences such offender to direct by the sentence that, in default of payment of the fine, the offender shall suffer imprisonment for a certain term, which shall be simple imprisonment. BNS 8(4): Reflects updated legal terminology and provisions in the new Bharatiya Nyaya Sanhita. IPC 66: Part of the older Indian Penal Code framework, now replaced by BNS 8(4).

BNS Section 8(5)

Definition: Imprisonment for Non-Payment of Fine, When Offence Punishable with Fine Only Section 8(5) of the Bharatiya Nyaya Sanhita (BNS) 2023 addresses the [158]situation where an offender is sentenced to a fine only and fails to pay the fine. The court may direct

[154] bprd.nic.in

[155] scholar.uwindsor.ca

[156] core.ac.uk

[157] core.ac.uk

[158] core.ac.uk

[159]**that, in default of payment of the fine, the offender shall suffer simple imprisonment for a certain term.**

Illustration: If a person is fined ₹5,000 for a minor offense and fails to pay the fine, the court may order that the person be imprisoned for a term in default of payment.

Example: Suppose a person is fined ₹2,000 for littering in a public place and does not pay the fine. The court may direct that the person serves simple imprisonment for a period, such as one month, until the fine is paid.

Comment: This section ensures that there is a consequence for failing [160]to pay a fine, even when the offense is only punishable by a fine. It provides a clear mechanism for dealing with non-compliance with financial penalties and helps enforce court orders.

Comparison: Section 67 of the Indian Penal Code (IPC) also addresses the consequences faced by individuals who fail to pay a fine imposed as part of their sentence: IPC Section 67: States that if the offense be [161]punishable with fine only, the imprisonment which the court imposes in [162]default of payment of the fine shall be simple, and the term for which the court directs the offender to be imprisoned in default of payment of a fine shall not exceed the following scale: [163]for any term not exceeding two months, if the fine shall not exceed fifty rupees, and for any term not exceeding four months, if the fine shall not exceed one hundred rupees, and for any term not exceeding six months in any other case. BNS 8(5): Reflects updated legal terminology and provisions in the new Bharatiya Nyaya Sanhita. IPC 67: Part of the older Indian Penal Code framework, now replaced by BNS 8(5).

---

[159] bprd.nic.in

[160]core.ac.uk

[161]devgan.in

[162]bprd.nic.in

[163]devgan.in

BNS Section 8(6)

Definition: Imprisonment to Terminate on Payment of Fine Section, Termination of imprisonment on payments of [164]proportional part of fine. 8(6) of the Bharatiya Nyaya Sanhita (BNS) 2023 states that: Imprisonment shall terminate whenever the [165]fine is either paid or levied by process of law. Proportional Termination: If, before the expiration of the term of imprisonment fixed in default of payment, such a proportion of the fine is paid or levied that the term of imprisonment suffered in default of payment is not less than proportional to the part of the fine still unpaid, the imprisonment shall terminate.

Illustration: If a person is sentenced to imprisonment for 4 months in default of payment of a ₹100 fine, and they pay ₹75 before the term expires, their imprisonment will terminate as the paid amount is proportional to the remaining fine.

Example: Suppose a person is fined ₹200 [166]and sentenced to 6 months of imprisonment in default of payment. If they pay ₹150 before the term expires, their imprisonment will terminate as the paid amount is proportional to the remaining fine.

Comment: This section ensures that imprisonment for non-payment of a fine is not indefinite and provides a fair mechanism for early release based on the proportion of the fine paid. It balances the enforcement of court orders with the rights of the offender.

Comparison: with IPC Sections 68 & 69Section 68 of the Indian Penal Code (IPC) states that: [167]The imprisonment which is imposed in default of payment of a fine shall terminate whenever that fine is either paid or levied by process of law. Section 69 of the IPC states that:If, before the expiration of the term of imprisonment fixed in default of payment, such

---

[164]www.bareactslive.com

[165]bprd.nic.in

[166]core.ac.uk

[167]bprd.nic.in

a proportion of the fine is paid or levied that the term of imprisonment suffered in default of payment is not less than proportional to the part of the fine still unpaid, the imprisonment shall terminate. BNS 8(6): Reflects updated legal terminology and provisions in the new Bharatiya Nyaya Sanhita. IPC 68 & 69: Part of the older [168]Indian Penal Code framework, now replaced by BNS 8(6).

BNS Section 8 (7)

Definition: Fine Leviable within Six Years, or During [169]Imprisonment. Death Not to Discharge Property from Liability. Section 8(7) [170]of the Bharatiya Nyaya Sanhita (BNS) 2023 states that: The fine, or any part thereof which remains unpaid, may be levied at any time within six years after the passing of the sentence. If the offender is liable to imprisonment for a longer period than six years, then the fine may be levied at any time before [171]the expiration of that period. [172]The death of the offender does not discharge from liability any property which would, after his death, be legally liable for his debts.

Illustration: If a person is fined ₹10,000 for a minor offense and fails to pay, the fine can be levied at any time within six years from the date of the sentence. If the person dies within this period, their property can still be used to pay off the fine.

Example: Suppose a person is fined ₹5,000 for littering and does not pay the fine. The court can enforce the fine at any time within six years. If the person passes away within this period, their estate will still be liable for the unpaid fine.

---

[168]devgan.in

[169]www.ilo.org

[170]bprd.nic.in

[171]core.ac.uk

[172]bprd.nic.in

Comment: This section ensures that fines remain enforceable for a reasonable period, allowing legal authorities to collect unpaid fines while also ensuring that the liability does not simply disappear upon the death of the offender. It balances the need for enforcement with the rights of the offender and their estate.

Comparison: Section 70 [173]of the Indian Penal Code (IPC) also addresses the same concept: IPC Section 70: States that the [174]fine, or any part thereof which remains unpaid, may be levied at any time within six years after the passing of the sentence. If the offender is liable to imprisonment for a longer period than six years, then at any time before [175]the expiration of that period. [176]The death of the offender does not discharge from liability any property which would, after his death, be legally liable for his debts. BNS 8(7): Reflects updated legal terminology and provisions in the new Bharatiya Nyaya Sanhita. IPC 70: Part of the older Indian Penal Code framework, now replaced by BNS 8(7).

BNS Section 9

Definition: [177]Limit of Punishment of Offence Made Up of Several Offences Section 9 of the Bharatiya Nyaya Sanhita (BNS) 2023 states that: Single Punishment: Where an offense is made up of parts, any of which parts is itself an offense, the offender shall not be punished with the punishment of more than one of such offenses, unless it is expressly provided otherwise. Multiple Offenses: Where an offense falls within two or more separate definitions of any law in force, [178]or where several acts, of which one or more would by itself or themselves constitute an offense, constitute, when combined, a different offense,

[173]core.ac.uk

[174]bprd.nic.in

[175]core.ac.uk

[176]bprd.nic.in

[177]pdfcookie.com

[178]pdfcookie.com

the offender shall not be punished with a more severe punishment than the court could award for any one of such offenses.

Illustration: If a person commits an act that constitutes both theft and assault, they should not be punished twice for the same act unless the law expressly provides for it.

Example: Suppose a person commits an act that involves both damaging property and causing hurt. The court can punish the person for either damaging property or causing hurt, but not both, unless the law specifically states otherwise.

Comment: This section ensures that offenders are not subjected to multiple punishments for a single act or a series of acts that constitute different offenses. It promotes fairness and prevents excessive punishment by allowing only one punishment for an offense made up of several parts.

Comparison [179]Section 71 of the Indian Penal Code (IPC) also addresses the same concept: IPC Section 71: States that [180]where anything which is an offense is made up of parts, any of which parts is itself an offense, the offender shall not be punished with the punishment of more than one of such offenses, unless it is so expressly provided. It also states that where an offense [181]falls within two or more separate definitions of any law in force, [182]or where several acts, of which one or more would by itself or themselves constitute an offense, constitute, when combined, a different offense, the offender shall not be punished with a more severe punishment than the court could award for any one of such offenses. BNS 9: Reflects updated legal terminology and provisions in the new Bharatiya Nyaya Sanhita. IPC 71: Part of the older Indian Penal Code framework, now replaced by BNS 9.

---

[179]Thesis submitted to shodhganga - shodhganga.inflibnet.ac.in

[180]pdfcookie.com

[181]Thesis Submitted to Shodhganga Repositor

[182]pdfcookie.com

BNS Section 10

Definition: Punishment of Person Guilty of One of Several Offences, the Judgment Stating That It Is Doubtful of Which Section 10 of the Bharatiya Nyaya Sanhita (BNS) 2023 states that in cases where a judgment is given that a person is guilty of one of several offenses specified in the judgment, but it is doubtful of which offense the person is guilty, the offender shall be punished for the offense for which the lowest punishment is provided, if the same punishment is not provided for all offenses.

Illustration: If a person is found guilty of either theft or assault, but it is unclear which specific offense they committed, the court will impose the punishment for the lesser offense, which is theft in this case.

Example: Suppose a person is convicted of either damaging property or causing hurt, but it is uncertain which specific act they committed. The court will punish the person for the lesser offense, which is damaging property.

Comment: This section ensures fairness in sentencing by preventing excessively harsh penalties in cases where there is uncertainty about the specific offense committed. It upholds the principle of proportionality in punishment and protects the rights of the accused.

Comparison: Section 72 of the Indian Penal Code (IPC) also addresses the same concept: IPC Section 72: States that in all cases where judgment is given that a person is guilty of one of several offenses specified in the judgment, but it is doubtful of which of these offenses the person is guilty, the offender shall be punished for the offense for which the lowest punishment is provided if the same punishment is not provided for all offenses. BNS 10: Reflects updated legal terminology and provisions in the new Bharatiya Nyaya Sanhita. IPC 72: Part of the older Indian Penal Code framework, now replaced by BNS 10.

BNS Section 11

Definition: Solitary Confinement Section 11 of the Bharatiya Nyaya Sanhita (BNS) 2023 addresses solitary [183]confinement as a form of punishment. It states that whenever [184]a person is convicted of an offense [185]for which the court has the power to sentence them [186]to rigorous imprisonment, the court may [187]order that the offender be [188]kept in solitary confinement for any portion of the imprisonment, not exceeding three months in total. The duration of solitary confinement is determined based on the length of the imprisonment: Not exceeding one month if the term of imprisonment does not exceed six months. Not exceeding two months if the term of imprisonment exceeds six [189]months but does not exceed one year. Not [190]exceeding three months if the term of imprisonment exceeds one year.

Illustration: If a person is sentenced to 8 months of rigorous imprisonment, the court may order that they be kept in solitary confinement for up to 2 months during their sentence.

Example: Suppose a person is sentenced to 3 years of imprisonment. [191]The court may order that they [192]be kept in solitary confinement for up to 3 months during their sentence.

Comment: Solitary confinement is a severe form of punishment that isolates the prisoner from other inmates, typically in a single cell with

---

[183]blog.scconline.com

[184]pdfcookie.com

[185]www.scribd.com

[186]pdfcookie.com

[187]blog.scconline.com

[188]pdfcookie.com

[189]erepository.uonbi.ac.ke

[190] www.bareactslive.com

[191] blog.scconline.com

[192]pdfcookie.com

limited or no interaction with others9. This section ensures that solitary confinement is used as a part of the overall sentence and sets clear limits on its duration to prevent excessive use.

Comparison: Section 73 of the Indian Penal Code (IPC) also addresses solitary [193]confinement as a form of punishment10. It states that whenever a [194]person is convicted of an offense [195]for which the court has the power to sentence them to rigorous imprisonment, the court [196]may order that the offender be kept in solitary confinement for any portion of the imprisonment, not exceeding three months in total, according to the same scale as mentioned above. BNS 11: Reflects updated legal terminology and provisions in the new Bharatiya Nyaya Sanhita. IPC 73: Part of the older Indian Penal Code framework, now replaced by BNS 11.

BNS Section 12

Definition: Limit of Solitary Confinement Section 12 of the Bharatiya Nyaya Sanhita (BNS) 2023 outlines the limits on solitary [197]confinement as a form of punishment. It states that: Duration: [198]Solitary confinement shall not exceed 14 days at a time. Intervals: There must be intervals between periods of solitary confinement of at least the same duration as the confinement itself. Extended Imprisonment: If the total imprisonment exceeds three months, solitary confinement shall not exceed 7 [199]days in any one month.

Illustration: If a person is sentenced to solitary confinement, they can be isolated for up to 14 days, followed by a break of at least 14 days before the next period of confinement can begin.

---

[193] blog.scconline.com

[194] pdfcookie.com

[195] www.scribd.com

[196] blog.scconline.com

[197] blog.scconline.com

[198] pdfcookie.com

[199] www.ijser.org

Example: Suppose a person is sentenced to 6 months of imprisonment, including solitary confinement. The court can impose solitary confinement for up to 7 days each month, with breaks [200]of at least 7 days between each period.

Comment: This section ensures that solitary confinement is used in a controlled and humane manner, preventing excessive isolation that could lead to severe mental and physical health issues. It balances the need for punishment with the [201]rights and well-being of the prisoner.

Comparison: Section 74 of the Indian Penal Code (IPC) also addresses the limits on solitary confinement and is similar to BNS 12: IPC Section 74: States that solitary confinement shall not exceed [202]14 days at a time, with intervals between periods of confinement of at least the same duration. If the total imprisonment exceeds three months, solitary confinement shall not exceed [203]7 days in any one month. BNS 12: Reflects updated legal terminology and provisions in the new Bharatiya Nyaya Sanhita. IPC 74: Part of the older Indian Penal Code framework, now replaced by BNS 12.

BNS Section 13

Definition: [204]Enhanced Punishment for Certain Offences After Previous Conviction Section 13 of the Bharatiya Nyaya Sanhita (BNS) 2023 provides for enhanced punishment for repeat offenders. It states that if a person has been previously convicted by a court in India for an offense punishable with imprisonment for three years or more, and they are subsequently convicted of another offense under the same chapters, they shall be subject to imprisonment for life or imprisonment for a term which may extend to ten years.

---

[200]www.scribd.com

[201] www.ijser.org

[202]pdfcookie.com

[203]www.ijser.org

[204] pdfcookie.com

Illustration: If a [205]person is convicted of a serious offense under Chapter X of BNS and sentenced to imprisonment for five years, and later commits another offense under the same chapter, they could face life imprisonment or imprisonment up to ten years.

Example: Suppose a person is convicted of theft (punishable with imprisonment for three years) and later commits another theft. The court may impose a harsher sentence, such as imprisonment for life or up to ten years, due to the previous conviction.

Comment: This section aims to deter repeat offenses by imposing stricter penalties on repeat offenders. It ensures that individuals who have previously been convicted of serious crimes face more severe consequences if they reoffend, thereby promoting public safety and justice.

Comparison: Section 75 of the Indian Penal Code (IPC) also addresses enhanced punishment for repeat offenders. It states that if a person has been previously convicted by a court in India for an offense punishable with imprisonment for three years or more, and they are subsequently convicted of another offense under the same chapters, they shall be subject to imprisonment for life or imprisonment for a term which may extend to ten years. BNS 13: Reflects updated legal terminology and provisions in the new Bharatiya Nyaya Sanhita. IPC 75: Part of the older Indian Penal Code framework, now replaced by BNS 13.

[205]pdfcookie.com

CHAPTER-III; GENERAL EXCEPTIONS

BNS Section 14

Definition: [206]Act Done by a Person Bound, or by Mistake of Fact Believing Himself Bound, by Law Section 14 of the Bharatiya Nyaya Sanhita (BNS) 2023 states that: No Offense: Nothing is an offense which is done by a person who is, or who by reason of a mistake of fact and not by reason of a mistake of law in good faith believes himself to be, bound by law to do it.

Illustration: (a) A soldier fires on a mob by the order of his superior officer, in conformity with the commands of the law. The soldier has committed no offense.

(b) An officer of a court, being ordered by that court to arrest Y, and after due enquiry, believing Z to be Y, arrests Z. The officer has committed no offense.

Example: Vinod, an officer of the court, was directed to arrest Rakesh. Vinod, after investigating, arrests Amit, mistaking him to be Rakesh. This act of Vinod was not illegal since the officer was acting under a factual mistake.

Comment: This section provides legal protection for individuals who act under a mistake of fact, believing in good faith that they are bound [207]by law to perform the act9. It ensures that such individuals are not criminally liable for their actions, promoting fairness and justice in the legal system.

Comparison: Section 76 [208]of the Indian Penal Code (IPC) also addresses the same concept: IPC Section 76: States that nothing is an offense which

[206] pdfcookie.com

[207]www.courts.state.va.us

[208]pdfcookie.com

is done by a person who is, or who by reason of a mistake of fact and not by reason of a mistake of law in good faith believes himself to be, bound by law to do it. BNS 14: Reflects updated legal terminology and provisions in the new Bharatiya Nyaya Sanhita. IPC 76: Part of the older Indian Penal Code framework, now replaced by BNS 14.

BNS Section 15

Definition: Act of Judge When Acting Judicially Section 15 of the Bharatiya Nyaya Sanhita (BNS) 2023 states that: No Offense: Nothing is an offense which is done by a Judge when acting judicially in the exercise of any power which is, or which in good faith he believes to be, given to him by law.

Illustration: A judge sentences a defendant to life imprisonment. The judge is [209]not liable for any offense because they are acting within their judicial capacity and in good faith.

Example: Suppose a judge orders the arrest of an individual based on a valid warrant. Even if the individual later turns out to be innocent, the judge is not liable for any offense because they acted in good faith and within their judicial authority.

Comment: This section provides judicial immunity to judges, ensuring that they are protected from criminal liability for actions taken in the course of their judicial duties. This protection is crucial for maintaining the independence and impartiality of the judiciary, allowing judges to make decisions without fear of personal repercussions.

Comparison: Section 77 [210]of the Indian Penal Code (IPC) also addresses the same concept: IPC Section 77: States that nothing is an offense which is done by a Judge when acting judicially in the exercise of any power which is, or which in good faith he believes to be, given to him by law. BNS 15: Reflects updated legal terminology and provisions in the new

[209]pdfcookie.com

[210]pdfcookie.com

Bharatiya Nyaya Sanhita. IPC 77: Part of the older Indian Penal Code framework, now replaced by BNS 15.

BNS Section 16

Definition: Act Done Pursuant to the Judgment or Order of Court Section 16 of the Bharatiya Nyaya Sanhita (BNS) 2023 states that: No Offense: Nothing which is done in pursuance of, or which is warranted by the judgment or order of, a Court; if done whilst such judgment or order remains in force, is an offense, notwithstanding the Court may have had no jurisdiction to pass such judgment or order, provided the person doing the act in good faith believes that the Court had such jurisdiction.

Illustration: A court orders the seizure of property belonging to an individual. Even if the court later turns out to lack jurisdiction, the person executing the [211]order is not liable for any offense as long as they acted in good faith, believing the court had the authority.

Example: Suppose a court issue an order to arrest an individual. The police officer, acting in good faith, carries out the arrest. Later, it is discovered that the court did not have jurisdiction. The officer is not criminally liable for the act done pursuant to the court order.

Comment: This section provides legal protection to individuals who act in accordance with a court order, even if the court later turns out to lack jurisdiction. It ensures that those who follow court orders in good faith are not held criminally liable, promoting adherence to judicial decisions and maintaining the rule of law.

Comparison: Section 78 of the Indian Penal Code (IPC) also addresses the same concept: IPC Section 78: States that nothing which is done in pursuance of, or which is warranted by the judgment or order of, a Court of Justice; if done whilst such judgment or order remains in force, is an offense, notwithstanding the Court may have had no jurisdiction to pass such judgment or order, provided the person doing the act in good faith

[211]pdfcookie.com

believes that the Court had such jurisdiction. BNS 16: Reflects updated legal terminology and provisions in the new Bharatiya Nyaya Sanhita. IPC 78: Part of the older Indian Penal Code framework, now replaced by BNS 16.

BNS Section 17

Definition: Act Done by a Person Justified, or by Mistake of Fact Believing Himself Justified, by Law Section 17 of the Bharatiya Nyaya Sanhita (BNS) 2023 states that: No Offense: Nothing is an offense which is done by any person who is justified by law, or who by reason of a mistake of fact and not by reason of a mistake of law in good faith, believes himself to be justified by law, in doing it.

Illustration: (a) A sees Z[212] commit what appears to A to be a murder. A, in the exercise, to the best of his judgment exerted in good faith, of the power which the law gives to all persons of apprehending murderers in the fact, seizes Z, in order to bring Z before the proper authorities. A has committed no offense, though it may turn out that Z was acting in self-defense.

Example: Vijay believed that Rakesh was brutally hitting another person and forcefully stopped him. Here, Vijay has committed no offense because he acted under a factual mistake in good faith, believing he was justified by law.

Comment: This section provides a legal defense for individuals who commit acts that would otherwise be offenses, as long as they are either justified by law or genuinely believe in good faith, due to a mistake of fact, that they are justified by law. It ensures that individuals are not criminally liable for actions taken under such beliefs, promoting fairness and justice in the legal system.

Comparison: Section 79 of the Indian Penal Code (IPC) also addresses the same concept: IPC Section 79: States that nothing is an offense which is done by any person who is justified by law, or who by reason of a

[212] pdfcookie.com

mistake of fact and not by reason of a mistake of law in good faith, believes himself to be justified by law, in doing it. BNS 17: Reflects updated legal terminology and provisions in the new Bharatiya Nyaya Sanhita. IPC 79: Part of the older Indian Penal Code framework, now replaced by BNS 17.

BNS Section 18

Definition: Accident in Doing a Lawful Act Section 18 of the Bharatiya Nyaya Sanhita (BNS) 2023 states that: No Offense: Nothing is an offense which is done by accident or misfortune, and without any criminal intention or knowledge in the doing of a lawful act in a lawful manner by lawful means and with proper care and caution.

Illustration: A is at work with a hatchet; the head flies off and kills a man who is standing by. Here, if there was no want of proper caution on the part of A, his act is excusable and not an offense.

Example: Vijay, while driving carefully and within the speed limit, accidentally hits a pedestrian who suddenly moved in front of his car. Here, Vijay has committed no crime, as he was following all traffic rules and had no intention to hit anyone.

Comment: This section provides a [213]defense for individuals who cause harm accidentally while performing a lawful act with due care and caution. It ensures that people are not criminally liable for unintended consequences that occur despite their responsible behavior.

Comparison: With IPC Section 80 of the Indian Penal Code (IPC) also addresses the same concept: IPC Section 80: States that nothing is an offense which is done by accident or misfortune, and without any criminal intention or knowledge in the doing of a lawful act in a lawful manner by lawful means and with proper care and caution. 18: Reflects updated legal terminology and provisions in the new Bharatiya Nyaya Sanhita. IPC 80: Part of the older Indian Penal Code framework, now replaced by BNS 18.

---

[213] pdfcookie.com

BNS Section 19

Definition: Act Likely to Cause Harm, but Done Without Criminal Intent, and to Prevent Other Harm Section 19 of the Bharatiya Nyaya Sanhita (BNS) 2023 states that: No Offense: Nothing is an offense merely by reason of its being done with the knowledge that it is likely to cause harm, if it be done without any criminal intention to cause harm, and in good faith for the purpose of preventing or avoiding other harm to person or property.

Illustration: A, the captain of a vessel, suddenly, and without any fault or negligence on his part, finds himself in such a position that, before he can stop his vessel, he must inevitably run down a [214]boat B, with twenty people on board, unless he changes his course and runs down a vessel C, with only two people on board. A change his course and runs down vessel C. A has committed no offense.

Example: Suppose a [215]doctor administers a drug to a patient to save their life, knowing that the drug might have side effects. If the doctor acts in good faith and without any criminal intent, they are not liable for any offense.

Comment: This section provides a defence for individuals who take actions that might cause harm, but do so to prevent a greater harm. It ensures that people are not criminally liable for unintended consequences if they act in good faith and without criminal intent.

Comparison: Section 81 of the Indian Penal Code (IPC) also addresses the same concept: IPC Section 81: States that nothing is an offense which is done by a person, and which is likely to cause harm, if it is done without any criminal intention to cause harm, and in good faith for the purpose of preventing or avoiding other harm to person or property. BNS 19: Reflects updated legal terminology and provisions in the new Bharatiya Nyaya

[214] www.bareactslive.com

[215] pdfcookie.com

Sanhita. IPC 81: Part of the older Indian Penal Code framework, now replaced by BNS 19.

BNS Section 20

Definition: Act of a Child Under Seven Years of Age Section 20 of the Bharatiya Nyaya Sanhita (BNS) 2023 states that: No Offense: Nothing is an offense which is done by a child under seven years of age.

Illustration: A child under seven years old accidentally breaks a neighbour's window while playing. The child cannot be held criminally liable for this act.

Example: Suppose a six-year-old child takes a toy from a store without paying. The child cannot be charged with theft because they are under seven years old.

Comment: This section is based on the principle of doli incapax, which means that children under seven years of age are presumed incapable of forming the necessary criminal intent to commit an offense. It recognizes that children at this age lack the mental capacity to understand the nature and consequences of their actions.

Comparison: Section 82 of the Indian Penal Code (IPC) also addresses the same concept: IPC Section 82: States that nothing is an offense which is done by a child under seven years of age. BNS 20: Reflects updated legal terminology and provisions in the new Bharatiya Nyaya Sanhita. IPC 82: Part of the older Indian Penal Code framework, now replaced by BNS 20.

BNS Section 21

Definition: Act of a Child Above Seven and Under Twelve of Immature Understanding Section 21 of the Bharatiya Nyaya Sanhita (BNS) [216]2023 states that: No Offense: Nothing is an offense which is

---

[216] pdfcookie.com

done by a child above seven years of age and under twelve, who has not attained sufficient maturity of understanding to judge the nature and consequences of their conduct on that occasion.

Illustration: A child aged nine years, who does not understand the consequences of setting a small fire, accidentally causes damage to property. This child cannot be held criminally liable if it is proven that they lacked the maturity to understand their actions.

Example: Suppose an eleven-year-old child, without understanding the danger, throws a stone that breaks a window. If it is shown that the child lacks the maturity to comprehend the consequences, they cannot be held criminally liable.

Comment: This section is based on the principle that children within this age range may not fully understand the nature and consequences of their actions. It ensures that such children are not unfairly punished for acts committed without mature understanding, promoting a more compassionate approach to juvenile justice.

Comparison: Section 83 of the Indian Penal Code (IPC) also addresses the same concept: IPC Section 83: States that nothing is an offense which is done by a child above seven years of age and under twelve, who has not attained sufficient maturity of understanding to judge the nature and consequences of their conduct on that occasion. BNS 21: Reflects updated legal terminology and provisions in the new Bharatiya Nyaya Sanhita. IPC 83: Part of the older Indian Penal Code framework, now replaced by BNS 21.

BNS Section 22

Definition: Act of a Person of Unsound Mind Section 22 of the Bharatiya Nyaya Sanhita (BNS) 2023 states that: No Offense: Nothing is an offense which is done by a person who, at the time of doing it, by reason of unsoundness of mind, [217]is incapable of knowing the nature of the act, or that he is doing what is either wrong or contrary to law.

---

[217] pdfcookie.com

Illustration: A person suffering from a severe mental disorder, who is unaware of the nature of their actions, accidentally causes damage to property. This person cannot be held criminally liable because they lack the capacity to understand their actions.

Example: Suppose someone with a mental illness, believing they are acting in self- defence, harms another person without understanding the wrongfulness of their actions. This person would not [218]be held criminally responsible under this section.

Comment: This section provides a defence for individuals who commit acts while suffering from unsoundness of mind, ensuring they are not criminally liable if they are incapable of understanding the nature of their actions or that what they are doing is wrong or illegal. It upholds the principle that criminal liability requires both the act (actus reus) and the guilty mind (mens rea).

Comparison: With IPC Section 84 of the Indian Penal Code (IPC) also addresses the same concept: IPC Section 84: States that nothing is an offense which is done by a person who, at the time of doing it, by reason of unsoundness of mind, is incapable of knowing the nature of the act, or that he is doing what is either wrong or contrary to law. BNS 22: Reflects updated legal terminology and provisions in the new Bharatiya Nyaya Sanhita. IPC 84: Part of the older Indian Penal Code framework, now replaced by BNS 22.

BNS Section 23

Definition: Act of a Person [219]Incapable of Judgment by Reason of Intoxication Caused Against His Will Section 23 of the Bharatiya Nyaya Sanhita (BNS) 2023 states that: No Offense: Nothing is an offense which is done by a person who, at the time of doing it, is, by reason of intoxication, incapable of knowing the nature of the act, or that he is doing what is either wrong, or contrary to law; provided

---

[218]law.emory.edu

[219]Ministry of Home Affairs. (2024). The Bharatiya Nyaya Sanhita, 2023. Retrieved from https://www.mha.gov.in/sites/default/files/250883_english_01042024.pdf

that the thing which intoxicated him was administered to him without his knowledge or against his will.

Illustration: A person is unknowingly given a drink that contains a strong sedative. While under the influence, they commit an act that [220]they would not have done if sober. This person cannot be held criminally liable because the intoxication was involuntary.

Example: Suppose someone is drugged without their knowledge and, while under the influence, they damage property. Since the intoxication was [221]against their will, they are not criminally responsible for the act.

Comment: This section provides a [222]defence for individuals who commit acts while involuntarily intoxicated, ensuring they are not criminally liable if they were incapable of understanding the nature or wrongfulness of their actions due to the intoxication. It recognizes that involuntary intoxication impairs judgment and should not be grounds for criminal liability.

Comparison: Section 85 [223]of the Indian Penal Code (IPC) also addresses the same concept: IPC Section 85: States that [224]nothing is an offense which is done by a person who, at the time of doing it, is, by reason of intoxication, incapable of knowing the nature of the act, or that he is doing what is either wrong, or contrary to law; provided that the thing which intoxicated him was administered to him without his knowledge or against his will. BNS 23: Reflects updated legal terminology and provisions in the new Bharatiya Nyaya Sanhita. IPC 85: Part of the older Indian Penal Code framework, now replaced by BNS 23.

---

[220]dsc.duq.edu

[221]docplayer.net

[222]digitalcommons.lmu.edu

[223]lawtimesjournal.in

[224]bprd.nic.in

BNS Section 24

Definition: [225] Offence requiring a particular intent or knowledge committed by one who is intoxicated.

Illustration: A person, while voluntarily intoxicated, commits an act that requires specific intent, such as theft. They will be treated as if they had the necessary intent, even though they were intoxicated.

Example: Suppose someone drinks alcohol voluntarily and then decides to drive. If they cause an accident, they will be held accountable as if they were sober, because driving requires a particular intent and knowledge.

Comment: This section addresses the legal responsibility of individuals who commit offenses requiring specific intent or knowledge while intoxicated. It establishes that voluntary intoxication does not exempt them from liability, except in cases where the intoxication was involuntary.

Comparison: Section 86 [226]of the Indian Penal Code (IPC) also addresses the same concept: IPC Section 86: States that [227]in cases where an act done is not an offense unless done with a particular knowledge or intent, a person who does the act in a state of intoxication shall be liable to be dealt with as if he had the same knowledge as he would have had if he had not been intoxicated, unless the thing which intoxicated him was administered to him without his knowledge or against his will. BNS 24: Reflects updated legal terminology and provisions in the new Bharatiya Nyaya Sanhita. IPC 86: Part of the older Indian Penal Code framework, now replaced by BNS 24.

---

[225] Ministry of Home Affairs. (2024). The Bharatiya Nyaya Sanhita, 2023. Retrieved from https://www.mha.gov.in/sites/default/files/250883_english_01042024.pdf

[226]lawtimesjournal.in

[227]bprd.nic.in

BNS Section 25

Definition: Act Not Intended and Not Known to Be Likely to Cause [228]Death or Grievous Hurt, Done by Consent Section 25 of the Bharatiya Nyaya Sanhita (BNS) 2023 states that: No Offense: Nothing which is not intended to cause death, or grievous hurt, and which is not known by the doer to be likely to cause death or grievous hurt, is an offense by reason of any harm which it may cause, or be intended by the doer to cause, to any person, above eighteen years of age, who has given consent, whether express or implied, to suffer that harm; or by reason of any harm which it may be known by the doer to be likely to cause to any such person who has consented to take the risk of that harm.

Illustration: A and Z agree to fence with each other. A accidentally injures Z, but A neither intended to cause harm nor [229]knew that the act was likely to cause grievous hurt. Z had consented to the risk of harm by agreeing to fence.

Example: Suppose a person consents to participate in a game of rugby, knowing there is a risk of injury. If they get hurt during the game, the player who caused the injury [230]is not liable for an offense, provided the act was not intended to cause grievous hurt and was [231]not known to be likely to do so.

Comment: This section provides a legal defence for acts that cause harm but are [232]done with the consent of the person harmed, as long as the harm was neither intended nor [233]known to be likely to cause death or grievous hurt. It emphasizes the importance of consent in determining criminal

---

[228] Ministry of Home Affairs. (2024). The Bharatiya Nyaya Sanhita, 2023. Retrieved from https://www.mha.gov.in/sites/default/files/250883_english_01042024.pdf

[229] www.lawfinderlive.com

[230] pdfcookie.com

[231] bprd.nic.in

[232] pdfcookie.com

[233] bprd.nic.in

liability and ensures that individuals are not held criminally responsible for consensual acts that result in unintended harm.

Comparison: Section 87 [234]of the Indian Penal Code (IPC) also addresses the same concept: IPC Section 87: States that [235]nothing which is not intended to cause death, or grievous hurt, and which is not known by the doer to be likely to cause death or grievous hurt, is an offense by reason of any harm which it may cause, or be intended by the doer to cause, to any person, above eighteen years of age, who has given consent, whether express or implied, to suffer that harm; or by reason of any harm which it may be known by the doer to be likely to cause to any such person who has consented to take the risk of that harm. BNS 25: Reflects updated legal terminology and provisions in the new Bharatiya Nyaya Sanhita. IPC 87: Part of the older Indian Penal Code framework, now replaced by BNS 25.

BNS Section 26

Definition: Act Not Intended to Cause Death, Done by Consent in Good Faith for Person's Benefit Section 26 of the Bharatiya Nyaya [236]Sanhita (BNS) 2023 states that: No Offense: Nothing which is not intended to cause death, is an offense by reason of any harm which it may cause, or be intended by the doer to cause, or be known by the doer to be likely to cause, to any person for whose benefit it is done in good faith, and who has given a consent, whether express or implied, to suffer that harm or to take the risk of that harm.

Illustration: A surgeon, knowing that a particular operation is likely to cause the death of the patient, but not intending to cause death, and having the patient's consent, performs the operation in good faith for the patient's benefit. A has committed no offense.

---

[234] lawtimesjournal.in

[235] bprd.nic.in

[236] Ministry of Home Affairs. (2024). The Bharatiya Nyaya Sanhita, 2023. Retrieved from https://www.mha.gov.in/sites/default/files/250883_english_01042024.pdf

Example: Suppose a patient consents to a high-risk surgery to remove a tumor. The surgeon, acting in [237]good faith and without intending to cause death, performs the surgery. Even if the patient dies, the surgeon is not liable for an offense [238]under this section.

Comment: This section provides a defence for acts done in good faith for the benefit of another person, with their consent, even if [239]there is a risk of harm. It emphasizes the importance of intent and consent in determining criminal liability, ensuring that individuals acting with good intentions and proper consent are not held criminally responsible for unintended consequences.

Comparison: With IPC Section 88Section 88 of the Indian Penal Code (IPC) also addresses the same concept: IPC Section 88: States [240]that nothing, which is not [241]intended to cause death, is an offense by reason of any harm which it may cause, or be intended by the doer to cause, or be known by the doer to be likely to cause, to any person for whose benefit it is done in good faith, and who has given a consent, whether express or implied, to suffer that harm or to take the risk of that harm. BNS 26: Reflects updated legal terminology and provisions in the new Bharatiya Nyaya Sanhita. IPC 88: Part of the older Indian Penal Code framework, now replaced by BNS 26.

BNS Section 27

Definition: Act Done in Good Faith for Benefit of [242]Child or Person, by or by Consent of Guardian Section 27 of the Bharatiya Nyaya Sanhita (BNS) 2023 states that:No Offense: Nothing which is done in good faith for the benefit of a person under twelve years of age, or of

---

[237] pdfcookie.com

[238]bprd.nic.in

[239] lawtimesjournal.in

[240] www.icsi.edu

[241]bprd.nic.in

[242] Ministry of Home Affairs. (2024). The Bharatiya Nyaya Sanhita, 2023. Retrieved from https://www.mha.gov.in/sites/default/files/250883_english_01042024.pdf

unsound mind, by or by consent, either express or implied, of the guardian or other person having lawful charge of that person, is an offense by reason of any harm which it may cause or be intended by the doer to cause, or be known by the doer to be likely to cause to that person.

Illustration: A, in good faith, for his child's benefit, without the child's consent, performs a minor surgery. A has committed no offense if the action is done for the child's benefit and with the guardian's consent.

Example: Suppose a parent gives consent for their child to undergo a medical procedure that is necessary for the child's health, even though the child does not fully understand the procedure. The medical professional performing the procedure is not liable for any offense as long as [243]it is done in good faith for the child's benefit.

Comment: This section provides a defence for acts done in good faith for the benefit of children or individuals of unsound mind with the consent of their guardians. It ensures that individuals acting with good intentions and proper consent are not held criminally responsible for unintended harm.

Comparison: Section 89 of the [244]Indian Penal Code (IPC) also addresses the same concept: IPC Section 89: States that [245]nothing which is done in good faith for the benefit of a person under twelve years of age, or [246]of unsound mind, by or by consent, either express or implied, of the guardian or other person having lawful charge of that person, is an offense by reason of any harm which it may cause or be intended by the doer to cause, or be known by the doer to be likely to cause to that person. BNS 27: Reflects updated legal terminology and provisions in the new Bharatiya Nyaya Sanhita. IPC 89: Part of the older Indian Penal Code framework, now replaced by BNS 27.

---

[243]bprd.nic.in

[244]lawtimesjournal.in

[245]bprd.nic.in

[246]pdfcookie.com

BNS Section 28

Definition: Consent Known to Be Given [247]Under Fear or Misconception Section 28 of the Bharatiya Nyaya Sanhita (BNS) 2023 states that: Consent Not Valid: A consent is not such a consent as it intended by any section of this Sanhita, if the consent is given by a person under fear of injury, or under a misconception of fact, and if the person doing the act knows, or has reason to believe, that the consent was given in consequence of such fear or misconception.

Illustration: A threatens to harm B if B does not sign a contract. B, fearing for their safety, signs the contract. B's [248]consent is not valid because it was given under fear of injury.

Example: Suppose a person is deceived into consenting to a financial transaction because they were given false information about the benefits. If the person who obtained the consent knew about the deception, the consent is not valid under this section.

Comment: This section ensures that consent obtained through fear or misconception is not legally valid. It protects individuals from being exploited or coerced into agreements or actions that they would not have willingly undertaken if they had not been misled or intimidated. It emphasizes the importance of genuine and informed consent in legal and social transactions.

Comparison: with IPC Section 90Section 90 of the Indian Penal Code (IPC) also addresses the same concept: IPC Section 90: States that a [249]consent is not such a consent as is intended by any section of this [250]Code, if the consent is given by a person under fear of injury, or under a misconception of fact, and if the person doing the act knows, or has reason to believe, that the consent was given in consequence of such fear

---

[247] Ministry of Home Affairs. (2024). The Bharatiya Nyaya Sanhita, 2023. Retrieved from https://www.mha.gov.in/sites/default/files/250883_english_01042024.pdf

[248]www.icsi.edu

[249]bprd.nic.in

[250] pdfcookie.com

or misconception. BNS 28: Reflects updated legal terminology and provisions in the new Bharatiya Nyaya Sanhita. IPC 90: Part of the older Indian Penal Code framework, now replaced by BNS 28.

BNS Section 29

Definition: Exclusion of Acts Which Are Offences [251]Independently of Harm Caused Section 29 of the Bharatiya Nyaya Sanhita (BNS) 2023 states that: No Exception: The exceptions in sections 25, 26, and 27 do not extend to acts which are offenses independently of any harm which they may cause, or be intended to cause, or be known to be likely to cause, to the person giving the consent, or on whose behalf the consent is given.

Illustration: Causing a miscarriage (unless done in good faith for the purpose of saving the life of the woman) is an offense independently of any harm it may cause. Therefore, it is not an offense "by reason of such harm," and the consent of the woman or her guardian does not justify the act.

Example: Suppose a person consents to a medical procedure that involves a high risk of harm. If the act itself is inherently illegal (e.g., causing a miscarriage without medical necessity), the consent does not make it lawful.

Comment: This section clarifies that certain acts remain criminal regardless of the harm caused or consent given. It ensures that illegal acts cannot be justified by consent if they are inherently wrong.

Comparison: Section 91 of the [252]Indian Penal Code (IPC) also addresses the same concept: IPC Section 91: States that the exceptions in sections 87, 88, [253]and 89 do not extend to acts which are offenses [254]independently

---

[251] Ministry of Home Affairs. (2024). The Bharatiya Nyaya Sanhita, 2023. Retrieved from https://www.mha.gov.in/sites/default/files/250883_english_01042024.pdf

[252] lawtimesjournal.in

[253] pdfcookie.com

[254] bprd.nic.in

of any harm which they may cause, or be intended to cause, or be known to be likely to cause, to the person giving the consent, or on whose behalf the consent is given. BNS 29: Reflects updated legal terminology and provisions in the new Bharatiya Nyaya Sanhita. IPC 91: Part of the older Indian Penal Code framework, now replaced by BNS 29.

BNS Section 30

Definition: Act Done in Good Faith for Benefit of a Person Without Consent Section 30 of the Bharatiya Nyaya Sanhita[255] (BNS) 2023 states that: No Offense: Nothing is an offense by reason of any harm which it may cause to a person for whose benefit it is done in good faith, even without that person's consent, if the circumstances are such that it is impossible for that person to signify consent, or if that person is incapable of giving consent, and has no guardian or other person in lawful charge of him from whom it is possible to obtain consent in time for the thing to be done with benefit. Provided that this exception shall not extend to:(a) the intentional causing of death, or the attempting to cause death;(b) the doing of anything which the person doing it knows to be likely to cause death.

Illustration: A doctor administers emergency treatment to an unconscious patient who cannot give consent. The treatment is done in good faith for the patient's benefit, and the doctor [256]is not liable for any harm caused.

Example: Suppose a person finds an unconscious individual in a life-threatening situation and performs a medical procedure to save their life without obtaining consent. [257]The act is done in good faith, and [258]the person is not criminally liable.

Comment: This section provides a legal defence for acts done in good faith for the benefit of a person who is unable to give consent and has no

---

[255] Ministry of Home Affairs. (2024). The Bharatiya Nyaya Sanhita, 2023. Retrieved from https://www.mha.gov.in/sites/default/files/250883_english_01042024.pdf

[256] pdfcookie.com

[257] www.icsi.edu

[258] bprd.nic.in

guardian to provide consent on their behalf. It ensures that individuals acting with good intentions are not held criminally responsible for unintended harm in such circumstances.

Comparison: Section 92 of the Indian Penal Code (IPC) also addresses the same concept : IPC Section 92: States that nothing is an offense by reason of any harm which it may cause to a person for whose benefit it is done in good faith, even without that person's consent, if the circumstances are such that it is impossible for that person to signify consent, or if that person is incapable of giving consent, and has no guardian or other person in lawful charge of him from whom it is possible to obtain consent in time for the thing to be done with benefit. Provided that this exception shall not extend to:(a) the intentional causing of death, or the attempting to cause death;(b) the doing of anything which the person doing it knows to be likely to cause death. BNS Reflects updated legal terminology and provisions in the new Bharatiya Nyaya Sanhita. IPC 92: Part of the older Indian Penal Code framework, now replaced by BNS 30.

BNS Section 31

Definition: Communication Made in Good Faith Section 31 of the [259]Bharatiya Nyaya Sanhita (BNS) 2023 states that: No Offense: No communication made in good faith is an offense by reason of any harm to the person to whom it is made, if it is made for the benefit of that person.

Illustration: A surgeon, in good faith, communicates to a patient his opinion that he cannot live. The patient dies in consequence of the shock. The surgeon has committed no offense, though he knew it to be likely that the communication might cause the patient's death.

Example: A doctor tells Vijay that he has a serious health problem that needs urgent care. Vijay gets a heart attack due to this shocking news.

[259] Ministry of Home Affairs. (2024). The Bharatiya Nyaya Sanhita, 2023. Retrieved from https://www.mha.gov.in/sites/default/files/250883_english_01042024.pdf

Here, the doctor told Vijay about his health in good faith and for Vijay's benefit. Here, the doctor has committed no offense.

Comment: This section provides protection for individuals who communicate honestly and with good intentions, even if the information causes unintended harm. It emphasizes the importance of intent behind the communication, ensuring that well-meaning individuals are not held criminally responsible for the consequences of their honest communication.

Comparison: [260]Section 93 of the Indian Penal Code (IPC) also addresses the same concept: IPC Section 93: States that [261]no communication made in good faith is an offense by reason of any harm to the person to whom it is made, if it is made for the benefit of that person. BNS 31: Reflects updated legal terminology and provisions in the new Bharatiya Nyaya Sanhita11.IPC 93: Part of the older Indian Penal Code framework, now replaced by BNS 31.

BNS Section 32

Definition: Act to Which a Person is Compelled by [262]Threats Section 32 of the Bharatiya Nyaya Sanhita (BNS) 2023 states that: No Offense: Except murder, and offences against the State punishable with death, nothing is an offense which is done by a person who is compelled to do it by threats, which, at the time of doing it, reasonably cause the apprehension that instant death to that person will otherwise be the consequence. Provided that the person doing the act did not of his own accord, or from a reasonable apprehension of harm to himself short of instant death, place himself in the situation by which he became subject to such constraint.

[260]lawtimesjournal.in

[261]bprd.nic.in

[262] Ministry of Home Affairs. (2024). The Bharatiya Nyaya Sanhita, 2023. Retrieved from https://www.mha.gov.in/sites/default/files/250883_english_01042024.pdf

Illustration: A person is threatened with immediate death if they do not commit a theft. They comply with the threat to save their life. This act is not considered an offense under this section.

Example: Suppose someone is kidnapped and threatened with death unless they rob a bank. The person, [263]under the fear of instant death, commits the robbery. This act is not considered an offense under this section.

Comment: This section provides a legal defence for individuals who commit acts under the threat of immediate death, except in cases of murder or offenses [264]against the State punishable with death. It ensures that individuals who act under duress, with a reasonable fear of instant death, [265]are not held criminally responsible for those acts.

Comparison: Section 94 of the Indian Penal Code (IPC) also addresses the same concept: IPC Section 94: States that [266]except murder, and offences against the State punishable with death, nothing is an offense which is done by a person who is compelled to do it by threats, which, at the time of doing it, reasonably cause the apprehension that instant death to that person will otherwise be the consequence. Provided the person doing the act did not of his own accord, or from a reasonable apprehension of harm to himself short of instant death, place himself in the situation by which he became subject to such constraint. BNS 32: Reflects updated legal terminology and provisions in the new Bharatiya Nyaya Sanhita. IPC 94: Part of the older Indian Penal Code framework, now replaced by BNS 32.

[263]www.lawfinderlive.com

[264] bprd.nic.in

[265] lawtimesjournal.in

[266] bprd.nic.in

BNS Section 33

Definition: Act Causing Slight Harm Section 33 of the [267]Bharatiya Nyaya Sanhita (BNS) 2023 states that: No Offense: Nothing is an offense by reason that it causes, or that it is intended to cause, or that it is known to be likely to cause, any harm, if that harm is so slight that no person of ordinary sense and temper would complain of such harm.

Illustration: While getting out of a bus, Rakesh slightly bumps into Vijay, causing a minor scratch. Since the harm is so slight, Rakesh has not committed any offense.

Example: Suppose someone accidentally steps on another person's foot, causing a small bruise. The harm is minimal and would not be complained about by a person of ordinary sense and temper, so it is not considered an offense under this section.

Comment: This section provides a legal defense for acts that cause minimal or slight harm, ensuring that trivial injuries or inconveniences are not subject to criminal liability. It acknowledges that not every small injury or inconvenience warrants legal action, promoting a practical approach to minor harms.

Comparison: with IPC Section 95Section 95 of the Indian Penal Code (IPC) also addresses the same concept: IPC Section 95: States that nothing is an offense [268]by reason that it causes, or that it is intended to cause, or that it is known to be likely to cause, any harm, if that harm is so slight that no person of ordinary sense and temper would complain of such harm. BNS 33: Reflects updated legal terminology and provisions in the new Bharatiya Nyaya Sanhita. IPC 95: Part of the older [269]Indian Penal Code framework, now replaced by BNS 33.

---

[267] Ministry of Home Affairs. (2024). The Bharatiya Nyaya Sanhita, 2023. Retrieved from https://www.mha.gov.in/sites/default/files/250883_english_01042024.pdf

[268] bprd.nic.in

[269]pdfcookie.com

BNS Section 34

Definition: Things done in private defence.

Illustration: A kidnapper confines a person in a locked room for four days without their consent. This act falls under wrongful confinement for more than three days.

Example: Suppose an individual is held against their will in a house for five days. The person responsible for the confinement can be charged under this section.

Comment: This section addresses the serious nature of wrongful confinement, especially when it extends beyond three days. It provides a clear legal framework for punishing such acts, emphasizing the protection of personal liberty and the severe consequences for those who violate it.

Comparison: Section 96 [270]of the Indian Penal Code (IPC) addresses the [271]right to private defence: IPC Section 96: States that nothing is an offense which is done in the exercise of the right of private defence. This means that actions taken in self-defence or defence of others are not considered offenses: BNS 34: Focuses on the punishment for wrongful confinement lasting three days or more. IPC 96

BNS Section 35

Definition: [272]Right of Private Défense of Body and of Property Section 35 of the Bharatiya Nyaya Sanhita (BNS) 2023 states that : Right to Defend: Every person has a right, subject to the restrictions contained in section 37, to defend:(a) his own body, and the body of any other person, against any offence affecting the human body;(b) the property, whether movable or immovable, of himself or of any other person, against any act which is an offence falling under the

---

[270]lawtimesjournal.in

[271] bprd.nic.in

[272] Ministry of Home Affairs. (2024). The Bharatiya Nyaya Sanhita, 2023. Retrieved from https://www.mha.gov.in/sites/default/files/250883_english_01042024.pdf

definition of theft, robbery, mischief or criminal trespass, or which is an attempt to commit theft, robbery, mischief or criminal trespass.

Illustration: Vijay sees someone attacking Priya and therefore pushes and hits the attacker. Here, Vijay has exercised [273]the right to private defence by [274]helping another person out of danger, and is therefore protected under the law.

Example: Suppose someone attempts to break into your house. You use reasonable force to stop them, protecting your property. This act is justified under the right of private defence.

Comment: This section ensures that individuals have the right to protect themselves and others from harm, as well as their property from theft, robbery, mischief, or criminal trespass. It emphasizes the importance of using reasonable force in such situations and sets limitations to prevent excessive use of force.

Comparison: Section 97 of the Indian Penal Code (IPC) also addresses the same concept: IPC Section 97: [275]States that every person has a right, subject to the restrictions contained in section 99, to defend:(a) [276]his own body, and the body of any other person, against any offence affecting the human body;(b) the property, whether movable or immovable, of himself or of any other person, against any act which is an offence falling under the definition of theft, robbery, mischief or criminal trespass, or which is an attempt to commit theft, robbery, mischief or criminal trespass. Reflects updated legal terminology and provisions in the new Bharatiya Nyaya Sanhita. IPC 97: Part of the older Indian Penal Code framework, now replaced by BNS 35.

[273] pdfcoffee.com

[274] www.ezylegal.in

[275] egyankosh.ac.in

[276] bprd.nic.in

BNS Section 36

Definition: Right of Private Defence Against [277]the Act of a Person of Unsound Mind, etc. Section 36 of the Bharatiya Nyaya Sanhita (BNS) 2023 states that : Right to Defend: When an act, which would otherwise be a certain offense, is not considered that offense due to the youth, lack of maturity of understanding, unsoundness of mind, or intoxication of the person doing the act, or due to any misconception on the part of that person, every person has the same right of private defense against that act as they would have if the act were that offense.

Illustration: Z, a person of unsound mind, attempts to kill A. Z is not guilty of any offense due to his unsound mind. However, [278]A has the same right of private defense as if Z were sane.

Example: A enters a house at night, which he is legally entitled to enter. Z, in good faith, mistakes A for a house-breaker and attacks A. Z commits no offense due to the misconception, but A has the same right of private defense as if Z were committing a house-breaking.

Comment: This section ensures that individuals have the right to defend themselves against acts that would normally be offenses, even if the person committing the act is not legally responsible due to youth, lack of understanding, unsound mind, intoxication, or misconception. It balances the need for self- defense with the recognition of diminished responsibility in certain situations.

Comparison: Section 98 [279]of the Indian Penal Code (IPC) also addresses the same concept: IPC Section 98: States that [280]when an act, which would otherwise be a certain offense, is not that offense due to the youth, lack of

---

[277] Ministry of Home Affairs. (2024). The Bharatiya Nyaya Sanhita, 2023. Retrieved from https://www.mha.gov.in/sites/default/files/250883_english_01042024.pdf

[278] bprd.nic.in

[279] egyankosh.ac.in

[280] bprd.nic.in

maturity of understanding, unsoundness of mind, intoxication of the person doing the act, or any misconception on the part of that person, every person has the same right of private defense against that act as they would have if the act were that offense. BNS 36: Reflects updated legal terminology and provisions in the new Bharatiya Nyaya Sanhita. IPC 98: Part of the older [281]Indian Penal Code framework, now replaced by BNS 36.

BNS Section 37

Definition: Act against which there is [282] no right to private defence, Extent to which the right may be exercised.

Illustration: A police officer, acting in good faith, detains a person for questioning. The detention does not cause any apprehension of death or grievous hurt. The person cannot [283]claim the right of private defense against this act.

Example: Suppose a public servant, such as a municipal officer, is performing their duties and accidentally causes minor harm to a citizen. The citizen cannot claim private defense as the act does not cause apprehension of death or grievous hurt.

Comment: This section clarifies the limitations on the right of private defense, ensuring that individuals cannot claim self- defense against acts by public servants acting in good faith or when there is time to seek protection from public authorities. It also emphasizes that the use of force in self-defense must be proportionate to the threat faced.

Comparison: Section 99 of the Indian Penal Code (IPC) also addresses the same concept: IPC Section 99: [284]States that there is no right of private defense against an act which does not reasonably cause the apprehension

---

[281] www.ezylegal.in

[282] Ministry of Home Affairs. (2024). The Bharatiya Nyaya Sanhita, 2023. Retrieved from https://www.mha.gov.in/sites/default/files/250883_english_01042024.pdf

[283] www.latestlaws.com

[284] www.ezylegal.in

of death or of grievous hurt, if done, or attempted to be done, by a public servant acting in good faith under color of his office, though that act may not be strictly justifiable by law. There is no right of private defense against an act which does not reasonably cause the apprehension of death or of grievous hurt, if done, or attempted to be done, by the direction of a public servant acting in good faith under color of his office, though that [285]direction may not be strictly justifiable by [286]law. There is no right of private defense in cases in which there is time to have recourse to the protection of the public authorities. The right of private defense in no case extends to the inflicting of more harm than it is necessary to inflict for the purpose of defense. BNS 37: Reflects updated legal terminology and provisions in the new Bharatiya Nyaya Sanhita. IPC 99: Part of the older Indian Penal Code framework, now replaced by BNS 37.

BNS Section 38

Definition: When the Right of [287]Private Defense of Property Extends to Causing Death Section 38 of the Bharatiya Nyaya Sanhita (BNS) 2023 states that: Right to Defend: The right of private defense of property extends, under the restrictions specified in section 37, to the voluntary causing of death or of any other harm to the assailant, if the offence which occasions the exercise of the right be of any of the descriptions hereinafter enumerated, namely:(a) such an assault as may reasonably cause the apprehension that death will otherwise be the consequence of such assault;(b) such an assault as may reasonably cause the apprehension that grievous hurt will otherwise be the consequence of such assault;(c) an assault with the intention of committing rape;(d) an assault with the intention of gratifying unnatural lust;(e) an assault with the intention of kidnapping or abducting;(f) an assault with the intention of wrongfully confining a

---

[285] bprd.nic.in

[286] egyankosh.ac.in

[287] Ministry of Home Affairs. (2024). The Bharatiya Nyaya Sanhita, 2023. Retrieved from https://www.mha.gov.in/sites/default/files/250883_english_01042024.pdf

person, under circumstances which may expose the person to the risk of death or grievous hurt, if the confinement is not prevented.

Illustration: A person breaks into a house with the intention of committing theft. The owner, fearing for their life, uses force that results in the death of the intruder. This act is justified under the right of private defense.

Example: Suppose someone attempts to kidnap a child, and the parent uses force to prevent the kidnapping, resulting in the death of the kidnapper. This act is justified under the right of private defense.

Comment: This section provides a legal justification for using force, including causing death, to protect property under specific circumstances. It emphasizes that the use of force must be reasonable and proportionate to the threat faced, and it must fall under the specified categories of assault.

Comparison: Section 100 of the Indian Penal Code (IPC) also addresses the same concept : IPC Section 100: States [288]that the right of private defense of the body extends, under the restrictions mentioned in the last preceding section, to the voluntary causing of death or of any other harm to the assailant, if the offence which occasions the exercise of the right be of any of the descriptions hereinafter enumerated, namely:(a) such an assault as may reasonably cause the apprehension that death will otherwise be the consequence of such assault;(b) such an assault as may reasonably cause the apprehension that grievous hurt will otherwise be the consequence of such assault;(c) an assault with the intention of committing rape;(d) an assault with the intention of gratifying unnatural lust;(e) an assault with the intention of kidnapping or abducting;(f) an assault with the intention of wrongfully confining a person, under circumstances which may expose the person to the risk of death or grievous hurt, if the confinement is not prevented. BNS 38: Reflects updated legal terminology and provisions in the new Bharatiya Nyaya Sanhita. IPC 100: Part of the older Indian Penal Code framework, now replaced by BNS 38.

---

[288] pdfcoffee.com

BNS Section 39

Definition: When Such [289]Right Extends to Causing Any Harm Other Than Death Section 39 of the Bharatiya Nyaya Sanhita (BNS) 2023 states that: Right to Defend: If the offense is not of the descriptions specified in section 38, the right of private defense of the body does not extend to the voluntary causing of death to the assailant, but does extend, under the restrictions mentioned in section 37, to the voluntary causing to the assailant of any harm other than death.

Illustration: Rakesh is screaming at Vijay. Vijay cannot use his right to private defense to kill Rakesh. However, Vijay can push Rakesh to stop him from causing further harm.

Example: Suppose someone tries to steal your bicycle. You can use reasonable force to stop them, but you cannot kill them under the right of private defense.

Comment: This section clarifies that [290]the right of private defense does not extend to causing death unless the situation falls under the severe criteria outlined in section 38. It ensures that individuals can protect themselves and others from harm without resorting to lethal force unless absolutely necessary.

Comparison: Section 101 [291]of the Indian Penal Code (IPC) also addresses the same concept: IPC Section 101: States that if the offense is not of the descriptions enumerated in the last preceding section, the right of private defense [292]of the body does not extend to the voluntary causing of death to the assailant, but does extend, under the restrictions mentioned in section 99, to the voluntary causing to the assailant of any harm other than death. BNS 39: Reflects updated legal terminology and provisions in

---

[289] Ministry of Home Affairs. (2024). The Bharatiya Nyaya Sanhita, 2023. Retrieved from https://www.mha.gov.in/sites/default/files/250883_english_01042024.pdf

[290] pdfcoffee.com

[291] egyankosh.ac.in

[292] bprd.nic.in

the new Bharatiya Nyaya Sanhita. IPC 101: Part of the older Indian Penal Code framework, now replaced by BNS 39.

BNS Section 40

Definition: [293]Commencement and Continuance of the Right of Private Defense of the Body Section 40 of the Bharatiya Nyaya Sanhita (BNS) 2023 states that: Commencement: The right of private defense of the body commences as soon as a reasonable apprehension of danger to the body arises from an attempt or threat to commit the offence, even if the offence has not yet been committed. Continuance: The right continues as long as such apprehension of danger to the body continues.

Illustration: If someone threatens to hit you with a stick, you have the right to defend yourself as soon as you reasonably fear the threat, even if they haven't actually swung the stick yet.

Example: Suppose someone tries to grab your bag forcefully, and you fear they might harm you. You can use reasonable force to prevent the theft and protect yourself.

Comment: This section ensures that individuals can act in self-defense as soon as they reasonably apprehend danger, even if the actual offense has not yet occurred. It emphasizes the importance of timely and proportionate response to threats.

Comparison: with IPC Section 102Section 102 of the Indian Penal Code (IPC) also addresses the same concept: IPC Section 102: States that the right of private defense [294]of the body commences as soon as a reasonable apprehension of danger to the body arises from an attempt or threat to commit the offence, though the offence may not have been committed; and it continues as long as such apprehension of danger to the body continues. BNS 40: Reflects updated legal terminology and provisions in the new

---

[293] Ministry of Home Affairs. (2024). The Bharatiya Nyaya Sanhita, 2023. Retrieved from https://www.mha.gov.in/sites/default/files/250883_english_01042024.pdf

[294] bprd.nic.in

Bharatiya Nyaya Sanhita. IPC 102: Part of the older Indian Penal Code framework, now replaced by BNS 40.

BNS Section 41

Definition: When the Right of Private Defense of Property [295]Extends to Causing Death Section 41 of the Bharatiya Nyaya Sanhita (BNS) 2023 states that: Right to Defend: The right of private defense of property extends, under the restrictions specified in section 37, to the voluntary causing of death or of any other harm to the wrong-doer, if the offence, the committing of which, or the attempting to commit which, occasions the exercise of the right, be an offence of any of the descriptions hereinafter enumerated, namely:(a) robbery;(b) house-breaking after sunset and before sunrise;(c) mischief by fire or any explosive substance committed on any building, tent, or vessel, which building, tent, or vessel is used as a human dwelling, or as a place for the custody of property;(d) theft, mischief, or house-trespass, under such circumstances as may reasonably cause apprehension that death or grievous hurt will otherwise be the consequence of such theft, mischief, or house-trespass.

Illustration: If someone breaks into your house at night with the intention of committing theft, and you apprehend that they might cause grievous hurt, you can use force that results in their death to protect your property.

Example: Suppose an individual attempts to set fire to your warehouse, which is used to store valuable goods. You can use force, including causing death, to stop them if you reasonably believe that the act could result in grievous hurt or death.

Comment: This section provides a legal justification for using lethal force to protect property under specific circumstances. It emphasizes that the use of such force must be reasonable and proportionate to the threat faced, and it must fall under the specified categories of offenses.

---

[295] Ministry of Home Affairs. (2024). The Bharatiya Nyaya Sanhita, 2023. Retrieved from https://www.mha.gov.in/sites/default/files/250883_english_01042024.pdf

Comparison: with IPC Section 103Section 103 of the Indian Penal Code (IPC) also addresses the same concept : IPC Section 103: [296]States that the right of private defense of property extends, under the restrictions mentioned in section 99, to the voluntary causing of death or of any other harm to the wrong-doer, if the offence, the committing of which, or the attempting to commit which, occasions the exercise of the right, be an offence of any of the descriptions hereinafter enumerated, namely:(a) robbery;(b) house-breaking by night;(c) mischief by fire committed on any building, tent, or vessel, which building, tent, or vessel is used as a human dwelling, or as a place for the custody of property;(d) theft, mischief, or house-trespass, under such circumstances as may reasonably cause apprehension that death or grievous hurt will otherwise be the consequence of such theft, mischief, or house-trespass. BNS 41: Reflects updated legal terminology and provisions in the new Bharatiya Nyaya Sanhita.IPC 103: Part of the older Indian Penal Code framework, now replaced by BNS 41.

BNS Section 42

Definition: When Such Right Extends to Causing Any Harm Other Than Death Section 42 of the [297]Bharatiya Nyaya Sanhita (BNS) 2023 states that: Right to Defend: If the offense, the committing of which, or the attempting to commit which, occasions the exercise of the right of private defense, be theft, mischief, or criminal trespass, not of any of the descriptions enumerated in section 41, that right does not extend to the voluntary causing of death, but does extend, subject to the restrictions mentioned in section 37, to the voluntary causing to the wrong-doer of any harm other than death.

Illustration: If someone tries to steal your car, you can use reasonable force to stop them, but you cannot kill them.

---

[296] pdfcoffee.com

[297] Ministry of Home Affairs. (2024). The Bharatiya Nyaya Sanhita, 2023. Retrieved from https://www.mha.gov.in/sites/default/files/250883_english_01042024.pdf

Example: Suppose a person attempts to vandalize your property. You can use force to prevent the damage, but you cannot use lethal force.

Comment: This section ensures that individuals can protect their property from theft, mischief, or trespass using reasonable force, but without causing death. It emphasizes proportionality in the use of force, ensuring that it is appropriate to the threat faced.

Comparison: Section 104 of the Indian Penal Code (IPC) also addresses the same concept : IPC Section 104: States that [298]if the offence, the committing of which, or the attempting to commit which, occasions the exercise of the right of private defense, be theft, mischief, or criminal trespass, not of any of the descriptions enumerated in the last preceding section, that right does not extend to the voluntary causing of death, but does extend, subject to the restrictions mentioned in section 99, to the voluntary causing to the wrong-doer of any harm other than death. BNS 42: Reflects updated legal terminology and provisions in the new Bharatiya Nyaya Sanhita. IPC 104: Part of the older Indian Penal Code framework, now replaced by BNS 42.

BNS Section 43

Definition: Commencement and [299]Continuance of the Right of Private Defense of Property Section 43 of the Bharatiya Nyaya Sanhita (BNS) 2023 states that: Commencement: The right of private defense of property commences when a reasonable apprehension of danger to the property arises. Continuance: Against Theft: Continues until the offender has affected his retreat with the property, or the assistance of the public authorities is obtained, or the property has been recovered. Against Robbery: Continues as long as the offender causes or attempts to cause death, hurt, or wrongful restraint, or as long as the fear of instant death, hurt, or personal restraint continues. Against Criminal Trespass or Mischief: Continues as long as the

[298] bprd.nic.in

[299] Ministry of Home Affairs. (2024). The Bharatiya Nyaya Sanhita, 2023. Retrieved from https://www.mha.gov.in/sites/default/files/250883_english_01042024.pdf

offender continues in the commission of criminal trespass or mischief. Against House-Breaking After Sunset and Before Sunrise: Continues as long as the house-trespass which has been begun by such house-breaking continues.

Illustration: If someone tries to steal your bicycle, you have the right to defend it as soon as you reasonably fear the theft. This right continues until the thief retreats with the bicycle or you recover it with the help of authorities.

Example: Suppose an intruder breaks into your house at night. You can use force to stop them, and this right continues as long as the intruder is committing the trespass.

Comment: This section ensures that individuals can act in defense of their property as soon as they reasonably apprehend danger. It also clarifies the duration of this right, depending on the nature of the offense [300]and the actions of the offender.

Comparison: Section 105 of the Indian Penal Code (IPC) also addresses the same concept: IPC Section 105: States that the right of private defense [301]of property commences when a reasonable apprehension of danger to the property arises. The right against theft continues until the offender has affected his retreat with the property, or [302]the assistance of the public authorities is obtained, or the property has been recovered. The right against robbery continues as long as the offender causes or attempts to cause death, hurt, or wrongful restraint, or as long as the fear of instant death, hurt, or [303]personal restraint continues. The right against criminal trespass or mischief continues as long as the offender continues in the commission of criminal trespass or mischief. The right against house breaking after sunset and before sunrise continues as long as the house-trespass which has been begun by such house-breaking continues BNS 43: Reflects updated legal terminology and provisions in the new Bharatiya

---

[300] www.nluo.ac.in

[301] egyankosh.ac.in

[302] bprd.nic.in

[303] egyankosh.ac.in

Nyaya Sanhita. IPC 105: Part of the older Indian Penal Code framework, now replaced by BNS 43.

BNS Section 44

Definition: Right of Private [304]Defense Against Deadly Assault When There Is Risk of Harm to Innocent Person Section 44 of the Bharatiya Nyaya Sanhita (BNS) 2023 states that: Right to Defend: If in the exercise of the right of private defense against an assault which reasonably causes the apprehension of death, the defender is so situated that he cannot effectually exercise that right without risk of harm to an innocent person, his right of private defense extends to the running of that risk.

Illustration: A person is [305]attacked by a mob that attempts to murder him. He cannot effectively defend himself without firing on the mob, and he cannot fire without risking harm to young children who are mingled with the mob. If he harms any of the children while defending himself, he commits no offence.

Example: Vijay is attacked by a mob, and he can only protect himself by risking harm to innocent bystanders. In this situation, Vijay's right of private defense extends to running the risk of harming the innocent bystanders.

Comment: This section acknowledges that in some situations, urgent action is necessary to prevent a deadly assault, even if it poses a risk to innocent persons. It ensures that individuals can defend themselves effectively without being held liable for unintended harm to by standers. **Comparison:** Section 106 of the Indian Penal Code (IPC) also addresses the same concept: IPC Section 106: States that if in the exercise of the right of private defence against an assault which reasonably causes the apprehension of death, the defender is so situated that he cannot effectually exercise that right without risk of harm to an innocent person, his right of

---

[304] Ministry of Home Affairs. (2024). The Bharatiya Nyaya Sanhita, 2023. Retrieved from https://www.mha.gov.in/sites/default/files/250883_english_01042024.pdf

[305]bprd.nic.in

private defence extends to the running of that risk. BNS 44: Reflects updated legal terminology and provisions in the new Bharatiya Nyaya Sanhita. IPC 106: Part of the older Indian Penal Code framework, now replaced by BNS 44.

CHAPTER-IV; OF ABETMENT, CRIMINAL CONSPIRACY AND ATTEMPT OF ABETMENT

BNS Section 45

Definition: Abetment of a Thing Section 45 of the [306]Bharatiya Nyaya Sanhita (BNS) 2023 states that: Abetment: A person abets the doing of a thing, who:(a) Instigates any person to do that thing;(b) Engages with one or more other persons in any conspiracy for the doing of that thing, if an act or illegal omission takes place in pursuance of that conspiracy, and in order to the doing of that thing;(c) Intentionally aids, by any act or illegal omission, the doing of that thing.

Illustration: A instigates B to commit theft. B commits the theft as a result of A's instigation.

Example: Suppose C and D conspire to commit a robbery. During the robbery, E intentionally aids them by providing a getaway vehicle.

Comment: This section defines the concept of abetment, which involves instigating, conspiring with, or aiding [307]in the commission of an offense. It highlights the different ways a person can be held responsible for abetting a crime, even if they do not directly commit the crime themselves.

Comparison: Section 107 [308]of the Indian Penal Code (IPC) also addresses the same concept: IPC Section 107: States that [309]a person abets the doing of a thing, who:(a) Instigates any person to do that thing;(b) Engages with one or more other persons in any conspiracy for the doing

[306] Ministry of Home Affairs. (2024). The Bharatiya Nyaya Sanhita, 2023. Retrieved from https://www.mha.gov.in/sites/default/files/250883_english_01042024.pdf

[307] pdfcookie.com

[308] egyankosh.ac.in

[309] bprd.nic.in

of that thing, if an act or illegal omission takes place in pursuance of that conspiracy, and in order to the doing of that thing;(c) Intentionally aids, by any act or illegal omission, the doing of that thing. BNS 45: Reflects updated legal terminology and provisions in the new Bharatiya Nyaya Sanhita. IPC 107: Part of the older Indian Penal Code framework, now replaced by BNS 45.

BNS Section 46

Definition: Abettor Section 46 of the[310] Bharatiya Nyaya Sanhita (BNS) 2023 defines an abettor as a person who abets an offense, meaning a person who:(a) Instigates any person to do that thing; or(b) Engages with one or more other persons in any conspiracy for the doing of that thing, if an act or illegal omission takes place in pursuance of that conspiracy, and in order to the doing of that thing; or(c) Intentionally aids, by any act or illegal omission, the doing of that thing.

Illustration: A encourages B to commit [311]theft. B commits the theft. A is an abettor because he instigated B to commit the offense.

Example: Suppose C and D plan to commit a fraud. E helps them by providing false documents. E is an abettor because he aided in the commission of the offense.

Comment: This section highlights the role of an abettor [312]in the commission of an offense, emphasizing that instigating, conspiring, or aiding in a crime makes a person legally responsible as an abettor. It underscores the importance of addressing not just the principal offender but also those who facilitate or encourage the crime.

---

[310] Ministry of Home Affairs. (2024). The Bharatiya Nyaya Sanhita, 2023. Retrieved from https://www.mha.gov.in/sites/default/files/250883_english_01042024.pdf

[311] bprd.nic.in

[312] hyderabadpolice.gov.in

Comparison: Section 108 of the Indian Penal Code (IPC) also defines an abettor: IPC Section 108: States [313]that a person abets an offense who:(a) [314]Instigates any person to do that thing; or(b) Engages with one or more other persons in any conspiracy for the doing of that thing, if an act or illegal omission takes place in pursuance of that conspiracy, and in order to the doing of that thing; or(c) Intentionally aids, by any act or illegal omission, the doing of that thing. BNS 46: Reflects updated legal terminology and provisions in the new Bharatiya Nyaya Sanhita. IPC 108: Part of the older Indian Penal Code framework, now replaced by BNS 46.

BNS Section 47

Definition: Abetment in India of Offences Outside India Section 47 [315]of the Bharatiya Nyaya Sanhita (BNS) 2023 states that: Abetment: A person abets an offence within the meaning of this Sanhita who, in India, abets the commission of any act without and beyond India which would constitute an offence if committed in India.

Illustration: A, in India, instigates B, a foreigner in country X, to commit a murder in that country. A is guilty of abetting murder.

Example: Vijay from India, instigates and aids Zack in Australia, to commit bank robbery. Here, Vijay is guilty of abetting robbery.

Comment: This section ensures that individuals in India can be held accountable for abetting crimes committed outside India, provided the act would be considered an offence if committed within India. It extends the jurisdiction of Indian law to acts that have cross-border implications.

Comparison: Section 108A of the [316]Indian Penal Code (IPC) also addresses the same concept: IPC Section 108A: States [317]that a person

---

[313] prsindia.org

[314] bprd.nic.in

[315] Ministry of Home Affairs. (2024). The Bharatiya Nyaya Sanhita, 2023. Retrieved from https://www.mha.gov.in/sites/default/files/250883_english_01042024.pdf

[316] hyderabadpolice.gov.in

[317] prsindia.org

abets an offence within the meaning of this Code who, in India, abets the commission of any act without and beyond India which would constitute an offence if committed in India. BNS 47: Reflects updated legal terminology and provisions in the new Bharatiya Nyaya Sanhita. IPC 108A: Part of the older Indian Penal Code framework, now replaced by BNS 47.

BNS Section 48

Definition: Abetment Outside India for Offence in India Section 48[318] of the Bharatiya Nyaya Sanhita (BNS) 2023 states that: Abetment: A person abets an offence within the meaning of this Sanhita who, without and beyond India, abets the commission of any act in India which would constitute an offence if committed in India.

Illustration: A, who is in the United States, instigates B, who is in India, to commit a robbery in India. A is guilty of abetting the robbery.

Example: Suppose C, residing in the UK, provides financial support and plans a cyber-attack on a bank in India. C is guilty of abetting the cyber-attack.

Comment: This section ensures that individuals who commit acts of abetment from outside India can be held accountable if the act would be considered an offence if committed within India. It extends the jurisdiction of Indian law to cross-border criminal activities.

Comparison: Section 108A of the [319]Indian Penal Code (IPC) also addresses the same concept: IPC Section 108A: [320]States that any person who instigates someone in India to commit an offence outside India shall be guilty of an offence. BNS 48: Reflects updated legal terminology and provisions in the new Bharatiya Nyaya Sanhita. IPC 108A: Part of the older Indian Penal Code framework, now replaced by BNS 48.

---

[318] Ministry of Home Affairs. (2024). The Bharatiya Nyaya Sanhita, 2023. Retrieved from https://www.mha.gov.in/sites/default/files/250883_english_01042024.pdf

[319] hyderabadpolice.gov.in

[320] indiankanoon.org

BNS Section 49

Definition: Punishment [321]of Abetment If act abetted is committed in consequence and where no express provision is made for its punishment Section 49 of the Bharatiya Nyaya Sanhita (BNS) 2023 addresses the punishment for abetment if the act abetted is committed in consequence and where no express provision is made for its punishment.

Illustration: If A instigates B to commit theft, and B commits the theft as a result of A's instigation, A is guilty of abetment under BNS 49.

Example: Suppose A encourages B to hack into a company's computer system, and B follows through with the hack. A is guilty of abetment and will face the same punishment as B for the act of hacking.

Comment: This section ensures that individuals who facilitate or encourage the commission of a crime are held accountable. It emphasizes that abettors are as culpable as those who commit the actual offense, promoting accountability and deterrence.

Classification of Offence and Punishment Classification: This offense is classified as a criminal offense due to the intent to facilitate the commission of a crime.

Punishment: The punishment for committing this offense under BNS 49 is the same as the punishment provided for the offense that was abetted.

Cognizable or Non-Cognizable, Bailable or Non-Bailable: This offense is cognizable, meaning the police can arrest the accused without a warrant.

Bailable: This offense is bailable, indicating that the accused can secure bail and be released from custody until the trial is completed.

Comparison: Section 109 of the [322]Indian Penal Code (IPC) also addresses the punishment for abetment Section 109: States that whoever abets any offense shall, if the act abetted is committed in consequence of

---

[321] Ministry of Home Affairs. (2024). The Bharatiya Nyaya Sanhita, 2023. Retrieved from https://www.mha.gov.in/sites/default/files/250883_english_01042024.pdf

[322] hyderabadpolice.gov.in

the abetment, and no express provision is made by this Code for the punishment of such abetment, be punished with the punishment provided for the offense.

Key Differences: BNS 49: Reflects updated legal terminology and provisions in the new Bharatiya Nyaya Sanhita. IPC 109: Part of the older Indian Penal Code framework, now replaced by BNS 49.

BNS Section 50

Definition: [323]Punishment of Abetment Section 50 of the Bharatiya Nyaya Sanhita (BNS) 2023 addresses the punishment for abetment if the person abetted does the act with a different intention from that of the abettor.

Illustration: If A encourages B to commit a [324]robbery with the intention of causing financial harm, but B commits the robbery with the intention of causing physical harm, A is still liable for abetment under BNS 50.

Example: Suppose A advises B to vandalize a property to protest against a policy, but B does it with the intention of stealing valuable items. A is guilty of abetment under BNS 50, as B's different intention does not absolve A of responsibility.

Comment: This section ensures that abettors are held accountable even if the person they abet acts with a different intention. It underscores the seriousness of abetment and the responsibility of instigating or facilitating a crime, regardless of the specific outcomes.

Classification of Offence and Punishment Classification: This offense is classified as a criminal offense due to the intent to facilitate the commission of a crime.

---

[323] Ministry of Home Affairs. (2024). The Bharatiya Nyaya Sanhita, 2023. Retrieved from https://www.mha.gov.in/sites/default/files/250883_english_01042024.pdf

[324] bprd.nic.in

Punishment: The punishment for committing this offense under BNS 50 is the same as the punishment provided for the [325]offense which would have been committed if the act had been done with the intention or knowledge of the abettor.

Cognizable or Non-Cognizable, Bailable or Non-Bailable: This offense is cognizable, meaning the police can arrest the accused without a warrant.

Bailable: This offense is bailable, indicating that the accused can secure bail and be released from custody until the trial is completed.

Comparison: Section 110 of the [326]Indian Penal Code (IPC) also addresses the punishment for abetment: IPC Section 110: States [327]that whoever abets the commission of an offense shall, if the person abetted does the act with a different intention or knowledge from that of the abettor, be punished with the punishment provided for the offense which would have been committed if the act had been done with the intention or knowledge of the abettor and with no other.

Key Differences: BNS 50: Reflects updated legal terminology and provisions in the new Bharatiya Nyaya Sanhita. IPC 110: Part of the older Indian Penal Code framework, now replaced by BNS 50.

BNS Section 51

Definition: Liability of Abettor When One Act [328]Abetted and Different Act Done Section 51 of the Bharatiya Nyaya Sanhita (BNS) 2023 addresses the liability of an abettor when the act committed by the person abetted is different from the one initially abetted but is a consequence of the abetment.

---

[325] wwrkds.net

[326] hyderabadpolice.gov.in

[327] prsindia.org

[328] Ministry of Home Affairs. (2024). The Bharatiya Nyaya Sanhita, 2023. Retrieved from https://www.mha.gov.in/sites/default/files/250883_english_01042024.pdf

Illustration: If A instigates B to commit theft, and B ends up committing assault instead, A is still liable for the assault as if they had directly abetted it.

Example: Suppose A encourages B to vandalize a property, but B ends up stealing from the property instead. A is liable for the theft as if they had directly abetted it.

Comment: This section ensures that abettors are held accountable for different but related acts resulting from their instigation. It highlights the principle that abetment encompasses not just the specific act instigated but also the probable consequences of that instigation.

Classification of Offence and Punishment Classification: This offense is classified as a criminal offense due to the [329]intent to facilitate the commission of a crime.

Punishment: The punishment for committing this offense under BNS 51 is the same as the punishment provided for the offense which was actually committed.

Cognizable or Non-Cognizable, Bailable or Non-Bailable: This offense is cognizable, meaning the police can arrest the accused without a warrant.

Bailable: This offense is bailable, indicating that the accused can secure bail and be released from custody until the trial is completed.

Comparison: Section 111 of the [330]Indian Penal Code (IPC) also addresses the liability of an abettor when the act committed by the person abetted [331]is different from the one initially abetted but is a consequence of the abetment: IPC Section 111: States [332]that when an act is abetted and a different act is done, the abettor is liable for the act done, in the same manner and to the same extent as if they had directly abetted it, provided

---

[329] bprd.nic.in

[330] hyderabadpolice.gov.in

[331] jajharkhand.in

[332] prsindia.org

[333]the act done was a probable consequence of the abetment and was committed under the influence of the instigation, or with the aid or in pursuance of the conspiracy which constituted the abetment.

Key Differences: BNS 51: Reflects updated legal terminology and provisions in the new Bharatiya Nyaya Sanhita. IPC 111: Part of the older Indian Penal Code framework, now replaced by BNS 51.

BNS Section 52

Definition: Abettor When [334]Liable to Cumulative Punishment for act abetted and for act done. Section 52 of the Bharatiya Nyaya Sanhita (BNS) 2023 addresses the liability of an abettor when the act abetted and the act done are distinct offenses.

Illustration: If A instigates B to resist a public servant's distress by force, and B, in resisting, also causes grievous hurt to the officer, A is liable for both the act of resisting and causing grievous hurt.

Example: Suppose A encourages B to [335]commit a robbery, and during the robbery, B also assaults a person. A is liable for both the robbery and the assault.

Comment: This section ensures that abettors are held accountable for different but related acts resulting from their instigation. It highlights the principle that abetment encompasses not just the specific act instigated but also the probable consequences of that instigation.

Classification of Offence and Punishment Classification: This offense is classified as a criminal offense due to the [336]intent to facilitate the commission of multiple crimes. **Punishment:** The punishment for

---

[333] bprd.nic.in

[334] Ministry of Home Affairs. (2024). The Bharatiya Nyaya Sanhita, 2023. Retrieved from https://www.mha.gov.in/sites/default/files/250883_english_01042024.pdf

[335] prsindia.org

[336] bprd.nic.in

committing this offense under BNS 52 is cumulative, meaning the abettor is liable to punishment for each of the offenses committed.

Cognizable or Non-Cognizable, Bailable or Non-Bailable: This offense is cognizable, meaning the police can arrest the accused without a warrant.

Bailable: This offense is bailable, indicating that the accused can secure bail and be released from custody until the trial is completed.

Comparison: Section 112 of the [337]Indian Penal Code (IPC) also addresses the liability of an abettor when the act abetted and the act done are distinct offenses' Section 112: States that if the act for which the abettor is liable under the last preceding section is committed in addition to the act abetted, and constitutes a distinct offense, the [338]abettor is liable to punishment for each of the offenses.

Key Differences: BNS 52: Reflects updated legal terminology and provisions in the new Bharatiya Nyaya Sanhita. IPC 112: Part of the older Indian Penal Code framework, now replaced by BNS 52.

BNS Section 53

Definition: **Liability of Abettor for an Effect [339]Caused by the Act Abetted Different from That Intended by the Abettor Section 53** of the Bharatiya Nyaya Sanhita (BNS) 2023 addresses the liability of an abettor when the effect caused by the act abetted is different from the effect intended by the abettor.

Illustration: If A [340]instigates B to cause grievous hurt to Z, but Z [341]dies as a result of the [342]grievous hurt, A is liable for Z's death if A knew that the grievous hurt could cause death.

---

[337] hyderabadpolice.gov.in

[338] bprd.nic.in

[339] Ministry of Home Affairs. (2024). The Bharatiya Nyaya Sanhita, 2023. Retrieved from https://www.mha.gov.in/sites/default/files/250883_english_01042024.pdf

[340] bprd.nic.in

[341] jlrjs.com

[342] bprd.nic.in

Example: Suppose A encourages B to set fire to a building intending to cause property damage, but the fire spreads and causes injury to people. If A knew that the fire could cause injury, A is liable for the injuries caused.

Comment: This section ensures that abettors are held accountable for consequences [343]that differ from their original intent if they knew the act abetted was likely to cause those consequences. It emphasizes the serious nature of abetment and the potential for unintended harm.

Classification of Offence and Punishment Classification: This offense is classified as a criminal offense due to the intent to facilitate the commission of a crime and the resulting harm. Punishment: The punishment for committing this offense under BNS 53 is the same as the punishment provided for the offense which was actually caused, provided the abettor knew that the act abetted was likely to cause that effect.

Cognizable or Non-Cognizable, Bailable or Non-Bailable: This offense is cognizable, meaning the police can arrest the accused without a warrant.

Bailable: This offense is bailable, indicating that the accused can secure bail and be released from custody until the trial is completed.

Comparison: Section 113 [344]of the Indian Penal Code (IPC) also addresses the [345]liability of an abettor for an effect caused by the act abetted different from that intended by the abettor: IPC Section 113: States that when an act is abetted with the intention on the part of the abettor of causing a particular effect, and an act for which the abettor is liable in consequence of the abetment, causes a different effect from that intended by the abettor, the abettor is liable for the effect caused, in the same manner and to the same extent as if he had abetted the [346]act with the intention of

[343] Favourable habitats for Coffea inter-specific hybridization in central New

Caled by Clin-2010

[344] hyderabadpolice.gov.in

[345] jajharkhand.in

[346] bprd.nic.in

causing that effect, provided he knew [347]that the act abetted was likely to cause that effect.

Key Differences: BNS 53: Reflects updated legal terminology and provisions in the new Bharatiya Nyaya Sanhita. IPC 113: Part of the older Indian Penal Code framework, now replaced by BNS 53.

BNS Section 54

Definition: Abettor Present When Offence Committed Section 54 [348]of the Bharatiya Nyaya Sanhita (BNS) 2023 addresses the liability of an abettor who is present when the offense is committed.

Illustration: If A instigates B to commit theft, and A is present when B actually commits the theft, A is [349]deemed to have committed the theft as well.

Example: Suppose A encourages B to assault someone, and A is present during the assault. A is treated as if they committed the assault themselves.

Comment: This section ensures that abettors [350]who are physically present during [351]the commission of an offense are held equally accountable. It underscores the principle that being present and involved in the crime implies shared responsibility.

Classification of Offence and Punishment Classification: This offense is classified as a criminal offense due to the intent to facilitate the commission of a crime.

Punishment: The punishment for committing this offense under BNS 54 is the same as the punishment provided for the offense which was actually committed.

---

[347] prsindia.org

[348] Ministry of Home Affairs. (2024). The Bharatiya Nyaya Sanhita, 2023. Retrieved from https://www.mha.gov.in/sites/default/files/250883_english_01042024.pdf

[349] jajharkhand.in

[350] Critical care organization, by Chang, Steven Y. M- 2005

[351] bprd.nic.in

Cognizable or Non-Cognizable, Bailable or Non-Bailable: This offense is cognizable, meaning the police can arrest the accused without a warrant.

Bailable: This offense is bailable, indicating that the accused can secure bail and be released from custody until the trial is completed.

Comparison: Section 114 of the [352]Indian Penal Code (IPC) also addresses the liability of an abettor who is present when the offense is committed: IPC Section 114: States [353]that whenever any person, who [354]would be liable to be punished as an abettor if absent, is present when the act or offense for which they would be punishable in consequence of the abetment is committed, they shall be deemed to have committed such act or offense.

Key Differences: BNS 54: Reflects updated legal terminology and provisions in the new Bharatiya Nyaya Sanhita. IPC 114: Part of the older Indian Penal Code framework, now replaced by BNS 54.

BNS Section 55

Definition: Abetment of Offence Punishable with Death or [355]Imprisonment for Life Section 55 of the Bharatiya Nyaya Sanhita (BNS) 2023 addresses the punishment for abetting an offense punishable with death or imprisonment for life.

Illustration: If A instigates B to commit murder, but B does not commit the murder, A is still liable for abetment.

Example: Suppose A encourages B to kidnap someone with the intent of demanding a ransom, but B does not go through with the kidnapping. A is still liable for abetment under BNS 55.

[352] hyderabadpolice.gov.in

[353] prsindia.org

[354] bprd.nic.in

[355] Ministry of Home Affairs. (2024). The Bharatiya Nyaya Sanhita, 2023. Retrieved from https://www.mha.gov.in/sites/default/files/250883_english_01042024.pdf

Comment: This section ensures that individuals who abet serious crimes, such as those [356]punishable by death or life imprisonment, are held accountable [357]even if the crime is not completed. It emphasizes the seriousness of abetment and its potential consequences.

Classification of Offence and Punishment Classification: This offense is classified as a criminal offense due to the intent to facilitate the commission of a serious crime.

Punishment: The punishment for committing this offense under BNS 55 is imprisonment of either description for a term which may extend to seven years, and the abettor shall also be liable to a fine. If any act causing harm is done in consequence of the abetment, the punishment increases to imprisonment of either description for a term which may extend to fourteen years, and the abettor shall also be liable to a fine.

Cognizable or Non-Cognizable, Bailable or Non-Bailable: This offense is cognizable, meaning the police can arrest the accused without a warrant.

Bailable: This offense is bailable, indicating that the accused can secure bail and be released from custody until the trial is completed.

Comparison: Section 115 of the [358]Indian Penal Code (IPC) also addresses the punishment for abetting an offense punishable with death or imprisonment for life: IPC Section 115: States [359]that whoever abets the commission of an offense punishable with death or imprisonment for life, shall, if that offense is not committed in consequence of the abetment, and no express provision is made by this [360]Code for the punishment of such abetment, be punished with imprisonment of either description for a term which may extend to seven years, and shall also be liable to fine.

---

[356] www.readbag.com

[357] bprd.nic.in

[358] hyderabadpolice.gov.in

[359] prsindia.org

[360] hyderabadpolice.gov.in

Key Differences: BNS 55: Reflects updated legal terminology and provisions in the new Bharatiya Nyaya Sanhita. IPC 115: Part of the older Indian Penal Code framework, now replaced by BNS 55.

BNS Section 56

Definition: Abetment of Offence Punishable with [361]Imprisonment Section 56 of the Bharatiya Nyaya Sanhita (BNS) 2023 addresses the punishment for abetting an offense punishable with imprisonment, even if the offense is not committed.

Illustration: If A instigates B to commit a crime punishable with imprisonment, but B does not commit the crime, A is still liable for abetment under BNS 56.

Example: Suppose A encourages B to commit fraud, but B decides not to go through with it. A is still liable for abetment under BNS 56.

Comment: This section ensures that individuals who abet crimes are held accountable even if the crime is not completed. It underscores the serious nature of abetment and the intent to facilitate criminal acts.

Classification of Offence and Punishment Classification: This offense is classified as a criminal offense due to the intent to facilitate the commission of a crime.

Punishment: The punishment for committing this offense under BNS 56 is imprisonment of any description provided for that offense for a term which may extend to one-fourth part of the longest term provided for that offense, or with such fine as is provided for that offense, or with both.

Cognizable or Non-Cognizable, Bailable or Non-Bailable: This offense is cognizable, meaning the police can arrest the accused without a warrant.

Bailable: This offense is bailable, indicating that the accused can secure bail and be released from custody until the trial is completed.

---

[361] Ministry of Home Affairs. (2024). The Bharatiya Nyaya Sanhita, 2023. Retrieved from https://www.mha.gov.in/sites/default/files/250883_english_01042024.pdf

Comparison: Section 116 of the [362]Indian Penal Code (IPC) also addresses the punishment for abetting an offense punishable with imprisonment Section 116: States that whoever abets an offense [363]punishable with imprisonment shall, if that offense is not committed in consequence of the abetment, and no express provision is made by this Code for the punishment of such abetment, be punished with imprisonment of any description provided for that offense for a term which may extend to one-fourth part of the longest term provided for that offense, or with such fine as is provided for that offense, or with both.

Key Differences: BNS 56: Reflects updated legal terminology and provisions in the new Bharatiya Nyaya Sanhita. IPC 116: Part of the older Indian Penal Code framework, now replaced by BNS 56.

BNS Section 57

Definition: Abetting Commission of Offence by [364]the Public or by More Than Ten Persons Section 57 of the Bharatiya Nyaya Sanhita (BNS) 2023 addresses the liability of an abettor who instigates the commission of an offense by the public or by a group of more than ten persons.

Illustration: If A affixes a placard in a public place instigating a sect consisting of more than ten members to meet at a certain time and [365]place for the purpose of attacking members of an adverse sect, A has committed the offense defined in this section.

Example: Suppose Vijay posts on his YouTube channel encouraging a [366]large number of people to gather at a specific location to vandalize property. Vijay would be charged under this section.

---

[362] hyderabadpolice.gov.in

[363] bprd.nic.in

[364] prsindia.org

[365] pdfcookie.com

[366] www.slideshare.net

Comment: This section ensures that individuals who instigate large groups to commit crimes are held accountable. It highlights the potential for greater harm and public disorder when crimes are instigated among larger groups, and underscores the seriousness of such abetment.

Classification of Offence and Punishment Classification: This offense is classified as a criminal offense due to the intent to instigate a group [367]to commit a crime.

Punishment: The punishment for committing this offense under BNS 57 is imprisonment of either description for a term which may extend to seven years and with a fine.

Cognizable or Non-Cognizable, Bailable or Non-Bailable: This offense is cognizable, meaning the police can arrest the accused without a warrant.

Bailable: This offense is bailable, indicating that the accused can secure bail and be released from custody until the trial is completed.

Comparison: Section 117 of the Indian Penal Code (IPC) also addresses the liability of an abettor who instigates the commission of an offense [368]by the public or by a group of more than ten persons: IPC Section 117: States [369]that whoever abets the commission of an offense by the public generally [370]or by any number or class of persons exceeding ten, shall be punished with imprisonment [371]of either description for a term which may extend to three years, [372]or with fine, or with both.

Key Differences: BNS 57: Reflects updated legal terminology and provisions in the new Bharatiya Nyaya Sanhita. IPC 117: Part of the older Indian Penal Code framework, now replaced by BNS 57.

---

[367] eparlib.nic.in

[368] prsindia.org

[369] indiankanoon.org

[370] adoc.pub

[371] eparlib.nic.in

[372] adoc.pub

BNS Section 58

Definition: Concealing Design to Commit Offence [373]Punishable with Death or Imprisonment for Life Section 58 of the Bharatiya Nyaya Sanhita (BNS) 2023 addresses the liability of an individual who conceals a design to commit an offense [374]punishable with death or imprisonment for life.

Illustration: If A knows that B is planning to commit a murder and A helps B by hiding this information from the authorities, A is liable under this section.

Example: Suppose A is aware that C is planning to commit a robbery that could result in someone's death, and A uses encryption to hide C's plan from the police. A is liable under this section.

Comment: This section ensures that individuals who conceal plans for serious crimes are held accountable. It underscores the importance of preventing crimes by holding those who facilitate such plans responsible.

Classification of Offence and Punishment Classification: This offense is classified as a criminal offense due to the intent to [375]facilitate the commission of a serious crime.

Punishment: The punishment for committing this offense under BNS 58 is: If the offense is committed: [376]Imprisonment of either description for a term which may extend to seven years, and the abettor [377]shall also be liable to a fine. If the offense is not committed: [378]Imprisonment of either

---

[373] Ministry of Home Affairs. (2024). The Bharatiya Nyaya Sanhita, 2023. Retrieved from https://www.mha.gov.in/sites/default/files/250883_english_01042024.pdf

[374] eparlib.nic.in

[375] www.bareactslive.com

[376] eparlib.nic.in

[377] adoc.pub

[378] eparlib.nic.in

description for a term which may extend to three years, and the abettor [379]shall also be liable to a fine.

Cognizable or Non-Cognizable, Bailable or Non-Bailable: This offense is cognizable, meaning the police can arrest the accused without a warrant.

Bailable: This offense is bailable, indicating that the accused can secure bail and be released from custody until the trial is completed.

Comparison: Section 118 of the Indian [380]Penal Code (IPC) also addresses the liability of an individual who conceals a design to commit an offense punishable with death or imprisonment for life: IPC Section 118: States that whoever, intending to facilitate or knowing [381]it to be likely that he will thereby [382]facilitate the commission of an offense [383]punishable with death or imprisonment for life, voluntarily conceals by any act or omission, the existence of a design to commit such offense or [384]makes any representation which he knows to be false respecting such design, shall be punished with imprisonment [385]of either description for a term which may extend to seven years, or with fine, or with both.

Key Differences: BNS 58: Reflects updated legal terminology and provisions in the new Bharatiya Nyaya Sanhita. IPC 118: Part of the older Indian Penal Code framework, now replaced by BNS 58.

---

[379] adoc.pub

[380] eparlib.nic.in

[381] pdfcookie.com

[382] www.bareactslive.com

[383] eparlib.nic.in

[384] pdfcookie.com

[385] eparlib.nic.in

BNS Section 59

Definition: Public Servant [386]Concealing Design to Commit [387]Offence Section 59 of the Bharatiya Nyaya Sanhita (BNS) 2023 addresses the liability of a public servant who conceals a design to commit an offense which it is their duty to prevent.

Illustration: If a police officer knows that a colleague is planning to commit a murder and hides this information from the authorities, the officer is liable under this section.

Example: Suppose a government official is aware of a plan to commit a large-scale fraud and uses encryption to hide this information from law enforcement. The official would be charged under this section

Comment: [388]This section ensures that public servants who fail in their duty to prevent crimes are held accountable. It emphasizes the responsibility of public servants to uphold the law and [389]prevent the commission of offenses.

Classification of Offence and Punishment Classification: This offense is classified as a criminal offense due to the breach of duty and intent to facilitate the commission of a crime.

Punishment: The punishment for committing this offense under BNS 59 is: If the offense is committed: [390]Imprisonment of any description provided for the offense, [391]for a term which may extend to one-half of the longest term of such imprisonment, or [392]with such fine as is provided for

---

[386] Ministry of Home Affairs. (2024). The Bharatiya Nyaya Sanhita, 2023. Retrieved from https://www.mha.gov.in/sites/default/files/250883_english_01042024.pdf

[387] prsindia.org

[388] scholar.sun.ac.za

[389] www.bareactslive.com

[390] pdfcookie.com

[391] adoc.pub

[392] pdfcookie.com

that offense, or with both. If the offense is [393]punishable with death or imprisonment for life: [394]Imprisonment of either description for a term which may extend to ten years. If the offense is not committed: Imprisonment of any description provided for the offense [395]for a term which may extend to one-half of the longest term of such imprisonment.

Cognizable or Non-Cognizable, Bailable or Non-Bailable: This offense is cognizable, meaning the police can arrest the accused without a warrant.

Bailable: This offense is bailable, indicating that the accused can secure bail and be released from custody until the trial is completed.

Comparison : Section 119 [396]of the Indian Penal Code (IPC) also addresses the liability of a public servant who conceals a [397]design to commit an offense which it is their duty to prevent : IPC Section 119: States that [398]whoever, being a public servant, intending to facilitate [399]or knowing it to be likely that he will thereby [400]facilitate the commission of an offense [401]which it is his duty as such public servant to prevent, voluntarily conceals, by any act or omission, the existence of a design to commit such offense, or makes any representation which he knows to be false respecting such design, [402]shall be punished with imprisonment of [403]either description for a term which may extend to seven years, or with fine, or with both.

---

[393] eparlib.nic.in

[394] pdfcookie.com

[395] adoc.pub

[396] eparlib.nic.in

[397] prsindia.org

[398] eparlib.nic.in

[399] pdfcookie.com

[400] www.bareactslive.com

[401] prsindia.org

[402]adoc.pub

[403] eparlib.nic.in

Key Differences: BNS 59: Reflects updated legal terminology and provisions in the new Bharatiya Nyaya Sanhita. IPC 119: Part of the older Indian Penal Code framework, now replaced by BNS 59.

BNS Section 60

Definition: Concealing Design to Commit Offence Punishable[404] with Imprisonment Section 60 of the Bharatiya Nyaya Sanhita (BNS) 2023 [405]addresses the liability of an individual who conceals a design to commit an offense punishable with imprisonment.

Illustration: If A knows that B is planning to commit a robbery and A helps B by hiding this information from the authorities, A is liable under this section.

Example: Suppose A is aware that C is planning to commit a fraud and uses encryption to hide C's plan from the police. A is liable under this section.

Comment: This section ensures that individuals who conceal plans for crimes are held accountable. It highlights the importance of preventing crimes by holding those who facilitate such plans responsible.

Classification of Offence and Punishment Classification: This offense is classified as a criminal offense due to the intent to [406]facilitate the commission of a crime.

Punishment: The punishment for committing this offense under BNS 60 is: If the offense is committed: [407]Imprisonment of the description provided for the offense, for a term which may extend to one-fourth of the longest term provided for that offense, or with such fine as is provided for that offense, or with both. If the offense is not committed: Imprisonment

[404] Ministry of Home Affairs. (2024). The Bharatiya Nyaya Sanhita, 2023. Retrieved from https://www.mha.gov.in/sites/default/files/250883_english_01042024.pdf

[405] prsindia.org

[406] www.bareactslive.com

[407] pdfcookie.com

of the description provided for the offense, [408]for a term which may extend to one-eighth of the longest term provided for that offense, or with such fine as is provided for that offense, or with both.

Cognizable or Non-Cognizable, Bailable or Non-Bailable: This offense is cognizable, meaning the police can arrest the accused without a warrant.

Bailable: This offense is bailable, indicating that the accused can secure bail and be released from custody until the trial is completed.

Comparison: Section 120 of the Indian [409]Penal Code (IPC) also addresses [410]the liability of an individual who conceals a design to commit an offense punishable with imprisonment Section 120: States that whoever, [411]intending to facilitate or knowing it to be likely that he will thereby [412]facilitate the commission of an offense punishable with imprisonment, voluntarily conceals, by any act or illegal omission, the existence of a design to commit such offense, [413]or makes any representation which he knows to be false respecting such design, shall, if the offense [414]be committed, be punished with imprisonment of [415]the description provided for the offense, for a term which may extend to one-fourth of the longest term provided for that offense, or with such fine as is provided for that offense, or with both. If the offense is not committed, the punishment is imprisonment of the description provided for the offense, [416]for a term which may extend to one-eighth of the longest term provided

---

[408] adoc.pub

[409] eparlib.nic.in

[410] prsindia.org

[411] pdfcookie.com

[412] www.bareactslive.com

[413] pdfcookie.com

[414] prsindia.org

[415] pdfcookie.com

[416] adoc.pub

for that offense, [417]or with such fine as is provided for that offense, or with both.

Key Differences: BNS 60: Reflects updated legal terminology and provisions in the new Bharatiya Nyaya Sanhita. IPC 120: Part of the older Indian Penal Code framework, now replaced by BNS 60.

BNS Section 61(1)

Definition: [418] Criminal Conspiracy definition Section 61(1) of Bharatiya Nyaya Sanhita (BNS) 2023 defines criminal conspiracy as follows: [419]When two or more persons agree to do, or cause to be done:(a) An illegal act; or(b) An act which is not illegal by illegal means.

Such an agreement is designated as a criminal conspiracy. However, no agreement except an agreement to commit an offense shall amount to a criminal conspiracy unless some act besides the agreement is done by one or more parties to such agreement in pursuance thereof.

Illustration: If A and B agree to rob a bank (an illegal act), their agreement constitutes a criminal conspiracy.

Example: Suppose A and C conspire to bribe a public official to secure a government contract (an illegal means to achieve a legal act). Their agreement is considered a criminal conspiracy.

Comment: The definition emphasizes that mere agreement is not enough to constitute a criminal conspiracy unless some act is done in furtherance of the agreement6. This ensures that individuals ae not penalized solely for discussing or planning a crime [420]without taking any concrete steps towards its commission.

---

[417] pdfcookie.com

[418] Ministry of Home Affairs. (2024). The Bharatiya Nyaya Sanhita, 2023. Retrieved from https://www.mha.gov.in/sites/default/files/250883_english_01042024.pdf

[419] advocatetanmoy.com

[420] abyssum.org

Classification of Offence and Punishment Classification: This offense is classified as a criminal offense due to the intent [421]to facilitate the commission of a crime.

Punishment: The punishment for committing this offense under BNS 61(1) is [422]imprisonment of either description for a term which may extend to 2 years to life, and the abettor [423]shall also be liable to a fine.

Cognizable or Non-Cognizable, Bailable or Non-Bailable: This offense is cognizable, meaning the police can arrest the accused without a warrant.

Bailable: This offense is bailable, indicating that the accused can secure bail and be released from custody until the trial is completed.

Comparison: Section 120A of the [424]Indian Penal Code (IPC) also addresses [425]the definition of criminal conspiracy: IPC Section 120A: States that when two or more persons agree to do, or cause to be done, an illegal act or an act which is not illegal by illegal means, such an agreement is designated a criminal conspiracy. The provision also specifies that no agreement except an agreement to commit an offense shall amount to a criminal conspiracy unless some act besides the agreement is done by one or more parties to such agreement in pursuance thereof.

Key Differences: BNS 61(1): Reflects updated legal terminology and provisions in the new Bharatiya Nyaya Sanhita. IPC 120A: Part of the older Indian Penal Code framework, now replaced by BNS 61(1).

---

[421] www.bareactslive.com

[422] eparlib.nic.in

[423] adoc.pub

[424] eparlib.nic.in

[425] advocatetanmoy.com

BNS Section 61(2)

Definition: Criminal Conspiracy Punishment[426] Section 61(2) of the Bharatiya Nyaya Sanhita (BNS) 2023 addresses the punishment for criminal conspiracy.

Illustration: If A and B conspire to commit a robbery (an offense punishable with imprisonment for life), they are liable under this section.

Example: Suppose A, B, and C plan to hack into a bank's computer system to steal money. Even if they are caught before executing the plan, they are liable under this section.

Comment: The section emphasizes that the punishment for criminal conspiracy is based on the severity of the intended offense. This ensures that conspirators are held accountable even if the crime is not completed.

Classification of Offence and Punishment Classification: This offense is classified as a criminal offense due to the [427]intent to facilitate the commission of a crime.

Punishment: The punishment for committing this offense under BNS 61(2) is: For [428]offenses punishable with death, imprisonment for life, [429]or rigorous imprisonment for a term of two years or upwards: The conspirator [430]shall be punished in the same manner as if he had abetted such offense. For other offenses: [431]The conspirator shall be punished with imprisonment [432]of either description for a term not exceeding six months, or with fine, or with both.

---

[426] Ministry of Home Affairs. (2024). The Bharatiya Nyaya Sanhita, 2023. Retrieved from https://www.mha.gov.in/sites/default/files/250883_english_01042024.pdf

[427] www.bareactslive.com

[428] tripakshalitigation.com

[429] prsindia.org

[430] pdfcookie.com

[431] adoc.pub

[432] eparlib.nic.in

Cognizable or Non-Cognizable, Bailable or Non-Bailable: This offense is cognizable, meaning the police can arrest the accused without a warrant.

Bailable: This offense is bailable, indicating that the accused can secure bail and be released from custody until the trial is completed.

Comparison: Section 120B of the Indian Penal Code (IPC) also addresses the punishment for criminal conspiracy : IPC Section 120B: States that whoever [433]is a party to a criminal conspiracy to commit an offense [434]punishable with death, imprisonment for life, [435]or rigorous imprisonment for a term of two years or upwards, [436]shall, where no express provision is made in [437]this Code for the punishment of such a conspiracy, be punished in the same manner as if he had abetted such offense. For other offenses, the punishment is [438]imprisonment of either description for a term not exceeding six months, or with fine, or with both.

Key Differences: BNS 61(2): Reflects updated legal terminology and provisions in the new Bharatiya Nyaya Sanhita. IPC 120B: Part of the older Indian Penal Code framework, now replaced by BNS 61(2).

BNS Section 62

Definition: Punishment for [439]Attempting to Commit Offences Punishable with Imprisonment Section 62 of the Bharatiya Nyaya Sanhita (BNS) 2023 addresses the punishment for attempting to commit offenses punishable with imprisonment for life or other imprisonment.

---

[433] prsindia.org

[434] pdfcookie.com

[435] eparlib.nic.in

[436] adoc.pub

[437] pdfcookie.com

[438] eparlib.nic.in

[439] Ministry of Home Affairs. (2024). The Bharatiya Nyaya Sanhita, 2023. Retrieved from https://www.mha.gov.in/sites/default/files/250883_english_01042024.pdf

Illustration: If A attempts to commit a robbery (an offense punishable with imprisonment for life) but is caught before completing the act, A is liable under this section.

Example: Suppose A tries to hack into a bank's computer system to steal money but fails to do so because the security system detects the attempt. A is liable under this section.

Comment: The section emphasizes that even an attempt to commit a crime is punishable, reflecting the seriousness of the intent behind the act. This ensures that individuals are held accountable for their actions even if they do not succeed in committing the full offense. **Classification of Offence and Punishment Classification:** This offense is classified as a criminal offense due to the intent to commit a crime.

Punishment: The punishment for committing this offense under BNS 62 is: For offenses punishable with imprisonment for life: [440]Imprisonment of any description provided for the offense, [441]for a term which may extend to [442]one-half of the imprisonment for life. For other offenses: Imprisonment of any description provided for the offense, [443]for a term which may extend to one-half of the longest term [444]of imprisonment provided for that offense, or with such fine as is provided for the offense, or with both.

Cognizable or Non-Cognizable, Bailable or Non-Bailable: This offense is cognizable, meaning the police can arrest the accused without a warrant.

Bailable: This offense is bailable, indicating that the accused can secure bail and be released from custody until the trial is completed.

---

[440] pdfcookie.com

[441] adoc.pub

[442] pdfcookie.com

[443] adoc.pub

[444]pdfcookie.com

Comparison: Section 511 of the [445]Indian Penal Code (IPC) also addresses the punishment for attempting to commit offenses [446]punishable with imprisonment for life or other imprisonment: IPC Section 511: States that [447]whoever attempts to commit an [448]offense punishable by this Code with imprisonment for life or imprisonment, or to cause such an offense [449]to be committed, and in such attempt does any act towards the commission of the offense, shall, where no express provision is made by this Code for the punishment of such attempt, be punished with imprisonment of any description provided for the offense, for a term which may extend to one-half of the imprisonment for life or, as the case may be, one-half of the longest term of [450]imprisonment provided for that offense, or with such fine as is provided for the offense, or with both.

Key Differences: BNS 62: Reflects updated legal terminology and provisions in the new Bharatiya Nyaya Sanhita. IPC 511: Part of the older Indian Penal Code framework, now replaced by BNS 62.

---

[445] eparlib.nic.in

[446] adoc.pub

[447] adoc.pub

[448] tripakshalitigation.com

[449] adoc.pub

[450] pdfcookie.com

CHAPTER-V; OF OFFENCES AGAINST WOMEN AND CHILD

BNS Section 63

Definition: Rape Definition[451] Section 63 of the Bharatiya Nyaya Sanhita (BNS) 2023 defines rape as: Rape: An act of sexual violation involving penetration or manipulation of the body without consent, through coercion, deception, or incapacity to consent. The section details various actions that constitute rape, including: Penetration with body parts or objects. Manipulation causing penetration.

Illustration: If a person forces another individual into a sexual act without their consent, it constitutes rape under BNS 63.

Example: Suppose someone uses physical force to engage in sexual activity with another person against their will. This act falls under BNS 63 as it involves non-consensual penetration.

Comment: This section ensures clarity in the definition of rape, focusing on the importance of consent. It aims to protect individuals from sexual violence by criminalizing non-consensual sexual acts.

Classification of Offence and Punishment Offence Classification: This offence is cognizable and non-bailable.

Punishment: The punishment for committing this offence under BNS 63 is [452]rigorous imprisonment for not less than ten years, which may extend to imprisonment for life, and a fine.

Cognizable or non-cognizable Cognizable: The police can arrest the accused without a warrant.

---

[451] en.wikipedia.org

[452] prsindia.org

Bailable or Non-Bailable: Non-Bailable Bail is not granted as a matter of right, and the accused can be released on bail only [453]at the discretion of the court.

Comparison: Section 375 [454]of the Indian Penal Code (IPC) also defines rape, detailing acts that constitute rape, including penetration without consent. However, there are some differences in the classification and punishment: IPC Section 375: Rape is a cognizable and non-bailable offence.

Punishment: The punishment under IPC Section 375 can vary, but it generally includes [455]imprisonment for a term which [456]shall not be less than seven years but which may extend to imprisonment for life and a fine.

Key Differences: BNS 63: Focuses on consent and the severity of the crime, ensuring stricter penalties. IPC 375: Provides a similar definition and classification but with a minimum imprisonment term of seven years.

BNS Section 64

Definition: Punishment for [457]Rape Section 64 of the Bharatiya Nyaya Sanhita (BNS) 2023 outlines the punishment for the crime of rape.

Illustration: If a man forces a woman to have sexual intercourse without her consent, he is committing rape under BNS 63 and is liable for punishment under BNS 64.

Example: Suppose a man coerces a woman into performing sexual acts against her will. This act falls under BNS 63 as rape, and the perpetrator will be punished under BNS 64.

---

[453] advocatetanmoy.com

[454] eparlib.nic.in

[455] eparlib.nic.in

[456] adoc.pub

[457] Ministry of Home Affairs. (2024). The Bharatiya Nyaya Sanhita, 2023. Retrieved from https://www.mha.gov.in/sites/default/files/250883_english_01042024.pdf

Comment: This section emphasizes the severe violation of a person's bodily autonomy and dignity that rape represents. It ensures stringent punishment to deter such heinous acts and protect individuals from sexual violence.

Classification of Offence and Punishment Classification: This offense is classified as a heinous criminal offense due to the severe violation of a person's bodily autonomy and dignity.

Punishment: The punishment for committing this offense under BNS 64 is: Sub-section (1): [458]Whoever, except in the cases provided for in sub-section (2), commits rape, shall be punished with rigorous imprisonment of either description for a term which shall not be less than ten years, but which may extend to imprisonment for life, and shall also be liable to a fine. Sub-section (2): Specifies harsher punishments for certain categories of offenders, such as police officers, public servants, and members of the armed forces, who commit rape under specific circumstances.

Cognizable or Non-Cognizable, Bailable or Non-Bailable: This offense is cognizable, meaning the police can arrest the accused without a warrant.

Non-Bailable: This offense is non-bailable, indicating [459]that the accused cannot secure bail and must remain in custody until the trial is completed.

Comparison: With IPC Section 376(1) & [460]376(2) Section 376 of the Indian Penal Code (IPC) also addresses the punishment for rape: IPC Section 376(1): States that [461]whoever, except in the cases provided for in sub-section (2), commits [462]rape, shall be punished with rigorous imprisonment of either description for a term which shall not be less than ten years, but which may extend to imprisonment for life, and shall also be liable to a fine. IPC Section 376(2): Specifies harsher punishments for certain categories of offenders, such as police officers, public servants, and

---

[458] eparlib.nic.in

[459] www.legalkart.com

[460] indiankanoon.org

[461] assets.publishing.service.gov.uk

[462] eparlib.nic.in

members of the armed forces, who commit rape under specific circumstances.

Key Differences: BNS 64: Reflects updated legal terminology and provisions in the new Bharatiya Nyaya Sanhita. IPC 376: Part of the older Indian Penal Code framework, now replaced by BNS 64.

BNS Section 65(1)

Definition: Punishment for Rape in [463]Certain Cases - Rape on a Woman Under Sixteen Years Section 65(1) of the Bharatiya Nyaya Sanhita (BNS) 2023 addresses the punishment for committing rape on a woman under sixteen years of age.

Illustration: [464]If a person commits rape on a girl who is fifteen years old, they are subject to the punishment outlined in BNS 65(1).

Example: Suppose an individual is found guilty of raping a fourteen-year-old girl. This act falls under BNS 65(1) and the offender will face the specified punishment.

Comment: This section emphasizes the severity of the crime [465]when the victim is a [466]minor under sixteen years of age. It aims to provide stringent punishment to deter such heinous acts and protect minors from sexual violence.

Classification of Offence and Punishment Offence Classification: This offence is cognizable and non-bailable.

Cognizable or Non-Cognizable Cognizable: The police can [467]arrest the accused without a warrant.

---

[463] Ministry of Home Affairs. (2024). The Bharatiya Nyaya Sanhita, 2023. Retrieved from https://www.mha.gov.in/sites/default/files/250883_english_01042024.pdf

[464] www.hindustantimes.com

[465] thc.nic.in

[466]pdfcoffee.com

[467] nalsarpro.org

Non-Bailable: Bail is not granted as a matter of right, and the accused can be released on bail only at the [468]discretion of the court.

Comparison: Section 376(3) [469]of the Indian Penal Code (IPC) also addresses the punishment for committing rape on a woman under sixteen years of age: IPC Section 376(3): States that whoever commits [470]rape on a woman under sixteen years of age shall be punished with rigorous imprisonment for a term which shall not be less than twenty years, but which may extend to imprisonment for life, which shall mean imprisonment for the remainder of that person's natural life, and shall also be liable to a fine.

Key Differences: BNS 65(1): Reflects updated legal terminology and provisions in the new Bharatiya Nyaya Sanhita. IPC 376(3): Part of the older Indian Penal Code framework, now replaced by BNS 65(1).

BNS Section 65 (2)

Definition: Punishment for rape in certain cases rape on a [471]woman under twelve years. of the Bharatiya Nyaya Sanhita, 2023, addresses the punishment for rape on a woman under twelve years of age.

Illustration: If a 30-year-old man is convicted of raping a 10-year-old girl, he would face a minimum of twenty years in prison, potentially extending to life imprisonment or even the death penalty, [472]depending on the severity of the case.

Example: In a recent case, a man was sentenced under BNS 65 (2) for raping a 9-year-old girl. The court imposed a life sentence and a substantial fine to cover the victim's medical and rehabilitation costs.

---

[468] icsiiip.in

[469] assets.publishing.service.gov.uk

[470] indiankanoon.org

[471] Ministry of Home Affairs. (2024). The Bharatiya Nyaya Sanhita, 2023. Retrieved from https://www.mha.gov.in/sites/default/files/250883_english_01042024.pdf

[472] www.legalkart.com

Comment: This section underscores the severe penalties for crimes against minors, reflecting the legal system's commitment to protecting vulnerable populations and deterring such heinous acts. Victim Support: The provision for fines to be directed towards the victim's medical and rehabilitation expenses highlights a victim-centric approach.

Classification of Offence and Punishment Offence Classification: [473]Whoever commits rape on a [474]woman under twelve years of age shall be punished with rigorous imprisonment for a term not less than twenty years, which may extend to life imprisonment (meaning imprisonment for the remainder of the [475]person's natural life), and with fine or with death. Fine: The fine imposed should be just and reasonable to cover the medical expenses and rehabilitation of the victim. Any fine imposed under this section shall be paid to the victim.

Classification of Offence Cognizable or Non-Cognizable: The offence is cognizable, meaning the police have the authority to arrest without a warrant and [476]start an investigation without the court's permission.

Bailable or Non-Bailable: The offence is non-bailable, indicating that bail is not a right and can only be granted at the discretion of the court.

Comparison: with IPC Section 376 (a) and (b)IPC Section 376 (a): Deals with [477]rape committed by a person in a position of trust or authority, such as a public servant, police officer, [478]or member of the armed forces. The punishment is rigorous imprisonment for a term not less than ten years, which may extend to life imprisonment, and with fine. IPC Section 376 (b): Pertains to rape committed by a person in a position of trust or authority, such as a public servant, police officer, or member of the armed

---

[473] www.hindustantimes.com

[474] ohrh.law.ox.ac.uk

[475] assets.publishing.service.gov.uk

[476] nalsarpro.org

[477] old.nmu.ac.in

[478] www.hindustantimes.com

forces, [479]on a woman under sixteen years of age. The punishment is rigorous imprisonment for a term not less than ten years, which may extend to life imprisonment, and with fine.

Key Differences: BNS 65 (2) specifically addresses victims under twelve years, whereas IPC 376 (b) addresses victims under sixteen years. Punishment Severity: BNS 65 (2) includes the possibility of the death penalty, reflecting a harsher stance compared to IPC 376 (a) and (b).

BNS Section 66

Definition: Punishment for [480]Causing Death or Resulting in Persistent Vegetative State of Victim Section 66 of the Bharatiya Nyaya Sanhita (BNS) 2023 addresses the punishment for causing death or resulting in a persistent vegetative state of the victim during the commission of an offense under sub-section (1) or sub-section (2) of section 64.

Illustration: If a man commits rape and, in the course of the act, inflicts injuries that cause the death of the woman or leave her in a persistent vegetative state, he is liable under BNS 66.

Example: Suppose a man assaults a woman during a sexual offense, causing severe brain damage that leaves her in a persistent vegetative state. This act falls under BNS 66 as it results in a severe and lasting impact on the victim.

Comment: This section emphasizes the severe consequences of causing death or a persistent vegetative state during the commission of a sexual offense. It ensures stringent punishment to deter such heinous acts and provide justice for the victims

Classification of Offence and Punishment Classification: This offense is classified as a heinous criminal offense due to the severe consequences of the act.

---

[479] indiankanoon.org

[480] assets.publishing.service.gov.uk

Punishment: The punishment for committing this offense under BNS 66 [481]is rigorous imprisonment for a term which shall [482]not be less than twenty years, but which may extend to imprisonment for life, which means imprisonment for the remainder of that person's natural life, or with death.

Cognizable or Non-Cognizable, Bailable or Non-Bailable: This offense is cognizable, meaning the police can arrest [483]the accused without a warrant.

Non-Bailable: This offense is non-bailable, indicating that the accused cannot secure bail and must remain in [484]custody until the trial is completed.

Comparison: Section 376A of the Indian Penal Code (IPC) also addresses the punishment for causing death or resulting in a persistent vegetative state of the victim: IPC Section 376A: States that whoever commits an offense punishable under sub-section (1) or sub-section (2) of section 376 and in the course of such commission inflicts an injury which causes the death of the woman or causes the woman to be in a persistent vegetative state, shall be punished with rigorous imprisonment for a term which shall not be less than twenty years, but which may extend to imprisonment for life, which means [485]imprisonment for the remainder of that person's natural life, or with death.

Key Differences: BNS 66: Reflects updated legal terminology and provisions in the new Bharatiya Nyaya Sanhita. IPC 376A: Part of the older Indian Penal Code framework, now replaced by BNS 66.

---

[481] www.legalkart.com

[482] assets.publishing.service.gov.uk

[483] nalsarpro.org

[484] www.legalkart.com

[485] assets.publishing.service.gov.uk

BNS Section 67

Definition: Sexual Intercourse by Husband Upon His Wife [486]During Separation Section 67 [487]of the Bharatiya Nyaya Sanhita (BNS) 2023 addresses the offense of sexual intercourse by a husband upon his wife during separation.

Illustration: If a [488]husband has sexual intercourse with his wife, who is living separately, without her consent, he is committing an offense under BNS 67.

Example: Suppose a husband forces his [489]wife, who is living separately under a decree of separation, to have [490]sexual intercourse without her consent. This act falls under BNS 67 as sexual intercourse by a husband upon his wife during separation.

Comment: This section emphasizes the importance of consent and bodily autonomy, even within a marriage. It ensures that a husband cannot [491]force his wife into sexual intercourse during a period of separation, recognizing the wife's right to refuse.

Classification of Offence and Punishment Classification: This offense is classified as a criminal offense due to the violation of the wife's bodily autonomy and consent.

Punishment: The punishment for committing this offense under BNS 67 is imprisonment of either description for a term which shall not be less than two years but which may extend to seven years, and the offender shall also be [492]liable to a fine.

---

[486] Ministry of Home Affairs. (2024). The Bharatiya Nyaya Sanhita, 2023. Retrieved from https://www.mha.gov.in/sites/default/files/250883_english_01042024.pdf

[487] prsindia.org

[488] indiankanoon.org

[489] eparlib.nic.in

[490] pdfcoffee.com

[491] indiankanoon.org

[492] assets.publishing.service.gov.uk

Cognizable or Non-Cognizable, Bailable or Non-Bailable: This offense is cognizable, meaning the police can [493]arrest the accused without a warrant.

Bailable: This offense is bailable, indicating that the accused can secure bail and be released from custody [494]until the trial is completed.

Comparison: Section 376B of the [495]Indian Penal Code (IPC) also addresses the offense of [496]sexual intercourse by a husband upon his wife during separation: IPC Section 376B: States that whoever has [497]sexual intercourse with his own wife, who is living separately, whether under a decree of separation or otherwise, without her consent, shall be punished with imprisonment of either description for a term which shall not be less than two years but which may extend to seven years, and shall also be liable to a fine.

Key Differences: BNS 67: Reflects updated legal terminology and provisions in the new Bharatiya Nyaya Sanhita. IPC 376B: Part of the older Indian Penal Code framework, now replaced by BNS 67.

BNS Section 68

Definition: [498]Sexual Intercourse by a Person in Authority Section 68 of the [499]Bharatiya Nyaya Sanhita (BNS) 2023 addresses the offense of sexual intercourse by a person in authority.

---

493 nalsarpro.org

494 www.legalkart.com

495 eparlib.nic.in

496 pdfcoffee.com

497 eparlib.nic.in

498 assets.publishing.service.gov.uk

499 Ministry of Home Affairs. (2024). The Bharatiya Nyaya Sanhita, 2023. Retrieved from https://www.mha.gov.in/sites/default/files/250883_english_01042024.pdf

Illustration: If a superintendent of a jail abuses his position to coerce a female inmate into having sexual intercourse with him, he is committing an offense under BNS 68.

Example: Suppose a hospital staff member uses his position to seduce a female patient under his care into having sexual intercourse. This act falls under BNS 68 as sexual intercourse by a person in authority.

Comment: This section emphasizes the abuse of [500]power and violation of trust that occurs when a person in authority coerces someone into sexual intercourse. It ensures that those in positions of power are held accountable for exploiting their authority.

Classification of Offence and Punishment Classification: This offense is classified as a criminal offense due to the abuse of power and violation of trust.

Punishment: The punishment for committing this offense under BNS 68 is [501]rigorous imprisonment of either description for a term which shall not be less than five years, but which may extend to ten years, and the offender shall also be liable to a fine.

Cognizable or Non-Cognizable, Bailable or Non-Bailable: This offense is cognizable, meaning the police can [502]arrest the accused without a warrant.

Bailable: This offense is bailable, indicating that the accused can secure bail and be released from [503]custody until the trial is completed.

Comparison: Section 376C[504] of the Indian Penal Code (IPC) also addresses the offense of sexual intercourse by a person in authority : IPC Section 376C: States that [505]whoever, being in a position of authority or in

---

[500] www.orfonline.org

[501] assets.publishing.service.gov.uk

[502] nalsarpro.org

[503] www.legalkart.com

[504] eparlib.nic.in

[505] ohrh.law.ox.ac.uk

a fiduciary relationship, or a public servant, or superintendent or manager of a jail, remand home or other place of custody established by or under any law for the time being in force, or a women's or children's institution, or on the management of a hospital or being on the staff of a hospital, abuses such position [506]or fiduciary relationship to induce or seduce any woman either in his custody or under his charge or present in the premises to have sexual intercourse with him, such sexual intercourse not amounting to the offense of rape, shall be punished with rigorous imprisonment of either description for a term which shall not be less than five years, but which may extend to ten years, and shall also be liable to a fine.

Key Differences: BNS 68: Reflects updated legal terminology and provisions in the new Bharatiya Nyaya Sanhita. IPC 376C: Part of the older Indian Penal Code framework, now replaced by BNS 68.

BNS Section 69

Definition: Sexual [507]Intercourse by Employing Deceitful Means, etc. Section 69 of the Bharatiya Nyaya Sanhita (BNS) 2023 addresses the offense of engaging in sexual intercourse by employing deceitful means or making false promises, particularly concerning marriage or employment.

Illustration: [508]If a person promises to marry someone without any intention of fulfilling that promise and engages in sexual intercourse with them, it constitutes an offense under BNS 69.

Example: Suppose an individual falsely promises a job promotion to someone in exchange for sexual favors. This act falls under BNS 69 as it involves deceitful means to engage in sexual intercourse.

---

506 eparlib.nic.in

507 Ministry of Home Affairs. (2024). The Bharatiya Nyaya Sanhita, 2023. Retrieved from https://www.mha.gov.in/sites/default/files/250883_english_01042024.pdf

508 sansad.in

Comment: [509]This section aims to protect individuals from being exploited through false promises or deceitful means. It emphasizes [510]the importance of genuine consent and criminalizes acts that manipulate or deceive individuals into sexual relations.

Classification of Offence and Punishment Offence Classification: This offense is cognizable and non-bailable.

Punishment: The punishment for committing this offense under BNS 69 is imprisonment of either description for a term which may extend to ten years and a fine.

Cognizable or non-cognizable Cognizable: The police can [511]arrest the accused without a warrant.

Bailable or non-Bailable: Bail is not granted as a matter of right, and the accused can be released on bail only [512]at the discretion of the court.

Comparison: With IPC Section Section 69 [513]of the Bharatiya Nyaya Sanhita (BNS) 2023 is a new provision.

BNS Section 70 (1)

Definition: Bharatiya Nyaya Sanhita, 2023, [514]addresses the punishment for Gang rape. BNS 70 (1) Punishment: Where a woman is raped by one or more persons constituting a group or acting in furtherance of a common intention, each of those persons shall be deemed to have committed the offence of rape and shall be punished with rigorous imprisonment for a term not less than twenty years,

[509] www.legalserviceindia.com

[510] www.legalkart.com

[511] nalsarpro.org

[512] icsiiip.in

[513] prsindia.org

[514] Ministry of Home Affairs. (2024). The Bharatiya Nyaya Sanhita, 2023. Retrieved from https://www.mha.gov.in/sites/default/files/250883_english_01042024.pdf

which may extend to life imprisonment [515](meaning imprisonment for the remainder of that person's natural life), and with fine.

Illustration: If three men are convicted of raping a woman together, each of them would face a minimum of twenty years in prison, potentially extending to life imprisonment, and a fine.

Example: In a recent case, a group of men were sentenced under BNS 70 (1) for gang-raping a woman. The court-imposed life sentences on all the perpetrators and substantial fines to cover the victim's medical and rehabilitation costs.

Comment: This section emphasizes the severe penalties for gang rape, reflecting the legal system's commitment to deterring such heinous acts and ensuring justice for the victims. The provision for fines to be directed towards the victim's medical and rehabilitation expenses highlights a victim-centric approach.

Classification of Offence Cognizable or Non-Cognizable: The offence is cognizable, meaning the police have the authority to arrest without a warrant and [516]start an investigation without the court's permission.

Bailable or Non-Bailable: The offence is non-bailable, indicating that bail is not a right and can only be granted at the discretion of the court.

Comparison: IPC Section 376D: Deals with gang rape, where a [517]woman is raped by one or more persons constituting a group or acting in furtherance of a common intention. The punishment is rigorous imprisonment for a term not less than twenty years, which may extend to life imprisonment, and with fine.

Key Differences: Both BNS 70 (1) and IPC 376D prescribe similar punishments for gang rape, emphasizing severe penalties and victim support. However, BNS 70 (1) is part of the newer [518]Bharatiya Nyaya

---

[515] www.legalkart.com

[516] nalsarpro.org

[517] eparlib.nic.in

[518]prsindia.org

Sanhita, which may include updated procedural aspects and victim support mechanisms.

BNS Section 70 (2)

Definition: Bharatiya Nyaya Sanhita, 2023, addresses [519] the punishment for gang rape on women under the age of eighteen. Text of BNS 70 (2) Punishment: Where a woman under eighteen years of age is raped by one or more persons constituting a group or acting in furtherance of a common intention, each of those persons shall be deemed to have committed the offence of rape and shall be punished with imprisonment for life, which shall mean imprisonment for the remainder of that person's natural life, and with fine, or with death.

Illustration: If a group of men are convicted of gang-raping a 17-year-old girl, each of them would face life imprisonment, potentially extending to the [520]death penalty, and a fine.

Example: In a recent case, a group of men were sentenced under BNS 70 (2) for gang-raping a 16-year-old girl. The court-imposed life sentences on all the perpetrators and substantial fines to cover the victim's medical and rehabilitation costs.

Comment: This section emphasizes the severe penalties for gang rape, especially when the victim is a minor, reflecting the legal system's commitment to deterring such heinous acts and ensuring justice for the victims. Victim Support: The provision for fines to be directed towards the victim's medical and rehabilitation expenses highlights a victim-centric approach.

Classification of Offence Cognizable or Non-Cognizable: The offence is cognizable, meaning the police have the authority to arrest without a warrant and [521]start an investigation without the court's permission.

---

[519] Ministry of Home Affairs. (2024). The Bharatiya Nyaya Sanhita, 2023. Retrieved from https://www.mha.gov.in/sites/default/files/250883_english_01042024.pdf

[520] thc.nic.in

[521] nalsarpro.org

Bailable or Non-Bailable: The offence is non-bailable, indicating that bail is not a right and can only be granted at the discretion of the court.

Comparison: IPC Section 376DB: Deals with [522]gang rape on a woman under sixteen years of age. The punishment is rigorous imprisonment for a term not less than twenty [523]years, which may extend to life imprisonment, and with fine or with death.

Key Differences: Both BNS 70 (2) and IPC 376DB prescribe severe punishments for gang rape on minors, emphasizing life [524]imprisonment or the death penalty. However, BNS 70 (2) specifically addresses victims under eighteen years, whereas IPC 376DB addresses victims under sixteen years.

BNS Section 71

Definition: Punishment for Repeat Offenders Section 71 [525]of the Bharatiya Nyaya Sanhita (BNS) 2023 addresses the punishment for repeat offenders who have been previously convicted of offenses under Sections 64, 65, 66, or 70 and are subsequently convicted of any of these offenses again.

Illustration: If a person was previously convicted of wrongful confinement under Section 65 and is later convicted again for the same offense, they would be subject to the punishment outlined in Section 71.

Example: Suppose an individual was previously convicted of gang rape under Section 70 and is later found guilty of committing gang rape again. This person would face the enhanced punishment under Section 71.

Comment: This section ensures that repeat offenders face enhanced penalties, reflecting the serious nature of repeated criminal behaviour. It aims to deter recidivism and provide justice for victims.

---

[522] prsindia.org

[523] ohrh.law.ox.ac.uk

[524] www.legalkart.com

[525] prsindia.org

Classification of Offence and Punishment Classification: This offense is classified as a criminal offense due to the serious nature of the repeated crime.

Punishment: The punishment for committing this offense under BNS 71 is imprisonment for life, which means imprisonment for the remainder of that person's natural life, or with death.

Cognizable or Non-Cognizable, Bailable or Non-Bailable: This offense is cognizable, meaning the police can [526]arrest the accused without a warrant.

Non-Bailable: This offense is non-bailable, indicating that the accused cannot secure bail and must remain [527]in custody until the trial is completed.

Comparison: Section 376E[528] of the Indian Penal Code (IPC) also addresses the punishment for repeat offenders: IPC Section 376E: States that whoever has been previously convicted of an offense punishable under Section 376, Section 376A, Section 376D, or [529]Section 376DB and is subsequently convicted of an offense [530]punishable under any of the said sections [531]shall be punished with imprisonment for life, which means [532]imprisonment for the remainder of that person's natural life, or with death.

Key Differences: BNS 71: Reflects updated legal terminology and provisions in the new Bharatiya Nyaya Sanhita. IPC 376E: Part of the older Indian Penal Code framework, now replaced by BNS 71.

---

[526] nalsarpro.org

[527] www.legalkart.com

[528] assets.publishing.service.gov.uk

[529] ohrh.law.ox.ac.uk

[530] assets.publishing.service.gov.uk

[531] eparlib.nic.in

[532] assets.publishing.service.gov.uk

BNS Section 72

Definition: Disclosure of Identity of Victim of Certain [533] Offences etc Section 72 of the Bharatiya Nyaya Sanhita (BNS) 2023 addresses the disclosure of the identity of victims of certain offenses. Voluntarily causing hurt or grievous hurt by dangerous weapons or means.

Illustration: If a newspaper [534]publishes the name or any details that could reveal the [535]identity of a victim of rape, the publisher is committing an offense under BNS 72.

Example: Suppose a media outlet releases a story about a sexual assault case and includes the victim's name and address. This act falls under BNS 72 as it discloses the victim's identity. **Comment:** This section ensures the protection of the victim's privacy and dignity by prohibiting the disclosure of their identity. It highlights the importance of maintaining confidentiality in sensitive cases to prevent further trauma and stigma.

Classification of Offence and Punishment Classification: This offense is classified as a criminal offense due to the potential harm and violation of privacy it causes to the victim. **Punishment:** The punishment for committing this offense under BNS 72 is [536]imprisonment of either description for a term which may extend to two years and the offender shall also be liable to a fine.

Cognizable or Non-Cognizable, Bailable or Non-Bailable: This offense is cognizable, meaning the police can arrest the accused without a warrant.

Bailable: This offense is bailable, indicating that the accused can secure bail and be released from custody until the trial is completed.

---

[533] Ministry of Home Affairs. (2024). The Bharatiya Nyaya Sanhita, 2023. Retrieved from https://www.mha.gov.in/sites/default/files/250883_english_01042024.pdf

[534] ohrh.law.ox.ac.uk

[535] pdfcoffee.com

[536] devgan.in

Comparison: With IPC Section 228A (1)/(2) Section 228A [537]of the Indian Penal Code (IPC) also addresses the disclosure of the[538] identity of the victim of certain offenses: IPC Section 228A (1): States that whoever prints or publishes the name or any matter which may make known the identity of any person against whom an offense [539]under Section 376, Section 376A, Section 376B, Section 376C, Section 376D, Section 376DA, or Section 376DB [540]is alleged or found to have been committed shall be punished with imprisonment of either description for a term which may extend to [541]two years, and [542]shall also be liable to a fine. IPC Section 228A (2): Provides exceptions for cases where the victim or their guardian gives written authorization to the disclosure, [543]or if the name is disclosed in the interest of justice for public good.

Key Differences: BNS 72: Reflects updated legal terminology and provisions in the new Bharatiya Nyaya Sanhita.IPC 228A (1)/(2): Word "minor' is replaced by 'child'. Part of the older Indian Penal Code framework, now replaced by BNS 72.

BNS Section 73

Definition: Printing or Publishing[544] Any Matter Relating to Court Proceedings Without Permission Section 73 of the Bharatiya Nyaya Sanhita (BNS) 2023 addresses the prohibition on printing or publishing any matter related to court proceedings without permission.

---

[537] eparlib.nic.in

[538] www.iitk.ac.in

[539] eparlib.nic.in

[540] www.iitk.ac.in

[541] 104

[542] devgan.in

[543] www.indiacode.nic.in

[544] Ministry of Home Affairs. (2024). The Bharatiya Nyaya Sanhita, 2023. Retrieved from https://www.mha.gov.in/sites/default/files/250883_english_01042024.pdf

Illustration: If a journalist publishes details of a court case involving a sexual assault without obtaining permission from the court, they are committing an offense under BNS 73.

Example: Suppose a media outlet releases a story about an ongoing trial for a sexual offense and includes sensitive information about the proceedings without the court's consent. This act falls under BNS 73 as it involves publishing court proceedings without permission.

Comment: This section ensures the protection of the judicial process's integrity and the privacy of the individuals involved. It emphasizes the importance of maintaining confidentiality in court proceedings to prevent prejudice and undue influence on the judicial process.

Classification of Offence and Punishment Classification: This offense is classified as a criminal offense due to the potential harm it can cause to the integrity of the judicial process and the privacy of the individuals involved.

Punishment: The punishment for committing this offense under BNS 73 is [545]imprisonment of either description for a term which may extend to two years and the offender shall also be liable to a fine.

Cognizable or Non-Cognizable, Bailable or Non-Bailable: This offense is cognizable, meaning the police can arrest the accused without a warrant.

Bailable: This offense is bailable, indicating that the accused can secure bail and be released from custody until the trial is completed.

Comparison: With IPC Section 228A (3)Section 228A [546](3) of the Indian Penal Code (IPC) also addresses the prohibition on printing or publishing any matter related to court proceedings without permission :IPC Section 228A (3): States that [547]whoever prints or publishes any matter in relation to any proceeding before a court with respect to an offense [548]referred to

[545] devgan.in

[546] www.bareactslive.com

[547] www.iitk.ac.in

[548] pdfcookie.com

in sub-section (1) [549]without the previous permission of such court shall be punished with imprisonment of either description for a term which may extend to two years and shall also be liable to a fine.

Key Differences: BNS 73: Reflects updated legal terminology and provisions in the new Bharatiya Nyaya Sanhita. IPC 228A (3): Part of the older Indian Penal Code framework, now replaced by BNS 73.

BNS Section 74

Definition: Assault or Use of Criminal [550]Force to Woman with Intent to Outrage Her Modesty Section 74 of the Bharatiya Nyaya Sanhita (BNS) 2023 addresses the offense of assaulting or using criminal force on a woman with the intent to outrage her modesty.

Illustration: If a man forcibly grabs a woman's hand in a crowded place with the intent to outrage her modesty, he is committing an offense under BNS 74.

Example: Suppose a person intentionally touches a woman inappropriately in a public setting, knowing it is likely to outrage her modesty. This act falls under BNS 74 as it involves using criminal force with the intent to outrage her modesty.

Comment: This section emphasizes the serious nature of assaulting or using criminal force on a woman with the intent to outrage her modesty. It underscores the importance of protecting women's dignity and ensuring accountability for such violations.

Classification of Offence and Punishment Classification: This offense is classified as a criminal offense due to the serious nature of the act and its impact on the victim's dignity and modesty.

Punishment: The punishment for committing this offense under BNS 74 is imprisonment of either description for a term which shall not be less

---

[549] www.iitk.ac.in

[550] Ministry of Home Affairs. (2024). The Bharatiya Nyaya Sanhita, 2023. Retrieved from https://www.mha.gov.in/sites/default/files/250883_english_01042024.pdf

than one year but which may extend to five years, and the offender shall also be liable to a fine.

Cognizable or Non-Cognizable, Bailable or Non-Bailable: This offense is cognizable, meaning the police can arrest the accused without a warrant.

Bailable: This offense is bailable, indicating that the accused can secure bail and be released from custody until the trial is completed.

Comparison: With IPC Section 354Section [551]354 of the Indian Penal Code (IPC) also addresses the offense of assaulting or using criminal force on a woman with the [552]intent to outrage her modesty : IPC Section 354: States that whoever assaults or uses criminal force to any woman, intending to [553]outrage or knowing it to be likely that he will thereby outrage her modesty, shall be punished with imprisonment of either description for a term which shall not be less than one year but which may extend to five years, and shall also be liable to a fine.

Key Differences: BNS 74: Reflects updated legal terminology and provisions in the new Bharatiya Nyaya Sanhita.IPC 354: Part of the older Indian Penal Code framework, now replaced by BNS 74.

BNS Section 75

Definition: Sexual Harassment Section 75 of the [554]Bharatiya Nyaya Sanhita (BNS) 2023 addresses the offense of sexual harassment.

Illustration: If a man makes unwelcome physical advances towards a woman, he is committing an offense under BNS 75.

Example: Suppose a man demands sexual favors from a colleague at work. This act falls under BNS 75 as sexual harassment.

---

[551] eparlib.nic.in

[552] devgan.in

[553] pdfcoffee.com

[554] Ministry of Home Affairs. (2024). The Bharatiya Nyaya Sanhita, 2023. Retrieved from https://www.mha.gov.in/sites/default/files/250883_english_01042024.pdf

Classification of Offence and Punishment Classification: This offense is classified as a criminal offense due to the violation of a person's dignity and autonomy.

Punishment: The punishment for committing this offense under BNS 75 is: For [555]physical contact and advances involving unwelcome and explicit sexual overtures, a demand or request for sexual favors, or showing pornography against the will of a woman: Rigorous imprisonment for a term which may extend to three years, or with fine, or with both. For making sexually colored remarks: Imprisonment of either description for a term which may extend to one year, or with fine, or with both.

Cognizable or Non-Cognizable, Bailable or Non-Bailable: This offense is cognizable, meaning the police can arrest the accused without a warrant.

Bailable: This offense is bailable, indicating that the accused can secure bail and be released from custody until the trial is completed.

Comparison: with IPC Section 354ASection 354A [556]of the Indian Penal Code (IPC) also addresses the offense of sexual harassment: IPC Section 354A: States that [557]a man committing any of the following acts—physical contact and advances involving unwelcome and explicit sexual overtures; a demand or request for sexual favors; showing pornography against the will of a woman; or making sexually colored remarks—shall be guilty of the offense of sexual harassment.

Key Differences: BNS 75: Reflects updated legal terminology and provisions in the new Bharatiya Nyaya Sanhita. IPC 354A: Part of the older Indian Penal Code framework, now replaced by BNS 75.

---

[555] devgan.in

[556] eparlib.nic.in

[557] devgan.in

BNS Section 76

Definition: Assault or Use of Criminal Force to Woman[558] with Intent to Disrobe Section 76 of the Bharatiya Nyaya Sanhita (BNS) 2023 addresses the offense of assaulting or using criminal force on a woman with the intent to disrobe or compel her to be naked.

Illustration: If a man forcibly tries to remove a woman's clothes in a public place, he is committing an offense under BNS 76.

Example: Suppose a person grabs a woman's dress with the intent to remove it without her consent. This act falls under BNS 76 as it involves using criminal force with the intent to disrobe.

Comment: BNS Section 76 reaffirms the commitment to protecting women's dignity and bodily integrity in a modern context. By clearly defining the offense and prescribing stringent punishments, it serves [559]as a strong deterrent against such violations. This reflects the evolving nature of legislation to be more responsive to contemporary issues, ensuring that legal measures remain effective in safeguarding individual rights and dignity.

Classification of Offence and Punishment Classification: This offense is classified as a criminal offense due to the serious violation of the woman's dignity and privacy.

Punishment: The punishment for committing this offense under BNS 76 is [560]imprisonment of either description for a term which shall not be less than three years but which may extend to seven years, and the offender shall also be liable to a fine.

Cognizable or Non-Cognizable, Bailable or Non-Bailable: This offense is cognizable, meaning the police can arrest the accused without a warrant.

---

558 Ministry of Home Affairs. (2024). The Bharatiya Nyaya Sanhita, 2023. Retrieved from https://www.mha.gov.in/sites/default/files/250883_english_01042024.pdf

559 eparlib.nic.in

560 devgan.in

Non-Bailable: This offense is non-bailable, indicating that the accused cannot secure bail and must remain in custody until the trial is completed.

Comparison: Section 354B of the Indian Penal Code (IPC) [561]also addresses the offense of assaulting or using criminal force on a woman with the intent to disrobe: IPC Section 354B: States that any man who assaults or uses criminal force to [562]any woman or abets such act with the intention of disrobing or compelling her to be naked, shall be punished with imprisonment of either description for a term which shall not be less than three years but which may extend to seven years, and shall also be liable to a fine.

Key Differences: BNS 76: Reflects updated legal terminology and provisions in the new Bharatiya Nyaya Sanhita 354B: Part of the older Indian Penal Code framework, now replaced by BNS 76.

BNS Section 77

Definition: Voyeurism Section 77 of the [563]Bharatiya Nyaya Sanhita (BNS) 2023 addresses the offense of voyeurism.

Illustration: If a man secretly watches a woman in her private moments without her consent, he is committing an offense under BNS 77.

Example: Suppose a person uses a hidden camera to record a woman in a private space without her knowledge. This act falls under BNS 77 as voyeurism.

Comment: This section highlights the importance of protecting individuals' privacy and dignity in an era where technology can easily be misused.

---

[561] eparlib.nic.in

[562] devgan.in

[563] Ministry of Home Affairs. (2024). The Bharatiya Nyaya Sanhita, 2023. Retrieved from https://www.mha.gov.in/sites/default/files/250883_english_01042024.pdf

Classification of Offence and Punishment Classification: This offense is classified as a criminal offense due to the violation of the victim's privacy and dignity.

Punishment: The punishment for committing this offense under BNS 77 is: For the first conviction: Imprisonment of either [564]description for a term which shall not be less than one year but which may extend to three years, and the offender shall also be liable to a fine. For a second or subsequent conviction: Imprisonment of either description for a term which shall not be less than three years but which may extend to seven years, and the offender shall also be liable to a fine.

Cognizable or Non-Cognizable, Bailable or Non-Bailable: This offense is cognizable, meaning the police can arrest the accused without a warrant.

Bailable: This offense is bailable, indicating that the accused can secure bail and be released from custody until the trial is completed.

Comparison: Section 354C [565]of the Indian Penal Code (IPC) also addresses the offense of voyeurism :IPC Section 354C: [566]States that any man who watches, or captures the image of a woman engaging in a private act in circumstances where she would usually have the expectation of not being observed, or disseminates such image, shall be punished on first conviction with imprisonment of either description for a term which shall not be less than one year but which may extend to three years, and shall also be liable to a fine, and be punished on a second or subsequent conviction with imprisonment of either description for a term which shall not be less than three years but which may extend to seven years, and shall also be liable to a fine.

Key Differences: BNS 77: Reflects updated legal terminology and provisions in the new Bharatiya Nyaya Sanhita. IPC 354C: Part of the older Indian Penal Code framework, now replaced by BNS 77.

---

[564] devgan.in

[565] eparlib.nic.in

[566] devgan.in

BNS Section 78

Definition: Stalking Section [567]78 of the Bharatiya Nyaya Sanhita (BNS) 2023 addresses the offense of stalking.

Illustration: If a man repeatedly follows a woman to her workplace without her consent, he is committing an offense under BNS 78.

Example: Suppose a person sends unwanted messages to another on social media, follows them to various locations, and makes repeated unwanted contact. This act falls under BNS 78 as stalking.

Comment: This section highlights the serious invasion of privacy and the distress caused by such actions. It aims to protect individuals from persistent harassment and ensure their safety.

Classification of Offence and Punishment Classification: This offense is classified as a criminal offense due to the invasion of the victim's privacy and causing fear or distress.

Punishment: The punishment for committing this offense under BNS 78 is: For the first conviction: Imprisonment of either description for a term which may extend to three years, and the offender shall also be liable to a fine. For a second or subsequent conviction: Imprisonment of either description for a term which may extend to five years, and the offender shall also be liable to a fine.

Cognizable or Non-Cognizable, Bailable or Non-Bailable: This offense is cognizable, meaning the police can arrest the accused without a warrant.

Bailable: This offense is bailable, indicating that the accused can secure bail and be released from custody until the trial is completed.

Comparison: Section 354D [568]of the Indian Penal Code (IPC) also addresses the offense of stalking: IPC Section 354D: States that [569]any man

---

[567] Ministry of Home Affairs. (2024). The Bharatiya Nyaya Sanhita, 2023. Retrieved from https://www.mha.gov.in/sites/default/files/250883_english_01042024.pdf

[568] eparlib.nic.in

[569] pdfcoffee.com

who follows a woman and contacts, or attempts to contact such woman to foster personal interaction repeatedly despite a clear indication of disinterest by such woman, or [570]monitors the use by a woman of the internet, email or any other form of electronic communication, commits the offense of stalking.

Key Differences: BNS 78: Reflects updated legal terminology and provisions in the new Bharatiya Nyaya Sanhita. IPC 354D: Part of the older Indian Penal Code framework, now replaced by BNS 78.

BNS Section 79

Definition: Word, Gesture, or Act Intended[571] to Insult the Modesty of a Woman Section 79 of the Bharatiya Nyaya Sanhita (BNS) 2023 addresses the offense of using words, gestures, or acts intended to insult the modesty of a woman.

Illustration: If a man makes lewd comments or gestures towards a woman in public, he is committing an offense under BNS 79.

Example: Suppose a person shouts inappropriate remarks at a woman in a crowded market. This act falls under BNS 79 as it involves using words or gestures to insult her modesty.

Comment: This section highlights the violation of a woman's dignity and modesty. It aims to protect women from verbal and non-verbal harassment and ensure their right to live with dignity.

Classification of Offence and Punishment Classification: This offense is classified as a criminal offense due to the violation of the woman's dignity and modesty.

---

[570] devgan.in

[571] Ministry of Home Affairs. (2024). The Bharatiya Nyaya Sanhita, 2023. Retrieved from https://www.mha.gov.in/sites/default/files/250883_english_01042024.pdf

Punishment: [572]The punishment for committing this offense under BNS 79 is simple imprisonment for a term which may extend to three years, and the offender [573]shall also be liable to a fine.

Cognizable or Non-Cognizable, Bailable or Non-Bailable: This offense is cognizable, meaning the police can arrest the accused without a warrant.

Bailable: This offense is bailable, indicating that the accused can secure bail and be released from custody until the trial is completed.

Comparison: Section 509 of the Indian Penal Code (IPC) also addresses the offense of using words, gestures, or acts intended to insult the modesty of a woman: IPC Section 509: States that whoever, intending to insult the modesty of any woman, utters any word, makes any sound or gesture, or exhibits any object, intending that such word or sound shall be heard, or that such gesture or object shall be seen, by such woman, or intrudes upon the privacy of such woman, [574]shall be punished with simple imprisonment for a term which may extend to three years, and shall also be liable to a fine.

Key Differences: BNS 79: Reflects updated legal terminology and provisions in the new Bharatiya Nyaya Sanhita. IPC 509: Part of the older Indian Penal Code framework, now replaced by BNS 79.

BNS Section 80

Definition: Dowry [575]Death Section 80 of the Bharatiya Nyaya Sanhita (BNS) 2023 addresses the offense of dowry death.

Illustration: If a woman dies due to burns or bodily injury within seven years of marriage, [576]and it is shown that she was subjected to cruelty or

---

[572] eparlib.nic.in

[573] devgan.in

[574] eparlib.nic.in

[575] Ministry of Home Affairs. (2024). The Bharatiya Nyaya Sanhita, 2023. Retrieved from https://www.mha.gov.in/sites/default/files/250883_english_01042024.pdf

[576] indiankanoon.org

harassment related to dowry demands, it is considered a dowry death under BNS 80.

Example: Suppose a woman dies under suspicious circumstances within seven years of marriage, and investigations reveal that she was subjected to severe [577]harassment by her husband and in-laws for dowry. This act falls under BNS 80 as a dowry death.

Comment: This section addresses the severe impact of dowry-related violence on victims and society. By defining the offense and prescribing strict punishments, it aims to deter such actions and provide justice for the victims.

Classification of Offence and Punishment Classification: This offense is classified as a criminal offense due to the severe impact on the victim and the societal implications of dowry-related violence.

Punishment: The punishment for committing this offense under BNS 80 is imprisonment for a term which shall not be less than [578]seven years but which may extend to [579]imprisonment for life.

Cognizable or Non-Cognizable, Bailable or Non-Bailable: This offense is cognizable, meaning the police can arrest the accused without a warrant.

Non-Bailable: This offense is non-bailable, indicating that the accused cannot secure bail and must remain in custody until the trial is completed.

Comparison: Section 304B[580] of the Indian Penal Code (IPC) also addresses the offense of dowry death: IPC Section 304B: States that where the death of a woman is caused by burns or bodily injury or occurs otherwise than under normal circumstances within seven years of her marriage and it is shown that soon before her death she was subjected to cruelty or harassment by her husband or any relative of her husband for, or in connection with, any demand for dowry, such death shall be called a "dowry death," and such husband or relative shall be deemed to have

---

[577] www.slic.org.in

[578] eparlib.nic.in

[579] devgan.in

[580] indiankanoon.org

caused her death. The punishment is [581]imprisonment for a term which shall not be less than seven years but which may extend to imprisonment for life.

Key Differences: BNS 80: Reflects updated legal terminology and provisions in the new Bharatiya Nyaya Sanhita. IPC 304B: Part of the older Indian Penal Code framework, now replaced by BNS 80.

BNS Section 81

Definition: Cohabitation Caused by Man Deceitfully [582]Inducing Belief of Lawful Marriage Section 81 of the Bharatiya Nyaya Sanhita (BNS) 2023 addresses the offense of cohabitation caused by a man deceitfully inducing a belief of lawful marriage.

Illustration: If a man deceives a woman into believing that they are lawfully married and convinces her to live with him, he is committing an offense under BNS 81.

Example: Suppose a man falsely claims to be married to a woman and persuades her to cohabit with him under this false pretense. This act falls under BNS 81 as it involves deceitful inducement of belief of lawful marriage.

Comment: This section emphasizes the serious nature of deceit in relationships and the harm it can cause to individuals. By addressing this issue and prescribing appropriate punishments, the BNS aims to protect individuals from fraudulent relationships and ensure justice.

Classification of Offence and Punishment Classification: This offense is classified as a criminal offense due to the deceitful nature of the act and the potential harm to the woman involved.

---

[581] devgan.in

[582] Ministry of Home Affairs. (2024). The Bharatiya Nyaya Sanhita, 2023. Retrieved from https://www.mha.gov.in/sites/default/files/250883_english_01042024.pdf

Punishment: The punishment for committing this offense under BNS 81 is [583]imprisonment of either description for a term which may extend to two years, and the offender shall also be liable to a fine.

Cognizable or Non-Cognizable, Bailable or Non-Bailable: This offense is cognizable, meaning the police can arrest the accused without a warrant.

Bailable: This offense is bailable, indicating that the accused can secure bail and be released from custody until the trial is completed.

Comparison: Section 493 [584]of the Indian Penal Code (IPC) also addresses the offense of cohabitation caused by a man deceitfully inducing a belief of lawful marriage: IPC Section 493: States that every man who by deceit causes any woman who is not lawfully married to him to believe that she is lawfully married to him and to cohabit or have sexual intercourse with him in that belief, shall be punished with imprisonment of either description for a term which may extend to two years, and[585] shall also be liable to a fine.

Key Differences: BNS 81: Reflects updated legal terminology and provisions in the new Bharatiya Nyaya Sanhita. IPC 493: Part of the older Indian Penal Code framework, now replaced by BNS 81.

BNS Section 82(1)

Definition: Marrying Again During Lifetime of [586]Husband or Wife Section 82(1) of the Bharatiya Nyaya Sanhita (BNS) 2023 addresses the offense of marrying again during the lifetime of a husband or wife.

Illustration: If a person marries another individual while their current spouse is still alive, they are committing an offense under BNS 82(1).

---

[583] devgan.in

[585] www.bareactslive.com

[586] Ministry of Home Affairs. (2024). The Bharatiya Nyaya Sanhita, 2023. Retrieved from https://www.mha.gov.in/sites/default/files/250883_english_01042024.pdf

Example: Suppose a man, who is already married, marries another woman without legally divorcing his first wife. This act falls under BNS 82(1) as it involves marrying again during the lifetime of his existing spouse.

Comment: This section underscores the importance of marital laws and the potential harm caused by violating them. By addressing this issue and prescribing appropriate punishments, the BNS aims to ensure the sanctity and legality of marriage institutions.

Classification of Offence and Punishment Classification: This offense is classified as a criminal offense due to the violation of marital laws and the potential harm to the parties involved.

Punishment: The punishment for committing this offense under BNS 82(1) is [587]imprisonment of either description for a term which may extend to seven years, and the offender shall also be liable to a fine.

Cognizable or Non-Cognizable, Bailable or Non-Bailable: This offense is cognizable, meaning the police can arrest the accused without a warrant.

Bailable: This offense is bailable, indicating that the accused can secure bail and be released from custody until the trial is completed.

Comparison: Section 494 of the [588]Indian Penal Code (IPC) also addresses the offense of marrying again during the lifetime of a husband or wife: IPC Section 494: States that [589]whoever, having a husband or wife living, marries in any case in which such marriage is void by reason of its taking place during the life of such husband or wife, shall be punished with imprisonment of either description for a term which may extend to seven years, and shall also be liable to a fine.

Key Differences: BNS 82(1): Reflects updated legal terminology and provisions in the new Bharatiya Nyaya Sanhita. IPC 494: Part of the older Indian Penal Code framework, now replaced by BNS 82(1).

---

[587] forest.jharkhand.gov.in

[588] www.bareactslive.com

[589] forest.jharkhand.gov.in

BNS Section 82(2)

Definition: Marrying Again During Lifetime of Husband or Wife with Concealment of Former Marriage Section 82(2)[590] of the Bharatiya Nyaya Sanhita (BNS) 2023 addresses the offense of marrying again during the lifetime of a husband or wife while concealing the existence of the former marriage from the person with whom the subsequent marriage is contracted.

Illustration: If a man who is already married marries another woman without informing her of his existing marriage, he is committing an offense under BNS 82(2).

Example: Suppose a man marries a woman without disclosing that he is already married to another woman. This act falls under BNS 82(2) as it involves marrying again during the lifetime of the first wife and concealing this fact from the second woman.

Comment: This section addresses the deceitful nature of such acts and the significant harm they cause to individuals. By defining the offense and prescribing appropriate punishments, the BNS aims to protect people from fraudulent marriages and ensure justice.

Classification of Offence and Punishment Classification: This offense is classified as a criminal offense due to the deceitful nature of the act and the potential harm to the individuals involved.

Punishment: The punishment for committing this offense under BNS 82(2) is imprisonment of either description for a term which may extend to ten years, and the offender shall also be liable to a fine.

Cognizable or Non-Cognizable, Bailable or Non-Bailable: This offense is cognizable, meaning the police can arrest the accused without a warrant.

Non-Bailable: This offense is non-bailable, indicating that the accused cannot secure bail and must remain in custody until the trial is completed.

---

590 Ministry of Home Affairs. (2024). The Bharatiya Nyaya Sanhita, 2023. Retrieved from https://www.mha.gov.in/sites/default/files/250883_english_01042024.pdf

Comparison: Section 495 of the Indian Penal Code (IPC) also addresses the offense of marrying again during the lifetime of a husband or wife with concealment of the former marriage: IPC Section 495: States [591]that whoever commits the offense [592]defined in the last preceding section having concealed from the person with whom the subsequent marriage is contracted the fact of the former marriage, shall be punished with imprisonment of either description for a term which may extend to ten years, and shall also be liable to a fine.

Key Differences: BNS 82(2): Reflects updated legal terminology and provisions in the new Bharatiya Nyaya Sanhita. IPC 495: Part of the older Indian Penal Code framework, now replaced by BNS 82(2).

BNS Section 83

Definition: Marriage Ceremony Fraudulently Gone Through Without Lawful Marriage Section 83[593] of the Bharatiya Nyaya Sanhita[594] (BNS) 2023 addresses the offense of going through a marriage ceremony fraudulently without a lawful marriage.

Illustration: If a man knowingly goes through a marriage ceremony with a woman, pretending to be lawfully married when he is not, he is committing an offense under BNS 83.

Example: Suppose a man, who is already married, conducts a marriage ceremony with another woman without disclosing his existing marriage. This act falls under BNS 83 as it involves fraudulently going through a marriage ceremony without lawful marriage.

Comment: This section emphasizes the severe implications of deceit in marital relationships and the harm it causes to the affected individuals. By

---

[591] devgan.in

[592] forest.jharkhand.gov.in

[593] www.livelaw.in

[594] Ministry of Home Affairs. (2024). The Bharatiya Nyaya Sanhita, 2023. Retrieved from https://www.mha.gov.in/sites/default/files/250883_english_01042024.pdf

addressing this issue and setting forth stringent punishments, the BNS aims to uphold the sanctity and legal integrity of marriage.

Classification of Offence and Punishment Classification: This offense is classified as a criminal offense due to the deceitful nature of the act and the potential harm to the individuals involved.

Punishment: The punishment for committing this offense under BNS 83 is imprisonment of either description for a term which may extend to seven years, and the offender shall also be liable to a fine.

Cognizable or Non-Cognizable, Bailable or Non-Bailable: This offense is cognizable, meaning the police can arrest the accused without a warrant.

Bailable: This offense is bailable, indicating that the accused can secure bail and be released from custody until the trial is completed.

Comparison: [595]Section 496 of the Indian Penal Code (IPC) also addresses the offense of [596]marriage ceremony fraudulently gone through without lawful marriage: IPC Section 496: States that whoever, dishonestly or with a fraudulent intention, goes through the ceremony of being married, knowing that he is not thereby lawfully married, shall be punished with imprisonment of either description for a term which may extend to seven years, and shall also be liable to a fine.

Key Differences: BNS 83: Reflects updated legal terminology and provisions in the new Bharatiya Nyaya Sanhita. IPC 496: Part of the older Indian Penal Code framework, now replaced by BNS 83.

BNS Section 84

Definition: Enticing or [597]Taking Away or Detaining with Criminal Intent a Married Woman Section 84 of the Bharatiya Nyaya Sanhita

---

[595] www.bareactslive.com

[596] forest.jharkhand.gov.in

[597] Ministry of Home Affairs. (2024). The Bharatiya Nyaya Sanhita, 2023. Retrieved from https://www.mha.gov.in/sites/default/files/250883_english_01042024.pdf

(BNS) 2023 addresses the offense of enticing, taking away, or detaining a married woman with criminal intent.

Illustration: If a man knowingly takes away a married woman with the intent of engaging in illicit intercourse, he is committing an offense under BNS 84.

Example: Suppose a man, aware that a woman is married, persuades her to leave her husband and live with him. This act falls under BNS 84 as it involves enticing or taking away a married woman with criminal intent.

Comment: This section emphasizes the significant impact of violating marital laws and the harm it causes to the individuals involved. By defining the offense and prescribing appropriate punishments, the BNS aims to protect marital relationships and ensure justice.

Classification of Offence and Punishment Classification: This offense is classified as a criminal offense due to the violation of marital laws and the potential harm to the individuals involved.

Punishment: The punishment for committing this offense under BNS 84 is [598]imprisonment of either description for a term which may extend to two years, and the offender shall also be liable to a fine.

Cognizable or Non-Cognizable, Bailable or Non-Bailable: This offense is cognizable, meaning the police can arrest the accused without a warrant.

Bailable: This offense is bailable, indicating that the accused can secure bail and be released from custody until the trial is completed.

Comparison: Section 498 of the Indian Penal Code (IPC) also addresses the offense of enticing, taking away, or [599]detaining with criminal intent a married woman: IPC Section 498: States that whoever takes or entices away any woman who is and whom he knows or has reason to believe to be the wife of any other man, from that man, or from any person having the care of her on behalf of that man, with intent that she may have illicit intercourse with any person, shall be punished with imprisonment of either

---

[598] forest.jharkhand.gov.in

[599] forest.jharkhand.gov.in

description for a term which may extend to two years, and shall also be liable to a fine.

Key Differences: BNS 84: Reflects updated legal terminology and provisions in the new Bharatiya Nyaya Sanhita. IPC 498: Part of the older Indian Penal Code framework, now replaced by BNS 84.

BNS Section 85

Definition: Husband or Relative of [600]Husband of a Woman Subjecting Her to Cruelty Section 85 of the Bharatiya Nyaya Sanhita (BNS) 2023 addresses the offense of a husband or relative of a husband subjecting a woman to cruelty.

Illustration: If a husband or his relative subjects a woman to physical, emotional, or financial abuse, they are committing an offense under BNS 85.

Example: Suppose a woman's husband and his family constantly demand dowry, physically abuse her, and blame her for not bringing enough wealth after marriage. This act falls under BNS 85 as it involves subjecting the woman to cruelty.

Comment: In this context includes both physical and mental harm. It is aimed at protecting spouses, particularly women, from any form of abuse that can cause substantial harm or distress, either physically or emotionally.

Classification of Offence and Punishment Classification: This offense is classified as a criminal offense due to its severe impact on the victim's well-being.

Punishment: The punishment for committing this offense under BNS 85 is imprisonment for a term which may extend to three years, and the offender shall also be liable to a fine. **Cognizable or Non-Cognizable,**

---

[600] Ministry of Home Affairs. (2024). The Bharatiya Nyaya Sanhita, 2023. Retrieved from https://www.mha.gov.in/sites/default/files/250883_english_01042024.pdf

Bailable or Non-Bailable: This offense is cognizable, meaning the police can arrest the accused without a warrant.

Non-Bailable: This offense is non-bailable, indicating that the accused cannot secure bail and must remain in custody until the trial is completed.

Comparison: Section 498A of the Indian Penal Code (IPC) also addresses the definition and punishment for cruelty: IPC Section 498A: States that whoever, being the [601]husband or the relative of the husband of a woman, subjects such woman to cruelty shall be punished with imprisonment for a term which may extend to three years, and shall also be liable to a fine.

Key Differences: BNS 85: Reflects updated legal terminology and provisions in the new Bharatiya Nyaya Sanhita. IPC 498A: Part of the older Indian Penal Code framework, now replaced by BNS 85.

BNS Section 86

Definition Cruelty Defined Section 86 of the Bharatiya Nyaya Sanhita (BNS) 2023 defines cruelty.

Illustration: If a husband or his relative subjects a woman to physical, emotional, or financial abuse, they are committing an offense under BNS 86.

Example: Suppose a woman's husband constantly belittles her, isolates her from friends and family, and controls all her financial resources. This act falls under BNS 86 as it involves subjecting the woman to cruelty.

Comment: This section emphasizes the recognition of both physical and mental harm as forms of cruelty. It aims to protect spouses, particularly women, from any form of abuse that can cause substantial harm or distress, either physically or emotionally.

Classification of Offence and Punishment Classification: This offense is classified as a criminal offense due to its severe impact on the victim's well-being.

---

[601] forest.jharkhand.gov.in

Punishment: The punishment for committing this offense under BNS 86 is imprisonment for a term which may extend to three years, and the offender shall also be liable to a fine.

Cognizable or Non-Cognizable, Bailable or Non-Bailable: This offense is cognizable, meaning the police can arrest the accused without a warrant.

Non-Bailable: This offense is non-bailable, indicating that the accused cannot secure bail and must remain in custody until the trial is completed.

Comparison: Section 498A of the Indian Penal Code (IPC) also addresses the definition and punishment for cruelty: IPC Section 498A: States that whoever, being the husband or the relative of the husband of a woman, subjects such woman to cruelty shall be punished with imprisonment for a term which may extend to three years, and shall also be liable to a fine.

Key Differences: BNS 86: Reflects updated legal terminology and provisions in the new Bharatiya Nyaya Sanhita. IPC 498A: Part of the older Indian Penal Code framework, now replaced by BNS 86.

BNS Section 87

Definition: Kidnapping or [602]Abducting in Order to Murder or for Ransom, etc. Section 87 of the Bharatiya Nyaya Sanhita (BNS) 2023 addresses the offense of kidnapping or abducting a person with the intent to murder or for ransom.

Illustration: If a person kidnaps another individual with the intention of killing them or demands a ransom for their release, they are committing an offense under BNS 87.

Example: Suppose someone abducts a person and demands a large sum of money from their family in exchange for their safe return. This act falls under BNS 87 as it involves kidnapping for ransom.

Comment: section is designed to address severe crimes involving kidnapping and abduction with the intent to cause harm or extort money.

---

[602] Ministry of Home Affairs. (2024). The Bharatiya Nyaya Sanhita, 2023. Retrieved from https://www.mha.gov.in/sites/default/files/250883_english_01042024.pdf

The stringent punishment reflects the gravity of such offenses and aims to deter potential offenders.

Classification of Offence and Punishment Classification: This offense is classified as a criminal offense due to the serious nature of the act and the potential harm to the victim.

Punishment: The punishment for committing this offense under BNS 87 is imprisonment for life or rigorous imprisonment for a term which may extend to ten years, and the offender [603]shall also be liable to a fine.

Cognizable or Non-Cognizable, Bailable or Non-Bailable: This offense is cognizable, meaning the police can arrest the accused without a warrant.

Non-Bailable: This offense is non-bailable, indicating that the accused cannot secure bail and must remain in custody until the trial is completed.

Comparison: Section 366 of the Indian Penal Code (IPC) addresses the offense of kidnapping, abducting, or inducing a woman to compel her marriage: IPC Section 366: States that whoever kidnaps or abducts any [604]woman with the intent that she may be compelled, or knowing it to be likely that she will be compelled, to marry any person against her will, or in order that she may be forced or seduced to illicit intercourse, shall be punished [605]with imprisonment for a term which [606]may extend to ten years, and shall also be liable to a fine.

Key Differences: BNS 87: Focuses on kidnapping or abduction with the intent to murder or for ransom, while IPC Section 366 specifically addresses kidnapping or abduction of women for forced marriage or illicit intercourse. BNS 87: Reflects updated legal terminology and provisions in the new Bharatiya Nyaya Sanhita. IPC 366: Part of the older Indian Penal Code framework, now replaced by BNS 87.

---

[603] forest.jharkhand.gov.in

[604] www.bareactslive.com

[605] www.iitk.ac.in

[606] www.bareactslive.com

BNS Section 88

Definition: Causing Miscarriage Section 88[607] of the Bharatiya Nyaya Sanhita (BNS) 2023 addresses the offense of causing miscarriage.

Illustration: If a person voluntarily causes a woman to miscarry without a valid medical reason, they are committing an offense under BNS 88.

Example: Suppose a man intentionally causes a woman to miscarry because he does not want the child. This act falls under BNS 88 as it involves causing miscarriage without lawful justification.

Comment: This section is aimed at protecting the health and rights of pregnant women by criminalizing the act of causing miscarriage without a valid reason. The law recognizes the physical and emotional trauma that such an act can cause to the woman.

Classification of Offence and Punishment Classification: This offense is classified as a criminal offense due to its serious nature and potential harm to the victim.

Punishment: The punishment for committing this offense under BNS 88 is [608]imprisonment of either description for a term which may extend to three years, and the offender shall also be liable to a fine. If the woman is "quick with child" (meaning the fetus is developed), the punishment can extend to seven years of imprisonment and a fine.

Cognizable or Non-Cognizable, Bailable or Non-Bailable: This offense is cognizable, meaning the police can arrest the accused without a warrant.

Bailable: This offense is bailable, indicating that the accused can secure bail and be released from custody until the trial is completed.

Comparison: Section 312 of the Indian Penal Code (IPC) also addresses the offense of causing miscarriage: IPC Section 312: States that whoever

---

[607] Ministry of Home Affairs. (2024). The Bharatiya Nyaya Sanhita, 2023. Retrieved from https://www.mha.gov.in/sites/default/files/250883_english_01042024.pdf

[608] forest.jharkhand.gov.in

voluntarily causes a[609] woman with child to miscarry, shall, if such miscarriage be not caused in good faith for the purpose of saving the life of the woman, [610]be punished with imprisonment of either description for a term which may extend to three years, and shall also be liable to a fine. If the woman is "quick with child," the punishment can extend to seven years of imprisonment and a fine.

Key Differences: BNS 88: Reflects updated legal terminology and provisions in the new Bharatiya Nyaya Sanhita. IPC 312: Part of the older [611]Indian Penal Code framework, now replaced by BNS 88.

BNS Section 89

Definition: Causing Miscarriage Without Woman's [612]Consent Section 89 of the Bharatiya Nyaya Sanhita (BNS) 2023 addresses the offense of causing miscarriage without the woman's consent.

Illustration: [613]If a person causes a woman to miscarry without her consent, whether she is in the early or advanced stages of pregnancy, they are committing an offense under BNS 89.

Example: Suppose a man intentionally causes a woman to miscarry without her knowledge or consent. This act falls under BNS 89 as it involves causing miscarriage without the woman's consent.

Comment: This section is aimed at protecting the autonomy and bodily integrity of women by criminalizing the act of causing miscarriage without their consent. It recognizes the severe physical and emotional trauma that such an act can cause to the woman.

---

[609] www.bareactslive.com

[610] forest.jharkhand.gov.in

[611] www.livelaw.in

[612] Ministry of Home Affairs. (2024). The Bharatiya Nyaya Sanhita, 2023. Retrieved from https://www.mha.gov.in/sites/default/files/250883_english_01042024.pdf

[613] www.bareactslive.com

Classification of Offence and Punishment Classification: This offense is classified as a criminal offense due to its serious nature and potential harm to the victim.

Punishment: The punishment for committing this offense under BNS 89 is imprisonment for life or imprisonment of either description for a term which may extend to ten years, and the offender [614]shall also be liable to a fine.

Cognizable or Non-Cognizable, Bailable or Non-Bailable: This offense is cognizable, meaning the police can arrest the accused without a warrant.

Non-Bailable: This offense is non-bailable, indicating that the accused cannot secure bail and must remain in custody until the trial is completed.

Comparison: Section 313 of the Indian Penal Code (IPC) also addresses the offense of causing miscarriage without the woman's consent: IPC Section 313: States that whoever commits the offense [615]defined in the last preceding section (causing miscarriage) without the consent of the woman, whether the woman is quick with child or not, shall be punished with imprisonment for life, or with imprisonment [616]of either description for a term which may extend to ten years, and shall also be liable to a fine.

Key Differences: BNS 89: Reflects updated legal terminology and provisions in the new Bharatiya Nyaya Sanhita.IPC 313: Part of the older [617]Indian Penal Code framework, now replaced by BNS 89.

BNS Section 90

Definition: Death Caused by Act Done[618] with Intent to Cause Miscarriage Section 90 of the Bharatiya Nyaya Sanhita (BNS) 2023

---

[614] forest.jharkhand.gov.in

[615] forest.jharkhand.gov.in

[616] odishapolicecidcb.gov.in

[617] www.bareactslive.com

[618] Ministry of Home Affairs. (2024). The Bharatiya Nyaya Sanhita, 2023. Retrieved from https://www.mha.gov.in/sites/default/files/250883_english_01042024.pdf

addresses the offense of causing death while attempting to cause a miscarriage.

Illustration: If a person performs an act with the intent to cause a miscarriage, and this act results in the death of the pregnant woman, they are committing an offense under BNS 90.

Example: Suppose a man administers a substance to a pregnant woman to induce a miscarriage, but the substance causes her death instead. This act falls under BNS 90 as it involves causing death while attempting to cause a miscarriage.

Comment: This section is aimed at addressing the severe consequences of actions taken with the intent to cause a miscarriage. It emphasizes the gravity of such offenses and the need to protect the lives of pregnant women.

Classification of Offence and Punishment Classification: This offense is classified as a criminal offense due to its serious nature and potential harm to the victim.

Punishment: The punishment for committing this offense under BNS 90 is imprisonment of either description for a term which may extend to ten years, and the offender shall also be liable to a fine. If the act is done without the woman's consent, the punishment can extend to imprisonment for life.

Cognizable or Non-Cognizable, Bailable or Non-Bailable: This offense is cognizable, meaning the police can arrest the accused without a warrant. Non-Bailable: This offense is non-bailable, indicating that the accused cannot secure bail and must remain in custody until the trial is completed.

Comparison: Section 314 of the Indian Penal Code (IPC) also addresses the offense of causing death while attempting to cause a miscarriage: IPC Section 314: States that whoever, with intent to cause the miscarriage of a woman with child, does any act which causes the death of [619]such woman, shall be punished with imprisonment of either description for a term

---

[619] forest.jharkhand.gov.in

[620]which may extend to ten years, and shall also be liable to a fine. If the act is done without the woman's consent, the punishment can extend to imprisonment for life.

Key Differences: BNS 90: Reflects updated legal terminology and provisions in the new Bharatiya Nyaya Sanhita. IPC 314: Part of the older Indian Penal Code framework, now replaced by BNS 90.

BNS Section 91

Definition: Act Done with Intent to Prevent [621]Child Being Born Alive or to Cause it to Die After Birth Section 91 of the Bharatiya Nyaya Sanhita (BNS) 2023 addresses the offense of causing harm with the intent to prevent a child from being born alive or to cause the child to die after birth.

Illustration: If a person intentionally causes an injury to a pregnant woman with the intent to kill the unborn child or prevent it from being born alive, they are committing an offense under BNS 91.

Example: Suppose a person administers a harmful substance to a pregnant woman with the intent to kill her unborn child. This act falls under BNS 91 as it involves an act done with intent to prevent the child from being born alive or to cause it to die after birth.

Comment: This section aims to protect the lives of unborn children and newborns from intentional harm. The law emphasizes the severe consequences of such actions and underscores the value of protecting vulnerable lives.

Classification of Offence and Punishment Classification: This offense is classified as a criminal offense due to the serious nature of the act and its potential harm to both the mother and the child.

---

[620] www.iitk.ac.in

[621] Ministry of Home Affairs. (2024). The Bharatiya Nyaya Sanhita, 2023. Retrieved from https://www.mha.gov.in/sites/default/files/250883_english_01042024.pdf

Punishment: The punishment for committing this offense under BNS 91 is [622]imprisonment of either description for a term which may extend to ten years, and the offender shall also be liable to a fine.

Cognizable or Non-Cognizable, Bailable or Non-Bailable: This offense is cognizable, meaning the police can arrest the accused without a warrant.

Bailable: This offense is non-bailable, indicating that the accused cannot secure bail and must remain in custody until the trial is completed.

Comparison: Section 315[623] of the Indian Penal Code (IPC) also addresses the offense of preventing a [624]child from being born alive or causing it to die after birth: IPC Section 315: States [625]that whoever before the birth of any child does any act with the intention of [626]preventing that child from being born alive or causing it to die after its birth, and does by such act prevent that child from being born alive or [627]cause it to die after its birth, shall be punished with imprisonment of either description for a term which may extend to ten years, or with fine, or with both.

Key Differences: BNS 91: Reflects updated legal terminology and provisions in the new Bharatiya Nyaya Sanhita. IPC 315: Part of the older Indian Penal Code framework, now replaced by BNS 91.

BNS Section 92

Definition: Causing Death of Quick Unborn [628]Child by Act Amounting to Culpable Homicide Section 92 of the Bharatiya Nyaya

---

[622] bprd.nic.in

[623] www.bareactslive.com

[624] bprd.nic.in

[625] prsindia.org

[626] bprd.nic.in

[627] odishapolicecidcb.gov.in

[628] Ministry of Home Affairs. (2024). The Bharatiya Nyaya Sanhita, 2023. Retrieved from https://www.mha.gov.in/sites/default/files/250883_english_01042024.pdf

Sanhita (BNS) 2023 addresses the offense of causing the death of a quick unborn child by an act amounting to culpable homicide.

Illustration: If a person performs an act knowing it could cause the death of a pregnant woman, and this act [629]results in the death of the unborn child, they are committing an offense under BNS 92.

Example: Suppose a person intentionally injures a pregnant woman, knowing that the injury could be fatal. The woman survives, but the unborn child dies as a result of the act. This act falls under BNS 92 as it involves [630]causing the death of a quick unborn child by an [631]act amounting to culpable homicide.

Comment: This section is aimed at protecting the lives of unborn children by criminalizing acts that result in their death due to culpable actions. It emphasizes the serious consequences of such acts and the need to hold the perpetrator accountable.

Classification of Offence and Punishment Classification: This offense is classified as a criminal offense due to its serious nature and potential harm to the victim.

Punishment: The punishment for committing this offense under BNS 92 is imprisonment of either description for a term which may extend to ten years, and the offender shall also be liable to a fine.

Cognizable or Non-Cognizable, Bailable or Non-Bailable: This offense is cognizable, meaning the police can arrest the accused without a warrant.

Bailable: This offense is bailable, indicating that the accused can secure bail and be released from custody until the trial is completed.

Comparison: Section 316 of the Indian Penal Code (IPC) also addresses the offense [632]of causing the death of a quick unborn child by an act

---

[629] www.freelaw.in

[630] odishapolicecidcb.gov.in

[631] bprd.nic.in

[632] odishapolicecidcb.gov.in

amounting to culpable homicide : IPC Section 316: States that [633]whoever does any [634]act under such circumstances, that if he thereby caused death he would be guilty of culpable homicide, and does by such act cause the death of a quick unborn child, shall be punished with imprisonment of either description for a term which may extend to ten years, and shall also be liable to a fine.

Key Differences: BNS 92: Reflects updated legal terminology and provisions in the new Bharatiya Nyaya Sanhita.IPC 316: Part of the older Indian Penal Code framework, now replaced by BNS 92.

BNS Section 93

Definition: Exposure and abandonment of child under twelve years, by parent or person having care of it.

Illustration: If a person performs an act knowing it could cause the death of a pregnant woman, and this act [635]results in the death of the unborn child, they are committing an offense under BNS 93. Additionally, if a parent or caregiver leaves a child under twelve years old in a place with the intention of abandoning them, they are also committing an offense under this section.

Example: Suppose a person intentionally injures a pregnant woman, knowing that the injury could be fatal. The woman survives, but the unborn child dies as a result of the act. This act falls under BNS 93 as it involves [636]causing the death of a quick unborn child by an [637]act amounting to culpable homicide. Another example is if a parent leaves their young child in a deserted area with no intention of returning, this act falls under the exposure and abandonment part of BNS 93.

---

[633] prsindia.org

[634] bprd.nic.in

[635] www.freelaw.in

[636] odishapolicecidcb.gov.in

[637] bprd.nic.in

Comment: This section is aimed at protecting both unborn children and young children from severe harm. The first part addresses the gravity of [638]causing the death of an unborn child through culpable actions, while the second part focuses on the protection of young children from abandonment and exposure.

Classification of Offence and Punishment Classification: This offense is classified as a criminal offense due to its serious nature and potential harm to the victim.

Punishment: The punishment for causing the death of a quick unborn child by an [639]act amounting to culpable homicide is imprisonment of either description for a term which may extend to ten years, and the offender shall also be liable to a fine. For the exposure and [640]abandonment of a child under twelve years, the punishment is [641]imprisonment of either description for a term which may extend to seven years, and the offender shall also be liable to a fine.

Cognizable or Non-Cognizable, Bailable or Non-Bailable: This offense is cognizable, meaning the police can arrest the accused without a warrant.

Bailable: This offense is bailable, indicating that the accused can secure bail and be released from custody until the trial is completed.

Comparison: Section 317[642] of the Indian Penal Code (IPC) also addresses the offense of exposure and [643]abandonment of a child under twelve years :IPC Section 317: States [644]that whoever being the father or mother of a child under the age of twelve years, or having the care of such child, shall expose or leave such child in any place with the intention of wholly abandoning such child, shall be punished with imprisonment of

---

638 odishapolicecidcb.gov.in

639 bprd.nic.in

640 www.slideshare.net

641 bprd.nic.in

642 www.bareactslive.com

643 www.slideshare.net

644 prsindia.org

either description for a term which may extend to seven years, or with fine, or with both.

Key Differences: BNS 93: Reflects updated legal terminology and provisions in the new Bharatiya Nyaya Sanhita.IPC 317: Part of the older Indian Penal Code framework, now replaced by BNS 93.

BNS Section 94

Definition: Concealment of Birth by Secret [645]Disposal of Dead Body Section 94 of the Bharatiya Nyaya Sanhita (BNS) 2023 addresses the offense of concealing the birth of a child by secretly disposing of the dead body.

Illustration: If a person secretly buries [646]or otherwise disposes of the dead body of a child, whether the child died before, during, or after birth, with the intent to conceal the birth, they are committing an offense under BNS 94.

Example: Suppose a woman gives birth to a stillborn child and, instead of reporting it, she secretly buries the body in an attempt to hide the birth. This act falls under BNS 94 as it involves concealing the birth by secret disposal of the dead body.

Comment: This section is aimed at addressing the serious issue of concealing [647]the birth of a child by disposing of the body in a secretive manner. [648]It emphasizes the need to protect the dignity and rights of the deceased child and ensure that such acts are appropriately penalized.

---

[645] Ministry of Home Affairs. (2024). The Bharatiya Nyaya Sanhita, 2023. Retrieved from https://www.mha.gov.in/sites/default/files/250883_english_01042024.pdf

[646] bprd.nic.in

[647] www.bareactslive.com

[648] www.freelaw.in

Classification of Offence and Punishment Classification: This offense is classified as a criminal offense due to its serious nature and potential [649]harm to the victim.

Punishment: The punishment for committing this offense under BNS 94 is imprisonment of either description for a term which may extend to two years, and the offender shall also be liable to a fine.

Cognizable or Non-Cognizable, Bailable or Non-Bailable: This offense is cognizable, meaning the police can arrest the accused without a warrant.

Bailable: This offense is bailable, indicating that the accused can secure bail and be released from custody until the trial is completed.

Comparison: Section 318 [650]of the Indian Penal Code (IPC) also addresses the offense of concealing the [651]birth of a child by secret disposal of the dead body: IPC Section 318: States [652]that whoever, by secretly burying or otherwise disposing of the dead body of a child whether such child die before or after or during its birth, intentionally conceals or endeavours to [653]conceal the birth of such child, shall be punished with imprisonment of either description for a term which may extend to two years, or with fine, or with both.

Key Differences: BNS 94: Reflects updated legal terminology and provisions in the new Bharatiya Nyaya Sanhita. IPC 318: Part of the older Indian Penal Code framework, now replaced by BNS 94.

[649] bprd.nic.in

[650] odishapolicecidcb.gov.in

[651] www.bareactslive.com

[652] prsindia.org

[653] bprd.nic.in

BNS Section 95

Definition: Hiring, employing [654] or Engaging a Child to Commit an Offence Section 95 of the Bharatiya Nyaya Sanhita (BNS) 2023 addresses the offense of hiring [655], or engaging a child to commit an offense.

Illustration: If a person hires a child to steal from a shop, they are committing an offense under BNS 95.

Example: Suppose an individual employs a child to deliver illegal substances. This act falls under BNS 95 as it involves engaging a child to commit an offense.

Comment: This section aims to protect children from being exploited and used in criminal activities. It emphasizes the importance of safeguarding the well-being of children and holding accountable those who involve minors in illegal acts.

Classification of Offence and Punishment Offence Classification: This offense is cognizable and non-bailable.

Punishment: The punishment for committing this offense under BNS 95 is imprisonment of either description for a term which shall not be less than three years but which may extend to ten years, and a fine. If the offense is committed, the person shall also be punished with the punishment provided for that offense as if the offense had been committed by such person themselves.

Cognizable or non-cognizable Cognizable: The police can arrest the accused without a warrant.

Bailable or non-Bailable Non Bailable: Bail is not granted as a [655]matter of right, and the accused can be released on bail only at the discretion of the court.

---

[654] Ministry of Home Affairs. (2024). The Bharatiya Nyaya Sanhita, 2023. Retrieved from https://www.mha.gov.in/sites/default/files/250883_english_01042024.pdf

[655] www.slideshare.net

BNS Section 96

Definition: Procuration of Child Section 96 of the Bharatiya Nyaya Sanhita (BNS) 2023 addresses the offense of procuring a child for illicit purposes.

Illustration: If a person induces a [656]child under the age of eighteen to go from one place to another or to perform [657]an act with the intent that the child [658]may be forced or seduced into [659]illicit intercourse with another person, they are committing an offense under BNS 96.

Example: Suppose an individual convinces a minor to travel to a different city with the intent of forcing them into prostitution. This act falls under BNS 96 as it involves procuring a child for illicit purposes.

Comment: This section is aimed at protecting children from exploitation and abuse. It criminalizes actions that involve enticing or coercing children into situations where they may be subjected to [660]sexual exploitation or forced into illicit activities.

Classification of Offence and Punishment Classification: This offense is classified as a criminal offense due to its serious nature and potential harm to the victim.

Punishment: The punishment for committing this offense under BNS 96 is imprisonment of either description for a term which may extend to ten years, and the offender shall also be liable to a fine.

Cognizable or Non-Cognizable, Bailable or Non-Bailable: This offense is cognizable, meaning the police can arrest the accused without a warrant.

Non-Bailable: This offense is non-bailable, indicating that the accused cannot secure bail and must remain in custody until the trial is completed.

---

[656] bprd.nic.in

[657] prsindia.org

[658] bprd.nic.in

[659] pdfcookie.com

[660] bprd.nic.in

Comparison: Section 366A of the [661]Indian Penal Code (IPC) also addresses the offense of procuring a minor girl for illicit purposes: IPC Section 366A: [662]States that whoever, by any means whatsoever, induces any minor girl under the age of eighteen years to go from any place or to do any act with intent that such girl may be, or knowing that it is likely that she will be, forced or seduced to illicit intercourse with another person shall be [663]punished with imprisonment of either description for a term which may extend to ten years, and shall also be liable to a fine.

Key Differences: BNS 96: Reflects updated legal terminology and provisions in the new Bharatiya Nyaya Sanhita, and is gender-neutral.IPC 366A: Part of the older Indian Penal Code framework, now replaced by BNS 96, and specifically addressed minor girl.

BNS Section 97

Definition: Kidnapping or Abducting[664] Child Under Ten Years with Intent to Steal Section 97 of the Bharatiya Nyaya Sanhita (BNS) 2023 addresses the offense of kidnapping or abducting a child under ten years with the intent to steal from the child's person.

Illustration: If a person kidnaps or abducts [665]a child under the age of ten with the intention of taking something valuable from the child, they are committing an offense under BNS 97.

Example: Suppose an individual forcibly takes a young child from a park with the intent to steal a piece of jewelry the child is wearing. This act falls under BNS 97 as it involves kidnapping or abducting a [666]child under ten years with the intent to steal.

---

[661] odishapolicecidcb.gov.in

[662] prsindia.org

[663] bprd.nic.in

[664] Ministry of Home Affairs. (2024). The Bharatiya Nyaya Sanhita, 2023. Retrieved from https://www.mha.gov.in/sites/default/files/250883_english_01042024.pdf

[665] bprd.nic.in

[666] odishapolicecidcb.gov.in

Comment: This section is aimed at protecting young children from being exploited and stolen from. It criminalizes the act of kidnapping or abducting a child with the specific intent to take something valuable from them, emphasizing the need to safeguard the well-being and security of minors.

Classification of Offence and Punishment Classification: This offense is classified as a criminal offense due to its serious nature and potential harm to the victim.

Punishment: The punishment for committing this offense under BNS 97 is [667]imprisonment of either description for a term which may extend to seven years, and the offender shall also be liable to a fine.

Cognizable or Non-Cognizable, Bailable or Non-Bailable: This offense is cognizable, meaning the police can arrest the accused without a warrant.

Non-Bailable: This offense is non-bailable, indicating that the accused cannot secure bail and must remain in custody until the trial is completed.

Comparison: Section 369 of the[668] Indian Penal Code (IPC) also addresses the offense of kidnapping or abducting a [669]child under ten years with the [670]intent to steal from its person : IPC Section 369: States [671]that whoever kidnaps or abducts any child under the age of ten years with the intention of taking dishonestly any movable property from the person of such child, shall be punished with imprisonment of either description for a term which may extend to seven years, and shall also be liable to a fine.

Key Differences: BNS 97: Reflects updated legal terminology and provisions in the new Bharatiya Nyaya Sanhita. IPC 369: Part of the older Indian Penal Code framework, now replaced by BNS 97.

---

[667] bprd.nic.in

[668] www.bareactslive.com

[669] odishapolicecidcb.gov.in

[670] bprd.nic.in

[671] prsindia.org

BNS Section 98

Definition: Selling Minor for Purposes of [672]Prostitution, etc. Section 98 of the Bharatiya Nyaya Sanhita (BNS) 2023 addresses the offense of selling, letting to hire, or otherwise disposing of a child for purposes of prostitution or illicit intercourse.

Illustration: [673]If a person sells a child to a brothel owner with the intent that the child will be used for prostitution, it constitutes an offense under BNS 98.

Example: Suppose an individual disposes of a minor to someone who runs an illegal brothel. This act falls under BNS 98 as it involves selling a child for immoral purposes.

Comment: This section aims to protect children from being exploited and used in prostitution or other immoral activities. It emphasizes the importance of safeguarding minors and holding accountable those who exploit them for such purposes.

Classification of Offence and Punishment Offence Classification: This offense is cognizable and non-bailable.

Punishment: The punishment for committing this offense under BNS 98 is [674]imprisonment of either description for a term which may extend to ten years, and a fine.

Cognizable or non-cognizable Cognizable: The police can arrest the accused without a warrant.

Bailable or non-Bailable: Non Bailable bail is not [675]granted as a matter of right, and the accused can be released on bail only at the discretion of the court.

---

[672] Ministry of Home Affairs. (2024). The Bharatiya Nyaya Sanhita, 2023. Retrieved from https://www.mha.gov.in/sites/default/files/250883_english_01042024.pdf

[673] www.bareactslive.com

[674] bprd.nic.in

[675] www.slideshare.net

Comparison: Section 372[676] of the Indian Penal Code (IPC) also addresses the offense of selling a [677]minor for purposes of prostitution or illicit intercourse. The key differences between BNS 98 and IPC Section 372 are: BNS 98: Reflects updated legal terminology and provisions in the new Bharatiya Nyaya Sanhita. IPC 372: Part of the older Indian Penal Code framework, now replaced by BNS 98.

BNS Section 99

Definition: Buying Minor for Purposes of [678]Prostitution, etc. Section 99 of the Bharatiya Nyaya Sanhita (BNS) 2023 addresses the offense of buying, hiring, or otherwise obtaining possession of a child for purposes of prostitution or illicit intercourse.

Illustration: If a person buys a child with the intent to use them for prostitution, it constitutes an offense under BNS 99.

Example: Suppose an individual hires a minor to work in a brothel. This act falls under BNS 99 as it involves obtaining possession of a child for immoral purposes.

Comment: This section aims to protect children from being exploited and used in prostitution or other immoral activities. It emphasizes the importance of safeguarding minors and holding accountable those who exploit them for such purposes.

Classification of Offence and Punishment Offence Classification: This offense is cognizable and non-bailable.

Punishment: The punishment for committing this offense under BNS 99 is [679]imprisonment of either description for a term which shall not be less than seven years but which may extend to fourteen years, and a fine.

---

[676] www.bareactslive.com

[677] odishapolicecidcb.gov.in

[678] Ministry of Home Affairs. (2024). The Bharatiya Nyaya Sanhita, 2023. Retrieved from https://www.mha.gov.in/sites/default/files/250883_english_01042024.pdf

[679] bprd.nic.in

Cognizable or Non- Cognizable Cognizable: The police can arrest the accused without a warrant.

Bailable or Non-Bailable: Non bailable bail is not [680]granted as a matter of right, and the accused can be released on bail only at the discretion of the court.

Comparison: With IPC Section 373 and Section 99 of the Bharatiya Nyaya Sanhita (BNS) 2023 is similar to [681]Section 373 of the Indian Penal Code (IPC), which also addresses the offense of buying, hiring, or otherwise obtaining possession of [682]a child for purposes of prostitution or illicit intercourse.

Key differences: Between BNS 99 and IPC Section 373 are: BNS 99: Reflects updated legal terminology and provisions in the new Bharatiya Nyaya Sanhita. IPC 373: Part of the older Indian Penal Code framework, now replaced by BNS 99.

[680] www.slideshare.net

[681] www.bareactslive.com

[682] prsindia.org

CHAPTER-VI; OF OFFENCES AFFECTING THE HUMAN BODY

BNS Section 100

Definition: Culpable Homicide Section 100 of the [683]Bharatiya Nyaya Sanhita (BNS) 2023 defines culpable homicide as causing death by doing an act with the intention of causing death, or with the intention of causing such bodily injury as is likely to cause death, or with the knowledge that the act is likely to cause death.

Illustration: [684]If a person lays sticks and turf over a pit [685]with the intention of causing death, or knowing [686]that death is likely to be caused, and someone falls into the pit and dies, the person who laid the sticks and turf has committed culpable homicide.

Example: Suppose A knows that there is a pit covered with sticks and turf, and [687]Z, believing the ground to be firm, treads on it, falls in, and is killed. A has committed the offense of culpable homicide.

Comment: This section emphasizes the seriousness of causing death through intentional actions or with [688]knowledge of the likely consequences. It highlights the need for accountability when such actions result in the loss of life.

---

[683] Ministry of Home Affairs. (2024). The Bharatiya Nyaya Sanhita, 2023. Retrieved from https://www.mha.gov.in/sites/default/files/250883_english_01042024.pdf

[684] www.bareactslive.com

[685] bprd.nic.in

[686] www.bareactslive.com

[687] www.indiacode.nic.in

[688] bprd.nic.in

Classification of Offence and Punishment Classification: This offense is classified as a criminal offense due to its serious nature and potential harm to the victim.

Punishment: The punishment for committing this offense under BNS 100 is imprisonment of either description for a term which may extend to ten years, and the offender shall also be liable to a fine.

Cognizable or Non-Cognizable, Bailable or Non-Bailable: This offense is cognizable, meaning the police can arrest the accused without a warrant.

Bailable: This offense is bailable, indicating that the accused can secure bail and be released from custody until the trial is completed.

Comparison Section [689]299 of the Indian Penal Code (IPC) also defines culpable homicide in a similar manner: IPC Section 299: States [690]that whoever causes death by doing an act with the intention of causing death, or with the intention of causing such bodily injury as is likely to cause death, or with the knowledge that he is likely by such act to cause death, commits the offense of culpable homicide.

Key Differences: BNS 100: Reflects updated legal terminology and provisions in the new Bharatiya Nyaya Sanhita. IPC 299: Part of the older Indian Penal Code framework, now replaced by BNS 100.

BNS Section 101

Definition: Murder [691]BNS Section 101 deals with the crime of murder. Murder is the intentional killing of a person with malice aforethought.

Illustration: A person plans and executes the killing of a business rival. This premeditated act falls under the category of murder as defined by BNS 101.

---

[689] odishapolicecidcb.gov.in

[690] prsindia.org

[691] Ministry of Home Affairs. (2024). The Bharatiya Nyaya Sanhita, 2023. Retrieved from https://www.mha.gov.in/sites/default/files/250883_english_01042024.pdf

Example: Suppose someone deliberately poisons a coworker to take over their position. This act of intentional killing qualifies as murder under BNS 101.

Comment: This section emphasizes the severe nature of premeditated and malicious acts leading to death. It underscores the importance of distinguishing murder from other forms of homicide, ensuring that the punishment matches the gravity of the crime.

Classification of Offence and Punishment Classification: Murder is classified as a heinous crime due to the [692]deliberate and malicious intent behind it.

Punishment: The punishment for murder under BNS 101 can range from life imprisonment to the death penalty.

Cognizable or Non-Cognizable, Bailable or Non-Bailable: Murder is a cognizable offense, meaning the police have the authority to arrest the accused without a warrant.

Bailable: Murder is non-bailable, indicating the accused cannot easily secure bail and must remain in custody until the trial concludes.

Comparison: [693]Section 300 of the Indian Penal Code (IPC) outlines the conditions under which an act of killing is classified as murder. It covers several scenarios, including: Intentional Killing: When the act is done with the intention of causing death. Infliction of Fatal Injuries: When the act is done with the intention of causing bodily injury that the [694]offender knows is likely to cause death. Extreme Indifference: [695]When the act is done with such disregard for human life that it is almost certain to cause death.

Key Differences: IPC Section 300: Details specific exceptions where culpable homicide is not considered murder, such as killing in self-defence or in a sudden heat of passion upon grave provocation. BNS 101: Takes a

[692] www.bareactslive.com

[693] blog.ipleaders.in

[694] blog.ipleaders.in

[695] blog.ipleaders.in

more rigid stance and does not provide such exceptions, focusing strictly on the act of murder and its punishment.

BNS Section 102

Definition: [696]**Culpable Homicide by Causing Death of Person Other** [697]**Than Person Whose Death Was Intended Section 102** of the Bharatiya Nyaya Sanhita (BNS) 2023 addresses the scenario where a person, by doing something they intend or know is likely to cause death, ends up causing the death of someone other than the intended victim. The culpability of the offense remains the same as if the intended person had died.

Illustration: A person shoots at someone intending to kill them, but misses and hits an innocent bystander, causing their death.

Example: Suppose someone plants a bomb to kill a specific target, but the bomb explodes and kills a passerby instead. Under BNS 102, the offender is held responsible as if they had killed the intended target.

Comment: This section addresses the severe nature of unintended deaths resulting from actions intended to cause [698]death. It ensures that individuals are held accountable for the full consequences of their actions, maintaining the same level of culpability as if the intended person had been killed.

Classification of Offence and Punishment Classification: This is classified as a serious criminal offense due to the intent and the resulting death.

Punishment: The punishment for culpable homicide under BNS 102 can range from life imprisonment to the death penalty, depending on the circumstances and severity of the act.

---

[696] www.alujaipur.ac.in

[697] Ministry of Home Affairs. (2024). The Bharatiya Nyaya Sanhita, 2023. Retrieved from https://www.mha.gov.in/sites/default/files/250883_english_01042024.pdf

[698] repository.up.ac.za

Cognizable or Non-Cognizable, Bailable or Non-Bailable: This offense is cognizable, meaning the police can arrest the accused without a warrant.

Bailable: This offense is non-bailable, indicating that the accused cannot easily secure bail and must remain in custody until the trial concludes.

Comparison: [699]Section 301 of the Indian Penal Code (IPC) also deals with culpable homicide by causing the death of a person other than the person whose death was intended. The key points of comparison are :IPC Section 301: It states that if a person does something with the intention of causing death or [700]knowing it to be likely to cause death, and by that act causes the death of any person whose death they neither intend nor know themselves to be likely to cause, the culpable homicide committed by the offender is of the description of which it would have been if they [701]had caused the death of the person whose death they intended or knew themselves to be likely to cause.

Key Differences: BNS 102: Similar to IPC Section 301, it maintains the same level of culpability as if the intended person had been killed.

BNS Section 103(1)

Definition: Punishment for Murder Section 103[702] of the Bharatiya Nyaya Sanhita (BNS) 2023 specifies the punishment for committing murder.

Illustration: If an individual deliberately and with premeditation kills another person, such as a calculated assassination of a rival, this falls under the purview of BNS 103.

---

[699] blog.ipleaders.in

[700] www.bareactslive.com

[701] blog.ipleaders.in

[702] Ministry of Home Affairs. (2024). The Bharatiya Nyaya Sanhita, 2023. Retrieved from https://www.mha.gov.in/sites/default/files/250883_english_01042024.pdf

Example: Consider a case where a person meticulously plans and executes the poisoning of their business competitor to gain an unfair advantage. This is considered murder under BNS 103.

Classification of Offence and Punishment Classification: This is classified as a heinous criminal offense due to the intentional and premeditated nature of the act.

Punishment: The punishment for murder under BNS 103 can be either death or life imprisonment. Life imprisonment in this context means [703]imprisonment for the remainder of the convict's natural life.

Cognizable or Non-Cognizable, Bailable or Non-Bailable: Murder is a cognizable [704]offense, which means that police can arrest the accused without a warrant.

Bailable: Murder is non-bailable, indicating that the accused cannot easily secure bail and must remain in custody until the trial is completed.

Comparison: [705]Section 302 of the Indian Penal Code (IPC) also specifies the punishment for murder: IPC Section 302: States that whoever commits murder shall be punished with death or imprisonment for life, and shall also be liable to a fine.

Key Differences: BNS 103: Similar to IPC Section 302 in that both specify death or life imprisonment as the punishment for murder. However, BNS 103 does not mention the imposition of a fine. IPC Section 302: Includes an additional provision for the possibility of a fine along with the death penalty or life imprisonment.

---

[703] www.bareactslive.com

[704] 519-520.cocolog-nifty.com

[705]blog.ipleaders.in

BNS Section 103 (2)

Definition: Punishment for Murder[706] **BNS 103(2)** further elaborates on the punishment for murder, specifically addressing particular circumstances that might warrant variations in sentencing. Here's the lowdown:

Illustration: A person commits murder with premeditation and intent. For instance, a jealous lover meticulously plans and executes the killing of their partner's new lover. This scenario fits under BNS 103 (2) as it involves deliberate intent.

Example: Suppose an individual ambushes and kills a rival gang member in a planned attack. This act of murder, with evident premeditation, would be considered under BNS 103 (2).

Comment: This section underscores the severity of premeditated murder, highlighting the deliberate and malicious intent behind such acts. By specifying strict punishments, the BNS aims to deter such heinous crimes and ensure justice for victims.

Classification of Offence and Punishment Classification: This is categorized as a heinous and serious offense due to the deliberate and malicious intent behind the act.

Punishment: Punishments under BNS 103 (2) can range from life imprisonment to the death penalty. Life imprisonment under this section means imprisonment for the convict's natural life.

Cognizable or Non-Cognizable, Bailable or Non-Bailable: This offense is cognizable, allowing police to arrest the accused without a warrant.

Bailable: This offense is non-bailable, implying that the accused cannot easily secure bail and must remain in custody until the trial is concluded.

---

[706] Ministry of Home Affairs. (2024). The Bharatiya Nyaya Sanhita, 2023. Retrieved from https://www.mha.gov.in/sites/default/files/250883_english_01042024.pdf

Comparison: [707]Section 302 of the Indian Penal Code (IPC) also [708]deals with the punishment for murder: IPC Section 302: States that anyone committing murder shall be punished with death, or life imprisonment, and may also be liable to a fine.

Key Differences: BNS 103 (2): Similar to IPC Section 302, it stipulates either death or life imprisonment as the punishment for murder but focuses [709]explicitly on the nature of the crime being premeditated and intentional. IPC Section 302: Includes an additional provision for the possibility of a fine in addition to the death penalty or life imprisonment.

BNS Section 104

Definition: Punishment for Murder by [710]Life-Convict Section 104 of the Bharatiya Nyaya Sanhita (BNS) 2023 deals with the punishment for murder committed by a person who is already serving a life sentence.

Illustration: A person serving a life sentence for a previous crime kills another inmate or a prison guard. This act falls under BNS 104.

Example: Suppose a life-convict in a high-security prison murders a fellow inmate. Under BNS 104, the convict could face the death penalty or be sentenced to life imprisonment without the possibility of parole.

Comment: This section addresses the gravity of offenses committed by individuals already serving life sentences, emphasizing the severe nature of such acts. By prescribing stringent punishments, the BNS aims to deter further criminal activity by life-convicts and maintain safety within the prison system.

---

[707] blog.ipleaders.in

[708] www.bareactslive.com

[709] blog.ipleaders.in

[710] Ministry of Home Affairs. (2024). The Bharatiya Nyaya Sanhita, 2023. Retrieved from https://www.mha.gov.in/sites/default/files/250883_english_01042024.pdf

Classification of Offence and Punishment Classification: This is classified as a serious criminal offense due to the gravity of the act and the status of the offender as a life-convict.

Punishment: The punishment for murder under BNS 104 can be either death or life imprisonment, which means [711]imprisonment for the remainder of the convict's natural life.

Cognizable or Non-Cognizable, Bailable or Non-Bailable: This offense is cognizable, meaning the police can arrest the accused without a warrant.

Bailable: This offense is non-bailable, indicating that the accused cannot easily secure bail and must remain in custody until the trial is completed.

Comparison: [712]Section 303 of the Indian Penal Code (IPC), which was repealed by the Supreme Court in the case of Mithu v. State of Punjab, also dealt with the punishment for murder by a life-convict.

Key differences: IPC Section 303: It mandated the death penalty for a life-convict who committed murder, without any discretion for the courts to consider mitigating circumstances.

BNS Section 105

Definition: While it also provides for the death penalty or life imprisonment, it incorporates provisions for considering mitigating circumstances, giving courts some discretion in sentencing. Punishment for Culpable Homicide[713] Not Amounting to Murder Section 105 of the Bharatiya Nyaya Sanhita (BNS) 2023 deals with the punishment for culpable homicide that does not amount to murder.

---

[711] www.bareactslive.com

[712] www.bareactslive.com

[713] Ministry of Home Affairs. (2024). The Bharatiya Nyaya Sanhita, 2023. Retrieved from https://www.mha.gov.in/sites/default/files/250883_english_01042024.pdf

Illustration: A person, in a fit of rage, hits someone with a heavy object, causing their death. The act was not premeditated, but it was [714]done with the knowledge that it could cause death.

Example: Suppose someone, during a heated argument, pushes another person who then falls and hits their head, resulting [715]in death. This act falls under BNS 105 as culpable homicide not amounting to murder.

Comment: This section addresses serious offenses that result in death but lack the premeditation characteristic of murder. It emphasizes the intent and knowledge behind the act, ensuring that appropriate punishment is meted out.

Classification of Offence and Punishment Classification: This is classified as a serious criminal offense due to the resulting death, even though it lacks the premeditation of murder.

Punishment: [716]The punishment for culpable homicide not amounting to murder under BNS 105 can be imprisonment for life or [717]imprisonment of either description for a term which shall not be less than five years but which may extend to ten years, and the offender may also be liable to a fine.

Cognizable or Non-Cognizable, Bailable or Non-Bailable: This offense is cognizable, meaning the police can arrest the accused without a warrant.

Bailable: This offense is bailable, indicating that the accused can secure bail and be released from custody until the trial is completed.

Comparison: [718]Section 304 of the Indian Penal Code (IPC) also deals with culpable homicide not amounting to murder: IPC Section 304: It divides culpable homicide not amounting to murder into two parts: Section

---

[714] www.bareactslive.com

[715] blog.ipleaders.in

[716] blog.ipleaders.in

[717] www.latestlaws.com

[718] blog.ipleaders.in

304(a): Deals with [719]causing death by negligence, which is punishable with imprisonment of either description for a term which may extend to two years, or with fine, or with both. Section 304(b): Deals with causing [720]death by a rash or negligent act not amounting to culpable homicide, which is punishable with imprisonment of either description for a term which may extend to six months, or with fine, or with both.

Key Differences: BNS 105: Focuses on the intent and knowledge behind the act, providing a range of imprisonment terms and the possibility of a fine. IPC Section 304: Differentiates between culpable homicide by negligence and culpable homicide by a rash or negligent act, with varying degrees of punishment.

BNS Section 106 (1)

Definition: Causing Death by [721]Negligence Section 106(1) of the Bharatiya Nyaya Sanhita (BNS) 2023 addresses the punishment for causing death by negligence.

Illustration: A person driving recklessly without following traffic rules hits a pedestrian, leading to the pedestrian's death. This act falls under BNS 106(1) as it involves negligence.

Example: Suppose a factory owner fails to maintain safety standards, resulting in a fatal accident for a worker. This would be considered causing death by negligence under BNS 106(1).

Comment: This section underscores the seriousness of negligent actions that result in death, highlighting the need for accountability even in the absence of intent to kill. By defining the offense and prescribing punishments, the BNS aims to promote responsible behavior and adherence to safety standards.

---

[719] www.bareactslive.com

[720] blog.ipleaders.in

[721] Ministry of Home Affairs. (2024). The Bharatiya Nyaya Sanhita, 2023. Retrieved from https://www.mha.gov.in/sites/default/files/250883_english_01042024.pdf

Classification of Offence and Punishment Classification: This is classified as a criminal offense due to the resulting death, even though there was no intent to kill.

Punishment: The punishment for causing death by negligence under BNS 106(1) can be imprisonment for a term which may extend to [722]two years, or with fine, or with both.

Cognizable or Non-Cognizable, Bailable or Non-Bailable: This offense is cognizable, meaning the police can arrest the accused without a warrant.

Bailable: This offense is bailable, indicating that the accused can secure bail and be released from custody until the trial is completed.

Comparison: [723]Section 304A of the Indian Penal Code (IPC) also deals with causing death by negligence: IPC Section 304A: States that whoever causes the death of any person by doing any rash or negligent act not amounting to culpable homicide shall be punished with imprisonment of either description for a term which may extend to [724]two years, or with fine, or with both.

Key Differences: BNS 106(1): Similar to IPC Section 304A in terms of the punishment and classification of the offense. Both sections focus on acts of negligence that result in death. IPC Section 304A: Provides for the same range of imprisonment and fine for causing death by negligence.

BNS Section 106 (2)

Definition: Causing Death by Negligence[725] Section 106(2) of the Bharatiya Nyaya Sanhita (BNS) 2023 addresses situations where death is caused due to negligence, but the specifics might differ slightly from the earlier sub-section. Let's explore this in detail:

---

[722] www.bareactslive.com

[723] blog.ipleaders.in

[724] www.bareactslive.com

[725] Ministry of Home Affairs. (2024). The Bharatiya Nyaya Sanhita, 2023. Retrieved from https://www.mha.gov.in/sites/default/files/250883_english_01042024.pdf

Illustration: Imagine a building contractor neglects to follow safety protocols while constructing a building, leading to its collapse and causing fatalities. This would fall under BNS 106(2) due to the gross negligence involved.

Example: A doctor performs surgery without following standard medical procedures, resulting in the patient's death. This act of gross negligence would be addressed under BNS 106(2).

Comment: This section underscores the seriousness of gross negligence leading to death, highlighting the need for accountability even when there is no intent to kill. By defining the offense and prescribing punishments, the BNS aims to promote responsible behavior and adherence to safety standards.

Classification of Offence and Punishment Classification: This is classified as a criminal offense due to the resulting death caused by the negligent actions.

Punishment: The punishment for causing death by negligence under BNS 106(2) can be imprisonment for a term which may extend to [726]two years, or with fine, or with both.

Cognizable or Non-Cognizable, Bailable or Non-Bailable: This offense is cognizable, meaning the police can arrest the accused without a warrant.

Bailable: This offense is bailable, indicating that the accused can secure bail and be released from custody until the trial is completed.

Comparison: Section 304A of [727]the Indian Penal Code (IPC) also deals with [728]causing death by negligence: IPC Section 304A: States that whoever causes the death of any person by doing any rash or negligent act not amounting to culpable homicide shall be punished with imprisonment of either description for a term which may extend to two years, or with fine, or with both.

---

[726] www.bareactslive.com

[727] blog.ipleaders.in

[728] www.bareactslive.com

Key Differences: BNS 106(2): Similar to IPC Section 304A in terms of punishment and classification, focusing on acts of gross negligence leading to death. IPC Section 304A: Provides for the same range of imprisonment and fine for causing death by negligence.

BNS Section 107

Definition: Abetment of Suicide of Child or Person of Unsound [729]Mind Section 107 of the Bharatiya Nyaya Sanhita (BNS) 2023 addresses the offense of abetting the suicide of a child or a person of unsound mind.

Illustration: A person convinces a minor to end their life by providing them with means to do so, such as a rope or medication.

Example: Suppose an adult manipulates a person with a mental illness into believing that suicide is the only way out of their problems, leading them to take their own life. This act falls under BNS 107.

Comment: This section emphasizes the gravity of exploiting the vulnerabilities of children and individuals with mental health conditions. By defining this serious offense and prescribing severe punishments, the BNS aims to protect these vulnerable groups from such harmful actions.

Classification of Offence and Punishment Classification: This is classified as a serious criminal offense due to the vulnerability of the victims and the severe consequences of the act.

Punishment: The punishment for abetting the suicide of a child or a person of unsound mind under BNS 107 can be death, imprisonment for life, or imprisonment for a term not exceeding ten years, along with a fine.

Cognizable or Non-Cognizable, Bailable or Non-Bailable: This offense is cognizable, meaning the police can arrest the accused without a warrant.

Bailable: This offense is non-bailable, indicating that the accused cannot easily secure bail and must remain in custody until the trial is completed.

---

[729] Ministry of Home Affairs. (2024). The Bharatiya Nyaya Sanhita, 2023. Retrieved from https://www.mha.gov.in/sites/default/files/250883_english_01042024.pdf

Comparison: Section 305 of [730]the Indian Penal Code (IPC) also deals with the abetment of suicide of a child or an insane person: IPC Section 305: States that whoever abets the suicide of a child (under 18 years of age) or an [731]insane person shall be punished with death, imprisonment for life, or imprisonment for a term not exceeding ten years, along with a fine.

Key Differences: BNS 107: Similar to IPC Section 305 in terms of the punishment and classification of the offense. Both sections focus on the vulnerability of the victims and the severe consequences of the act. IPC Section 305: Replaced by BNS 107 with effect from July 1, 2024, but the essence remains the same.

BNS Section108

Definition: Abetment of Suicide Section 108 of the [732]Bharatiya Nyaya Sanhita (BNS) 2023 deals with the offense of abetting a person's suicide.

Illustration: A person harasses their neighbor relentlessly, leading the neighbor to take their own life. This harasser is liable under BNS 108 for abetment of suicide.

Example: Suppose someone repeatedly blackmails another person, causing them immense psychological distress, and the distressed individual eventually commits suicide. The blackmailer can be charged under BNS 108 for abetment of suicide.

Comment: This section underscores the grave consequences of driving someone to take their own life. By defining this serious offense and prescribing severe punishments, the BNS aims to deter such harmful actions and ensure justice for victims.

---

[730] www.bareactslive.com

[731] www.bareactslive.com

[732] Ministry of Home Affairs. (2024). The Bharatiya Nyaya Sanhita, 2023. Retrieved from https://www.mha.gov.in/sites/default/files/250883_english_01042024.pdf

Classification of Offence and Punishment Classification: This is classified as a serious criminal offense due to the grave consequences of driving someone to suicide.

Punishment: The punishment for abetment of suicide under BNS 108 can be imprisonment for a term which may extend to ten years, and the offender shall also be liable to a fine.

Cognizable or Non-Cognizable, Bailable or Non-Bailable: This offense is cognizable, meaning the police can arrest the accused without a warrant.

Bailable: This offense is non-bailable, indicating that the accused cannot easily secure bail and must remain in custody until the trial is completed.

Comparison: Section 306 of the Indian Penal Code (IPC) also deals with the abetment of suicide: IPC Section 306: States that if any person commits suicide, whoever abets the commission of such suicide shall be punished with imprisonment [733]of either description for a term which may extend to ten years, and shall also be liable to a fine.

Key Differences: BNS 108: Similar to IPC Section 306 in terms of punishment and classification of the offense. Both sections address the severe impact of pushing someone to take their own life. IPC Section 306: Provides the same range of imprisonment and fine for abetment of suicide.

BNS Section 109

Definition: Attempt to Murder Section 109 [734]of the Bharatiya Nyaya Sanhita (BNS) 2023 deals with the offense of attempting to commit murder.

Illustration: A person attempts to shoot someone with a firearm but misses. This act, although unsuccessful, is classified as an attempt to murder.

---

[733] blog.ipleaders.in

[734] Ministry of Home Affairs. (2024). The Bharatiya Nyaya Sanhita, 2023. Retrieved from https://www.mha.gov.in/sites/default/files/250883_english_01042024.pdf

Example: Suppose an individual tries to poison another person's drink, but the victim survives after immediate medical intervention. This would be considered an attempt to murder under BNS 109.

Comment: This section underscores the severe nature of attempting to take someone's life, highlighting the serious criminal intent behind such acts. By defining the offense and prescribing stringent punishments, the BNS aims to deter such harmful actions and ensure justice.

Classification of Offence and Punishment Classification: [735]Attempt to murder is classified as a serious criminal offense due to the intent to take a life.

Punishment: The punishment for an attempt to murder under BNS 109 can be imprisonment for life, or imprisonment of either description for a term which may extend to ten years, and the offender shall also be liable to a fine.

Cognizable or Non-Cognizable, Bailable or Non-Bailable: This offense is cognizable, meaning the police can arrest the accused without a warrant.

Bailable: This offense is non-bailable, indicating that the accused cannot easily secure bail and must remain in custody until the trial is completed.

Comparison: Section 307 of the I[736]ndian Penal Code (IPC) also deals with the attempt to murder: IPC Section 307: [737]States that whoever does any act with such intention or knowledge, and under such circumstances, that, if they by that act [738]caused death, they would be guilty of murder, shall be punished with imprisonment of either description for a term which may extend to ten years, and shall also be liable to a fine. If hurt is caused to any person by such act, the offender shall be liable to imprisonment for

[735] hcs.gov.in

[736] blog.ipleaders.in

[737] blog.ipleaders.in

[738] hcs.gov.in

life, or [739]imprisonment of either description for a term which may extend to ten years, and shall also be liable to a fine.

Key Differences: BNS 109: Similar to IPC Section 307 in terms of punishment and classification of the offense. Both sections address the serious nature of attempting to take someone's life. IPC Section 307: Provides the same range of imprisonment and fine for attempt to murder.

BNS Section 110

Definition: Attempt to Commit [740]Culpable Homicide Section 110 of the Bharatiya Nyaya Sanhita (BNS) 2023 addresses the offense of attempting to commit culpable homicide.

Illustration: A person attacks another with a blunt weapon, intending to cause serious [741]harm but not necessarily death. The victim survives, and the attacker is charged under BNS 110 for attempt to commit culpable homicide.

Example: Suppose someone stabs another person during a fight, aiming to seriously injure them but not [742]to kill. The victim survives, making this an attempt to commit culpable homicide under BNS 110.

Comment: This section focuses on the intent behind the act, ensuring that individuals who attempt to cause serious harm or potential death are held accountable. It highlights the importance of intent and provides a clear legal framework for punishing such acts.

---

[739] adoc.pub

[740] Ministry of Home Affairs. (2024). The Bharatiya Nyaya Sanhita, 2023. Retrieved from https://www.mha.gov.in/sites/default/files/250883_english_01042024.pdf

[741] hcs.gov.in

[742] blog.ipleaders.in

Classification of Offence and Punishment Classification: Attempt to [743]commit culpable homicide is classified as a serious criminal offense due to the [744]intent to cause serious harm or potential death.

Punishment: The punishment for an attempt to commit culpable homicide under BNS 110 can be imprisonment of either description for a term which may extend to seven years, and the offender [745]shall also be liable to a fine.

Cognizable or Non-Cognizable, Bailable or Non-Bailable: This offense is cognizable, meaning the police can arrest the accused without a warrant.

Bailable: This offense is bailable, indicating that the accused can secure bail and be released from custody until the trial is completed.

Comparison: Section 308 [746]of the Indian Penal Code (IPC) also deals with attempt to commit culpable homicide: IPC Section 308: [747]States that whoever does any act with such intention or knowledge, and under [748]such circumstances, that if they by that act caused death they would be guilty of culpable homicide not amounting to murder, shall be punished with imprisonment of either description for a term which may extend to three years, or with fine, or with both; and if hurt is caused to any person by such act, the offender shall be punished with imprisonment of either description for a term which may extend to seven years, or with fine, or with both.

Key Differences: BNS 110: Focuses on the [749]intent and knowledge behind the act, providing a clear range of punishment terms and the possibility of a fine. IPC Section 308: Differentiates between attempts causing hurt and those that do not, with varying degrees of punishment.

---

[743] adoc.pub

[744] blog.ipleaders.in

[745] adoc.pub

[746] www.bareactslive.com

[747] blog.ipleaders.in

[748] hcs.gov.in

[749] core.ac.uk

BNS Section 111

Definition: Organized Crime Section[750] 111 of the Bharatiya Nyaya Sanhita (BNS) 2023 addresses the offense of organized crime.

Illustration: A group of individuals collaborates to carry out a series of bank robberies, using violence and threats to intimidate bank staff and customers.

Example: Suppose a criminal syndicate engages in human trafficking, using coercion and violence to transport and exploit individuals for forced labor or prostitution. This would be considered organized crime under BNS 111.

Comment: This section emphasizes the severe and coordinated nature of organized crime, highlighting the danger it poses to society. By defining the offense and prescribing stringent punishments, the BNS aims to deter such activities and ensure justice.

Classification of Offence and Punishment Classification: This is classified as a serious criminal offense due to the organized and often violent nature of the activities involved.

Punishment: The punishment for organized crime under BNS 111 can include imprisonment for life, [751]imprisonment for a term which may extend to ten years, and the offender shall also be liable to a fine.

Cognizable or Non-Cognizable, Bailable or Non-Bailable: This offense is cognizable, meaning the police can arrest the accused without a warrant.

Bailable: This offense is non-bailable, indicating that the accused cannot easily secure bail and must remain in custody until the trial is completed.

Comparison: Section 310 of the Indian Penal Code (IPC) deals with criminal conspiracy: IPC Section 310: States that whoever is a [752]party to

---

[750] Ministry of Home Affairs. (2024). The Bharatiya Nyaya Sanhita, 2023. Retrieved from https://www.mha.gov.in/sites/default/files/250883_english_01042024.pdf

[751] adoc.pub

[752] blog.ipleaders.in

a criminal [753]conspiracy to commit an offense punishable with imprisonment for life, or imprisonment for a term which may extend to ten years, or with imprisonment of either description for a term which may extend to seven years, [754]or with fine, shall be punished with imprisonment [755]of either description for a term which may extend to ten years, and shall also be liable to a fine.

Key Differences: BNS 111: Focuses on organized crime involving multiple unlawful activities conducted by groups acting in concert. IPC Section 310: Focuses on criminal conspiracy to commit offenses punishable with imprisonment for life or other serious terms.

BNS Section 112

Definition: Petty Organized Crime Section 112 of the [756]Bharatiya Nyaya Sanhita (BNS) 2023 addresses the offense of petty organized crime.

Illustration: A group of individuals collaborates to carry out a series of small-scale thefts from vehicles, snatching valuables from pedestrians, and pickpocketing in crowded areas.

Example: Suppose a gang engages in unauthorized selling of tickets for public transport, or sells question papers for public examinations. These acts fall under petty organized crime as per BNS 112.

Comment: This section highlights the organized nature of smaller-scale criminal activities and their impact on society. By addressing these offenses and setting forth punishments, the BNS aims to curb such activities and uphold public order.

Classification of Offence and Punishment Classification: This is classified as a criminal offense due to the organized nature of the activities,

---

[753] pdfcookie.com

[754] adoc.pub

[755] blog.ipleaders.in

[756] Ministry of Home Affairs. (2024). The Bharatiya Nyaya Sanhita, 2023. Retrieved from https://www.mha.gov.in/sites/default/files/250883_english_01042024.pdf

even though they are on a smaller scale compared to major organized crime.

Punishment: The punishment for petty organized [757]crime under BNS 112 can be imprisonment for a term which shall not be less than one year but which may extend to seven years, and the offender [758]shall also be liable to a fine.

Cognizable or Non-Cognizable, Bailable or Non-Bailable: This offense is cognizable, meaning the police can arrest the accused without a warrant.

Bailable: This offense is bailable, indicating that the accused can secure bail and be released from custody until the trial is completed.

Comparison: Section 399 of the Indian Penal Code (IPC) deals with making preparation to commit an offense punishable [759]with imprisonment for life : IPC Section 399: States that whoever makes any preparation [760]to commit an offense punishable with imprisonment for life, or with imprisonment for a term which may extend to ten years, or with imprisonment of either description for a term which may extend to seven years, or with fine, shall be [761]punished with imprisonment of either description for a term which may extend to seven years, and shall also be liable to a fine.

Key Differences: BNS 112: Focuses on petty organized crime involving smaller-scale criminal activities conducted by groups or gangs. IPC Section 399: Focuses on making preparations to commit serious offenses [762]punishable with imprisonment for life or other significant terms.

---

[757] lawbhoomi.com

[758] adoc.pub

[759] blog.ipleaders.in

[760] adoc.pub

[761] pdfcookie.com

[762] adoc.pub

BNS Sections 113

Definition: Terrorist Act Section 113 of the [763]Bharatiya Nyaya Sanhita (BNS) 2023 defines and addresses the offense of a terrorist act.

Illustration: [764]A group of individuals detonates a bomb in a crowded market with the intent to cause fear and disrupt public order.

Example: Suppose a terrorist organization uses chemical weapons to attack a public gathering, aiming to cause mass casualties and spread terror among the population. This act falls under BNS 113.

Comment: This section emphasizes the severe impact of terrorist acts on public safety and national security. By defining such offenses and prescribing stringent punishments, the BNS aims to deter these harmful activities and ensure justice.

Classification of Offence and Punishment Classification: This is classified as a serious criminal offense due to the severe impact on public safety and national security.

Punishment: The punishment for committing a terrorist act under BNS 113 can be imprisonment for life, death penalty, [765]or imprisonment for a term which may extend to twenty years, along with a fine.

Cognizable or Non-Cognizable, Bailable or Non-Bailable: This offense is cognizable, meaning the police can arrest the accused without a warrant.

Bailable: This offense is non-bailable, indicating that the accused cannot easily secure bail and must remain in custody until the trial is completed.

Comparison: Section 121[766] of the Indian Penal Code (IPC) deals with waging, or attempting to wage war, or abetting the waging of war against

---

[763] Ministry of Home Affairs. (2024). The Bharatiya Nyaya Sanhita, 2023. Retrieved from https://www.mha.gov.in/sites/default/files/250883_english_01042024.pdf

[764] blog.ipleaders.in

[765] pdfcookie.com

[766] blog.ipleaders.in

the Government of India : IPC Section 121: States that whoever wages war against the Government of India, [767]or attempts to wage such war, or abets the waging of such war, shall be punished with imprisonment for life, [768]or imprisonment of either description for a term which may extend to ten years, and shall also be liable to a fine.

Key Differences: BNS 113: Focuses on acts intended to threaten the unity, integrity, sovereignty, security, or economic security of India, or to strike terror in the people. IPC Section 121: Focuses on [769]waging or attempting to wage war against the Government of India.

BNS Section 114

Definition: [770]Hurt Section 114 of the Bharatiya Nyaya Sanhita (BNS) 2023 defines and addresses the offense of hurt, which is the infliction of physical pain or injury to another person.

Illustration: A person slaps another during an argument, causing physical pain and a visible bruise. This act is considered hurt under BNS 114.

Example: Suppose someone hits their neighbor with a stick, causing a cut on the arm. This would be categorized as hurt under BNS 114.

Comment: This section emphasizes the intentional infliction of physical pain or injury, highlighting the importance of addressing and punishing such acts to ensure public order and individual safety.

Classification of Offence and Punishment Classification: Hurt [771]is classified as a criminal offense due to the intentional infliction of physical pain or injury. Punishment: The punishment for causing hurt under BNS

---

[767] adoc.pub

[768] hcs.gov.in

[769] adoc.pub

[770] Ministry of Home Affairs. (2024). The Bharatiya Nyaya Sanhita, 2023. Retrieved from https://www.mha.gov.in/sites/default/files/250883_english_01042024.pdf

[771] blog.ipleaders.in

114 can be [772]imprisonment for a term which may extend to one year, or with fine, or with both.

Cognizable or Non-Cognizable, Bailable or Non-Bailable: This offense is non-cognizable, meaning the police cannot arrest the accused without a warrant.

Bailable: This offense is bailable, indicating that the accused can secure bail and be released from custody until the trial is completed.

Comparison: Section [773]319 of the Indian Penal Code (IPC) defines hurt: IPC Section 319: States that whoever causes bodily pain, disease, or infirmity to any person is said to cause hurt.

Key Differences: BNS 114: Similar to IPC Section 319 in defining the offense of hurt and specifying punishment. Both sections focus on the infliction of physical pain or injury. IPC Section 319: Aligns with BNS 114 in terms of defining and addressing the offense of hurt.

BNS 115 (1)

Definition: [774]Voluntarily Causing Hurt Section 115(1) of the Bharatiya Nyaya Sanhita (BNS) 2023 deals with the offense of voluntarily causing hurt to another person.

Illustration: A person punches another during an argument, causing physical pain and injury. This act falls under BNS 115(1) as voluntarily causing hurt.

Example: Suppose someone throws a stone at another person, intending to cause pain or injury, and the victim gets a bruise. This would be classified as voluntarily causing hurt under BNS 115(1).

---

772 adoc.pub

773 blog.ipleaders.in

774 Ministry of Home Affairs. (2024). The Bharatiya Nyaya Sanhita, 2023. Retrieved from https://www.mha.gov.in/sites/default/files/250883_english_01042024.pdf

Classification of Offence and Punishment Classification: This is classified as a criminal offense due to the intentional infliction of pain or injury.

Punishment: [775]The punishment for voluntarily causing hurt under BNS 115(1) can be imprisonment for a term which may extend to one year, or with fine, or with both.

Cognizable or Non-Cognizable, Bailable or Non-Bailable: This offense is cognizable, meaning the police can arrest the accused without a warrant.

Bailable: This offense is bailable, indicating that the accused can secure bail and be released from custody until the trial is completed.

Comparison: [776]Section 321 of the Indian Penal Code (IPC) defines voluntarily causing hurt: IPC Section 321: States that whoever does any act with the intention of [777]thereby causing hurt to any person, or with the knowledge that he is likely thereby to cause hurt to any person, and does thereby cause hurt to any person, is said "voluntarily to cause hurt."

Key Differences: BNS 115(1): Similar to IPC Section 321 in defining and addressing the offense of voluntarily causing hurt, with specific punishment terms. IPC Section 321: Aligns with BNS 115(1) in terms of defining and addressing the offense of voluntarily causing hurt.

BNS Section 115 (2)

Definition: [778]Punishment for Voluntarily Causing Hurt Section 115(2) of the Bharatiya Nyaya Sanhita (BNS) 2023 deals specifically with the punishment for voluntarily causing hurt.

---

[775] hcs.gov.in

[776] blog.ipleaders.in

[777] pdfcookie.com

[778] Ministry of Home Affairs. (2024). The Bharatiya Nyaya Sanhita, 2023. Retrieved from https://www.mha.gov.in/sites/default/files/250883_english_01042024.pdf

Illustration: If a person intentionally strikes another with a stick, resulting in visible bruises and pain, this act is categorized under BNS 115(2) as voluntarily causing hurt.

Example: Suppose an individual punches someone during an altercation, causing a black eye and some swelling. This would be classified under BNS 115(2).

Comment: This section emphasizes the intentional nature of causing physical pain or injury. By defining the offense and prescribing punishments, the BNS aims to deter such acts and ensure accountability.

Classification of Offence and Punishment Classification: Voluntarily causing hurt is classified as a criminal offense [779]due to the intentional nature of the act.

Punishment: The punishment for voluntarily causing hurt under BNS 115(2) can be [780]imprisonment for a term which may extend to one year, or with fine, or with both.

Cognizable or Non-Cognizable, Bailable or Non-Bailable: This offense is non-cognizable, meaning the police cannot arrest the accused without a warrant.

Bailable: This offense is bailable, indicating that the accused can secure bail and be released from custody until the trial is completed.

Comparison: [781]Section 323 of the Indian Penal Code (IPC) deals with the punishment for voluntarily causing hurt: IPC Section 323: States that [782]whoever, except in the cases provided for by Section 334, voluntarily causes hurt shall be punished with imprisonment of either description for a term which may extend to one year, or with fine which may extend to one thousand rupees, or with both.

---

[779] hcs.gov.in

[780] adoc.pub

[781] blog.ipleaders.in

[782] pdfcookie.com

Key Differences: BNS 115(2): Similar to IPC Section 323 in defining and addressing the punishment for voluntarily causing hurt, specifying punishment terms and conditions. IPC Section 323: Aligns with BNS 115(2) in terms of defining and addressing the offense of voluntarily causing hurt with specified punishment terms.

BNS Section 116

Definition: Grievous Hurt Definition Section 116 of the [783]Bharatiya Nyaya Sanhita (BNS) 2023 defines grievous hurt and lays out the related punishments and classifications.

Illustration: If someone attacks another person with a weapon, resulting in severe injuries like fractures or deep wounds, this would be classified as grievous hurt under BNS 116.

Example: Suppose an individual severely beats another person, causing multiple fractures and a prolonged recovery period. This act would be considered grievous hurt under BNS 116.

Comment: This section emphasizes the serious nature of severe injuries inflicted intentionally. By defining grievous hurt and specifying punishments, the BNS aims to deter such acts and ensure justice for the victims.

Classification of Offence and Punishment Classification: Grievous hurt is classified as a serious criminal offense due to the severe nature of the injuries inflicted.

Punishment: [784]The punishment for causing grievous hurt under BNS 116 can be [785]imprisonment for a term which may extend to seven years, and the offender shall also be liable to a fine.

---

[783] Ministry of Home Affairs. (2024). The Bharatiya Nyaya Sanhita, 2023. Retrieved from https://www.mha.gov.in/sites/default/files/250883_english_01042024.pdf

[784] blog.ipleaders.in

[785] adoc.pub

Cognizable or Non-Cognizable, Bailable or Non-Bailable: This offense is cognizable, meaning the police can arrest the accused without a warrant.

Bailable: This offense is bailable, indicating that the accused can secure bail and be released from custody until the trial is completed.

Comparison: [786]Section 320 of the Indian Penal Code (IPC) defines grievous hurt : IPC Section 320: States that the following kinds of hurt only are designated as "grievous": Emasculation [787]Permanent privation of the sight of either eye Permanent privation of the hearing of either ear Privation of any member or joint Destruction or permanent impairing of the powers of any member or joint Permanent disfiguration of the head or face Fracture or dislocation of a bone or tooth Any hurt which endangers life or which causes the victim to be in severe bodily pain for twenty days or more, or unable to follow their ordinary pursuits for twenty days or more.

Key Differences: BNS 116: Provides a broader definition of grievous hurt and specifies a punishment. IPC Section 320: Defines grievous hurt with a detailed list of specific injuries and conditions that qualify.

BNS Section 117 (1)

Definition: Voluntarily Causing Grievous Hurt[788] Punishment Section 117(1) of the Bharatiya Nyaya Sanhita (BNS) 2023 deals with the punishment for voluntarily causing grievous hurt.

Illustration: If someone intentionally attacks another person with a weapon, causing a severe fracture, this act falls under BNS 117(1) as voluntarily causing grievous hurt.

Example: Suppose an individual uses a metal rod to repeatedly hit someone during a fight, resulting in multiple broken bones and long-term

---

[786] blog.ipleaders.in

[787] pdfcookie.com

[788] Ministry of Home Affairs. (2024). The Bharatiya Nyaya Sanhita, 2023. Retrieved from https://www.mha.gov.in/sites/default/files/250883_english_01042024.pdf

injuries. This would be categorized under BNS 117(1) as voluntarily causing grievous hurt.

Comment: This section emphasizes the severe and intentional nature of the injuries inflicted. By defining this serious offense and prescribing strict punishments, the BNS aims to deter such harmful actions and ensure justice for the victims.

Classification of Offence and Punishment Classification: Voluntarily causing grievous hurt is classified as a serious criminal offense due to the severe and intentional nature of the injuries inflicted.

Punishment: The punishment for [789]voluntarily causing grievous hurt under BNS 117(1) can be [790]imprisonment for a term which may extend to ten years, and the offender shall also be liable to a fine.

Cognizable or Non-Cognizable, Bailable or Non-Bailable: This offense is cognizable, meaning the police can arrest the accused without a warrant.

Bailable: This offense is non-bailable, indicating that the accused cannot easily secure bail and must remain in custody until the trial is completed.

Comparison: [791]Section 322 of the Indian Penal Code (IPC) defines [792]voluntarily causing grievous hurt: IPC Section 322: States that whoever voluntarily causes hurt, if the hurt which he intends to cause or knows himself to be likely to cause is grievous hurt, and if the hurt which he causes is grievous hurt, is said "voluntarily to cause grievous hurt."

Key Differences: BNS 117(1): Similar to IPC Section 322 in defining and addressing the punishment for[793] voluntarily causing grievous hurt, specifying punishment terms and conditions. IPC Section 322: Aligns with BNS 117(1) in terms of defining and addressing the offense of voluntarily causing grievous hurt with specified punishment terms.

---

[789] myneta.info

[790] adoc.pub

[791] blog.ipleaders.in

[792] pdfcookie.com

[793] myneta.info

BNS Section 117(2)

Definition: Punishment for Voluntarily Causing Grievous Hurt Section 117(2)[794] of the Bharatiya Nyaya Sanhita (BNS) 2023 specifies the punishment for the offense of voluntarily causing grievous hurt.

Illustration: If someone intentionally stabs another person, causing deep wounds and significant blood loss, this act is classified under BNS 117(2) as voluntarily causing grievous hurt.

Example: Suppose an individual attacks someone with a knife during a conflict, resulting in severe injuries such as fractured bones and permanent disfigurement. This would be categorized under BNS 117(2).

Comment: This section highlights the severe and intentional nature of the injuries inflicted. By defining this serious offense and prescribing strict punishments, the BNS aims to deter such harmful actions and ensure justice for the victims.

Classification of Offence and Punishment Classification: Voluntarily causing grievous hurt [795]is classified as a serious criminal offense due to the severe and intentional nature of the injuries inflicted.

Punishment: The punishment for voluntarily causing grievous hurt under BNS 117(2) can be [796]imprisonment for a term which may extend to ten years, and the offender shall also be liable to a fine.

Cognizable or Non-Cognizable, Bailable or Non-Bailable: This offense is cognizable, meaning [797]the police can arrest the accused without a warrant.

Bailable: This offense is non-bailable, indicating that the accused cannot easily secure bail and must remain in custody until the trial is completed.

---

[794] Ministry of Home Affairs. (2024). The Bharatiya Nyaya Sanhita, 2023. Retrieved from https://www.mha.gov.in/sites/default/files/250883_english_01042024.pdf

[795] blog.ipleaders.in

[796] odishapolicecidcb.gov.in

[797] blog.ipleaders.in

Comparison: [798]Section 325 of the Indian Penal Code (IPC) deals with the punishment for voluntarily causing grievous hurt: IPC Section 325: States that [799]whoever, except in the case provided for by Section 335, voluntarily causes grievous hurt shall be punished with imprisonment of either description for a term which may extend to seven years, and shall also be liable to a fine.

Key Differences: [800]BNS 117(2): Similar to IPC Section 325 in defining and addressing the punishment for voluntarily causing grievous hurt, but BNS 117(2) allows for imprisonment for a term which may extend to ten years. IPC Section 325: Specifies a term of imprisonment which may extend to seven years, along with a fine.

BNS Section 117 (3)

Definition: [801]Voluntarily Causing Grievous Hurt Section 117(3) of the Bharatiya Nyaya Sanhita (BNS) 2023 addresses the offense of voluntarily causing grievous hurt and outlines the related punishments.

Illustration: An individual intentionally burns another person, causing severe injuries such as third-degree burns. This act is classified under BNS 117(3) as voluntarily causing grievous hurt.

Example: Suppose a person throws acid on someone's face, resulting in permanent disfigurement and long-term medical treatment. This would be categorized under BNS 117(3).

Comment: This section highlights the severe and intentional nature of the injuries inflicted. By defining this serious offense and prescribing strict punishments, the BNS aims to deter such harmful actions and ensure justice for the victims.

---

[798] blog.ipleaders.in

[799] odishapolicecidcb.gov.in

[800] blog.ipleaders.in

[801] Ministry of Home Affairs. (2024). The Bharatiya Nyaya Sanhita, 2023. Retrieved from https://www.mha.gov.in/sites/default/files/250883_english_01042024.pdf

Classification of Offence and Punishment Classification: [802]Voluntarily causing grievous hurt is classified as a serious criminal offense due to the severe and intentional nature of the injuries inflicted.

Punishment: The punishment for voluntarily causing grievous hurt under BNS 117(3) can be [803]imprisonment for a term which may extend to ten years, and the offender shall also be liable to a fine.

Cognizable or Non-Cognizable, Bailable or Non-Bailable: This offense is cognizable, meaning the [804]police can arrest the accused without a warrant.

Bailable: This offense is non-bailable, indicating that the accused cannot easily secure bail and must remain in custody until the trial is completed.

Comparison with IPC[805] Sections of the Indian Penal Code (IPC) that deal with similar offenses include IPC Section 326 (Voluntarily causing grievous hurt by dangerous weapons or means):IPC Section 326: States that whoever voluntarily causes grievous hurt by means of any instrument for shooting, stabbing or cutting, or any instrument which, used as a weapon of offense, is likely to cause death, or by means of fire or any heated substance, or by means of any poison or any corrosive substance, or by means of any explosive substance, or by means of any substance which it is deleterious to the human body to inhale, to swallow, or to receive into the blood, or by means of any animal, shall be punished with imprisonment for life, or with imprisonment of either description for a term which may extend to ten years, and shall also be liable to fine.

Key Differences: BNS 117(3): Similar to IPC Section 326 in terms of defining and addressing the [806]punishment for voluntarily causing grievous hurt, specifying punishment terms and conditions. IPC Section 326:

[802] www.bareactslive.com

[803] odishapolicecidcb.gov.in

[804] blog.ipleaders.in

[805] www.bareactslive.com

[806] blog.ipleaders.in

Provides detailed methods of inflicting grievous hurt and prescribes punishment terms.

BNS Section 117 (4)

Definition: [807]Voluntarily Causing Grievous Hurt Section 117(4) of the Bharatiya Nyaya Sanhita (BNS) 2023 further elaborates on the offense of voluntarily causing grievous hurt, particularly in contexts that may involve aggravated circumstances.

Illustration: If someone throws acid on another person, causing permanent disfigurement and severe injuries, this act is classified under BNS 117(4) as voluntarily causing grievous hurt.

Example: Suppose an individual uses a heavy, blunt object to hit someone on the head multiple times, leading to a severe concussion and long-term brain damage. This would be categorized under BNS 117(4).

Comment: This section underscores the gravity of aggravated circumstances when causing grievous hurt. By defining such offenses and prescribing stringent punishments, the BNS aims to deter such harmful actions and ensure justice for the victims.

Classification of Offence and Punishment Classification: Voluntarily causing grievous hurt is classified as a serious criminal offense due to the severe and intentional nature of the injuries inflicted.

Punishment: [808]The punishment for voluntarily causing grievous hurt under BNS 117(4) can be imprisonment for a term which may extend to ten years, and the offender shall also be liable to a fine.

Cognizable or Non-Cognizable, Bailable or Non-Bailable: This offense is cognizable, meaning [809]the police can arrest the accused without a warrant.

---

[807] Ministry of Home Affairs. (2024). The Bharatiya Nyaya Sanhita, 2023. Retrieved from https://www.mha.gov.in/sites/default/files/250883_english_01042024.pdf

[808] odishapolicecidcb.gov.in

[809] blog.ipleaders.in

Bailable: This offense is non-bailable, indicating that the accused cannot easily secure bail and must remain in custody until the trial is completed.

Comparison [810]Section 326 of the Indian Penal Code (IPC) deals with [811]voluntarily causing [812]grievous hurt by dangerous weapons or means : IPC Section 326: States that whoever voluntarily causes grievous hurt by means of any instrument for shooting, stabbing or cutting, or any instrument which, used as a weapon of offense, is likely to cause death, or by means of fire or any heated substance, or by means of any poison or any corrosive substance, or by means of any explosive substance, or by means of any substance which it is deleterious to the human body to inhale, to swallow, or to receive into the blood, or by means of any animal, shall be punished with imprisonment for life, or with imprisonment of either description for a term which may extend to ten years, and shall also be liable to fine.

Key Differences: BNS 117(4): Similar to IPC Section 326 in defining and addressing the [813]punishment for voluntarily causing grievous hurt, specifying punishment terms and conditions. IPC Section 326: Provides detailed methods of inflicting grievous hurt and prescribes punishment terms, including imprisonment for life or up to ten years along with a fine.

BNS Section 118 (1)

Definition: Voluntarily Causing [814]Hurt or Grievous Hurt by Dangerous Weapons or Means Section 118(1) of the Bharatiya Nyaya Sanhita (BNS) 2023 addresses the offense of voluntarily causing hurt or grievous hurt using dangerous weapons or means.

---

[810] www.bareactslive.com

[811] blog.ipleaders.in

[812] odishapolicecidcb.gov.in

[813] blog.ipleaders.in

[814] Ministry of Home Affairs. (2024). The Bharatiya Nyaya Sanhita, 2023. Retrieved from https://www.mha.gov.in/sites/default/files/250883_english_01042024.pdf

Illustration: A person intentionally strikes another with a sword, causing deep cuts and severe injuries. This act is classified under BNS 118(1) as voluntarily causing hurt or grievous hurt by dangerous weapons.

Example: Suppose an individual throws acid on someone, resulting in severe burns and [815]disfigurement. This would be categorized under BNS 118(1) as grievous hurt by dangerous means.

Comment: This section highlights the severe nature of using dangerous weapons or means to inflict hurt. By defining this serious offense and prescribing strict punishments, the BNS aims to deter such harmful actions and ensure justice for victims.

Classification of Offence and Punishment Classification: Voluntarily causing hurt or [816]grievous hurt by dangerous weapons or means is classified as a serious criminal offense due to the use of dangerous and potentially lethal implements.

Punishment: The punishment for this offense under BNS 118(1) can be imprisonment for a term which may extend to ten years, and the offender shall also be liable to a fine.

Cognizable or Non-Cognizable, Bailable or Non-Bailable: This offense is cognizable, meaning [817]the police can arrest the accused without a warrant.

Bailable: This offense is non-bailable, indicating that the accused cannot easily secure bail and must remain in custody until the trial is completed.

Comparison: Section 324 of the Indian Penal Code (IPC) deals with [818]voluntarily causing hurt by dangerous weapons or means : IPC Section 324: States that [819]whoever, except in the case provided for by Section 334, voluntarily causes hurt by means of any instrument for shooting, stabbing

---

[815] www.bareactslive.com

[816] odishapolicecidcb.gov.in

[817] blog.ipleaders.in

[818] blog.ipleaders.in

[819] odishapolicecidcb.gov.in

or cutting, or any instrument which, used as a weapon of offense, is likely to cause death, or by means of fire or any heated substance, or by means of any poison or any corrosive substance, or by means of any explosive substance, or by means of any substance which it is deleterious to the human body to inhale, to swallow, or to receive into the blood, or by means of any animal, shall be punished it imprisonment of either description for a term which may extend to three years, or with fine, or with both.

Key Differences: BNS 118(1): Specifies the use of dangerous weapons or means, providing a punishment term which may extend to ten years. IPC Section 324: Focuses on various dangerous means of causing hurt, prescribing imprisonment for a term which may extend to three years, along with a fine.

BNS Section 118 (2)

Definition: Voluntarily causing hurt or grievous hurt by dangerous weapons or means.

Illustration: If a person serving a life sentence in prison kills another inmate or a prison staff member, this act falls under BNS 118(2) as murder by a life-convict.

Example: Suppose an individual who is serving a life sentence for a previous murder charges another inmate and kills them. This would be categorized under BNS 118(2) as murder by a life-convict.

Comment: This section emphasizes the gravity of committing another murder while already serving a life sentence. By defining this serious offense and prescribing the harshest punishments, the BNS aims to deter such extreme actions and ensure maximum accountability for the offenders.

Classification of Offence and Punishment Classification: Murder by a life-convict is classified as a very serious criminal offense due to the pre-existing life sentence and the gravity of committing another murder.

Punishment: The punishment for murder by a life-convict under BNS 118(2) can be death penalty or imprisonment for life, which means the remainder of the convict's natural life. **Cognizable or Non-Cognizable,**

Bailable or Non-Bailable: This offense is cognizable, [820]meaning the police can arrest the accused without a warrant.

Bailable: This offense is non-bailable, indicating that the accused cannot easily secure bail and must remain in custody until the trial is completed.

Comparison: [821]Section 326 of the Indian Penal Code (IPC) deals with voluntarily causing grievous hurt by dangerous weapons or means: IPC Section 326: States that whoever [822]voluntarily causes grievous hurt by means of any instrument for shooting, stabbing or cutting, or any instrument which, used as a weapon of offense, is likely to cause [823]death, or by means of fire or any heated substance, or by means of any poison or any corrosive substance, or by means of any explosive substance, or by means of any substance which it is deleterious to the human body to inhale, to swallow, or to receive into the blood, or by means of any animal, shall be punished with imprisonment for life, or with imprisonment of either description for a term which may extend to ten years, and shall also be liable to fine.

Key Differences: BNS 118(2): Focuses on the punishment for murder committed by a life-convict, with options for the death penalty or life imprisonment. IPC Section 326: Addresses voluntarily causing grievous hurt by dangerous means, prescribing imprisonment for life or up to ten years, along with a fine.

BNS Section 119 (1)

Definition: [824]**Voluntarily Causing Hurt or Grievous Hurt to Extort Property or Constrain to an Illegal Act Section 119(1)** of the Bharatiya Nyaya Sanhita (BNS) 2023 addresses the offense of voluntarily causing

---

[820] blog.ipleaders.in

[821] www.bareactslive.com

[822] blog.ipleaders.in

[823] www.nmu.ac.in

[824] Ministry of Home Affairs. (2024). The Bharatiya Nyaya Sanhita, 2023. Retrieved from https://www.mha.gov.in/sites/default/files/250883_english_01042024.pdf

hurt or grievous hurt to extort property or to constrain someone to commit an illegal act.

Illustration: If someone threatens another person with physical harm unless they hand over their valuables, this act falls under BNS 119(1) as voluntarily causing hurt to extort property.

Example: Suppose an individual injures someone and demands money in return for not reporting the incident to the authorities. This would be categorized under BNS 119(1) as causing hurt to extort property.

Comment: This section ensures that acts of coercion and violence for extortion or illegal purposes are penalized. It highlights the seriousness of using physical harm to force compliance or obtain property.

Classification of Offence and Punishment Classification: Voluntarily causing hurt or grievous hurt to extort property or constrain to an illegal act is classified as a serious criminal offense due to the coercive nature of the act.

Punishment: The punishment for this offense under BNS 119(1) can be imprisonment of either description for a term which may extend to ten years, and the offender shall also be liable to a fine.

Cognizable or Non-Cognizable, Bailable or Non-Bailable: This offense is cognizable, meaning [825]the police can arrest the accused without a warrant.

Bailable: This offense is bailable, indicating that the accused can secure bail and be released from custody until the trial is completed.

Comparison: [826]Section 327 of the Indian Penal Code (IPC), which has been replaced by BNS 119(1), dealt with voluntarily causing hurt to extort property or to constrain to an illegal act: IPC Section 327: States that whoever voluntarily causes hurt for the purpose of extorting from the sufferer, or from any person interested in the sufferer, any property or valuable security, or of constraining the sufferer or any person interested

---

[825] blog.ipleaders.in

[826] www.bareactslive.com

in such sufferer to do anything which is illegal or which may facilitate the commission of an offence, shall be punished with imprisonment of either description for a term which may extend to seven years, and shall also be liable to a fine.

Key Differences: BNS 119 (1): Specifies imprisonment for a term which may extend to ten years, compared to IPC Section 327 which specified imprisonment for up to seven years. IPC Section 327: Provided a similar framework but with a shorter term of imprisonment.

BNS Section 119 (2)

Definition: Voluntarily Causing [827]Hurt or Grievous Hurt to Extort Property or Constrain to an Illegal Act Section 119(2) of the Bharatiya Nyaya Sanhita (BNS) 2023 addresses the offense of voluntarily causing hurt or grievous hurt for the purpose of extorting property or forcing someone to commit an illegal act.

Illustration: Imagine a situation where a person is threatened and beaten until they hand over [828]their bank details and passwords. This act falls under BNS 119(2) as voluntarily causing hurt to extort property.

Example: Suppose an individual inflicts severe injuries on a business owner to force them to sign over their company's assets. This would be categorized under BNS 119(2) as causing grievous hurt to extort property.

Comment: This section ensures that acts of coercion and violence for extortion or illegal purposes are penalized. It highlights the seriousness of using physical harm to force compliance or obtain property.

Classification of Offence and Punishment Classification: Voluntarily causing hurt or grievous hurt to extort property or constrain to an illegal act is classified as a serious criminal offense due to the coercive and violent nature of the act.

---

[827] Ministry of Home Affairs. (2024). The Bharatiya Nyaya Sanhita, 2023. Retrieved from https://www.mha.gov.in/sites/default/files/250883_english_01042024.pdf

[828] odishapolicecidcb.gov.in

Punishment: The punishment for this offense under BNS 119(2) can be imprisonment for life, or imprisonment for a term which may extend to ten years, and the offender shall also be liable to a fine.

Cognizable or Non-Cognizable, Bailable or Non-Bailable: [829]This offense is cognizable, meaning the police can arrest the accused without a warrant.

Bailable: This offense is non-bailable, indicating that the accused cannot easily secure bail and must remain in custody until the trial is completed.

Comparison: With IPC Section 329 Section 329 of the Indian Penal Code (IPC) deals with voluntarily [830]causing grievous hurt to extort property, or to constrain to an illegal act.

BNS 120 (1)

Definition: Voluntarily [831]Causing Hurt or Grievous Hurt to Extort Confession or to Compel Restoration of Property Section 120(1) of the Bharatiya Nyaya Sanhita (BNS) 2023 addresses the offense of voluntarily causing hurt or grievous hurt to extort a confession or to compel the restoration of property.

Illustration: [832]A person physically assaults another to force them to confess to a theft or return stolen goods. This act falls under BNS 120(1) as voluntarily causing hurt to extort a confession.

Example: Suppose an individual tortures someone to make them admit to a crime or to force them to hand over property believed to be stolen. This would be categorized under BNS 120(1).

Comment: This section ensures that acts of coercion and violence for extorting confessions or forcing the restoration of property are penalized.

---

[829] blog.ipleaders.in

[830] odishapolicecidcb.gov.in

[831] Ministry of Home Affairs. (2024). The Bharatiya Nyaya Sanhita, 2023. Retrieved from https://www.mha.gov.in/sites/default/files/250883_english_01042024.pdf

[832] odishapolicecidcb.gov.in

It emphasizes the seriousness of using physical harm to force compliance or obtain property.

Classification of Offence and Punishment Classification: Voluntarily causing hurt or grievous hurt to extort confession or compel restoration of property is classified as a serious criminal offense due to the coercive and violent nature of the act.

Punishment: The punishment for this offense under BNS 120(1) can be imprisonment of either description for a term which may extend to ten years, and the offender shall also be liable to a fine.

Cognizable or Non-Cognizable, Bailable or Non-Bailable: This offense is cognizable, meaning [833]the police can arrest the accused without a warrant.

Bailable: This offense is bailable, indicating that the accused can secure bail and be released from custody until the trial is completed.

Comparison: Section 330 of the Indian Penal Code (IPC), which has been replaced by BNS 120(1), dealt with [834]voluntarily causing hurt to extort confession or to compel restoration of property : IPC Section 330: [835]States that whoever voluntarily causes [836]hurt for the purpose of extorting from the sufferer, or from any person interested in the sufferer, any confession or any information which may lead to the detection of an offense or misconduct, or for the purpose of constraining the sufferer or any person interested in the sufferer to restore or to cause the restoration of any property or valuable security or to satisfy any claim or demand, or to give information which may lead to the restoration of any property or valuable security, shall be punished with imprisonment of either description for a term which may extend to seven years, and shall also be liable to a fine.

Key Differences: BNS 120(1): Specifies imprisonment for a term which may extend to ten years, compared to IPC Section 330 which specified

---

[833] blog.ipleaders.in

[834] odishapolicecidcb.gov.in

[835] www.nmu.ac.in

[836] odishapolicecidcb.gov.in

imprisonment for up to seven years. IPC Section 330: Provided a similar framework but with a shorter term of imprisonment

BNS Section 120 (2)

Definition: Voluntarily [837]Causing Grievous Hurt to Extort Confession or to Compel Restoration of Property Section 120(2) of the Bharatiya Nyaya Sanhita (BNS) 2023 addresses the offense of voluntarily causing grievous hurt to extort a confession or to compel the restoration of property.

Illustration: If a person inflicts severe injuries on another to force them to confess to a crime or return stolen property, this act falls under BNS 120(2) as [838]voluntarily causing grievous hurt to extort confession or [839]compel restoration of property.

Example: Suppose an individual tortures someone by breaking their bones to make them admit to a theft or return stolen goods. This act would be categorized under BNS 120(2).

Comment: This section emphasizes the severe physical harm and coercive nature of such acts, ensuring that those who inflict [840]grievous hurt for extortion or compulsion face serious consequences.

Classification of Offence and Punishment Classification: Voluntarily causing grievous hurt to extort confession or compel restoration of property is classified as a serious criminal offense due to the severe physical harm and coercive nature of the act.

Punishment: The punishment for this offense under BNS 120(2) can be imprisonment of either description for a term which may extend to ten years, and the offender shall also be liable to a fine.

---

[837] Ministry of Home Affairs. (2024). The Bharatiya Nyaya Sanhita, 2023. Retrieved from https://www.mha.gov.in/sites/default/files/250883_english_01042024.pdf

[838] odishapolicecidcb.gov.in

[839] www.bareactslive.com

[840] odishapolicecidcb.gov.in

Cognizable or Non-Cognizable, Bailable or Non-Bailable: This offense is cognizable, meaning [841]the police can arrest the accused without a warrant.

Bailable: This offense is non-bailable, indicating that the accused cannot easily secure bail and must remain in custody until the trial is completed.

Comparison: [842]Section 331 of the Indian Penal Code (IPC), which has been replaced by BNS 120(2), dealt with voluntarily causing grievous hurt to extort confession or to compel restoration of property : IPC Section 331: [843]States that whoever voluntarily causes [844]grievous hurt for the purpose of extorting from the sufferer, or from any person interested in the sufferer, any confession or any information which may lead to the detection of an offense or misconduct, or for the purpose of constraining the sufferer or any person interested in such sufferer to restore or to cause the restoration of any property or valuable security, or to satisfy any claim or demand, or to give information which may lead to the restoration of any property or valuable security, shall be punished with imprisonment of either description for a term which may extend to ten years, and shall also be liable to a fine.

Key Differences: BNS 120(2): Specifies the same range of punishment as IPC Section 331, providing a framework to address the severity of the coercive and harmful act. IPC Section 331: Provided a similar framework with the same term of imprisonment and fine for causing grievous hurt to extort confession or compel restoration of property.

---

[841] blog.ipleaders.in

[842] odishapolicecidcb.gov.in

[843] www.nmu.ac.in

[844] odishapolicecidcb.gov.in

BNS Section 121(1)

Definition: [845]Voluntarily Causing Hurt to Deter Public Servant from His Duty Section 121(1) of the Bharatiya Nyaya Sanhita (BNS) 2023 addresses the offense of voluntarily causing hurt to a public servant to deter them from performing their duties.

Illustration: A person attacks a police officer to prevent the officer from making an arrest. This act falls under BNS 121(1) as [846]voluntarily causing hurt to deter a public servant from their duty.

Example: Suppose an individual punches a tax officer to stop them from conducting an audit. This would be categorized under BNS 121(1).

Classification of Offence and Punishment Classification: [847]Voluntarily causing hurt to deter a public servant from their duty is classified as a serious criminal offense due to the intentional obstruction of lawful duties.

Punishment: The punishment for this offense under BNS 121(1) can be [848]imprisonment of either description for a term which may extend to three years, and the offender shall also be liable to a fine.

Cognizable or Non-Cognizable, Bailable or Non-Bailable: This offense is cognizable, meaning the police can arrest the accused without a warrant.

Bailable: This offense is bailable, indicating that the accused can secure bail and be released from custody until the trial is completed.

[845] Ministry of Home Affairs. (2024). The Bharatiya Nyaya Sanhita, 2023. Retrieved from https://www.mha.gov.in/sites/default/files/250883_english_01042024.pdf

[846] odishapolicecidcb.gov.in

[847] odishapolicecidcb.gov.in

[848] bprd.nic.in

Comparison: Section 332[849] of the Indian Penal Code (IPC), which has been replaced by BNS 121(1), dealt with [850]voluntarily causing [851]hurt to deter a public servant from his duty: IPC Section 332: [852]States that whoever voluntarily causes hurt to any person being a public servant in the discharge of their duty as such public servant, or with intent to prevent or deter that person or any other public servant from discharging their duty as such public servant, or in consequence of anything done or attempted to be done by that person in the lawful discharge of their duty as such public servant, shall be punished with imprisonment of either description for a term which may extend to three years, or with fine, or with both.

Key Differences: BNS 121(1): Specifies imprisonment for a term which may extend to three years, similar to IPC Section 332, with the addition of a fine. IPC Section 332: Provided a similar framework with the same term of imprisonment and fine for causing hurt to deter a public servant from their duty.

BNS Section 121(2)

Definition: Voluntarily [853]Causing Grievous Hurt to Deter Public Servant from His Duty Section 121(2) of the Bharatiya Nyaya Sanhita (BNS) 2023 addresses the offense of voluntarily causing grievous hurt to a public servant to deter them from performing their duties.

Illustration: If a person inflicts severe injuries on a police officer to prevent them from making an arrest, this act falls under BNS 121(2) as voluntarily causing grievous hurt to deter a public servant from their duty.

---

[849] www.bareactslive.com

[850] odishapolicecidcb.gov.in

[851] odishapolicecidcb.gov.in

[852] old.nmu.ac.in

[853] Ministry of Home Affairs. (2024). The Bharatiya Nyaya Sanhita, 2023. Retrieved from https://www.mha.gov.in/sites/default/files/250883_english_01042024.pdf

Example: Suppose an individual attacks a tax officer, causing serious injuries to stop them from conducting an audit. This would be categorized under BNS 121(2).

Classification of Offence and Punishment Classification: Voluntarily causing grievous hurt to deter a public servant from their duty is classified as a serious criminal offense due to the severe physical harm and obstruction of lawful duties.

Punishment: The punishment for this offense under BNS 121(2) can be [854]imprisonment of either description for a term which may extend to ten years, and the offender shall also be liable to a fine.

Cognizable or Non-Cognizable, Bailable or Non-Bailable: This offense is cognizable, meaning the police can arrest the accused without a warrant.

Bailable: This offense is non-bailable, indicating that the accused cannot easily secure bail and must remain in custody until [855]the trial is completed.

Comparison: Section 333 of the Indian Penal Code (IPC), which has been replaced by BNS 121(2), dealt with voluntarily causing grievous hurt to deter a [856]public servant from his duty : IPC Section 333: [857]States that whoever voluntarily causes grievous hurt to any person being a public servant in the discharge of their duty as such public servant, or with intent to prevent or deter that person or any other public servant from discharging their duty as such public servant, or in consequence of anything done or attempted to be done by that person in the lawful discharge of their duty as such public servant, shall be punished with imprisonment of either description for a term which may extend to ten years, and shall also be liable to a fine.

Key Differences: BNS 121(2): Specifies the same range of punishment as IPC Section 333, providing a framework to address the severity of the coercive and harmful act. IPC Section 333: Provided a similar framework

---

[854] bprd.nic.in

[855] www.indiacode.nic.in

[856] bprd.nic.in

[857] old.nmu.ac.in

with the same term of imprisonment and fine for [858]causing grievous hurt to deter a public servant from their duty.

BNS Section 122 (1)

Definition: Voluntarily Causing Hurt on Provocation Section[859] 122(1) of the Bharatiya Nyaya Sanhita (BNS) 2023 addresses the offense of voluntarily causing hurt on grave and sudden provocation.

Illustration: If someone insults another person in a highly provocative manner, and the insulted person reacts immediately by hitting the insulter, this act falls under BNS 122(1) as [860]voluntarily causing hurt on provocation.

Example: Suppose an individual is provoked by a severe insult and responds by slapping the person who insulted them. This would be categorized under BNS 122(1) as causing hurt on provocation.

Comment: This section addresses impulsive acts of violence that occur in response to provocation. It recognizes the human tendency to react impulsively under extreme provocation but still holds individuals accountable for their actions.

Classification of Offence and Punishment Classification: [861]Voluntarily causing hurt on provocation is classified as a misdemeanour due to the impulsive nature of the act.

Punishment: The punishment for this offense under BNS 122(1) can be [862]imprisonment of either description for a term which may extend to one month, or with a fine which may extend to five thousand rupees, or with both.

---

[858] odishapolicecidcb.gov.in

[859] bprd.nic.in

[860] www.bareactslive.com

[861] odishapolicecidcb.gov.in

[862] bprd.nic.in

Cognizable or Non-Cognizable, Bailable or Non-Bailable: This offense is non-cognizable, meaning the police cannot arrest the accused without a warrant.

Bailable: This offense is bailable, indicating that the accused can secure bail and be released from custody until the trial is completed4.

Comparison: Section 334 [863]of the Indian Penal Code (IPC), which has been replaced by BNS 122(1), dealt with voluntarily causing hurt on provocation :IPC Section 334: States that whoever voluntarily causes [864]hurt on grave and sudden provocation, if he neither intends nor knows himself to be likely to cause hurt to any person other than the person who gave the provocation, shall be punished with imprisonment of either description for a term which may extend to one month, or with fine which may extend to five hundred rupees, or with both.

Key Differences: BNS 122(1): [865]Specifies imprisonment for a term which may extend to one month, with a fine which may extend to five thousand rupees, compared to IPC Section 334 which specified imprisonment for up to one month and a fine up to five hundred rupees. IPC Section 334: Provided a similar framework but with a lower fine amount.

BNS Section 122(2)

Definition: Voluntarily[866] Causing Grievous Hurt on Provocation Section 122(2) of the Bharatiya Nyaya Sanhita (BNS) 2023 deals with the offense of voluntarily causing grievous hurt in response to grave and sudden provocation.

Illustration: If a person is severely provoked and, in the heat of the moment, attacks another individual with a weapon causing serious

---

[863] odishapolicecidcb.gov.in

[864] bprd.nic.in

[865] bprd.nic.in

[866] Ministry of Home Affairs. (2024). The Bharatiya Nyaya Sanhita, 2023. Retrieved from https://www.mha.gov.in/sites/default/files/250883_english_01042024.pdf

injuries, this act falls under BNS 122(2) as voluntarily causing grievous hurt on provocation.

Example: Suppose an [867]individual is provoked by a severe insult and reacts by striking the insulter with a heavy object, resulting in broken bones. This would be classified under BNS 122(2) as causing grievous hurt on provocation.

Comment: This section addresses severe physical harm caused impulsively in response to provocation. It acknowledges the impulsive nature of the act but still holds individuals accountable for the serious injuries inflicted.

Classification of Offence and Punishment Classification: [868]Voluntarily causing grievous hurt on provocation is classified as a serious criminal offense due to the severity of the injuries caused.

Punishment: The [869]punishment for this offense under BNS 122(2) can be imprisonment of either description for a term which may extend to four years, or with a fine which may extend to ten thousand rupees, or with both.

Cognizable or Non-Cognizable, Bailable or Non-Bailable: This offense is cognizable, meaning the police can arrest the accused without a warrant.

Bailable: This offense is bailable, indicating that the accused can secure bail and be released from custody until the trial is completed.

Comparison: [870]Section 335 of the Indian Penal Code (IPC), [871]which has been replaced by BNS 122(2), dealt with voluntarily causing grievous hurt on provocation : IPC Section 335: [872]States that whoever voluntarily causes grievous hurt on grave and sudden provocation, if they neither

---

[867] www.bareactslive.com

[868] odishapolicecidcb.gov.in

[869] bprd.nic.in

[870] odishapolicecidcb.gov.in

[871] www.indiacode.nic.in

[872] old.nmu.ac.in

intend nor know themselves to be likely to cause [873]grievous hurt to any person other than the person who gave the provocation, shall be punished with imprisonment of either description for a term which may extend to four years, or with fine which may extend to two thousand rupees, or with both.

Key Differences: BNS 122(2): Specifies imprisonment for a term which may extend to four years, with a fine which may extend to ten thousand rupees, compared to IPC Section 335 which specified imprisonment for up to four years and a fine up to two thousand rupees. IPC Section 335: Provided a similar framework but with a lower fine amount.

BNS Section 123

Definition: Causing Harm by [874]Means of Poison, etc., with Intent to Commit an Offence Section 123 of the Bharatiya Nyaya Sanhita (BNS) 2023 addresses the offense of causing harm by means of poison or other harmful substances with the intent to commit an offense.

Illustration: A person poisons another's food, intending to incapacitate them in order to commit theft. This act falls under BNS 123.

Example: Suppose an individual mixes a sedative into someone's drink to render them unconscious and then proceeds to rob their house. This would be categorized under BNS 123 as causing harm by means of poison with intent to commit an offense.

Comment: This section ensures that acts involving the use of harmful substances with criminal intent are penalized. It highlights the seriousness of using poison or similar means to incapacitate or harm someone in order to commit further offenses.

Classification of Offence and Punishment Classification: This is classified as a serious criminal offense due to the use of harmful substances and the intent to commit another crime.

---

[873] bprd.nic.in

[874] Ministry of Home Affairs. (2024). The Bharatiya Nyaya Sanhita, 2023. Retrieved from https://www.mha.gov.in/sites/default/files/250883_english_01042024.pdf

Punishment: The punishment for this offense under BNS 123 can be imprisonment of either description for a term which may extend to ten years, and the offender shall also be liable to a fine.

Cognizable or Non-Cognizable, Bailable or Non-Bailable: This offense is cognizable, meaning the police can arrest the accused without a warrant.

Bailable: This offense is bailable, indicating that the accused can secure bail and be released from custody until the trial is completed.

Comparison: [875]Section 328 of the Indian Penal Code (IPC) deals with [876]causing hurt by means of poison, etc., with intent to commit an offense: IPC Section 328: States that whoever administers to or causes to be taken by any person any poison or any stupefying, in toxic ting, or unwholesome drug, or other thing with intent to cause hurt, or with intent to commit or to facilitate the commission of an offense, or knowing it to be likely that he will thereby cause hurt, shall be punished with imprisonment of either description for a term which may extend to ten years, and shall also be liable to a fine.

Key Differences: BNS 123: Similar to IPC Section 328 in terms of the punishment and classification of the offense, focusing on the use of poison or harmful substances with intent to commit an offense. IPC Section 328: Aligns with BNS 123, providing a similar framework with the same range of imprisonment and fine for causing harm by means of poison, etc.

BNS Section 124 (1)

Definition: Voluntarily Causing Grievous Hurt by Use of Acid, etc. Section 124(1)[877] of the Bharatiya Nyaya Sanhita (BNS) 2023 addresses the offense of voluntarily causing grievous hurt by using acid or similar harmful substances.

---

[875] www.bareactslive.com

[876] bprd.nic.in

[877]Ministry of Home Affairs. (2024). The Bharatiya Nyaya Sanhita, 2023. Retrieved from https://www.mha.gov.in/sites/default/files/250883_english_01042024.pdf

Illustration: A person throws acid on another, causing severe burns and permanent disfigurement. This act falls under BNS 124(1) as voluntarily causing grievous hurt by the use of acid.

Example: Suppose an individual uses a corrosive chemical to attack someone, resulting in life-altering injuries. This would be categorized under BNS 124(1) as grievous hurt caused by acid.

Comment: This section addresses the severe and often life-altering consequences of attacks using acid or similar substances. It emphasizes the need for stringent penalties to deter such heinous acts and provide justice for the victims.

Classification of Offence and Punishment Classification: This is classified as a serious criminal offense due to the severe nature and lasting impact of the injuries inflicted. **Punishment:** The punishment for this offense under BNS 124(1) can be imprisonment of either description for a term which may extend to ten years and which shall not be less than seven years, and the offender shall also be liable to a fine.

Cognizable or Non-Cognizable, Bailable or Non-Bailable: This offense is cognizable, meaning the police can arrest the accused without a warrant.

Bailable: This offense is non-bailable, indicating that the accused cannot easily secure bail and must remain in custody until the trial is completed.

Comparison: Section 326A of the [878]Indian Penal Code (IPC) deals with [879]voluntarily causing grievous hurt by [880]use of acid: IPC Section 326A: States that whoever causes permanent or partial damage or deformity to, or burns or maims or disfigures or disables, any part or parts of the body of a person or causes grievous hurt by throwing acid on or by administering acid to that person, or by using any other means with the intention of causing or with the knowledge that he is likely to cause such injury or hurt, shall be punished with imprisonment of either description for a term which shall not be less than ten years but which may extend to

---

[878] odishapolicecidcb.gov.in

[879] www.indiacode.nic.in

[880] bprd.nic.in

life imprisonment, and with fine. The fine imposed shall be just and reasonable to meet the medical expenses of the treatment of the victim, and any fine imposed under this section shall be paid to the victim.

Key Differences: BNS 124(1): Specifies imprisonment for a term which may extend to ten years and which shall not be less than seven years, along with a fine. IPC Section 326A: Prescribes a minimum imprisonment of ten years which may extend to life, along with a fine that is specifically intended to cover the medical expenses of the victim and be paid to the victim.

BNS 124(2)

Definition: Voluntarily [881]Causing Grievous Hurt by Throwing or Attempting to Throw Acid Section 124(2) of the Bharatiya Nyaya Sanhita (BNS) 2023 deals with the offense of voluntarily causing grievous hurt by throwing or attempting to throw acid.

Illustration: If a person throws acid on another individual, resulting in severe burns and permanent disfigurement, this act falls under BNS 124(2) as [882]voluntarily causing grievous hurt by throwing acid.

Example: Suppose someone attempts to throw acid on another person but is stopped before succeeding. Even the attempt alone would be categorized under BNS 124(2).

Comment: This section emphasizes the severe and often irreversible nature of injuries caused by acid attacks. It ensures stringent penalties to deter such heinous acts and provide justice for victims.

Classification of Offence and Punishment Classification: Voluntarily causing grievous hurt by [883]throwing or attempting to throw acid is

---

[881] Ministry of Home Affairs. (2024). The Bharatiya Nyaya Sanhita, 2023. Retrieved from https://www.mha.gov.in/sites/default/files/250883_english_01042024.pdf

[882] bprd.nic.in

[883] www.bareactslive.com

classified as a serious criminal offense due to the severe and often irreversible nature of the injuries caused.

Punishment: The punishment for this offense under BNS 124(2) can be [884]imprisonment of either description for a term which shall not be less than ten years but which may extend to life imprisonment, and the offender shall also be liable to a fine.

Cognizable or Non-Cognizable, Bailable or Non-Bailable: This offense is cognizable, meaning the police can arrest the accused without a warrant.

Bailable: This offense is non-bailable, indicating that the accused cannot easily secure bail and must remain in custody until the trial is completed.

Comparison: [885]Section 326B of the Indian Penal Code (IPC) deals with [886]voluntarily causing grievous hurt by throwing or attempting to [887]throw acid: IPC Section 326B: States that [888]whoever throws or attempts to throw acid on any person or attempts to administer acid to any person, or attempts to use any other means with the intention of causing permanent or partial damage or deformity, or burns or maims or disfigures or disables, any part or parts of the body of such person, shall be punished with imprisonment of either description for a term which shall not be less than ten years but which may extend to life imprisonment, and with fine. The fine imposed shall be just and reasonable to meet the medical expenses of the treatment of the victim, and any fine imposed under this section shall be paid to the victim.

Key Differences: BNS 124(2): Specifies imprisonment for a term which shall not be less than ten years and which may extend to life imprisonment, along with a fine. IPC Section 326B: Provides a similar framework with the same range of imprisonment and a fine intended to cover the medical expenses of the victim and be paid to the victim.

---

[884] bprd.nic.in

[885] odishapolicecidcb.gov.in

[886] www.indiacode.nic.in

[887] www.bareactslive.com

[888] bprd.nic.in

BNS Section 125

Definition: Act Endangering Life or [889]Personal Safety of Others Section 125 of the Bharatiya Nyaya Sanhita (BNS) 2023 addresses acts that endanger the life or personal safety of others.

Illustration: If a person recklessly drives through a crowded marketplace, endangering the lives of pedestrians, this act falls under BNS 125 as an act endangering life or personal safety.

Example: Suppose an individual sets off fireworks in a densely populated area without taking safety precautions, causing panic and potential harm to people. This would be categorized under BNS 125 as an act endangering personal safety.

Comment: This section underscores the importance of ensuring public safety and holding individuals accountable for reckless or negligent actions that put others at risk.

Classification of Offence and Punishment Classification: This is classified as a criminal offense due to the potential harm and risk posed to others.

Punishment: The punishment for this offense under BNS 125 can be imprisonment for a term which may extend to three months, or with fine which may extend to five [890]hundred rupees, or with both.

Cognizable or Non-Cognizable, Bailable or Non-Bailable: This offense is non-cognizable, meaning the police cannot arrest the accused without a warrant.

Bailable: This offense is bailable, indicating that the accused can secure bail and be released from custody until the trial is completed.

---

[889] Ministry of Home Affairs. (2024). The Bharatiya Nyaya Sanhita, 2023. Retrieved from https://www.mha.gov.in/sites/default/files/250883_english_01042024.pdf

[890] odishapolicecidcb.gov.in

Comparison: Section 336 of the Indian Penal Code (IPC) deals with acts [891]endangering life or personal safety of others: IPC Section 336: States that whoever does any act so rashly or negligently as to endanger human life or the personal safety of others, shall be punished with imprisonment of either description for a term which may extend to three months, or with fine which may extend to two hundred [892]and fifty rupees, or with both.

Key Differences: BNS 125: Specifies a fine which may extend to five hundred rupees, compared to IPC Section 336 which specified a fine up to two hundred and fifty rupees. IPC Section 336: Provided a similar framework with a shorter maximum fine amount.

BNS Section 125A

Definition: Where [893]Hurt is Caused Section 125A of the Bharatiya Nyaya Sanhita (BNS) 2023 addresses situations where hurt is caused due to rash or negligent acts, extending the scope from Section 125 to cases where actual injury occurs.

Illustration: A person drives recklessly and hits a pedestrian, causing injury. This act falls under BNS 125A as an act where hurt is caused.

Example: Suppose an individual sets off fireworks recklessly, causing burns to nearby people. This would be categorized under BNS 125A.

Comment: This section ensures accountability for rash or negligent actions that result in physical harm to others. It highlights the importance of public safety and holding individuals responsible for injuries caused by their reckless behaviour.

Classification of Offence and Punishment Classification: This is classified as a criminal offense due to the physical harm inflicted on others.

---

[891] bprd.nic.in

[892] odishapolicecidcb.gov.in

[893] Ministry of Home Affairs. (2024). The Bharatiya Nyaya Sanhita, 2023. Retrieved from https://www.mha.gov.in/sites/default/files/250883_english_01042024.pdf

Punishment: The punishment for this offense under BNS 125A can be [894]imprisonment for a term which may extend to six months, or with fine which may extend to one thousand rupees, or with both.

Cognizable or Non-Cognizable, Bailable or Non-Bailable: This offense is cognizable, meaning the police can arrest the accused without a warrant.

Bailable: This offense is bailable, indicating that the accused can secure bail and be released from custody until the trial is completed.

Comparison: Section 337 [895]of the Indian Penal Code (IPC) deals with causing hurt by act endangering life or personal safety of others : IPC Section 337: States that whoever causes hurt to any person by doing any act so rashly or negligently as to endanger human life or the personal safety of others, shall be punished with imprisonment of either description for a term which may extend to six months, or with fine which may extend to five hundred rupees, or with both.

Key Differences: BNS 125A: [896]Specifies a fine which may extend to one thousand rupees, compared to IPC Section 337 which specified a fine up to five hundred rupees. IPC Section 337: Provided a similar framework with a lower maximum fine amount.

BNS Section 125B

Definition: Where Grievous Hurt is Caused[897] Section 125B of the Bharatiya Nyaya Sanhita (BNS) 2023 deals with situations where grievous hurt is caused due to rash or negligent acts.

Illustration: A person drives a vehicle recklessly, resulting in an accident that causes serious injuries like broken bones to a pedestrian. This act falls under BNS 125B as causing grievous hurt.

---

[894] bprd.nic.in

[895] odishapolicecidcb.gov.in

[896] bprd.nic.in

[897] Ministry of Home Affairs. (2024). The Bharatiya Nyaya Sanhita, 2023. Retrieved from https://www.mha.gov.in/sites/default/files/250883_english_01042024.pdf

Example: [898]Suppose someone fires a gun negligently in a public place, hitting an innocent bystander and causing severe injury. This would be categorized under BNS 125B as causing grievous hurt.

Comment: This section ensures accountability for reckless or negligent actions that result in severe physical injuries to others. It highlights the importance of public safety and the responsibility individuals bear for their actions.

Classification of Offence and Punishment Classification: This is classified as a serious criminal offense due to the severe nature of the injuries inflicted.

Punishment: [899]The punishment for this offense under BNS 125B can be imprisonment for a term which may extend to two years, or with fine which may extend to one thousand rupees, or with both.

Cognizable or Non-Cognizable, Bailable or Non-Bailable: This offense is cognizable, meaning the police can arrest the accused without a warrant.

Bailable: This offense is bailable, indicating that the accused can secure bail and be released from custody until the trial is completed.

Comparison: [900]Section 338 of the Indian Penal Code (IPC) [901]deals with causing grievous hurt by[902] act endangering life or personal safety of others : IPC Section 338: States that whoever causes grievous hurt to any person by doing any act so rashly or negligently as to endanger human life [903]or the personal safety of others, shall be punished with imprisonment of either description for a term which may extend to two years, or with fine which may extend to one thousand rupees, or with both.

---

[898]bprd.nic.in

[899] bprd.nic.in

[900]blog.ipleaders.in

[901] adrindia.org

[902] odishapolicecidcb.gov.in

[903] odishapolicecidcb.gov.in

Key Differences: BNS 125B: Specifies a similar range of punishment as IPC Section 338, focusing on the severity of the injuries and the negligent or rash nature of the act. IPC Section 338: Aligns with BNS 125B in terms of punishment and classification of the offense.

BNS Section 126(1)

Definition: Wrongful Restraint[904] Section 126(1) of the Bharatiya Nyaya Sanhita (BNS) 2023 addresses the offense of wrongful restraint, which involves unlawfully preventing someone from moving freely.

Illustration: If a person blocks the only exit of a room to prevent another person from leaving, this act falls under BNS 126(1) as wrongful restraint.

Example: Suppose an individual stands in front of a car, refusing to let the driver proceed. This would be categorized as wrongful restraint under BNS 126(1).

Comment: This section emphasizes the importance of allowing individuals the freedom to move without unlawful restrictions. It ensures accountability for actions that unlawfully impede someone's movement.

Classification of Offence and Punishment Classification: Wrongful restraint is classified as a criminal offense due to the unlawful restriction of an individual's freedom of movement.

Punishment: The punishment for wrongful restraint under BNS 126(1) can be [905]imprisonment for a term which may extend to one [906]month, or with fine which may extend to five hundred rupees, or with both.

Cognizable or Non-Cognizable, Bailable or Non-Bailable: This offense is non-cognizable, meaning the police cannot arrest the accused without a warrant.

---

[904] Ministry of Home Affairs. (2024). The Bharatiya Nyaya Sanhita, 2023. Retrieved from https://www.mha.gov.in/sites/default/files/250883_english_01042024.pdf

[905] blog.ipleaders.in

[906] odishapolicecidcb.gov.in

Bailable: This offense is bailable, indicating that the accused can secure bail and be released from custody until the trial is completed.

Comparison: [907]Section 339 of the Indian Penal Code (IPC) deals with wrongful restraint: IPC Section 339: States that whoever voluntarily obstructs any person so as to prevent that person from proceeding in any direction in which that person has a right to proceed, is said wrongfully to restrain that person.

Key Differences: BNS 126(1): Similar to IPC Section 339 in defining wrongful restraint and specifying punishment. Both sections address the unlawful prevention of someone's free movement. IPC Section 339: Provides a framework for addressing wrongful restraint with similar definitions and classifications.

BNS Section 126 (2)

Definition: Punishment for Wrongful[908] Restraint Section 126(2) of the Bharatiya Nyaya Sanhita (BNS) 2023 addresses the punishment for the offense of wrongful restraint.

Illustration: A person unlawfully blocks another individual's car from leaving [909]a parking lot, preventing them from moving freely. This act falls under BNS 126(2) [910]as wrongful restraint.

Example: Suppose someone locks the gate of a building, preventing the residents from exiting. This would be categorized as wrongful restraint under BNS 126(2).

Comment: This section ensures that individuals who unlawfully prevent others from moving freely are held accountable. It emphasizes the importance of personal freedom and the consequences of obstructing it.

---

[907] blog.ipleaders.in

[908] www.ima-india.org

[909] apnews-int.appspot.com

[910] blog.ipleaders.in

Classification of Offence and Punishment Classification: Wrongful restraint is classified as a criminal offense due to the unlawful prevention of an individual's free movement.

Punishment: The punishment for wrongful restraint under BNS 126(2) can be imprisonment for a term which may extend to one [911]month, or with fine which may extend to five hundred rupees, or with both.

Cognizable or Non-Cognizable, Bailable or Non-Bailable: This offense is non-cognizable, meaning the police cannot arrest the accused without a warrant.

Bailable: This offense is bailable, indicating that the accused can secure bail and be released from custody until the trial is completed.

Comparison: [912]Section 341 of the Indian Penal Code (IPC) deals with the [913]punishment for wrongful restraint: IPC Section 341: States that whoever wrongfully restrains any person shall be punished with imprisonment of either description for a term which may extend to one [914]month, or with fine which may extend to five hundred rupees, or with both.

Key Differences: BNS 126(2): Similar to IPC Section 341 in defining the punishment for wrongful restraint, with both specifying [915]imprisonment for a term which may extend to one [916]month, or a fine which may extend to five hundred rupees, or both. IPC Section 341: Aligns closely with BNS 126(2), providing a similar framework for the punishment of wrongful restraint.

---

[911] odishapolicecidcb.gov.in

[912] blog.ipleaders.in

[913] blog.ipleaders.in

[914] odishapolicecidcb.gov.in

[915] blog.ipleaders.in

[916] odishapolicecidcb.gov.in

BNS Section 127 (1)

Definition: Wrongful Confinement[917] Section 127(1) of the Bharatiya Nyaya Sanhita (BNS) 2023 addresses the offense of wrongful confinement, which involves unlawfully restraining a person in such a manner that they cannot move freely.

Illustration: A person locks another individual in a room without their consent, preventing them from leaving. This act falls under BNS 127(1) as wrongful confinement.

Example: Suppose an individual is locked in a warehouse by someone who then leaves the premises, making it impossible for the confined person to escape. This would be categorized as wrongful confinement under BNS 127(1).

Comment: This section emphasizes the importance of personal freedom and ensures accountability for actions that unlawfully impede someone's movement.

Classification of Offence and Punishment Classification: Wrongful confinement is classified as a criminal offense due to the unlawful restriction of an individual's freedom of movement. Punishment: The punishment for wrongful confinement under BNS 127(1) can be imprisonment for a term which may extend to one year, or with fine, or with both.

Cognizable or Non-Cognizable, Bailable or Non-Bailable: This offense is cognizable, meaning the police can arrest the accused without a warrant.

Bailable: This offense is bailable, indicating that the accused can secure bail and be released from custody until the trial is completed.

Comparison: Section 340 of the Indian Penal Code (IPC) deals with wrongful confinement Section 340: [918]States that whoever wrongfully

---

[917] Ministry of Home Affairs. (2024). The Bharatiya Nyaya Sanhita, 2023. Retrieved from https://www.mha.gov.in/sites/default/files/250883_english_01042024.pdf

[918] blog.ipleaders.in

restrains [919]any person in such a manner as to prevent that person from proceeding beyond certain circumscribing limits is said "wrongfully to [920]confine" that person.

Key Differences: BNS 127(1): Similar to IPC Section 340 in defining wrongful confinement and specifying punishment. Both sections address the unlawful restriction of someone's freedom of movement. IPC Section 340: Provides a framework for addressing wrongful confinement with similar definitions and classifications.

BNS Section 127 (2)

Definition: Punishment for [921]Wrongful Confinement Section 127(2) of the Bharatiya Nyaya Sanhita (BNS) 2023 deals with the punishment for the offense of wrongful confinement.

Illustration: A person unlawfully confines another in a room, locking the door and preventing them from leaving. This act falls under BNS 127(2) as wrongful confinement.

Example: Suppose someone traps another person in a cellar without their consent, making it impossible for them to escape. This would be categorized as wrongful confinement under BNS 127(2).

Comment: This section ensures that individuals who unlawfully confine others are held accountable. It emphasizes the importance of personal freedom and the consequences of restricting it unlawfully.

Classification of Offence and Punishment Classification: Wrongful confinement is classified as a criminal offense due to the unlawful restriction of an individual's freedom of movement.

---

[919] blog.ipleaders.in

[920] prsindia.org

[921] Ministry of Home Affairs. (2024). The Bharatiya Nyaya Sanhita, 2023. Retrieved from https://www.mha.gov.in/sites/default/files/250883_english_01042024.pdf

Punishment: The punishment for wrongful confinement under BNS 127(2) [922]can be imprisonment for a term which may extend to one year, or with fine, or with both.

Cognizable or Non-Cognizable, Bailable or Non-Bailable: This offense is cognizable, meaning the police can arrest the accused without a warrant.

Bailable: This offense is bailable, indicating that the accused can secure bail and be released from custody until the trial is completed.

Comparison: Section [923]342 of the Indian Penal Code (IPC) deals with the punishment for wrongful confinement: IPC Section 342: States that whoever wrongfully confines any person shall be punished with imprisonment of either description for a term which may extend to one year, or with fine, or with both.

Key Differences: BNS 127(2): Similar to IPC Section 342 in defining the punishment for wrongful confinement, [924]with both specifying imprisonment for a term which may extend to one year, or a fine, or both. IPC Section 342.

BNS Section 127(3)

Definition: Wrongful Confinement for Three or More Days Section 127(3)[925] of the Bharatiya Nyaya Sanhita (BNS) 2023 addresses the offense of wrongful confinement that lasts for three or more days.

Illustration: A person unlawfully confines another individual in a room for more than three [926]days, preventing them from leaving and accessing basic necessities. This act falls under BNS 127(3) as wrongful confinement for three or more days.

---

[922] blog.ipleaders.in

[923] blog.ipleaders.in

[924] blog.ipleaders.in

[925] Ministry of Home Affairs. (2024). The Bharatiya Nyaya Sanhita, 2023. Retrieved from https://www.mha.gov.in/sites/default/files/250883_english_01042024.pdf

[926] blog.ipleaders.in

Example: Suppose someone locks an employee in a storage room for four days as a form of punishment. This would be categorized under BNS 127(3) as wrongful confinement for three or more days.

Comment: This section emphasizes the seriousness of prolonged unlawful confinement, ensuring strict penalties for those who unlawfully restrict another's freedom for extended periods.

Classification of Offence and Punishment Classification: Wrongful confinement for three or more days is classified as a serious criminal offense due to the prolonged and unlawful restriction of an individual's freedom.

Punishment: The punishment for wrongful confinement under BNS 127(3) can be imprisonment for a term which may extend to three years, and the offender shall also be liable to a fine.

Cognizable or Non-Cognizable, Bailable or Non-Bailable: This offense is cognizable, meaning the police can arrest the accused without a warrant.

Bailable: This offense is bailable, indicating that the accused can secure bail and be released from custody until the trial is completed.

Comparison: [927]Section 343 of the Indian Penal Code (IPC) deals with [928]wrongful confinement for three or more days: IPC Section 343: States that whoever wrongfully confines any person for [929]three days or more, shall be punished with imprisonment of either description for a term which may extend to two years, or with fine, or with both.

Key Differences: BNS 127(3): Specifies imprisonment for a term which may extend to three years, along with a fine. IPC Section 343: Provides a similar framework but with a shorter maximum term of imprisonment (up to two years).

---

[927] blog.ipleaders.in

[928] blog.ipleaders.in

[929] www.wipo.int

BNS Section 127 (4)

Definition: Wrongful Confinement for[930] Ten or More Days Section 127(4) of the Bharatiya Nyaya Sanhita (BNS) 2023 addresses the offense of wrongful confinement that lasts for ten or more days.

Illustration: A person unlawfully confines another individual in a basement for more than ten [931]days, restricting their movement and access to basic needs. This act falls under BNS 127(4) as wrongful confinement for ten or more days.

Example: Suppose someone abducts a person and keeps them locked in a remote cabin for twelve days. This would be categorized as wrongful confinement for ten or more days under BNS 127(4).

Comment: This section emphasizes the severity of prolonged unlawful confinement, ensuring strict penalties for those who unlawfully restrict another's freedom for extended periods.

Classification of Offence and Punishment Classification: Wrongful confinement for ten or more days is classified as a serious criminal offense due to the prolonged and unlawful restriction of an individual's freedom.

Punishment: The punishment for wrongful confinement under BNS 127(4) can be imprisonment for a term which may extend to seven years, and the offender shall also be liable to a fine.

Cognizable or Non-Cognizable, Bailable or Non-Bailable: This offense is cognizable, meaning the police can arrest the accused without a warrant.

Bailable: This offense is non-bailable, indicating that the accused cannot easily secure bail and must remain in custody until the trial is completed.

Comparison: Section 344 of the Indian Penal Code (IPC) deals with wrongful confinement for ten or more days: IPC Section 344: States that

---

[930] Ministry of Home Affairs. (2024). The Bharatiya Nyaya Sanhita, 2023. Retrieved from https://www.mha.gov.in/sites/default/files/250883_english_01042024.pdf

[931] blog.ipleaders.in

whoever wrongfully confines any person for ten [932]days or more, shall be punished with imprisonment of either description for a term which may extend to three years, and shall also be liable to a fine.

Key Differences: BNS 127(4): Specifies imprisonment for a term which may extend to seven years, along with a fine. IPC Section 344: Provides a similar framework but with a shorter maximum term of imprisonment (up to three years).

BNS Section 127 (5)

Definition: Wrongful Confinement of Person [933]for Whose Liberation Writ Has Been Issued Section 127(5) of the Bharatiya Nyaya Sanhita (BNS) 2023 addresses the offense of wrongful confinement of a person for whose liberation a writ has been issued.

Illustration: If a person is unlawfully confined despite a court issuing a writ for their release, the act of continuing to confine them falls under BNS 127(5).

Example: Suppose an individual is detained in a facility despite a court order for their release. The authorities' refusal to comply with the writ and release the person would be categorized under BNS 127(5).

Comment: This section underscores the seriousness of ignoring judicial orders and ensures strict penalties for unlawfully continuing to confine someone despite a writ for their release.

Classification of Offence and Punishment Classification: [934]Wrongful confinement of a person for whose liberation a writ has been issued is classified as a serious criminal offense due to the blatant disregard for judicial orders and the unlawful restriction of an individual's freedom.

---

[932] prsindia.org

[933] Ministry of Home Affairs. (2024). The Bharatiya Nyaya Sanhita, 2023. Retrieved from https://www.mha.gov.in/sites/default/files/250883_english_01042024.pdf

[934] blog.ipleaders.in

Punishment: The punishment for this offense under BNS 127(5) can be imprisonment for a term which may extend to two years, and the offender shall also be liable to a fine.

Cognizable or Non-Cognizable, Bailable or Non-Bailable: This offense is cognizable, meaning the police can arrest the accused without a warrant.

Bailable: This offense is bailable, indicating that the accused can secure bail and be released from custody until the trial is completed.

Comparison: Section 345 of the Indian Penal Code (IPC) deals with wrongful confinement of a person for whose liberation a writ has been issued: IPC Section 345: [935]States that whoever keeps any person in wrongful [936]confinement, knowing that a writ for the liberation of that person has been duly issued, shall be punished with imprisonment of either description for a term which may extend to two years, and shall also be liable to a fine.

Key Differences: BNS 127(5): Specifies the same range of punishment as IPC Section 345, providing a framework to address the unlawful confinement of a person despite a writ for their release. IPC Section 345: Aligns with BNS 127(5), providing a similar framework with the same term of imprisonment and fine.

BNS Section 127(6)

Definition: Wrongful Confinement in Secret [937]Section 127(6) of the Bharatiya Nyaya Sanhita (BNS) 2023 addresses the offense of wrongful confinement in secret, which involves confining someone in such a manner that their confinement is hidden from others.

Illustration: A person locks another individual in a hidden basement room, unknown to others, making it impossible for the confined person to

---

[935]blog.ipleaders.in

[936] blog.ipleaders.in

[937] Ministry of Home Affairs. (2024). The Bharatiya Nyaya Sanhita, 2023. Retrieved from https://www.mha.gov.in/sites/default/files/250883_english_01042024.pdf

be discovered or rescued. This act falls under BNS 127(6) as wrongful confinement in secret.

Example: Suppose someone kidnaps a person and keeps them hidden in an isolated cabin without any communication with the outside world, ensuring that no one knows about the confinement. This would be categorized as wrongful confinement in secret under BNS 127(6).

Comment: This section emphasizes the severity of concealing someone's confinement, making it challenging for the confined person to be found or rescued. It ensures strict penalties [938]for those who commit such acts, highlighting the importance of individual freedom and safety.

Classification of Offence and Punishment Classification: Wrongful confinement in secret is classified as a serious criminal offense due to the hidden nature and the difficulty in rescuing the confined individual.

Punishment: The punishment for [939]wrongful confinement under BNS 127(6) can be imprisonment for a term which may extend to two years, and the offender shall also be liable to a fine.

Cognizable or Non-Cognizable, Bailable or Non-Bailable: This offense is cognizable, meaning the police can arrest the accused without a warrant.

Bailable: This offense is bailable, indicating that the accused can secure bail and be released from custody until the trial is completed.

Comparison: Section 346 of the Indian Penal Code (IPC) deals with wrongful confinement in secret :IPC Section 346: States that whoever wrongfully confines any person in such a manner as to indicate an intention that the confinement of such person may not be known to any person interested in the person so confined, or to any public servant or as to indicate that the place of such confinement may not be known to or discovered by any such person or public [940]servant, shall be punished with

[938] www.omct.org

[939] blog.ipleaders.in

[940] odishapolicecidcb.gov.in

imprisonment of either description for a term which may extend to two years, [941]and shall also be liable to a fine.

Key Differences: BNS 127(6): Specifies the same range of punishment as IPC Section 346, providing a framework to address the severity of wrongful confinement in secret. IPC Section 346: Aligns closely with BNS 127(6), providing a similar framework with the same term of imprisonment and fine.

BNS Section 127 (7)

Definition: Wrongful Confinement to Extort[942] Property, or Constrain to Illegal Act Section 127(7) of the Bharatiya Nyaya Sanhita (BNS) 2023 addresses the offense of wrongful confinement with the intent to extort property or constrain someone to commit an illegal act.

Illustration: A person unlawfully confines another individual and demands money for their release. This act falls under BNS 127(7) as wrongful confinement to extort property.

Example: Suppose an individual locks someone in a room and forces them to sign illegal documents under the threat of continued confinement. This would be categorized under BNS 127(7) as wrongful confinement to constrain to an illegal act.

Comment: This section highlights the serious nature of using confinement as a means to extort property or coerce someone into committing an illegal act. It ensures accountability for such coercive and unlawful actions.

Classification of Offence and Punishment Classification: [943]Wrongful confinement to extort property or [944]constrain to an illegal act is classified

---

[941] blog.ipleaders.in

[942]Ministry of Home Affairs. (2024). The Bharatiya Nyaya Sanhita, 2023. Retrieved from https://www.mha.gov.in/sites/default/files/250883_english_01042024.pdf

[943] blog.ipleaders.in

[944] odishapolicecidcb.gov.in

as a serious criminal offense due to the coercive and unlawful nature of the act.

Punishment: The punishment for this offense under BNS 127(7) can be [945]imprisonment for a term which may extend to three years, and the offender shall also be liable to a fine.

Cognizable or Non-Cognizable, Bailable or Non-Bailable: This offense is cognizable, meaning the police can arrest the accused without a warrant.

Bailable: This offense is non-bailable, indicating that the accused cannot easily secure bail and must remain in custody until the trial is completed.

Comparison: [946]Section 347 of the Indian Penal Code (IPC) deals with [947]wrongful confinement to extort property, or constrain to illegal act: IPC Section 347: States that whoever wrongfully confines any person for the purpose of extorting from the person confined or any person interested in the person confined any [948]property or valuable security, or of constraining the person confined or any person interested in such person to do anything illegal or to [949]facilitate the commission of an offense, shall be punished with imprisonment of either description for a term which may extend to three years, and shall also be liable to a fine.

Key Differences: BNS 127(7): Similar to IPC Section 347 in defining the offense and specifying punishment. Both address the unlawful and coercive nature of wrongful confinement to extort property or [950]constrain to an illegal act. IPC Section 347: Provides a similar framework with the same term of imprisonment and fine for such offenses.

---

[945] blog.ipleaders.in

[946] www.bareactslive.com

[947] blog.ipleaders.in

[948] odishapolicecidcb.gov.in

[949] blog.ipleaders.in

[950] www.bareactslive.com

BNS Section 127 (8)

Definition: Wrongful Confinement[951] to Extort Confession, or Compel Restoration of Property Section 127(8) of the Bharatiya Nyaya Sanhita (BNS) 2023 addresses the offense of wrongful confinement with the intent to extort a confession or compel the restoration of property.

Illustration: If a person unlawfully [952]confines another individual and demands a confession to a crime in exchange for their release, this act falls under BNS 127(8).

Example: Suppose an individual locks someone in a room and forces them to admit to a theft or return stolen goods under threat of continued confinement. This[953] would be categorized as wrongful confinement to extort confession or compel restoration of property under BNS 127(8).

Comment: This section highlights the serious nature of using confinement to extort confessions or compel the restoration of property, ensuring accountability for such coercive and unlawful[954] actions.

Classification of Offence and Punishment Classification: Wrongful confinement to extort confession or compel[955] restoration of property is classified as a serious criminal offense due to the coercive and unlawful nature of the act.

Punishment: The punishment for this offense under BNS 127(8) can be imprisonment for a term which may extend to three years, and the offender shall also be liable to a fine.

Cognizable or Non-Cognizable, Bailable or Non-Bailable: This offense is cognizable, meaning the police can arrest the accused without a warrant.

---

[951] Ministry of Home Affairs. (2024). The Bharatiya Nyaya Sanhita, 2023. Retrieved from https://www.mha.gov.in/sites/default/files/250883_english_01042024.pdf

[952] blog.ipleaders.in

[953] blog.ipleaders.in

[954] blog.ipleaders.in

[955] blog.ipleaders.in

Bailable: This offense is non-bailable, indicating that the accused cannot easily secure bail and must remain in custody until the trial is completed.

Comparison: [956]Section 348 of the Indian Penal Code (IPC) deals with [957]wrongful confinement to extort confession, or compel restoration of property: IPC Section 348: States that whoever wrongfully confines any person for the purpose of extorting from the person confined or any person interested in the person confined any confession or any information which may lead to the detection of an offense or misconduct, or for the purpose of constraining the person confined or any person interested in such person to restore or to cause the restoration of any property or valuable security, or to satisfy any claim or demand, or to give information which may lead to the restoration of any property or valuable security, shall be punished with imprisonment of either description for a term which may extend to three years, and shall also be liable to a fine.

Key Differences: BNS 127(8): Similar to IPC Section 348 in defining the offense and specifying punishment.[958] Both address the unlawful and coercive nature of wrongful confinement to extort confession or compel restoration of property. IPC Section 348: Provides a similar framework with the same term of imprisonment and fine for such offenses.

BNS Section 128

Definition: Force[959] Section 128 of the Bharatiya Nyaya Sanhita (BNS) 2023 defines the concept of "force" and outlines the circumstances under which it is considered to be used against another person.

Illustration: If a person pushes another, causing them to move or fall, this act constitutes the use of force.

---

956 www.bareactslive.com

957 odishapolicecidcb.gov.in

958 www.bareactslive.com

959 Ministry of Home Affairs. (2024). The Bharatiya Nyaya Sanhita, 2023. Retrieved from https://www.mha.gov.in/sites/default/files/250883_english_01042024.pdf

Example: Suppose someone throws a rock, causing it to hit another person. This would be considered using force under BNS 128.

Comment: This section clarifies the definition and application of force, emphasizing the circumstances in which it can be considered a criminal act.

Classification of Offence and Punishment Classification: The use of force is classified as a criminal offense when it is done unlawfully or without consent.

Punishment: The punishment for using force can vary depending on the severity and [960]context of the act, but it generally includes imprisonment and/or fine.

Cognizable or Non-Cognizable, Bailable or Non-Bailable: This offense is cognizable, meaning the police can arrest the accused without a warrant.

Bailable: This offense is bailable, indicating that the accused can secure bail and be released from custody until the trial is completed.

Comparison: Section 349 of the Indian Penal Code (IPC) also defines the concept of "force": IPC Section 349[961]: States that a person is said to use force to another if they cause motion, change of motion, or cessation of motion to that other, or if they cause to any substance such motion, or change of motion, or cessation of motion as brings that substance into contact with any part of that other's body, or with anything which that other is wearing or carrying, or with anything so situated that such contact affects that other's sense of feeling.

Key Differences: BNS 128: Similar to IPC Section 349 in defining the concept of force, with both addressing the use of force in causing motion or contact2.IPC Section 349: Provides a detailed framework for understanding force, including the ways it can be applied (through bodily power, disposing substances, or inducing animals to move)

[960] main.sci.gov.in

[961] main.sci.gov.in

BNS Section 129

Definition: Criminal[962] Force Section 129 of the Bharatiya Nyaya Sanhita (BNS) 2023 defines the offense of "criminal force" and outlines the associated circumstances and punishments.

Illustration: If a person pushes another to steal their wallet, this act is considered criminal force.

Example: Suppose someone forcibly grabs a person's arm to prevent them from calling for help while committing[963] a robbery. This use of force with intent to commit an offense falls under BNS 129 as criminal force.

Comment: This section clarifies the definition and application of criminal force, emphasizing the circumstances under which force becomes a criminal act due to its intent and effect.

Classification of Offence and Punishment Classification: Criminal force is classified as a criminal offense because it involves[964] using force with a criminal intent.

Punishment: The punishment for criminal force under BNS 129 can be [965]imprisonment for a term which may extend to three months, or with fine which may extend to five hundred rupees, or with both.

Cognizable or Non-Cognizable, Bailable or Non-Bailable: This offense is non-cognizable, meaning the police cannot arrest the accused without a warrant.

Bailable: This offense is bailable, indicating that the accused can secure bail and be released from custody until the trial is completed.

---

[962] Ministry of Home Affairs. (2024). The Bharatiya Nyaya Sanhita, 2023. Retrieved from https://www.mha.gov.in/sites/default/files/250883_english_01042024.pdf

[963] odishapolicecidcb.gov.in

[964] odishapolicecidcb.gov.in

[965] msbrijuniversity.ac.in

Comparison: Section 350 of the [966]Indian Penal Code (IPC) defines criminal force : IPC Section 350: States that [967]whoever intentionally uses force to any person, without that person's consent, in order to commit an offense or intending by the use of such force to cause, or knowing it to be likely that by the use of such force he will [968]cause injury, fear, or annoyance to [969]the person to whom the force is used, is said to use criminal force to that other.

Key Differences: BNS 129: Similar to IPC Section 350 in defining criminal force and specifying punishment. Both address the use of force with criminal intent, causing injury, fear, or annoyance. IPC Section 350: Provides a detailed framework for understanding criminal force, including the intentions behind using such force.

BNS Section 130

Definition: Assault[970] Section 130 of the Bharatiya Nyaya Sanhita (BNS) 2023 defines the offense of "assault" and outlines the associated circumstances and punishments.

Illustration: If a person raises their hand to strike another, but does not actually make contact, this act is considered assault under BNS 130.

Comment: This section clarifies the definition and application of assault, emphasizing the circumstances under which causing apprehension of harm becomes a criminal act.

Example: Suppose someone brandishes a weapon in a threatening manner towards another person, causing the victim to fear immediate harm. This would be categorized as assault under BNS 130.

[966] main.sci.gov.in

[967] msbrijuniversity.ac.in

[968] odishapolicecidcb.gov.in

[969] msbrijuniversity.ac.in

[970] Ministry of Home Affairs. (2024). The Bharatiya Nyaya Sanhita, 2023. Retrieved from https://www.mha.gov.in/sites/default/files/250883_english_01042024.pdf

Classification of Offence and Punishment Classification: Assault is classified as a criminal offense [971]due to the act of causing apprehension of harm.

Punishment: [972]The punishment for assault under BNS 130 can be imprisonment for a term which may extend to three months, or with fine which may extend to five hundred rupees, or with both.

Cognizable or Non-Cognizable, Bailable or Non-Bailable: This offense is non-cognizable, meaning the police cannot arrest the accused without a warrant.

Bailable: This offense is bailable, indicating that the accused can secure bail and be released from custody until the trial is completed.

Comparison: Section 351 [973]of the Indian Penal Code (IPC) defines assault: IPC Section 351: States that [974]whoever makes any gesture or any preparation intending or knowing it to be likely that such gesture or preparation will cause any person present to apprehend that he who makes that gesture or preparation is about to use criminal force to that person, is said to commit an assault.

Key Differences: BNS 130: Similar to IPC Section 351 in defining assault and specifying punishment. Both address the act of causing apprehension of harm through gestures or preparations Section 351: Provides a detailed framework for understanding assault, including the intentions behind making threatening gestures or preparations.

BNS Section 131

Definition: Punishment[975] for Assault or Criminal Force Otherwise Than on Grave Provocation Section 131 of the Bharatiya Nyaya

[971] www.jetir.org

[972] msbrijuniversity.ac.in

[973] main.sci.gov.in

[974] msbrijuniversity.ac.in

[975] Ministry of Home Affairs. (2024). The Bharatiya Nyaya Sanhita, 2023. Retrieved from https://www.mha.gov.in/sites/default/files/250883_english_01042024.pdf

Sanhita (BNS) 2023 deals with the punishment for assault or criminal force that is not committed under grave provocation.

Illustration: If a person slaps another during a casual argument without any grave provocation, this act is considered assault under BNS 131.

Example: Suppose someone pushes another person out of annoyance in a queue. This would be categorized as assault or criminal force otherwise than on grave provocation under BNS 131.

Comment: This section clarifies the consequences of using force or causing apprehension of harm in situations where there is no grave provocation. It emphasizes the importance of maintaining order and accountability in social interactions.

Classification of Offence and Punishment Classification: Assault or criminal force otherwise than on grave provocation is classified as a criminal offense due to the intentional use of force or threat.

Punishment: The punishment for this offense under BNS 131 can be imprisonment for a term which may extend to three months, or with fine which may extend to five hundred rupees, or with both.

Cognizable or Non-Cognizable, Bailable or Non-Bailable: This offense is non-cognizable, meaning the police cannot arrest the accused without a warrant.

Bailable: This offense is bailable, indicating that the accused can secure bail and be released from custody until the trial is completed.

Comparison: Section 352[976] of the Indian Penal Code (IPC) deals with the [977]punishment for assault or criminal force otherwise than on grave provocation: IPC Section 352: States that whoever assaults or uses criminal force to any person otherwise than on grave and sudden provocation given by that [978]person, shall be punished with imprisonment

[976] main.sci.gov.in

[977] odishapolicecidcb.gov.in

[978] msbrijuniversity.ac.in

of either description for a term which may extend to three months, or with fine which may extend to five hundred rupees, or with both.

Key Differences: BNS 131: Similar to IPC Section 352 in defining and addressing the [979]punishment for assault or criminal force otherwise than on grave provocation. Both specify [980]imprisonment for a term which may extend to three months, or a fine which may extend to five hundred rupees, or both. IPC Section 352: Aligns closely with BNS 131, providing a similar framework [981]for the punishment of such offenses.

BNS Section 132

Definition: Assault or Criminal Force to [982]Deter Public Servant from Discharge of His Duty Section 132 of the Bharatiya Nyaya Sanhita (BNS) 2023 deals with the offense of assault or use of criminal force to deter a public servant from the discharge of their duty.

Illustration: If a person pushes a police officer to prevent them from making an arrest, this act falls under BNS 132 as assault or criminal force to deter a public servant from their duty.

Example: Suppose an individual threatens a tax officer with physical harm to stop them from conducting an audit. This would be categorized under BNS 132.

Comment: This section highlights the seriousness of obstructing lawful duties of public servants through the use of force or threats. It underscores the need for accountability in maintaining law and order.

Classification of Offence and Punishment Classification: Assault or criminal force to deter a public servant from their duty is classified as a

---

[979] odishapolicecidcb.gov.in

[980] msbrijuniversity.ac.in

[981] main.sci.gov.in

[982] Ministry of Home Affairs. (2024). The Bharatiya Nyaya Sanhita, 2023. Retrieved from https://www.mha.gov.in/sites/default/files/250883_english_01042024.pdf

serious criminal offense due to the obstruction of lawful duties and the use of force or threats.

Punishment: The punishment for this offense under BNS 132 can be imprisonment of either description for a term which may extend to [983]two years, or with fine, or with both.

Cognizable or Non-Cognizable, Bailable or Non-Bailable: This offense is cognizable, meaning the police can arrest the accused without a warrant.

Bailable: This offense is bailable, indicating that the accused can secure bail and be released from custody until the trial is completed.

Comparison: [984]Section 353 of the Indian Penal Code (IPC) deals with assault or criminal force to [985]deter public servant from discharge of his duty: IPC Section 353: States that whoever assaults or uses criminal force to any person being a public servant in the execution of their duty as such public servant, or with intent to prevent or deter that person from discharging their duty as such public servant, or in consequence of anything done or attempted to be done by that person in the lawful discharge of their duty as such public servant, shall be punished with imprisonment of either description for a term which may extend to two years, or with fine, or with both.

Key Differences: BNS 132: Similar to IPC Section 353 in defining the offense and specifying punishment. Both address the unlawful use of force or threats to deter a public servant from their duty. IPC Section 353: Provides a similar framework [986]with the same term of imprisonment and fine for such offenses.

---

[983] msbrijuniversity.ac.in

[984] main.sci.gov.in

[985] odishapolicecidcb.gov.in

[986] odishapolicecidcb.gov.in

BNS Section 133

Definition: Assault or Criminal [987]Force with Intent to Dishonor Person, Otherwise Than on Grave Provocation Section 133 of the Bharatiya Nyaya Sanhita (BNS) 2023 addresses the offense of using assault or criminal force with the intent to dishonor a person without grave provocation.

Illustration: If a person slaps another in public to humiliate them, this act is considered assault or criminal force with intent to dishonor under BNS 133.Example: Suppose someone forcibly pulls off another person's headscarf in public, intending to disgrace them. This would fall under BNS 133.

Example: Suppose someone forcibly pulls off another person's headscarf in public, intending to disgrace them. This would fall under BNS 133.

Comment: This section highlights the serious nature of actions intended to dishonor or humiliate others, ensuring accountability for such harmful behavior. It reflects a commitment to upholding dignity and respect in social interactions.

Classification of Offence and Punishment Classification: Assault or criminal force with intent to dishonor is classified as a serious criminal offense due to the malicious intent and potential social harm.

Punishment: The punishment for this offense under BNS 133 can be [988]imprisonment for a term which may extend to two years, or with fine, or with both.

Cognizable or Non-Cognizable, Bailable or Non-Bailable: This offense is cognizable, meaning the police can arrest the accused without a warrant.

Bailable: This offense is bailable, indicating that the accused can secure bail and be released from custody until the trial is completed.

---

[987] Ministry of Home Affairs. (2024). The Bharatiya Nyaya Sanhita, 2023. Retrieved from https://www.mha.gov.in/sites/default/files/250883_english_01042024.pdf

[988] msbrijuniversity.ac.in

Comparison: Section 355 [989]of the Indian Penal Code (IPC) deals with [990]assault or criminal force with intent to dishonor person, otherwise than on grave provocation Section 355: States that [991]whoever assaults or uses criminal force to any person, intending thereby to dishonor that [992]person, otherwise than on grave and sudden provocation given by that person, shall be punished with imprisonment of either description for a term which may extend to two years, or with fine, or with both.

Key Differences: BNS 133: Similar to IPC Section 355 in defining and addressing the [993]punishment for assault or criminal force with intent to dishonor a person without grave provocation. Both specify [994]imprisonment for a term which may extend to two years, or a fine, or both IPC Section 355: Provides a similar framework with the same term of imprisonment and fine for such offenses.

BNS Section 134

Definition: Assault or [995]Criminal Force in Attempt to Commit Theft of Property Carried by a Person Section 134 of the Bharatiya Nyaya Sanhita (BNS) 2023 addresses the offense of using assault or criminal force to attempt to commit theft of property carried by a person.

Illustration: If a person forcefully snatches a bag from [996]someone's shoulder, this act is considered assault or criminal force in an attempt to commit theft under BNS 134.

---

[989] main.sci.gov.in

[990] odishapolicecidcb.gov.in

[991] main.sci.gov.in

[992] www.indiacode.nic.in

[993] odishapolicecidcb.gov.in

[994] msbrijuniversity.ac.in

[995] Ministry of Home Affairs. (2024). The Bharatiya Nyaya Sanhita, 2023. Retrieved from https://www.mha.gov.in/sites/default/files/250883_english_01042024.pdf

[996] msbrijuniversity.ac.in

Example: Suppose someone grabs a phone from another person's hand by using physical force. This would be categorized as assault or criminal force in an attempt to commit theft under BNS 134.

Comment: This section addresses the aggressive and unlawful nature of using force to attempt theft, ensuring accountability for such actions. It emphasizes the importance of protecting individuals from physical aggression aimed at theft.

Classification of Offence and Punishment Classification: Assault or criminal force in an attempt to commit theft is classified as a serious criminal offense due to the aggressive and unlawful nature of the act.

Punishment: The punishment for this offense under BNS 134 can be imprisonment for a term which may extend to two years, or with fine, or with both.

Cognizable or Non-Cognizable, Bailable or Non-Bailable: This offense is cognizable, meaning the police can arrest the accused without a warrant.

Bailable: This offense is bailable, indicating that the accused can secure bail and be released from custody until the trial is completed.

Comparison: Section 356[997] of the Indian Penal Code (IPC) deals with [998]assault or criminal force in an [999]attempt to commit theft of property carried by a person :IPC Section 356: States that whoever assaults or uses criminal force to any person, in attempting to commit theft on any property which that person is then wearing or carrying, shall be punished with imprisonment of either description for a term which may extend to two years, or with fine, or with both.

Key Differences: BNS 134: Similar to IPC Section 356 in defining the offense and specifying punishment. Both address the use of force to attempt theft of property carried by a person. IPC Section 356: Provides a

---

[997] main.sci.gov.in

[998] msbrijuniversity.ac.in

[999] main.sci.gov.in

similar framework with the same term of imprisonment and fine for such offenses.

BNS Section 135

Definition: Assault or Criminal Force [1000]in Attempt to Wrongfully Confine a Person Section 135 of the Bharatiya Nyaya Sanhita (BNS) 2023 addresses the offense of using assault or criminal force to attempt to wrongfully confine a person.

Illustration: If a person physically restrains another to force them into a locked room, this act is considered assault or criminal force in an attempt to wrongfully confine under BNS 135.

Example: Suppose someone grabs another person and drags them towards a car, intending to lock them inside against their will. This would be categorized as assault or criminal force in an attempt to wrongfully confine under BNS 135.

Comment: This section emphasizes the violation of personal liberty involved in using force or threats to confine someone against their will. It ensures accountability for such serious offenses.

Classification of Offence and Punishment Classification: Assault or criminal force in an attempt to wrongfully confine a person is classified as a serious criminal offense due to the violation of personal liberty and the use of force or threats.

Punishment: The punishment for this offense under BNS 135 can be imprisonment for a term which may extend to one year, or with fine, or with both.

Cognizable or Non-Cognizable, Bailable or Non-Bailable: This offense is non-cognizable, meaning the police cannot arrest the accused without a warrant.

[1000] Ministry of Home Affairs. (2024). The Bharatiya Nyaya Sanhita, 2023. Retrieved from https://www.mha.gov.in/sites/default/files/250883_english_01042024.pdf

Bailable: This offense is bailable, indicating that the accused can secure bail and be released from custody until the trial is completed.

Comparison: Section 357 [1001]of the Indian Penal Code (IPC) deals with [1002]assault or criminal force in attempt to wrongfully confine a person: IPC Section 357: States that whoever assaults or uses criminal force to any person, in attempting wrongfully to confine that person, shall be punished with imprisonment of either description for a term which may extend to one year, or with fine, or with both.

Key Differences: BNS 135: Similar to IPC Section 357 in defining the offense and specifying punishment. Both address the use of force to attempt to wrongfully confine a person. IPC Section 357: Provides a similar framework with the same term of imprisonment and fine for such offenses.

BNS Section 136

Definition: Assault or[1003] Criminal Force on Grave Provocation Section 136 of the Bharatiya Nyaya Sanhita (BNS) 2023 addresses the offense of assault or use of criminal force committed under grave provocation.

Illustration: [1004]If a person, upon receiving a sudden and severe insult, reacts by pushing the insulter, this act is considered assault on grave provocation under BNS 136.

Example: Suppose someone is verbally provoked with harsh insults and, in the heat of the moment, slaps the provocateur. This would be categorized as assault on grave provocation under BNS 136.

[1001]main.sci.gov.in

[1002] msbrijuniversity.ac.in

[1003] Ministry of Home Affairs. (2024). The Bharatiya Nyaya Sanhita, 2023. Retrieved from https://www.mha.gov.in/sites/default/files/250883_english_01042024.pdf

[1004] odishapolicecidcb.gov.in

Comment: This section acknowledges the mitigating factor of provocation while still recognizing the offense. It ensures that individuals reacting to grave provocation are held accountable, but with consideration of the circumstances.

Classification of Offence and Punishment Classification: Assault or criminal force on grave provocation is classified as a criminal offense but acknowledges the mitigating factor of provocation.

Punishment: The punishment for this offense under BNS 136 can be [1005]imprisonment for a term which may extend to one month, or with fine which may extend to five hundred rupees, or with both.

Cognizable or Non-Cognizable, Bailable or Non-Bailable: This offense is non-cognizable, meaning the police cannot arrest the accused without a warrant.

Bailable: This offense is bailable, indicating that the accused can secure bail and be released from custody until the trial is completed.

Comparison: Section[1006] 358 of the Indian Penal Code (IPC) [1007]deals with assault or criminal force on grave provocation: IPC Section 358: States that [1008]whoever assaults or uses criminal force to any [1009]person on grave and sudden provocation given by that person, shall be punished with imprisonment of either description for a term which may extend to one month, or with fine which may extend to two hundred rupees, or with both.

Key Differences: BNS 136: Specifies a higher [1010]fine which may extend to five hundred rupees, compared to IPC Section 358 which specified a fine up to two hundred rupees. IPC Section 358: Provided a similar framework but with a lower maximum fine amount.

[1005] msbrijuniversity.ac.in

[1006] main.sci.gov.in

[1007] odishapolicecidcb.gov.in

[1008] main.sci.gov.in

[1009] odishapolicecidcb.gov.in

[1010] msbrijuniversity.ac.in

BNS Section 137(1)

Definition: Kidnapping [1011]Section 137 (1) of the Bharatiya Nyaya Sanhita (BNS) 2023 defines the offense of kidnapping and outlines the associated circumstances and punishments.

Illustration: If a person forcibly takes another individual and transports them [1012]beyond the borders of India without their consent, this act is considered kidnapping from India under BNS 137 (1).

Example: Suppose someone abducts a child and takes them out of the country without the consent of the child's legal guardian. This would be categorized as [1013]kidnapping from lawful guardianship under BNS 137 (1).

Comment: This section highlights the severe violation of personal liberty involved in kidnapping, ensuring strict penalties for such offenses. It underscores the importance of protecting individuals from being unlawfully taken or transported.

Classification of Offence and Punishment Classification: Kidnapping is classified as a serious criminal offense due to the severe violation of personal liberty and safety.

Punishment: [1014]The punishment for kidnapping under BNS 137 (1) can be imprisonment for life, or with fine, or with both.

Cognizable or Non-Cognizable, Bailable or Non-Bailable: This offense is cognizable, meaning the police can arrest the accused without a warrant.

Bailable: This offense is non-bailable, indicating that the accused cannot secure bail and must remain in custody until the trial is completed.

[1011]Ministry of Home Affairs. (2024). The Bharatiya Nyaya Sanhita, 2023. Retrieved from https://www.mha.gov.in/sites/default/files/250883_english_01042024.pdf

[1012] lawtimesjournal.in

[1013] pdfcookie.com

[1014] moam.info

Comparison: Section 359 [1015]of the Indian Penal Code (IPC) defines kidnapping: IPC Section 359: States that kidnapping is of two kinds: [1016]kidnapping from India and kidnapping from lawful guardianship. [1017]Kidnapping from India involves taking a person beyond the country's borders without their consent or the consent of someone legally authorized to act on their behalf. Kidnapping from lawful guardianship involves taking or enticing a child or a person of unsound mind out of the keeping of their lawful guardian without consent.

Key Differences: BNS 137 (1): Similar to IPC Section 359 in defining kidnapping and specifying punishment. Both address the act of taking a person without consent and the severe penalties associated with it. IPC Section 359: Provides a detailed framework for understanding kidnapping, including the different forms and the associated legal consequences.

BNS Section 137(1)A

Definition: Kidnapping[1018] from India Section 137 (1)A of the Bharatiya Nyaya Sanhita (BNS) 2023 deals specifically with the offense of kidnapping from India.

Illustration: If a person forcibly takes another individual and transports them beyond the borders of India without their consent, this act is considered kidnapping from India under BNS 137 (1) A.

Example: Suppose someone abducts a minor and takes them out of India without the consent of the minor's parents or legal guardians. This would be categorized as kidnapping from India under BNS 137 (1) A.

Comment: This section underscores the severe violation of personal liberty and safety involved in kidnapping, ensuring strict penalties for such

---

[1015] highcourtchd.gov.in

[1016] www.latestlaws.com

[1017] moam.info

[1018] Ministry of Home Affairs. (2024). The Bharatiya Nyaya Sanhita, 2023. Retrieved from https://www.mha.gov.in/sites/default/files/250883_english_01042024.pdf

offenses. It highlights the critical importance of protecting individuals from being unlawfully taken or transported beyond national borders.

Classification of Offence and Punishment Classification: Kidnapping from India is classified as a serious criminal offense due to the severe violation of personal liberty and safety.

Punishment: The punishment for kidnapping from India under BNS 137 (1)A can be [1019]imprisonment for life, or with fine, or with both.

Cognizable or Non-Cognizable, Bailable or Non-Bailable: This offense is cognizable, meaning the police can arrest the accused without a warrant.

Bailable: This offense is non-bailable, indicating that the accused cannot secure bail and must remain in custody until the trial is completed.

Comparison: Section 360[1020] of the Indian Penal Code (IPC) defines kidnapping from India: IPC Section 360: States that[1021] whoever conveys any person beyond the limits of India without the consent of that person, or of some person legally authorized to consent on behalf of that [1022]person, is said to kidnap that person from India.

Key Differences: BNS 137 (1)A: Similar to IPC Section 360 in defining the offense and specifying punishment. Both address the act of conveying a person beyond India's borders without consent and the severe penalties associated with it. IPC Section 360: Provides a detailed framework for understanding kidnapping from India, including the need for consent from the person or their legal guardian.

[1019] moam.info

[1020] highcourtchd.gov.in

[1021] awtimesjournal.in

[1022] moam.info

BNS Section 137 (1)B

Definition: Kidnapping from Lawful Guardianship Section[1023] 137 (1)B of the Bharatiya Nyaya Sanhita (BNS) 2023 deals specifically with the offense of kidnapping from lawful guardianship.

Illustration: If a person takes a child away from their lawful guardian without permission, this act is considered [1024]kidnapping from lawful guardianship under BNS 137 (1) B.

Example: Suppose someone entices a child to leave their home and come with them, [1025]without the consent of the child's parents or legal guardians. This would be categorized as [1026]kidnapping from lawful guardianship under BNS 137 (1) B.

Comment: This section highlights the severe violation of personal liberty and the potential harm to the victim involved in kidnapping from lawful guardianship. It ensures strict penalties for such offenses, underscoring the importance of protecting [1027]minors and individuals of unsound mind from being unlawfully taken.

Classification of Offence and Punishment Classification: Kidnapping [1028]from lawful guardianship is classified as a serious criminal offense due to the severe violation of personal liberty and the potential harm to the victim.

Punishment: The [1029]punishment for kidnapping from lawful guardianship under BNS 137 (1)B can be [1030]imprisonment for a term

---

[1023] Ministry of Home Affairs. (2024). The Bharatiya Nyaya Sanhita, 2023. Retrieved from https://www.mha.gov.in/sites/default/files/250883_english_01042024.pdf

[1024] pdfcookie.com

[1025] awtimesjournal.in

[1026] pdfcookie.com

[1027] lawtimesjournal.in

[1028] www.lawfinderlive.com

[1029] www.lawfinderlive.com

[1030] highcourtchd.gov.in

which may extend to seven years, and the offender shall also be liable to a fine.

Cognizable or Non-Cognizable, Bailable or Non-Bailable: This offense is cognizable, meaning the police can arrest the accused without a warrant.

Bailable: This offense is bailable, indicating that the accused can secure bail and be released from custody until the trial is completed.

Comparison: [1031]Section 361 of the Indian Penal Code (IPC) defines kidnapping from lawful guardianship: IPC Section 361: States that [1032]whoever takes or entices any minor under sixteen years of age if a male, or under eighteen years of age if a female, or any person of unsound mind, out of the keeping of the lawful guardian of such minor or person of unsound mind, without the consent of such guardian, is said to kidnap such minor or person from lawful guardianship.

Key Differences: BNS 137 (1)B: Similar to IPC Section 361 in defining the offense and specifying punishment. Both address the act of taking a minor or person of unsound mind from their lawful guardian without consent. IPC Section 361: Provides a detailed framework for understanding kidnapping from lawful guardianship, including the age and mental status of the victim.

BNS Section 137(2)

Definition: Punishment[1033] for Kidnapping Section 137 (2) of the Bharatiya Nyaya Sanhita (BNS) 2023 deals with the punishment for the offense of kidnapping.

Illustration: If a person kidnaps a child and demands a ransom for their release, this act is considered kidnapping and falls under BNS 137 (2) for punishment.

[1031] www.lawfinderlive.com

[1032] highcourtchd.gov.in

[1033] Ministry of Home Affairs. (2024). The Bharatiya Nyaya Sanhita, 2023. Retrieved from https://www.mha.gov.in/sites/default/files/250883_english_01042024.pdf

Example: Suppose someone takes a minor away from their lawful guardian without consent and hides them. This would be categorized under BNS 137 (2) as kidnapping, warranting punishment.

Comment: This section underscores the severe violation of personal liberty involved in kidnapping, ensuring strict penalties for such offenses. It highlights the critical importance of protecting individuals, especially minors, from being unlawfully taken or detained.

Classification of Offence and Punishment Classification: Kidnapping is classified as a serious criminal offense due to the severe violation of personal liberty and potential harm to the victim.

Punishment: The punishment for kidnapping under BNS 137 (2) can be [1034]imprisonment for life, or imprisonment for a[1035] term which may extend to ten years, and the offender shall also be liable to a fine.

Cognizable or Non-Cognizable, Bailable or Non-Bailable: This offense is cognizable, meaning the police can arrest the accused without a warrant.

Bailable: This offense is non-bailable, indicating that the accused cannot secure bail and must remain in custody until the trial is completed.

Comparison: [1036]Section 363 of the Indian Penal Code (IPC) deals with the punishment for kidnapping: IPC Section 363: States that [1037]whoever kidnaps any person from India or from lawful guardianship shall be punished with imprisonment of either description for a term which may extend to seven years, and shall also be liable to a fine.

Key Differences: BNS 137 (2): Specifies imprisonment [1038]for life or for a term which may extend to ten years, along with a fine. IPC Section 363:

[1034] moam.info

[1035] highcourtchd.gov.in

[1036] www.bareactslive.com

[1037] highcourtchd.gov.in

[1038] moam.info

Provides for [1039]imprisonment for a term which may extend to seven years and a fine.

BNS Section 138

Definition: Abduction[1040] Section 138 of the Bharatiya Nyaya Sanhita (BNS) 2023 addresses the offense of abduction and outlines the circumstances and punishments associated with it.

Illustration: If a person forcibly takes another individual to a different location against their will, this act is considered abduction under BNS 138.

Example: Suppose someone deceives another person into getting into their car and then drives them to an unknown location, preventing them from leaving. This would be categorized as abduction under BNS 138.

Comment: This section emphasizes the serious violation of personal liberty and the potential harm to the victim involved in abduction. It ensures that individuals who commit such acts face stringent penalties.

Classification of Offence and Punishment Classification: Abduction is classified as a serious criminal offense due to the violation of personal liberty and the potential for harm to the victim.

Punishment: The punishment for abduction under BNS 138 can vary, but generally includes imprisonment for a term which may extend to seven years, and the offender shall also be liable to a fine.

Cognizable or Non-Cognizable, Bailable or Non-Bailable: This offense is cognizable, meaning the police can arrest the accused without a warrant.

Bailable: This offense is bailable, indicating that the accused can secure bail and be released from custody until the trial is completed.

Comparison: Section 362 of the Indian Penal Code (IPC) defines abduction: IPC Section 362: States that [1041]whoever by force compels or

---

[1039] highcourtchd.gov.in

[1040] Ministry of Home Affairs. (2024). The Bharatiya Nyaya Sanhita, 2023. Retrieved from https://www.mha.gov.in/sites/default/files/250883_english_01042024.pdf

[1041] www.lawfinderlive.com

by any deceitful means induces any person to go from any place, is said to abduct that person.

Key Differences: BNS 138: Similar to IPC Section 362 in defining abduction and specifying punishment. Both sections address the act of compelling or inducing someone to move from one place to another without their consent. IPC Section 362: Provides a detailed framework for understanding abduction, including the use of force or deceitful means.

BNS Section 139:

Definition: Kidnapping or Maiming a Child[1042] for Purposes of Begging Section 139 of the Bharatiya Nyaya Sanhita (BNS) 2023 addresses the offense of kidnapping or maiming a child for the purposes of begging.

Illustration: If a person kidnaps a child and maims them to make them appear more sympathetic and thus, more successful at begging, this act falls under BNS 139.

Example: Suppose someone takes a child away from their lawful guardianship, harms them in a way that results in a disability, and then uses the child to beg on the streets. This would be categorized as kidnapping or maiming a child for the purposes of begging under BNS 139.

Comment: This section emphasizes the severe violation of personal liberty and the exploitation of vulnerable children involved in such acts. It ensures that individuals who commit such heinous crimes face stringent penalties.

Classification of Offence and Punishment Classification: Kidnapping or maiming a child for purposes of begging is classified as a very serious criminal offense due to the severe violation of personal liberty and the exploitation of vulnerable children.

[1042] Ministry of Home Affairs. (2024). The Bharatiya Nyaya Sanhita, 2023. Retrieved from https://www.mha.gov.in/sites/default/files/250883_english_01042024.pdf

Punishment: The [1043]punishment for this offense under BNS 139 can be rigorous imprisonment for a term which [1044]shall not be less than ten years but which may extend to life imprisonment, and the offender shall also be liable to a fine.

Cognizable or Non-Cognizable, Bailable or Non-Bailable: This offense is cognizable, meaning the police can arrest the accused without a warrant.

Bailable: This offense is non-bailable, indicating that the accused cannot secure bail and must remain in custody until the trial is completed.

Comparison: [1045]Section 363A of the Indian Penal Code (IPC) deals with kidnapping or maiming a minor for purposes of begging: IPC Section 363A: States that whoever kidnaps any minor or, not being the lawful guardian of a minor, obtains the custody of the minor, in order that such minor may be employed or used for the purpose of begging shall be punished with imprisonment of either description for a term which may extend to ten years, and shall also be liable to a fine. Whoever maims any minor in order that such minor may be employed or used for the purposes of begging shall be punished with imprisonment for life, and shall also be liable to a fine.

Key Differences: BNS 139: Specifies rigorous imprisonment and a fine for kidnapping or maiming a child for purposes of begging, with imprisonment potentially extending to life.IPC Section 363A: Provides imprisonment for up to ten years and a fine for kidnapping, and life imprisonment and a fine for maiming.

BNS Section 140 (1)

Definition: Kidnapping or Abducting[1046] in Order to Murder, etc. Section 140 (1) of the Bharatiya Nyaya Sanhita (BNS) 2023 addresses

---

1043 highcourtchd.gov.in

1044 moam.info

1045 moam.info

1046 Ministry of Home Affairs. (2024). The Bharatiya Nyaya Sanhita, 2023. Retrieved from https://www.mha.gov.in/sites/default/files/250883_english_01042024.pdf

the offense of kidnapping or abducting a person with the intent to murder or put them in danger of being murdered.

Illustration: If a person kidnaps another individual with the intention of murdering them or putting them in a situation where they are likely to be murdered, this act falls under BNS 140 (1).

Example: Suppose someone abducts a person [1047]and takes them to a remote location with the intent to kill them. This would be categorized as kidnapping or abducting in order to murder under BNS 140 (1).

Comment: This section emphasizes the severe violation of personal liberty and the potential for causing death involved in kidnapping or abducting with such malicious intent. It ensures stringent penalties for individuals who commit such heinous acts.

Classification of Offence and Punishment Classification: Kidnapping or abducting in order to murder is classified as a very serious criminal offense due to the severe violation of personal liberty and the potential for causing death.

Punishment: [1048]The punishment for this offense under BNS 140 (1) can be imprisonment for life, or rigorous imprisonment for a term which may extend to ten years, and the offender [1049]shall also be liable to a fine.

Cognizable or Non-Cognizable, Bailable or Non-Bailable: This offense is cognizable, meaning the police can arrest the accused without a warrant.

Bailable: This offense is non-bailable, indicating that the accused cannot secure bail and must remain in custody until the trial is completed.

Comparison: Section 364 of the [1050]Indian Penal Code (IPC) defines [1051]kidnapping or abducting in order to murder: IPC Section 364: States that whoever kidnaps or abducts any person in order that such person may

---

[1047] highcourtchd.gov.in

[1048] moam.info

[1049] highcourtchd.gov.in

[1050] www.bareactslive.com

[1051] highcourtchd.gov.in

be murdered or may be so disposed of as to be put in danger of being murdered, shall be punished with imprisonment for life or rigorous imprisonment for a term which may extend to ten years, and shall also be liable to a fine.

Key Differences: BNS 140 (1): Similar to IPC Section 364 in defining the offense and specifying punishment. Both address the act of kidnapping [1052]or abducting with the intent to murder or put the person in danger of being murdered. IPC Section 364: Provides a detailed framework for understanding the offense, including the intent and the associated legal consequences.

BNS Section 140 (2)

Definition: Kidnapping[1053] for Ransom, etc. Section 140 (2) of the Bharatiya Nyaya Sanhita (BNS) 2023 addresses the offense of kidnapping for ransom or other coercive purposes.

Illustration: If a person kidnaps someone and demands a ransom for their release, this act falls under BNS 140 (2).

Example: Suppose someone abducts a person and threatens to harm them unless a ransom is paid. This would be categorized as kidnapping for ransom under BNS 140 (2).

Comment: This section underscores the severe violation of personal liberty involved in kidnapping for ransom, ensuring stringent penalties for such heinous acts. It reflects the critical importance of protecting individuals from being unlawfully taken or detained for coercive purposes.

Classification of Offence and Punishment Classification: [1054]Kidnapping for ransom is classified as a very serious criminal offense

---

[1052] www.latestlaws.com

[1053] Ministry of Home Affairs. (2024). The Bharatiya Nyaya Sanhita, 2023. Retrieved from https://www.mha.gov.in/sites/default/files/250883_english_01042024.pdf

[1054] moam.info

due to the severe violation of personal liberty and the potential for causing harm to the victim.

Punishment: The punishment for kidnapping for ransom under BNS 140 (2) can be death, imprisonment for life, or rigorous imprisonment for a term which may extend to ten years, and the offender [1055]shall also be liable to a fine.

Cognizable or Non-Cognizable, Bailable or Non-Bailable: This offense is cognizable, meaning the police can arrest the accused without a warrant.

Bailable: This offense is non-bailable, indicating that the accused cannot secure bail and must remain in custody until the trial is completed.

Comparison: [1056]Section 364A of the Indian Penal Code (IPC) deals with kidnapping for ransom: IPC Section 364A: States that [1057]whoever kidnaps or abducts any person or keeps a person in detention after such kidnapping or abduction and threatens to cause death or hurt to such person, or by his conduct gives rise to a reasonable apprehension that such person may be put to death or hurt, or causes hurt or death to such person in order to compel the Government or any foreign State or international inter-governmental organization or any other person to do or abstain from doing any act or to pay a ransom, shall be punished with death, imprisonment for life, or rigorous imprisonment for a term which may extend to ten years, and [1058]shall also be liable to a fine.

Key Differences: BNS 140 (2): Similar to IPC Section 364A in defining the offense and specifying punishment. Both address the act of kidnapping or abducting with the intent to extort money or compel an action. IPC Section 364A: [1059]Provides a detailed framework for understanding the offense, including the intent and the associated legal consequences.

[1055] highcourtchd.gov.in

[1056] www.rgnul.ac.in

[1057] highcourtchd.gov.in

[1058] moam.info

[1059] moam.info

BNS Section 140(3)

Definition: Kidnapping or Abducting with Intent Secretly and Wrongfully to Confine Person Section 140 (3)[1060] of the Bharatiya Nyaya Sanhita (BNS) 2023 addresses the offense of kidnapping or abducting a person with the intent to secretly and wrongfully confine them.

Illustration: If a person kidnaps another and takes them to a hidden location with the intention of keeping them confined against their will, this act falls under BNS 140 (3).

Example: Suppose someone abducts a person and locks them in a secluded basement to prevent them from being found. This would be categorized as kidnapping or abducting with intent to secretly and wrongfully confine under BNS 140 (3).

Comment: This section underscores the severe violation of personal liberty involved in secretly and wrongfully confining someone. It ensures that individuals who commit such acts face stringent penalties.

Classification of Offence and Punishment Classification: Kidnapping or abducting with intent to secretly and wrongfully confine a person is classified as a serious criminal offense due to the severe violation of personal liberty.

Punishment: The punishment for this offense under BNS 140 (3) can be [1061]imprisonment for a term which may extend to seven years, and the offender shall also be liable to a fine.

Cognizable or Non-Cognizable, Bailable or Non-Bailable: This offense is cognizable, meaning the police can arrest the accused without a warrant.

Bailable: This offense is non-bailable, indicating that the accused cannot easily secure bail and must remain in custody until the trial is completed.

[1060]Ministry of Home Affairs. (2024). The Bharatiya Nyaya Sanhita, 2023. Retrieved from https://www.mha.gov.in/sites/default/files/250883_english_01042024.pdf

[1061] highcourtchd.gov.in

Comparison: [1062]Section 365 of the Indian Penal Code (IPC) deals with [1063]kidnapping or abducting with intent secretly and wrongfully to confine person: IPC Section 365: States that [1064]whoever kidnaps or abducts any person with intent to cause that person to be secretly and wrongfully confined, shall be punished with imprisonment of either description for a term which may extend to seven years, and shall also be liable to a fine.

Key Differences: BNS 140 (3): Similar to IPC Section 365 in defining the offense and specifying punishment. Both address the act of kidnapping or abducting with the intent to secretly and wrongfully confine the person. IPC Section 365: Provides a detailed framework for understanding the offense, including the intent and the associated legal consequences.

BNS Section 140 (4)

Definition: Kidnapping or Abducting in Order to Subject Person to Grievous Hurt, Slavery, etc. Section 140 (4)[1065] of the Bharatiya Nyaya Sanhita (BNS) 2023 addresses the offense of kidnapping or abducting a person with the intent to subject them to grievous hurt, slavery, or other forms of exploitation.

Illustration: If a person kidnaps another individual with the intention of inflicting serious injury, forcing them into slavery, or subjecting them to unnatural acts, this act falls under BNS 140 (4).

Example: Suppose someone abducts a person and confines them in a hidden location, intending to cause severe physical harm or force them into servitude. This would be categorized [1066]as kidnapping or abducting

---

[1062] www.bareactslive.com

[1063] moam.info

[1064] highcourtchd.gov.in

[1065] Ministry of Home Affairs. (2024). The Bharatiya Nyaya Sanhita, 2023. Retrieved from https://www.mha.gov.in/sites/default/files/250883_english_01042024.pdf

[1066] highcourtchd.gov.in

in order to subject the [1067]person to grievous hurt, slavery, etc., under BNS 140 (4).

Comment: Kidnapping or abducting with the intent to subject a person to grievous hurt, slavery, or other forms of exploitation is classified as a very serious criminal offense due to the severe violation of personal liberty and the potential for causing significant harm.

Classification of Offence and Punishment Classification: Kidnapping or abducting with the intent to subject a person to grievous hurt, slavery, or other forms of exploitation is classified as a very serious criminal offense due to the severe violation of personal liberty and the potential for causing significant harm.

Punishment: The punishment for this offense under BNS 140 (4) can be [1068]imprisonment of either description for a term which may extend to ten years, and the offender shall also be liable to a fine.

Cognizable or Non-Cognizable, Bailable or Non-Bailable: This offense is cognizable, meaning the police can arrest the accused without a warrant.

Bailable: This offense is non-bailable, indicating that the accused cannot secure bail and must remain in custody until the trial is completed.

Comparison: [1069]Section 367 of the Indian Penal Code (IPC) deals with [1070]kidnapping or abducting in order to subject [1071]a person to grievous hurt, slavery, etc. :IPC Section 367: States that whoever kidnaps or abducts any person in order that such person may be subjected, or may be so disposed of as to be put in danger of being subjected to grievous hurt, or slavery, or to the unnatural lust of any person, or knowing it to be likely that such person will be so subjected or disposed of, shall be punished with

[1067] moam.info

[1068] highcourtchd.gov.in

[1069] www.bareactslive.com

[1070] nalsarpro.org

[1071] www.caritasindia.org

imprisonment of either description for a term which may extend to ten years, and shall also be liable to a fine.

Key Differences: BNS 140 (4): Similar to IPC Section 367 in defining the offense and specifying punishment. Both address the act of kidnapping or abducting with the intent to subject the person to grievous hurt, slavery, or other forms of exploitation. IPC Section 367: Provides a detailed framework for understanding the offense, including the intent and the associated legal consequences.

BNS Section 141

Definition: Importation of Girl or Boy[1072] from Foreign Country Section 141 of the Bharatiya Nyaya Sanhita (BNS) 2023 addresses the offense of importing a girl under the age of twenty-one years or a boy under the age of eighteen years from a foreign country with the intent to force or seduce them into illicit intercourse.

Illustration: If a person brings a girl from another country into India with the intention of forcing her into prostitution or other forms of illicit intercourse, this act falls under BNS 141.

Example: Suppose someone smuggles a young girl from a neighboring country into India and plans to exploit her sexually. This would be categorized as importing a girl for illicit purposes under BNS 141.

Comment: This section emphasizes the severe nature of importing minors for illicit purposes, highlighting the significant harm and violation of personal liberty involved. It underscores the importance of stringent penalties to deter such offenses and protect vulnerable individuals from exploitation. The alignment with IPC Section 366B ensures consistency in addressing these serious crimes, reinforcing the legal framework to combat human trafficking and related offenses.

Classification of Offence and Punishment Classification: Importation of a girl or boy for illicit purposes is classified as a very serious criminal

---

[1072] Ministry of Home Affairs. (2024). The Bharatiya Nyaya Sanhita, 2023. Retrieved from https://www.mha.gov.in/sites/default/files/250883_english_01042024.pdf

offense due to the severe violation of personal liberty and [1073]the potential for causing significant harm.

Punishment: The punishment for this offense under BNS 141 can be imprisonment for a term which may extend to ten years, and the offender shall also be liable to a fine.

Cognizable or Non-Cognizable, Bailable or Non-Bailable: This offense is cognizable, meaning the police can arrest the accused without a warrant.

Bailable: This offense is non-bailable, indicating that the accused cannot secure bail and must remain in custody until the trial is completed.

Comparison: Section 366B of the Indian Penal Code (IPC) deals with the importation of [1074]a girl from a foreign country for illicit purposes: IPC Section 366B: States that [1075]whoever imports into India from any country outside India any girl under the age of twenty-one years [1076]with intent that she may be, or knowing it to be likely that she will be, forced or seduced to illicit intercourse with another person, shall be [1077]punished with imprisonment for a term which may extend to ten years, and shall also be liable to a fine.

Key Differences: BNS 141: Similar to IPC Section 366B in defining the offense and specifying punishment. Both address the act of importing minors into India for illicit purposes. IPC Section 366B: Provides a detailed framework for understanding the offense, including the intent and the associated legal consequences.

[1073] devgan.in

[1074] www.caritasindia.org

[1075] prsindia.org

[1076] nalsarpro.org

[1077] odishapolicecidcb.gov.in

BNS Section 142

Definition: Wrongfully[1078] Concealing or Keeping in Confinement, Kidnapped or Abducted Person Section 142 of the Bharatiya Nyaya Sanhita (BNS) 2023 addresses the offense of wrongfully concealing or keeping in confinement a person who has been kidnapped or abducted.

Illustration: [1079]If a person knows that someone has been kidnapped and then hides or confines that person to prevent their discovery, this act falls under BNS 142.

Example: Suppose someone abducts a person and then another individual, aware of the abduction, hides the victim in a secret location to avoid detection. This would be categorized as [1080]wrongfully concealing or keeping in confinement under BNS 142.

Comment: This section underscores the severe violation of personal liberty involved in concealing or confining a kidnapped or abducted [1081]person. It ensures accountability for those who assist in such acts by hiding the victims.

Classification of Offence and Punishment Classification: Wrongfully concealing or keeping in confinement a kidnapped or abducted person is classified as a serious criminal offense due to the severe [1082]violation of personal liberty and the potential for causing harm to the victim.

Punishment: The punishment for this offense under BNS 142 is the same as if the person had kidnapped or abducted the victim with the same intention or knowledge, or for the same purpose as that with or for which they conceal or detain the person in confinement.

[1078] Ministry of Home Affairs. (2024). The Bharatiya Nyaya Sanhita, 2023. Retrieved from https://www.mha.gov.in/sites/default/files/250883_english_01042024.pdf

[1079] prsindia.org

[1080] nalsarpro.org

[1081] nalsarpro.org

[1082] nalsarpro.org

Cognizable or Non-Cognizable, Bailable or Non-Bailable: This offense is cognizable, meaning the police can arrest the accused without a warrant.

Bailable: This offense is non-bailable, indicating that the accused cannot secure bail and must remain in custody until the trial is completed.

Comparison: [1083]Section 368 of the Indian Penal Code (IPC) deals with [1084]wrongfully concealing or keeping in confinement, kidnapped or abducted person: IPC Section 368: States that whoever, knowing that any person has been kidnapped or has been abducted, wrongfully conceals or confines such person, shall be punished in the same manner as if he had kidnapped or abducted such person with the same intention or knowledge, or for the same purpose as that with or for which he conceals or detains such person in confinement.

Key Differences: BNS 142: Similar to IPC Section 368 in defining the offense and specifying punishment. Both address the act of wrongfully concealing or keeping in confinement a kidnapped or abducted person. IPC Section 368: Provides a detailed framework for understanding the offense, including the intent and the associated legal consequences.

BNS Section 143

Definition: Trafficking[1085] of Person Section 143 of the Bharatiya Nyaya Sanhita (BNS) 2023 addresses the offense of trafficking a person for exploitation.

Illustration: If a person recruits, transports, harbors, transfers, or receives another person using threats, force, coercion, abduction, fraud, deception, abuse of power, or inducement, this act falls under BNS 143.

[1083] www.bareactslive.com

[1084] nalsarpro.org

[1085] Ministry of Home Affairs. (2024). The Bharatiya Nyaya Sanhita, 2023. Retrieved from https://www.mha.gov.in/sites/default/files/250883_english_01042024.pdf

Example: Suppose someone lures a person with the promise of a job, transports them to another location, and then forces them into labor or prostitution. This would be categorized as trafficking under BNS 143.

Comment: This section underscores the severe violation of personal liberty and the potential for causing significant harm involved in trafficking. It ensures that individuals who commit such acts face stringent penalties.

Classification of Offence and Punishment Classification: Trafficking of a person is classified as a very serious criminal offense due to the severe violation of personal liberty and [1086]the potential for causing significant harm.

Punishment: The punishment for trafficking under BNS 143 can be rigorous imprisonment for a term which may extend to ten years, and the offender shall also be liable to a fine. For trafficking multiple persons or children, the punishment can be [1087]rigorous imprisonment for 10 years to life imprisonment, and the offender [1088]shall also be liable to a fine.

Cognizable or Non-Cognizable, Bailable or Non-Bailable: This offense is cognizable, meaning the police can arrest the accused without a warrant.

Bailable: This offense is non-bailable, indicating that the accused cannot secure bail and must remain in custody until the trial is completed.

Comparison: Section 370 of the Indian Penal Code (IPC) also deals with trafficking of persons: IPC Section 370: States that [1089]whoever, for the purpose of exploitation, recruits, transports, harbors, transfers, or receives a person or persons, by using threats, force, coercion, abduction, fraud, deception, abuse of power, or inducement, commits the offense of trafficking. The punishment for trafficking under IPC Section 370 can be imprisonment for a term which may extend to seven years, and the offender shall also be liable to a fine.

[1086] nalsarpro.org

[1087] odishapolicecidcb.gov.in

[1088] nalsarpro.org

[1089] nalsarpro.org

Key Differences: BNS 143: Similar to IPC Section 370 in defining the offense and specifying punishment. Both address the act of trafficking with the intent to exploit the victim10.IPC Section 370: Provides a detailed framework for understanding the offense, including the intent and the associated legal consequences.

BNS Section 144

Definition: Exploitation[1090] of a Trafficked Person Section 144 of the Bharatiya Nyaya Sanhita (BNS) 2023 addresses the offense of exploiting a trafficked person.

Illustration: If a person knowingly engages a trafficked child for sexual exploitation, this act falls under BNS 144.

Example: Suppose someone is aware that a child has been trafficked and then forces the child into prostitution. This would be categorized as [1091]exploitation of a trafficked person under BNS 144.

Comment: This section emphasizes the severe nature of exploiting trafficked persons and underscores the legal system's commitment to protecting vulnerable.

Classification of Offence and Punishment Classification: Exploitation of a trafficked person is classified as a very serious criminal offense due to the severe violation of personal liberty and the potential for causing significant harm[1092].

Punishment: The punishment for exploiting a trafficked child under BNS 144 can be rigorous imprisonment for a term which shall not be less than five years, but which may extend to ten years, and the offender shall also be liable to a fine. For trafficking adults, the punishment can be rigorous

---

[1090] Ministry of Home Affairs. (2024). The Bharatiya Nyaya Sanhita, 2023. Retrieved from https://www.mha.gov.in/sites/default/files/250883_english_01042024.pdf

[1091] nalsarpro.org

[1092] nalsarpro.org

imprisonment for a term which shall not be less than three years, but which may extend to seven years, and the offender shall also be liable to a fine.

Cognizable or Non-Cognizable, Bailable or Non-Bailable: This offense is cognizable, meaning the police can arrest the accused without a warrant.

Bailable: This offense is non-bailable, indicating that the accused cannot secure bail and must remain in custody until the trial is completed.

Comparison: Section 370A of the Indian Penal Code (IPC) also deals with the exploitation of trafficked persons: IPC Section 370A: States that [1093]whoever, knowingly or having reason to believe that a minor has been trafficked, engages such minor for sexual exploitation in any manner, shall be punished with rigorous imprisonment for a term which shall not be less than five years, but which may extend to seven years, and shall also be liable to a fine.

Key Differences: BNS 144: Similar to IPC Section 370A in defining the offense and specifying punishment. Both address the act of exploiting trafficked individuals.IPC Section 370A: Provides a detailed framework for understanding the offense, including the intent and the associated legal consequences.

BNS Section 145

Definition: Habitual Dealing in Slaves Section 145[1094] of the Bharatiya Nyaya Sanhita (BNS) 2023 addresses the offense of habitual dealing in slaves.

Illustration: If a person regularly engages in the buying, selling, or trafficking of individuals as slaves, this act falls under BNS 145.

Example: Suppose someone habitually imports individuals from another country, sells them, and forces them into servitude. This would be categorized as habitual dealing in slaves under BNS 145.

[1093] nalsarpro.org

[1094] Ministry of Home Affairs. (2024). The Bharatiya Nyaya Sanhita, 2023. Retrieved from https://www.mha.gov.in/sites/default/files/250883_english_01042024.pdf

Comment: This section underscores the heinous nature of habitual dealing in slaves and reflects the strong legal measures in place to combat human trafficking. It emphasizes the commitment to upholding human rights and ensuring that individuals who engage in such exploitative practices face severe penalties. By updating the legal terminology and provisions, BNS 145 aims to effectively address and deter modern forms of slavery, reinforcing the protection of human dignity and liberty.

Classification of Offence and Punishment Classification: Habitual dealing in slaves is classified as a very serious criminal offense due to the severe violation of human rights and the potential for causing significant harm.

Punishment: The punishment for habitual dealing in slaves under BNS 145 can be imprisonment for life, or [1095]imprisonment of either description for a term not exceeding ten years, and the offender [1096]shall also be liable to a fine.

Cognizable or Non-Cognizable, Bailable or Non-Bailable: This offense is cognizable, meaning the police can arrest the accused without a warrant.

Bailable: This offense is non-bailable, indicating that the accused cannot secure bail and must remain in custody until the trial is completed.

Comparison: [1097]Section 371 of the Indian Penal Code (IPC) also deals with habitual dealing in slaves: IPC Section 371: States that [1098]whoever habitually imports, exports, removes, buys, sells, traffics, or deals in slaves, shall be punished with imprisonment for life, or imprisonment of either description for a term not exceeding ten years, and shall also be liable to a fine.

Key Differences: BNS 145: Similar to IPC Section 371 in defining the offense and specifying punishment. Both address the act of habitual dealing in slaves. IPC Section 371: Provides a detailed framework for

---

[1095] odishapolicecidcb.gov.in

[1096] nalsarpro.org

[1097] www.bareactslive.com

[1098] nalsarpro.org

understanding the offense, including the intent and the associated legal consequences.

BNS Section 146

Definition: Unlawful[1099] Compulsory Labor Section 146 of the Bharatiya Nyaya Sanhita (BNS) 2023 addresses the offense of compelling any person to labor against their will.

Illustration: If an employer forces an employee to work without their consent, using threats or coercion, this act falls under BNS 146.

Example: Suppose a factory owner makes a worker continue working overtime without pay, threatening to fire them if they refuse. This would be categorized as unlawful compulsory labor under BNS 146.

Comment: This section underscores the importance of personal freedom and dignity by criminalizing the act of compelling someone to work against their will. It ensures that individuals who engage in such coercive practices face appropriate legal consequences.

Classification of Offence and Punishment Classification: Unlawful compulsory labor is classified as a serious criminal offense due to the violation of personal freedom and dignity.

Punishment: The punishment for this offense under BNS 146 can be [1100]imprisonment of either description for a term which may extend to one year, and/or a fine.

Cognizable or Non-Cognizable, Bailable or Non-Bailable: This offense is cognizable, meaning the police can arrest the accused without a warrant.

Bailable: This offense is bailable, indicating that the accused can secure bail and be released from custody until the trial is completed.

[1099] Ministry of Home Affairs. (2024). The Bharatiya Nyaya Sanhita, 2023. Retrieved from https://www.mha.gov.in/sites/default/files/250883_english_01042024.pdf

[1100] nalsarpro.org

Comparison: [1101]Section 374 of the Indian Penal Code (IPC) also deals with unlawful compulsory labor: IPC Section 374: States that [1102]whoever unlawfully compels any person to labor against the will of that person, shall be punished with imprisonment of either description for a term which may extend to one year, and/or a fine.

Key Differences: BNS 146: Similar to IPC Section 374 in defining the offense and specifying punishment6. Both address the act of compelling someone to work against their will. IPC Section 374: Provides a detailed framework for understanding the offense, including the intent and the associated legal consequences.

[1101] nalsarpro.org

[1102] odishapolicecidcb.gov.in

CHAPTER-VII; OF OFFENCES AGAINST THE STATE

BNS Section 147

Definition: Waging, or [1103]Attempting to Wage War, or Abetting Waging of War, Against the Government of India Section 147 of the Bharatiya Nyaya Sanhita (BNS) 2023 addresses the offense of waging, attempting to wage, or abetting the waging of war against the Government of India.

Illustration: [1104]If a person joins an insurrection against the Government of India, they have committed the offense defined in this section.

Example: Suppose an individual actively participates in a rebellion aimed at overthrowing the government. This act would be categorized as waging war against the Government of India under BNS 147.

Comment: This section underscores the severe threat to national security and public order posed by acts of waging war against the government. It ensures that such acts are met with the most stringent penalties.

Classification of Offence and Punishment Classification: Waging, attempting to wage, or abetting the waging of war against the Government of India is classified as a very serious criminal offense due to the severe threat it poses to national security and public order.

[1103] Ministry of Home Affairs. (2024). The Bharatiya Nyaya Sanhita, 2023. Retrieved from https://www.mha.gov.in/sites/default/files/250883_english_01042024.pdf

[1104] prsindia.org

Punishment: The punishment for this offense under BNS 147 can be [1105]death, or imprisonment for life, and the offender [1106]shall also be liable to a fine.

Cognizable or Non-Cognizable, Bailable or Non-Bailable: This offense is cognizable, meaning the police can arrest the accused without a warrant.

Bailable: This offense is non-bailable, indicating that the accused cannot secure bail and must remain in custody until the trial is completed.

Comparison: Section 121 of the Indian Penal Code (IPC) also deals with waging, attempting to wage, or abetting the waging of [1107]war against the Government of India: IPC Section 121: States that whoever wages war against the Government of India, or attempts to wage such war, or abets the waging of such war, shall be punished with death, or imprisonment for life, and shall also be liable to a fine.

Key Differences: BNS 147: Similar to IPC Section 121 in defining the offense and specifying punishment. Both address the act of waging war against the Government of India.IPC Section 121: Provides a detailed framework for understanding the offense, including the intent and the associated legal consequences.

BNS Section 148

Definition: Conspiracy to Commit Offences Punishable[1108] by Section 147 Section 148 of the Bharatiya Nyaya Sanhita (BNS) 2023 addresses the offense of conspiring to commit offenses punishable by Section 147, which involves waging, attempting to wage, or abetting the waging of war against the Government of India.

[1105] odishapolicecidcb.gov.in

[1106] nalsarpro.org

[1107] prsindia.org

[1108]Ministry of Home Affairs. (2024). The Bharatiya Nyaya Sanhita, 2023. Retrieved from https://www.mha.gov.in/sites/default/files/250883_english_01042024.pdf

Illustration: [1109]If a group of individuals plans to overthrow the government by force, even if they haven't taken any concrete steps yet, this act falls under BNS 148.

Example: Suppose a group of people conspire to attack government buildings and overthrow the government. Even if they haven't executed their plan, the mere act of conspiring is punishable under BNS 148.

Comment: This section highlights the severe threat to national security and public order posed by conspiracy to [1110]commit offenses against the Government of India. It ensures stringent penalties for individuals who engage in such conspiracies, reflecting the importance of maintaining stability and security.

Classification of Offence and Punishment Classification: Conspiracy to commit offenses punishable by Section 147 is classified as a very serious criminal offense due to the severe threat it poses to national security and public order.

Punishment: The punishment for this offense under BNS 148 can be [1111]imprisonment for life, or imprisonment of either description [1112]which may extend to ten years, and the offender shall also be liable to a fine.

Cognizable or Non-Cognizable, Bailable or Non-Bailable: This offense is cognizable, meaning the police can arrest the accused without a warrant.

Bailable: This offense is non-bailable, indicating that the accused cannot secure bail and must remain in custody until the trial is completed.

Comparison: [1113]Section 121A of the Indian Penal Code (IPC) also deals with conspiracy to commit offenses punishable by Section 121, which involves waging, attempting to wage, or abetting the waging of [1114]war

---

[1109] prsindia.org

[1110] prsindia.org

[1111] odishapolicecidcb.gov.in

[1112] nalsarpro.org

[1113] nalsarpro.org

[1114] prsindia.org

against the Government of India: IPC Section 121A: States that whoever conspires to commit any of the offenses punishable by Section 121, or conspires to overawe, by means of criminal force or the show of criminal force, the Central Government or any State Government, shall be punished with imprisonment for life, or imprisonment of either description which may extend to ten years, and shall also be liable to a fine.

Key Differences: BNS 148: Similar to IPC Section 121A in defining the offense and specifying punishment. Both address the act of conspiring to wage war against the Government of India. IPC Section 121A: Provides a detailed framework for understanding the offense, including the intent and the associated legal consequences.

BNS Section 149

Definition: Collecting Arms, etc., with Intention[1115] of Waging War Against the Government of India. Section 149 of the Bharatiya Nyaya Sanhita (BNS) 2023 addresses the offense of collecting arms, ammunition, or otherwise preparing to wage war against the Government of India.

Illustration: If a group of individuals gathers weapons and military supplies [1116]with the intention of overthrowing the government, this act falls under BNS 149.

Example: Suppose a group of people amasses firearms, explosives, and other military equipment with the plan to attack government installations and destabilize the government. This would be categorized as collecting arms with the intention of waging war under BNS 149.

Comment: This section highlights the severe threat to national security and public order posed by the preparation to wage [1117]war against the government. It ensures that such acts are met with stringent penalties.

[1115] Ministry of Home Affairs. (2024). The Bharatiya Nyaya Sanhita, 2023. Retrieved from https://www.mha.gov.in/sites/default/files/250883_english_01042024.pdf

[1116] prsindia.org

[1117] prsindia.org

Classification of Offence and Punishment Classification: Collecting arms [1118]with the intention of waging war is classified as a very serious criminal offense due to the severe threat it poses to national security and public order.

Punishment: The punishment for this offense under BNS 149 can be [1119]imprisonment for life, or imprisonment of either description for a term not exceeding ten years, and the offender [1120]shall also be liable to a fine.

Cognizable or Non-Cognizable, Bailable or Non-Bailable: This offense is cognizable, meaning the police can arrest the accused without a warrant.

Bailable: This offense is non-bailable, indicating that the accused cannot secure bail and must remain in custody until the trial is completed.

Comparison: [1121]Section 122 of the Indian Penal Code (IPC) also deals with collecting arms, etc., [1122]with the intention of waging war against the Government of India : IPC Section 122: States that whoever collects men, arms, [1123]or ammunition or otherwise prepares to wage war with the intention of either waging or being prepared to wage war against the Government of India, shall be punished with imprisonment for life, or imprisonment of either description for a term not exceeding ten years, and shall also be liable to a fine.

Key Differences: BNS 149: Similar to IPC Section 122 in defining the offense and specifying punishment. Both address [1124]the act of collecting arms with the intent to wage war against the Government of India. IPC Section 122: Provides a detailed framework for understanding the offense, including the intent and the associated legal consequences.

[1118] prsindia.org

[1119] odishapolicecidcb.gov.in

[1120] nalsarpro.org

[1121] odishapolicecidcb.gov.in

[1122] www.bareactslive.com

[1123] odishapolicecidcb.gov.in

[1124] odishapolicecidcb.gov.in

BNS Section 150

Definition: Concealing[1125] with Intent to Facilitate Design to Wage War Section 150 of the Bharatiya Nyaya Sanhita (BNS) 2023 addresses the offense of concealing with the intent to facilitate a design to wage war against the Government of India.

Illustration: If a person hides [1126]information about a planned insurrection against the government, knowing that this concealment will help the conspirators, this act falls under BNS 150.

Example: Suppose an individual learns about a group planning to overthrow the government and decides to keep this information secret, believing it will help the group succeed. This would be categorized as concealing[1127] with intent to facilitate a design to wage war under BNS 150.

Comment: This section highlights the severe threat to national security and public order posed by concealing information about plans to wage war. It ensures that such acts are met with stringent penalties, reflecting the importance of maintaining stability and security.

Classification of Offence and Punishment Classification: [1128]Concealing with intent to facilitate a design to wage war is classified as a very serious criminal offense due to the severe threat it poses to national security and public order.

Punishment: [1129]The punishment for this offense under BNS 150 can be imprisonment of either description for a term which may extend to ten years, and the offender shall also be liable to a fine.

[1125] Ministry of Home Affairs. (2024). The Bharatiya Nyaya Sanhita, 2023. Retrieved from https://www.mha.gov.in/sites/default/files/250883_english_01042024.pdf

[1126] odishapolicecidcb.gov.in

[1127] odishapolicecidcb.gov.in

[1128] odishapolicecidcb.gov.in

[1129] odishapolicecidcb.gov.in

Cognizable or Non-Cognizable, Bailable or Non-Bailable: This offense is cognizable, meaning the police can arrest the accused without a warrant.

Bailable: This offense is non-bailable, indicating that the accused cannot secure bail and must remain in custody until the trial is completed.

Comparison: [1130]Section 123 of the Indian Penal Code (IPC) also deals with concealing with intent to facilitate a design to wage war against the Government of India:IPC Section 123: States that whoever, by any act, or by any illegal omission, conceals the existence of a design to wage war against the Government of India, intending by such concealment to facilitate, or knowing it to be likely that such concealment will facilitate, the waging of such war, shall be punished with imprisonment of either description for a term which may extend to ten years, and shall also be liable to a fine.

Key Differences: BNS 150: Similar to IPC Section 123 in defining the offense and specifying punishment. Both address the act of concealing information to facilitate a design to wage war against the Government of India. IPC Section 123: Provides a detailed framework for understanding the offense, including the intent and the associated legal consequences.

BNS Section 151

Definition: [1131]Assaulting President, Governor, etc., with Intent to Compel or Restrain the Exercise of Any Lawful Power Section 151 of the Bharatiya Nyaya Sanhita (BNS) 2023 addresses the offense of assaulting or intimidating the President of India, the Governor of a State, or any other person holding a similar position, with the intent to compel or restrain the exercise of their lawful powers.

Illustration: If a person physically attacks or threatens the President of India to prevent them from signing a bill into law, this act falls under BNS 151.

[1130] odishapolicecidcb.gov.in

[1131] Ministry of Home Affairs. (2024). The Bharatiya Nyaya Sanhita, 2023. Retrieved from https://www.mha.gov.in/sites/default/files/250883_english_01042024.pdf

Example: Suppose an individual attempts to forcefully restrain the Governor of a State to stop [1132]them from issuing an executive order. This would be categorized as assaulting with intent to compel or restrain lawful power under BNS 151.

Comment: This section underscores the severe threat to national security and public order posed by the assault or intimidation of high-ranking officials to influence their lawful duties. It ensures that such acts are met with stringent penalties.

Classification of Offence and Punishment Classification: Assaulting or intimidating a high-ranking official to influence their lawful duties is classified as a very serious criminal offense due to the severe threat it poses to national security and public order.

Punishment: [1133]The punishment for this offense under BNS 151 can be imprisonment of either description for a term which may extend to seven years, and the offender shall also be liable to a fine.

Cognizable or Non-Cognizable, Bailable or Non-Bailable: This offense is cognizable, meaning the police can arrest the accused without a warrant.

Bailable: This offense is non-bailable, indicating that the accused cannot secure bail and must remain in custody until the trial is completed.

Comparison: Section 124 of the [1134]Indian Penal Code (IPC) also deals with assaulting President, Governor, etc., with intent to compel or restrain the exercise of any lawful power: IPC Section 124: States that whoever, with the intention of inducing or compelling the President of India, or Governor of any State, to exercise or refrain from exercising in any manner any of the lawful powers of such President or Governor, [1135]assaults or wrongfully restrains, or attempts wrongfully to restrain, or overawes, by means of criminal force or the show of criminal force, or

---

[1132] odishapolicecidcb.gov.in

[1133] odishapolicecidcb.gov.in

[1134] odishapolicecidcb.gov.in

[1135] www.bareactslive.com

attempts so to overawe, such [1136]President or Governor, shall be punished with imprisonment of either description for a term which may extend to seven years, and shall also be liable to a fine.

Key Differences: BNS 151: Similar to IPC Section 124 in defining the offense and specifying punishment. Both address the act of assaulting or intimidating high-ranking officials to influence their lawful duties. IPC Section 124: Provides a detailed framework for understanding the offense, including the intent and the associated legal consequences.

BNS Section 152

Definition: Act Endangering Sovereignty, [1137]Unity, and Integrity of India Section 152 of the Bharatiya Nyaya Sanhita (BNS) 2023 addresses the offense of endangering the sovereignty, unity, and integrity of India through various means.

Illustration: If a person spreads propaganda or incites violence with the intent to create unrest and disrupt the unity of the country, this act falls under BNS 152.

Example: Suppose an individual uses social media to spread false information and incite people to rebel against the government, aiming to create chaos and weaken the nation's unity. This would be categorized as an act endangering sovereignty, unity, and integrity under BNS 152.

Comment: This section underscores the severe threat to national security and public order posed by acts that endanger the sovereignty, unity, and integrity of India. It ensures that such acts are met with stringent penalties, reflecting the importance of maintaining stability and security.

Classification of Offence and Punishment Classification: Endangering the sovereignty, unity, and integrity of India is classified as a very serious criminal offense due to the severe threat it poses to national security and public order.

[1136] odishapolicecidcb.gov.in

[1137] Ministry of Home Affairs. (2024). The Bharatiya Nyaya Sanhita, 2023. Retrieved from https://www.mha.gov.in/sites/default/files/250883_english_01042024.pdf

Punishment: The [1138]punishment for this offense under BNS 152 can be imprisonment for life, or imprisonment of either description for a term which may extend to seven years, and the offender shall also be liable to a fine.

Cognizable or Non-Cognizable, Bailable or Non-Bailable: This offense is cognizable, meaning the police can arrest the accused without a warrant.

Bailable: This offense is non-bailable, indicating that the accused cannot secure bail and must remain in custody until the trial is completed.

Comparison: [1139]Section 124A of the Indian Penal Code (IPC) also deals with acts endangering the sovereignty, unity, and integrity of India: IPC Section 124A: States that whoever, by words, either spoken or written, or by signs, or by visible representation, or by any other means, brings or attempts to bring into hatred or contempt, or excites or attempts to excite disaffection towards the Government established by law in India, shall be punished with imprisonment for life, or imprisonment of either description for a term which may extend to three years, and shall also be liable to a fine.

Key Differences: BNS 152: Similar to IPC Section 124A in defining the offense and specifying punishment. Both address acts that endanger the sovereignty, unity, and integrity of India. IPC Section 124A: Focuses on bringing hatred, contempt, or disaffection towards the government, while BNS 152 emphasizes broader threats to national security and public order.

BNS Section 153

Definition: Waging War[1140] Against Government of Any Foreign State at Peace with Government of India. Section 153 of the Bharatiya Nyaya Sanhita (BNS) 2023 addresses the offense of waging war

---

[1138] odishapolicecidcb.gov.in

[1139] odishapolicecidcb.gov.in

[1140] Ministry of Home Affairs. (2024). The Bharatiya Nyaya Sanhita, 2023. Retrieved from https://www.mha.gov.in/sites/default/files/250883_english_01042024.pdf

against the government of any foreign state that is at peace with the Government of India.

Illustration: If a group of individuals plans and executes an attack on a foreign embassy or consulate in India, aiming to overthrow the government of that foreign state, this act falls under BNS 153.

Example: Suppose a group of people conspire to attack the embassy of a friendly nation, intending to destabilize that country's government. This would be categorized as [1141]waging war against a foreign state at peace with India under BNS 153.

Comment: This section emphasizes the severe threat to international relations and national security posed by acts of waging war against a foreign state at peace [1142]with India. It ensures that such acts are met with stringent penalties, reflecting the importance of maintaining peaceful diplomatic relations and global stability.

Classification of Offence and Punishment Classification: [1143]Waging war against a foreign state at peace with India is classified as a very serious criminal offense due to the severe threat it poses to international relations and national security.

Punishment: The [1144]punishment for this offense under BNS 153 can be imprisonment for life, or imprisonment of either description for a term which may extend to seven years, and the offender shall also be liable to a fine.

Cognizable or Non-Cognizable, Bailable or Non-Bailable: This offense is cognizable, meaning the police can arrest the accused without a warrant.

Bailable: This offense is non-bailable, indicating that the accused cannot secure bail and must remain in custody until the trial is completed.

[1141] odishapolicecidcb.gov.in

[1142] odishapolicecidcb.gov.in

[1143] odishapolicecidcb.gov.in

[1144] odishapolicecidcb.gov.in

Comparison: [1145]Section 125 of the Indian Penal Code (IPC) also deals [1146]with waging war against any Asiatic Power in alliance with or at peace with the Government of India : IPC Section 125: States that whoever wages war against the Government of any Asiatic Power in alliance or at peace with the Government of India, or attempts to wage such war, or abets the waging of such war, shall be punished with imprisonment for life, or imprisonment of either description for a term which may extend to seven years, and shall also be liable to a fine.

Key Differences: BNS 153: Similar to IPC Section 125 in defining the offense and specifying punishment. Both address the act of waging war against a foreign state at peace with India. IPC Section 125: Focuses on waging war [1147]against any Asiatic Power in alliance or at peace with the Government of India, while BNS 153 uses broader terminology to include any foreign state at peace with India.

BNS Section 154

Definition: Committing[1148] Depredation on Territories of Foreign State at Peace with Government of India Section 154 of the Bharatiya Nyaya Sanhita (BNS) 2023 addresses the offense of committing depredation on the territories of any foreign state that is at peace with the Government of India.

Illustration: If a group of individuals raids and loots properties in a foreign country that is at peace with India, this act falls under BNS 154.

Example: Suppose a group of people plans and executes an attack on a foreign village, stealing valuable resources and causing destruction. This would be categorized as committing depredation under BNS 154.

[1145] www.bareactslive.com

[1146] odishapolicecidcb.gov.in

[1147] www.bareactslive.com

[1148] Ministry of Home Affairs. (2024). The Bharatiya Nyaya Sanhita, 2023. Retrieved from https://www.mha.gov.in/sites/default/files/250883_english_01042024.pdf

Comment: This section emphasizes the severe threat to international relations and national security posed by acts of committing depredation on territories of foreign states at peace with India. It ensures that such acts are met with stringent penalties, reflecting the importance of maintaining peaceful diplomatic relations and global stability.

Classification of Offence and Punishment Classification: Committing depredation on the territories of a foreign state at peace with India is classified as a very serious criminal offense due to the severe threat it poses to international relations and national security.

Punishment: [1149]The punishment for this offense under BNS 154 can be imprisonment of either description for a term which may extend to seven years, and the offender shall also be liable to a fine and forfeiture of any property used or intended to be used in committing such depredation, or acquired by such depredation.

Cognizable or Non-Cognizable, Bailable or Non-Bailable: This offense is cognizable, meaning the police can arrest the accused without a warrant.

Bailable: This offense is non-bailable, indicating that the accused cannot secure bail and must remain in custody until the trial is completed.

Comparison: [1150]Section 126 of the Indian Penal Code (IPC) also deals with committing depredation on territories of a power at peace with the Government of India: IPC Section 126: States that whoever commits depredation, or makes [1151]preparations to commit depredation, on the territories of any power in alliance or at peace with the Government of [1152]India, shall be punished with imprisonment of either description for a term which may extend to seven years, and shall also be liable to a fine and forfeiture of any property used or intended to be used in committing such depredation, or acquired by such depredation.

[1149] odishapolicecidcb.gov.in

[1150] odishapolicecidcb.gov.in

[1151] www.wipo.int

[1152] odishapolicecidcb.gov.in

Key Differences: BNS 154: Similar to IPC Section 126 in defining the offense and specifying punishment. Both address the act of committing depredation on territories of a foreign state at peace with India. IPC Section 126: [1153]Focuses on committing depredation on territories of any power in alliance or at peace with the Government of India, while BNS 154 uses broader terminology to include any foreign state at peace with India.

BNS Section 155

Definition: Receiving [1154]Property Taken by War or Depredation Mentioned in Sections 153 and 154.Section 155 of the Bharatiya Nyaya Sanhita (BNS) 2023 addresses the offense of receiving property that was taken by war or depredation as mentioned in Sections 153 and 154.

Illustration: If a person knowingly accepts goods stolen during an attack on a foreign state at peace with India, this act falls under BNS 155.

Example: Suppose an individual receives a shipment of valuable artifacts that were looted during a raid on a foreign village. Knowing the origin of these items, the individual is committing an offense under BNS 155.

Comment: This section highlights the serious implications of [1155]receiving property taken by war or depredation on international relations and national security. It ensures that individuals who engage in such acts face stringent penalties, reflecting the importance of upholding international law and preventing the circulation of unlawfully acquired property.

Classification of Offence and Punishment Classification: [1156]Receiving property taken by war or depredation is classified as a serious criminal

---

[1153] odishapolicecidcb.gov.in

[1154] Ministry of Home Affairs. (2024). The Bharatiya Nyaya Sanhita, 2023. Retrieved from https://www.mha.gov.in/sites/default/files/250883_english_01042024.pdf

[1155] odishapolicecidcb.gov.in

[1156] odishapolicecidcb.gov.in

offense due to its implications on international relations and national security.

Punishment: [1157]The punishment for this offense under BNS 155 can be imprisonment of either description for a term which may extend to seven years, and the offender shall also be liable to a fine and forfeiture of the property so received.

Cognizable or Non-Cognizable, Bailable or Non-Bailable: This offense is cognizable, meaning the police can arrest the accused without a warrant.

Bailable: This offense is non bailable, indicating that the accused cannot secure bail and must remain in custody until the trial is completed.

Comparison: Section 127 of the Indian Penal Code (IPC) also deals with receiving property taken by war or [1158]depredation mentioned in Sections 125 and 126:IPC Section 127: States that [1159]whoever receives any property knowing the same to have been taken in the commission of any of the offenses mentioned in sections 125 and 126, shall be punished with imprisonment of either description for a term which may extend to seven years, and shall also be liable to a fine and forfeiture of the property so received.

Key Differences: BNS 155: Similar to IPC Section 127 in defining the offense and specifying punishment. Both address the act of receiving property taken by war or depredation. IPC Section 127: Focuses on [1160]receiving property taken during acts of war or depredation as specified in Sections 125 and 126, while BNS 155 uses broader terminology to include any property taken in the commission of offenses mentioned in Sections 153 and 154.

[1157] odishapolicecidcb.gov.in

[1158] www.bareactslive.com

[1159] odishapolicecidcb.gov.in

[1160] odishapolicecidcb.gov.in

BNS Section 156

Definition: Public [1161]Servant Voluntarily Allowing Prisoner of State or War to Escape Section 156 of the Bharatiya Nyaya Sanhita (BNS) 2023 addresses the offense of a public servant voluntarily allowing a prisoner of state or war to escape.

Illustration: If a prison guard intentionally opens the cell door of a high-profile prisoner of war and lets them walk out without any resistance, this act falls under BNS 156.

Example: Suppose a jail warden, who is responsible for the custody of a captured enemy combatant, deliberately helps the prisoner escape by providing them with a key to the cell. This would be categorized as an offense under BNS 156.

Comment: [1162]This section underscores the severe threat to national security and public order posed by a public servant allowing a prisoner of state or war to escape. It ensures that such acts are met with stringent penalties, reflecting the importance of maintaining custody and control over high-profile prisoners.

Classification of Offence and Punishment Classification: This offense is classified as a very serious criminal offense due to the severe threat it poses to national security and public order.

Punishment: The [1163]punishment for this offense under BNS 156 can be imprisonment for life, or imprisonment of either description for a term which may extend to ten years, and the offender shall also be liable to a fine.

Cognizable or Non-Cognizable, Bailable or Non-Bailable: This offense is cognizable, meaning the police can arrest the accused without a warrant.

[1161] Ministry of Home Affairs. (2024). The Bharatiya Nyaya Sanhita, 2023. Retrieved from https://www.mha.gov.in/sites/default/files/250883_english_01042024.pdf

[1162] odishapolicecidcb.gov.in

[1163] odishapolicecidcb.gov.in

Bailable: This offense is non-bailable, indicating that the accused cannot secure bail and must remain in custody until the trial is completed.

Comparison: Section 128 of the Indian Penal Code (IPC) also deals with public servants voluntarily allowing prisoners of state or war to escape: IPC Section 128: States that [1164]whoever, being a public servant and having the custody of any State prisoner or prisoner of war, voluntarily allows such prisoner to escape from any place in which such prisoner is confined, shall be punished with imprisonment for life, or imprisonment of either description for a term which may extend to ten years, and shall also be liable to a fine.

Key Differences: BNS 156: Similar to IPC Section 128 in defining the offense and specifying punishment. Both address the act of a public servant allowing a prisoner to escape. IPC Section 128: Focuses on the same offense but is part of the older legal framework, which has now been updated and incorporated into BNS 156.

BNS Section 157

Definition: Public Servant Negligently[1165] Suffering Such Prisoner to Escape Section 157 of the Bharatiya Nyaya Sanhita (BNS) 2023 deals with the offense of a public servant negligently allowing a prisoner to escape.

Illustration: If a jailor, through negligence, leaves a prison cell unlocked, resulting in the escape of a high-profile prisoner, this act falls under BNS 157.

Example: Suppose a prison guard fails to secure the cell door of a convicted murderer properly, and the prisoner escapes. This would be categorized as negligent conduct under BNS 157.

[1164] odishapolicecidcb.gov.in

[1165] Ministry of Home Affairs. (2024). The Bharatiya Nyaya Sanhita, 2023. Retrieved from https://www.mha.gov.in/sites/default/files/250883_english_01042024.pdf

Comment: [1166]This section emphasizes the severe threat to public safety posed by the negligent conduct of public servants in charge of prisoners. It ensures that such acts of negligence are met with appropriate penalties to maintain accountability and deter futXure lapses.

Classification of Offence and Punishment Classification: This offense is classified as a serious criminal offense due to the severe threat it poses to public safety.

Punishment: [1167]The punishment for this offense under BNS 157 can be imprisonment of either description for a term which may extend to three years, and the offender shall also be liable to a fine.

Cognizable or Non-Cognizable, Bailable or Non-Bailable: This offense is cognizable, meaning the police can arrest the accused without a warrant.

Bailable: This offense is bailable, indicating that the accused can secure bail and be released from custody until the trial is completed.

Comparison: [1168]Section 129 of the Indian Penal Code (IPC) deals with the same situation: IPC Section 129: States that whoever, being a public servant and having the custody of any State prisoner or prisoner of war, negligently suffers such prisoner to escape from any place in which such prisoner is confined, shall be punished with imprisonment of either description for a term which may extend to three years, and shall also be liable to a fine.

Key Differences: BNS 157: Similar to IPC Section 129 in defining the offense and specifying punishment. Both address the act of negligently allowing a prisoner to escape. IPC Section 129: Focuses on the same offense but is part of the older legal framework, which has now been updated and incorporated into BNS 157.

[1166] odishapolicecidcb.gov.in

[1167] odishapolicecidcb.gov.in

[1168] odishapolicecidcb.gov.in

BNS Section 158

Definition: Aiding Escape[1169] of, Rescuing or Harbouring Such Prisoner Section 158 of the Bharatiya Nyaya Sanhita (BNS) 2023 addresses the offense of aiding the escape of, rescuing, or harbouring a prisoner of state or war who has escaped from lawful custody.

Illustration: If a person knowingly provides shelter to a prisoner of war who has escaped from a detention facility, this act falls under BNS 158.

Example: Suppose an individual helps a captured enemy combatant escape from a military prison by providing them with food, shelter, and transportation. This would be categorized as harbouring under BNS 158.

Comment: This section highlights the severe threat to national security and public order posed by aiding the escape of, rescuing, or harbouring escaped prisoners. It ensures that such acts are met with stringent penalties to prevent any compromise in custody and control over prisoners.

Classification of Offence and Punishment Classification: This offense is classified as a very serious criminal offense due to the severe threat it poses to national security and public order.

Punishment: [1170]The punishment for this offense under BNS 158 can be imprisonment for life, or imprisonment of either description for a term which may extend to ten years, and the offender shall also be liable to a fine.

Cognizable or Non-Cognizable, Bailable or Non-Bailable: This offense is cognizable, meaning the police can arrest the accused without a warrant.

Bailable: This offense is non-bailable, indicating that the accused cannot secure bail and must remain in custody until the trial is completed.

[1169] Ministry of Home Affairs. (2024). The Bharatiya Nyaya Sanhita, 2023. Retrieved from https://www.mha.gov.in/sites/default/files/250883_english_01042024.pdf

[1170] bprd.nic.in

Comparison: [1171]Section 130 of the Indian Penal Code (IPC) also deals with aiding the escape of, rescuing, or harbouring such prisoner: IPC Section 130: States that [1172]whoever knowingly aids or assists any State prisoner or prisoner of war in escaping from lawful custody, or rescues or attempts to rescue any such prisoner, or harbours or conceals any such prisoner who has escaped from lawful custody, or offers or attempts to offer any resistance to the recapture of such prisoner, shall be punished with imprisonment for life, or imprisonment of either description for a term which may extend to ten years, and shall also be liable to a fine.

Key Differences: BNS 158: Similar to IPC Section 130 in defining the offense and specifying punishment. Both address the act of aiding the escape of, rescuing, or harbouring a prisoner. IPC Section 130: Part of the older legal framework, while BNS 158 is the updated version in the new Bharatiya Nyaya Sanhita.

[1171] orest.jharkhand.gov.in

[1172] bprd.nic.in

CHAPTER-VIII: OF OFFENCES RELATING TO THE ARMY, NAVY AND AIR FORCE

BNS Section 159

Definition: [1173]Abetting Mutiny, or Attempting to Seduce a Soldier, Sailor or Airman from His Duty Section 159 of the Bharatiya Nyaya Sanhita (BNS) 2023 addresses the offense of abetting mutiny or attempting to seduce a soldier, sailor, or airman from his duty.

Illustration: [1174]If a person persuades a soldier to desert their post or incites a group of soldiers to rebel against their commanding officers, this act falls under BNS 159.

Example: Suppose an individual spreads propaganda among sailors, encouraging them to mutiny against their captain. This would be categorized as attempting to seduce a sailor from his duty under[1175] BNS 159.

Comment: This section underscores the severe threat to military discipline and national security posed by abetting mutiny or attempting to seduce military personnel from their duty. It ensures that such acts are met with stringent penalties to maintain order and discipline within the armed forces.

Classification of Offence and Punishment Classification: This offense is classified as a very serious criminal offense due to the severe threat it poses to military discipline and national security.

[1173] bprd.nic.in

[1174] bprd.nic.in

[1175] bprd.nic.in

Punishment: The [1176]punishment for this offense under BNS 159 can be imprisonment for life, or imprisonment of either description for a term which may extend to ten years, and the offender shall also be liable to a fine.

Cognizable or Non-Cognizable, Bailable or Non-Bailable: This offense is cognizable, meaning the police can arrest the accused without a warrant.

Bailable: This offense is non-bailable, indicating that the accused cannot secure bail and must remain in custody until the trial is completed.

Comparison: [1177]Section 131 of the Indian Penal Code (IPC) also deals with abetting mutiny [1178]or attempting to seduce a soldier, sailor, or airman from his duty:IPC Section 131: States that whoever abets the committing of mutiny by an officer, soldier, sailor, or airman, in the Army, Navy, or Air Force of the Government of India, or attempts to seduce any such officer, soldier, sailor, or airman from his allegiance or his duty, shall be punished with imprisonment for life, or imprisonment of either description for a term which may extend to ten years, and shall also be liable to a fine.

Key Differences: BNS 159: Similar to IPC Section 131 in defining the offense and specifying punishment. Both address the act of abetting mutiny or attempting to seduce a soldier, sailor, or airman from his duty. IPC Section 131: Part of the older legal framework, while BNS 159 is the updated version in the new Bharatiya Nyaya Sanhita.

BNS Section 160

Definition: Abetment[1179] of Mutiny, if Mutiny is Committed in Consequence Thereof Section 160 of the Bharatiya Nyaya Sanhita (BNS) 2023 addresses the offense of abetting mutiny if the mutiny is committed in consequence thereof.

[1176] bprd.nic.in

[1177] forest.jharkhand.gov.in

[1178] bprd.nic.in

[1179] Ministry of Home Affairs. (2024). The Bharatiya Nyaya Sanhita, 2023. Retrieved from https://www.mha.gov.in/sites/default/files/250883_english_01042024.pdf

Illustration: [1180]If a person instigates a group of soldiers to rebel against their commanding officers, and the soldiers actually commit mutiny as a result, this act falls under BNS 160.

Example: Suppose an individual spreads propaganda among soldiers, encouraging them to overthrow their superiors. If the soldiers act on this instigation and mutiny occurs, the instigator would be charged under BNS 160.

Comment: This section underscores the severe threat to military discipline and national security posed by abetting mutiny. It ensures that such acts are met with the highest level of penalties, reflecting the critical importance of maintaining order and discipline within the armed forces.

Classification of Offence and Punishment Classification: This offense is classified as a very serious criminal offense due to the severe threat it poses to military discipline and national security.

Punishment: [1181]The punishment for this offense under BNS 160 can be death, or imprisonment for life, or imprisonment of either description for a term which may extend to ten years, and the offender shall also be liable to a fine.

Cognizable or Non-Cognizable, Bailable or Non-Bailable: This offense is cognizable, meaning the police can arrest the accused without a warrant.

Bailable: This offense is non-bailable, indicating that the accused cannot secure bail and must remain in custody until the trial is completed.

Comparison: Section 132 [1182]of the Indian Penal Code (IPC) also deals with abetment of mutiny [1183]if mutiny is committed in consequence thereof: IPC Section 132: States that whoever abets the committing of mutiny by an officer, soldier, sailor, or airman in the Army, Navy, or Air Force of the Government of India, shall, if mutiny be committed in consequence of that abetment, be punished with death, or imprisonment

---

[1180] bprd.nic.in

[1181] bprd.nic.in

[1182] forest.jharkhand.gov.in

[1183] bprd.nic.in

for if, or imprisonment of either description for a term which may extend to ten years, and shall also be liable to a fine.

Key Differences: BNS 160: Similar to IPC Section 132 in defining the offense and specifying punishment. Both address the act of abetting mutiny if mutiny is committed in consequence thereof. IPC Section 132: Part of the older legal framework, while BNS 160 is the updated version in the new Bharatiya Nyaya Sanhita.

BNS Section 161

Definition: Abetment of Assault[1184] by Soldier, Sailor or Airman on His Superior Officer when in execution of his office Section 161 of the Bharatiya Nyaya Sanhita (BNS) 2023 addresses the offense of abetting an assault by a soldier, sailor, or airman on their superior officer while the officer is executing their duties.

Illustration: If a person encourages or instigates a soldier to attack their commanding officer during a military operation, this act falls under BNS 161.

Example: Suppose an individual persuades a sailor to physically assault their captain while the captain is performing official duties on the ship. This would be categorized as abetment of assault under BNS 161.

Comment: This section underscores the severe impact on military discipline and hierarchy posed by abetting assault on superior officers. It ensures that such acts are met with appropriate penalties to maintain the order and authority necessary within the armed forces.

Classification of Offence and Punishment Classification: This offense is classified as a serious criminal offense due to the severe impact on military discipline and hierarchy.

[1184] Ministry of Home Affairs. (2024). The Bharatiya Nyaya Sanhita, 2023. Retrieved from https://www.mha.gov.in/sites/default/files/250883_english_01042024.pdf

Punishment: [1185]The punishment for this offense under BNS 161 can be imprisonment of either description for a term which may extend to three years, and the offender shall also be liable to a fine.

Cognizable or Non-Cognizable, Bailable or Non-Bailable: This offense is cognizable, meaning the police can arrest the accused without a warrant.

Bailable: This offense is non-bailable, indicating that the accused cannot secure bail and must remain in custody until the trial is completed.

Comparison: [1186]Section 133 of the Indian Penal Code (IPC) also deals with abetment of assault by a soldier, sailor, or airman on their superior officer: IPC Section 133: States that [1187]whoever abets an assault by an officer, soldier, sailor, or airman, in the Army, Navy, or Air Force of the Government of India, on any superior officer being in the execution of his office, shall be punished with imprisonment of either description for a term which may extend to three years, and shall also be liable to a fine.

Key Differences: BNS 161: Similar to IPC Section 133 in defining the offense and specifying punishment. Both address the act of abetting assault on a superior officer. IPC Section 133: Part of the older legal framework, while BNS 161 is the updated version in the new Bharatiya Nyaya Sanhita.

BNS Section 162

Definition: Abetment of Such [1188]Assault, if the Assault is Committed Section 162 of the Bharatiya Nyaya Sanhita (BNS) 2023 addresses the offense of abetting an assault by a soldier, sailor, or airman on their superior officer, if the assault is committed.

[1185] bprd.nic.in

[1186] forest.jharkhand.gov.in

[1187] bprd.nic.in

[1188] Ministry of Home Affairs. (2024). The Bharatiya Nyaya Sanhita, 2023. Retrieved from https://www.mha.gov.in/sites/default/files/250883_english_01042024.pdf

Illustration: If a person encourages or instigates a soldier to attack their commanding officer during a military operation, and the soldier actually commits the assault, this act falls under BNS 162.

Example: Suppose an individual persuades a sailor to physically assault their captain while the captain is performing official duties on the ship. If the sailor follows through and assaults the captain, the instigator would be charged under BNS 162.Classification of Offence and Punishment

Classification: This offense is classified as a serious criminal offense due to the severe impact on military discipline and hierarchy.

Punishment: The punishment for this offense under BNS 162 can be [1189]imprisonment of either description for a term which may extend to seven years, and the offender shall also be liable to a fine.

Cognizable or Non-Cognizable, Bailable or Non-Bailable: This offense is cognizable, meaning the police can arrest the accused without a warrant.

Bailable: This offense is non-bailable, indicating that the accused cannot secure bail and must remain in custody until the trial is completed.

Comparison [1190]Section 134 of the Indian Penal Code (IPC) also deals with abetment of such assault if the [1191]assault is committed : IPC Section 134: States that [1192]whoever abets an assault by an officer, soldier, sailor, or airman, in the Army, Navy, or Air Force of the Government of India, on any superior officer being in the execution of his office, shall, if such assault be committed in consequence of that abetment be punished with imprisonment of either description for a term which may extend to seven years, and shall also be liable to a fine.

Key Differences: BNS 162: Similar to IPC Section 134 in defining the offense and specifying punishment. Both address the act of abetting an assault on a superior officer. IPC Section 134: Part of the older legal

---

[1189] bprd.nic.in

[1190] orest.jharkhand.gov.in

[1191] districts.ecourts.gov.in

[1192] bprd.nic.in

framework, while BNS 162 is the updated version in the new Bharatiya Nyaya Sanhita.

BNS Section 163

Definition: Abetment of [1193]Desertion of Soldier, Sailor or Airman Section 163 of the Bharatiya Nyaya Sanhita (BNS) 2023 addresses the offense of abetting the desertion of a soldier, sailor, or airman from the Army, Navy, or Air Force of the Government of India.

Illustration: If a person persuades or assists a soldier to leave their post without permission, this act falls under BNS 163.

Example: Suppose an individual convinces a sailor to abandon their ship duties and not return. This would be categorized as abetment of desertion under BNS 163.

Comment: This section emphasizes the impact of abetting desertion on military discipline and operational capability. It ensures that such acts are met with appropriate penalties to maintain order and functionality within the armed forces.

Classification of Offence and Punishment Classification: This offense is classified as a serious criminal offense due to its impact on military discipline and operational capability.

Punishment: The [1194]punishment for this offense under BNS 163 can be imprisonment of either description for a term which may extend to two years, and the offender shall also be liable to a fine.

Cognizable or Non-Cognizable, Bailable or Non-Bailable: This offense is cognizable, meaning the police can arrest the accused without a warrant.

Bailable: This offense is bailable, indicating that the accused can secure bail and be released from custody until the trial is completed.

[1193] Ministry of Home Affairs. (2024). The Bharatiya Nyaya Sanhita, 2023. Retrieved from https://www.mha.gov.in/sites/default/files/250883_english_01042024.pdf

[1194] bprd.nic.in

Comparison: Section 135 [1195]of the Indian Penal Code (IPC) also deals with abetment of desertion of a soldier, sailor, or airman: IPC Section 135: States that [1196]whoever abets the desertion of any officer, soldier, sailor, or airman, in the Army, Navy, or Air Force of the Government of India, shall be punished with imprisonment of either description for a term which may extend to two years, and shall also be liable to a fine.

Key Differences: BNS 163: Similar to IPC Section 135 in defining the offense and specifying punishment. Both address [1197]the act of abetting desertion. IPC Section 135: Part of the older legal framework, while BNS 163 is the updated version in the new Bharatiya Nyaya Sanhita.

BNS Section 164

Definition: Harbouring [1198]Deserter Section 164 of the Bharatiya Nyaya Sanhita (BNS) 2023 addresses the offense of harbouring a deserter from the military services.

Illustration: If a person knowingly provides shelter to a soldier who has deserted their post, this act falls under BNS 164.

Example: Suppose an individual allows a sailor who has abandoned their ship duties to stay at their home. This would be categorized as harbouring a deserter under BNS 164.

Classification of Offence and Punishment Classification: This offense is classified as a serious criminal offense due to its impact on military discipline and operational capability.

1195 forest.jharkhand.gov.in

1196 bprd.nic.in

1197 bprd.nic.in

1198 Ministry of Home Affairs. (2024). The Bharatiya Nyaya Sanhita, 2023. Retrieved from https://www.mha.gov.in/sites/default/files/250883_english_01042024.pdf

Punishment: [1199]The punishment for this offense under BNS 164 can be imprisonment of either description for a term which may extend to two years, or a fine, or both.

Cognizable or Non-Cognizable, Bailable or Non-Bailable: This offense is cognizable, meaning the police can arrest the accused without a warrant.

Bailable: This offense is bailable, indicating that the accused can secure bail and be released from custody until the trial is completed.

Comparison: Section 136 [1200]of the Indian Penal Code (IPC) also deals with harbouring a deserter: IPC Section 136: States that [1201]whoever, knowing or having reason to believe that an officer, soldier, sailor, [1202]or airman, in the Army, Navy, or Air Force of the Government of India, has deserted, harbours such officer, soldier, sailor, or airman, shall be punished with imprisonment of either description for a term which may extend to two years, or with a fine, or both.

Key Differences: BNS 164: Similar to IPC Section 136 in defining the offense and specifying punishment. Both address the act of harbouring a deserter. IPC Section 136: Part of the older legal framework, while BNS 164 is the updated version in the new Bharatiya Nyaya Sanhita.

BNS Section 165

Definition: Deserter Concealed on Board Master Merchant[1203] Vessel Through Negligence Section 165 of the Bharatiya Nyaya Sanhita (BNS) 2023 addresses the offense of a deserter being concealed on board a merchant vessel due to the negligence of the master or person in charge of the vessel.

[1199]bprd.nic.in

[1200] forest.jharkhand.gov.in

[1201] odishapolicecidcb.gov.in

[1202] bprd.nic.in

[1203] Ministry of Home Affairs. (2024). The Bharatiya Nyaya Sanhita, 2023. Retrieved from https://www.mha.gov.in/sites/default/files/250883_english_01042024.pdf

Illustration: If a soldier deserts their post and hides [1204]on a merchant vessel, and the master of the vessel fails to detect the deserter due to neglecting their duty, this act falls under BNS 165.

Example: Suppose a sailor abandons their ship and hides in the cargo hold. The captain, through negligence in performing routine checks, fails to discover the sailor. This would be categorized as a violation of BNS 165.

Comment: This section underscores the impact of harbouring deserters on military discipline and operational capability. It ensures that such acts are met with appropriate penalties to maintain order and functionality within the armed forces.

Classification of Offence and Punishment Classification: This offense is classified as a minor criminal offense due to its less severe impact compared to other military-related offenses.

Punishment: The punishment for this offense under BNS 165 can be a fine not exceeding three thousand rupees.

Cognizable or Non-Cognizable, Bailable or Non-Bailable: This offense is non-cognizable, meaning the police cannot arrest the accused without a warrant.

Bailable: This offense is bailable, indicating that the accused can secure bail and be released from custody until the trial is completed.

Comparison: Section 137 of the [1205]Indian Penal Code (IPC) also deals with the same offense: IPC Section 137: States that [1206]the master or person in charge of a merchant vessel, on board of which any deserter from the Army, Navy, or Air Force of the Government of India is concealed, shall, though ignorant of such concealment, be liable to a penalty not exceeding [1207]five hundred rupees, if he might have known of such concealment but

---

[1204] bprd.nic.in

[1205] forest.jharkhand.gov.in

[1206] bprd.nic.in

[1207] forest.jharkhand.gov.in

for some neglect of his duty as such master or person in charge, or but for some want of discipline on board of the vessel.

Key Differences: BNS 165: Similar to IPC Section 137 in defining the offense and specifying punishment. Both address the act of concealing a deserter on a merchant vessel through negligence. IPC Section 137: Part of the older legal framework, while BNS 165 is the updated version in the new Bharatiya Nyaya Sanhita.

BNS Section 166

Definition: Abetment of Act of [1208]Insubordination by Soldier, Sailor or Airman Section 166 of the Bharatiya Nyaya Sanhita (BNS) 2023 addresses the offense of abetting an act of insubordination by a soldier, sailor, or airman.

Illustration: [1209]If a person encourages or instigates a soldier to disobey orders from their commanding officer, this act falls under BNS 166.

Example: Suppose an individual persuades a sailor to refuse to follow the captain's commands during a critical operation. This would be categorized as abetment of insubordination under BNS 166.

Comment: This section emphasizes the impact of abetting insubordination on military discipline and hierarchy. It ensures that such acts are met with appropriate penalties to maintain order and authority within the armed forces.

Classification of Offence and Punishment Classification: This offense is classified as a serious criminal offense due to its impact on military discipline and hierarchy.

[1208]Ministry of Home Affairs. (2024). The Bharatiya Nyaya Sanhita, 2023. Retrieved from https://www.mha.gov.in/sites/default/files/250883_english_01042024.pdf

[1209] bprd.nic.in

Punishment: [1210]The punishment for this offense under BNS 166 can be imprisonment of either description for a term which may extend to two years, or a fine, or both.

Cognizable or Non-Cognizable, Bailable or Non-Bailable: This offense is cognizable, meaning the police can arrest the accused without a warrant.

Bailable: This offense is bailable, indicating that the accused can secure bail and be released from custody until the trial is completed.

Comparison: [1211]Section 138 of the Indian Penal Code (IPC) also deals with [1212]abetment of act of insubordination by a soldier, sailor, or airman: IPC Section 138: States that whoever abets an act of insubordination by an officer, soldier, sailor, or airman, in the Army, Navy, or Air Force of the Government of India, shall, if such act of insubordination be committed in consequence of that abetment, be punished with imprisonment of either description for a term which may extend to six months, or a fine, or both.

Key Differences: BNS 166: Similar to IPC Section 138 in defining the offense and specifying punishment. Both address the act of abetting insubordination. IPC Section 138: [1213]Part of the older legal framework, while BNS 166 is the updated version in the new Bharatiya Nyaya Sanhita.

BNS Section 167

Definition: Persons Subject to [1214]Certain Acts Section 167 of the Bharatiya Nyaya Sanhita (BNS) 2023 specifies that individuals subject to the Army Act, 1950, the Indian Navy (Discipline) Act, 1934, or the Air Force Act, 1950, are not subject to punishment under this Sanhita for offenses defined in this Chapter.

[1210] bprd.nic.in

[1211] forest.jharkhand.gov.in

[1212] bprd.nic.in

[1213] bprd.nic.in

[1214] Ministry of Home Affairs. (2024). The Bharatiya Nyaya Sanhita, 2023. Retrieved from https://www.mha.gov.in/sites/default/files/250883_english_01042024.pdf

Illustration: [1215]If a soldier commits an offense defined in this Chapter of the BNS, they will be subject to the relevant military act (Army Act, Navy Act, or Air Force Act) rather than the BNS.

Example: Suppose an airman disobeys orders and is found guilty of insubordination. Instead of being punished under BNS, they would be [1216]subject to the Air Force Act, 1950.

Comment: [1217]This section is more of a procedural guideline rather than an offense with a specific punishment. It directs individuals to the relevant military acts for handling offenses, ensuring that military personnel are governed by the appropriate legal framework.

Classification of Offence and Punishment Classification: This section is more of a procedural guideline rather than an offense with a specific punishment.

Punishment: No specific punishment is outlined in this section as it directs individuals to the relevant military acts for offenses.

Cognizable or Non-Cognizable, Bailable or Non-Bailable: Not applicable as this section does not define an offense.

Bailable: Not applicable as this section does not define an offense.

Comparison: [1218]Section 139 of the Indian Penal Code (IPC) also deals with persons subject to certain acts: IPC Section 139: States that [1219]no person subject to the Army Act, 1950, the Indian Navy (Discipline) Act, 1934, [1220]or the Air Force Act, 1950, is subject to punishment under this Code for any of the offenses defined in this.

Key Differences: BNS 167: Similar to IPC Section 139 in specifying that military personnel are subject to their respective military acts rather than

---

[1215] bprd.nic.in

[1216] bprd.nic.in

[1217] bprd.nic.in

[1218] forest.jharkhand.gov.in

[1219]bprd.nic.in

[1220] www.bareactslive.com

the BNS or IPC for offenses defined in this Chapter910. IPC Section 139: Part of the older legal framework, while BNS 167 is the updated version in the new Bharatiya Nyaya Sanhita.

BNS Section 168

Definition: Wearing [1221]Garb or Carrying Token Used by Soldier, Sailor or Airman Section 168 of the Bharatiya Nyaya Sanhita (BNS) 2023 addresses the offense of wearing military garb or carrying tokens used by soldiers, sailors, or airmen without authorization.

Illustration: [1222]If a person who is not a member of the military wears a military uniform or carries a military badge with the intention of deceiving others into believing they are a soldier, sailor, or airman, this act falls under BNS 168.

Example: Suppose an individual wears an army uniform and carries a military ID card to gain access to a restricted military area. This would be categorized as an offense under BNS 168.

Comment: This section highlights the importance of maintaining the integrity and trust associated with military uniforms and tokens. It ensures that unauthorized use is met with penalties to prevent deception and misuse.

Classification of Offence and Punishment Classification: This offense is classified as a minor criminal offense due to its less severe impact compared to other military-related offenses.

Punishment: [1223]The punishment for this offense under BNS 168 can be [1224]imprisonment of either description for a term which may extend to three months, or a fine which may extend to two thousand rupees, or both.

[1221] Ministry of Home Affairs. (2024). The Bharatiya Nyaya Sanhita, 2023. Retrieved from https://www.mha.gov.in/sites/default/files/250883_english_01042024.pdf

[1222] mdpi.com

[1223]www.rockpebblesindia.in

[1224] ceorajasthan.nic.in

Cognizable or Non-Cognizable, Bailable or Non-Bailable: This offense is cognizable, meaning the police can arrest the accused without a warrant.

Bailable: This offense is bailable, indicating that the accused can secure bail and be released from custody until the trial is completed.

Comparison: With IPC Section 140Section 140 of the Indian Penal Code (IPC) also deals [1225]with the same offense: IPC Section 140: States that whoever, not being a soldier, sailor, or airman in the Military, Naval, or Air service of the Government of India, wears any garb or carries any token resembling any garb or token used by such a soldier, sailor, or airman with the intention that it may be believed that he is such a soldier, sailor, or airman, shall be punished with imprisonment of either description for a term which may extend to three months, or with a [1226]fine which may extend to five hundred rupees, or with both.

Key Differences: BNS 168: Similar to IPC Section 140 in defining the offense and specifying punishment. Both address the act of wearing military garb or carrying tokens without authorization. IPC Section 140: Part of the older legal framework, while BNS 168 is the updated version in the new Bharatiya Nyaya Ssanhita.

[1225] pdfcookie.com

[1226] ceorajasthan.nic.in

CHAPTER-IX; OF OFFENCES RELATING TO ELECTIONS

BNS Section 169

Definition: Candidate, [1227]Electoral Right Defined Section 169 of the Bharatiya Nyaya Sanhita (BNS) 2023 defines the terms "candidate" and "electoral right" for the purposes of this chapter.

Illustration: [1228]A person who has been nominated as a candidate for an election is considered a "candidate" under this section.

Example: If someone is running for a local government position and has been officially nominated, they are recognized as a candidate under BNS 169.

Classification of Offence and Punishment Classification: [1229]This section is more of a definitional provision rather than an offense with a specific punishment.

Punishment: No specific punishment is outlined in this section as it merely provides definitions.

Cognizable or Non-Cognizable, Bailable or Non-Bailable: [1230]Not applicable as this section does not define an offense.

Bailable: Not applicable as this section does not define an offense.

1227 Ministry of Home Affairs. (2024). The Bharatiya Nyaya Sanhita, 2023. Retrieved from https://www.mha.gov.in/sites/default/files/250883_english_01042024.pdf

1228 pdfcookie.com

1229 pdfcookie.com

1230 editorialsamarth.blogspot.com

Comparison: Section 171A [1231]of the Indian Penal Code (IPC) also defines "candidate" and "electoral right": IPC Section 171A: States that for the purposes of this chapter, a "[1232]candidate" means a person who has been nominated as a candidate at any election, and "electoral right" means the right of a person to stand, or not to stand as, or to withdraw from being, a candidate or to vote or refrain from voting at any election.

Key Differences: BNS 169: Similar to IPC Section 171A in defining the terms "candidate" and "electoral right." IPC Section 171A: Part of the older legal framework, while BNS 169 is the updated version in the new Bharatiya Nyaya Sanhita.

BNS Section 170

Definition: Bribery [1233]Section 170 of the Bharatiya Nyaya Sanhita (BNS) 2023 addresses the offense of bribery in relation to electoral rights.

Illustration: If a person gives money to a voter with the intention of influencing their vote, this act falls under BNS 170.

Example: Suppose an individual offers a [1234]gratification to a person to vote for a particular candidate or to reward them for having voted for that candidate. This would be categorized as bribery under BNS 170.

Comment: This section is more of a definitional provision rather than an offense with a specific punishment. It provides clarity [1235]on who is considered a candidate and what constitutes electoral rights.

[1231] ceorajasthan.nic.in

[1232] pdfcookie.com

[1233] Ministry of Home Affairs. (2024). The Bharatiya Nyaya Sanhita, 2023. Retrieved from https://www.mha.gov.in/sites/default/files/250883_english_01042024.pdf

[1234] pdfcookie.com

[1235] pdfcookie.com

Classification of Offence and Punishment Classification: This offense is classified as a serious criminal offense due to its potential to undermine the integrity [1236]of the electoral process.

Punishment: [1237]The punishment for this offense under BNS 170 can be [1238]imprisonment of either description for a term which may extend to seven years, and the offender [1239]shall also be liable to a fine.

Cognizable or Non-Cognizable, Bailable or Non-Bailable: This offense is cognizable, meaning the police can arrest the accused without a warrant.

Bailable: This offense is non-bailable, indicating that the accused cannot secure bail and must remain in custody until the trial is completed.

Comparison: Section 171B [1240]of the Indian Penal Code (IPC) also deals with bribery in relation to electoral rights: IPC Section 171B: States that whoever gives or accepts gratification with the intention of influencing someone's electoral right or rewarding them for having exercised such a right commits the offense of bribery. The punishment under IPC Section 171B can be imprisonment of either description for a term which may extend to one year, or a fine, or both.

Key Differences: BNS 170: Similar to IPC Section 171B in defining the offense and specifying punishment. Both address the act of bribery in relation to electoral rights. IPC Section 171B: Part of the older legal framework, while BNS 170 is the updated version in the new Bharatiya Nyaya Sanhita.

[1236] pdfcookie.com

[1237] www.rockpebblesindia.in

[1238] ceorajasthan.nic.in

[1239] indiankanoon.org

[1240] ceorajasthan.nic.in

BNS Section 171

Definition: Undue Influence at Elections[1241] Section 171 of the Bharatiya Nyaya Sanhita (BNS) 2023 addresses the offense of undue influence at elections.

Illustration: If a person threatens a voter with harm or tries to influence their vote by promising them a benefit, this act falls under BNS 171.

Example: Suppose an individual threatens a candidate's family member with injury if the candidate does not withdraw from the election. This would be categorized as undue influence under BNS 171.

Comment: This section emphasizes the serious nature of undue influence at elections, which can undermine the integrity of the electoral process. It ensures that individuals who engage in such acts face stringent penalties.

Classification of Offence and Punishment Classification: This offense is classified as a serious criminal offense due to its potential to undermine the integrity of the electoral process.

Punishment: [1242]The punishment for this offense under BNS 171 can be [1243]imprisonment of either description for a term which may extend to three years, and the offender [1244]shall also be liable to a fine.

Cognizable or Non-Cognizable, Bailable or Non-Bailable: This offense is cognizable, meaning the police can arrest the accused without a warrant.

Bailable: This offense is non-bailable, indicating that the accused cannot secure bail and must remain in custody until the trial is completed.

[1241] Ministry of Home Affairs. (2024). The Bharatiya Nyaya Sanhita, 2023. Retrieved from https://www.mha.gov.in/sites/default/files/250883_english_01042024.pdf

[1242] www.rockpebblesindia.in

[1243] ceorajasthan.nic.in

[1244] indiankanoon.org

Comparison: Section 171C of the [1245]Indian Penal Code (IPC) also deals with [1246]undue influence at elections: IPC Section 171C: States that whoever voluntarily interferes or attempts to interfere with the free exercise of any electoral right commits the offense of undue influence at an election. The punishment under IPC Section 171C can be imprisonment of either description for a term which may extend to one year, or a fine, or both.

Key Differences: BNS 171: Similar to IPC Section 171C in defining the offense and specifying punishment. Both address the act of undue influence at elections. IPC Section 171C: Part of the older legal framework, while BNS 171 is the updated version in the new Bharatiya Nyaya Sanhita.

BNS Section 172

Definition: Personation[1247] at Elections Section 172 of the Bharatiya Nyaya Sanhita (BNS) 2023 addresses the offense of personation at elections.

Illustration: [1248]If a person applies for a voting paper in the name of another person (whether living or dead) or in a fictitious name, or votes more than once in the same election, this act falls under BNS 172.

Example: Suppose an individual votes using a deceased person's name or votes twice in the same election. This would be categorized as personation under BNS 172.

Comment: This section underscores the serious nature of personation at elections, which can undermine the integrity of the electoral process. It ensures that individuals who engage in such acts face stringent penalties.

[1245] ceorajasthan.nic.in

[1246] pdfcookie.com

[1247] Ministry of Home Affairs. (2024). The Bharatiya Nyaya Sanhita, 2023. Retrieved from https://www.mha.gov.in/sites/default/files/250883_english_01042024.pdf

[1248] pdfcookie.com

Classification of Offence and Punishment Classification: This offense is classified as a serious criminal offense due to its potential to undermine the integrity of the electoral process.

Punishment: [1249]The punishment for this offense under BNS 172 can be [1250]imprisonment of either description for a term which may extend to three years, and the offender [1251]shall also be liable to a fine.

Cognizable or Non-Cognizable, Bailable or Non-Bailable: This offense is cognizable, meaning the police can arrest the accused without a warrant.

Bailable: This offense is non-bailable, indicating that the accused cannot secure bail and must remain in custody until the trial is completed.

Comparison: Section 171D [1252]of the Indian Penal Code (IPC) also deals with personation at elections: IPC Section 171D: States that anyone who [1253]applies for a voting paper in someone else's name or uses a fictitious name to vote, or votes more than once in the same election, and anyone who helps or encourages [1254]such actions, commits the offense of personation at an election. The punishment under IPC Section 171D can be [1255]imprisonment of either description for a term which may extend to one year, or a fine, or both.

Key Differences: BNS 172: Similar to IPC Section 171D in defining the offense and specifying punishment. Both address the act of personation at elections. IPC Section 171D: Part of the older legal framework, while BNS 172 is the updated version in the new Bharatiya Nyaya Sanhita.

[1249] www.rockpebblesindia.in

[1250] ceorajasthan.nic.in

[1251] indiankanoon.org

[1252] ceorajasthan.nic.in

[1253] wbsec.gov.in

[1254] www.bareactslive.com

[1255] ceorajasthan.nic.in

BNS Section 173

Definition: Punishment[1256] for Bribery Section 173 of the Bharatiya Nyaya Sanhita (BNS) 2023 outlines the punishment for committing the offense of bribery.

Illustration: If a person offers money to a public official to influence their decision or action, this act falls under BNS 173.

Example: Suppose an individual gives a sum of money to a traffic police officer to avoid a fine for over speeding. This would be categorized as bribery under BNS 173.

Comment: This section emphasizes the serious nature of bribery, which can undermine public trust and integrity. It ensures that individuals who engage in such acts face stringent penalties.

Classification of Offence and Punishment Classification: This offense is classified as a serious criminal offense due to its potential to undermine public trust and integrity.

Punishment: The punishment for this offense under BNS 173 can be [1257]imprisonment of either description for a term which may extend to one year, or a fine, or both1. However, if the bribery involves treating (providing food, drink, entertainment, or provision), it is punishable with a fine only.

Cognizable or Non-Cognizable, Bailable or Non-Bailable: [1258]This offense is cognizable, meaning the police can arrest the accused without a warrant.

Bailable: This [1259]offense is bailable, indicating that the accused can secure bail and be released from custody until the trial is completed.

[1256] Ministry of Home Affairs. (2024). The Bharatiya Nyaya Sanhita, 2023. Retrieved from https://www.mha.gov.in/sites/default/files/250883_english_01042024.pdf

[1257] ceorajasthan.nic.in

[1258] ceorajasthan.nic.in

[1259] ceorajasthan.nic.in

Comparison: Section 171E of the Indian Penal Code (IPC) also deals with the punishment for bribery: IPC [1260]Section 171E: States that whoever commits the offense of bribery shall be punished with imprisonment of either description for a term which may extend to one year, or a fine, or both. However, bribery by treating is punishable with a fine only.

Key Differences: BNS 173: Similar to IPC Section 171E in [1261]defining the offense and specifying punishment. Both address the act of bribery and its consequences. IPC Section 171E: Part of the older legal framework, while BNS 173 is the updated version in the new Bharatiya Nyaya Sanhita.

BNS Section 174

Definition: Punishment[1262] for Undue Influence or Personation at an Election Section 174 of the Bharatiya Nyaya Sanhita (BNS) 2023 outlines the punishment for committing the offenses of undue influence or personation at an election.

Illustration: If a person threatens a voter to influence their vote or impersonates another voter to cast a vote, this act falls under BNS 174.

Example: Suppose an individual threatens a voter with harm if they do not vote for a particular candidate, or someone votes using another person's identity. These actions would be categorized as undue influence or personation under BNS 174.

Comment: This section emphasizes the serious nature of undue influence or personation at elections, which can undermine the integrity of the electoral process. It ensures that individuals who engage in such acts face stringent penalties.

[1260] ceorajasthan.nic.in

[1261] ceorajasthan.nic.in

[1262] Ministry of Home Affairs. (2024). The Bharatiya Nyaya Sanhita, 2023. Retrieved from https://www.mha.gov.in/sites/default/files/250883_english_01042024.pdf

Classification of Offence and Punishment Classification: This offense is classified as a serious criminal offense due to its potential to undermine the integrity of the electoral process.

Punishment: [1263]The punishment for this offense under BNS 174 can be [1264]imprisonment of either description for a term which may extend to one year, or a fine, or both.

Cognizable or Non-Cognizable, Bailable or Non-Bailable: This offense is cognizable, meaning the police can arrest the accused without a warrant.

Bailable: This offense is bailable, indicating that the accused can secure bail and [1265]be released from custody until the trial is completed.

Comparison: Section 171F of the Indian Penal Code (IPC) also deals with the [1266]punishment for undue influence or personation at an election: IPC Section 171F: States that whoever commits the offense of undue influence or personation at an election shall be punished with imprisonment of either description for a term which may extend to one year, or a fine, or both.

Key Differences: BNS 174: Similar to IPC Section 171F in defining the offense and specifying punishment. Both address the act of undue influence or personation at elections. IPC Section 171F: Part of the older legal framework, while BNS 174 is the updated version in the new Bharatiya Nyaya Sanhita.

[1263] www.rockpebblesindia.in

[1264] ceorajasthan.nic.in

[1265] wbsec.gov.in

[1266] ceorajasthan.nic.in

BNS Section 175

Definition: [1267]False Statement in Connection with an Election Section 175 of the Bharatiya Nyaya Sanhita (BNS) 2023 addresses the offense of making false statements in connection with an election.

Illustration: If a person knowingly makes or publishes a false statement about a candidate's personal character or conduct with the intent to affect the election result, this act falls under BNS 175.

Example: Suppose an individual spreads a false rumor about a candidate's criminal background to dissuade voters from supporting that candidate. This would be categorized as a false statement under BNS 175.Classification of Offence and Punishment

Comment: This section emphasizes the serious nature of making false statements in [1268]connection with an election, which can undermine the integrity of the electoral process. It ensures that individuals who engage in such acts face stringent penalties.

Classification: This offense is classified as a serious criminal offense due to its potential to undermine the integrity of the electoral process.

Punishment: [1269]The punishment for this offense under BNS 175 can be [1270]imprisonment of either description for a term which may extend to one year, or a fine.

Cognizable or Non-Cognizable, Bailable or Non-Bailable: This offense is non-cognizable, meaning the police cannot arrest the accused without a warrant.

Bailable: This offense is bailable, indicating that the accused can secure bail and be released from custody until the trial is completed.

[1267] Ministry of Home Affairs. (2024). The Bharatiya Nyaya Sanhita, 2023. Retrieved from https://www.mha.gov.in/sites/default/files/250883_english_01042024.pdf

[1268] wbsec.gov.in

[1269] www.rockpebblesindia.in

[1270] ceorajasthan.nic.in

Comparison: Section 171G of the Indian Penal Code (IPC) also deals with false statements in connection with an election: IPC Section 171G: States that [1271]whoever with intent to affect the result of an election makes or publishes any statement purporting to be a statement of fact which is false and which he either knows or believes to be false or does not believe to be true, in relation to the personal character or conduct of any candidate shall be punished with imprisonment of either description for a term which may extend to one year, or a fine, or both.

Key Differences: BNS 175: Similar to IPC Section 171G in defining the offense and specifying punishment. [1272]Both address the act of making false statements in connection with an election. IPC Section 171G: Part of the older legal framework, while BNS 175 is the updated version in the new Bharatiya Nyaya Sanhita.

BNS Section 176

Definition: Illegal[1273] Payment in Connection with an Election Section 176 of the Bharatiya Nyaya Sanhita (BNS) 2023 addresses the offense of making illegal payments in connection with an election.

Illustration: If a person incurs expenses for a public meeting, advertisement, or publication to promote a candidate's election without the candidate's authorization, this act falls under BNS 176.

Example: Suppose an individual pays for a rally to support a candidate without obtaining the candidate's written approval. This would be categorized as an illegal payment under BNS 176.

Comment: This section addresses the issue of unauthorized expenses in elections, emphasizing the importance of transparency and fairness. By penalizing illegal payments, it aims to maintain the integrity of the electoral process.

[1271] pdfcookie.com

[1272] pdfcookie.com

[1273] Ministry of Home Affairs. (2024). The Bharatiya Nyaya Sanhita, 2023. Retrieved from https://www.mha.gov.in/sites/default/files/250883_english_01042024.pdf

Classification of Offence and Punishment Classification: This offense is classified as a minor criminal offense due to its less severe impact compared to other election-related offenses.[1274]

Punishment: [1275]The punishment for this offense under BNS 176 [1276]can be a fine which may extend to ten thousand rupees.

Cognizable or Non-Cognizable, Bailable or Non-Bailable: This offense is non-cognizable, meaning the police cannot arrest the accused without a warrant.

Bailable: This offense is bailable, indicating that the accused can secure bail and be released from custody until the trial is completed.

Comparison: Section 171H of the Indian Penal Code (IPC) also deals with [1277]illegal payments in connection with an election : IPC Section 171H: States that [1278]whoever without the general or special authority in writing of a candidate incurs or [1279]authorizes expenses on account of the holding of any public meeting, or upon any advertisement, circular or publication, or in any other way whatsoever for the purpose of promoting or procuring the election of such candidate, shall be punished with a fine which may extend to five hundred rupees.

Key Differences: BNS 176: Similar to IPC Section 171 H in defining the offense and specifying punishment. Both address the act of making [1280]illegal payments in connection with an election. IPC Section 171H: Part of the older legal framework, while BNS 176 is the updated version in the new Bharatiya Nyaya Sanhita.

[1274] pdfcookie.com

[1275] www.rockpebblesindia.in

[1276] ceorajasthan.nic.in

[1277] pdfcookie.com

[1278] ceorajasthan.nic.in

[1279] wbsec.gov.in

[1280] pdfcookie.com

BNS Section 177

Definition: Failure[1281] to Keep Election Accounts Section 177 of the Bharatiya Nyaya Sanhita (BNS) 2023 addresses the offense of failing to keep election accounts as required by law.

Illustration: If a candidate or their agent is required by law to maintain a record of all election-related expenses but fails to do so, this act falls under BNS 177.

Example: Suppose a candidate does not keep a detailed account of the funds spent on campaign advertisements and rallies as mandated by election laws. This would be categorized as a failure to keep election accounts under BNS 177.

Comment: This section addresses the administrative nature of maintaining election accounts, emphasizing the importance of transparency and accountability in the electoral process. By penalizing the failure to keep election accounts, [1282]it aims to uphold the integrity of elections.

Classification of Offence and Punishment Classification: This offense is classified as a minor criminal offense due to its administrative nature.

Punishment: The punishment for this offense under BNS 177 [1283]can be a fine which may extend to five thousand rupees.

Cognizable or Non-Cognizable, Bailable or Non-Bailable: This offense is non-cognizable, meaning the police cannot arrest the accused without a warrant.

Bailable: This offense is bailable, indicating that the accused can secure bail and be released from custody until the trial is completed.

[1281] Ministry of Home Affairs. (2024). The Bharatiya Nyaya Sanhita, 2023. Retrieved from https://www.mha.gov.in/sites/default/files/250883_english_01042024.pdf

[1282] www.rockpebblesindia.in

[1283] ceorajasthan.nic.in

Comparison: Section 171I of the Indian Penal Code (IPC) also deals with the failure to keep election accounts: IPC Section 171I: States that whoever, [1284]being required by any law for the time being in force or any rule having the force of law to keep accounts of expenses incurred at or in connection with an election, [1285]fails to keep such accounts shall be punished with a fine which may extend to five hundred rupees.

Key Differences: BNS 177: Similar to IPC Section 171I in defining the offense and specifying punishment. Both address the act of failing to keep election accounts. IPC Section 171I: Part of the older legal framework, while BNS 177 is the updated version in the new Bharatiya Nyaya Sanhita.

[1284] pdfcookie.com

[1285] ceorajasthan.nic.in

CHAPTER-X; OF OFFENCES RELATING TO COIN, CURRENCY -NOTES, BANK-NOTES, AND GOVERNMENT STAMPS

BNS Section 178

Definition: Counterfeiting[1286] Coin, Government Stamps, Currency-Notes or Bank- Notes Section 178 of the Bharatiya Nyaya Sanhita (BNS) 2023 addresses the offense of counterfeiting coin, government stamps, currency-notes, or bank-notes.

Illustration: [1287]If a person creates fake currency notes or coins, or knowingly participates in the process of creating counterfeit currency, this act falls under BNS 178.

Example: Suppose an individual uses sophisticated printing equipment to produce fake currency notes that resemble genuine ones. This would be categorized as counterfeiting under BNS 178.

Comment: This section highlights the serious nature of counterfeiting, which can undermine the financial system and public trust. It ensures that individuals who engage in such acts face stringent penalties.

Classification of Offence and Punishment Classification: This offense is classified as a serious criminal offense due to its potential to undermine the financial system and public trust.

Punishment: [1288]The punishment for this offense under BNS 178 can be imprisonment for life, or imprisonment of either description for a term

[1286] Ministry of Home Affairs. (2024). The Bharatiya Nyaya Sanhita, 2023. Retrieved from https://www.mha.gov.in/sites/default/files/250883_english_01042024.pdf

[1287] bprd.nic.in

[1288] bprd.nic.in

which may extend to ten years, and [1289]the offender shall also be liable to a fine.

Cognizable or Non-Cognizable, Bailable or Non-Bailable: This offense is cognizable, meaning the police can arrest the accused without a warrant.

Bailable: This offense is non-bailable, indicating that the accused cannot secure bail and must remain in custody until the trial is completed.

Comparison: Sections 230 to 232, 246 to 249, 255, and 489A [1290]of the Indian Penal Code (IPC) also address various aspects of counterfeiting: IPC Section 230 to 232: These sections deal with counterfeiting coins and government stamps. IPC Section 246 to 249: These sections address counterfeiting currency-notes and bank-notes. IPC Section 255: This section provides general provisions regarding counterfeiting. IPC Section 489A: States that whoever counterfeits, or knowingly performs any part of the process of counterfeiting, any currency-note or bank-note, shall be punished with imprisonment for [1291]life, or imprisonment of either description for a term which may extend to ten years, and shall also be liable to a fine.

Key Differences: BNS 178: Similar to IPC Sections 230 to 232, 246 to 249, 255, and 489A in defining the offense and specifying punishment. Both address the act of counterfeiting coins, government stamps, currency-notes, or bank-notes. IPC Sections 230 to 232, 246 to 249, 255, 489A: Part of the older legal framework, while BNS 178 is the updated version in the new Bharatiya Nyaya Sanhita.

BNS Section 179

Definition: [1292]Using as Genuine, Forged or Counterfeit Coin, Government Stamp, Currency-Notes or Bank-Notes Section 179 of

---

[1289] www.pakistani.org

[1290] advocatetanmoy.com

[1291] bprd.nic.in

[1292] Ministry of Home Affairs. (2024). The Bharatiya Nyaya Sanhita, 2023. Retrieved from https://www.mha.gov.in/sites/default/files/250883_english_01042024.pdf

the Bharatiya Nyaya Sanhita (BNS) 2023 addresses the offense of using forged or counterfeit coins, government stamps, currency-notes, or bank-notes as genuine.

Illustration: [1293]If a person knowingly uses or traffics counterfeit currency or stamps, believing or knowing them to be fake, this act falls under BNS 179.

Example: Suppose an individual knowingly uses counterfeit currency notes to make purchases or trades them with others. This would be categorized as using forged or counterfeit currency under BNS 179.

Comment: This section underscores the serious nature of using forged or counterfeit currency and stamps, which can undermine the financial system and public trust. It ensures that individuals who engage in such acts face stringent penalties

Classification of Offence and Punishment Classification: This offense is classified as a serious criminal offense due to its potential to undermine the financial system and public trust.

Punishment: [1294]The punishment for this offense under BNS 179 can be imprisonment for life, or imprisonment of either description for a term which may extend to ten years, and [1295]the offender shall also be liable to a fine.

Cognizable or Non-Cognizable, Bailable or Non-Bailable: This offense is cognizable, meaning the police can arrest the accused without a warrant.

Bailable: This offense is non-bailable, indicating that the accused cannot secure bail and must remain in custody until the trial is completed.

Comparison: Sections 237 to 241, 250, 251, 254, 258, 260, and 489B [1296]of the Indian Penal Code (IPC) also address various aspects of counterfeiting and using forged currency: IPC Section 237: Import or

---

[1293] bprd.nic.in

[1294] bprd.nic.in

[1295] www.pakistani.org

[1296] advocatetanmoy.com

export of counterfeit coin. IPC Section 238: Making or possessing instruments for counterfeiting coin. IPC Section 239: Making or possessing instruments for counterfeiting government stamps. IPC Section 240: [1297]Making or possessing instruments for counterfeiting currency-notes or bank-notes. IPC Section 241: Using as genuine, forged or counterfeit coin, government stamp, currency-notes or bank-notes. IPC Section 250: Using as genuine, forged or counterfeit coin, government stamp, currency-notes or bank-notes, knowing them to be forged or counterfeit. IPC Section 251: Using as genuine, forged or counterfeit coin, government stamp, currency-notes or bank-notes, with the intent to deceive any person. IPC Section 254: Using as genuine, forged or counterfeit coin, government stamp, currency-notes or bank-notes, with the intent to defraud the Government. IPC Section 258: Using as genuine, forged or counterfeit coin, government stamp, currency-notes or bank-notes, with the intent to defraud any person. IPC Section 260: Using as genuine, forged or counterfeit coin, government stamp, currency-notes or bank-notes, with the intent to defraud the public. IPC Section 489B: Using as genuine, forged or counterfeit coin, government stamp, currency-notes or bank-notes, with the intent to defraud the public.

Key Differences: BNS 179: [1298]Similar to IPC Sections 237 to 241, 250, 251, 254, 258, 260, and 489B in defining the offense and specifying punishment. Both address the act of using forged or counterfeit currency and stamps. IPC Sections 237 to 241, 250, 251, 254, 258, 260, 489B: Part of the older legal framework, while BNS 179 is the updated version in the new Bharatiya Nyaya Sanhita.

BNS Section 180

Definition: [1299]Possession of Forged or Counterfeit Coin, Government Stamp, Currency-Notes or Bank-Notes Section 180 of the Bharatiya

---

[1297] bprd.nic.in

[1298] bprd.nic.in

[1299] Ministry of Home Affairs. (2024). The Bharatiya Nyaya Sanhita, 2023. Retrieved from https://www.mha.gov.in/sites/default/files/250883_english_01042024.pdf

Nyaya Sanhita (BNS) 2023 addresses the offense of possessing forged or counterfeit coins, government stamps, currency-notes, or bank-notes.

Illustration: If a person knowingly has in their possession counterfeit currency or stamps, with [1300]the intent to use them as genuine, this act falls under BNS 180.

Example: Suppose an individual is found with a batch of fake currency notes that they intended to use for transactions. This would be categorized as possession of forged or counterfeit currency[1301] under BNS 180.

Classification of Offence and Punishment Classification: This offense is classified as a serious criminal offense due to its potential to undermine the financial system and public trust.

Punishment: [1302]The punishment for this offense under BNS 180 can be [1303]imprisonment of either description for a term which may extend to seven years, or a fine, or both.

Cognizable or Non-Cognizable, Bailable or Non-Bailable: This offense is cognizable, meaning the police can arrest the accused without a warrant.

Bailable: This offense is non-bailable, indicating that the accused cannot secure bail and must remain in custody until the trial is completed.

Comparison: [1304]Sections 242, 243, 252, 253, 259, and 489C of the Indian Penal Code (IPC) also address various aspects of possessing forged or counterfeit currency and stamps: IPC Section 242: Possession of counterfeit coin by a [1305]person who knew it[1306] to be counterfeit when they became possessed of it. IPC Section 243: Possession of counterfeit coin

---

[1300] bprd.nic.in

[1301] bprd.nic.in

[1302] bprd.nic.in

[1303] advocatetanmoy.com

[1304] advocatetanmoy.com

[1305] scholar.ufs.ac.za

[1306] advocatetanmoy.com

by a person who did not know it to be counterfeit when they became possessed of it. IPC Section 252: Possession of counterfeit coin by a person who obtained it innocently. IPC Section 253: Possession of counterfeit coin by a person who obtained it dishonestly. IPC Section 259: Possession of counterfeit coin by a person who obtained it dishonestly and without knowing it to be counterfeit. IPC Section 489C: Using as genuine, forged or counterfeit coin, government stamp, currency-notes or bank-notes, [1307]with the intent to defraud the public.

Key Differences: BNS 180: Similar to IPC Sections 242, 243, 252, 253, 259, and 489C in defining the offense and specifying punishment. Both address the act of possessing forged or counterfeit[1308] currency and stamps. IPC Sections 242, 243, 252, 253, 259, 489C: Part of the older legal framework, while BNS 180 is the updated version in the new Bharatiya Nyaya Sanhita.

BNS Section 181

Definition: Making or Possessing Instruments[1309] or Materials for Forging or Counterfeiting Section 181 of the Bharatiya Nyaya Sanhita (BNS) 2023 addresses the offense of making, mending, buying, selling, disposing of, or possessing any machinery, die, instrument, or material intended for forging or counterfeiting coins, government stamps, currency-notes, or bank-notes.

Illustration: [1310]If a person creates or possesses equipment specifically designed to produce counterfeit currency, this act falls under BNS 181.

Example: Suppose an individual is found with a printing press and dies used to create fake currency notes. This would be categorized as making or possessing instruments for counterfeiting under BNS 181.

[1307] bprd.nic.in

[1308] bprd.nic.in

[1309] Ministry of Home Affairs. (2024). The Bharatiya Nyaya Sanhita, 2023. Retrieved from https://www.mha.gov.in/sites/default/files/250883_english_01042024.pdf

[1310] bprd.nic.in

Comment: This section underscores the serious nature of making or possessing instruments for counterfeiting, which can undermine the financial system and public trust. It ensures that individuals who engage in such acts face stringent penalties.

Classification of Offence and Punishment Classification: This offense is classified as a serious criminal offense due to its potential to undermine the financial system and public trust.

Punishment: [1311]The punishment for this offense under BNS 181 can be imprisonment for life, or imprisonment of either description for a term which may extend to ten years, and [1312]the offender shall also be liable to a fine.

Cognizable or Non-Cognizable, Bailable or Non-Bailable: This offense is cognizable, meaning the police can arrest the accused without a warrant.

Bailable: This offense is non-bailable, indicating that the accused cannot secure bail and must remain in custody until the trial is completed.

Comparison: Sections 233 to 235, 256, 257, and 489D [1313]of the Indian Penal Code (IPC) also address various aspects of making or possessing instruments for counterfeiting: IPC Section 233: Making or mending, or performing any part of the process of making or mending, or buying, selling or disposing of, any die or instrument for the purpose of being used, or knowing or having reason to believe that it is intended to be used, for counterfeiting coin. IPC Section 234: Making or mending, or performing any part of the process of making or mending, or buying, selling or disposing of, any die or instrument for the purpose of being used, or knowing or having reason to believe that it is intended to be used, for counterfeiting government stamp. IPC Section 235: Making or mending, or performing any part of the process of making or mending, or buying, selling or disposing of, any die or instrument for the purpose of being used, or knowing or having reason to believe that it is intended to be used, for

[1311] bprd.nic.in

[1312] www.pakistani.org

[1313] advocatetanmoy.com

counterfeiting currency-notes or bank-notes. IPC Section 256: Making or mending, or performing any part of the process of making or mending, or buying, selling or disposing of, any die or instrument for the purpose of being used, or knowing or having reason to believe that it is intended to be used, for counterfeiting coin, knowing it to be counterfeit. IPC Section 257: [1314]Making or mending, or performing any part of the process of making or mending, or buying, selling or disposing of, any die or instrument for the purpose of being used, or knowing or having reason to believe that it is intended to be used, for counterfeiting government stamp, knowing it to be counterfeit. IPC Section 489D: Making or possessing instruments or materials for forging or counterfeiting currency-notes or bank-notes.

Key Differences: BNS 181: Similar to IPC Sections 233 to 235, 256, 257, and 489D in defining the offense and specifying punishment. Both address [1315]the act of making or possessing instruments for counterfeiting coins, government stamps, currency-notes, or bank-notes. IPC Sections 233 to 235, 256, 257, 489D: Part of the older legal framework, while BNS 181 is the updated version in the new Bharatiya Nyaya Sanhita.

BNS Section 182

Definition: Making[1316] or Using Documents Resembling Currency-Notes or Bank-Notes Section 182 of the Bharatiya Nyaya Sanhita (BNS) 2023 addresses the offense of making, using, or delivering documents that resemble currency-notes or bank-notes with the intent to deceive.

Illustration: [1317]If a person creates or uses documents that closely resemble genuine currency-notes or bank-notes, this act falls under BNS 182.

[1314] bprd.nic.in

[1315] bprd.nic.in

[1316] Ministry of Home Affairs. (2024). The Bharatiya Nyaya Sanhita, 2023. Retrieved from https://www.mha.gov.in/sites/default/files/250883_english_01042024.pdf

[1317] bprd.nic.in

Example: Suppose an individual prints fake currency notes and [1318]attempts to use them for transactions. This would be categorized as making or using documents resembling currency-notes under BNS 182.

Comment: This section underscores the serious nature of making or using documents that resemble currency-notes or bank-notes, which can undermine the financial system and public trust. It ensures that individuals who engage in such acts face stringent penalties.

Classification of Offence and Punishment Classification: This offense is classified as a serious criminal offense due to its potential to undermine the financial system and public trust.

Punishment: The punishment for this offense under BNS 182 can be a [1319]fine which may extend to three hundred rupees.

Cognizable or Non-Cognizable, Bailable or Non-Bailable: This offense is cognizable, meaning the police can arrest the accused without a warrant.

Bailable: This offense is bailable, indicating that the accused can secure bail and be released from custody until the trial is completed.

Comparison: Section 489E of the Indian Penal Code (IPC) also addresses the offense of [1320]making or using documents resembling currency-notes or bank-notes : IPC Section 489E: States that whoever makes, or causes to be made, or uses for any purpose whatsoever, or delivers to any person, any document purporting to be, or in any way resembling, or so nearly resembling as to be calculated to deceive, any currency-note or bank-note shall be punished with a fine [1321]which may extend to one hundred rupees.

Key Differences: BNS 182: Similar to IPC Section 489E in defining the offense and specifying punishment. Both address [1322]the act of making or using documents resembling currency-notes or bank-notes. IPC Section

---

[1318] bprd.nic.in

[1319] advocatetanmoy.com

[1320] bprd.nic.in

[1321] advocatetanmoy.com

[1322] bprd.nic.in

489E: Part of the older legal framework, while BNS 182 is the updated version in the new Bharatiya Nyaya Sanhita.

BNS Section 183

Definition: Effacing [1323]Writing from Substance Bearing Government Stamp Section 183 of the Bharatiya Nyaya Sanhita (BNS) 2023 addresses the offense of effacing writing from a substance bearing a government stamp or removing a stamp from a document with the intent to cause loss to the government.

Illustration: If a person fraudulently removes a revenue stamp from a document to use it on another document, this act falls under BNS 183.

Example: Suppose an individual erases the writing on a document that has a government stamp and then uses the same stamp on a different document to avoid paying the required fee. This would be categorized as effacing writing from a substance bearing a government stamp under BNS 183.

Comment: This section underscores the serious nature of effacing writing from a substance bearing a [1324]government stamp or removing a stamp from a document [1325]with the intent to defraud the government. It ensures that such acts are met with stringent penalties to protect government revenue.

Classification of Offence and Punishment Classification: This offense is classified as a serious criminal offense due to its potential to defraud the government.

[1323] Ministry of Home Affairs. (2024). The Bharatiya Nyaya Sanhita, 2023. Retrieved from https://www.mha.gov.in/sites/default/files/250883_english_01042024.pdf

[1324] advocatetanmoy.com

[1325] advocatetanmoy.com

Punishment: The punishment for this offense under BNS 183 can be [1326]imprisonment of either description for a term which may extend to three years, or a fine, or both.

Cognizable or Non-Cognizable, Bailable or Non-Bailable: This offense is cognizable, meaning the police can arrest the accused without a warrant.

Bailable: This offense is bailable, indicating that the accused can secure bail and be released from custody until the trial is completed.

Comparison: [1327]Section 261 of the [1328]Indian Penal Code (IPC) also addresses the offense of effacing writing from a substance bearing a government stamp or removing a stamp from a document with the intent to cause loss to the government : IPC Section 261: States that whoever, fraudulently or with intent to cause loss to [1329]the government, removes or effaces from any substance, bearing any stamp issued by the government for the purpose of revenue, any writing or document for which such stamp has been used, or removes from any writing or document a stamp which has been used for such writing or document, in order that such stamp may be used for a different writing or document, shall be punished with imprisonment of either description for a term which may extend to three years, or with a fine, or both.

Key Differences: BNS 183: Similar to IPC Section 261 in defining the offense and specifying punishment. Both address the act of effacing writing from a substance bearing a government stamp or removing a stamp from a document with the intent[1330] to cause loss to the government. IPC Section 261: Part of the older legal framework, while BNS 183 is the updated version in the new Bharatiya Nyaya Sanhita.

[1326] advocatetanmoy.com

[1327] advocatetanmoy.com

[1328] www.bareactslive.com

[1329] forest.jharkhand.gov.in

[1330] advocatetanmoy.com

BNS Section 184

Definition: Using [1331]Government Stamp Known to Have Been Before Used Section 184 of the Bharatiya Nyaya Sanhita (BNS) 2023 addresses the offense of using a government stamp that is known to have been previously used.

Illustration: If a person knowingly uses a revenue stamp that has already been used on another document, this act falls under BNS 184.

Example: Suppose an individual finds a used revenue stamp and decides to use it on a new document to avoid paying the required fee. This would be categorized as using a government [1332]stamp known to have been before used under BNS 184.

Comment: This section emphasizes the serious nature of using [1333]a government stamp known to have been previously used, which can defraud the government. It ensures that such acts are met with appropriate penalties to protect government revenue.

Classification of Offence and Punishment Classification: This offense is classified as a serious criminal offense due to its potential to defraud the government.

Punishment: [1334]The punishment for this offense under BNS 184 can be imprisonment of either description for a term which may extend to two years, or a fine, or both.

Cognizable or Non-Cognizable, Bailable or Non-Bailable: This offense is cognizable, meaning the police can arrest the accused without a warrant.

Bailable: This offense is bailable, indicating that the accused can secure bail and be released from custody until the trial is completed.

[1331] Ministry of Home Affairs. (2024). The Bharatiya Nyaya Sanhita, 2023. Retrieved from https://www.mha.gov.in/sites/default/files/250883_english_01042024.pdf

[1332] advocatetanmoy.com

[1333] advocatetanmoy.com

[1334] advocatetanmoy.com

Comparison: [1335]Section 262 of the Indian Penal Code (IPC) also addresses the offense of [1336]using a government stamp known to have been before used: IPC Section 262: States that whoever, fraudulently or with intent to cause loss to the Government, uses for any purpose a stamp issued by Government for the purpose of revenue, which he knows to have been before used, shall be punished with imprisonment of either description for a term which may extend to two years, or with a fine, or both.

Key Differences: BNS 184: [1337]Similar to IPC Section 262 in defining the offense and specifying punishment. Both address the act of using a government stamp known to have been before used. IPC Section 262: Part of the older legal framework, while BNS 184 is the updated version in the new Bharatiya Nyaya Sanhita.

BNS Section 185

Definition: Erasure of Mark [1338]Denoting that Stamp has been Used Section 185 of the Bharatiya Nyaya Sanhita (BNS) 2023 addresses the offense of erasing or removing marks from government revenue stamps that denote their previous use.

Illustration: If a person fraudulently removes a mark from a revenue stamp to reuse it on another document, this act falls under BNS 185.

Example: Suppose an individual erases the mark on a used revenue stamp and then uses it on a new document to avoid paying the required fee. This would be categorized as erasing the mark [1339]denoting that the stamp has been used under BNS 185.

Comment: This section emphasizes the serious nature of erasing or removing marks from government revenue stamps, which can defraud the

---

[1335] www.bareactslive.com

[1336] advocatetanmoy.com

[1337] advocatetanmoy.com

[1338] Ministry of Home Affairs. (2024). The Bharatiya Nyaya Sanhita, 2023. Retrieved from https://www.mha.gov.in/sites/default/files/250883_english_01042024.pdf

[1339] www.bareactslive.com

government. It ensures that such acts are met with stringent penalties to protect government revenue.

Classification of Offence and Punishment Classification: This offense is classified as a serious criminal offense due to its potential to defraud the government.

Punishment: The punishment for this offense under BNS 185 can be [1340]imprisonment of either description for a term which may extend to three years, or a fine, or both.

Cognizable or Non-Cognizable, Bailable or Non-Bailable: This offense is cognizable, meaning the police can arrest the accused without a warrant.

Bailable: This offense is bailable, indicating that the accused can secure bail and be released from custody until the trial is completed.

Comparison: [1341]Section 263 of the Indian Penal Code (IPC) also addresses the offense of erasing or removing marks from government revenue stamps that denote their previous use: IPC Section 263: States that [1342]whoever, fraudulently or with intent to cause loss to the Government, erases or removes from a stamp issued by [1343]the Government for the purpose of revenue, any mark, put or impressed upon such stamp for the purpose of denoting that the same has been used, or knowingly has in his possession or sells or disposes of any such stamp from which such mark has been erased or removed, or sells or disposes of any such stamp which he knows to have been used, shall be punished with imprisonment of either description for a term which may extend to three years, or with a fine, or both.

Key Differences: BNS 185: Similar to IPC Section 263 in defining the offense and specifying punishment. Both address the act of erasing or removing marks from government revenue stamps that denote their

---

[1340] advocatetanmoy.com

[1341] www.bareactslive.com

[1342] advocatetanmoy.com

[1343] forest.jharkhand.gov.in

previous use. IPC Section 263: Part of the older legal framework, while BNS 185 is the updated version in the new Bharatiya Nyaya Sanhita.

BNS Section 186

Definition: Prohibition of Fictitious Stamps[1344] Section 186 of the Bharatiya Nyaya Sanhita (BNS) 2023 addresses the offense of making, dealing in, possessing, or using fictitious stamps.

Illustration: If a person creates or uses stamps that falsely purport to be[1345] issued by the government for postal purposes, this act falls under BNS 186.

Example: Suppose an individual prints fake stamps resembling official government-issued stamps and uses them to send mail. This would be categorized as using fictitious stamps under BNS 186.

Comment: This section underscores the serious nature of making, dealing in, possessing, or using fictitious stamps, which can undermine the postal system and public trust. It ensures that such acts are met with penalties to protect the integrity of official postal services.

Classification of Offence and Punishment Classification: This offense is classified as a serious criminal offense due to its potential to undermine the postal system and public trust.

Punishment: The punishment for this offense under BNS 186 can be a [1346]fine which may extend to two hundred rupees.

Cognizable or Non-Cognizable, Bailable or Non-Bailable: This offense is cognizable, meaning the police can arrest the accused without a warrant.

Bailable: This offense is bailable, indicating that the accused can secure bail and be released from custody until the trial is completed.

[1344] Ministry of Home Affairs. (2024). The Bharatiya Nyaya Sanhita, 2023. Retrieved from https://www.mha.gov.in/sites/default/files/250883_english_01042024.pdf

[1345] forest.jharkhand.gov.in

[1346] advocatetanmoy.com

Comparison: [1347]Section 263A of the Indian Penal Code (IPC) also addresses the offense of making, dealing in, possessing, or using fictitious stamps: IPC Section 263A: States that whoever [1348]makes, knowingly utters, deals in or sells any fictitious stamp, or knowingly uses for any postal purpose any fictitious stamp, or has in his possession, without lawful excuse, any fictitious stamp, or makes or, without lawful excuse, has in his possession any die, plate, instrument or materials for making any fictitious stamp, shall be punished with a [1349]fine which may extend to two hundred rupees.

Key Differences: BNS 186: Similar to IPC Section 263A in defining the offense and specifying punishment. Both address the act of making, dealing in, possessing, or using fictitious stamps6.IPC Section 263A: Part of the older legal framework, while BNS 186 is the updated version in the new Bharatiya Nyaya Sanhita.

BNS Section 187

Definition: Person Employed in Mint Causing Coin[1350] to Be of Different Weight or Composition from That Fixed by Law Section 187 of the Bharatiya Nyaya Sanhita (BNS) 2023 addresses the offense of a person employed in a mint causing coins to be of a different weight or composition from that fixed by law.

Illustration: If a mint employee intentionally alters the [1351]weight or composition of coins during the minting process, this act falls under BNS 187.

Example: Suppose a worker at a mint decides to use less metal in the coins to save costs, resulting in coins that are lighter than the legally specified

---

[1347] blog.ipleaders.in

[1348] odishapolicecidcb.gov.in

[1349] advocatetanmoy.com

[1350] Ministry of Home Affairs. (2024). The Bharatiya Nyaya Sanhita, 2023. Retrieved from https://www.mha.gov.in/sites/default/files/250883_english_01042024.pdf

[1351] blog.ipleaders.in

weight. This would be categorized as causing coins [1352]to be of a different weight or composition under BNS 187.

Comment: This [1353]section emphasizes the serious nature of causing coins to be of a different weight or composition from that fixed by law, which can undermine the integrity of the currency system. It ensures that individuals who engage in such acts face stringent penalties.

Classification of Offence and Punishment Classification: This offense is classified as a serious criminal offense due to its potential to undermine the integrity of the currency system.

Punishment: [1354]The punishment for this offense under BNS 187 can be imprisonment of either description for a term which may extend to seven years, and the offender shall also be liable to a fine.

Cognizable or Non-Cognizable, Bailable or Non-Bailable: This offense is cognizable, meaning the police can arrest the accused without a warrant.

Bailable: This offense is non-bailable, indicating that the accused cannot secure bail and must remain in custody until the trial is completed.

Comparison: [1355]Section 244 of the Indian Penal Code (IPC) also addresses the offense of a person employed in a mint causing coins [1356]to be of a different weight or composition from that fixed by law: IPC Section 244: States that whoever, being employed in any mint lawfully established in [1357]India, does any act, or omits what he is legally bound to do, with the intention of causing any coin issued from that mint to be of a different weight or composition from the weight or composition fixed by law, shall be punished with imprisonment of either description for a term which may extend to seven years, and shall also be liable to a fine.

1352 advocatetanmoy.com

1353 advocatetanmoy.com

1354 advocatetanmoy.com

1355 www.bareactslive.com

1356 advocatetanmoy.com

1357 odishapolicecidcb.gov.in

Key Differences: BNS 187: Similar to IPC Section 244 in defining the offense and specifying punishment. Both address the act of altering [1358]the weight or composition of coins by a mint employee. IPC Section 244: Part of the older legal framework, while BNS 187 is the updated version in the new Bharatiya Nyaya Sanhita.

BNS Section 188

Definition: Unlawfully [1359]Taking Coining Instrument from Mint Section 188 of the Bharatiya Nyaya Sanhita (BNS) 2023 addresses the offense of unlawfully taking coining instruments from a mint.

Illustration: If a [1360]person without lawful authority takes out any coining tool or instrument from a [1361]mint lawfully established in India, this act falls under BNS 188.

Example: Suppose an individual working at a mint secretly removes a coining die or press to use it for unauthorized purposes. This would be categorized as unlawfully taking coining instruments under BNS 188.

Comment: This section emphasizes the serious nature of unlawfully taking coining instruments from a mint, which can undermine the integrity of the currency system. It ensures that individuals who engage in such acts face stringent penalties.

Classification of Offence and Punishment Classification: This offense is classified as a serious criminal offense due to its potential to undermine the integrity of the currency system.

[1358] blog.ipleaders.in

[1359] Ministry of Home Affairs. (2024). The Bharatiya Nyaya Sanhita, 2023. Retrieved from https://www.mha.gov.in/sites/default/files/250883_english_01042024.pdf

[1360] blog.ipleaders.in

[1361] odishapolicecidcb.gov.in

Punishment: The punishment for this offense under BNS 188 can be [1362]imprisonment of either description for a term which may extend to seven years, and the offender shall also be liable to a fine.

Cognizable or Non-Cognizable, Bailable or Non-Bailable: This offense is cognizable, meaning the police can arrest the accused without a warrant.

Bailable: This offense is non-bailable, indicating that the accused cannot secure bail and must remain in custody until the trial is completed.

Comparison: [1363]Section 245 of the Indian Penal Code (IPC) also addresses the offense of unlawfully taking coining instruments from a mint: IPC Section 245: States that [1364]whoever, without lawful authority, takes out of any mint, lawfully established in India[1365], any coining tool or instrument, shall be punished with imprisonment of either description for a term which may extend to seven years, and shall also be liable to a fine.

Key Differences: BNS 188: Similar to IPC Section 245 in defining the offense and specifying punishment. Both address the act[1366] of unlawfully taking coining instruments from a mint. IPC Section 245: Part of the older legal framework, while BNS 188 is the updated version in the new Bharatiya Nyaya Sanhita.

[1362] advocatetanmoy.com

[1363] www.bareactslive.com

[1364] advocatetanmoy.com

[1365] odishapolicecidcb.gov.in

[1366] odishapolicecidcb.gov.in

CHAPTER-XI; OF OFFENCES AGAINST THE PUBLIC TRANQUILLITY

BNS Section 189 (1

Definition: Unlawful Assembly Section 189 of the Bharatiya Nyaya Sanhita (BNS) 2023 addresses the offense of unlawful assembly[1367].

Illustration: If a group of five or more people gathers with the common intention of committing an offense, resisting legal process, or causing public disturbance, this assembly is considered unlawful under BNS 1892.

Example: Suppose a group of individuals assembles with the intent to forcefully disrupt a government function or resist the execution of a court order. This would be categorized as an unlawful assembly under BNS 189.

Comment: This section emphasizes the potential disruption to public order and safety caused by unlawful assemblies. By penalizing such acts, it aims to maintain peace and legal order in society.

Classification of Offence and Punishment Classification: This offense is classified as a serious criminal offense due to its potential to disrupt public order and safety.

Punishment: The punishment[1368] for this offense under BNS 189 can be imprisonment of either description for a term which may extend to six months, or a fine, or both.

Cognizable or Non-Cognizable, Bailable or Non-Bailable: This offense is cognizable, meaning the police can arrest the accused without a warrant.

[1367] indiacode.nic.in

[1368] advocatetanmoy.com

Bailable: This offense is bailable, indicating that the accused can secure bail and be released from custody until the trial is completed.

Comparison: Section 141 of the Indian Penal Code[1369] (IPC) also addresses the offense of unlawful assembly: IPC Section 141: States that an [1370]assembly of five or more persons is designated an "unlawful assembly" if the common object of the persons composing that assembly is to commit any offense, resist the execution of any law, or cause a breach of the peace. Punishment: [1371]The punishment for this offense under IPC Section 141 can be imprisonment of either description for a term which may extend to six months, or a fine, or both.

Key Differences: BNS 189(1): Similar to IPC Section 141 in defining the offense and specifying punishment. Both address the act of unlawful assembly with the common object of committing an offense, resisting legal process, or causing public disturbance. IPC Section 141: Part of the older legal framework, while BNS 189 is the updated version in the new Bharatiya Nyaya Sanhita.

BNS Section189 (2)

Definition: Unlawful Assembly - Being Member of Unlawful Assembly Section 189(2) of the Bharatiya Nyaya Sanhita (BNS) 2023 addresses the offense of [1372]being a member of an unlawful assembly.

Illustration: If a group of five or more people gathers with the common intention of committing an offense, and a person joins and participates in this assembly, their participation is considered an offense under BNS 189(2).

Example: Suppose a person joins a group that has assembled to protest illegally and disrupt public order, knowing the group's common intent.

[1369] blog.ipleaders.in

[1370] indiacode.nic.in

[1371] advocatetanmoy.com

[1372] www.refworld.org

This would be categorized as being a member of an unlawful assembly under BNS 189(2).

Comment: This section emphasizes the serious nature of being a member of an unlawful assembly, which can disrupt public order and safety. By penalizing such acts, it aims to maintain peace and legal order in society.

Classification of Offence and Punishment Classification: This offense is classified as a serious criminal offense due to its potential to disrupt public order and safety.

Punishment: The punishment for this offense under BNS 189(2) can be imprisonment[1373] of either description for a term which may extend to six months, or a fine, or both.

Cognizable or Non-Cognizable, Bailable or Non-Bailable: This offense is cognizable, meaning the police can arrest the accused without a warrant.

Bailable: This offense is bailable, indicating that the accused can secure bail and be released from custody until the trial is completed.

Comparison: Section 142 of the Indian Penal Code[1374] (IPC) also addresses the offense of being a member of an unlawful assembly[1375]: IPC Section 142: States that whoever[1376], being aware of facts which render any assembly an unlawful assembly, intentionally joins that assembly, or continues in it, is said to be a member of an unlawful assembly.

Punishment: The punishment[1377] for this offense under IPC Section 142 can be imprisonment of either description for a term which may extend to six months, or a fine, or both.

Key Differences: BNS 189(2): Similar to IPC Section 142 in defining the offense and specifying punishment. Both address the act of being[1378] a

---

[1373] advocatetanmoy.com

[1374] blog.ipleaders.in

[1375] www.refworld.org

[1376] indiacode.nic.in

[1377] advocatetanmoy.com

[1378] www.refworld.org

member of an unlawful assembly with the common object of committing an offense, resisting legal process, or causing public disturbance. IPC Section 142: Part of the older legal framework, while BNS 189(2) is the updated version in the new Bharatiya Nyaya Sanhita.

BNS Section 189(3)

Definition: Unlawful Assembly - Joining or Continuing in Unlawful Assembly, knowing it has been Commanded to Disperse[1379] Section 189(3) of the Bharatiya Nyaya Sanhita (BNS) 2023 addresses the offense of joining[1380] or continuing in an unlawful assembly after[1381] it has been commanded to disperse.

Illustration: If a group of people is ordered by the police to disperse and they continue to assemble or join the group, this act falls under BNS 189(3).

Example: Suppose a group is protesting without permission and the police command them to disperse, but some individuals continue to gather and refuse to leave. This would be categorized as joining[1382] or continuing in an unlawful assembly under BNS 189(3).

Comment: This section emphasizes the serious nature of continuing in an unlawful assembly after being commanded to disperse, which can disrupt public order and safety. By penalizing such acts, it aims to maintain peace and legal order in society.

Classification of Offence and Punishment Classification: This offense is classified as a serious criminal offense due to its potential to disrupt public order and safety.

[1379] indiacode.nic.in

[1380] www.refworld.org

[1381] indiacode.nic.in

[1382] www.refworld.org

Punishment: The punishment for this offense under BNS 189(3) can be imprisonment[1383] of either description for a term which may extend to six months, or a fine, or both.

Cognizable or Non-Cognizable, Bailable or Non-Bailable: This offense is cognizable, meaning the police can arrest the accused without a warrant.

Bailable: This offense is bailable, indicating that the accused can secure bail and be released from custody until the trial is completed.

Comparison: Section 145 of the Indian Penal Code[1384] (IPC) also deals with the offense of joining[1385] or continuing in unlawful assembly knowing it has been commanded to disperse: IPC Section 145: States that whoever joins or continues in an unlawful assembly, knowing that such unlawful assembly has been commanded in the manner prescribed by law to disperse, shall be punished with imprisonment of either description for a term which may extend to two years, or with a fine, or with both.

Key Differences: BNS 189(3): Similar to IPC Section 145 in defining the offense and specifying punishment. Both address the act of joining[1386] or continuing in an unlawful assembly knowing it has been commanded to disperse[1387]. IPC Section 145: Provides a longer maximum term of imprisonment (up to two years) compared to BNS 189(3) which specifies up to six months.

BNS Section 189(4)

Definition: Unlawful Assembly - Joining Unlawful Assembly Armed with Deadly Weapon Section 189(4) of the Bharatiya Nyaya Sanhita (BNS) 2023 addresses the offense of joining an unlawful assembly while being armed with a deadly weapon.

[1383] advocatetanmoy.com

[1384] blog.ipleaders.in

[1385] indiacode.nic.in

[1386] www.refworld.org

[1387] indiacode.nic.in

Illustration: If a person knowingly joins a group that has been declared an unlawful assembly and carries a weapon capable of causing death or serious injury, this act falls under BNS 189(4).

Example: Suppose an individual joins a protest that has been declared unlawful and brings a firearm or a knife. This would be categorized as joining[1388] an unlawful assembly armed with a deadly weapon under BNS 189(4).

Comment: This section emphasizes the severe potential harm and escalation of violence that can arise when individuals join unlawful assemblies while armed with deadly weapons. By penalizing such acts, it aims to maintain public safety and legal order.

Classification of Offence and Punishment Classification: This offense is classified as a serious criminal offense due to its potential to cause significant harm and escalate violence.

Punishment: The punishment for this offense under BNS 189(4) can be imprisonment[1389] of either description for a term which may extend to two years, or a fine, or both.

Cognizable or Non-Cognizable, Bailable or Non-Bailable: This offense is cognizable, meaning the police can arrest the accused without a warrant.

Bailable: This offense is bailable, indicating that the accused can secure bail and be released from custody until the trial is completed.

Comparison: Section 144 of the Indian Penal Code[1390] (IPC) also addresses the offense of joining[1391] an unlawful assembly armed with a deadly weapon: IPC Section 144: States that whoever[1392], being armed with any deadly weapon, or with anything which, used as a weapon of

---

1388 www.refworld.org

1389 advocatetanmoy.com

1390 blog.ipleaders.in

1391 www.refworld.org

1392 indiacode.nic.in

offense, is likely[1393] to cause death, is a member of an unlawful[1394] assembly, shall be punished with imprisonment of either description for a term which may extend to two years, or with a fine, or with both.

Key Differences: BNS 189(4): Similar to IPC Section 144 in defining the offense and specifying punishment. Both address the act of joining an unlawful assembly while armed[1395] with a deadly weapon. IPC Section 144: Part of the older legal framework, while BNS 189(4) is the updated version in the new Bharatiya Nyaya Sanhita.

BNS Definition 189(5)

Definition: Unlawful Assembly - Joining or Continuing in Unlawful Assembly After Command to Disperse Section 189(5) of the Bharatiya Nyaya Sanhita (BNS) 2023 addresses the offense of knowingly[1396] joining or continuing in an assembly of five or more persons after it has been commanded to disperse.

Illustration: If a group of five or more people is lawfully commanded to disperse by the authorities, and a person knowingly joins or continues to be part of that assembly, this act falls under BNS 189(5).

Example: Suppose a protest has been declared unlawful, and the police order the protesters to disperse. If an individual, aware of the command, still joins the protest or remains with the group, this would be categorized as joining[1397] or continuing in an unlawful assembly under BNS 189(5).

Comment: This section emphasizes the serious nature of joining or continuing in an unlawful assembly after being commanded to disperse, which can disrupt public order and safety. By penalizing such acts, it aims to maintain peace and legal order in society.

[1393] advocatetanmoy.com

[1394] indiacode.nic.in

[1395] www.refworld.org

[1396] indiacode.nic.in

[1397] www.refworld.org

Classification of Offence and Punishment Classification: This offense is classified as a serious criminal offense due to its potential to disrupt public order and safety.

Punishment: The punishment for this offense under BNS 189(5) can be imprisonment[1398] of either description for a term which may extend to six months, or a fine, or both.

Cognizable or Non-Cognizable, Bailable or Non-Bailable: This offense is cognizable, meaning the police can arrest the accused without a warrant.

Bailable: This offense is bailable, indicating that the accused can secure bail and be released from custody until the trial is completed.

Comparison: Section 151 of the Indian Penal Code[1399] (IPC) also addresses the offense of knowingly joining or continuing in an assembly of five or more persons after it has been commanded to disperse : IPC Section 151: States that whoever knowingly[1400] joins or continues in any assembly of five or more persons likely to cause a disturbance of the public peace, after such assembly has been lawfully commanded to disperse, shall be punished with imprisonment of either description for a term which may extend to six months, or with a fine, or with both.

Key Differences: BNS 189(5): Similar to IPC Section 151 in defining the offense and specifying punishment. Both address the act of knowingly joining or continuing in an assembly after it has been commanded to disperse. IPC Section 151: Part of the older legal framework, while BNS 189(5) is the updated version in the new Bharatiya Nyaya Sanhita.

BNS Section 189(6)

Definition: Unlawful Assembly - Hiring or Conniving at Hiring of Persons to Join Unlawful Assembly Section 189(6) of the Bharatiya

---

[1398] advocatetanmoy.com

[1399] blog.ipleaders.in

[1400] indiacode.nic.in

Nyaya Sanhita (BNS) 2023 addresses the offense of hiring or conniving[1401] at hiring persons to join an unlawful[1402] assembly.

Illustration: If an individual hires others to join an assembly that has been declared unlawful, or if they connive at such hiring, they are committing an offense under BNS 189(6).

Example: Suppose a person pays others to join a protest that has been declared unlawful, knowing the assembly's unlawful nature. This would be categorized as hiring or conniving[1403] at hiring under BNS 189(6).

Comment: This section emphasizes the potential escalation of unlawful activities and disruption of public order caused by hiring or conniving at hiring persons to join an unlawful[1404] assembly. By penalizing such acts, it aims to maintain public peace and safety.

Classification of Offence and Punishment Classification: This offense is classified as a serious criminal offense due to its potential to escalate unlawful activities and disrupt public order.

Punishment: The punishment[1405] for this offense under BNS 189(6) can be imprisonment of either description for a term which may extend to two years, or a fine, or both.

Cognizable or Non-Cognizable, Bailable or Non-Bailable: This offense is cognizable, meaning the police can arrest the accused without a warrant.

Bailable: This offense is bailable, indicating that the accused can secure bail and be released from custody until the trial is completed.

Comparison: With IPC Section 150Section 150 of the Indian Penal Code (IPC) also addresses the offense of hiring or conniving at hiring persons to join an unlawful assembly : IPC Section 150: States that whoever[1406]

[1401] www.refworld.org

[1402] www.lawfinderlive.com

[1403] www.refworld.org

[1404] www.lawfinderlive.com

[1405] advocatetanmoy.com

[1406] pdfcookie.com

hires or engages or employs, or promotes, or connives at the hiring, engagement[1407], or employment of any person to join or become a member of any unlawful assembly, shall be punishable as a member of such unlawful assembly, and for any offense which[1408] may be committed by any such person as a member of such unlawful assembly in pursuance of such hiring, engagement[1409], or employment, in the same manner as if he had been a member of such unlawful assembly, or himself had committed such offense.

Key Differences: BNS 189(6): Similar to IPC Section 150 in defining the offense and specifying punishment. Both address the act of hiring or conniving at hiring persons to join an unlawful[1410] assembly. IPC Section 150: Part of the older legal framework, while BNS 189(6) is the updated version in the new Bharatiya Nyaya Sanhita.

BNS Section 189(7)

Definition: Unlawful Assembly - Harbouring Persons Hired for an Unlawful Assembly Section 189(7) of the Bharatiya Nyaya Sanhita (BNS) 2023 addresses the offense of harboring persons who have been hired to join an unlawful assembly.

Illustration: If a person knowingly provides shelter to individuals who have been hired to join an unlawful assembly, this act falls under BNS 189(7).

Example: Suppose someone hires a group of individuals to join a protest that has been declared unlawful and then offers them a place to stay to avoid detection by authorities. This would be categorized as harboring persons hired for an unlawful assembly under BNS 189(7).

Comment: This section emphasizes the serious nature of harboring persons hired for an unlawful assembly, which can escalate unlawful

---

[1407] www.refworld.org

[1408] indiacode.nic.in

[1409] www.refworld.org

[1410] www.lawfinderlive.com

activities and disrupt public order. By penalizing such acts, it aims to maintain peace and safety in society.

Classification of Offence and Punishment Classification: This offense is classified as a serious criminal offense due to its potential to escalate unlawful activities and disrupt public order.

Punishment: The punishment[1411] for this offense under BNS 189(7) can be imprisonment of either description for a term which may extend to one year, or a fine, or both.

Cognizable or Non-Cognizable, Bailable or Non-Bailable: This offense is cognizable, meaning the police can arrest the accused without a warrant.

Bailable: This offense is bailable, indicating that the accused can secure bail and be released from custody until the trial is completed.

Comparison: Section 157 of the Indian Penal Code[1412] (IPC) also addresses the offense of harboring persons[1413] hired for an unlawful assembly : IPC Section 157: States that whoever harbors, receives, or assembles any persons knowing that such persons have been hired, engaged[1414], or employed, or are to be hired, engaged, or employed[1415], to join or become members of any unlawful assembly, shall be punished with imprisonment of either description for a term which may extend to six months, or with a fine, or with both.

Key Differences: BNS 189(7): Specifies a longer maximum term of imprisonment (up to one year) compared to IPC Section 157, which specifies up to six months. IPC Section 157: Part of the older legal framework, while BNS 189(7) is the updated version in the new Bharatiya Nyaya Sanhita.

[1411] advocatetanmoy.com

[1412] blog.ipleaders.in

[1413] indiacode.nic.in

[1414] www.refworld.org

[1415] ndiacode.nic.in

BNS Section 189(8,9)

Definition: Unlawful Assembly - Being Hired to Take Part in an Unlawful Assembly or Riot, or to Go Armed Section 189(8,9) of the Bharatiya Nyaya Sanhita (BNS) 2023 addresses the offenses of being hired[1416] to take part in an unlawful assembly or riot and being hired to go armed.

Illustration: If a person[1417] accepts payment to join an unlawful assembly or riot, or to carry a weapon during such an assembly, this act falls under BNS 189(8,9).

Example: Suppose an individual is paid to participate in a riot and to carry a weapon to intimidate others. This would be categorized as being hired[1418] to take part in an unlawful assembly or riot, or to go armed[1419] under BNS 189(8,9).

Comment: These sections highlight the severe implications of hiring individuals to partake in unlawful activities, which can escalate violence and disrupt public order. Penalizing these actions helps maintain societal peace and safety.

Classification of Offence and Punishment Classification: These offenses are classified as serious criminal offenses due to their potential to escalate violence and disrupt public order.

Punishment: The punishment[1420] for these offenses under BNS 189(8, 9) can be imprisonment of either description for a term which may extend to six months, or a fine, or both.

[1416] appforest.jharkhand.gov.in

[1417] www.ilo.org

[1418] appforest.jharkhand.gov.in

[1419] www.ilo.org

[1420] appforest.jharkhand.gov.in

Cognizable or Non-Cognizable, Bailable or Non-Bailable: These offenses are cognizable, meaning the police can arrest the accused without a warrant.

Bailable: These offenses are bailable, indicating that the accused can secure bail and be released from custody until the trial is completed.

Comparison: Section 158 of the Indian Penal Code (IPC) also addresses the offenses of being hired to take part in an unlawful assembly or riot, and being hired to go armed: IPC Section 158: States that whoever is hired to take part in an unlawful assembly or riot, or to go armed, knowing it to be unlawful or to be a riot, or knowing it to be likely to cause a breach of the peace, shall be punished with imprisonment of either description for a term which may extend to six months, or with a fine, or with both.

Key Differences: BNS 189(8, 9): Similar to IPC Section 158 in defining the offenses and specifying punishment. Both address the acts of being hired to take part in an unlawful assembly or riot, and being hired to go armed. IPC Section 158: Part of the older legal framework, while BNS 189(8, 9) is the updated version in the new Bharatiya Nyaya Sanhita.

BNS Section 190

Definition: Every Member of Unlawful Assembly Guilty of Offence Committed in Prosecution of Common Object Section 190 of the Bharatiya Nyaya Sanhita (BNS) 2023 states that every member[1421] of an unlawful assembly is guilty of an offense committed in prosecution[1422] of the common object of the assembly.

Illustration: If a group of individuals forms an unlawful assembly with the common intent to vandalize property, and one member of the group commits arson, all members of the assembly are held accountable for the act of arson under BNS 190.

Example: Suppose a crowd of protestors gathers illegally and decides to destroy public property. If one protestor sets a building on fire, every

---

[1421] hyderabadpolice.gov.in

[1422] appforest.jharkhand.gov.in

member of that unlawful assembly can be prosecuted for arson under BNS 190.

Comment: This section emphasizes the serious nature of holding all members of an unlawful assembly accountable for actions taken in pursuit of their common objective. It ensures collective responsibility and deterrence against participating in unlawful assemblies.

Classification of Offence and Punishment Classification: This offense is classified as a serious criminal offense because it holds all members of the assembly accountable for actions taken in pursuit of their common objective.

Punishment: The punishment for this offense under BNS 190 is the same as that for the principal offense committed by any member of the assembly in pursuit of the common objective. For example, if the principal offense is arson, the punishment is the same as that for arson.

Cognizable or Non-Cognizable, Bailable or Non-Bailable: This offense is cognizable, meaning the police can arrest any member of the unlawful assembly without a warrant.

Bailable: This offense is generally non-bailable, indicating that members cannot easily secure bail and must remain in custody until the trial is completed, depending on the severity of the principal offense.

Comparison: Section 149 of the Indian Penal Code (IPC) also deals with the liability of every [1423]member of an unlawful assembly for offenses committed in prosecution[1424] of the common object : IPC Section 149: States that if an offense is committed by any member of an unlawful assembly in prosecution of the common object of that assembly, or such as the members of that assembly knew to be likely to be committed in prosecution of that object, every person who, at the time of the committing of that offense, is a member of the same assembly, is guilty of that offense.

Key Differences: BNS 190: Similar to IPC Section 149 in defining the offense and specifying punishment. Both sections hold all members of an

---

[1423] hyderabadpolice.gov.in

[1424] appforest.jharkhand.gov.in

unlawful assembly accountable for offenses committed in pursuit of their common objective. IPC Section 149: Part of the older legal framework, while BNS 190 is the updated version in the new Bharatiya Nyaya Sanhita.

BNS Section 191(1)

Definition: Rioting - Offence Defined Section 191(1) of the Bharatiya Nyaya Sanhita (BNS) 2023 defines the offense of rioting.

Illustration: If a group of people forms an unlawful assembly and uses force or violence to achieve their common objective, every member of that assembly is guilty of rioting.

Example: Suppose a group of protesters gathers unlawfully and starts throwing stones at a police station to protest a decision. Every member of that group is guilty of rioting under BNS 191(1).

Comment: This section highlights the significant public disorder and harm[1425] that can result from rioting. It ensures that every member of an unlawful[1426] assembly using force or violence is held accountable for their actions.

Classification of Offence and Punishment Classification: This offense is classified as a serious criminal offense due to its potential to cause significant public disorder and harm.

Punishment: The punishment for rioting under BNS 191(1) can be imprisonment[1427] of either description for a term which may extend to two years, or a fine, or both.

Cognizable or Non-Cognizable, Bailable or Non-Bailable: This offense is cognizable, meaning the police can arrest the accused without a warrant.

Bailable: This offense is bailable, indicating that the accused can secure bail and be released from custody until the trial is completed.

[1425] www.academia.edu

[1426] hyderabadpolice.gov.in

[1427] appforest.jharkhand.gov.in

Comparison: With IPC Section 146Section 146 of the Indian Penal Code (IPC) also defines the offense of rioting: IPC Section 146: States that whenever force or violence is used by an unlawful assembly, or by any member thereof, in prosecution of the common object of such assembly, every member of such assembly is guilty of the offence of rioting.

Key Differences: BNS 191(1): Similar to IPC Section 146 in defining the offense and specifying punishment. Both sections hold every member[1428] of an unlawful assembly accountable for rioting. IPC Section 146: Part of the older legal framework, while BNS 191(1) is the updated version in the new Bharatiya Nyaya Sanhita.

BNS Section 191(2)

Definition: Rioting - Punishment for Rioting Section 191(2) of the Bharatiya Nyaya Sanhita (BNS) 2023 outlines the punishment for the offense of rioting.

Illustration: If a group of people forms an unlawful assembly and uses force or violence in pursuit of their common objective, every member of the group is liable for the offense of rioting and its punishment.

Example: Suppose a group of protestors gathers illegally and starts damaging public property. Every participant in this group can be punished for rioting under BNS 191(2).

Classification of Offence and Punishment Classification: This offense is classified as a serious criminal offense due to its potential to cause public disorder and harm.

Punishment: The punishment for rioting under BNS 191(2) can be imprisonment[1429] of either description for a term which may extend to two years, or a fine, or both.

Cognizable or Non-Cognizable, Bailable or Non-Bailable: This offense is cognizable, meaning the police can arrest the accused without a warrant.

[1428] hyderabadpolice.gov.in

[1429] appforest.jharkhand.gov.in

Bailable: This offense is bailable, indicating that the accused can secure bail and be released from custody until the trial is completed.

Comparison: Section 147 of the Indian Penal Code (IPC) also deals with the punishment for the offense of rioting: IPC Section 147: States that whoever is guilty of rioting shall be punished with imprisonment of either description for a term which may extend to two years, or with a fine, or with both.

Key Differences: BNS 191(2): Similar to IPC Section 147 in defining the punishment for rioting. Both sections hold participants of an unlawful assembly accountable for the offense of rioting. IPC Section 147: Part of the older legal framework, while BNS 191(2) is the updated version in the new Bharatiya Nyaya Sanhita.

BNS Section 191(3)

Definition: Rioting - Being Armed with Deadly Weapon Section 191(3) of the Bharatiya Nyaya Sanhita (BNS) 2023 addresses the offense of participating in a riot while being armed with a deadly weapon.

Illustration: If a person participates in a riot and carries a weapon capable of causing death or serious injury, this act falls under BNS 191(3).

Example: Suppose an individual joins a riot and carries a firearm or a large knife, making them and the assembly more dangerous. This would be categorized as rioting while being armed with a deadly weapon under BNS 191(3).

Comment: This section emphasizes the serious nature of rioting, which can cause public disorder and harm. It ensures that every participant in an unlawful assembly using force or violence is held accountable.

Classification of Offence and Punishment Classification: This offense is classified as a very serious criminal offense due to its potential to cause significant harm and escalate violence.

Punishment: The punishment for this offense under BNS 191(3) can be imprisonment of either description for a term which may extend to three years, or a fine, or both.

Cognizable or Non-Cognizable, Bailable or Non-Bailable: This offense is cognizable, meaning the police can arrest the accused without a warrant.

Bailable: This offense is non-bailable, indicating that the accused cannot secure bail and must remain in custody until the trial is completed.

Comparison: Section 148 of the Indian Penal Code (IPC) also deals with the offense of rioting while being armed with a deadly weapon: IPC Section 148: States that whoever is guilty of rioting, being armed with a deadly weapon or with anything which, used as a weapon of offense, is likely to cause death, shall be punished with imprisonment of either description for a term which may extend to three years, or with a fine, or with both.

Key Differences: BNS 191(3): Similar to IPC Section 148 in defining the offense and specifying punishment. Both address the act of participating in a riot while being armed with a deadly weapon. IPC Section 148: Part of the older legal framework, while BNS 191(3) is the updated version in the new Bharatiya Nyaya Sanhita.

BNS Section 192

Definition: Wantonly Giving Provocation with Intent to Cause Riot Section 192 of the Bharatiya Nyaya Sanhita (BNS) 2023 addresses the offense of wantonly giving provocation with the intent to cause a riot if rioting be committed if not committed.

Illustration: If a person intentionally provokes another person or group with the knowledge or intention that such provocation will likely lead to a riot, this act falls under BNS 192.

Example: Suppose an individual makes inflammatory remarks about a religious group, knowing that it could incite violence and lead to a riot. If a riot occurs as a result, the individual can be charged under BNS 192.

Comment: This section emphasizes the serious nature of provoking actions that can lead to riots, which can incite public disorder and violence. It ensures that individuals who engage in such acts face stringent penalties.

Classification of Offence and Punishment Classification: This offense is classified as a serious criminal offense due to its potential to incite public disorder and violence.

Punishment: The punishment for this offense under BNS 192 can be imprisonment of either description for a term which may extend to one year, or a fine, or both if a riot occurs. If no riot occurs, the punishment can be imprisonment of either description for a term which may extend to six months, or a fine, or both.

Cognizable or Non-Cognizable, Bailable or Non-Bailable: This offense is cognizable, meaning the police can arrest the accused without a warrant.

Bailable: This offense is bailable, indicating that the accused can secure bail and be released from custody until the trial is completed.

Comparison: Section 153 of the Indian Penal Code (IPC) also addresses the offense of wantonly giving provocation with the intent to cause a riot: IPC Section 153: States that whoever malignantly, or with the knowledge[1430] that his words or actions are likely to cause a breach of the peace[1431], by doing anything which is illegal, gives provocation to any person intending or knowing it to be likely that such provocation[1432] will cause the offense of rioting to be committed, shall be punished with imprisonment of either description for a term which may extend to one year, or with a fine, or with both.

Key Differences: BNS 192: Similar to IPC Section 153 in defining the offense and specifying punishment. Both address the act of wantonly giving provocation with the intent to cause a riot. IPC Section 153: Part of the older legal framework, while BNS 192 is the updated version in the new Bharatiya Nyaya Sanhita.

[1430] hyderabadpolice.gov.in

[1431] www.hrw.org

[1432] appforest.jharkhand.gov.in

BNS Section 193(1)

Definition: Liability of Owner, Occupier, etc., of Land on Which an Unlawful Assembly or Riot Takes Place Section 193(1) of the Bharatiya Nyaya Sanhita (BNS) 2023 addresses the liability of the owner, occupier, or any person having an interest in the land where an unlawful[1433] assembly or riot takes place.

Illustration: If a protest turns into a riot on a privately owned property, the owner or occupier of that property is responsible for taking action to prevent the riot and reporting it to the authorities.

Example: Suppose a group of people gathers on a piece of land and starts rioting. The owner of the land, knowing about the riot, fails to inform the police or take steps to stop it. The owner can be held liable under BNS 193(1).

Comment: This section emphasizes the responsibility of property owners or occupiers to take measures to prevent unlawful assemblies or riots on their land and to report them to the authorities. It ensures accountability and encourages proactive action to maintain public order.

Classification of Offence and Punishment Classification: This offense is classified as a minor criminal offense due to its focus on the responsibility of property owners rather than direct participation in the riot.

Punishment: The punishment for this offense under BNS 193(1) can be a fine not exceeding[1434] one thousand rupees.

Cognizable or Non-Cognizable, Bailable or Non-Bailable: This offense is non-cognizable, meaning the police cannot arrest the accused without a warrant.

Bailable: This offense is bailable, indicating that the accused can secure bail and be released from custody until the trial is completed.

[1433] appforest.jharkhand.gov.in

[1434] pdfcookie.com

Comparison: Section 154 of the Indian Penal Code[1435] (IPC) also addresses the liability of the owner or occupier of land on which an unlawful assembly or riot takes place : IPC Section 154: States that whenever any unlawful assembly or riot takes place, the owner or occupier of the land upon which such unlawful assembly is held, or such riot is committed, and any person having or claiming an interest in such land, shall be punishable with a fine not exceeding[1436] one thousand rupees, if he or his agent or manager, knowing that such offense is being or has been committed, or having reason to believe it is likely to be committed, do not give the earliest notice thereof in his or their power to the officer[1437] in charge at the nearest police station, and do not, in the case of his or their having reason to believe that it was about to be committed, use all lawful means in his or their power to prevent it and, in the event of its taking place, do not use all lawful means in his or their power to disperse it.

Key Differences: BNS 193(1): Similar to IPC Section 154 in defining the liability and specifying punishment. Both sections hold property owners accountable for failing to prevent or report unlawful assemblies or riots. IPC Section 154: Part of the older legal framework, while BNS 193(1) is the updated version in the new Bharatiya Nyaya Sanhita.

BNS Section 193(2)

Definition: Liability of Person for Whose Benefit Riot is Committed Section 193(2) of the Bharatiya Nyaya Sanhita (BNS) 2023 addresses the liability of a person for whose benefit a riot is committed.

Illustration: If a riot occurs on a piece of land and the owner of the land benefits from it, the owner can be held liable under BNS 193(2).

Example: Suppose a group of people commits a riot to protest against a decision that affects a particular piece of land. If the owner of the land

---

[1435] appforest.jharkhand.gov.in

[1436] pdfcookie.com

[1437] prsindia.org

benefits from the outcome of the riot, they can be held liable under BNS 193(2).

Comment: This section emphasizes the responsibility of individuals who benefit from riots, ensuring accountability for actions that escalate public disorder and violence.

Classification of Offence and Punishment Classification: This offense is classified as a minor criminal offense due to its focus on holding individuals accountable for benefiting from a riot.

Punishment: The punishment for this offense under BNS 193(2) can be a fine not exceeding one [1438]thousand rupees.

Cognizable or Non-Cognizable, Bailable or Non-Bailable: This offense is non-cognizable, meaning the police cannot arrest the accused without a warrant.

Bailable: This offense is bailable, indicating that the accused can secure bail and be released from custody until the trial is completed.

Comparison: Section 155 of the Indian Penal Code[1439] (IPC) also addresses the liability of a person for whose benefit a riot is committed: IPC Section 155: It states that if a riot is committed for the benefit of someone who owns or occupies the land where it occurs, claims any interest in the land, is involved in a dispute that led to the riot, or has accepted or benefited from it, they will be fined. If their agent or manager has reason to believe that the riot is likely to occur or that the unlawful assembly that caused it is likely to occur, they must use all legal means within their power to stop the riot or assembly from occurring.

Key Differences: BNS 193(2): Similar to IPC Section 155 in defining the liability and specifying punishment. Both sections hold individuals accountable for benefiting from a riot. IPC Section 155: Part of the older legal framework, while BNS 193(2) is the updated version in the new Bharatiya Nyaya Sanhita.

[1438] pdfcookie.com

[1439] appforest.jharkhand.gov.in

BNS Section 193(3)

Definition: Liability of Agent of Owner or Occupier for Whose Benefit Riot is Committed Section 193(3) of the Bharatiya Nyaya Sanhita (BNS) 2023 addresses the liability of the agent of an owner or occupier for whose benefit a riot is committed.

Illustration: If an agent of a landowner benefits from a riot that takes place on the owner's land and fails to take steps to prevent or report it, the agent is liable under BNS 193(3).

Example: Suppose an agent managing a property knows that a riot is likely to occur for the benefit of the property owner and does nothing to prevent or report it. The agent can be held accountable under BNS 193(3).

Comment: This section emphasizes the responsibility of agents to prevent or report riots committed for the benefit of the owner or occupier of the land. It ensures accountability and encourages proactive action to maintain public order.

Classification of Offence and Punishment Classification: This offense is classified as a minor criminal offense due to its focus on the responsibility of agents rather than direct participation in the riot.

Punishment: The punishment for this offense under BNS 193(3) can be a fine not exceeding one[1440] thousand rupees.

Cognizable or Non-Cognizable, Bailable or Non-Bailable: This offense is non-cognizable, meaning the police cannot arrest the accused without a warrant

Bailable: This offense is bailable, indicating that the accused can secure bail and be released from custody until the trial is completed.

Comparison: Section 156 of the Indian Penal Code[1441] (IPC) also addresses the liability of the agent of an owner or occupier for whose benefit a riot is committed: IPC Section 156: States that whenever a riot is

---

[1440] pdfcookie.com

[1441] appforest.jharkhand.gov.in

committed for the benefit or on behalf of any person who is the owner or occupier of any land respecting which such riot takes place or who claims any interest in such land, or in the subject of any dispute which gave rise to the riot, or who has accepted or derived any benefit therefrom, such agent or manager shall be punishable with a fine not exceeding one thousand rupees, if he, knowing that such offense is being or has been committed, or having reason to believe that it is likely to be committed, does not give the earliest notice thereof in his power[1442] to the officer in charge at the nearest police station, and does not use all lawful means in his power to prevent it, and for suppressing and dispersing the same.

Key Differences: BNS 193(3): Similar to IPC Section 156 in defining the liability and specifying punishment. Both sections hold agents accountable for failing to prevent or report riots committed for the benefit of the owner or occupier. IPC Section 156: Part of the older legal framework, while BNS 193(3) is the updated version in the new Bharatiya Nyaya Sanhita.

BNS Section194 (1)

Definition: Affray – Defined Section 194(1) of the Bharatiya Nyaya Sanhita (BNS) 2023 defines the offense of affray.

Illustration: When two or more persons[1443] engage in a fight in a public place, disturbing the public peace, they are said to commit an affray.

Example: If two individuals start fighting in a crowded market, causing panic and disruption, they are committing an affray under BNS 194(1).

Comment: This section underscores the impact of fighting in public places, which can disturb public peace. It ensures that individuals who engage in such acts face appropriate penalties to maintain order.

Classification of Offence and Punishment Classification: This offense is classified as a minor criminal offense due to its impact on public order.

[1442] prsindia.org

[1443] bprd.nic.in

Punishment: The punishment for committing an affray under BNS 194(1) can be imprisonment of either description for a term which may extend to one month, or a fine which may extend to one thousand rupees, or both.

Cognizable or Non-Cognizable, Bailable or Non-Bailable: This offense is cognizable, meaning the police can arrest the accused without a warrant.

Bailable: This offense is bailable, indicating that the accused can secure bail and be released from custody until the trial is completed.

Comparison: Section 159 of the Indian Penal Code[1444] (IPC) also addresses the offense of affray: IPC Section 159: States that whoever[1445] commits an affray shall be punished with imprisonment of either description for a term which may extend to one month, or with a fine, or with both.

Key Differences: BNS 194(1): Similar to IPC Section 159 in defining the offense and specifying punishment. Both sections address the act of disturbing public peace through fighting in a public place. IPC Section 159: Part of the older legal framework, while BNS 194(1) is the updated version in the new Bharatiya Nyaya Sanhita.

BNS Section 194(2

Definition: Punishment for Affray Section 194(2) of the Bharatiya Nyaya Sanhita (BNS) 2023 outlines the punishment for the offense of affray.

Illustration: If two or more persons engage in a fight in a public place, causing a disturbance to public peace, they are liable to punishment under BNS 194(2).

Example: Suppose two individuals start a fistfight in a busy shopping area, causing panic and disruption. They would be punished for affray under BNS 194(2).

[1444] bhu.ac.in

[1445] bprd.nic.in

Comment: This section underscores the impact of fighting in public places, which can disturb public peace. It ensures that individuals who engage in such acts face appropriate penalties to maintain order.

Classification of Offence and Punishment Classification: This offense is classified as a minor criminal offense due to its impact on public order.

Punishment: The punishment for committing an affray under BNS 194(2) can be imprisonment of either description for a term which may extend to one month, or a fine, or both.

Cognizable or Non-Cognizable, Bailable or Non-Bailable: This offense is cognizable, meaning the police can arrest the accused without a warrant.

Bailable: This offense is bailable, indicating that the accused can secure bail and be released from custody until the trial is completed.

Comparison: Section 160 of the Indian Penal Code[1446] (IPC) also addresses the punishment for the offense of affray: IPC Section 160: States that whoever commits an affray shall[1447] be punished with imprisonment of either description for a term which may extend to one month, or with a fine which may extend to one hundred rupees[1448], or with both.

Key Differences: BNS 194(2): Similar to IPC Section 160 in defining the punishment for affray. Both sections address the act[1449] of disturbing public peace through fighting in a public place and outline similar penalties. IPC Section 160: Part of the older legal framework, while BNS 194(2) is the updated version in the new Bharatiya Nyaya Sanhita.

[1446] www.indiacode.nic.in

[1447] bprd.nic.in

[1448] odishapolicecidcb.gov.in

[1449] bprd.nic.in

BNS Section 195(1)

Definition: Assaulting or Obstructing Public Servant When Suppressing Riot, etc. Section 195(1) of the Bharatiya Nyaya Sanhita (BNS) 2023 addresses the offense of assaulting or obstructing a public servant while they are trying to disperse an unlawful assembly, suppress a riot, or handle an affray.

Illustration: If a person physically attacks or hinders a police officer[1450] who is trying to control a riot, they are committing an offense under BNS 195(1).

Example: Suppose during a protest, a demonstrator throws a stone at a police officer attempting to restore order. This act would fall under BNS 195(1).

Comment: This section emphasizes the serious nature of assaulting or obstructing public servants, which can undermine public order and safety. It ensures that individuals who engage in such acts face stringent penalties.

Classification of Offence and Punishment Classification: This offense is classified as a serious criminal offense due to its potential to undermine public order and safety.

Punishment: The punishment[1451] for this offense under BNS 195(1) can be imprisonment of either description for a term which may extend to three years, or a fine which shall not be less than twenty-five thousand rupees, or both.

Cognizable or Non-Cognizable, Bailable or Non-Bailable: This offense is cognizable, meaning the police can arrest the accused without a warrant.

Bailable: This offense is bailable, indicating that the accused can secure bail and be released from custody until the trial is completed.

[1450] www.livelaw.in

[1451] bprd.nic.in

Comparison: Section 152 of the Indian Penal Code [1452](IPC) also addresses the offense of assaulting or obstructing a public servant while they are trying to disperse[1453] an unlawful assembly, suppress a riot, or handle an affray: IPC Section 152: States that whoever assaults or threatens to assault, or obstructs or attempts to obstruct, any public servant in the discharge of his duty as such public servant, in endeavoring to disperse an unlawful assembly, or to suppress a riot or affray, or uses[1454], or threatens, or attempts to use criminal force to such public servant, shall be punished with imprisonment of either description for a term which may extend to three years, or with a fine, or with both.

Key Differences: BNS 195(1): Similar to IPC Section 152 in defining the offense and specifying punishment. Both sections address the act of interfering with public servants performing their duties.IPC Section 152: Part of the older legal framework, while BNS 195(1) is the updated version in the new Bharatiya Nyaya Sanhita.

BNS Section 195(2)

Definition: Assaulting or Obstructing Public Servant When Suppressing Riot, etc. Section 195(2) of the Bharatiya Nyaya Sanhita (BNS) 2023 addresses the offense of assaulting or obstructing a public servant while they are trying to disperse an unlawful assembly, suppress a riot, or handle an affray.

Illustration: If a person physically attacks or hinders a police officer[1455] who is trying to control a riot, they are committing an offense under BNS 195(2).

Example: Suppose during a protest, a demonstrator throws a stone at a police officer attempting to restore order. This act would fall under BNS 195(2).

1452 bhu.ac.in

1453 bprd.nic.in

1454 odishapolicecidcb.gov.in

1455 www.livelaw.in

Comment: This section emphasizes the serious nature of assaulting or obstructing public servants, which can undermine public order and safety. It ensures that individuals who engage in such acts face stringent penalties.

Classification of Offence and Punishment Classification: This offense is classified as a serious criminal offense due to its potential to undermine public order and safety.

Punishment: The punishment[1456] for this offense under BNS 195(2) can be imprisonment of either description for a term which may extend to three years, or a fine which shall not be less than twenty-five thousand rupees, or both.

Cognizable or Non-Cognizable, Bailable or Non-Bailable: This offense is cognizable, meaning the police can arrest the accused without a warrant.

Bailable: This offense is bailable, indicating that the accused can secure bail and be released from custody until the trial is completed.

Comparison: Section 152 of the Indian Penal Code (IPC) also addresses the offense of assaulting or obstructing a public servant while they are trying to disperse an unlawful assembly, suppress a riot[1457], or handle an affray: IPC Section 152: States that whoever assaults or threatens to assault, or obstructs or attempts to obstruct, any public servant in the discharge of his duty as such public servant, in endeavoring to disperse an unlawful assembly, or to suppress a riot or affray, or uses, or threatens, or attempts to use criminal force to such public servant, shall be punished with imprisonment of either description for a term which may extend to three years, or with a fine, or with both.

Key Differences: BNS 195(2): Similar to IPC Section 152 in defining the offense and specifying punishment. Both sections address the act of interfering with public servants performing their duties. IPC Section 152: Part of the older legal framework, while BNS 195(2) is the updated version in the new Bharatiya Nyaya Sanhita.

[1456] bprd.nic.in

[1457] odishapolicecidcb.gov.in

BNS Section 196

Definition: Promoting Enmity Between Different Groups Section 196 of the Bharatiya Nyaya Sanhita (BNS) 2023 addresses the offense of promoting[1458] enmity between different groups on grounds of religion, race, place of birth, residence, language, etc., ad doing acts prejudicial to the maintenance of harmony.

Illustration: If someone makes a speech or posts content online that incites hatred or enmity between different religious or racial groups, they are committing an offense under BNS 196.

Example: Suppose a person spreads false information about a particular community, claiming they are responsible for a crime, and this leads to violence or unrest. This act falls under BNS 196.

Comment: This section emphasizes the serious nature of promoting enmity between different groups, which can disrupt public order and harmony. It ensures that individuals who engage in such acts face stringent penalties.

Classification of Offence and Punishment Classification: This offense is classified as a serious criminal offense due to its potential to disrupt public order and harmony.

Punishment: The punishment for committing[1459] this offense under BNS 196 can be imprisonment of either description for a term which may extend to three years, or a fine which shall not be less than twenty-five thousand rupees, or both.

Cognizable or Non-Cognizable, Bailable or Non-Bailable: This offense is cognizable, meaning the police can arrest the accused without a warrant.

Bailable: This offense is bailable, indicating that the accused can secure bail and be released from custody until the trial is completed.

[1458] r2pasiapacific.org

[1459] bprd.nic.in

Comparison: Section 153A of the Indian Penal Code[1460] (IPC) also addresses the offense of promoting[1461] enmity between different groups: IPC Section 153A: States that whoever[1462], by words, either spoken or written, or by signs or by visible representations, promotes or attempts to promote[1463], on grounds of religion, race, place of birth, residence, language, caste or community or any other ground whatsoever, disharmony or feelings of enmity, hatred or ill-will between different religious, racial, language or regional groups or castes or communities, shall be punished with imprisonment of either description for a term which may extend to three years, or with a fine, or with both.

Key Differences: BNS 196: Similar to IPC Section 153A in defining the offense and specifying punishment. Both sections address the act of promoting enmity and disrupting harmony between different groups. IPC Section 153A: Part of the older legal framework, while BNS 196 is the updated version in the new Bharatiya Nyaya Sanhita.

BNS Section 197

Definition: Imputations, Assertions Prejudicial to National Integration Section 197 of the Bharatiya Nyaya Sanhita (BNS) 2023 addresses the offense of making imputations or assertions that are prejudicial to national integration.

Illustration: If someone spreads false information that a particular religious group is disloyal to the Constitution of India[1464], they are committing an offense under BNS 197.

[1460] odishapolicecidcb.gov.in

[1461] r2pasiapacific.org

[1462] ijrcs.org

[1463] bprd.nic.in

[1464] qdoc.tips

Example: Suppose a person publishes a statement claiming that members[1465] of a specific community cannot uphold the sovereignty and integrity of India. This act falls under BNS 197.

Comment: This section emphasizes the serious nature of making imputations or assertions that disrupt national unity and harmony. It ensures that individuals who engage in such acts face stringent penalties.

Classification of Offence and Punishment Classification: This offense is classified as a serious criminal offense due to its potential to disrupt national unity and harmony.

Punishment: The punishment for committing this offense under BNS 197 can be imprisonment of either description for a term which may extend to three years, or a fine which shall not be less than twenty-five thousand rupees, or both.

Cognizable or Non-Cognizable, Bailable or Non-Bailable: This offense is cognizable, meaning the police can arrest the accused without a warrant.

Bailable: This offense is bailable, indicating that the accused can secure bail and be released from custody until the trial is completed.

Comparison: Section 153B of the Indian Penal Code[1466] (IPC) also addresses the offense of making imputations or assertions prejudicial to national integration : IPC Section 153B: States that whoever[1467], by words either spoken or written or by signs or by visible representations or otherwise, makes or publishes any imputation that any class of persons cannot, by reason of their being members of any religious, racial, language or regional group or caste or community, bear true faith and allegiance to the Constitution of India as by law established or uphold the sovereignty and integrity of India[1468], or asserts, counsels, advises, propagates or publishes that any class of persons shall, by reason of their being members of any religious, racial, language or regional group or caste or community,

---

[1465] bprd.nic.in

[1466] bhu.ac.in

[1467] bprd.nic.in

[1468] ijrcs.org

be denied, or deprived of their rights as citizens of India, or makes or publishes any assertion[1469], counsel, plea or appeal concerning the obligation of any class of persons, by reason of their being members of any religious, racial, language or regional group or caste or community, and such assertion, counsel, plea or appeal causes or is likely to cause disharmony or feelings of enmity, hatred or ill-will between different religious, racial, language or regional groups or castes or communities, shall be punished with imprisonment of either description for a term which may extend to three years, or with a fine, or with both.

Key Differences: BNS 197: Similar to IPC Section 153B in defining the offense and specifying punishment. Both sections address the act of making statements that disrupt national harmony. IPC Section 153B: Part of the older legal framework, while BNS 197 is the updated version in the new Bharatiya Nyaya Sanhita.

BNS Section 197(1D)

Definition: Making or Publishing False or Misleading Information Section 197 (1 D) of the Bharatiya Nyaya Sanhita (BNS) 2023 addresses the offense of making or publishing false or misleading information that jeopardizes the sovereignty, unity, integrity, or security of India.

Illustration: If someone spreads a false rumor that a particular[1470] community is planning a coup to overthrow the government, they are committing an offense under BNS 197 (1 D).

Example: Suppose a person posts a fake news article claiming that a specific religious group is plotting to disrupt national elections. This act falls under BNS 197 (1 D).

Comment: This section emphasizes the serious nature of spreading false or misleading information that can harm national security and public order. It ensures that individuals who engage in such acts face stringent penalties.

[1469] bprd.nic.in

[1470] bprd.nic.in

Classification of Offence and Punishment Classification: This offense is classified as a serious criminal offense due to its potential to cause significant harm to national security and public order.

Punishment: The punishment for committing this offense under BNS 197 (1 D) can be imprisonment[1471] of either description for a term which may extend to three years, or a fine which shall not be less than twenty-five thousand rupees, or both.

Cognizable or Non-Cognizable, Bailable or Non-Bailable: This offense is cognizable, meaning the police can arrest the accused without a warrant.

Bailable: This offense is bailable, indicating that the accused can secure bail and be released from custody until the trial is completed.

Comparison: New Section addresses the offense of making or publishing false or misleading information that jeopardizes the sovereignty, unity, integrity, or security of India : IPC Section 153B: States that whoever[1472], by words, either spoken or written, or by signs or by visible representations, promotes or attempts to promote[1473], on grounds of religion, race, place of birth, residence, language, caste or community or any other ground whatsoever, disharmony or feelings of enmity, hatred or ill-will between different religious, racial, language or regional groups or castes or communities, shall be punished with imprisonment of either description for a term which may extend to three years, or with a fine, or with both.

Key Differences: BNS 197 (1 D): Similar to IPC Section 153B in defining the offense and specifying punishment. Both sections address the act of spreading false or misleading information that disrupts national harmony. IPC Section 153B: Part of the older legal framework, while BNS 197 (1 D) is the updated version in the new Bharatiya Nyaya Sanhita.

[1471] bprd.nic.in

[1472] ijrcs.org

[1473] bprd.nic.in

CHAPTER-XII; OF OFFENCES BY OR RELATING TO PUBLIC SERVANTS

BNS Section 198

Definition: Public Servant Disobeying Law, with Intent to Cause Injury to Any Person Section 198 of the Bharatiya Nyaya Sanhita (BNS) 2023 addresses the offense of a public servant knowingly disobeying any direction of the law[1474] with the intent to cause injury[1475] to any person.

Illustration: If a police officer, who is legally required to file a complaint, deliberately refuses to do so, knowing that this refusal will cause harm to the complainant, they are committing an offense under BNS 198.

Example: Suppose a government official is directed by law to provide essential services to a community but intentionally neglects this duty, causing harm to the community members. This act falls under BNS 198.

Comment: This section emphasizes the serious nature of a public servant disobeying the law with the intent to cause harm. It highlights the potential to undermine public trust and the need for accountability.

Classification of Offence and Punishment Classification: This offense is classified as a serious criminal offense due to its potential to cause significant harm to individuals and undermine public trust in public servants.

Punishment: The punishment for committing this offense under BNS 198 can be simple imprisonment for a term which may extend to one year, or a fine, or both.

[1474] bhu.ac.in

[1475] bprd.nic.in

Cognizable or Non-Cognizable, Bailable or Non-Bailable: This offense is cognizable, meaning the police can arrest the accused without a warrant.

Bailable: This offense is bailable, indicating that the accused can secure bail and be released from custody until the trial is completed.

Comparison: Section 166 of the Indian Penal Code (IPC) also addresses the offense of a public servant disobeying the law with the intent to cause injury[1476] to any person : IPC Section 166: States that whoever, being a public servant, knowingly disobeys any direction of the law as to the way in which he is to conduct himself as such public servant, intending to cause, or knowing it to be likely that he will by such disobedience, cause injury to any person, shall be punished with simple imprisonment for a term which may extend to one year, or with a fine, or with both.

Key Differences: BNS 198: Similar to IPC Section 166 in defining the offense and specifying punishment. Both sections address the act of a public servant disobeying the law with the intent to cause harm. IPC Section 166: Part of the older legal framework, while BNS 198 is the updated version in the new Bharatiya Nyaya Sanhita.

BNS Section 199

Definition: Public Servant Disobeying Direction Under Law Section 199 of the Bharatiya Nyaya Sanhita (BNS) 2023 addresses the offense of a public servant knowingly disobeying any direction of the law.

Illustration: If a police officer, who is legally required to file a complaint, deliberately refuses to do so, knowing that this refusal will cause harm to the complainant, they are committing an offense under BNS 199.

Example: Suppose a government official is directed by law to provide essential services to a community but intentionally neglects this duty, causing harm to the community members. This act falls under BNS 199.

[1476] bprd.nic.in

Comment: This section emphasizes the serious nature of a public servant disobeying the law. It highlights the potential to cause significant harm and undermine public trust, ensuring accountability.

Classification of Offence and Punishment Classification: This offense is classified as a serious criminal offense due to its potential to cause significant harm to individuals and undermine public trust in public servants.

Punishment: The punishment for committing this offense under BNS 199 can be rigorous[1477] imprisonment for a term which may extend to one year, or a fine, or both.

Cognizable or Non-Cognizable, Bailable or Non-Bailable: This offense is cognizable, meaning the police can arrest the accused without a warrant.

Bailable: This offense is bailable, indicating that the accused can secure bail and be released from custody until the trial is completed.

Comparison: Section 166A of the Indian Penal Code (IPC) also addresses the offense of a public servant disobeying the law: IPC Section 166A: States that whoever[1478], being a public servant, knowingly disobeys any direction of the law which prohibits him from requiring the attendance at any place of any person for the purpose of investigation into an offence or any other matter[1479], or knowingly disobeys, to the prejudice of any person, any other direction of the law regulating the manner in which he shall conduct such investigation, or fails to record any information given to him under sub-section (1) of section 154 of the Code of Criminal Procedure[1480], 1973, in relation to cognizable offence punishable under section 326A, section 326B, section 354, section 354B, section 370, section 370A, section 376, section 376A, section 376AB[1481], section 376B, section 376C, section 376D, section 376DA, section 376DB, section 376E or section

---

[1477] bhu.ac.in

[1478] bprd.nic.in

[1479] devgan.in

[1480] bhu.ac.in

[1481] devgan.in

509, shall be punished with simple imprisonment for a term which may extend to one year, or with a fine, or with both.

Key Differences: BNS 199: Similar to IPC Section 166A in defining the offense and specifying punishment. Both sections address the act of a public servant disobeying the law. IPC Section 166A: Part of the older legal framework, while BNS 199 is the updated version in the new Bharatiya Nyaya Sanhita.

BNS Section 200

Definition: Punishment for Non-Treatment of Victim Section 200 of the Bharatiya Nyaya Sanhita (BNS) 2023 addresses the offense of non-treatment of a victim by a hospital or medical facility.

Illustration: If a hospital administrator, knowing that a patient requires urgent medical care, deliberately refuses to provide treatment, they are committing an offense under BNS 200.

Example: Suppose a person is brought to a hospital with a severe injury, and the hospital staff, despite having the necessary resources, refuses to treat the patient due to negligence or bias. This act falls under BNS 200.

Comment: This section emphasizes the serious nature of refusing medical care to those in need, highlighting the potential harm such actions can cause. It ensures that individuals responsible for such refusals face appropriate penalties.

Classification of Offence and Punishment Classification: This offense is classified as a serious criminal offense due to its potential to cause significant harm to individuals in need of medical care.

Punishment: The punishment for committing this offense under BNS 200 can be imprisonment[1482] for a term which may extend to one year, or a fine, or both.

[1482] en.wikipedia.org

Cognizable or Non-Cognizable, Bailable or Non-Bailable: This offense is non-cognizable, meaning the police cannot arrest the accused without a warrant.

Bailable: This offense is bailable, indicating that the accused can secure bail and be released from custody until the trial is completed.

Comparison: Section 166B of the Indian Penal Code (IPC) also addresses the offense of non-treatment of a victim: IPC Section 166B: States that whoever, being in charge of a hospital, public or private, whether run by the Central Government, the State Government, local bodies or any other person, contravenes the provisions of section 357C of the Code of Criminal Procedure, 1973, shall be punished with imprisonment for a term which may extend to one year, or with a fine, or with both.

Key Differences: BNS 200: Similar to IPC Section 166B in defining the offense and specifying punishment. Both sections address the act of non-treatment of a victim by a hospital. IPC Section 166B: Part of the older legal framework, while BNS 200 is the updated version in the new Bharatiya Nyaya Sanhita.

BNS Section 201

Definition: Public Servant Framing an Incorrect Document with Intent to Cause Injury Section 201 of the Bharatiya Nyaya Sanhita (BNS) 2023 addresses the offense of a public servant[1483] knowingly framing an incorrect document with the intent[1484] to cause injury to any person.

Illustration: If a government clerk, responsible for preparing official documents, deliberately alters the content of a document to falsely implicate someone in a crime, they are committing an offense under BNS 201.

[1483] moam.info

[1484] moam.info

Example: Suppose a public servant, tasked with preparing a report, intentionally includes false information that leads to the wrongful arrest of an individual. This act falls under BNS 201.

Comment: This section emphasizes the serious nature of a public servant framing an incorrect document with the intent to cause harm. It highlights the potential to cause significant harm to individuals and undermine public trust in public servants[1485].

Classification of Offence and Punishment Classification: This offense is classified as a serious criminal offense due to its potential to cause significant harm to individuals and undermine public trust in public servants.

Punishment: The punishment for committing this offense under BNS 201 can be imprisonment of either description for a term which may extend to three years, or a fine, or both.

Cognizable or Non-Cognizable, Bailable or Non-Bailable: This offense is cognizable, meaning the police can arrest the accused without a warrant.

Bailable: This offense is bailable, indicating that the accused can secure bail and be released from custody until the trial is completed.

Comparison: Section 167 of the Indian Penal Code [1486](IPC) also addresses the offense of a public servant framing an incorrect document with intent to cause injury: IPC Section 167: States that whoever[1487], being a public servant, and being[1488], as such public servant, charged with the preparation or translation of any document or electronic record, frames, prepares or translates that document or electronic record in a manner which he knows or believes to be incorrect, intending thereby to cause or knowing it to be likely that he may thereby cause injury to any person,

---

[1485] moam.info

[1486] en.wikipedia.org

[1487] www.bareactslive.com

[1488] moam.info

shall be punished with imprisonment[1489] of either description for a term which may extend to three years, or with a fine, or with both.

Key Differences: BNS 201: Similar to IPC Section 167 in defining the offense and specifying punishment. Both sections address the act of a public servant framing incorrect documents with the intent to cause harm. IPC Section 167: Part of the older legal framework, while BNS 201 is the updated version in the new Bharatiya Nyaya Sanhita.

BNS Section 202

Definition: Public Servant Unlawfully Engaging in Trade Section 202 of the Bharatiya Nyaya Sanhita (BNS) 2023 addresses the offense of a public servant[1490] unlawfully engaging in trade.

Illustration: If a government official, who is legally prohibited from engaging in private trade, starts a business and conducts trade activities, they are committing an offense under BNS 202.

Example: Suppose a public servant, who is not allowed to have private business interests, opens a shop and sells goods for personal profit. This act falls under BNS 202.

Comment: This section emphasizes the serious nature of a public servant engaging in trade unlawfully, which can undermine public trust and the integrity of public service.

Classification of Offence and Punishment Classification: This offense is classified as a serious criminal offense due to its potential to undermine public trust and the integrity of public service.

Punishment: The punishment for committing this offense under BNS 202 can be simple[1491] imprisonment for a term which may extend to one year, or a fine, or both.

[1489] en.wikipedia.org

[1490] moam.info

[1491] en.wikipedia.org

Cognizable or Non-Cognizable, Bailable or Non-Bailable: This offense is non-cognizable, meaning the police cannot arrest the accused without a warrant.

Bailable: This offense is bailable, indicating that the accused can secure bail and be released from custody until the trial is completed.

Comparison: Section 168 of the Indian Penal Code[1492] (IPC) also addresses the offense of a public servant[1493] unlawfully engaging in trade: IPC Section 168: States that whoever, being a public servant, and being legally bound as such public servant not to engage in trade, engages in trade, shall be punished with simple imprisonment for a term which may extend to one year, or with a fine, or with both.

Key Differences: BNS 202: Similar to IPC Section 168 in defining the offense and specifying punishment. Both sections address the act of a public servant unlawfully engaging in trade. IPC Section 168: Part of the older legal framework, while BNS 202 is the updated version in the new Bharatiya Nyaya Sanhita.

BNS Section 203

Definition: Public Servant Unlawfully Buying or Bidding for Property Section 203 of the Bharatiya Nyaya Sanhita (BNS) 2023 addresses the offense of a public servant unlawfully buying or bidding for property.

Illustration: If a government official, who is legally prohibited from purchasing property, buys land in their own name or in the name of another person, they are committing an offense under BNS 203.

Example: Suppose a public servant, who is not allowed to engage in private property transactions, participates in an auction and wins a bid for a piece of property. This act falls under BNS 203.

[1492] pdfcookie.com

[1493] moam.info

Comment: This section underscores the significance of upholding public trust and the integrity of public service by prohibiting public servants from engaging in unlawful property transactions.

Classification of Offence and Punishment Classification: This offense is classified as a serious criminal offense due to its potential to undermine public trust and the integrity of public service.

Punishment: The punishment for committing this offense under BNS 203 can be simple imprisonment for a term which may extend to two years, or a fine, or both. Additionally, the property[1494], if purchased, shall be confiscated.

Cognizable or Non-Cognizable, Bailable or Non-Bailable: This offense is non-cognizable, meaning the police cannot arrest the accused without a warrant.

Bailable: This offense is bailable, indicating that the accused can secure bail and be released from custody until the trial is completed.

Comparison: Section 169 of the Indian Penal Code [1495](IPC) also addresses the offense of a public servant unlawfully buying or bidding for property: IPC Section 169: States that whoever, being a public servant, and being legally[1496] bound as such public servant, not to purchase or bid for certain property, purchases or bids for that property, either in his own name or in the name of another, or jointly, or in shares with others, shall be punished with simple imprisonment for a term which may extend to two years, or with a fine, or with both.

Key Differences: BNS 203: Similar to IPC Section 169 in defining the offense and specifying punishment. Both sections address the act of a public servant unlawfully buying or bidding for property. IPC Section 169: Part of the older legal framework, while BNS 203 is the updated version in the new Bharatiya Nyaya Sanhita.

[1494] moam.info

[1495] pdfcookie.com

[1496] moam.info

BNS Section 204

Definition: Personating a Public Servant Section 204 of the Bharatiya Nyaya Sanhita (BNS) 2023 addresses the offense of personating a public servant.

Illustration: If a person falsely presents themselves as a police officer and uses this false identity to influence or deceive others, they are committing an offense under BNS 204.

Example: Suppose an individual pretends to be a government official to gain access to a restricted area or to intimidate someone. This act falls under BNS 204.

Comment: This section emphasizes the serious nature of personating a public servant, which can undermine public trust and authority. It ensures that individuals who engage in such acts face appropriate penalties.

Classification of Offence and Punishment Classification: This offense is classified as a serious criminal offense due to its potential to undermine public trust and authority.

Punishment: The punishment for committing this offense under BNS 204 can be imprisonment of either description for a term which may extend to two years, or a fine, or both.

Cognizable or Non-Cognizable, Bailable or Non-Bailable: This offense is cognizable, meaning the police can arrest the accused without a warrant.

Bailable: This offense is bailable, indicating that the accused can secure bail and be released from custody until the trial is completed.

Comparison: Section 170 of the Indian Penal Code (IPC) also addresses the offense of personating a public servant: IPC Section 170: States that whoever pretends to hold any office as a public servant, knowing that he does not hold such office, or falsely personates[1497] any other person holding such office, and in such assumed character does or attempts to do any act under color of such office, shall be punished with imprisonment of

---

[1497] moam.info

either description for a term which may extend to two years, or with a fine, or with both.

Key Differences: BNS 204: Similar to IPC Section 170 in defining the offense and specifying punishment. Both sections address the act of personating a public servant. IPC Section 170: Part of the older legal framework, while BNS 204 is the updated version in the new Bharatiya Nyaya Sanhita.

BNS Section 205

Definition: Wearing Garb or Carrying Token Used by Public Servant with Fraudulent Intent Section 205 of the Bharatiya Nyaya Sanhita (BNS) 2023 addresses the offense of wearing garb[1498] or carrying tokens used by a public servant with the intent to commit fraud.

Illustration: If a person, not being a police officer, wears a police uniform to gain access to restricted areas or to intimidate others, they are committing an offense under BNS 205.

Example: Suppose an individual dresses up as a government official and uses a fake ID badge to enter a secure government building. This act falls under BNS 205.

Comment: This section underscores the serious nature of wearing garb or carrying tokens used by a public servant with fraudulent intent, which can undermine public trust and authority.

Classification of Offence and Punishment Classification: This offense is classified as a serious criminal offense due to its potential to undermine public trust and authority.

Punishment: The punishment for committing this offense under BNS 205 can be imprisonment of either description for a term which may extend to two years, or a fine, or both.

Cognizable or Non-Cognizable, Bailable or Non-Bailable: This offense is cognizable, meaning the police can arrest the accused without a warrant.

[1498] moam.info

Bailable: This offense is bailable, indicating that the accused can secure bail and be released from custody until the trial is completed.

Comparison: Section 171 of the Indian Penal Code (IPC) also addresses the offense of wearing garb or carrying tokens used by a public servant with the intent to commit fraud : IPC Section 171: States that whoever, not being a public servant, wears any garb[1499] or carries any token resembling any garb or token used by such a public servant with the intention that it may be believed that he is such a public servant, shall be punished with imprisonment of either description for a term which may extend to three months, or with a fine, or with both.

Key Differences: BNS 205: Provides for a harsher punishment (up to two years) compared to IPC Section 171 (up to three months). IPC Section 171: Part of the older legal framework, while BNS 205 is the updated version in the new Bharatiya Nyaya Sanhita.

[1499] indiankanoon.org

CHAPTER-XIII: OF CONTEMPTS OF THE LAWFUL AUTHORITY OF PUBLIC SERVANTS

BNS Section 206

Definition: Absconding to Avoid Service of Summons or Other Proceeding Description: Section 206 of the Bharatiya Nyaya Sanhita (BNS) 2023 addresses the act of absconding to avoid being served with a summons, notice, or order issued by a public servant[1500] legally competent to do so.

Illustration: If a person learns that a court has issued a summons and deliberately leaves their residence or hides to avoid receiving it, they are committing an offense under BNS 206.

Example: Suppose an individual receives a notice to appear in court and decides to leave town without informing the authorities to evade the summons. This act falls under BNS 206.

Comment: This section aims to ensure that individuals cannot evade legal responsibilities by avoiding the service of legal documents, thereby obstructing the legal process.

Classification of Offence and Punishment: Classification: This offense is classified as a serious criminal offense due to its potential to undermine the legal process.

Punishment: The punishment for committing this offense under BNS 206 can be: Simple Imprisonment: Up to one month. Fine: Up to five thousand rupees. Both: Imprisonment and fine can be imposed together. If the summons or notice is to attend in person[1501] or produce a document in

---

[1500] moam.info

[1501] moam.info

court, the punishment can be: Simple Imprisonment: Up to six months. Fine: Up to ten thousand rupees. Both: Imprisonment and fine can be imposed together.

Cognizable or Non-Cognizable, Bailable or Non-Bailable: This offense is cognizable, meaning the police can arrest the accused without a warrant.

Bailable: This offense is bailable, indicating that the accused can secure bail and be released from custody until the trial is completed.

Comparison: IPC Section 172: Deals with the offense of absconding to avoid service of summons or other legal processes, similar to BNS 206.

Key Differences: BNS 206: Provides for a harsher punishment (up to six months imprisonment and a higher fine) compared to IPC Section 172 (up to one month imprisonment and a lower fine). IPC Section 172: Part of the older legal framework, while BNS 206 is the updated version in the new Bharatiya Nyaya Sanhita.

BNS Section 207

Definition: Preventing Service of Summons or Other Proceeding, or Preventing Publication There of Section 207 of the Bharatiya Nyaya Sanhita (BNS) 2023 addresses the offense of preventing the service of any summons, notice, or order from a public servant, or preventing the lawful publication of any such document.

Illustration: If a person tears up a summons issued by a court before it can be delivered to the intended recipient, they are committing an offense under BNS 207.

Example: Suppose an individual intercepts and destroys a legal notice meant for their neighbor, to prevent them from responding to a court proceeding. This act falls under BNS 207.

Comment: This section emphasizes the serious nature of preventing the service of legal documents, which can obstruct justice and undermine the legal process. It ensures that individuals who engage in such acts face appropriate penalties.

Classification of Offence and Punishment Classification: This offense is classified as a serious criminal offense due to its potential to obstruct justice and undermine the legal process.

Punishment: The punishment for committing this offense under BNS 207 can be simple [1502]imprisonment for a term which may extend to six months, or a fine which may[1503] extend to five thousand rupees, or both.

Cognizable or Non-Cognizable, Bailable or Non-Bailable: This offense is non-cognizable, meaning the police cannot arrest the accused without a warrant.

Bailable: This offense is bailable, indicating that the accused can secure bail and be released from custody until the trial is completed.

Comparison: Section 173 of the Indian Penal Code (IPC) also addresses the offense of preventing[1504] the service of summons or other proceeding, or preventing the publication thereof : IPC Section 173: States that whoever in any manner intentionally prevents the serving on himself, or on any other person, of any summons, notice or order proceeding from any public servant legally competent, as such public servant, to issue such summons, notice or order, or intentionally prevents the lawful affixing to any place of any such summons, notice or order, or intentionally removes any such summons, notice or order from any place to which it is lawfully affixed, or intentionally prevents the lawful making of any proclamation, under the authority of any public servant legally competent, as such public servant, to direct such proclamation to be made, shall be punished with simple imprisonment for a term which may extend to six months, or with a fine which may extend to five hundred rupees, or with both.

Key Differences: BNS 207: Provides for a higher fine (up to five thousand rupees). IPC 173: Limits the fine to a maximum of five hundred rupees.

[1502] en.wikipedia.org

[1503] moam.info

[1504] moam.info

BNS Section 208

Definition: Non-Attendance in Obedience to an Order from Public Servant Section 208 of the Bharatiya Nyaya Sanhita (BNS) 2023 addresses the offense of failing to attend in obedience to a summons, notice, order, or proclamation proceeding from any public servant legally competent to issue it.

Illustration: If a person receives a lawful order to appear before a public servant and intentionally fails to attend without any valid excuse, they are committing an offense under BNS 208.

Example: Suppose an individual is summoned to appear before a court as a witness and deliberately ignores the summons. This act falls under BNS 208.

Comment: This section emphasizes the importance of complying with lawful orders from public servants, as non-attendance can obstruct justice and undermine the authority of public officials.

Classification of Offence and Punishment Classification: This offense is classified as a minor criminal offense due to its potential to obstruct justice and undermine the authority of public servants.

Punishment: The punishment for committing this offense under BNS 208 can be simple [1505]imprisonment for a term which may extend to one month, or a fine which may extend to one thousand rupees, or both. If the order requires attendance in person or by agent, or to produce a document or an electronic record in a Court, the punishment can be simple imprisonment for a term which may extend to six months, or a fine which may extend to five thousand rupees, or both.

Cognizable or Non-Cognizable, Bailable or Non-Bailable: This offense is non-cognizable, meaning the police cannot arrest the accused without a warrant.

[1505] en.wikipedia.org

Bailable: This offense is bailable, indicating that the accused can secure bail and be released from custody until the trial is completed.

Comparison: Section 174 of the Indian Penal Code (IPC) also addresses the offense of failing to attend in obedience[1506] to a summons, notice, order, or proclamation: IPC Section 174: States that whoever, being legally bound to attend in person or by an agent at a certain place and time in obedience to a summons, notice, order, or proclamation proceeding from any public servant legally competent, as such public servant, to issue the same, intentionally omits to attend at that place or time, or departs from the place where he is bound to attend before the expiration of the time for which he is bound to attend, shall be punished with simple imprisonment for a term which may extend to one month, or with a fine which may extend to five hundred rupees, or with both. If the order requires attendance in person or by agent, or to produce a document or an electronic record in a Court, the punishment can be simple imprisonment for a term which may extend to six months, or with a fine which may extend to one thousand rupees, or with both.

Key Differences: BNS 208: Provides for a higher fine (up to one thousand rupees and up to five thousand rupees for specific orders). IPC 174: Limits the fine to a maximum of five hundred rupees and one thousand rupees for specific orders.

BNS Section 209

Definition: Non-appearance in Response to a Proclamation under Section 84 of Bharatiya Nagarik Suraksha Sanhita, 2023 Section 209 of the Bharatiya Nyaya Sanhita (BNS) 2023 addresses the act of failing to appear[1507] at the specified place and time as required by a proclamation published under Section 84 of the Bharatiya Nagarik Suraksha Sanhita, 2023.

[1506] moam.info

[1507] www.bareactslive.com

Illustration: If a person is summoned to appear in court and deliberately avoids showing up at the specified time and place, they are committing an offense under this section.

Example: Suppose an individual receives a court summons and decides to ignore it, not showing up at the court on the designated date. This act falls under BNS 209.

Comment: This section ensures that individuals cannot evade legal responsibilities by ignoring court summonses, thereby obstructing the legal process and undermining the rule of law.

Classification of Offence and Punishment of Classification: Yes, police can arrest without a warrant.

Bailable: Yes, the accused can be released on bail.

Punishment: Simple Imprisonment: Up to three years2.Fine: Applicable. Community Service: May be imposed. Severe Punishment: If a declaration is made pronouncing the individual as a proclaimed[1508] offender, the punishment can extend to seven years of imprisonment and a fine.

Comparison: IPC Section 174A: Deals with non-appearance in response to a proclamation under Section 82 of the Code of Criminal Procedure[1509], 1973.

Key Differences: BNS 209: Updated legal framework with provisions for community service and potentially harsher penalties. IPC Section 174A: Part of the older legal framework, with similar penalties but without provisions for community service.

BNS Section 210

Definition: Omission to Produce Document or Electronic Record to Public Servant by Person, Legally Bound to Produce It Section 210 of the Bharatiya Nyaya Sanhita (BNS) 2023 addresses the offense of

---

1508 www.bareactslive.com

1509 odishapolicecidcb.gov.in

failing to produce[1510] a document or electronic record to a public servant by a person who is legally bound to produce it.

Illustration: If a person is required by law to present certain documents to a government official for an investigation and intentionally fails to do so, they are committing an offense under BNS 210.

Example: Suppose an individual, legally required to submit financial records to a tax officer, deliberately withholds these documents. This act falls under BNS 210.

Comment: This section emphasizes the importance of complying with legal requirements to produce documents or electronic records. Failing to do so can obstruct justice and undermine administrative processes.

Classification of Offence and Punishment Classification: This offense is classified as a minor criminal offense due to its potential to obstruct justice and undermine administrative processes.

Punishment: The punishment for committing this offense under BNS 210 can be simple [1511]imprisonment for a term which may extend to one month, or a fine which may extend to one thousand rupees, or both. If the document or electronic record is required to be produced in a Court, the punishment can be simple imprisonment for a term which may extend to six months, or a fine which may extend to five thousand rupees, or both.

Cognizable or Non-Cognizable, Bailable or Non-Bailable: This offense is non-cognizable, meaning the police cannot arrest the accused without a warrant.

Bailable: This offense is bailable, indicating that the accused can secure bail and be released from custody until the trial is completed.

Comparison: Section 175 of the Indian Penal Code (IPC) also addresses the offense of failing to produce a document or electronic record to a public servant : IPC Section 175: States that whoever[1512], being legally

---

[1510] www.bareactslive.com

[1511] en.wikipedia.org

[1512] odishapolicecidcb.gov.in

bound to produce or deliver up any document to any public servant, as such, intentionally omits so to produce or deliver up the same, shall be punished with simple imprisonment for a term which may extend to one month, or with a fine which may extend to five hundred rupees, or with both. If the document is required to be produced in a court, the punishment can be simple imprisonment for a term which may extend to six months, or with a fine which may extend to one thousand rupees, or with both.

Key Differences: BNS 210: Provides for a higher fine (up to one thousand rupees for general cases and up to five thousand rupees for court cases). IPC 175: Limits the fine to a maximum of five hundred rupees for general cases and one thousand rupees for court cases.

BNS Section 211

Definition: Omission to Give Notice or Information to Public Servant by Person Legally Bound to Give It Section 211 of the Bharatiya Nyaya Sanhita (BNS) 2023 addresses the offense of failing to give notice or information to a public servant by a person who is legally bound to give it.

Illustration: If a person is legally required to report a notifiable disease to health authorities and intentionally fails to do so, they are committing an offense under BNS 211.

Example: Suppose a factory owner is legally obligated to inform the authorities about a hazardous chemical spill but deliberately withholds this information. This act falls under BNS 211.

Comment: This section emphasizes the importance of complying with legal requirements to provide notice or information to public servants. Failing to do so can cause significant harm to public health and safety.

Classification of Offence and Punishment Classification: This offense is classified as a serious criminal offense due to its potential to cause significant harm to public health and safety.

Punishment: The punishment for committing this offense under BNS 211 can be simple imprisonment[1513] for a term which may extend to six months, or a fine which may[1514] extend to one thousand rupees, or both. If the information is required for investigation of an offense or for conduct of public business, the punishment can be simple imprisonment for a term which may extend to one year, or a fine which may extend to five thousand rupees, or both.

Cognizable or Non-Cognizable, Bailable or Non-Bailable: This offense is non-cognizable, meaning the police cannot arrest the accused without a warrant.

Bailable: This offense is bailable, indicating that the accused can secure bail and be released from custody until the trial is completed.

Comparison: Section 176 of the Indian Penal Code[1515] (IPC) also addresses the offense of failing to give notice[1516] or information to a public servant: IPC Section 176: States that whoever, being legally bound to give any notice or information to any public servant, as such, intentionally omits to give such notice or information, shall[1517] be punished with simple imprisonment for a term which may extend to one month[1518], or with a fine which may extend to five hundred rupees, or with both. If the notice or information is required for investigation of an offense or for the conduct of public business, the punishment can be simple imprisonment[1519] for a term which may extend to six months, or with a fine which may extend to one thousand rupees, or with both.

Key Differences: BNS 211: Provides for a higher fine (up to one thousand rupees for general cases and up to five thousand rupees for specific cases).

[1513] en.wikipedia.org

[1514] odishapolicecidcb.gov.in

[1515] en.wikipedia.org

[1516] odishapolicecidcb.gov.in

[1517] en.wikipedia.org

[1518] odishapolicecidcb.gov.in

[1519] en.wikipedia.org

IPC 176: Limits the fine to a maximum of five hundred rupees for general cases and one thousand rupees for specific cases.

BNS Section 212

Definition: Furnishing False Information Section 212 of the Bharatiya Nyaya Sanhita (BNS) 2023 addresses the offense of furnishing false information to a public servant.

Illustration: If a person knowingly provides incorrect details in a legal document submitted to a government office, they are committing an offense under BNS 212.

Example: Suppose an individual submits a false address on a government form to avoid tax obligations. This act falls under BNS 212.

Comment: This section underscores the serious nature of providing false information, which can mislead public servants and disrupt legal and administrative processes. Ensuring accurate information is crucial to upholding the integrity of these processes.

Classification of Offence and Punishment Classification: This offense is classified as a serious criminal offense due to its potential to mislead public servants and disrupt legal and administrative processes.

Punishment: The punishment for committing this offense under BNS 212 can be simple imprisonment[1520] for a term which may extend to six months, or a fine[1521] which may extend to ten thousand rupees, or both. If the false information is given in connection with the commission of an offense or to obstruct justice, the punishment can be simple imprisonment for a term which may extend to two years, or a fine which may extend to fifty thousand rupees, or both.

Cognizable or Non-Cognizable, Bailable or Non-Bailable: This offense is non-cognizable, meaning the police cannot arrest the accused without a warrant.

[1520] en.wikipedia.org

[1521] odishapolicecidcb.gov.in

Bailable: This offense is bailable, indicating that the accused can secure bail and be released from custody until the trial is completed.

Comparison: Section 177 of the Indian Penal Code[1522] (IPC) also addresses the offense of furnishing[1523] false information : IPC Section 177: States that whoever, being legally bound to furnish information on any subject to any public servant, as such, furnishes, as true, information on the subject which he knows or has reason to believe to be false, shall be punished with simple imprisonment for a term which may extend to six months, or with a fine which may extend to one thousand rupees, or with both. If the false information is given to obstruct justice or in relation to the commission of an offense, the punishment can be simple imprisonment for a term which may extend to two years, or with a fine, or with both.

Key Differences: BNS 212: Provides for higher fines (up to ten thousand rupees for general cases and up to fifty thousand rupees for specific cases). IPC 177: Limits the fine to a maximum of one thousand rupees for general cases and does not specify a higher fine for specific cases.

BNS Section 213

Definition: Refusing Oath or Affirmation When Duly Required[1524] by Public Servant to Make It Section 213 of the Bharatiya Nyaya Sanhita (BNS) 2023 addresses the offense of refusing to take an oath or make an affirmation when lawfully required to do so by a public servant.

Illustration: If a witness in a court case is required to take an oath before giving testimony and they refuse, they are committing an offense under BNS 213.

Example: Suppose a person is called to testify in a legal proceeding and is asked to swear an oath to tell the truth, but they refuse to do so. This act falls under BNS 213.

[1522] en.wikipedia.org

[1523] odishapolicecidcb.gov.in

[1524] Ministry of Home Affairs. (2024). The Bharatiya Nyaya Sanhita, 2023. Retrieved from https://www.mha.gov.in/sites/default/files/250883_english_01042024.pdf

Comment: This section emphasizes the importance of taking an oath or affirmation in legal proceedings. Refusing to do so can disrupt the legal process and undermine the integrity of the proceedings.

Classification of Offence and Punishment Classification: This offense is classified as a minor criminal offense due to its potential to disrupt legal processes.

Punishment: The punishment for committing this offense under BNS 213 can be simple imprisonment[1525] for a term which may extend to six months, or a fine[1526] which may extend to five thousand rupees, or both.

Cognizable or Non-Cognizable, Bailable or Non-Bailable: This offense is non-cognizable, meaning the police cannot arrest the accused without a warrant.

Bailable: This offense is bailable, indicating that the accused can secure bail and be released from custody until the trial is completed.

Comparison: With IPC Section 178Section 178 of the Indian Penal Code[1527] (IPC) also addresses the offense of refusing to take an oath[1528] or make an affirmation : IPC Section 178: States that whoever refuses to bind himself by an oath or affirmation to state the truth when required by a public servant or a Court of Justice, shall[1529] be punished with simple imprisonment for a term which may extend to six months, or with a fine[1530] which may extend to one thousand rupees, or with both.

Key Differences: BNS 213: Provides for a higher fine (up to five thousand rupees) compared to IPC Section 178 (up to one thousand rupees). IPC 178: Limits the fine to a maximum of one thousand rupees.

[1525] en.wikipedia.org

[1526] odishapolicecidcb.gov.in

[1527] en.wikipedia.org

[1528] odishapolicecidcb.gov.in

[1529] en.wikipedia.org

[1530] odishapolicecidcb.gov.in

BNS Section 214

Definition: Refusing to Answer Public Servant Authorized to Question Section 214 of the Bharatiya Nyaya Sanhita (BNS) 2023 addresses the offense of refusing to answer a public servant who is legally authorized to question.

Illustration: If a person, during a police investigation, is asked specific questions by an officer and they refuse to provide answers without any lawful excuse, they are committing an offense under BNS 214.

Example: Suppose an individual is being questioned by a customs officer regarding the contents of their luggage and they intentionally refuse to respond. This act falls under BNS 214.

Comment: This section highlights the importance of cooperating with public servants during investigations and other official processes. Refusing to answer questions can hinder investigations and disrupt legal procedures.

Classification of Offence and Punishment Classification: This offense is classified as a minor criminal offense due to its potential to hinder official investigations and legal processes.

Punishment: The punishment for committing this offense under BNS 214 can be simple imprisonment[1531] for a term which may extend to six months, or a fine[1532] which may extend to five thousand rupees, or both.

Cognizable or Non-Cognizable, Bailable or Non-Bailable: This offense is non-cognizable, meaning the police cannot arrest the accused without a warrant.

Bailable: This offense is bailable, indicating that the accused can secure bail and be released from custody until the trial is completed.

[1531] en.wikipedia.org

[1532] odishapolicecidcb.gov.in

Comparison: Section 179 of the Indian Penal Code[1533] (IPC) also addresses the offense of refusing to answer a public servant authorized to question: IPC Section 179: States that whoever[1534], being legally bound to state the truth on any subject to any public servant, refuses to answer any question demanded of him touching the subject, shall[1535] be punished with simple imprisonment for a term which may extend to six months, or with a fine[1536] which may extend to one thousand rupees, or with both.

Key Differences: BNS 214: Provides for a higher fine (up to five thousand rupees) compared to IPC Section 179 (up to one thousand rupees). IPC 179: Limits the fine to a maximum of one thousand rupees.

BNS Section 215

Definition: Refusing to Sign Statement Section 215 of the Bharatiya Nyaya Sanhita (BNS) 2023 addresses the offense of refusing to sign a statement when legally required to do so by a public servant.

Illustration: If a person is legally required to sign a statement after giving a deposition to a public servant and they refuse, they are committing an offense under BNS 215.

Example: Suppose an individual provides a statement to the police as part of an investigation but refuses to sign the document afterward. This act falls under BNS 215.

Comment: This section emphasizes the importance of signing statements when legally required. Refusing to do so can hinder legal processes and affect the integrity of investigations.

Classification of Offence and Punishment Classification: This offense is classified as a minor criminal offense due to its potential to hinder legal processes.

[1533] en.wikipedia.org

[1534] odishapolicecidcb.gov.in

[1535] en.wikipedia.org

[1536] odishapolicecidcb.gov.in

Punishment: The punishment for committing this offense under BNS 215 can be simple imprisonment[1537] for a term which may extend to three months, or a fine[1538] which may extend to five thousand rupees, or both.

Cognizable or Non-Cognizable, Bailable or Non-Bailable: This offense is non-cognizable, meaning the police cannot arrest the accused without a warrant.

Bailable: This offense is bailable, indicating that the accused can secure bail and be released from custody until the trial is completed.

Comparison: Section 180 of the Indian Penal Code[1539] (IPC) also addresses the offense of refusing[1540] to sign a statement: IPC Section 180: States that whoever refuses to sign any statement made by him, when required to do so by a public servant legally competent to require that he shall sign that statement, shall be punished with simple imprisonment for a term which may extend to three months, or with a fine which may extend to five hundred rupees, or with both.

Key Differences: BNS 215: Provides for a higher fine (up to five thousand rupees) compared to IPC Section 180 (up to five hundred rupees). IPC 180: Limits the fine to a maximum of five hundred rupees.

BNS Section 216:

Definition: False Statement on Oath or Affirmation to Public Servant or Person Authorized[1541] to Administer an Oath or Affirmation Section 216 of the Bharatiya Nyaya Sanhita (BNS) 2023 addresses the offense of making a false statement on oath or affirmation to a public

---

[1537] en.wikipedia.org

[1538] odishapolicecidcb.gov.in

[1539] en.wikipedia.org

[1540] odishapolicecidcb.gov.in

[1541] Ministry of Home Affairs. (2024). The Bharatiya Nyaya Sanhita, 2023. Retrieved from https://www.mha.gov.in/sites/default/files/250883_english_01042024.pdf

servant or any person authorized to administer an oath or affirmation.

Illustration: If a person, while giving a sworn statement to a public servant, knowingly provides false information, they are committing an offense under BNS 216.

Example: Suppose an individual swears under oath in court that they[1542] did not witness a crime, knowing this statement to be false. This act falls under BNS 216.

Comment: This section emphasizes the serious nature of making false statements[1543] under oath, which can mislead public servants and disrupt legal processes. Ensuring truthful statements is crucial to the integrity of these processes.

Classification of Offence and Punishment Classification: This offense is classified as a serious criminal offense due to its potential to mislead public servants and disrupt legal processes.

Punishment: The punishment for committing this offense under BNS 216 can be imprisonment[1544] of either description for a term which may extend to three years, or a fine, or both.

Cognizable or Non-Cognizable, Bailable or Non-Bailable: This offense is cognizable, meaning the police can arrest the accused without a warrant.

Bailable: This offense is bailable, indicating that the accused can secure bail and be released from custody until the trial is completed.

Comparison: Section 181 of the Indian Penal Code (IPC) also addresses the offense of making a false statement[1545] on oath or affirmation to a public servant[1546] or person authorized to administer an oath or

---

[1542] austlii.edu.au

[1543] thesaurus.yourdictionary.com

[1544] en.wikipedia.org

[1545] odishapolicecidcb.gov.in

[1546] www.wipo.int

affirmation: IPC Section 181: States that whoever[1547], being legally bound by an oath or affirmation to state the truth on any subject to any public servant or other person authorized by law to administer such oath or affirmation, makes, to such public servant or other person as aforesaid, a statement which is false, and which he either knows or believes to be false or does not believe to be true, shall be punished with imprisonment of either description for a term which may extend to three years, or with a fine, or with both.

Key Differences: BNS 216: Updated version in the Bharatiya Nyaya Sanhita. IPC 181: Part of the older Indian Penal Code.

BNS Section 217

Definition: False Information, with Intent to Cause Public Servant to Use His Lawful Power to the Injury of Another Person Section 217 of the Bharatiya Nyaya Sanhita (BNS) 2023 addresses the offense of providing false information with the intent to cause a public servant to use their lawful power to the injury of another person.

Illustration: If a person falsely reports to a police officer that their neighbor is involved in illegal activities, intending for the officer to take action against the neighbor, they are committing an offense under BNS 217.

Example: Suppose an individual fabricates evidence and presents it to a tax officer, aiming to get a rival investigated for tax evasion. This act falls under BNS 217.

Comment: This section highlights the potential harm and misuse of public resources that can result[1548] from providing false information to public servants. Ensuring truthful information is crucial to maintaining justice and public trust.

[1547] odishapolicecidcb.gov.in

[1548] www.loc.gov

Classification of Offence and Punishment Classification: This offense is classified as a serious criminal offense due to its potential to harm individuals and misuse public resources.

Punishment: The punishment for committing this offense under BNS 217 can be imprisonment[1549] of either description for a term which may extend to six months, or a fine which may extend to ten thousand rupees, or both. If the false information is given with intent to cause a public servant to use their lawful power to the injury or annoyance of any person, the punishment can be imprisonment of either description for a term which may extend to two years, or a fine which may extend to twenty thousand rupees, or both.

Cognizable or Non-Cognizable, Bailable or Non-Bailable: This offense is cognizable, meaning the police can arrest the accused without a warrant.

Bailable: This offense is bailable, indicating that the accused can secure bail and be released from custody until the trial is completed.

Comparison: Section 182 of the Indian Penal Code[1550] (IPC) also addresses the offense of providing false information with intent to cause a public servant to use their lawful[1551] power to the injury of another person : IPC Section 182: States that whoever gives to any public servant any information which he knows or believes to be false, intending thereby to cause, or knowing it to be likely that he will thereby cause, such public servant to do or omit anything which such public servant ought not to do or omit if the true state of facts respecting which such information is given were known by him, shall be punished with imprisonment of either description for a term which may extend to six months, or with a fine which may extend to one thousand rupees, or with both.

Key Differences: BNS 217: Provides for higher fines (up to ten thousand rupees for general cases and up to twenty thousand rupees for specific cases). IPC 182: Limits the fine to a maximum of one thousand rupees.

1549 en.wikipedia.org

1550 en.wikipedia.org

1551 odishapolicecidcb.gov.in

BNS Section 218

Definition: Resistance to the Taking of Property by the Lawful Authority of a Public Servant[1552] Section 218 of the Bharatiya Nyaya Sanhita (BNS) 2023 addresses the offense of resisting the taking of property by a public servant who is lawfully authorized to take it.

Illustration: If a public servant is lawfully seizing property under a court order and the owner physically prevents the public servant from carrying out the seizure, they are committing an offense under BNS 218.

Example: Suppose a person obstructs a tax officer who is attempting to confiscate assets due to unpaid taxes, acting under the authority of a court order. This act falls under BNS 218.

Comment: This section emphasizes the importance of complying with lawful actions taken by public servants. Resisting such actions can obstruct justice and disrupt lawful administrative processes.

Classification of Offence and Punishment Classification: This offense is classified as a serious criminal offense due to its potential to obstruct justice and lawful administrative processes.

Punishment: The punishment for committing this offense under BNS 218 can be imprisonment[1553] of either description for a term which may extend to six months, or a fine[1554] which may extend to five thousand rupees, or both.

Cognizable or Non-Cognizable, Bailable or Non-Bailable: This offense is non-cognizable, meaning the police cannot arrest the accused without a warrant.

Bailable: This offense is bailable, indicating that the accused can secure bail and be released from custody until the trial is completed.

[1552] Ministry of Home Affairs. (2024). The Bharatiya Nyaya Sanhita, 2023. Retrieved from https://www.mha.gov.in/sites/default/files/250883_english_01042024.pdf

[1553] en.wikipedia.org

[1554] odishapolicecidcb.gov.in

Comparison: Section 183 of the Indian Penal Code[1555] (IPC) also addresses the offense of resisting the taking of property by a public servant: IPC Section 183: States that whoever[1556] offers any resistance to the taking of any property by the lawful authority of any public servant, knowing or having reason to believe that the said public servant is acting in the exercise of his lawful powers, shall be punished with imprisonment of either description for a term which may extend to six months, or with a fine which may extend to five hundred rupees, or with both.

Key Differences: BNS 218: Provides for a higher fine (up to five thousand rupees) compared to IPC Section 183 (up to five hundred rupees). IPC 183: Limits the fine to a maximum of five hundred rupees.

BNS Section 219

Definition: Obstructing Sale of Property Offered by Authority of Public Servant[1557] for Sale Section 219 of the Bharatiya Nyaya Sanhita (BNS) 2023 addresses the offense of obstructing the sale of property that has been lawfully offered for sale by the authority of a public servant.

Illustration: If a public servant is auctioning a property due to legal proceedings and an individual disrupts the auction, preventing the sale, they are committing an offense under BNS 219.

Example: Suppose a person deliberately creates a disturbance at a court-ordered auction, causing the auction to be halted. This act falls under BNS 219.

Comment: This section highlights the potential interference with legal processes and public auctions caused by obstructing the sale of property. Ensuring smooth and lawful auctions is crucial to maintaining justice.

[1555] odishapolicecidcb.gov.in

[1556] bprd.nic.in

[1557] Ministry of Home Affairs. (2024). The Bharatiya Nyaya Sanhita, 2023. Retrieved from https://www.mha.gov.in/sites/default/files/250883_english_01042024.pdf

Classification of Offence and Punishment Classification: This offense is classified as a serious criminal offense due to its potential to interfere with legal processes and public auctions.

Punishment: The punishment for committing this offense under BNS 219 can be imprisonment of either description for a term which may extend to six months, or a fine which may extend to five thousand rupees, or both.

Cognizable or Non-Cognizable, Bailable or Non-Bailable: This offense is non-cognizable, meaning the police cannot arrest the accused without a warrant.

Bailable: This offense is bailable, indicating that the accused can secure bail and be released from custody until the trial is completed.

Comparison: Section 184 of the Indian Penal Code[1558] (IPC) also addresses the offense of obstructing the sale of property offered by the authority of a public servant[1559] : IPC Section 184: States that whoever intentionally obstructs the sale of any property[1560] offered for sale by the lawful authority[1561] of any public servant, shall be punished with imprisonment of either description for a term which may extend to one month, or with a fine which may extend to five hundred rupees, or with both.

Key Differences: BNS 219: Provides for a higher term of imprisonment (up to six months) and a higher fine (up to five thousand rupees) compared to IPC Section 184.IPC 184: Limits the term of imprisonment to a maximum of one month and the fine to a maximum of five hundred rupees.

[1558] odishapolicecidcb.gov.in

[1559] www.bareactslive.com

[1560] www.indiacode.nic.in

[1561] bprd.nic.in

BNS Section 220

Definition: Illegal Purchase or Bid for Property Offered for Sale by Authority of Public Servant[1562] Section 220 of the Bharatiya Nyaya Sanhita (BNS) 2023 addresses the offense of illegally purchasing or bidding for property that has been lawfully offered for sale by the authority of a public servant.

Illustration: If a public servant is auctioning a property due to legal proceedings and an individual, who is not legally allowed to bid, participates in the auction and wins, they are committing an offense under BNS 220.

Example: Suppose a person, who is legally prohibited from purchasing property due to a conflict of interest, bids on a piece of property at a government auction and wins. This act falls under BNS 220.

Comment: This section underscores the importance of maintaining public trust and fairness in the auction process. Illegally purchasing or bidding for property can undermine these principles.

Classification of Offence and Punishment Classification: This offense is classified as a serious criminal offense due to its potential to undermine public trust and fairness in the auction process.

Punishment: The punishment for committing this offense under BNS 220 can be imprisonment of either description for a term which may extend to two years, or a fine which may extend to ten thousand rupees, or both.

Cognizable or Non-Cognizable, Bailable or Non-Bailable: This offense is non-cognizable, meaning the police cannot arrest the accused without a warrant.

Bailable: This offense is bailable, indicating that the accused can secure bail and be released from custody until the trial is completed.

[1562] Ministry of Home Affairs. (2024). The Bharatiya Nyaya Sanhita, 2023. Retrieved from https://www.mha.gov.in/sites/default/files/250883_english_01042024.pdf

Comparison: Section 185 of the Indian Penal Code[1563] (IPC) also addresses the offense of illegally purchasing or bidding for property[1564] offered for sale by the authority of a public servant: IPC Section 185: States that whoever, at any sale of property held by the lawful authority of a public servant, purchases or bids for any property on account of any other person whom he knows to be under disability to bid for or purchase that property, shall be punished with imprisonment of either description for a term which may extend to two years, or with a fine, or with both.

Key Differences: BNS 220: Provides a clearer framework for the legal repercussions of illegally purchasing or bidding for property. IPC 185: Part of the older Indian Penal Code.

BNS Section 221

Definition: Obstructing Public Servant in Discharge of Public[1565] Functions Section 221 of the Bharatiya Nyaya Sanhita (BNS) 2023 addresses the offense of obstructing a public servant in the discharge of their public functions.

Illustration: If a person intentionally hinders a police officer from conducting a lawful search, they are committing an offense under BNS 221.

Example: Suppose an individual blocks the entrance to a building to prevent a health inspector from performing an inspection. This act falls under BNS 221.

Comment: This section emphasizes the serious nature of obstructing public servants in the discharge of their duties, which can disrupt public order and hinder the execution of lawful duties.

[1563] odishapolicecidcb.gov.in

[1564] bprd.nic.in

[1565] Ministry of Home Affairs. (2024). The Bharatiya Nyaya Sanhita, 2023. Retrieved from https://www.mha.gov.in/sites/default/files/250883_english_01042024.pdf

Classification of Offence and Punishment Classification: This offense is classified as a serious criminal offense due to its potential to disrupt public order and hinder the execution of lawful duties.

Punishment: The punishment for committing this offense under[1566] BNS 221 can be imprisonment of either description for a term which may extend to three months, or a fine which may extend to five thousand rupees, or both.

Cognizable or Non-Cognizable, Bailable or Non-Bailable: This offense is cognizable, meaning the police can arrest the accused without a warrant.

Bailable: This offense is bailable, indicating that the accused can secure bail and be released from custody until the trial is completed.

Comparison: Section 186 of the Indian Penal Code[1567] (IPC) also addresses the offense of obstructing a public servant[1568] in the discharge of their public functions: IPC Section 186: States that whoever[1569] voluntarily obstructs any public servant in the discharge of his public functions shall be punished with imprisonment of either description for a term which may extend to three months, or with a fine which may extend to five hundred rupees, or with both.

Key Differences: BNS 221: Provides for a higher fine (up to five thousand rupees) compared to IPC Section 186 (up to five hundred rupees). IPC 186: Limits the fine to a maximum of five hundred rupees.

BNS Section 222

Definition: Omission to Assist Public Servant When Bound[1570] by Law to Give Assistance Section 222 of the Bharatiya Nyaya Sanhita (BNS)

[1566] bprd.nic.in

[1567] odishapolicecidcb.gov.in

[1568] www.lawfinderlive.com

[1569] bprd.nic.in

[1570] Ministry of Home Affairs. (2024). The Bharatiya Nyaya Sanhita, 2023. Retrieved from https://www.mha.gov.in/sites/default/files/250883_english_01042024.pdf

2023 addresses the offense of failing to assist a public servant when legally bound to do so.

Illustration: If a person witnesses a public servant, such as a police officer, in need of assistance during an arrest and legally required to help, but intentionally refuses to assist, they are committing an offense under BNS 222.

Example: Suppose an individual is present during a public emergency and is requested by a firefighter to help operate a hose, but they refuse to comply. This act falls under BNS 222.

Comment: This section underscores the importance of providing assistance to public servants when legally required, as failing to do so can hinder their ability to perform their duties effectively.

Classification of Offence and Punishment Classification: This offense is classified as a serious criminal offense due to its potential to hinder public servants from effectively performing their duties.

Punishment: The punishment[1571] for committing this offense under BNS 222 can be imprisonment of either description for a term which may extend to one month, or a fine which may extend to one thousand rupees, or both.

Cognizable or Non-Cognizable, Bailable or Non-Bailable: This offense is non-cognizable, meaning the police cannot arrest the accused without a warrant.

Bailable: This offense is bailable, indicating that the accused can secure bail and be released from custody until the trial is completed.

Comparison: Section 187 of the Indian Penal Code[1572] (IPC) also addresses the offense of failing to assist a public servant when legally bound to do so: IPC Section 187: States that whoever[1573], being bound by law to render or furnish assistance to any public servant in the execution

---

[1571] bprd.nic.in

[1572] odishapolicecidcb.gov.in

[1573] bprd.nic.in

of his public duty, intentionally omits to give such assistance, shall be punished with imprisonment of either description for a term which may extend to one month, or with a fine which may extend to two hundred rupees, or with both.

Key Differences: BNS 222: Provides for a higher fine (up to one thousand rupees) compared to IPC Section 187 (up to two hundred rupees). IPC 187: Limits the fine to a maximum of two hundred rupees.

BNS Section 223

Definition: Disobedience to Order Duly Promulgated by Public Servant[1574] Section 223 of the Bharatiya Nyaya Sanhita (BNS) 2023 addresses the offense of disobeying an order lawfully[1575] promulgated by a public servant.

Illustration: If a public servant issues a curfew order to maintain public safety, and a person willfully violates this order, they are committing an offense under BNS 223.

Example: Suppose a local government imposes a ban on public gatherings due to a health emergency, and an individual organizes a large public event in defiance of this order. This act falls under BNS 223.

Comment: This section underscores the importance of complying with orders from public servants to maintain public order and safety. Disobedience can lead to serious consequences and disrupt societal harmony.

Classification of Offence and Punishment Classification: This offense is classified as a serious criminal offense due to its potential to disrupt public order and safety.

[1574] Ministry of Home Affairs. (2024). The Bharatiya Nyaya Sanhita, 2023. Retrieved from https://www.mha.gov.in/sites/default/files/250883_english_01042024.pdf

[1575] www.indiacode.nic.in

Punishment: The punishment[1576] for committing this offense under BNS 223 can be imprisonment of either description for a term which may extend to six months, or a fine which may extend to five thousand rupees, or both. If such disobedience causes or tends to cause danger to human life, health, or safety, or causes or tends to cause a riot or affray, the punishment can be imprisonment of either description for a term which may extend to two years, or a fine, or both.

Cognizable or Non-Cognizable, Bailable or Non-Bailable: This offense is cognizable, meaning the police can arrest the accused without a warrant.

Bailable: This offense is bailable, indicating that the accused can secure bail and be released from custody until the trial is completed.

Comparison: Section 188 of the Indian Penal Code[1577] (IPC) also addresses the offense of disobeying an order duly promulgated by a public servant: IPC Section 188: States that whoever[1578], knowing that, by an order promulgated by a public servant lawfully empowered to promulgate such order, he is directed to abstain from a certain act, or to take certain order with certain property in his possession or under his management, disobeys such direction, shall, if such disobedience causes or tends to cause obstruction, annoyance or injury, or risk of obstruction, annoyance or injury, to any person lawfully employed, be punished with imprisonment of either description for a term which may extend to one month, or with a fine which may extend to two hundred rupees, or with both; and if such disobedience[1579] causes or tends to cause danger to human life, health or safety, or causes or tends to cause a riot or affray, shall be punished with imprisonment of either description for a term which may extend to six months, or with a fine which may extend to one thousand rupees, or with both.

Key Differences: BNS 223: Provides for higher fines (up to five thousand rupees for general cases and no specific limit mentioned for severe cases).

[1576] bprd.nic.in

[1577] www.bareactslive.com

[1578] bprd.nic.in

[1579] indianrailways.gov.in

IPC 188: Limits the fine to a maximum of two hundred rupees for general cases and one thousand rupees for severe cases.

BNS Section 224

Definition: Threat of Injury to Public Servant[1580] Section 224 of the Bharatiya Nyaya Sanhita (BNS) 2023 addresses the offense of threatening to cause injury to a public servant with the intent to deter or influence them in the discharge of their official duties.

Illustration: If a person threatens a tax officer with harm to prevent them from conducting an audit, they are committing an offense under BNS 224.

Example: Suppose an individual sends a threatening letter to a judge, warning them to rule in a particular way or face consequences. This act falls under BNS 224.

Comment: This section underscores the serious nature of threatening public servants, which can intimidate them and obstruct justice. Ensuring the safety and integrity of public servants is crucial for maintaining law and order.

Classification of Offence and Punishment Classification: This offense is classified as a serious criminal offense due to its potential to intimidate public servants and obstruct justice.

Punishment: The punishment for committing this offense under BNS 224 can be imprisonment of either description for a term which may extend to two years, or a fine, or both.

Cognizable or Non-Cognizable, Bailable or Non-Bailable: This offense is cognizable, meaning the police can arrest the accused without a warrant.

Bailable: This offense is bailable, indicating that the accused can secure bail and be released from custody until the trial is completed.

[1580] Ministry of Home Affairs. (2024). The Bharatiya Nyaya Sanhita, 2023. Retrieved from https://www.mha.gov.in/sites/default/files/250883_english_01042024.pdf

Comparison: Section 189 of the Indian Penal Code[1581] (IPC) also addresses the offense of threatening to cause injury[1582] to a public servant: IPC Section 189: States that whoever holds out any threat of injury to any public servant, or to any person in whom he believes that public servant to be interested, shall be punished with imprisonment of either description for a term which may extend to two years, or with a fine, or with both.

Key Differences: BNS 224: Updated version in the Bharatiya Nyaya Sanhita. IPC 189: Part of the older Indian Penal Code.

BNS Section 225

Definition: Threat of Injury to Induce Person to Refrain from Applying for Protection[1583] Section 225 of the Bharatiya Nyaya Sanhita (BNS) 2023 addresses the offense of threatening to cause injury to a person with the intent to induce them to refrain from applying for protection.

Illustration: If a person threatens another individual with harm to prevent them from reporting a crime to the police, they are committing an offense under BNS 225.

Example: Suppose an individual tells their neighbor that they will harm them if they go to the authorities for protection against harassment. This act falls under BNS 225.

Comment: This section highlights the potential harm and intimidation that can result from threatening individuals to prevent them from seeking protection. Ensuring safety and justice for individuals is crucial.

Classification of Offence and Punishment Classification: This offense is classified as a serious criminal offense due to its potential to intimidate individuals and obstruct justice.

[1581] odishapolicecidcb.gov.in

[1582] bprd.nic.in

[1583] Ministry of Home Affairs. (2024). The Bharatiya Nyaya Sanhita, 2023. Retrieved from https://www.mha.gov.in/sites/default/files/250883_english_01042024.pdf

Punishment: The punishment for committing this offense under BNS 225 can be imprisonment of either description for a term which may extend to one year, or a fine which may extend to five thousand rupees, or both.

Cognizable or Non-Cognizable, Bailable or Non-Bailable: This offense is non-cognizable, meaning the police cannot arrest the accused without a warrant.

Bailable: This offense is bailable, indicating that the accused can secure bail and be released from custody until the trial is completed.

Comparison: Section 190 of the Indian Penal Code[1584] (IPC) also addresses the offense of threatening to cause injury to induce a person[1585] to refrain from applying for protection: IPC Section 190: States that whoever holds out any threat of injury to any person with the intent to induce that person to refrain[1586] from making a legal application for protection against any injury or threat of injury, shall be punished with imprisonment of either description for a term which may extend to one year, or with a fine, or with both.

Key Differences: BNS 225: Updated version in the Bharatiya Nyaya Sanhita. IPC 190: Part of the older Indian Penal Code.

BNS Section 226

Definition: Attempt to Commit Suicide to Compel or Restrain[1587] from Applying or Restrain of Lawful Power Section 226 of the Bharatiya Nyaya Sanhita (BNS) 2023 addresses the offense of attempting to commit suicide with the intent to compel or restrain any public servant from discharging their official duty.

[1584] odishapolicecidcb.gov.in

[1585] bprd.nic.in

[1586] www.indiacode.nic.in

[1587] Ministry of Home Affairs. (2024). The Bharatiya Nyaya Sanhita, 2023. Retrieved from https://www.mha.gov.in/sites/default/files/250883_english_01042024.pdf

Illustration: If a person attempts suicide to force a police officer to drop charges against them, it constitutes an offense under BNS 226.

Example: Suppose an individual threatens to commit suicide unless a judge dismisses a case against them. This act falls under BNS 226 as it involves attempting suicide to influence a public servant's actions.

Comment: This section aims to protect public servants from being manipulated or coerced through threats of suicide. It emphasizes the importance of maintaining the integrity of public duties and ensuring that public servants can perform their roles without undue pressure.

Classification of Offence and Punishment Offence Classification: This offense is cognizable and bailable.

Punishment: The punishment for committing this offense under BNS 226 is simple imprisonment for a term which may extend to one year, or a fine, or both, or with community service.

Cognizable or Non-Cognizable, Bailable or Non-Bailable: The police can arrest the accused without a warrant.

Bailable: Bail is granted as a matter of right, and the accused can be released on bail.

Comparison: Section 226 of the Bharatiya Nyaya Sanhita (BNS) 2023 is a new provision that does not have a direct equivalent in the older Indian Penal Code (IPC). It specifically addresses the issue of attempting suicide to influence public servants and provides penalties for such acts.

CHAPTER-XIV; OF FALSE EVIDENCE AND OFFENCES AGAINST PUBLIC JUSTICE

BNS Section 227

Definition: Giving False Evidence[1588] Section 227 of the Bharatiya Nyaya Sanhita (BNS) 2023 addresses the offense of giving false evidence under oath or affirmation.

Illustration: If a person, during a legal proceeding, swears to tell the truth and then knowingly provides false information, they are committing an offense under BNS 227.

Example: Suppose an individual testifies in court that they witnessed a robbery when, in fact, they did not. This act falls under BNS 227.

Comment: This section underscores the serious implications of giving false evidence, which can mislead the court and obstruct justice. Maintaining truthful testimony is crucial for the integrity of the legal system.

Classification of Offence and Punishment Classification: This offense is classified as a serious criminal offense due to its potential to mislead the court and obstruct justice.

Punishment: The punishment[1589] for committing this offense under BNS 227 can be imprisonment of either description for a term which may extend to seven years, and the offender shall also be liable to a fine.

Cognizable or Non-Cognizable, Bailable or Non-Bailable: This offense is cognizable, meaning the police can arrest the accused without a warrant.

[1588] Ministry of Home Affairs. (2024). The Bharatiya Nyaya Sanhita, 2023. Retrieved from https://www.mha.gov.in/sites/default/files/250883_english_01042024.pdf

[1589] bprd.nic.in

Bailable: This offense is non-bailable, indicating that the accused cannot easily secure bail and must remain in custody until the trial is completed.

Comparison: Section 191 of the Indian Penal Code[1590] (IPC) defines the offense of giving false evidence: IPC Section 191: States that whoever[1591], being legally bound by an oath or affirmation to state the truth on any subject to any public servant or other person authorized by law to administer such oath or affirmation, makes, to such public servant or other person as aforesaid, a statement which is false, and which he either knows or believes to be false or does not believe to be true, is said to give false evidence.

Key Differences: BNS 227: Provides for a term of imprisonment which may extend to seven years and a fine. IPC 191: Part of the older Indian Penal Code, defining the concept without specifying the punishment directly but linking it to related sections.

BNS Section 228

Definition: Fabricating False Evidence Section 228 of the Bharatiya Nyaya Sanhita (BNS) 2023 addresses the offense of fabricating false evidence with the intent to mislead public servants or judicial proceedings.

Illustration: If a person creates a fake document to support a false claim in a legal case, they are committing an offense under BNS 228.

Example: Suppose an individual forges a contract to show that a property transaction took place, intending to deceive the court. This act falls under BNS 228.

Comment: This section underscores the serious implications of fabricating false evidence, which can obstruct justice and mislead judicial proceedings. Maintaining truthful evidence is crucial for the integrity of the legal system.

[1590] odishapolicecidcb.gov.in

[1591] bprd.nic.in

Classification of Offence and Punishment Classification: This offense is classified as a serious criminal offense due to its potential to obstruct justice and mislead judicial proceedings.

Punishment: The punishment for committing this offense under BNS 228 can be imprisonment[1592] of either description for a term which may extend to seven years, and the offender shall[1593] also be liable to a fine.

Cognizable or Non-Cognizable, Bailable or Non-Bailable: This offense is cognizable, meaning the police can arrest the accused without a warrant.

Bailable: This offense is non-bailable, indicating that the accused cannot easily secure bail and must remain in custody until the trial is completed.

Comparison: Section 192 of the Indian Penal Code (IPC) also addresses the offense of fabricating false evidence: IPC Section 192: States that whoever[1594] causes any circumstance to exist or makes any false entry in any book or record, or makes[1595] any document containing a false statement, intending that such circumstance, false entry[1596], or false statement may appear in evidence in a judicial proceeding, or in a proceeding taken by law before a public servant as such, or before an arbitrator, and that such circumstance, false entry, or false statement, so appearing in evidence, may cause any person who in such proceeding is to form an opinion upon the evidence, to entertain an erroneous opinion touching any point material to the result of such proceeding, is said "to fabricate false evidence".

Key Differences: BNS 228: Provides for a term of imprisonment which may extend to seven years and a fine. IPC 192: Defines the act of fabricating false evidence but doesn't specify the punishment directly, linking it to related sections.

[1592] blog.scconline.com

[1593] blog.ipleaders.in

[1594] blog.scconline.com

[1595] forest.jharkhand.gov.in

[1596] www.refworld.org

BNS Section 229

Definition: Punishment for False Evidence Section 229 of the Bharatiya Nyaya Sanhita (BNS) 2023 addresses the punishment for giving false evidence[1597] under oath or affirmation.

Illustration: If a person knowingly provides false testimony in a court of law, they are committing an offense under BNS 229.

Example: Suppose an individual lies under oath during a trial, falsely accusing someone of a crime they did not commit. This act falls under BNS 229.

Comment: This section underscores the serious implications of giving false evidence, which can mislead the court and obstruct justice. Ensuring truthful testimony is crucial for the integrity of the legal system.

Classification of Offence and Punishment Classification: This offense is classified as a serious criminal offense due to its potential to mislead the court and obstruct justice.

Punishment: The punishment for committing this offense under BNS 229 can be imprisonment[1598] of either description for a term which may extend to seven years, and the offender shall also be liable[1599] to a fine.

Cognizable or Non-Cognizable, Bailable or Non-Bailable: This offense is cognizable, meaning the police can arrest the accused without a warrant.

Bailable: This offense is non-bailable, indicating that the accused cannot easily secure bail and must remain in custody until the trial is completed.

Comparison: Section 193 of the Indian Penal Code (IPC) also addresses the punishment for giving false evidence: IPC Section 193: States that whoever[1600] intentionally gives false evidence in any stage of a judicial proceeding, or fabricates false evidence for the purpose of being used in

---

[1597] blog.ipleaders.in

[1598] blog.scconline.com

[1599] blog.ipleaders.in

[1600] blog.scconline.com

any stage of a judicial proceeding, shall be punished with imprisonment of either description for a term which may extend to seven years, and shall also be liable to a fine; and whoever intentionally gives or fabricates false evidence in any other case, shall be punished with imprisonment of either description for a term which may extend to three years, and shall also be liable to a fine.

Key Differences: BNS 229: Provides for a uniform punishment of up to seven years' imprisonment and a fine. IPC 193: Differentiates between judicial proceedings and other cases, providing a maximum of seven years' imprisonment for judicial proceedings and three years for other cases.

BNS Section 230

Definition: Giving or Fabricating False Evidence[1601] with Intent to Procure Conviction of Capital Offence Section 230 of the Bharatiya Nyaya Sanhita (BNS) 2023 addresses the offense of giving or fabricating false evidence with the intent to procure the conviction of a person for a capital offense.

Illustration: If a person fabricates evidence to falsely implicate another individual in a crime punishable by death, they are committing an offense under BNS 230.

Example: Suppose an individual plants forged documents and creates false testimony to frame someone for murder, intending for them to receive a death sentence. This act falls under BNS 230.

Comment: This section underscores the grave consequences of fabricating evidence that could lead to wrongful convictions and potential executions. It highlights the importance of integrity within the legal system and ensures that those who attempt to manipulate justice through deceit face severe penalties.

[1601] Ministry of Home Affairs. (2024). The Bharatiya Nyaya Sanhita, 2023. Retrieved from https://www.mha.gov.in/sites/default/files/250883_english_01042024.pdf

Classification of Offence and Punishment Classification: This offense is classified as a very serious criminal offense due to its potential to lead to the wrongful conviction and possible execution of an innocent person.

Punishment: The punishment for committing this offense under BNS 230 can be imprisonment[1602] for life, or imprisonment of either[1603] description for a term which may extend to ten years, and the offender shall also be liable to a fine[1604].

Cognizable or Non-Cognizable, Bailable or Non-Bailable: This offense is cognizable, meaning the police can arrest the accused without a warrant.

Bailable: This offense is non-bailable, indicating that the accused cannot secure bail and must remain in custody until the trial is completed.

Comparison: Section 194 of the Indian Penal Code[1605] (IPC) also addresses the offense of giving[1606] or fabricating false evidence with intent to procure the conviction[1607] of a capital offense: IPC Section 194: States that whoever gives or fabricates false evidence, intending thereby to cause, or knowing it to be likely that he will thereby cause, any person to be convicted of an offense which is capital by the law for the time being in force in India[1608], shall be punished with imprisonment for life, or with rigorous imprisonment for a term which may extend to ten years[1609], and shall also be liable to a fine; and if an innocent person[1610] be thereby convicted and executed, the person who gives such false evidence shall be punished with death.

[1602] bprd.nic.in

[1603] blog.scconline.com

[1604] blog.ipleaders.in

[1605] www.bareactslive.com

[1606] odishapolicecidcb.gov.in

[1607] bprd.nic.in

[1608] blog.ipleaders.in

[1609] blog.scconline.com

[1610] forest.jharkhand.gov.in

Key Differences: BNS 230: Provides for life imprisonment or a term up to ten years and a fine. IPC 194: Includes the provision that if an innocent person is executed as a result of the false evidence[1611], the person who fabricated the evidence may face the death penalty.

BNS Section 231

Definition: Giving or Fabricating False Evidence with Intent to Procure[1612] Conviction of Offence Punishable with Imprisonment for Life or Imprisonment Section 231 of the Bharatiya Nyaya Sanhita (BNS) 2023 addresses the offense of giving or fabricating false evidence with the intent to procure the conviction of a person for an offense punishable with imprisonment for life or imprisonment.

Illustration: If a person creates false evidence to falsely implicate another individual in a crime punishable by life imprisonment, they are committing an offense under BNS 231.

Example: Suppose an individual fabricates witness statements and other evidence to frame someone for a serious crime such as kidnapping, intending for them to receive a life sentence. This act falls under BNS 231.

Comment: This section highlights the severe implications of giving or fabricating false evidence[1613], which can lead to the wrongful conviction and severe punishment of an innocent person. Ensuring the integrity of evidence is crucial for justice.

Classification of Offence and Punishment Classification: This offense is classified as a very serious criminal offense due to its potential to lead to the wrongful conviction and severe punishment of an innocent person.

[1611] devgan.in

[1612] Ministry of Home Affairs. (2024). The Bharatiya Nyaya Sanhita, 2023. Retrieved from https://www.mha.gov.in/sites/default/files/250883_english_01042024.pdf

[1613] odishapolicecidcb.gov.in

Punishment: The punishment for committing this offense under BNS 231 can be imprisonment[1614] of either description for a term which may extend to ten years, and the offender shall also be liable to a fine[1615].

Cognizable or Non-Cognizable, Bailable or Non-Bailable: This offense is cognizable, meaning the police can arrest the accused without a warrant.

Bailable: This offense is non-bailable, indicating that the accused cannot easily secure bail and must remain in custody until the trial is completed.

Comparison: Section 195 of the Indian Penal Code (IPC) also addresses the offense of giving or fabricating false evidence[1616] with intent to procure the conviction[1617] of an offense punishable with imprisonment[1618] for life or imprisonment: IPC Section 195: States that whoever gives or fabricates false evidence, intending thereby to cause, or knowing it to be likely that he will thereby cause, any person to be convicted of an offense which is punishable with imprisonment for life, or imprisonment, shall be punished as a person convicted of that offense would be liable[1619] to be punished.

Key Differences: BNS 231: Specifies a maximum term of imprisonment of up to ten years and a fine. IPC 195: Specifies that the punishment will be the same as that of the offense for which the false evidence was intended to procure a conviction.

BNS Section 232

Definition: Threatening Any Person to Give False Evidence[1620] Section 232 of the Bharatiya Nyaya Sanhita (BNS) 2023 addresses the offense

---

[1614] blog.scconline.com

[1615] blog.ipleaders.in

[1616] odishapolicecidcb.gov.in

[1617] bprd.nic.in

[1618] devgan.in

[1619] blog.ipleaders.in

[1620] Ministry of Home Affairs. (2024). The Bharatiya Nyaya Sanhita, 2023. Retrieved from https://www.mha.gov.in/sites/default/files/250883_english_01042024.pdf

of threatening any person to give false evidence or to withhold true evidence.

Illustration: If a person threatens another individual with harm unless they testify falsely in court, they are committing an offense under BNS 232.

Example: Suppose an individual tells a witness that they will harm their family if they do not lie on the stand and say that they saw something that never happened. This act falls under BNS 232.

Comment: This section highlights the potential harm and intimidation that can result from threatening individuals to give false evidence. It aims to protect the integrity of the judicial process by deterring such coercion.

Classification of Offence and Punishment Classification: This offense is classified as a very serious criminal offense due to its potential to obstruct justice and intimidate witnesses.

Punishment: The punishment for committing this offense under BNS 232 can be imprisonment[1621] of either description for a term which may extend to seven years, and the offender shall also be liable to a fine[1622].

Cognizable or Non-Cognizable, Bailable or Non-Bailable: This offense is cognizable, meaning the police can arrest the accused without a warrant.

Bailable: This offense is non-bailable, indicating that the accused cannot secure bail easily and must remain in custody until the trial is completed.

Comparison: Section 195A of the Indian Penal Code (IPC) also addresses the offense of threatening[1623] any person to give false evidence: IPC Section 195A: States that whoever threatens another with any injury to their person, reputation, or property, or to the person or reputation of anyone in whom that person is interested, with the intent to cause that person to give false evidence, shall be[1624] punished with imprisonment of

---

[1621] blog.scconline.com

[1622] blog.ipleaders.in

[1623] bprd.nic.in

[1624] blog.ipleaders.in

either description for a term which may extend to seven years, or with a fine[1625], or with both; and if innocent, they will receive punishment corresponding to the intended consequence of the false evidence.

Key Differences: BNS 232: Provides a detailed framework for the punishment of threatening someone to give false evidence. IPC 195A: Contains similar provisions but is part of the older Indian Penal Code framework.

BNS Section 233

Definition: Using Evidence Known to be False Section[1626] 233 of the Bharatiya Nyaya Sanhita (BNS) 2023 addresses the offense of using evidence that a person knows to be false.

Illustration: If a lawyer presents a document in court, knowing it to be forged, they are committing an offense under BNS 233.

Example: Suppose an individual submits a fake bank statement as evidence in a financial dispute case, knowing that the statement is falsified. This act falls under BNS 233.

Comment: This section highlights the severe implications of using false evidence, which can mislead judicial proceedings and obstruct justice. Ensuring the integrity of evidence is crucial for maintaining trust in the legal system.

Classification of Offence and Punishment Classification: This offense is classified as a serious criminal offense due to its potential to mislead judicial proceedings and obstruct justice.

[1625] blog.ipleaders.in

[1626] Ministry of Home Affairs. (2024). The Bharatiya Nyaya Sanhita, 2023. Retrieved from https://www.mha.gov.in/sites/default/files/250883_english_01042024.pdf

Punishment: The punishment for committing this offense under BNS 233 can be imprisonment[1627] of either description for a term which may extend to seven years, and the offender shall also be liable to a fine[1628].

Cognizable or Non-Cognizable, Bailable or Non-Bailable: This offense is cognizable, meaning the police can arrest the accused without a warrant.

Bailable: This offense is non-bailable, indicating that the accused cannot secure bail and must remain in custody until the trial is completed.

Comparison: Section 196 of the Indian Penal Code[1629] (IPC) also addresses the offense of using evidence known to be false: IPC Section 196: States that whoever[1630] corruptly uses or attempts to use as true[1631] or genuine evidence any evidence which he knows to be false or fabricated shall be punished in the same manner as if he gave or fabricated false evidence.

Key Differences: BNS 233: Provides a clear framework for the punishment of using false evidence, with specific terms of imprisonment and fines. IPC 196: Links the punishment to the same penalties as giving or fabricating false evidence, without specifying separate terms.

BNS Section 234

Definition: Issuing or Signing False Certificate[1632] Section 234 of the Bharatiya Nyaya Sanhita (BNS) 2023 addresses the offense of issuing or signing a false certificate.

1627 blog.scconline.com

1628 blog.ipleaders.in

1629 blog.scconline.com

1630 blog.ipleaders.in

1631 bprd.nic.in

1632 Ministry of Home Affairs. (2024). The Bharatiya Nyaya Sanhita, 2023. Retrieved from https://www.mha.gov.in/sites/default/files/250883_english_01042024.pdf

Illustration: If a person, authorized to issue a certificate of a particular qualification, knowingly signs a certificate for someone who has not met the required standards, they are committing an offense under BNS 234.

Example: Suppose a doctor issue a false medical certificate stating that a person is fit to work, knowing that the person has a serious health condition that disqualifies them. This act falls under BNS 234.

Comment: This section emphasizes the serious nature of issuing or signing false certificates, which can mislead authorities and institutions and harm public trust. Maintaining accurate certification is crucial for ensuring integrity and public confidence.

Classification of Offence and Punishment Classification: This offense is classified as a serious criminal offense due to its potential to mislead authorities and institutions and to harm public trust.

Punishment: The punishment for committing this offense under BNS 234 can be imprisonment[1633] of either description for a term which may extend to three years, and the offender shall also be liable to a fine[1634].

Cognizable or Non-Cognizable, Bailable or Non-Bailable: This offense is cognizable, meaning the police can arrest the accused without a warrant.

Bailable: This offense is bailable, indicating that the accused can secure bail and be released from custody until the trial is completed.

Comparison: Section 197 of the Indian Penal Code (IPC) also addresses the offense of issuing[1635] or signing a false certificate: IPC Section 197: States that whoever[1636] issues or signs any certificate required by law to be issued or signed or relating[1637] to any fact of which such certificate is by law admissible in evidence, and which he knows or believes to be false in

[1633] blog.scconline.com

[1634] blog.ipleaders.in

[1635] www.refworld.org

[1636] blog.ipleaders.in

[1637] bprd.nic.in

any material point, shall be punished in the same manner as if he gave false evidence.

Key Differences: BNS 234: Provides a clear framework for the punishment[1638] of issuing or signing a false certificate, specifying a term of imprisonment and a fine. IPC 197: Links the punishment to the same penalties as giving false evidence, without specifying separate terms.

BNS Section 235

Definition: Using as True a Certificate Known to be False[1639] Section 235 of the Bharatiya Nyaya Sanhita (BNS) 2023 addresses the offense of using a certificate that a person knows to be false as if it were true.

Illustration: If a person presents a forged educational certificate for a job application, knowing it to be false, they are committing an offense under BNS 235.

Example: Suppose an individual applies for a government job and submits a fake degree certificate, fully aware that the certificate is not genuine. This act falls under BNS 235.

Comment: This section emphasizes the serious nature of using false certificates, which can deceive authorities and institutions and undermine public trust. Ensuring the authenticity of certificates is crucial for maintaining integrity and public confidence.

Classification of Offence and Punishment Classification: This offense is classified as a serious criminal offense due to its potential to deceive authorities and institutions and to undermine public trust.

[1638] www.refworld.org

[1639] Ministry of Home Affairs. (2024). The Bharatiya Nyaya Sanhita, 2023. Retrieved from https://www.mha.gov.in/sites/default/files/250883_english_01042024.pdf

Punishment: The punishment for committing this offense under BNS 235 can be imprisonment[1640] of either description for a term which may extend to three years, and the offender shall also be liable to a fine[1641].

Cognizable or Non-Cognizable, Bailable or Non-Bailable: This offense is cognizable, meaning the police can arrest the accused without a warrant.

Bailable: This offense is bailable, indicating that the accused can secure bail and be released from custody until the trial is completed.

Comparison: Section 198 of the Indian Penal Code (IPC) also addresses the offense of using a certificate known to be false[1642]: IPC Section 198: States that whoever uses[1643] or attempts to use as true a certificate known to be false in any material point shall be punished in the same manner as if they gave false evidence.

Key Differences: BNS 235: Provides a clear framework for the punishment of using a false certificate, specifying a term of imprisonment and a fine. IPC 198: Links the punishment to the same penalties as giving false evidence, without specifying separate terms.

BNS Section 236

Definition: False Statement Made in Declaration Which is by Law Receivable[1644] as Evidence Section 236 of the Bharatiya Nyaya Sanhita (BNS) 2023 addresses the offense of making a false statement in a declaration that is by law receivable as evidence.

[1640] blog.scconline.com

[1641] blog.ipleaders.in

[1642] bprd.nic.in

[1643] blog.ipleaders.in

[1644] Ministry of Home Affairs. (2024). The Bharatiya Nyaya Sanhita, 2023. Retrieved from https://www.mha.gov.in/sites/default/files/250883_english_01042024.pdf

Illustration: If a person makes a sworn declaration in an affidavit that is intended[1645] to be used as evidence in court, and the statement is knowingly false, they are committing an offense under BNS 236.

Example: Suppose an individual files an affidavit claiming they were present at a specific location during an incident, while knowing they were actually elsewhere. This act falls under BNS 236.

Comment: This section highlights the severe implications of making false statements in declarations that are receivable as evidence, which can mislead judicial proceedings and obstruct justice. Maintaining truthful declarations is crucial for the integrity of the legal system.

Classification of Offence and Punishment Classification: This offense is classified as a serious criminal offense due to its potential to mislead judicial proceedings and obstruct justice.

Punishment: The punishment for committing this offense under BNS 236 can be imprisonment[1646] of either description for a term which may extend to seven years, and the offender shall also be liable to a fine[1647].

Cognizable or Non-Cognizable, Bailable or Non-Bailable: This offense is cognizable, meaning the police can arrest the accused without a warrant.

Bailable: This offense is non-bailable, indicating that the accused cannot secure bail easily and must remain in custody until the trial is completed.

Comparison: with IPC Section 199Section 199 of the Indian Penal Code (IPC) also addresses the offense of making a false statement in a declaration[1648] which is by law receivable as evidence: IPC Section 199: States that whoever, in any declaration made or subscribed by him, which declaration any Court of Justice or any public servant is bound[1649] or authorized by law to receive as evidence of any fact, makes any statement

[1645] forest.jharkhand.gov.in

[1646] blog.scconline.com

[1647] blog.ipleaders.in

[1648] blog.scconline.com

[1649] devgan.in

which is false, and which he either knows or believes to be false or does not believe to be true, shall be punished[1650] in the same manner as if he gave false evidence.

Key Differences: BNS 236: Provides a clear framework for the punishment of making a false statement in a declaration receivable as evidence, specifying a term of imprisonment[1651] and a fine. IPC 199: Links the punishment to the same penalties as giving false evidence, without specifying separate terms.

BNS Section 237

Definition: Using as True Such Declaration Knowing It to Be False[1652] Section 237 of the Bharatiya Nyaya Sanhita (BNS) 2023 addresses the offense of using a declaration known to be false as if it were true.

Illustration: If a person presents a falsified income statement to secure a loan, knowing it to be false, they are committing an offense under BNS 237.

Example: Suppose an individual submits a fake employment verification letter to obtain housing benefits, fully aware that the document is fraudulent. This act falls under BNS 237.

Comment: This section underscores the serious implications of using false declarations, which can deceive authorities and institutions and undermine public trust. Ensuring the authenticity of declarations is crucial for maintaining integrity.

Classification of Offence and Punishment Classification: This offense is classified as a serious criminal offense due to its potential to deceive authorities and institutions and undermine public trust.

[1650] blog.ipleaders.in

[1651] bprd.nic.in

[1652] Ministry of Home Affairs. (2024). The Bharatiya Nyaya Sanhita, 2023. Retrieved from https://www.mha.gov.in/sites/default/files/250883_english_01042024.pdf

Punishment: The punishment for committing this offense under BNS 237 can be imprisonment[1653] of either description for a term which may extend to seven years, and the offender shall also be liable to a fine[1654].

Cognizable or Non-Cognizable, Bailable or Non-Bailable: This offense is cognizable, meaning the police can arrest the accused without a warrant.

Bailable: This offense is non-bailable, indicating that the accused cannot secure bail and must remain in custody until the trial is completed.

Comparison: Section 200 of the Indian Penal Code[1655] (IPC) also addresses the offense of using a declaration known to be false: IPC Section 200: States that whoever[1656] corruptly uses or attempts to use any such declaration as true, knowing the same to be false in any material point, shall be punished in the same manner as if they gave false evidence.

Key Differences: BNS 237: Provides a clear framework for the punishment of using a false declaration, specifying a term of imprisonment and a fine. IPC 200: Links the punishment to the same penalties as giving false evidence, without specifying separate terms.

BNS Section 238

Definition: Causing Disappearance of Evidence, or Giving False Information[1657] to Screen Offender Section 238 of the Bharatiya Nyaya Sanhita (BNS) 2023 addresses the offense of causing the disappearance of evidence or giving false information with the intent to screen an offender from legal punishment.

[1653] blog.scconline.com

[1654] blog.ipleaders.in

[1655] www.bareactslive.com

[1656] blog.ipleaders.in

[1657] Ministry of Home Affairs. (2024). The Bharatiya Nyaya Sanhita, 2023. Retrieved from https://www.mha.gov.in/sites/default/files/250883_english_01042024.pdf

Illustration: If a person burns clothes stained with blood to prevent them from being used as evidence in a murder case, they are committing an offense under BNS 238.

Example: Suppose an individual lies to the police, providing a false alibi for a friend who committed a robbery, with the intent to protect the friend from arrest. This act falls under BNS 238.

Comment: This section highlights the serious implications of causing the disappearance[1658] of evidence or giving false information[1659] to screen an offender, which can obstruct justice and aid offenders in evading legal consequences.

Classification of Offence and Punishment Classification: This offense is classified as a serious criminal offense due to its potential to obstruct justice and aid offenders in evading legal consequences.

Punishment: The punishment for committing this offense under BNS 238 can vary: If the offense screened is punishable by death or imprisonment for life: The punishment can be imprisonment[1660] of either description for a term which may extend to ten years, and the offender shall also be liable to a fine. If the offense screened is punishable with less severe penalties: The punishment can be imprisonment of either description for a term which may extend to seven years, and the offender shall also be liable to a fine. If the offense screened is only punishable with a fine: The punishment can be imprisonment of either description for a term which may extend to three years, and the offender shall also be liable to a fine.

Cognizable or Non-Cognizable, Bailable or Non-Bailable: This offense is cognizable, meaning the police can arrest the accused without a warrant.

Bailable: Depending on the severity of the offense being screened, this offense can be bailable or non-bailable.

[1658] blog.ipleaders.in

[1659] devgan.in

[1660] blog.ipleaders.in

Comparison: Section 201 of the Indian Penal Code[1661] (IPC) also addresses the offense of causing the disappearance[1662] of evidence or giving false information[1663] to screen an offender: IPC Section 201: States that whoever, knowing or having reason to believe that an offense has been committed, causes any evidence of the commission of that offense to disappear, with the intention of screening the offender from legal punishment, or gives any information respecting the offense which he knows or believes to be false, shall be punished: If the offense is punishable with death: With imprisonment of either description for a term which may extend to ten years[1664], and shall also be liable to a fine. If the offense is punishable with life imprisonment: With imprisonment of either description for a term which may extend to seven years, and shall also be liable to a fine. If the offense is punishable with less severe penalties: With imprisonment of either description for a term which may extend to three years, or with a fine, or with both.

Key Differences: BNS 238: Provides a clear framework for varying punishments based on the severity of the offense being screened, including a three-tier punishment structure. IPC 201: Similar framework with specific terms of imprisonment and fines linked to the severity of the offense.

BNS Section 239

Definition: Intentional Omission to Give Information of Offense by Person Bound[1665] to Inform Section 239 of the Bharatiya Nyaya Sanhita (BNS) 2023 addresses the offense of intentionally omitting to give information of an offense by a person who is legally bound to inform.

1661 www.bareactslive.com

1662 blog.ipleaders.in

1663 devgan.in

1664 copyright.gov.in

1665 Ministry of Home Affairs. (2024). The Bharatiya Nyaya Sanhita, 2023. Retrieved from https://www.mha.gov.in/sites/default/files/250883_english_01042024.pdf

Illustration: If a government employee knows that a crime has been committed in their department but deliberately chooses not to report it, they are committing an offense under BNS 239.

Example: Suppose a person witnesses their neighbor committing a theft and, although legally required to report such incidents, decides not to inform the authorities. This act falls under BNS 239.

Classification of Offence and Punishment Classification: This offense is classified as a serious criminal offense due to its potential to obstruct justice and allow offenders to evade legal consequences.

Punishment: The punishment for committing this offense under BNS 239 can be imprisonment of either description for a term which may extend to six months, or a fine[1666] which may extend to five thousand rupees, or both.

Cognizable or Non-Cognizable, Bailable or Non-Bailable: This offense is non-cognizable, meaning the police cannot arrest the accused without a warrant.

Bailable: This offense is bailable, indicating that the accused can secure bail and be released from custody until the trial is completed.

Comparison: Section 202 of the Indian Penal Code[1667] (IPC) also addresses the offense of intentionally omitting to give information of an offense by a person[1668] bound to inform: IPC Section 202: States that whoever[1669], knowing or having reason to believe that an offense has been committed, intentionally omits to give any information respecting that offense which he is legally[1670] bound to give, shall be punished with imprisonment of either description for a term which may extend to six months, or with a fine, or with both; or if the offense is punishable[1671] with death, imprisonment for life, or imprisonment up to ten years, shall be

---

[1666] copyright.gov.in

[1667] www.bareactslive.com

[1668] blog.ipleaders.in

[1669] devgan.in

[1670] copyright.gov.in

[1671] www.slideshare.net

punished with imprisonment of either description for a term which may extend to one year, or with a fine, or with both.

Key Differences: BNS 239: Provides a clear framework for the punishment of intentional omission to give information, specifying a term of imprisonment and a fine. IPC 202: Differentiates between the severity of the offenses, providing higher punishments for more severe cases.

BNS Section 240

Definition: Giving False Information Respecting an Offense Committed[1672] Section 240 of the Bharatiya Nyaya Sanhita (BNS) 2023 addresses the offense of giving false information[1673] about an offense that has been committed.

Illustration: If a person reports to the police that a theft has occurred at their house when no such incident took place, they are committing an offense under BNS 240.

Example: Suppose an individual falsely informs the authorities that their car was stolen to claim insurance money. This act falls under BNS 240.

Comment: This section emphasizes the serious implications of intentionally omitting to give information of an offense, which can obstruct justice and allow offenders to evade legal consequences.

Classification of Offence and Punishment Classification: This offense is classified as a serious criminal offense due to its potential to mislead law enforcement and waste public resources.

Punishment: The punishment for committing this offense under BNS 240 can be imprisonment of either description for a term which may extend to six months, or a fine which may[1674] extend to five thousand rupees, or both.

[1672] Ministry of Home Affairs. (2024). The Bharatiya Nyaya Sanhita, 2023. Retrieved from https://www.mha.gov.in/sites/default/files/250883_english_01042024.pdf

[1673] blog.ipleaders.in

[1674] copyright.gov.in

Cognizable or Non-Cognizable, Bailable or Non-Bailable: This offense is non-cognizable, meaning the police cannot arrest the accused without a warrant.

Bailable: This offense is bailable, indicating that the accused can secure bail and be released from custody until the trial is completed.

Comparison: Section 203 of the Indian Penal Code[1675] (IPC) also addresses the offense of giving[1676] false information respecting an offense committed: IPC Section 203: States that whoever, knowing or having reason to believe that an offense has been committed, gives any information respecting that offense which[1677] he knows or believes to be false, shall be punished with imprisonment of either description for a term which may extend to two years, or with a fine, or with both.

Key Differences: BNS 240: Specifies a maximum term of imprisonment of up to six months and a fine of up to five thousand rupees. IPC 203: Specifies a maximum term of imprisonment of up to two years and includes the possibility of a fine or both.

BNS Section 241

Definition: Destruction of Document or Electronic Record[1678] to Prevent Its Production as Evidence Section 241 of the Bharatiya Nyaya Sanhita (BNS) 2023 addresses the offense of destroying or hiding a document or electronic record that one is legally required to produce[1679] as evidence in court or before a public servant, with the intent to prevent its use as evidence.

Illustration: If a company executive destroys emails that contain incriminating evidence about financial fraud, knowing that these emails

[1675] www.bareactslive.com

[1676] devgan.in

[1677] blog.ipleaders.in

[1678] Ministry of Home Affairs. (2024). The Bharatiya Nyaya Sanhita, 2023. Retrieved from https://www.mha.gov.in/sites/default/files/250883_english_01042024.pdf

[1679] copyright.gov.in

could be demanded in a court case, they are committing an offense under BNS 241.

Example: Suppose an individual shreds a contract that proves they breached an agreement, after being informed that the document might be needed in a legal proceeding. This act falls under BNS 241.

Comment: This section highlights the serious implications of destroying or hiding documents or electronic records that are legally required as evidence, which can obstruct justice and hinder the legal process.

Classification of Offence and Punishment Classification: This offense is classified as a serious criminal offense due to its potential to obstruct justice and hinder the legal process.

Punishment: The punishment for committing this offense under BNS 241 can be imprisonment[1680] of either description for a term which may extend to three years, or a fine which may extend to five thousand rupees[1681], or both.

Cognizable or Non-Cognizable, Bailable or Non-Bailable: This offense is cognizable, meaning the police can arrest the accused without a warrant.

Bailable: This offense is bailable, indicating that the accused can secure bail and be released from custody until the trial is completed.

Comparison: Section 204 of the Indian Penal Code[1682] (IPC) also addresses the offense of destroying or hiding a document[1683] or electronic record to prevent its production as evidence: IPC Section 204: States that whoever[1684] secretes or destroys any document[1685] or electronic record which he may be lawfully compelled to produce as evidence in a Court of Justice, or in any proceeding lawfully held before a public servant, as such,

---

1680 blog.ipleaders.in

1681 copyright.gov.in

1682 www.bareactslive.com

1683 prsindia.org

1684 copyright.gov.in

1685 devgan.in

or obliterates or renders illegible the whole or any part of such document or electronic record with the intention of preventing the same from being produced or used as evidence before such Court or public servant as aforesaid, or after he shall have been lawfully summoned or required to produce the same for that pupose, shall be punished[1686] with imprisonment of either description for a term which may extend to two years, or with a fine, or with both.

Key Differences: BNS 241: Specifies a maximum term of imprisonment of up to three years and a fine of up to five thousand rupees. IPC 204: Specifies a maximum term of imprisonment of up to two years and includes the possibility of a fine[1687] or both.

BNS Section 242

Definition: False Personation for Purpose of Act or Proceeding in Suit or Prosecution[1688] Section 242 of the Bharatiya Nyaya Sanhita (BNS) 2023 addresses the offense of falsely personating another person for the purpose of any act or proceeding in a suit or criminal prosecution.

Illustration: If a person pretends to be someone else and makes a false statement in court, they are committing an offense under BNS 242.

Example: Suppose an individual falsely claims to be a witness and provides false testimony in a criminal trial. This act falls under BNS 242.

Comment: This section underscores the serious implications of falsely personating another individual in legal proceedings, which can obstruct justice and mislead the court. It emphasizes the necessity of maintaining integrity in the judicial process by enforcing stringent penalties for such offenses.

[1686] blog.ipleaders.in

[1687] devgan.in

[1688] Ministry of Home Affairs. (2024). The Bharatiya Nyaya Sanhita, 2023. Retrieved from https://www.mha.gov.in/sites/default/files/250883_english_01042024.pdf

Classification of Offence and Punishment Classification: This offense is classified as a serious criminal offense due to its potential to obstruct justice and mislead legal proceedings.

Punishment: The punishment for committing this offense under BNS 242 can be imprisonment[1689] of either description for a term which may extend to three years, or a fine, or both.

Cognizable or Non-Cognizable, Bailable or Non-Bailable: This offense is non-cognizable, meaning the police cannot arrest the accused without a warrant.

Bailable: This offense is bailable, indicating that the accused can secure bail and be released from custody until the trial is completed.

Comparison: Section 205 of the Indian Penal Code[1690] (IPC) also addresses the offense of false personation for the purpose of any act or proceeding in a suit or criminal prosecution: IPC Section 205: States that whoever[1691] falsely personates another, and in such assumed character makes any admission or statement, or confesses judgment, or causes any process to be issued or becomes bail or security, or does any other act in any suit or criminal prosecution, shall be punished with imprisonment[1692] of either description for a term which may extend to three years, or with a fine, or with both.

Key Differences: BNS 242: Provides a clear framework for the punishment of false personation, specifying a term of imprisonment and a fine. IPC 205: Similar framework with specific terms of imprisonment and fines linked to the severity of the offense.

[1689] blog.ipleaders.in

[1690] www.bareactslive.com

[1691] devgan.in

[1692] blog.ipleaders.in

BNS Section 243

Definition: Fraudulent Removal or Concealment of Property to Prevent Its Seizure as Forfeited or in Execution[1693] Section 243 of the Bharatiya Nyaya Sanhita (BNS) 2023 addresses the offense of fraudulently removing, concealing, transferring, or delivering property to prevent its seizure as forfeited or in execution of a court order.

Illustration: If a person hides their valuable assets to avoid them being seized by the court as part of a legal judgment, they are committing an offense under BNS 243.

Example: Suppose an individual transfers ownership of their property to a relative to prevent it from being taken by creditors. This act falls under BNS 243.

Comment: This section emphasizes the serious implications of fraudulently removing or concealing property to prevent its seizure, which can obstruct justice and allow individuals to evade legal consequences.

Classification of Offence and Punishment Classification: This offense is classified as a serious criminal offense due to its potential to obstruct justice and evade legal consequences.

Punishment: The punishment for committing this offense under BNS 243 can be imprisonment[1694] of either description for a term which may extend to two years, or a fine, or both.

Cognizable or Non-Cognizable, Bailable or Non-Bailable: This offense is cognizable, meaning the police can arrest the accused without a warrant.

Bailable: This offense is bailable, indicating that the accused can secure bail and be released from custody until the trial is completed.

[1693] Ministry of Home Affairs. (2024). The Bharatiya Nyaya Sanhita, 2023. Retrieved from https://www.mha.gov.in/sites/default/files/250883_english_01042024.pdf

[1694] blog.ipleaders.in

Comparison: Section 206 of the Indian Penal Code[1695] (IPC) also addresses the offense of fraudulent[1696] removal or concealment of property to prevent its seizure: IPC Section 206: States that whoever fraudulently removes, conceals, transfers, or delivers any property or interest therein, intending to prevent it from being taken as a forfeiture or in satisfaction of a fine, under a sentence pronounced by a court, or from being taken in execution of a decree or order[1697], shall be punished with imprisonment of either description for a term which may extend to two years, or with a fine, or with both.

Key Differences: BNS 243: Similar to IPC Section 206 in defining the offense and specifying punishment. Both address fraudulent[1698] removal or concealment of property to prevent its seizure as forfeited or in execution of a court order. IPC 206: Part of the older legal framework, while BNS 243 is the updated version in the new Bharatiya Nyaya Sanhita.

BNS Section 244

Definition: Fraudulent Claim to Property to Prevent Its Seizure as Forfeited or in Execution[1699] Section 244 of the Bharatiya Nyaya Sanhita (BNS) 2023 addresses the offense of fraudulently claiming property to prevent its seizure as forfeited or in execution of a court order.

Illustration: If a person falsely claims ownership of a property that is subject to seizure by the court, they are committing an offense under BNS 244.

Example: Suppose an individual, knowing that a court has ordered the seizure of a property, fraudulently claims that they are the rightful owner to prevent the seizure. This act falls under BNS 244.

[1695] www.bareactslive.com

[1696] cms.rajyasabha.nic.in

[1697] www.indiacode.nic.in

[1698] cms.rajyasabha.nic.in

[1699] Ministry of Home Affairs. (2024). The Bharatiya Nyaya Sanhita, 2023. Retrieved from https://www.mha.gov.in/sites/default/files/250883_english_01042024.pdf

Comment: This section emphasizes the serious implications of fraudulently claiming property to prevent its seizure, which can obstruct justice and allow individuals to evade legal consequences.

Classification of Offence and Punishment Classification: This offense is classified as a serious criminal offense due to its potential to obstruct justice and evade legal consequences.

Punishment: The punishment for committing this offense under BNS 244 can be imprisonment[1700] of either description for a term which may extend to two years, or a fine, or both.

Cognizable or Non-Cognizable, Bailable or Non-Bailable: This offense is cognizable, meaning the police can arrest the accused without a warrant.

Bailable: This offense is bailable, indicating that the accused can secure bail and be released from custody until the trial is completed.

Comparison: Section 207 of the Indian Penal Code[1701] (IPC) also addresses the offense of fraudulent[1702] claim to property to prevent its seizure: IPC Section 207: States that whoever fraudulently accepts, receives, or claims any property or any interest therein, knowing that they have no right or rightful claim to such property or interest, or practices any deception touching any right to any property or any interest therein, intending thereby to prevent that property or interest therein from being taken as a forfeiture or in satisfaction of a fine, under a sentence which has been pronounced, or which they know to be likely to be pronounced[1703] by a Court or other competent authority, or from being taken in execution of a decree or order which has been made, or which[1704] they know to be likely to be made by a Court in a civil suit, shall be punished with imprisonment

---

[1700] blog.ipleaders.in

[1701] www.bareactslive.com

[1702] devgan.in

[1703] cms.rajyasabha.nic.in

[1704] prsindia.org

of either description[1705] for a term which may extend to two years, or with a fine, or with both.

Key Differences: BNS 244: Similar to IPC Section 207 in defining the offense and specifying punishment. Both address fraudulent claims to property to prevent its lawful seizure. IPC 207: Part of the older legal framework, while BNS 244 is the updated version in the new Bharatiya Nyaya Sanhita.

BNS Section 245

Definition: Fraudulently Suffering Decree for Sum Not Due[1706] Section 245 of the Bharatiya Nyaya Sanhita (BNS) 2023 addresses the offense of fraudulently causing or suffering a decree or order to be passed against oneself for a sum not due or for a larger sum than is due, or for any property or interest in property to which one is not entitled.

Illustration: If a person knowingly allows a court to pass a judgment against them for a debt they do not owe, they are committing an offense under BNS 245.

Example: Suppose an individual, aware that they do not owe any money to a creditor, allows a court to pass a decree for a large sum in favor of that creditor. This act falls under BNS 245.

Comment: This section emphasizes the serious implications of fraudulently causing or suffering a decree for a sum not due, which can mislead the court and evade legal responsibilities.

Classification of Offence and Punishment Classification: This offense is classified as a serious criminal offense due to its potential to mislead the court and evade legal responsibilities.

[1705] cms.rajyasabha.nic.in

[1706] Ministry of Home Affairs. (2024). The Bharatiya Nyaya Sanhita, 2023. Retrieved from https://www.mha.gov.in/sites/default/files/250883_english_01042024.pdf

Punishment: The punishment for committing this offense under BNS 245 can be imprisonment[1707] of either description for a term which may extend to two years, or a fine, or both.

Cognizable or Non-Cognizable, Bailable or Non-Bailable: This offense is cognizable, meaning the police can arrest the accused without a warrant.

Bailable: This offense is bailable, indicating that the accused can secure bail and be released from custody until the trial is completed.

Comparison: Section 208 of the Indian Penal Code[1708] (IPC) also addresses the offense of fraudulently suffering a decree[1709] for a sum not due: IPC Section 208: States that whoever[1710] fraudulently causes or suffers a decree or order to be passed against them at the suit of any person for a sum not due or for a larger sum than is due to such person, or for any property or interest in property to which such person is not entitled, or fraudulently causes or suffers a decree or order to be executed against them after[1711] it has been satisfied, shall be punished with imprisonment of either description for a term which may extend to two years, or with a fine, or with both.

Key Differences: BNS 245: Similar to IPC Section 208 in defining the offense and specifying punishment. IPC 208: Part of the older legal framework, while BNS 245 is the updated version in the new Bharatiya Nyaya Sanhita.

[1707] blog.ipleaders.in

[1708] www.bareactslive.com

[1709] blog.ipleaders.in

[1710] devgan.in

[1711] odishapolicecidcb.gov.in

BNS Section 246

Definition: Dishonestly Making False Claim in Court[1712] Section 246 of the Bharatiya Nyaya Sanhita (BNS) 2023 addresses the offense of dishonestly making a false claim[1713] in court.

Illustration: If a person knowingly makes a false claim about ownership of property in court, they are committing an offense under BNS 246.

Example: Suppose an individual falsely claims in court that they are the rightful owner of a piece of land, knowing that this claim is untrue. This act falls under BNS 246.

Comment: This section emphasizes the serious implications of dishonestly making false claims in court, which can mislead the court and disrupt justice.

Classification of Offence and Punishment Classification: This offense is classified as a serious criminal offense due to its potential to mislead the court and disrupt justice.

Punishment: The punishment for committing this offense under BNS 246 can be imprisonment of either description for a term which may extend to two years, or a fine, or both.

Cognizable or Non-Cognizable, Bailable or Non-Bailable: This offense is non-cognizable, meaning the police cannot arrest the accused without a warrant.

Bailable: This offense is bailable, indicating that the accused can secure bail and be released from custody until the trial is completed.

Comparison: Section 209 of the Indian Penal Code[1714] (IPC) also addresses the offense of dishonestly making a false claim in court: IPC Section 209: States that whoever fraudulently or dishonestly, or with intent

---

[1712] Ministry of Home Affairs. (2024). The Bharatiya Nyaya Sanhita, 2023. Retrieved from https://www.mha.gov.in/sites/default/files/250883_english_01042024.pdf

[1713] blog.ipleaders.in

[1714] www.bareactslive.com

to injure or annoy[1715] any person, makes in a Court of Justice any claim which he knows to be false, shall be punished with imprisonment of either description for a term which may extend to two years, or with a fine, or with both.

Key Differences: BNS 246: Similar to IPC Section 209 in defining the offense and specifying punishment. IPC 209: Part of the older legal framework, while BNS 246 is the updated version in the new Bharatiya Nyaya Sanhita.

BNS Section 247

Definition: Fraudulently Obtaining Decree for Sum Not Due[1716] Section 247 of the Bharatiya Nyaya Sanhita (BNS) 2023 addresses the offense of fraudulently obtaining a decree or order against any person for a sum not due, or for a larger sum than is due, or for any property or interest in property to which one is not entitled.

Illustration: If a person knowingly obtains a court decree for a debt they do not owe, they are committing an offense under BNS 247.

Example: Suppose an individual, aware that they do not owe any money to a creditor, fraudulently obtains a court decree for a large sum in favor of that creditor. This act falls under BNS 247.

Comment: This section emphasizes the serious implications of fraudulently obtaining a decree for a sum not due, which can mislead the court and evade legal responsibilities.

Classification of Offence and Punishment Classification: This offense is classified as a serious criminal offense due to its potential to mislead the court and evade legal responsibilities.

[1715] devgan.in

[1716] Ministry of Home Affairs. (2024). The Bharatiya Nyaya Sanhita, 2023. Retrieved from https://www.mha.gov.in/sites/default/files/250883_english_01042024.pdf

Punishment: The punishment for committing this offense under BNS 247 can be imprisonment of either description for a term which may extend to two years, or a fine, or both.

Cognizable or Non-Cognizable, Bailable or Non-Bailable: This offense is cognizable, meaning the police can arrest the accused without a warrant.

Bailable: This offense is bailable, indicating that the accused can secure bail and be released from custody until the trial is completed.

Comparison: Section 210 of the Indian Penal Code[1717] (IPC) also addresses the offense of fraudulently obtaining a decree for a sum not due: IPC Section 210: States that whoever [1718]fraudulently obtains a decree or order against any person for a sum not due, or for a larger sum than is due, or for any property or interest in property to which they are not entitled, or fraudulently causes a decree or order to be executed against any person after it has been satisfied, or fraudulently suffers or permits any such act to be done in their name, shall be punished with imprisonment of either description for a term which may extend to two years, or with a fine, or with both.

Key Differences: BNS 247: Similar to IPC Section 210 in defining the offense and specifying punishment. IPC 210: Part of the older legal framework, while BNS 247 is the updated version in the new Bharatiya Nyaya Sanhita.

BNS Section 248

Definition: False Charge of Offence Made with Intent to Injure[1719] Section 248 of the Bharatiya Nyaya Sanhita (BNS) 2023 addresses the offense of making a false charge of an offense with the intent to injure someone.

[1717] www.bareactslive.com

[1718] advocatetanmoy.com

[1719] Ministry of Home Affairs. (2024). The Bharatiya Nyaya Sanhita, 2023. Retrieved from https://www.mha.gov.in/sites/default/files/250883_english_01042024.pdf

Illustration: If a person knowingly makes a false accusation against another individual, intending to harm their reputation or cause them distress, they are committing an offense under BNS 248.

Example: Suppose an individual falsely accuses their neighbor of theft, knowing that the neighbor did not commit the crime, with the intent to damage their neighbor's reputation. This act falls under BNS 248.

Comment: This section emphasizes the serious implications of making false charges with intent to injure, which can cause[1720] significant harm to the accused.

Classification of Offence and Punishment Classification: This offense is classified as a serious criminal offense due to its potential to cause significant harm to the accused.

Punishment: The punishment[1721] for committing this offense under BNS 248 can be imprisonment of either description for a term which may extend to five years, or a fine which may extend to two lakh rupees, or both.

Cognizable or Non-Cognizable, Bailable or Non-Bailable: This offense is cognizable, meaning the police can arrest the accused without a warrant.

Bailable: This offense is bailable, indicating that the accused can secure bail and be released from custody until the trial is completed.

Comparison: Section 211 of the Indian Penal Code[1722] (IPC) also addresses the offense of making a false charge of an offense with the intent to injure: IPC Section 211: States that whoever[1723], with intent to cause injury to any person, institutes or causes to be instituted any criminal proceeding against that person, or falsely charges any person with having committed an offense, knowing that there is no just or lawful ground for such proceeding or charge against that person, shall be punished with imprisonment of either description for a term which may extend to two

---

[1720] mdpi.com

[1721] advocatetanmoy.com

[1722] www.indiacode.nic.in

[1723] devgan.in

years, or with a fine, or with both. If the false charge is for an offense punishable with death, imprisonment for life, or imprisonment for seven years or upwards, the punishment can extend to seven years.

Key Differences: BNS 248: Provides a more severe punishment with imprisonment up to five years and a fine up to two lakh rupees. IPC 211: Part of the older legal framework, with imprisonment up to two years and a fine, and up to seven years for more serious offenses.

BNS Section 249

Definition: Harbouring Offender Section 249 of the Bharatiya Nyaya Sanhita (BNS) 2023 addresses the offense of harbouring or concealing a person whom one knows[1724] or has reason to believe to be an offender, with the intention of screening them from legal punishment.

Illustration: If a person knowingly provides shelter to a criminal to help them evade arrest, they are committing an offense under BNS 249.

Example: Suppose an individual hides a friend who has committed a theft, knowing that the friend is wanted by the police. This act falls under BNS 249.

Comment: This section highlights the serious implications of harbouring an offender, which can obstruct justice and protect criminals from legal consequences.

Classification of Offence and Punishment Classification: This offense is classified as a serious criminal offense due to its potential to obstruct justice and protect criminals.

Punishment: The punishment for committing this offense under BNS 249 varies based on the severity of the offense committed by the offender: If the offense is punishable with death: Imprisonment of either description for a term which may extend to five years, and a fine. If the offense is punishable with imprisonment for life, or with imprisonment which may extend to ten years: Imprisonment of either description for a term which

[1724] advocatetanmoy.com

may extend to three years, and a fine. If the offense is punishable with imprisonment which may extend to one year, and not to ten years: Imprisonment of the description provided for the offense for a term which may extend to one-fourth part of the longest term of imprisonment provided for the offense, or with a fine.

Cognizable or Non-Cognizable, Bailable or Non-Bailable: This offense is cognizable, meaning the police can arrest the accused without a warrant.

Bailable: This offense is bailable, indicating that the accused can secure bail and be released from custody until the trial is completed.

Comparison: Section 212 of the Indian Penal Code[1725] (IPC) also addresses the offense of harbouring an offender: IPC Section 212: States that whoever[1726] harbours or conceals a person whom they know or have reason to believe to be the offender, with the intention of screening them from legal punishment, shall be punished similarly to BNS 249, with imprisonment and fines based on the severity of the offense committed by the offender.

Key Differences: BNS 249: Updated version in the new Bharatiya Nyaya Sanhita, with specific provisions for different types of offenses. IPC 212: Part of the older legal framework, now replaced by BNS 249.

BNS Section 250

Definition: Taking Gift, etc., to Screen an Offender from Punishment[1727] Section 250 of the Bharatiya Nyaya Sanhita (BNS) 2023 addresses the offense of accepting or attempting to obtain any gratification or restitution of property to screen an offender from legal punishment.

[1725] main.sci.gov.in

[1726] advocatetanmoy.com

[1727] Ministry of Home Affairs. (2024). The Bharatiya Nyaya Sanhita, 2023. Retrieved from https://www.mha.gov.in/sites/default/files/250883_english_01042024.pdf

Illustration: If a person accepts a bribe to hide a criminal's identity or to prevent their arrest, they are committing an offense under BNS 250.

Example: Suppose an individual receives a large sum of money from a friend to not report their involvement in a crime. This act falls under BNS 250.

Comment: This section highlights the serious implications of accepting or attempting to obtain any gratification to screen an offender, which can undermine the legal system and protect criminals from legal consequences.

Classification of Offence and Punishment Classification: This offense is classified as a serious criminal offense due to its potential to undermine the legal system and protect criminals.

Punishment: The punishment for committing this offense under BNS 250 varies based on the severity of the offense committed by the offender: If the offense is punishable with death: Imprisonment of either description for a term which may extend to seven years, and a fine. If the offense carries a life sentence in jail or a sentence that can last up to ten years: imprisonment of any kind for a maximum of three years, together with a fine. If the offense has a maximum sentence of one year in prison rather than ten years: imprisonment of the kind specified for the offense for a period of time that could equal one-fourth of the maximum sentence stipulated for the offense, a fine, or both.

Cognizable or Non-Cognizable, Bailable or Non-Bailable: This offense is cognizable, meaning the police can arrest the accused without a warrant.

Bailable: This offense is bailable, indicating that the accused can secure bail and be released from custody until the trial is completed.

Comparison: Section 213 of the Indian Penal Code[1728] (IPC) also addresses the offense of taking a gift[1729], etc., to screen an offender from punishment: IPC Section 213: States that whoever accepts or attempts to obtain, or agrees to accept, any gratification for himself or any other

---

[1728] main.sci.gov.in

[1729] advocatetanmoy.com

person, or any restitution of property to himself or any other person, in consideration of his concealing an offense or of his screening any person from legal punishment for any offense, or of his not proceeding against any person for the purpose of bringing him to legal punishment shall be punished with imprisonment of either description for a term which may extend to seven years, or with a fine, or with both.

Key Differences: BNS 250: Updated version in the new Bharatiya Nyaya Sanhita, with specific provisions for different types of offenses. IPC 213: Part of the older legal framework, now replaced by BNS 250.

BNS Section 251

Definition: Offering Gift or Restoration of Property in Consideration[1730] of Screening Offender Section 251 of the Bharatiya Nyaya Sanhita (BNS) 2023 addresses the offense of offering or agreeing to offer any gratification or restoring property to screen an offender from legal punishment.

Illustration: If a person offers money to a witness to prevent them from testifying against a criminal, they are committing an offense under BNS 251.

Example: Suppose an individual gives a valuable gift to a police officer to avoid the arrest of a friend who committed a crime. This act falls under BNS 251.

Comment: This section highlights the serious implications of offering or agreeing to offer any gratification to screen an offender, which can obstruct justice and protect criminals from legal consequences.

Classification of Offence and Punishment Classification: This offense is classified as a serious criminal offense due to its potential to obstruct justice and protect criminals.

[1730] Ministry of Home Affairs. (2024). The Bharatiya Nyaya Sanhita, 2023. Retrieved from https://www.mha.gov.in/sites/default/files/250883_english_01042024.pdf

Punishment: The punishment for committing this offense under BNS 251[1731] varies based on the severity of the offense committed by the offender: If the offense is punishable with death: Imprisonment of either description for a term which may extend to seven years, and a fine. If the offense is punishable with imprisonment for life, or with imprisonment which may extend to ten years: Imprisonment of either description for a term which may extend to three years, and a fine. If the offense is punishable with imprisonment not extending to ten years: Imprisonment of the description provided for the offense for a term which may extend to one-fourth part of the longest term of imprisonment provided for the offense, or with a fine, or both.

Cognizable or Non-Cognizable, Bailable or Non-Bailable: This offense is cognizable, meaning the police can arrest the accused without a warrant.

Bailable: This offense is bailable, indicating that the accused can secure bail and be released from custody until the trial is completed.

Comparison: Section 214 of the Indian Penal Code (IPC)[1732] also addresses the offense of offering a gift or restoration of property in consideration of screening an offender: IPC Section 214: States that whoever[1733] gives or causes, or offers or agrees to give or cause, any gratification to any person, or restores or causes the restoration of any property to any person, in consideration of that person's concealing[1734] an offense, or of his screening any person from legal punishment for any offense, or of his not proceeding against any person for the purpose of bringing him to legal punishment, shall be punished with imprisonment of either description for a term which may extend to seven years, or with a fine, or with both.

[1731] Ministry of Home Affairs. (2024). The Bharatiya Nyaya Sanhita, 2023. Retrieved from https://www.mha.gov.in/sites/default/files/250883_english_01042024.pdf

[1732] main.sci.gov.in

[1733] devgan.in

[1734] advocatetanmoy.com

Key Differences: BNS 251: Updated version in the new Bharatiya Nyaya Sanhita, with specific provisions for different types of offenses. IPC 214: Part of the older legal framework, now replaced by BNS 251.

BNS Section 252

Definition: Taking Gift to Help to Recover Stolen Property[1735] Section 252 of the Bharatiya Nyaya Sanhita (BNS) 2023 addresses the offense of taking or agreeing to take any gratification under the pretense of helping to recover stolen property, without making efforts to apprehend and convict the offender.

Illustration: If a person accepts a bribe to help someone recover stolen property but does not take any action to catch the thief, they are committing an offense under BNS 252.

Example: Suppose an individual receives a large sum of money from a victim to help recover stolen jewelry but does nothing to find the thief. This act falls under BNS 252.

Comment: This section highlights the serious implications of taking or agreeing to take any gratification to help recover stolen property without making efforts to catch the offender, which can obstruct justice and exploit victims.

Classification of Offence and Punishment Classification: This offense is classified as a serious criminal offense due to its potential to obstruct justice and exploit victims.

Punishment: The punishment for committing this offense under BNS 252 can be imprisonment of either description for a term which may extend to two years, or a fine, or both.

Cognizable or Non-Cognizable, Bailable or Non-Bailable: This offense is cognizable, meaning the police can arrest the accused without a warrant.

[1735] Ministry of Home Affairs. (2024). The Bharatiya Nyaya Sanhita, 2023. Retrieved from https://www.mha.gov.in/sites/default/files/250883_english_01042024.pdf

Bailable: This offense is bailable, indicating that the accused can secure bail and be released from custody until the trial is completed.

Comparison: Section 215 of the Indian Penal Code[1736] (IPC) also addresses the offense of taking a gift to help[1737] recover stolen property: IPC Section 215: States that whoever takes or agrees to take any gratification under pretense or on account of helping any person to recover any movable property of which they have been deprived by any offense punishable under this Code, shall, unless they use all means in their power to cause the offender to be apprehended and convicted of the offense, be punished with imprisonment of either description for a term which may extend to two years, or with a fine, or with both.

Key Differences: BNS 252: Updated version in the new Bharatiya Nyaya Sanhita, with specific provisions for different types of offenses. IPC 215: Part of the older legal framework, now replaced by BNS 252.

BNS Section 253

Definition: Harbouring Offender Who Has Escaped from Custody or Whose Apprehension Has Been Ordered[1738] Section 253 of the Bharatiya Nyaya Sanhita (BNS) 2023 addresses the offense of knowingly harbouring or concealing an offender who has escaped from lawful custody or whose apprehension has been ordered by a public servant.

Illustration: If a person provides shelter to a criminal who has escaped from jail, knowing that the person is wanted by the authorities, they are committing an offense under BNS 253.

Example: Suppose an individual hides a friend who has escaped from police custody, with the intention of preventing their arrest. This act falls under BNS 253.

[1736] main.sci.gov.in

[1737] advocatetanmoy.com

[1738] Ministry of Home Affairs. (2024). The Bharatiya Nyaya Sanhita, 2023. Retrieved from https://www.mha.gov.in/sites/default/files/250883_english_01042024.pdf

Comment: This section highlights the serious implications of harbouring an offender, which can obstruct justice and protect criminals from legal consequences.

Classification of Offence and Punishment Classification: This offense is classified as a serious criminal offense due to its potential to obstruct justice and protect criminals.

Punishment: The punishment for committing this offense under BNS 253 varies based on the severity of the offense committed by the offender: If the crime carries a death sentence: imprisonment of any kind for a maximum of seven years, along with a fine. If the offense carries a life sentence or a ten-year sentence in prison: imprisonment for a maximum of three years in each type of jail, with or without a fine. If the offense carries a maximum sentence of ten years in prison: imprisonment of the kind specified for the offense for a period of time that could equal one-fourth of the maximum sentence stipulated for the offense, a fine, or both.

Cognizable or Non-Cognizable, Bailable or Non-Bailable: This offense is cognizable, meaning the police can arrest the accused without a warrant.

Bailable: This offense is bailable, indicating that the accused can secure bail and be released from custody until the trial is completed.

Comparison: Section 216 of the Indian Penal Code[1739] (IPC) also addresses the offense of harbouring an offender[1740] who has escaped from custody or whose apprehension has been ordered: IPC Section 216: States that whoever, knowing that a person[1741] convicted of or charged with an offense is in lawful custody, escapes from such custody, or whenever a public servant orders a certain person to be apprehended for an offense, and harbours or conceals that person with the intention of preventing their apprehension, shall be punished with imprisonment of either description for a term which may extend to seven years, and shall also be liable to a fine.

[1739] main.sci.gov.in

[1740] advocatetanmoy.com

[1741] devgan.in

Key Differences: BNS 253: Updated version in the new Bharatiya Nyaya Sanhita, with specific provisions for different types of offenses. IPC 216: Part of the older legal framework, now replaced by BNS 253.

BNS Section 254

Definition: Penalty for Harbouring Robbers or Dacoits[1742] Section 254 of the Bharatiya Nyaya Sanhita (BNS) 2023 addresses the offense of knowingly harbouring or concealing individuals who are about to commit or have recently committed robbery or dacoity, with the intention of facilitating the crime or screening them from punishment.

Illustration: If a person provides shelter to a group of robbers knowing they have just committed a robbery, with the intent to help them evade arrest, they are committing an offense under BNS 254.

Example: Suppose an individual hides a friend who has committed a dacoity, knowing that the authorities are searching for them. This act falls under BNS 254.

Comment: This section highlights the serious implications of harbouring robbers or dacoits, which can obstruct justice and protect criminals from legal consequences.

Classification of Offence and Punishment Classification: This offense is classified as a serious criminal offense due to its potential to obstruct justice and protect criminals.

Punishment: The punishment for committing this offense under BNS 254 is rigorous imprisonment for a term which may extend to seven years, and the offender shall also be liable to a fine.

Cognizable or Non-Cognizable, Bailable or Non-Bailable: This offense is cognizable, meaning the police can arrest the accused without a warrant.

Bailable: This offense is bailable, indicating that the accused can secure bail and be released from custody until the trial is completed.

[1742] Ministry of Home Affairs. (2024). The Bharatiya Nyaya Sanhita, 2023. Retrieved from https://www.mha.gov.in/sites/default/files/250883_english_01042024.pdf

Comparison: Section 216A of the Indian Penal Code[1743] (IPC) also addresses the offense of harbouring[1744] robbers or dacoits: IPC Section 216A: States that whoever, knowing or having reason to believe that any persons are about to commit or have recently committed robbery or dacoity, harbours them or any of them, with the intention of facilitating the commission of such robbery or dacoity or of screening them or any of them from punishment, shall be punished with rigorous imprisonment for a term which may extend to seven years, and shall also be liable to a fine.

Key Differences: BNS 254: Updated version in the new Bharatiya Nyaya Sanhita, with specific provisions for different types of offenses. IPC 216A: Part of the older legal framework, now replaced by BNS 254.

BNS Section 255

Definition: Public Servant Disobeying Direction of Law with Intent to Save Person from Punishment or Property from Forfeiture[1745] Section 255 of the Bharatiya Nyaya Sanhita (BNS) 2023 addresses the offense committed by a public servant who knowingly disobeys any direction of the law with the intent to save a person from legal punishment or to save property from forfeiture.

Illustration: If police officer deliberately ignores a court order to arrest a suspect because they have a personal connection to the suspect, they are committing an offense under BNS 255.

Example: Suppose a public servant, such as a judge, intentionally disregards legal procedures to prevent the seizure of property that belongs to a friend or family member. This act falls under BNS 255.

Comment: This section emphasizes the serious implications of a public servant disobeying the direction of the law, which can undermine the integrity of the legal system and public trust.

[1743] main.sci.gov.in

[1744] advocatetanmoy.com

[1745] Ministry of Home Affairs. (2024). The Bharatiya Nyaya Sanhita, 2023. Retrieved from https://www.mha.gov.in/sites/default/files/250883_english_01042024.pdf

Classification of Offence and Punishment Classification: This offense is classified as a serious criminal offense due to its potential to undermine the integrity of the legal system and public trust.

Punishment: The punishment for committing[1746] this offense under BNS 255 is imprisonment of either description for a term which may extend to two years, or a fine, or both.

Cognizable or Non-Cognizable, Bailable or Non-Bailable: This offense is cognizable, meaning the police can arrest the accused without a warrant.

Bailable: This offense is bailable, indicating that the accused can secure bail and be released from custody until the trial is completed.

Comparison: Section 217 of the Indian Penal Code[1747] (IPC) also addresses the offense of a public servant disobeying the direction[1748] of the law with the intent to save a person[1749] from punishment or property from forfeiture: IPC Section 217: States that whoever, being a public servant, knowingly disobeys any direction of the law as to the way in which he is to conduct himself as such public servant, intending thereby to save, or knowing it to be likely that he will thereby save, any person from legal punishment, or subject him to a less punishment than that to which he is liable, or with intent to save, or knowing that he is likely thereby to save, any property from forfeiture or any charge to which it is liable by law, shall be punished with imprisonment of either description for a term which may extend to two years, or with a fine, or with both.

Key Differences: BNS 255: Updated version in the new Bharatiya Nyaya Sanhita, with specific provisions for different types of offenses. IPC 217: Part of the older legal framework, now replaced by BNS 255.

[1746] advocatetanmoy.com

[1747] www.bareactslive.com

[1748] www.bareactslive.com

[1749] devgan.in

BNS Section 256

Definition: Public Servant Framing Incorrect Record or Writing with Intent to Save Person from Punishment or Property from Forfeiture[1750] Section 256 of the Bharatiya Nyaya Sanhita (BNS) 2023 addresses the offense committed by a public servant who knowingly prepares incorrect records or writings with the intent to save a person from legal punishment or to save property from forfeiture.

Illustration: If police officer deliberately alters an arrest report to falsely show that a suspect was not present at the crime scene, they are committing an offense under BNS 256.

Example: Suppose a public servant, such as a clerk in a court, intentionally falsifies a document to prevent the seizure of property that belongs to a friend or family member[1751]. This act falls under BNS 256.

Comment: This section emphasizes the serious implications of a public servant[1752] disobeying the direction of the law, which can undermine the integrity of the legal system and public trust.

Classification of Offence and Punishment Classification: This offense is classified as a serious criminal offense due to its potential to undermine the integrity of the legal system and public trust.

Punishment: The punishment for committing this offense under BNS 256 is imprisonment[1753] of either description for a term which may extend to three years, or a fine, or both.

Cognizable or Non-Cognizable, Bailable or Non-Bailable: This offense is cognizable, meaning the police can arrest the accused without a warrant.

[1750] Ministry of Home Affairs. (2024). The Bharatiya Nyaya Sanhita, 2023. Retrieved from https://www.mha.gov.in/sites/default/files/250883_english_01042024.pdf

[1751] docplayer.net

[1752] devgan.in

[1753] devgan.in

Bailable: This offense is bailable, indicating that the accused can secure bail and be released from custody until the trial is completed.

Comparison: Section 218 of the Indian Penal Code[1754] (IPC) also addresses the offense of a public servant framing incorrect records or writings with the intent to save a person[1755] from punishment or property from forfeiture: IPC Section 218: States that whoever, being a public servant, and being as such public servant, charged with the preparation of any record or other writing, frames that record or writing in a manner which he knows to be incorrect, with intent to cause, or knowing it to be likely that he will thereby cause, loss or injury to the public or to any person, or with intent thereby to save, or knowing it to be likely that he will thereby save, any person from legal punishment, or with intent to save, or knowing that he is likely thereby to save, any property from forfeiture or other charge to which it is liable by law, shall be punished with imprisonment of either description for a term which may extend to three years, or with a fine, or with both.

Key Differences: BNS 256: Updated version in the new Bharatiya Nyaya Sanhita, with specific provisions for different types of offenses. IPC 218: Part of the older legal framework, now replaced by BNS 256.

BNS Section 257

Definition: Public Servant Corruptly Making Report, etc., Contrary to Law[1756] Section 257 of the Bharatiya Nyaya Sanhita (BNS) 2023 addresses the offense committed by a public servant who corruptly or maliciously makes or pronounces any report, order, verdict, or decision in any stage of a judicial proceeding, knowing it to be contrary to law.

[1754] www.bareactslive.com

[1755] devgan.in

[1756] Ministry of Home Affairs. (2024). The Bharatiya Nyaya Sanhita, 2023. Retrieved from https://www.mha.gov.in/sites/default/files/250883_english_01042024.pdf

Illustration: If a judge knowingly issues a verdict that contradicts established legal principles to favor a friend, they are committing an offense under BNS 257.

Example: Suppose a public servant, such as a magistrate, deliberately makes a false report to dismiss charges against a relative. This act falls under BNS 257.

Comment: This section emphasizes the serious implications of a public servant corruptly making a report or decision contrary to law, which can undermine the integrity of the judicial system and public trust.

Classification of Offence and Punishment Classification: This offense is classified as a serious criminal offense due to its potential to undermine the integrity of the judicial system and public trust.

Punishment: The punishment for committing this offense under BNS 257 is imprisonment of either description for a term which may extend to seven years, or a fine, or both.[1757]

Cognizable or Non-Cognizable, Bailable or Non-Bailable: This offense is non-cognizable, meaning the police cannot arrest the accused without a warrant.

Bailable: This offense is bailable, indicating that the accused can secure bail and be released from custody until the trial is completed.

Comparison: Section 219 of the Indian Penal Code[1758] (IPC) also addresses the offense of a public servant corruptly making a report, etc., contrary to law: IPC Section 219: States that whoever, being a public servant, corruptly or maliciously makes or pronounces in any stage of a judicial proceeding, any report, order, verdict, or decision which he knows to be contrary to law, shall be punished with imprisonment[1759] of either description for a term which may extend to seven years, or with a fine, or with both.

[1757] advocatetanmoy.com

[1758] www.bareactslive.com

[1759] devgan.in

Key Differences: BNS 257: Updated version in the new Bharatiya Nyaya Sanhita, with specific provisions for different types of offenses. IPC 219: Part of the older legal framework, now replaced by BNS 257.

BNS Section 258

Definition: Commitment for Trial or Confinement by Person Having Authority Who Knows That He Is Acting Contrary[1760] to Law Section 258 of the Bharatiya Nyaya Sanhita (BNS) 2023 addresses the offense committed by a public servant who knowingly commits or keeps a person in confinement for trial or confinement, knowing that they are acting contrary to law.

Illustration: If police officer knowingly detains a suspect without legal grounds, they are committing an offense under BNS 258.

Example: Suppose a magistrate intentionally commits a person to trial without proper legal authority, knowing that the action is illegal. This act falls under BNS 258.

Comment: This section emphasizes the serious implications of a public servant[1761] knowingly acting contrary to law, which can undermine the integrity of the legal system and public trust.

Classification of Offence and Punishment Classification: This offense is classified as a serious criminal offense due to its potential to undermine the integrity of the legal system and public trust.

Punishment: The punishment for committing this offense under BNS 258 is imprisonment of either description for a term which may extend to seven years, or a fine, or both.[1762]

Cognizable or Non-Cognizable, Bailable or Non-Bailable: This offense is cognizable, meaning the police can arrest the accused without a warrant.

[1760] Ministry of Home Affairs. (2024). The Bharatiya Nyaya Sanhita, 2023. Retrieved from https://www.mha.gov.in/sites/default/files/250883_english_01042024.pdf

[1761] devgan.in

[1762] devgan.in

Bailable: This offense is bailable, indicating that the accused can secure bail and be released from custody until the trial is completed.

Comparison: Section 220 of the Indian Penal Code[1763] (IPC) also addresses the offense of commitment for trial or confinement by a person having authority who knows that they are acting contrary to law: IPC Section 220: States that whoever, being in any office which gives[1764] them legal authority to commit persons for trial or to confinement, or to keep persons in confinement, corruptly or maliciously commits any person for trial or to confinement, or keeps any person in confinement, in the exercise of that authority knowing that in so doing they are acting contrary to law, shall be punished with imprisonment of either description for a term which may extend to seven years, or with a fine, or with both[1765].

Key Differences: BNS 258: Updated version in the new Bharatiya Nyaya Sanhita, with specific provisions for different types of offenses. IPC 220: Part of the older legal framework, now replaced by BNS 258.

BNS Section 259

Definition: Intentional Omission to Apprehend on Part of Public Servant Bound to Apprehend[1766] Section 259 of the Bharatiya Nyaya Sanhita (BNS) 2023 addresses the offense committed by a public servant who intentionally fails to apprehend or aids in the escape of a person they are legally bound to apprehend or keep in confinement.

Illustration: If a police officer, knowing that a suspect is liable to be apprehended for a serious crime, intentionally decides not to arrest them or even helps them escape, they are committing an offense under BNS 259.

[1763] www.bareactslive.com

[1764] patnahighcourt.gov.in

[1765] devgan.in

[1766] Ministry of Home Affairs. (2024). The Bharatiya Nyaya Sanhita, 2023. Retrieved from https://www.mha.gov.in/sites/default/files/250883_english_01042024.pdf

Example: Suppose a public servant, such as a jailer, intentionally allows a prisoner charged with a capital offense to escape. This act falls under BNS 259.

Comment: This section highlights the serious implications of a public servant intentionally failing to apprehend or aiding in the escape of a person they are legally bound to apprehend, which can undermine the integrity of the legal system and public trust.

Classification of Offence and Punishment Classification: This offense is classified as a serious criminal offense due to its potential to undermine the integrity of the legal system and public trust.

Punishment: The punishment for committing this offense under BNS 259 varies based on the severity of the offense: If the person under detention was accused of, or likely to be found guilty of, a crime carrying a death sentence, they could face imprisonment of any kind for up to seven years, with or without a fine. If the individual under detention was accused of, or likely to be found guilty of, a crime carrying a life sentence or a term that might go up to ten years in prison: imprisonment for a maximum of three years in each type of jail, with or without a fine.[1767] For any other offense: Imprisonment of either description for a term which may extend to two years, with or without a fine.

Cognizable or Non-Cognizable, Bailable or Non-Bailable: This offense is cognizable, meaning the police can arrest the accused without a warrant.

Bailable: This offense is bailable, indicating that the accused can secure bail and be released from custody until the trial is completed.

Comparison: Section 221 of the Indian Penal Code[1768] (IPC) also addresses the offense of intentional omission to apprehend on the part of a public servant bound to apprehend: IPC Section 221: explains that if a public servant who is legally required to arrest or detain someone who is accused of committing a crime, willfully fails to do so, willfully allows that person to escape, or willfully assists that person in escaping or

---

[1767] devgan.in

[1768] www.bareactslive.com

attempting to escape from that confinement, they will be punished as follows: Imprisonment of either description for a term which may extend to seven years, with or without a fine, if the person in confinement, or who ought to have been apprehended, was charged with, or liable to be apprehended for, an offense punishable with death. Imprisonment of either description for a term which may extend to three years, with or without a fine, if the person in confinement, or who ought to have been apprehended, was charged with, or liable to be apprehended for, an offense punishable with imprisonment for life or imprisonment for a term which may extend to ten years. Imprisonment of either description for a term which may extend to two years, with or without a fine, for any other offense.[1769]

Key Differences: BNS 259: Updated version in the new Bharatiya Nyaya Sanhita, with specific provisions for different types of offenses. IPC 221: Part of the older legal framework, now replaced by BNS 259.

BNS Section 260

Definition: Intentional Omission to Apprehend on Part of Public Servant Bound to Apprehend Person Under Sentence or Lawfully Committed[1770] Section 260 of the Bharatiya Nyaya Sanhita (BNS) 2023 addresses the offense committed by a public servant who intentionally fails to apprehend or aids in the escape of a person they are legally bound to apprehend or keep in confinement.

Illustration: If a police officer, knowing that a suspect is under a court sentence for a serious crime, intentionally decides not to arrest them or even helps them escape, they are committing an offense under BNS 260.

Example: Suppose a public servant, such as a jailer, intentionally allows a prisoner who has been lawfully committed to custody to escape[1771]. This act falls under BNS 260.

[1769] devgan.in

[1770] Ministry of Home Affairs. (2024). The Bharatiya Nyaya Sanhita, 2023. Retrieved from https://www.mha.gov.in/sites/default/files/250883_english_01042024.pdf

[1771] www.bareactslive.com

Comment: This section highlights the serious implications of a public servant intentionally failing to apprehend or aiding in the escape of a person they are legally bound to apprehend, which can undermine the integrity of the legal system and public trust.

Classification of Offence and Punishment Classification: This offense is classified as a serious criminal offense due to its potential to undermine the integrity of the legal system and public trust.

Punishment: The punishment for committing this offense under BNS 260 varies based on the severity of the offense: If the person in confinement was under a sentence of death: imprisonment of any kind for a maximum of fourteen years, with or without a fine, or imprisonment for life. Imprisonment of either kind for a period that may extend to seven years, with or without a fine, if the person in confinement was facing life in prison or imprisonment for ten years or more. Any other offense carries a maximum sentence of three years in prison of any kind, with or without a fine. [1772]

Cognizable or Non-Cognizable Bailable or Non-Bailable Cognizable: This offense is cognizable, meaning the police can arrest the accused without a warrant.

Bailable: This offense is bailable, indicating that the accused can secure bail and be released from custody until the trial is completed.

Comparison: Section 222 of the Indian Penal Code[1773] (IPC) also addresses the offense of intentional omission to apprehend on the part of a public servant bound to apprehend a person under sentence or lawfully committed: IPC Section 222: explains that if a public servant who is legally required to apprehend or confine someone who has been sentenced by a court of justice for any offense or who is lawfully in custody willfully fails to do so, willfully allows that person to escape, or willfully assists that person in escaping or attempting to escape from such confinement, they will be punished as follows: imprisonment for life or imprisonment of any kind for a maximum of fourteen years, with or without a fine, if the

---

[1772] devgan.in

[1773] www.bareactslive.com

individual being held or who should have been caught is facing a death sentence. If the person in confinement or who should have been apprehended is subject to a court sentence, or a commutation of such a sentence, to imprisonment for life, imprisonment for ten years, or upwards, they may be imprisoned for a period of imprisonment of any kind for a maximum of seven years, with or without a fine. For every other offense, imprisonment of any kind for a maximum of three years, with or without a fine.[1774]

Key Differences: BNS 260: Updated version in the new Bharatiya Nyaya Sanhita, with specific provisions for different types of offenses. IPC 222: Part of the older legal framework, now replaced by BNS 260.

BNS Section 261

Definition: Escape from Confinement or Custody Negligently Suffered by Public Servant Section[1775] 261 of the Bharatiya Nyaya Sanhita (BNS) 2023 addresses the offense committed by a public servant who negligently allows a person in their custody to escape.

Illustration: If a jailer forgets to lock a cell door and a prisoner escapes, they are committing an offense under BNS 261.

Example: Suppose a police officer, responsible for transporting a suspect, leaves the suspect unattended in a vehicle, and the suspect escapes. This act falls under BNS 261.

Comment: This section highlights the serious implications of negligently allowing an escape, which can undermine public trust and the integrity of the legal system.

Classification of Offence and Punishment Classification: This offense is classified as a criminal offense due to its potential to undermine public trust and the integrity of the legal system.

[1774] devgan.in

[1775] Ministry of Home Affairs. (2024). The Bharatiya Nyaya Sanhita, 2023. Retrieved from https://www.mha.gov.in/sites/default/files/250883_english_01042024.pdf

Punishment: The punishment for committing this offense under BNS 261 is simple imprisonment for a term which may extend to two years, or a fine, or both.[1776]

Cognizable or Non-Cognizable, Bailable or Non-Bailable: This offense is non-cognizable, meaning the police cannot arrest the accused without a warrant.

Bailable: This offense is bailable, indicating that the accused can secure bail and be released from custody until the trial is completed.

Comparison: Section 223 of the Indian Penal Code[1777] (IPC) also addresses the offense of escape from confinement or custody negligently suffered by a public servant: IPC Section 223: It states that if a public servant who is legally required to confine someone who has been charged with or convicted of a crime or who has been lawfully placed in custody allows that person to escape, they will be punished with simple imprisonment for a maximum of two years, a fine, or both.[1778]

Key Differences: BNS 261: Updated version in the new Bharatiya Nyaya Sanhita, with specific provisions for different types of offenses. IPC 223: Part of the older legal framework, now replaced by BNS 261.

BNS Section 262

Definition: Resistance or Obstruction by a Person to His Lawful Apprehension[1779] Section 262 of the Bharatiya Nyaya Sanhita (BNS) 2023 addresses the offense committed by a person who intentionally offers resistance or illegal obstruction to their lawful apprehension for any offense with which they are charged or convicted, or attempts to escape from lawful custody.

[1776] devgan.in

[1777] www.bareactslive.com

[1778] devgan.in

[1779] Ministry of Home Affairs. (2024). The Bharatiya Nyaya Sanhita, 2023. Retrieved from https://www.mha.gov.in/sites/default/files/250883_english_01042024.pdf

Illustration: If an individual, knowing they are charged with theft, physically resists arrest by a police officer, they are committing an offense under BNS 262.

Example: Suppose a person, who has been convicted of fraud, tries to break free from police custody during transport to the court. This act falls under BNS 262.

Comment: This section highlights the serious implications of resisting lawful apprehension, which can undermine the legal system and public order.

Classification of Offence and Punishment Classification: This offense is classified as a criminal offense due to its potential to undermine the legal system and public order.

Punishment: The punishment for committing this offense under BNS 262 is imprisonment of either description for a term which may extend to two years, or a fine, or both.[1780]

Cognizable or Non-Cognizable, Bailable or Non-Bailable: This offense is cognizable, meaning the police can arrest the accused without a warrant.

Bailable: This offense is bailable, indicating that the accused can secure bail and be released from custody until the trial is completed.

Comparison: Section 224 of the Indian Penal Code[1781] (IPC) also addresses the offense of resistance or obstruction by a person to their lawful apprehension: IPC Section 224: It states that anyone who willfully resists or illegally obstructs the lawful apprehension of themselves for any offense for which they are charged or convicted, or who flees or attempts to flee from any custody for which they are lawfully detained for any such offense, faces a maximum sentence of two years in either type of imprisonment, a fine, or both.[1782]

[1780] devgan.in

[1781] www.bareactslive.com

[1782] devgan.in

Key Differences: BNS 262: Updated version in the new Bharatiya Nyaya Sanhita, with specific provisions for different types of offenses. IPC 224: Part of the older legal framework, now replaced by BNS 262.

BNS Section 263

Definition: Resistance or Obstruction to Lawful Apprehension of Another Person[1783] Section 263 of the Bharatiya Nyaya Sanhita (BNS) 2023 addresses the offense committed by a person who intentionally offers resistance or illegal obstruction to the lawful apprehension of another person for an offense, or attempts to rescue another person from lawful custody.

Illustration: If an individual, knowing that their friend is being lawfully arrested for theft, physically intervenes to prevent the arrest, they are committing an offense under BNS 263.

Example: Suppose a person tries to break into a police station to free a relative who has been lawfully detained for a serious crime. This act falls under BNS 263.

Comment: This section underscores the serious implications of obstructing lawful apprehension, which can undermine public order and the integrity of the legal system.

Classification of Offence and Punishment Classification: This offense is classified as a criminal offense due to its potential to undermine public order and the legal system.

Punishment: According to BNS 263, the penalty for this infraction is either a fine, a period of imprisonment of any kind up to two years, or both. If the person who is to be apprehended, rescued, or attempted to be rescued is charged with, or likely to be apprehended for, an offense that carries a life sentence or a term of imprisonment that can last up to ten years, they

[1783] Ministry of Home Affairs. (2024). The Bharatiya Nyaya Sanhita, 2023. Retrieved from https://www.mha.gov.in/sites/default/files/250883_english_01042024.pdf

will be punished with either type of imprisonment for a maximum of three years, in addition to a fine.[1784]

Cognizable or Non-Cognizable, Bailable or Non-Bailable: This offense is cognizable, meaning the police can arrest the accused without a warrant.

Bailable: This offense is bailable, indicating that the accused can secure bail and be released from custody until the trial is completed.

Comparison: Section 225 of the Indian Penal Code[1785] (IPC) also addresses the offense of resistance or obstruction to lawful apprehension of another person: IPC Section 225: It states that anyone who willfully resists or unlawfully obstructs the lawful arrest of another person for a crime, or who attempts to free another person from custody where that person is lawfully detained for a crime, faces a maximum sentence of two years in either type of jail, a fine, or both. If the individual is to be captured, or the individual who was saved or attempted to be saved, is accused of or at risk of being caught for a crime that carries a life sentence or a term of imprisonment that can last up to ten years. The punishment is either type of imprisonment that can last up to three years, along with a fine.[1786]

Key Differences: BNS 263: Updated version in the new Bharatiya Nyaya Sanhita, with specific provisions for different types of offenses. IPC 225: Part of the older legal framework, now replaced by BNS 263.

BNS Section 264

Definition: Omission to Apprehend, or Sufferance of Escape, on Part of Public Servant, in Cases Not Otherwise Provided for[1787] Section 264 of the Bharatiya Nyaya Sanhita (BNS) 2023 addresses the offense committed by a public servant[1788] who intentionally or negligently

---

[1784] devgan.in

[1785] www.bareactslive.com

[1786] devgan.in

[1787] Ministry of Home Affairs. (2024). The Bharatiya Nyaya Sanhita, 2023. Retrieved from https://www.mha.gov.in/sites/default/files/250883_english_01042024.pdf

[1788] devgan.in

fails to apprehend or allows a person to escape from confinement in cases not covered by other specific sections.

Illustration: If a public servant, such as a police officer, intentionally fails to arrest a suspect who is known to have committed a crime, they are committing an offense under BNS 264.

Example: Suppose a jailer, who is responsible for keeping a prisoner in custody, negligently leaves the prison gate unlocked, allowing the prisoner to escape. This act falls under BNS 264.

Comment: This section highlights the significant impact of a public servant's intentional or negligent actions in allowing an escape, which can undermine public trust and the integrity of the legal system. The framework under BNS 264 ensures that both intentional and negligent omissions are appropriately penalized, reinforcing the importance of accountability.

Classification of Offence and Punishment Classification: This offense is classified as a criminal offense due to its potential to undermine public trust and the integrity of the legal system.

Punishment: The punishment for committing this offense under BNS 264 varies based on the nature[1789] of the act: If the act is intentional: Imprisonment of either description for a term which may extend to three years, or a fine, or both. If the act is negligent: Simple imprisonment for a term which may extend to two years, or a fine[1790], or both.

Cognizable or Non-Cognizable, Bailable or Non-Bailable: This offense is cognizable, meaning the police can arrest the accused without a warrant.

Bailable: This offense is bailable, indicating that the accused can secure bail and be released from custody until the trial is completed.

Comparison: Section 225A of the Indian Penal Code[1791] (IPC) also addresses the offense of omission to apprehend or sufferance of escape on

---

[1789] assets.publishing.service.gov.uk

[1790] advocatetanmoy.com

[1791] Ministry of Home Affairs. (2024). The Bharatiya Nyaya Sanhita, 2023. Retrieved from https://www.mha.gov.in/sites/default/files/250883_english_01042024.pdf

the part of a public servant in cases not otherwise provided for: IPC Section 225A: explains that if a public servant who is legally required to apprehend or confine someone who is not covered by sections 221, 222, or 223 of any current law fails to do so or allows that person to escape from confinement, they will be punished: If the behavior is deliberate: either type of imprisonment with a maximum sentence of three years, a fine, or both. [1792]If the act is negligent: Simple imprisonment for a term which may extend to two years, or with a fine, or with both.

Key Differences: BNS 264: Updated version in the new Bharatiya Nyaya Sanhita, with specific provisions for different types of offenses. IPC 225A: Part of the older legal framework, now replaced by BNS 264.

BNS Section 265

Definition: Resistance or Obstruction to Lawful Apprehension or Escape or Rescue in Cases Not Otherwise Provided[1793] for Section 265 of the Bharatiya Nyaya Sanhita (BNS) 2023 addresses the offense committed by a person who intentionally offers resistance or illegal obstruction to their own or another person's lawful apprehension, escapes from lawful custody, or attempts to rescue another person from lawful custody in cases not covered by other specific sections.

Illustration: If an individual, knowing they are charged with a crime, physically resists arrest by a police officer, they are committing an offense under BNS 265.

Example: Suppose a person tries to break into a police station to free a relative who has been lawfully detained for a serious crime[1794]. This act falls under BNS 265.

[1792] advocatetanmoy.com

[1793] Ministry of Home Affairs. (2024). The Bharatiya Nyaya Sanhita, 2023. Retrieved from https://www.mha.gov.in/sites/default/files/250883_english_01042024.pdf

[1794] repository.jmls.edu

Classification of Offence and Punishment Classification: This offense is classified as a criminal offense due to its potential to undermine public order and the legal system.

Punishment: The punishment for committing this offense under BNS 265 is imprisonment of either description for a term which may extend to six months, or a fine[1795], or both.

Cognizable or Non-Cognizable, Bailable or Non-Bailable: This offense is cognizable, meaning the police can arrest the accused without a warrant.

Bailable: This offense is bailable, indicating that the accused can secure bail and be released from custody until the trial is completed.

Comparison: Section 225B of the Indian Penal Code[1796] (IPC) also addresses the offense of resistance or obstruction to lawful apprehension, escape, or rescue in cases not otherwise provided for: IPC Section 225B: States that whoever, in any case not provided for in section 224 or section 225 or in any other law for the time being in force, intentionally offers any resistance or illegal obstruction to the lawful apprehension of himself or of any other person, or escapes or attempts to escape from any custody in which he is lawfully detained, or rescues or attempts to rescue any other person from any custody in which that person is lawfully detained, shall be punished with imprisonment of either description for a term which may extend to six months, or with a fine[1797], or with both.

Key Differences: BNS 265: Updated version in the new Bharatiya Nyaya Sanhita, with specific provisions for different types of offenses. IPC 225B: Part of the older legal framework, now replaced by BNS 265.

[1795] advocatetanmoy.com

[1796] devgan.in

[1797] advocatetanmoy.com

BNS Section 266

Definition: Violation of Condition of Remission of Punishment Section 266[1798] of the Bharatiya Nyaya Sanhita (BNS) 2023 addresses the offense committed by a person who knowingly violates any condition attached to their conditional remission of punishment.

Illustration: If a person, who was granted conditional remission of their sentence on the condition that they do not leave the city without permission, travels out of the city without seeking permission, they are committing an offense under BNS 266.

Example: Suppose an individual was released on parole with the condition that they must report to the police station every week[1799]. If they fail to do so, they are violating the conditions of their remission and committing an offense under BNS 266.

Comment: This section underscores the importance of adhering to the conditions of remission to maintain the integrity of the legal system and public trust.

Classification of Offence and Punishment Classification: This offense is classified as a criminal offense due to its potential to undermine the integrity of the legal system[1800] and public trust.

Punishment: The punishment for committing this offense under BNS 266 is: If the person has not yet served any part of their original sentence: The punishment to which they were originally sentenced. If the person has already served part of their original sentence: The remainder of the original sentence.

Cognizable or Non-Cognizable, Bailable or Non-Bailable: This offense is cognizable, meaning the police can arrest the accused without a warrant.

[1798] Ministry of Home Affairs. (2024). The Bharatiya Nyaya Sanhita, 2023. Retrieved from https://www.mha.gov.in/sites/default/files/250883_english_01042024.pdf

[1799] assets.publishing.service.gov.uk

[1800] www.bareactslive.com

Bailable: This offense is non-bailable, indicating that the accused cannot secure bail and must remain in custody until the trial is completed.

Comparison: Section 227 of the Indian Penal Code[1801] (IPC) also addresses the offense of violation of the condition of remission of punishment: IPC Section 227: It states that if someone accepts a conditional remission of punishment and then willfully violates any of the conditions under which the remission was granted, they will be punished with the original punishment, if they have already received none of it, and with as much of the punishment as they have not already received.[1802]

Key Differences: BNS 266: Updated version in the new Bharatiya Nyaya Sanhita, with specific provisions for different types of offenses. IPC 227: Part of the older legal framework, now replaced by BNS 266.

BNS Section 267

Definition: Intentional Insult or Interruption to Public Servant Sitting in Judicial Proceeding[1803] Section 267 of the Bharatiya Nyaya Sanhita (BNS) 2023 addresses the offense committed by a person who intentionally offers any insult or causes any interruption to a public servant while they are sitting in any stage of a judicial proceeding.

Illustration: If an individual, during a court hearing, loudly insults a judge or interrupts the proceedings by shouting, they are committing an offense under BNS 267.

Example: Suppose a person attending a trial stands up and starts making derogatory remarks about the public prosecutor, disrupting the court's proceedings. This act falls under BNS 267.

Comment: This section underscores the importance of maintaining decorum and respect in judicial proceedings. Disruptions can undermine

---

[1801] devgan.in

[1802] advocatetanmoy.com

[1803] Ministry of Home Affairs. (2024). The Bharatiya Nyaya Sanhita, 2023. Retrieved from https://www.mha.gov.in/sites/default/files/250883_english_01042024.pdf

the integrity of the judicial process and public order, highlighting the need for strict penalties.

Classification of Offence and Punishment Classification: This offense is classified as a criminal offense due to its potential to undermine the integrity of the judicial process and public order.

Punishment: The punishment for committing this offense under BNS 267 is simple imprisonment for a term which may extend to six months, or a fine which may extend to five thousand rupees, or both.[1804]

Cognizable or Non-Cognizable, Bailable or Non-Bailable: This offense is non-cognizable, meaning the police cannot arrest the accused without a warrant.

Bailable: This offense is bailable, indicating that the accused can secure bail and be released from custody until the trial is completed.

Comparison: Section 228 of the Indian Penal Code[1805] (IPC) also addresses the offense of intentional insult or interruption to a public servant sitting in a judicial proceeding: IPC Section 228: Declares that anyone who willfully insults or disturbs a public servant during any phase of a legal proceeding faces a maximum sentence of six months in simple imprisonment, a maximum fine of one thousand rupees, or both.[1806]

Key Differences: BNS 267: Updated version in the new Bharatiya Nyaya Sanhita, with specific provisions for different types of offenses. IPC 228: Part of the older legal framework, now replaced by BNS 267.

BNS Section 268

Definition: Personation of Assessor Section 268 of the Bharatiya Nyaya Sanhita (BNS) 2023 addresses the offense committed by a person who intentionally causes or knowingly allows themselves to be

---

[1804] advocatetanmoy.com

[1805] www.bareactslive.com

[1806] advocatetanmoy.com

empaneled or sworn as an assessor[1807] in a case where they are not legally entitled to be, and then voluntarily serves in that role.

Illustration: If an individual, knowing they are not qualified, falsely represents themselves to be eligible and gets selected as an assessor in a court case, they are committing an offense under BNS 268.

Example: Suppose a person, who is not a legal expert, manages to get empaneled as an assessor in a high-profile case by providing false credentials. This act falls under BNS 268.

Comment: This section underscores the serious implications of personation in the judicial process, which can undermine the integrity and fairness of legal proceedings.

Classification of Offence and Punishment Classification: This offense is classified as a criminal offense due to its potential to undermine the integrity of the judicial process.

Punishment: The punishment for committing this offense under BNS 268 is imprisonment of either description for a term which may extend to two years, or a fine[1808], or both.

Cognizable or Non-Cognizable, Bailable or Non-Bailable: This offense is non-cognizable, meaning the police cannot arrest the accused without a warrant.

Bailable: This offense is bailable, indicating that the accused can secure bail and be released from custody until the trial is completed.

Comparison: Section 229 of the Indian Penal Code (IPC) also addresses the offense of personation of a juror or assessor: IPC Section 229: States that whoever, by personation or otherwise[1809], intentionally causes or knowingly suffers himself to be returned, empaneled, or sworn as a juror or assessor in any case in which he knows that he is not entitled by law to be so returned, empaneled, or sworn, or knowing himself to have been so

---

[1807] prsindia.org

[1808] advocatetanmoy.com

[1809] devgan.in

returned, empaneled, or sworn contrary to law, shall voluntarily serve on such jury or as such assessor, shall be punished with imprisonment of either description for a term which may extend to two years, or with a fine, or with both.[1810]

Key Differences: BNS 268: Updated version in the new Bharatiya Nyaya Sanhita, with specific provisions for different types of offenses. IPC 229: Part of the older legal framework, now replaced by BNS 268.

BNS Section 269

Definition: Failure by Person Released on Bail or Bond to Appear in Court[1811] Section 269 of the Bharatiya Nyaya Sanhita (BNS) 2023 addresses the offense committed by a person who, having been charged with an offense and released on bail or bond, fails to appear in court without sufficient cause.

Illustration: If an individual, who was released on bail with the condition to appear in court on a specific date, fails to show up without a valid reason, they are committing an offense under BNS 269.

Example: Suppose a person released on bail for a theft charge does not appear in court as required because they forgot the date. This act falls under BNS 269.

Comment: This section underscores the importance of adhering to bail conditions to maintain the integrity of the legal process and public order.

Classification of Offence and Punishment Classification: This offense is classified as a criminal offense due to its potential to undermine the legal process and public order. Punishment: The punishment for committing this offense under BNS 269 is imprisonment of either description for a term which may extend to one year, or a fine[1812], or both.

[1810] advocatetanmoy.com

[1811] Ministry of Home Affairs. (2024). The Bharatiya Nyaya Sanhita, 2023. Retrieved from https://www.mha.gov.in/sites/default/files/250883_english_01042024.pdf

[1812] advocatetanmoy.com

Cognizable or Non-Cognizable, Bailable or Non-Bailable: This offense is cognizable, meaning the police can arrest the accused without a warrant.

Bailable: This offense is bailable, indicating that the accused can secure bail and be released from custody until the trial is completed.

Comparison: Section 229A of the Indian Penal Code (IPC) also addresses the offense of failure by a person released on bail or bond to appear in court: IPC Section 229A: States that whoever, having been charged with an offense and released on bail or on bond without sureties, fails without sufficient cause (the burden of proving which shall lie upon him), to appear in court in accordance with the terms of the bail or bond, shall be punished with imprisonment of either description for a term which may extend to one year, or with a fine, or with both.[1813]

Key Differences: BNS 269: Updated version in the new Bharatiya Nyaya Sanhita, with specific provisions for different types of offenses. IPC 229A: Part of the older legal framework, now replaced by BNS 269.

[1813] prsindia.org

CHAPTER-XV; OF OFFENCES AFFECTING THE PUBLIC HEALTH, SAFETY, CONVENIENCE, DECENCY AND MORALS

BNS Section 270

Definition: Public Nuisance[1814] Section 270 of the Bharatiya Nyaya Sanhita (BNS) 2023 addresses the offense of public nuisance. A person is guilty of a public nuisance if they do any act or are guilty of an illegal omission which causes any common injury, danger, or annoyance to the public or to the people in general who dwell or occupy property in the vicinity.

Illustration: If an individual dumps garbage in a public park, causing inconvenience and health hazards to the public, they are committing an offense under BNS 270.

Example: Suppose a factory releases pollutants into a river, affecting the water supply and health of nearby residents. This act falls under BNS 270.

Comment: This section highlights the significant impact of public nuisances, which can harm public health, safety, and order. It underscores the importance of maintaining public spaces and resources free from activities that could endanger or annoy the community.

Classification of Offence and Punishment Classification: This offense is classified as a criminal offense due to its potential to harm public health, safety, and order.

[1814] Ministry of Home Affairs. (2024). The Bharatiya Nyaya Sanhita, 2023. Retrieved from https://www.mha.gov.in/sites/default/files/250883_english_01042024.pdf

Punishment: The punishment for committing this offense under BNS 270 is simple imprisonment for a term which may extend to six months, or a fine which may extend to five thousand rupees[1815], or both.

Cognizable or Non-Cognizable, Bailable or Non-Bailable: This offense is cognizable, meaning the police can arrest the accused without a warrant.

Bailable: This offense is bailable, indicating that the accused can secure bail and be released from custody until the trial is completed.

Comparison: Section 268 of the Indian Penal Code (IPC) also addresses the offense of public nuisance: IPC Section 268: States that a person is guilty of a public nuisance who does any act or is guilty of an illegal omission which causes any common injury[1816], danger, or annoyance to the public or to the people in general who dwell or occupy[1817] property in the vicinity. A common nuisance is not excused on the ground that it causes some convenience or advantage.

Key Differences: BNS 270: Updated version in the new Bharatiya Nyaya Sanhita, with specific provisions for different types of offenses.IPC 268: Part of the older legal framework, now replaced by BNS 270.

BNS Section 271

Definition: Negligent Act Likely to Spread Infection of Disease Dangerous to Life[1818] Section 271 of the Bharatiya Nyaya Sanhita (BNS) 2023 addresses the offense committed by a person who unlawfully or negligently does any act which is, and which he knows or has reason to believe to be, likely to spread the infection of any disease dangerous to life.

[1815] advocatetanmoy.com

[1816] advocatetanmoy.com

[1817] devgan.in

[1818] Ministry of Home Affairs. (2024). The Bharatiya Nyaya Sanhita, 2023. Retrieved from https://www.mha.gov.in/sites/default/files/250883_english_01042024.pdf

Illustration: If a person, knowing they are infected with a contagious disease, fails to take necessary precautions and interacts with others, they are committing an offense under BNS 271.

Example: Suppose a food handler, who is aware they have a highly contagious disease, continues to work without informing their employer or taking any preventive measures. This act falls under BNS 271.

Comment: This section underscores the importance of preventing the spread of dangerous diseases to protect public health and safety. Negligent acts that risk public health are taken seriously and penalized to ensure compliance and responsibility.

Classification of Offence and Punishment Classification: This offense is classified as a criminal offense due to its potential to harm public health and safety.

Punishment: The punishment for committing this offense under BNS 271 is imprisonment of either description for a term which may extend to six months, or a fine[1819], or both.

Cognizable or Non-Cognizable, Bailable or Non-Bailable: This offense is cognizable, meaning the police can arrest the accused without a warrant.

Bailable: This offense is bailable, indicating that the accused can secure bail and be released from custody until the trial is completed.

Comparison: with IPC Section 269Section 269 of the Indian Penal Code (IPC) also addresses the offense of negligent acts likely to spread infection of disease dangerous to life: IPC Section 269: States that whoever unlawfully or negligently does any act which is, and which he knows or has reason to believe to be, likely to spread the infection of any disease dangerous to life, shall be punished with imprisonment of either description for a term which may extend to six months, or with a fine, or with both.[1820]

[1819] advocatetanmoy.com

[1820] advocatetanmoy.com

Key Differences: BNS 271: Updated version in the new Bharatiya Nyaya Sanhita, with specific provisions for different types of offenses. IPC 269: Part of the older legal framework, now replaced by BNS 271.

BNS Section 272

Definition: Malignant Act Likely to Spread Infection of Disease Dangerous to Life[1821] Section 272 of the Bharatiya Nyaya Sanhita (BNS) 2023 addresses the offense committed by a person who malignantly does any act which is, and which he knows or has reason to believe to be, likely to spread the infection of any disease dangerous to life.

Illustration: If a person, knowing they are infected with a highly contagious disease, intentionally coughs or sneezes in a crowded area without taking any precautions, they are committing an offense under BNS 272.

Example: Suppose an individual with a known case of tuberculosis knowingly spits in a public place, potentially spreading the infection to others. This act falls under BNS 272.

Comment: This section underscores the serious implications of acting malignantly in ways that spread dangerous diseases, which can cause significant harm to public health and safety.

Classification of Offence and Punishment Classification: This offense is classified as a criminal offense due to its potential to cause significant harm to public health and safety.

Punishment: The punishment for committing this offense under BNS 272 is imprisonment of either description for a term which may extend to two years, or a fine[1822], or both.

[1821] Ministry of Home Affairs. (2024). The Bharatiya Nyaya Sanhita, 2023. Retrieved from https://www.mha.gov.in/sites/default/files/250883_english_01042024.pdf

[1822] Ministry of Home Affairs. (2024). The Bharatiya Nyaya Sanhita, 2023. Retrieved from https://www.mha.gov.in/sites/default/files/250883_english_01042024.pdf

Cognizable or Non-Cognizable, Bailable or Non-Bailable: This offense is cognizable, meaning the police can arrest the accused without a warrant.

Bailable: This offense is bailable, indicating that the accused can secure bail and be released from custody until the trial is completed.

Comparison: Section 270 of the Indian Penal Code (IPC) also addresses the offense of malignant acts likely to spread infection of disease dangerous to life: IPC Section 270: Declares that anybody who intentionally commits an act that is, or that he knows or has reason to think is, likely to transmit the infection of any disease that is harmful to life faces a maximum sentence of two years in jail of any kind, a fine, or both. [1823]

Key Differences: BNS 272: Updated version in the new Bharatiya Nyaya Sanhita, with specific provisions for different types of offenses. IPC 270: Part of the older legal framework, now replaced by BNS 272.

BNS Section 273

Definition: Disobedience to Quarantine Rule Section 273 of the Bharatiya Nyaya Sanhita (BNS) 2023 addresses the offense committed by a person who knowingly disobeys any rule made by the Government for putting any mode of transport into a state of quarantine, or for regulating the intercourse of such transport in a state[1824] of quarantine, or for regulating the intercourse between places where an infectious disease prevails and other places[1825].

Illustration: If an individual, aware of a government-imposed quarantine rule, deliberately travels from an area with a known infectious disease[1826] to another area without following the required quarantine procedures, they are committing an offense under BNS 273.

[1823] advocatetanmoy.com

[1824] prsindia.org

[1825] advocatetanmoy.com

[1826] devgan.in

Example: Suppose a person returns from a country with a high incidence of a contagious disease and ignores the mandatory quarantine rules, instead choosing to visit public places. This act falls under BNS 273.

Comment: This section underscores the critical importance of adhering to quarantine rules to prevent the spread of infectious diseases and protect public health.

Classification of Offence and Punishment Classification: This offense is classified as a criminal offense due to its potential to spread infectious diseases and endanger public health.

Punishment: The punishment for committing this offense under BNS 273 is imprisonment of either description for a term which may extend to six months, or a fine[1827], or both.

Cognizable or Non-Cognizable, Bailable or Non-Bailable: This offense is non-cognizable, meaning the police cannot arrest the accused without a warrant.

Bailable: This offense is bailable, indicating that the accused can secure bail and be released from custody until the trial is completed.

Comparison: Section 271 of the Indian Penal Code (IPC) also addresses the offense of disobedience to quarantine rules: IPC Section 271: It states that anyone who willfully violates any rule created and issued by the government to place a vessel in quarantine, to regulate the interaction of vessels in quarantine with the shore or with other vessels, or to regulate the interaction between areas where an infectious disease is prevalent and other areas will be punished with either type of imprisonment for a maximum of six months, a fine, or both.[1828]

Key Differences: BNS 273: Updated version in the new Bharatiya Nyaya Sanhita, with specific provisions for different types of offenses. IPC 271: Part of the older legal framework, now replaced by BNS 273.

[1827] cdnbbsr.s3waas.gov.in

[1828] devgan.in

BNS Section 274

Definition: Adulteration of Food or Drink Intended for Sale[1829] Section 274 of the Bharatiya Nyaya Sanhita (BNS) 2023 addresses the offense of adulterating any article of food or drink so as to make it noxious, with the intention to sell it as food or drink, or knowing it is likely to be sold as such.

Illustration: If a food manufacturer knowingly adds harmful chemicals to a food product to increase its shelf life, intending to sell it to consumers, they are committing an offense under BNS 274.

Example: Suppose a vendor mixes water and coloring into milk to sell it as pure milk. This act falls under BNS 274.

Comment: This section underscores the critical importance of ensuring food and drink safety for the public. Adulteration poses significant health risks, and stringent penalties are essential to deter such harmful practices.

Classification of Offence and Punishment Classification: This offense is classified as a criminal offense due to its potential to harm public health and safety.

Punishment: The punishment for committing this offense under BNS 274 is imprisonment of either description for a term which may extend to six months, or a fine which may extend to five thousand rupees, or both.[1830]

Cognizable or Non-Cognizable, Bailable or Non-Bailable: This offense is non-cognizable, meaning the police cannot arrest the accused without a warrant.

Bailable: This offense is bailable, indicating that the accused can secure bail and be released from custody until the trial is completed.

[1829] Ministry of Home Affairs. (2024). The Bharatiya Nyaya Sanhita, 2023. Retrieved from https://www.mha.gov.in/sites/default/files/250883_english_01042024.pdf

[1830] cdnbbsr.s3waas.gov.in

Comparison: Section 272 of the Indian Penal Code[1831] (IPC) also addresses the offense of adulteration of food or drink intended for sale:IPC Section 272: It says that anyone who tampers with food or drink to make it noxious, plans to sell it as such, or knows it will be sold as such will be punished with either type of imprisonment for up to six months, a fine of up to one thousand rupees, or both[1832].

Key Differences: BNS 274: Updated version in the new Bharatiya Nyaya Sanhita, with specific provisions for different types of offenses. IPC 272: Part of the older legal framework, now replaced by BNS 274.

BNS Section 275

Definition: Sale of Noxious Food or Drink[1833] Section 275 of the Bharatiya Nyaya Sanhita (BNS) 2023 addresses the offense of selling, offering, or exposing for sale any food or drink that is noxious or unfit for consumption, knowing or having reason to believe that it is harmful.

Illustration: If a vendor knowingly sells milk that has been contaminated with harmful bacteria, they are committing an offense under BNS 275.

Example: Suppose a shopkeeper sells expired canned food, aware that it could cause food poisoning. This act falls under BNS 275.

Comment: This section underscores the critical importance of ensuring food and drink safety for the public. The sale of noxious food or drink poses[1834] significant health risks, and stringent penalties are essential to deter such harmful practices.

[1831] pdfcookie.com

[1832] cdnbbsr.s3waas.gov.in

[1833] Ministry of Home Affairs. (2024). The Bharatiya Nyaya Sanhita, 2023. Retrieved from https://www.mha.gov.in/sites/default/files/250883_english_01042024.pdf

[1834] pdfcookie.com

Classification of Offence and Punishment Classification: This offense is classified as a criminal offense due to its potential to harm public health and safety.

Punishment: The punishment for committing this offense under BNS 275 is imprisonment of either description for a term which may extend to six months, or a fine which may extend to five thousand rupees[1835], or both.

Cognizable or Non-Cognizable, Bailable or Non-Bailable: This offense is non-cognizable, meaning the police cannot arrest the accused without a warrant.

Bailable: This offense is bailable, indicating that the accused can secure bail and be released from custody until the trial is completed.

Comparison: Section 273 of the Indian Penal Code[1836] (IPC) also addresses the offense of sale of noxious food or drink: IPC Section 273: According to this, anyone who sells, offers, or exposes for sale as food or drink any item that has been rendered or has become noxious, or is in a state unfit for food or drink, knowing or having reason to believe that it is noxious as food or drink, faces a maximum sentence of six months in either type of jail, a maximum fine of one thousand rupees[1837], or both.

Key Differences: BNS 275: Updated version in the new Bharatiya Nyaya Sanhita, with specific provisions for different types of offenses. IPC 273: Part of the older legal framework, now replaced by BNS 275.

BNS Section 276

Definition: Adulteration of Drugs Section 276 of the Bharatiya Nyaya Sanhita (BNS) 2023 addresses the offense of adulterating any drug or medical preparation in such a manner as to lessen its efficacy, change

---

1835 cdnbbsr.s3waas.gov.in

1836 www.bareactslive.com

1837 cdnbbsr.s3waas.gov.in

its operation[1838], or make it noxious, with the intention to sell it or knowing it is likely to be sold for medicinal purposes[1839].

Illustration: If a pharmaceutical company knowingly adds a harmful substance to a drug to cut costs, intending to sell it as a legitimate medication, they are committing an offense under BNS 276.

Example: Suppose a manufacturer dilutes a life-saving drug with a cheaper, ineffective substance, knowing it will be sold to patients. This act falls under BNS 276.

Comment: This section underscores the critical importance of ensuring the safety and efficacy of drugs for public health. Adulteration of drugs poses significant risks, and stringent penalties are essential to deter such harmful practices.

Classification of Offence and Punishment Classification: This offense is classified as a criminal offense due to its potential to harm public health and safety.

Punishment: The punishment for committing this offense under BNS 276 is imprisonment of either description for a term which may extend to one year, or a fine which may extend to five thousand rupees, or both.[1840]

Cognizable or Non-Cognizable, Bailable or Non-Bailable: This offense is cognizable, meaning the police can arrest the accused without a warrant.

Bailable: This offense is bailable, indicating that the accused can secure bail and be released from custody until the trial is completed.

Comparison: Section 274 of the Indian Penal Code[1841] (IPC) also addresses the offense of adulteration of drugs: IPC Section 274: It states that anyone who adulterates a drug or medical preparation in a way that reduces its effectiveness, alters its mechanism of action, or makes it toxic with the intention of selling it or using it for a medicinal purpose—or

---

[1838] devgan.in

[1839] cdnbbsr.s3waas.gov.in

[1840] cdnbbsr.s3waas.gov.in

[1841] devgan.in

knowing that it will be sold or used for a medicinal purpose—will be punished with either type of imprisonment for a maximum of six months, a fine of up to one thousand rupees, or both[1842].

Key Differences: BNS 276: Updated version in the new Bharatiya Nyaya Sanhita, with specific provisions for different types of offenses. IPC 274: Part of the older legal framework, now replaced by BNS 276.

BNS Section 277

Definition: Sale of Adulterated Drugs Section 277 of the Bharatiya Nyaya Sanhita (BNS) 2023 addresses the offense of selling, offering, or exposing for sale any drug or medical preparation that has been adulterated in such a manner as to lessen its efficacy, change its operation, or make it noxious[1843], with the knowledge that it has been adulterated[1844].

Illustration: If a pharmacist knowingly sells a medication that has been diluted with a non-medicinal substance[1845], they are committing an offense under BNS 277.

Example: Suppose a drug manufacturer adds a harmful substance to a cough syrup to increase its volume and sells it as a pure medication. This act falls under BNS 277.

Comment: This section highlights the critical importance of ensuring the safety and efficacy of drugs for public health. The sale of adulterated drugs poses significant risks, making stringent penalties essential to deter such harmful practices.

[1842] cdnbbsr.s3waas.gov.in

[1843] devgan.in

[1844] www.bareactslive.com

[1845] www.freepatentsonline.com

Classification of Offence and Punishment Classification: This offense is classified as a criminal offense due to its potential to harm public health and safety[1846].

Punishment: The punishment for committing this offense under BNS 277 is imprisonment of either description for a term which may extend to six months, or a fine which may extend to five thousand rupees, or both.[1847]

Cognizable or Non-Cognizable, Bailable or Non-Bailable: This offense is cognizable, meaning the police can arrest the accused without a warrant.

Bailable: This offense is bailable, indicating that the accused can secure bail and be released from custody until the trial is completed.

Comparison: Section 275 of the Indian Penal Code (IPC) also addresses the offense of sale of adulterated drugs: IPC Section 275: States that whoever sells, or offers or exposes for sale, any drug or medical preparation that has been adulterated in such a manner as to lessen its efficacy, change its operation, or make it noxious, knowing it to be adulterated[1848], shall be punished with imprisonment of either description for a term which may extend to six months, or with a fine which may extend to one thousand rupees, or with both[1849].

Key Differences: BNS 277: Updated version in the new Bharatiya Nyaya Sanhita, with specific provisions for different types of offenses. IPC 275: Part of the older legal framework, now replaced by BNS 277.

BNS Section 278

Definition: Sale of Drug as a Different Drug or Preparation[1850] Section 278 of the Bharatiya Nyaya Sanhita (BNS) 2023 addresses the offense

---

[1846] cdnbbsr.s3waas.gov.in

[1847] cdnbbsr.s3waas.gov.in

[1848] devgan.in

[1849] cdnbbsr.s3waas.gov.in

[1850] Ministry of Home Affairs. (2024). The Bharatiya Nyaya Sanhita, 2023. Retrieved from https://www.mha.gov.in/sites/default/files/250883_english_01042024.pdf

of knowingly selling, offering, or exposing for sale, or issuing from a dispensary for medicinal purposes, any drug or medical preparation as a different drug or medical preparation.

Illustration: If a pharmacist sells a generic drug but labels it as a brand-name drug, they are committing an offense under BNS 278.

Example: Suppose a medical store owner sells a cheaper substitute for a prescribed medication, claiming it is the prescribed drug. This act falls under BNS 278.

Comment: This section emphasizes the serious implications of misrepresenting drugs, which can deceive consumers and harm public health.

Classification of Offence and Punishment Classification: This offense is classified as a criminal offense due to its potential to deceive consumers and harm public health.

Punishment: The punishment for committing this offense under BNS 278 is imprisonment of either description for a term which may extend to six months, or a fine which may extend to five thousand rupees, or both[1851].

Cognizable or Non-Cognizable, Bailable or Non-Bailable: This offense is cognizable, meaning the police can arrest the accused without a warrant.

Bailable: This offense is bailable, indicating that the accused can secure bail and be released from custody until the trial is completed.

Comparison: Section 276 of the Indian Penal Code[1852] (IPC) also addresses the offense of selling a drug as a different drug or preparation: IPC Section 276: States that whoever knowingly sells, or offers or exposes for sale, or issues from a dispensary for medicinal purposes, any drug or medical preparation, as a different drug or medical preparation, shall be punished with imprisonment of either description for a term which may

---

[1851] cdnbbsr.s3waas.gov.in

[1852] www.bareactslive.com

extend to six months[1853], or with a fine which may extend to one thousand rupees, or with both.

Key Differences: BNS 278: Updated version in the new Bharatiya Nyaya Sanhita, with specific provisions for different types of offenses. IPC 276: Part of the older legal framework, now replaced by BNS 278.

BNS Section 279

Definition: Fouling Water of Public Spring or Reservoir[1854] Section 279 of the Bharatiya Nyaya Sanhita (BNS) 2023 addresses the offense of voluntarily corrupting or fouling the water of any public spring or reservoir, so as to render it less fit for the purpose for which it is ordinarily used.

Illustration: If a factory discharges untreated industrial waste into a public reservoir, they are committing an offense under BNS 279.

Example: Suppose a person intentionally dumps chemicals into a public spring, knowing it will contaminate the water supply. This act falls under BNS 279.

Comment: This section underscores the serious implications of fouling public water sources, which can harm public health and safety.

Classification of Offence and Punishment Classification: This offense is classified as a criminal offense due to its potential to harm public health and safety[1855].

Punishment: The punishment for committing this offense under BNS 279 is imprisonment of either description for a term which may extend to six months, or a fine which may extend to five thousand rupees, or both.

Cognizable or Non-Cognizable, Bailable or Non-Bailable: This offense is cognizable, meaning the police can arrest the accused without a warrant.

[1853] cdnbbsr.s3waas.gov.in

[1854] Ministry of Home Affairs. (2024). The Bharatiya Nyaya Sanhita, 2023. Retrieved from https://www.mha.gov.in/sites/default/files/250883_english_01042024.pdf

[1855] cdnbbsr.s3waas.gov.in

Bailable: This offense is bailable, indicating that the accused can secure bail and be released from custody until the trial is completed.

Comparison: Section 277 of the Indian Penal Code[1856] (IPC) also addresses the offense of fouling water of public spring or reservoir: IPC Section 277: States that whoever voluntarily corrupts or fouls the water of any public spring or reservoir, so as to render it less fit for the purpose for which it is ordinarily used, shall be punished with imprisonment[1857] of either description for a term which may extend to three months, or with a fine which may extend to five hundred rupees[1858], or with both.

Key Differences: BNS 279: Updated version in the new Bharatiya Nyaya Sanhita, with specific provisions for different types of offenses. IPC 277: Part of the older legal framework, now replaced by BNS 279.

BNS Section 280

Definition: Making Atmosphere Noxious to Health[1859] Section 280 of the Bharatiya Nyaya Sanhita (BNS) 2023 addresses the offense of voluntarily vitiating the atmosphere in any place so as to make it noxious to the health of persons in general dwelling or carrying on business in the neighbourhood or passing along a public way.

Illustration: If a factory releases toxic fumes into the air, affecting the health of residents and businesses in the surrounding area, they are committing an offense under BNS 280.

Example: Suppose a person burns large quantities of waste in a residential area, causing air pollution that affects the health of people living nearby. This act falls under BNS 280.

[1856] www.bareactslive.com

[1857] devgan.in

[1858] cdnbbsr.s3waas.gov.in

[1859] Ministry of Home Affairs. (2024). The Bharatiya Nyaya Sanhita, 2023. Retrieved from https://www.mha.gov.in/sites/default/files/250883_english_01042024.pdf

Comment: This section underscores the serious implications of vitiating the atmosphere, which can harm public health and safety.

Classification of Offence and Punishment Classification: This offense is classified as a criminal offense due to its potential to harm public health and safety.

Punishment: The punishment for committing this offense under BNS 280 is a fine which may extend to one thousand rupees[1860].

Cognizable or Non-Cognizable, Bailable or Non-Bailable: This offense is non-cognizable, meaning the police cannot arrest the accused without a warrant.

Bailable: This offense is bailable, indicating that the accused can secure bail and be released from custody until the trial is completed.

Comparison: Section 278 of the Indian Penal Code[1861] (IPC) also addresses the offense of making the atmosphere noxious to health: IPC Section 278: States that whoever voluntarily vitiates the atmosphere in any place so as to make it noxious to the health of persons in general dwelling or carrying on business in the neighbourhood or passing along a public way, shall be punished[1862] with a fine which may extend to five hundred rupees[1863].

Key Differences: BNS 280: Updated version in the new Bharatiya Nyaya Sanhita, with specific provisions for different types of offenses. IPC 278: Part of the older legal framework, now replaced by BNS 280.

[1860] cdnbbsr.s3waas.gov.in

[1861] www.bareactslive.com

[1862] devgan.in

[1863] cdnbbsr.s3waas.gov.in

BNS Section 281

Definition: Rash Driving or Riding on a Public Way[1864] Section 281 of the Bharatiya Nyaya Sanhita (BNS) 2023 addresses the offense of driving or riding any vehicle on a public way in a manner so rash or negligent as to endanger human life, or to be likely to cause hurt or injury to any other person.

Illustration: If a driver speeds through a crowded market area, ignoring traffic signals and pedestrians, they are committing an offense under BNS 281.

Example: Suppose a motorcyclist weaves in and out of traffic at high speeds, causing other drivers to swerve and potentially causing accidents. This act falls under BNS 281.

Comment: This section emphasizes the serious implications of rash or negligent driving, which can endanger public safety.

Classification of Offence and Punishment Classification: This offense is classified as a criminal offense due to its potential to endanger public safety.

Punishment: The punishment for committing this offense under BNS 281 is imprisonment of either description for a term which may extend to six months, or a fine which may extend to one thousand rupees, or both.[1865]

Cognizable or Non-Cognizable, Bailable or Non-Bailable: This offense is cognizable, meaning the police can arrest the accused without a warrant.

Bailable: This offense is bailable, indicating that the accused can secure bail and be released from custody until the trial is completed.

Comparison: Section 279 of the Indian Penal Code[1866] (IPC) also addresses the offense of rash driving or riding on a public way: IPC

[1864] Ministry of Home Affairs. (2024). The Bharatiya Nyaya Sanhita, 2023. Retrieved from https://www.mha.gov.in/sites/default/files/250883_english_01042024.pdf

[1865] cdnbbsr.s3waas.gov.in

[1866] www.bareactslive.com

Section 279: States that whoever drives any vehicle, or rides, on any public way in a manner so rash or negligent as to endanger human life, or to be likely to cause hurt or injury to any other person, shall be punished with imprisonment [1867]of either description for a term which may extend to six months, or with a fine which may extend to one thousand rupees, or with both[1868].

Key Differences: BNS 281: Updated version in the new Bharatiya Nyaya Sanhita, with specific provisions for different types of offenses. IPC 279: Part of the older legal framework, now replaced by BNS 281.

BNS Section 282

Definition: Rash Navigation of Vessel[1869] Section 282 of the Bharatiya Nyaya Sanhita (BNS) 2023 addresses the offense of navigating any vessel in a manner so rash or negligent as to endanger human life, or to be likely to cause hurt or injury to any other person.

Illustration: If a boat captain speeds through a crowded waterway, ignoring other vessels and swimmers, they are committing an offense under BNS 282.

Example: Suppose a ferry operator navigates recklessly in stormy weather, causing the ferry to capsize and endangering passengers. This act falls under BNS 282.

Comment: This section emphasizes the serious implications of rash or negligent navigation, which can endanger public safety.

Classification of Offence and Punishment Classification: This offense is classified as a criminal offense due to its potential to endanger public safety.

[1867] devgan.in

[1868] cdnbbsr.s3waas.gov.in

[1869] Ministry of Home Affairs. (2024). The Bharatiya Nyaya Sanhita, 2023. Retrieved from https://www.mha.gov.in/sites/default/files/250883_english_01042024.pdf

Punishment: The punishment for committing this offense under BNS 282 is imprisonment of either description for a term which may extend to six months, or a fine which may extend to ten thousand rupees, or both.[1870]

Cognizable or Non-Cognizable, Bailable or Non-Bailable: This offense is cognizable, meaning the police can arrest the accused without a warrant.

Bailable: This offense is bailable, indicating that the accused can secure bail and be released from custody until the trial is completed.

Comparison: Section 280 of the Indian Penal Code[1871] (IPC) also addresses the offense of rash navigation of a vessel: IPC Section 280: States that whoever navigates any vessel in a manner so rash or negligent as to endanger human life, or to be likely to cause hurt or injury to any other person, shall be punished with imprisonment of either description for a term which may extend to six months[1872], or with a fine which may extend to one thousand rupees, or with both[1873].

Key Differences: BNS 282: Updated version in the new Bharatiya Nyaya Sanhita, with specific provisions for different types of offenses. IPC 280: Part of the older legal framework, now replaced by BNS 282.

BNS Section 283

Definition: Exhibition of False Light, Mark or Buoy[1874] Section 283 of the Bharatiya Nyaya Sanhita (BNS) 2023 addresses the offense of exhibiting any false light, mark, or buoy, intending or knowing it to be likely that such exhibition will mislead any navigator.

[1870] cdnbbsr.s3waas.gov.in

[1871] www.bareactslive.com

[1872] devgan.in

[1873] cdnbbsr.s3waas.gov.in

[1874] Ministry of Home Affairs. (2024). The Bharatiya Nyaya Sanhita, 2023. Retrieved from https://www.mha.gov.in/sites/default/files/250883_english_01042024.pdf

Illustration: If a lighthouse operator places a false light on the shore, intending to mislead ships into dangerous waters, they are committing an offense under BNS 283.

Example: Suppose a harbor worker places an incorrect buoy in a shipping channel, knowing it could cause ships to navigate incorrectly. This act falls under BNS 283.

Comment: This section emphasizes the serious implications of exhibiting false navigational aids, which can endanger maritime safety.

Classification of Offence and Punishment Classification: This offense is classified as a criminal offense due to its potential to endanger maritime safety.

Punishment: The punishment for committing this offense under BNS 283 is imprisonment of either description for a term which may extend to seven years,[1875] and a fine which shall not be less than ten thousand rupees[1876].

Cognizable or Non-Cognizable, Bailable or Non-Bailable: This offense is cognizable, meaning the police can arrest the accused without a warrant.

Bailable: This offense is bailable, indicating that the accused can secure bail and be released from custody until the trial is completed.

Comparison: Section 281 of the Indian Penal Code[1877] (IPC) also addresses the offense of exhibiting false light, mark, or buoy: IPC Section 281: States that whoever exhibits any false light, mark, or buoy, intending or knowing it to be likely that such exhibition will mislead any navigator, shall be punished with imprisonment of either description for a term which may extend to seven years, or with a fine, or with both[1878].

Key Differences: BNS 283: Updated version in the new Bharatiya Nyaya Sanhita, with specific provisions for different types of offenses. IPC 281: Part of the older legal framework, now replaced by BNS 283.

[1875] forest.jharkhand.gov.in

[1876] prsindia.org

[1877] www.bareactslive.com

[1878] forest.jharkhand.gov.in

BNS Section 284

Definition: Conveying Person by Water for Hire in Unsafe or Overloaded Vessel[1879] Section 284 of the Bharatiya Nyaya Sanhita (BNS) 2023 addresses the offense of knowingly or negligently conveying, or causing to be conveyed for hire, any person by water in any vessel, when that vessel is in such a state or so loaded as to endanger the life of that person.

Illustration: If a boat operator knowingly allows passengers to board an overloaded vessel that is not seaworthy, they are committing an offense under BNS 284.

Example: Suppose a ferry service owner allows a boat to sail despite knowing it has significant damage and is overloaded with passengers. This act falls under BNS 284.

Comment: This section emphasizes the serious implications of conveying people in unsafe or overloaded vessels, which can endanger public safety.

Classification of Offence and Punishment Classification: This offense is classified as a criminal offense due to its potential to endanger public safety.

Punishment: The punishment for committing this offense under BNS 284 is imprisonment of either description for a term which may extend to six months, or a fine which may extend to five thousand rupees, or both[1880].

Cognizable or Non-Cognizable, Bailable or Non-Bailable: This offense is cognizable, meaning the police can arrest the accused without a warrant.

Bailable: This offense is bailable, indicating that the accused can secure bail and be released from custody until the trial is completed.

[1879] Ministry of Home Affairs. (2024). The Bharatiya Nyaya Sanhita, 2023. Retrieved from https://www.mha.gov.in/sites/default/files/250883_english_01042024.pdf

[1880] forest.jharkhand.gov.in

Comparison: Section 282 of the Indian Penal Code[1881] (IPC) also addresses the offense of conveying a person by water for hire in an unsafe or overloaded vessel: IPC Section 282: States that whoever knowingly or negligently conveys, or causes to be conveyed for hire, any person by water in any vessel, when that vessel is in such a state[1882] or so loaded as to endanger the life of that person, shall be punished with imprisonment of either description for a term which may extend to six months[1883], or with a fine which may extend to one thousand rupees, or with both.

Key Differences: BNS 284: Updated version in the new Bharatiya Nyaya Sanhita, with specific provisions for different types of offenses. IPC 282: Part of the older legal framework, now replaced by BNS 284.

BNS Section 285

Definition: Danger or Obstruction in Public Way or Line of Navigation[1884] Section 285 of the Bharatiya Nyaya Sanhita (BNS) 2023 addresses the offense of causing danger, obstruction, or injury to any person in any public way or public line of navigation by doing any act or by omitting to take order with any property in one's possession or under one's charge.

Illustration: If a construction company leaves debris on a public road, causing an accident, they are committing an offense under BNS 285.

Example: Suppose a shop owner places a large signboard on a sidewalk, obstructing pedestrian traffic and causing people to trip. This act falls under BNS 285.

Comment: This section highlights the serious implications of causing danger or obstruction in public spaces, which can endanger public safety.

[1881] www.bareactslive.com

[1882] forest.jharkhand.gov.in

[1883] legislative.gov.in

[1884] Ministry of Home Affairs. (2024). The Bharatiya Nyaya Sanhita, 2023. Retrieved from https://www.mha.gov.in/sites/default/files/250883_english_01042024.pdf

Classification of Offence and Punishment Classification: This offense is classified as a criminal offense due to its potential to endanger public safety.

Punishment: The punishment for committing this offense under BNS 285 is a fine which may extend to five thousand rupees.

Cognizable or Non-Cognizable, Bailable or Non-Bailable: This offense is cognizable, meaning the police can arrest the accused without a warrant.

Bailable: This offense is bailable, indicating that the accused can secure bail and be released from custody until the trial is completed.

Comparison: Section 283 of the Indian Penal Code[1885] (IPC) also addresses the offense of causing danger, obstruction, or injury in a public way[1886] or line of navigation: IPC Section 283: States that whoever, by doing any act, or by omitting to take order with any property in his possession or under his charge, causes danger, obstruction, or injury to any person in any public way or public line of navigation, shall be punished with a fine which may extend to two hundred rupees[1887].

Key Differences: BNS 285: Updated version in the new Bharatiya Nyaya Sanhita, with specific provisions for different types of offenses. IPC 283: Part of the older legal framework, now replaced by BNS 285.

BNS Section 286

Definition: Negligent Conduct with Respect to Poisonous Substance[1888] Section 286 of the Bharatiya Nyaya Sanhita (BNS) 2023 addresses the offense of negligently handling a poisonous substance in a manner that endangers human life or is likely to cause hurt or injury to any person, or knowingly or negligently failing to take sufficient

---

1885 www.bareactslive.com

1886 www.readbag.com

1887 forest.jharkhand.gov.in

1888 Ministry of Home Affairs. (2024). The Bharatiya Nyaya Sanhita, 2023. Retrieved from https://www.mha.gov.in/sites/default/files/250883_english_01042024.pdf

precautions to guard against probable danger from such a substance[1889].

Illustration: If a chemical plant worker leaves a container of toxic chemicals unsealed, allowing harmful fumes to escape and endanger nearby residents, they are committing an offense under BNS 286.

Example: Suppose a farmer stores pesticides in an unmarked container, and a child accidentally ingests the substance, causing serious harm. This act falls under BNS 286.

Comment: This section highlights the serious implications of negligent conduct with poisonous substances, which can endanger public health and safety[1890].

Classification of Offence and Punishment Classification: This offense is classified as a criminal offense due to its potential to endanger public health and safety.

Punishment: The punishment for committing this offense under BNS 286 is imprisonment of either description for a term which may extend to six months, or a fine which may extend to five thousand rupees[1891], or both.

Cognizable or Non-Cognizable, Bailable or Non-Bailable: This offense is cognizable, meaning the police can arrest the accused without a warrant.

Bailable: This offense is bailable, indicating that the accused can secure bail and be released from custody until the trial is completed.

Comparison: Section 284 of the Indian Penal Code[1892] (IPC) also addresses the offense of negligent conduct with respect to a poisonous substance: IPC Section 284: Declares that anyone who uses a poisonous substance in a way that is so careless or reckless as to endanger human life or be likely to hurt or injure someone else, or who wilfully or carelessly fails to take the necessary precautions with any poisonous substance in his

---

[1889] prsindia.org

[1890] www.network.bepress.com

[1891] forest.jharkhand.gov.in

[1892] www.bareactslive.com

possession to guard against any probable danger to human life from such a poisonous substance, faces a maximum sentence of six months in prison of any kind, a maximum fine of one thousand rupees, or both[1893].

Key Differences: BNS 286: Updated version in the new Bharatiya Nyaya Sanhita, with specific provisions for different types of offenses. IPC 284: Part of the older legal framework, now replaced by BNS 286.

BNS Section 287

Definition: Negligent Conduct with Respect to Fire or Combustible Matter[1894] Section 287 of the Bharatiya Nyaya Sanhita (BNS) 2023 addresses the offense of negligently handling fire or combustible matter in a manner that endangers human life or is likely to cause hurt or injury to any person, or knowingly or negligently failing to take sufficient precautions to guard against probable danger from such fire or combustible matter.

Illustration: If a person leaves a lit candle unattended in a crowded room, causing a fire that endangers people, they are committing an offense under BNS 287.

Example: Suppose a factory worker improperly stores flammable chemicals, leading to a fire that injures employees. This act falls under BNS 287.

Comment: This section emphasizes the serious implications of negligently handling fire or combustible matter, which can endanger public safety.

Classification of Offence and Punishment Classification: This offense is classified as a criminal offense due to its potential to endanger public safety.

[1893] forest.jharkhand.gov.in

[1894] Ministry of Home Affairs. (2024). The Bharatiya Nyaya Sanhita, 2023. Retrieved from https://www.mha.gov.in/sites/default/files/250883_english_01042024.pdf

Punishment: The punishment for committing this offense under BNS 287 is imprisonment of either description for a term which may extend to six months, or a fine which may extend to two thousand rupees, or both.

Cognizable or Non-Cognizable, Bailable or Non-Bailable: This offense is cognizable, meaning the police can arrest the accused without a warrant.

Bailable: This offense is bailable, indicating that the accused can secure bail and be released from custody until the trial is completed.

Comparison: Section 285 of the Indian Penal Code[1895] (IPC) also addresses the offense of negligent conduct with respect to fire or combustible matter: IPC Section 285: The law stipulates that anyone who recklessly or carelessly handles fire or a combustible object in a way that endangers human life or is likely to cause harm or injury to another person, or who willfully or carelessly fails to take the necessary precautions with a fire or combustible object in his possession to prevent any potential threat to human life from such a fire or combustible object, faces a maximum sentence of six months in prison, a fine of up to one thousand rupees, or both[1896].

Key Differences: BNS 287: Updated version in the new Bharatiya Nyaya Sanhita, with specific provisions for different types of offenses. IPC 285: Part of the older legal framework, now replaced by BNS 287.

BNS Section 288

Definition: Negligent Conduct with Respect to Explosive Substance[1897] Section 288 of the Bharatiya Nyaya Sanhita (BNS) 2023 addresses the offense of negligently handling an explosive substance in a manner that endangers human life or is likely to cause hurt or injury to any person, or knowingly or negligently failing to take sufficient

[1895] www.bareactslive.com

[1896] forest.jharkhand.gov.in

[1897] Ministry of Home Affairs. (2024). The Bharatiya Nyaya Sanhita, 2023. Retrieved from https://www.mha.gov.in/sites/default/files/250883_english_01042024.pdf

precautions to guard against probable danger from such a substance[1898].

Illustration: If a construction worker leaves dynamite unattended at a site without proper safety measures, they are committing an offense under BNS 288.

Example: Suppose a fireworks manufacturer stores explosive materials without proper containment, leading to an accidental explosion that injures nearby workers. This act falls under BNS 288.

Comment: This section emphasizes the serious implications of negligently handling explosive substances, which can endanger public safety.

Classification of Offence and Punishment Classification: This offense is classified as a criminal offense due to its potential to endanger public safety.

Punishment: The punishment for committing this offense under BNS 288 is imprisonment of either description for a term which may extend to six months, or a fine which may extend to five thousand rupees, or both[1899].

Cognizable or Non-Cognizable, Bailable or Non-Bailable: This offense is cognizable, meaning the police can arrest the accused without a warrant.

Bailable: This offense is bailable, indicating that the accused can secure bail and be released from custody until the trial is completed.

Comparison: Section 286 of the Indian Penal Code[1900] (IPC) also addresses the offense of negligent conduct with respect to explosive substances: IPC Section 286: It states that anyone who uses an explosive substance in a way that is so careless or reckless as to endanger human life or be likely to hurt or injure another person, or who willfully or carelessly fails to take the necessary precautions with any explosive substance in his possession to guard against any probable danger to human life from that

---

[1898] forest.jharkhand.gov.in

[1899] forest.jharkhand.gov.in

[1900] www.bareactslive.com

substance, faces a maximum sentence of six months in prison of any kind, a maximum fine of one thousand rupees, or both[1901].

Key Differences: BNS 288: Updated version in the new Bharatiya Nyaya Sanhita, with specific provisions for different types of offenses. IPC 286: Part of the older legal framework, now replaced by BNS 288.

BNS Section 289

Definition: Negligent Conduct with Respect to Machinery[1902] Section 289 of the Bharatiya Nyaya Sanhita (BNS) 2023 addresses the offense of negligently handling machinery in a manner that endangers human life or is likely to cause hurt or injury to any person, or knowingly or negligently failing to take sufficient precautions to guard against probable danger from such machinery.

Illustration: If a factory worker leaves a running machine unattended without proper safety measures, causing it to malfunction and injure another worker, they are committing an offense under BNS 289.

Example: Suppose a construction site supervisor fails to ensure that heavy machinery is properly maintained, leading to an accident that injures a worker. This act falls under BNS 289.

Comment: This section emphasizes the serious implications of negligently handling machinery, which can endanger public safety.

Classification of Offence and Punishment Classification: This offense is classified as a criminal offense due to its potential to endanger public safety.

Punishment: The punishment for committing this offense under BNS 289 is imprisonment of either description for a term which may extend to six months, or a fine which may extend to five thousand rupees, or both[1903].

[1901] forest.jharkhand.gov.in

[1902] Ministry of Home Affairs. (2024). The Bharatiya Nyaya Sanhita, 2023. Retrieved from https://www.mha.gov.in/sites/default/files/250883_english_01042024.pdf

[1903] forest.jharkhand.gov.in

Cognizable or Non-Cognizable, Bailable or Non-Bailable: This offense is cognizable, meaning the police can arrest the accused without a warrant.

Bailable: This offense is bailable, indicating that the accused can secure bail and be released from custody until the trial is completed.

Comparison: Section 287 of the Indian Penal Code[1904] (IPC) also addresses the offense of negligent conduct with respect to machinery: IPC Section 287: Declares that anyone who uses machinery in a way that is so careless or reckless as to endanger human life or to be likely to hurt or injure another person, or who willfully or carelessly fails to take the necessary precautions with any machinery that is in his possession or under his care to guard against any probable danger to human life from such machinery, faces a maximum sentence of six months in either type of jail, a maximum fine of one thousand rupees, or both[1905].

Key Differences: BNS 289: Updated version in the new Bharatiya Nyaya Sanhita, with specific provisions for different types of offenses. IPC 287: Part of the older legal framework, now replaced by BNS 289.

BNS Section 290

Definition: Negligent Conduct with Respect to Pulling Down, Repairing or Constructing Buildings[1906], etc. Section 290 of the Bharatiya Nyaya Sanhita (BNS) 2023 addresses the offense of negligently handling the process of pulling down, repairing, or constructing buildings, which endangers human life or is likely to cause hurt or injury to any person, or knowingly or negligently failing to take sufficient precautions to guard against probable danger from such activities[1907].

[1904] www.bareactslive.com

[1905] forest.jharkhand.gov.in

[1906] Ministry of Home Affairs. (2024). The Bharatiya Nyaya Sanhita, 2023. Retrieved from https://www.mha.gov.in/sites/default/files/250883_english_01042024.pdf

[1907] forest.jharkhand.gov.in

Illustration: If a construction company fails to secure a building properly while demolishing it, causing debris to fall and injure pedestrians, they are committing an offense under BNS 290.

Example: Suppose a repair crew working on a bridge neglects to put up safety barriers, leading to an accident that injures a passerby. This act falls under BNS 290.

Comment: This section highlights the serious implications of negligent construction practices, which can endanger public safety.

Classification of Offence and Punishment Classification: This offense is classified as a criminal offense due to its potential to endanger public safety.

Punishment: The punishment for committing this offense under BNS 290 is imprisonment of either description for a term which may extend to six months, or a fine which may extend to five thousand rupees, or both[1908].

Cognizable or Non-Cognizable, Bailable or Non-Bailable: This offense is cognizable, meaning the police can arrest the accused without a warrant.

Bailable: This offense is bailable, indicating that the accused can secure bail and be released from custody until the trial is completed.

Comparison: Section 288 of the Indian Penal Code [1909](IPC) also addresses the offense of negligent conduct with respect to pulling down, repairing, or constructing buildings: IPC Section 288: It stipulates that anyone who willfully or carelessly fails to take the necessary precautions to ensure that no building or part of a building collapses, posing a risk to human life, will be punished with either type of imprisonment for a maximum of six months, a fine of up to one thousand rupees, or both[1910].

Key Differences: BNS 290: Updated version in the new Bharatiya Nyaya Sanhita, with specific provisions for different types of offenses. IPC 288: Part of the older legal framework, now replaced by BNS 290.

[1908] forest.jharkhand.gov.in

[1909] www.bareactslive.com

[1910] forest.jharkhand.gov.in

BNS Section 291

Definition: Negligent Conduct with Respect to Animal[1911] Section 291 of the Bharatiya Nyaya Sanhita (BNS) 2023 addresses the offense of negligently handling animals in a manner that endangers human life or is likely to cause grievous hurt, or knowingly or negligently failing to take sufficient precautions to guard against probable danger from such animals[1912].

Illustration: If a person leaves a dangerous dog unattended in a public park, and the dog attacks someone, they are committing an offense under BNS 291.

Example: Suppose a farmer fails to properly secure a bull in a field, and the bull escapes and causes an accident on a nearby road. This act falls under BNS 291.

Comment: This section underscores the serious implications of negligently handling animals, which can endanger public safety.

Classification of Offence and Punishment Classification: This offense is classified as a criminal offense due to its potential to endanger public safety.

Punishment: The punishment for committing this offense under BNS 291 is imprisonment of either description for a term which may extend to six months, or a fine which may extend to five thousand rupees, or both.[1913]

Cognizable or Non-Cognizable, Bailable or Non-Bailable: This offense is cognizable, meaning the police can arrest the accused without a warrant.

Bailable: This offense is bailable, indicating that the accused can secure bail and be released from custody until the trial is completed.

[1911] Ministry of Home Affairs. (2024). The Bharatiya Nyaya Sanhita, 2023. Retrieved from https://www.mha.gov.in/sites/default/files/250883_english_01042024.pdf

[1912] prsindia.org

[1913] forest.jharkhand.gov.in

Comparison: Section 289 of the Indian Penal Code (IPC)[1914] also addresses the offense of negligent conduct with respect to animals: IPC Section 289: It states that anyone who willfully or carelessly fails to take the necessary precautions with any animal in his possession to prevent any likely threat to human life or serious injury from the animal will be punished with either type of imprisonment for a maximum of six months, a fine of up to one thousand rupees, or both[1915].

Key Differences: BNS 291: Updated version in the new Bharatiya Nyaya Sanhita, with specific provisions for different types of offenses. IPC 289: Part of the older legal framework, now replaced by BNS 291.

BNS Section 292

Definition: Punishment for Public Nuisance in Cases Not Otherwise Provided For[1916] Section 292 of the Bharatiya Nyaya Sanhita (BNS) 2023 addresses the offense of committing a public nuisance in cases not otherwise punishable by the Sanhita.

Illustration: If someone dumps garbage in a public park, causing inconvenience and health hazards to the public, they are committing an offense under BNS 292.

Example: Suppose a person plays loud music late at night in a residential area, disturbing the peace and causing annoyance to the residents. This act falls under BNS 292.

Comment: This section highlights the significant impact of public nuisances, which can cause inconvenience and harm to the community.

Classification of Offence and Punishment Classification: This offense is classified as a criminal offense due to its potential to cause public inconvenience and harm.

[1914] www.bareactslive.com

[1915] forest.jharkhand.gov.in

[1916] Ministry of Home Affairs. (2024). The Bharatiya Nyaya Sanhita, 2023. Retrieved from https://www.mha.gov.in/sites/default/files/250883_english_01042024.pdf

Punishment: The punishment for committing this offense under BNS 292 is a fine which may extend to one thousand rupees. [1917]

Cognizable or Non-Cognizable, Bailable or Non-Bailable: This offense is non-cognizable, meaning the police cannot arrest the accused without a warrant.

Bailable: This offense is bailable, indicating that the accused can secure bail and be released from custody until the trial is completed.

Comparison: Section 290 of the Indian Penal Code[1918] (IPC) also addresses the offense of public nuisance in cases not otherwise provided for: IPC Section 290: States that whoever commits a public nuisance in any case not otherwise punishable by this Code, shall be punished with a fine which may extend to two hundred rupees[1919].

Key Differences: BNS 292: Updated version in the new Bharatiya Nyaya Sanhita, with a higher fine limit of one thousand rupees. IPC 290: Part of the older legal framework, now replaced by BNS 292.

BNS Section 293

Definition: Continuance of Nuisance After Injunction to Discontinue[1920] Section 293 of the Bharatiya Nyaya Sanhita (BNS) 2023 addresses the offense of continuing a public nuisance after being ordered by a public servant with lawful authority to discontinue such nuisance.

Illustration: If a factory continues to emit harmful pollutants into the air despite receiving an official order to stop, they are committing an offense under BNS 293.

[1917] forest.jharkhand.gov.in

[1918] www.bareactslive.com

[1919] devgan.in

[1920] Ministry of Home Affairs. (2024). The Bharatiya Nyaya Sanhita, 2023. Retrieved from https://www.mha.gov.in/sites/default/files/250883_english_01042024.pdf

Example: Suppose a restaurant repeatedly plays loud music late at night after being instructed by local authorities to cease, disturbing the neighborhood peace. This act falls under BNS 293.

Comment: This section emphasizes the serious implications of continuing a public nuisance, which can cause public inconvenience and harm.

Classification of Offence and Punishment Classification: This offense is classified as a criminal offense due to its potential to cause public inconvenience and harm.

Punishment: The punishment for committing this offense under BNS 293 is simple imprisonment for a term which may extend to six months, or a fine which may extend to five thousand rupees, or both[1921].

Cognizable or Non-Cognizable, Bailable or Non-Bailable: This offense is cognizable, meaning the police can arrest the accused without a warrant.

Bailable: This offense is bailable, indicating that the accused can secure bail and be released from custody until the trial is completed.

Comparison: Section 291 of the Indian Penal Code[1922] (IPC) also addresses the offense of continuing a public nuisance after an injunction: IPC Section 291: States that whoever repeats or continues a public nuisance, having been enjoined by any public servant who has lawful authority to issue such injunction not to repeat or continue such nuisance, shall be punished with simple imprisonment for a term which may extend to six months, or with a fine, or with both[1923].

Key Differences: BNS 293: Updated version in the new Bharatiya Nyaya Sanhita, with a specific fine limit of five thousand rupees. IPC 291: Part of the older legal framework, now replaced by BNS 293.

[1921] devgan.in

[1922] www.bareactslive.com

[1923] devgan.in

BNS Section 294

Definition: Sale, etc., of Obscene Books[1924], etc. Section 294 of the Bharatiya Nyaya Sanhita (BNS) 2023 addresses the offense of selling, distributing, or publicly exhibiting obscene materials.

Illustration: If a bookstore sells books containing explicit content that is deemed obscene, they are committing an offense under BNS 294.

Example: Suppose an online platform distributes videos that are lascivious or appeal to prurient interests without proper age restrictions. This act falls under BNS 294.

Comment: This section highlights the significant impact of distributing obscene materials, which can corrupt public morals and decency.

Classification of Offence and Punishment Classification: This offense is classified as a criminal offense due to its potential to corrupt public morals and decency.

Punishment: The punishment for committing this offense under BNS 294 is imprisonment of either description for a term which may extend to six months, or a fine which may extend to five thousand rupees, or both[1925].

Cognizable or Non-Cognizable, Bailable or Non-Bailable: This offense is cognizable, meaning the police can arrest the accused without a warrant.

Bailable: This offense is bailable, indicating that the accused can secure bail and be released from custody until the trial is completed.

Comparison: Section 292 of the Indian Penal Code[1926] (IPC) also addresses the offense of selling, distributing, or publicly exhibiting obscene materials: IPC Section 292: States that whoever sells, lets to hire, distributes, publicly exhibits or in any manner puts into circulation, or for purposes of sale, hire, distribution, public exhibition or circulation, makes,

---

[1924] Ministry of Home Affairs. (2024). The Bharatiya Nyaya Sanhita, 2023. Retrieved from https://www.mha.gov.in/sites/default/files/250883_english_01042024.pdf

[1925] devgan.in

[1926] indiankanoon.org

produces or has in his possession any obscene book, pamphlet, paper, drawing, painting, representation or figure or any other obscene object whatsoever[1927], shall be punished with imprisonment of either description for a term which may extend to six months, or with a fine which may extend to two thousand rupees, or with both[1928].

Key Differences: BNS 294: Updated version in the new Bharatiya Nyaya Sanhita, with a higher fine limit of five thousand rupees and inclusion of electronic content. IPC 292: Part of the older legal framework, now replaced by BNS 294.

BNS Section 295

Definition: Sale, etc., of Obscene Objects to Young Person[1929] Section 295 of the Bharatiya Nyaya Sanhita (BNS) 2023 addresses the offense of selling, distributing, or publicly exhibiting obscene materials to a child.

Illustration: If a shopkeeper sells a pornographic magazine to a minor, they are committing an offense under BNS 295.

Example: Suppose an online platform distributes explicit content to users under the age of eighteen[1930] without proper age verification. This act falls under BNS 295.

Comment: This section underscores the importance of protecting minors from exposure to obscene materials, which can have a detrimental impact on their moral and psychological development. The stringent penalties for repeat offenses reflect the seriousness with which the law views the corruption of minors' morals. The updated provisions in BNS 295, with a specific focus on children under eighteen years old and higher penalties

---

[1927] indiankanoon.org

[1928] devgan.in

[1929] Ministry of Home Affairs. (2024). The Bharatiya Nyaya Sanhita, 2023. Retrieved from https://www.mha.gov.in/sites/default/files/250883_english_01042024.pdf

[1930] www.wipo.int

for repeat offenses, highlight the commitment to safeguarding the well-being of young individuals in society

Classification of Offence and Punishment Classification: This offense is classified as a criminal offense due to its potential to corrupt the morals of minors[1931].

Punishment: According to BNS 295, the penalty for this infraction is either a fine of up to two thousand rupees or imprisonment of any kind for a maximum of three years, or both on a first conviction. Punishment for a second or subsequent conviction consists of a fine of up to five thousand rupees and imprisonment of any kind for a maximum of seven years[1932].

Cognizable or Non-Cognizable, Bailable or Non-Bailable: This offense is cognizable, meaning the police can arrest the accused without a warrant.

Bailable: This offense is bailable, indicating that the accused can secure bail and be released from custody until the trial is completed.

Comparison: Section 293 of the Indian Penal Code[1933] (IPC) also addresses the offense of selling, distributing, or publicly exhibiting obscene materials to young persons: IPC Section 293: States that whoever sells, lets to hire, distributes, publicly exhibits or in any manner puts into circulation, or for purposes of sale, hire, distribution, public exhibition or circulation, makes, produces or has in his possession any obscene book, pamphlet, paper, drawing, painting, representation or figure or any other obscene object whatsoever[1934], to any person under the age of twenty years, shall be punished with imprisonment of either description for a term which may extend to three years[1935], or with a fine which may extend to two thousand rupees, or with both[1936].

[1931] indiankanoon.org

[1932] devgan.in

[1933] www.bareactslive.com

[1934] indiankanoon.org

[1935] odishapolicecidcb.gov.in

[1936] devgan.in

Key Differences: BNS 295: Updated version in the new Bharatiya Nyaya Sanhita, with a specific focus on children under eighteen years old and higher penalties for repeat offenses. IPC 293: Part of the older legal framework, now replaced by BNS 295.

BNS Section 296

Definition: Obscene Acts and Songs Section 296 of the Bharatiya Nyaya Sanhita (BNS) 2023 addresses the offense of performing obscene acts or singing, reciting, or uttering obscene songs, ballads, or words in public places, causing annoyance to others.

Illustration: If a person performs an obscene dance in a public park, causing discomfort to the people around, they are committing an offense under BNS 296.

Example: Suppose an individual loudly sings explicit songs with offensive lyrics in a busy market, disturbing the public. This act falls under BNS 296.

Comment: This section emphasizes the importance of maintaining public decency and order. Obscene acts and songs can disturb and offend the community, highlighting the need for legal measures to prevent such behaviors. The penalties under BNS 296 reflect the seriousness of these offenses, ensuring that public spaces remain respectful and conducive to all members of society. The updated provisions in BNS 296 provide clarity and specific guidelines to address various forms of obscene conduct, reinforcing the commitment to uphold community standards and public morality.

Classification of Offence and Punishment Classification: This offense is classified as a criminal offense due to its potential to disturb public decency and order.

Punishment: The punishment for committing this offense under BNS 296 is imprisonment of either description for a term which may extend to three months, or a fine which may extend to one thousand rupees, or both.[1937]

Cognizable or Non-Cognizable, Bailable or Non-Bailable: This offense is cognizable, meaning the police can arrest the accused without a warrant.

Bailable: This offense is bailable, indicating that the accused can secure bail and be released from custody until the trial is completed.

Comparison: Section 294 of the Indian Penal Code[1938] (IPC) also addresses the offense of performing obscene acts or singing, reciting, or uttering obscene songs, ballads, or words in public places, causing annoyance to others: IPC Section 294: States that whoever, to the annoyance of others, does any obscene act in any public place, or sings[1939], recites, or utters any obscene song, ballad, or words, in or near any public place, shall be punished with imprisonment of either description for a term which may extend to three months, or with a fine[1940], or with both.

Key Differences: BNS 296: Updated version in the Bharatiya Nyaya Sanhita, with specific provisions for different types of offenses. IPC 294: Part of the older Indian Penal Code framework, now replaced by BNS 296.

BNS Section 297

Definition: Keeping Lottery Office Section 297 of the Bharatiya Nyaya Sanhita (BNS) 2023 addresses the offense of keeping an office or place for the purpose of drawing any lottery that is not a State lottery or a lottery authorized by the State Government[1941].

[1937] devgan.in

[1938] en.wikipedia.org

[1939] devgan.in

[1940] pdfcookie.com

[1941] devgan.in

Illustration: If someone operates a lottery office without the necessary authorization from the State Government, they are committing an offense under BNS 297.

Example: Suppose a person sets up a lottery booth in a market to sell tickets for a private lottery. This act falls under BNS 297.

Comment: This section emphasizes the importance of regulating lottery activities to prevent illegal gambling and protect public trust. Unauthorized lotteries can exploit individuals and undermine the integrity of lawful gambling operations.

Classification of Offence and Punishment Classification: This offense is classified as a criminal offense due to its potential to exploit public trust and encourage illegal gambling.

Punishment: The punishment for committing this offense under BNS 297 is imprisonment of either description for a term which may extend to six months, or a fine which may extend to five thousand rupees, or both[1942].

Cognizable or Non-Cognizable, Bailable or Non-Bailable: This offense is cognizable, meaning the police can arrest the accused without a warrant.

Bailable: This offense is bailable, indicating that the accused can secure bail and be released from custody until the trial is completed.

Comparison: Section 294A of the Indian Penal Code[1943] (IPC) also addresses the offense of keeping a lottery office: IPC Section 294A: States that whoever keeps any office or place for the purpose of drawing any lottery not being a State lottery or a lottery authorized by the State Government, shall be punished with imprisonment of either description for a term which may extend to six months, or with a fine which may extend to one thousand rupees, or with both[1944].

[1942] devgan.in

[1943] en.wikipedia.org

[1944] devgan.in

Key Differences: BNS 297: Updated version in the new Bharatiya Nyaya Sanhita, with a higher fine limit of five thousand rupees.IPC 294A: Part of the older legal framework, now replaced by BNS 297.

CHAPTER-XVI; OF OFFENCES RELATING TO RELIGION

BNS Section 298

Definition: Injuring or Defiling Place of Worship with Intent to Insult the Religion of Any Class[1945] Section 298 of the Bharatiya Nyaya Sanhita (BNS) 2023 addresses the offense of intentionally destroying, damaging, or defiling any place of worship or any object held sacred by any class of persons with the intention of insulting the religion of that class or with the knowledge that such destruction, damage, or defilement is likely to be considered an insult by that class.

Illustration: If someone vandalizes a church, mosque, or temple with the intent to insult the religion of the followers, they are committing an offense under BNS 298.

Example: Suppose an individual defaces a religious statue in a public park, knowing that it is considered sacred by a particular community. This act falls under BNS 298.

Comment: This section underscores the potential to incite religious disharmony and cause emotional distress to the affected community

Classification of Offence and Punishment Classification: This offense is classified as a criminal offense due to its potential to incite religious disharmony and cause emotional distress to the affected community.

[1945] Ministry of Home Affairs. (2024). The Bharatiya Nyaya Sanhita, 2023. Retrieved from https://www.mha.gov.in/sites/default/files/250883_english_01042024.pdf

Punishment: The punishment for committing this offense under BNS 298 is imprisonment of either description for a term which may extend to two years, or a fine, or both[1946].

Cognizable or Non-Cognizable, Bailable or Non-Bailable: This offense is cognizable, meaning the police can arrest the accused without a warrant.

Bailable: This offense is bailable, indicating that the accused can secure bail and be released from custody until the trial is completed.

Comparison: Section 295 of the Indian Penal Code[1947] (IPC) also addresses the offense of injuring or defiling a place of worship with the intent to insult the religion of any[1948] class: IPC Section 295: States that whoever intentionally destroys, damages, or defiles any place of worship or any object held sacred by any class of persons with the intention of thereby insulting the religion of that class, or with the knowledge that any class of persons is likely to consider such destruction, damage, or defilement as an insult to their religion, shall be punished[1949] with imprisonment of either description for a term which may extend to two years, or with a fine, or with both.

Key Differences: BNS 298: Updated version in the new Bharatiya Nyaya Sanhita, with specific provisions for different types of offenses. IPC 295: Part of the older legal framework, now replaced by BNS 298.

BNS Section 299

Definition: Deliberate and Malicious Acts Intended to Outrage Religious Feelings of Any [1950]Class Section 299 of the Bharatiya Nyaya Sanhita (BNS) 2023 addresses the offense of deliberately and

[1946] devgan.in

[1947] en.wikipedia.org

[1948] odishapolicecidcb.gov.in

[1949] devgan.in

[1950] Ministry of Home Affairs. (2024). The Bharatiya Nyaya Sanhita, 2023. Retrieved from https://www.mha.gov.in/sites/default/files/250883_english_01042024.pdf

maliciously acting to outrage the religious feelings of any class by insulting its religion or religious beliefs[1951].

Illustration: If someone publicly makes derogatory remarks about a religious group's beliefs, intending to insult and provoke them, they are committing an offense under BNS 299.

Example: Suppose an individual distributes pamphlets with offensive content about a particular religion, knowing it will outrage the followers of that religion. This act falls under BNS 299.

Comment: This section highlights the balance between freedom of expression and the need to protect communities from actions designed to provoke and insult their religious sentiments.

Classification of Offence and Punishment Classification: This offense is classified as a criminal offense due to its potential to incite religious disharmony and cause emotional distress to the affected community.

Punishment: The punishment for committing this offense under BNS 299 is imprisonment of either description for a term which may extend to three years, or a fine, or both.[1952]

Cognizable or Non-Cognizable, Bailable or Non-Bailable: This offense is cognizable, meaning the police can arrest the accused without a warrant.

Bailable: This offense is bailable, indicating that the accused can secure bail and be released from custody until the trial is completed.

Comparison: Section 295A of the Indian Penal Code[1953] (IPC) also addresses the offense of deliberately and maliciously acting to outrage the religious feelings of any class by insulting its religion or religious beliefs: IPC Section 295A: Declares that anyone who intentionally and maliciously tries to offend the religious sentiments of any group of Indian citizens through written or spoken words, signs, or other visible

---

[1951] odishapolicecidcb.gov.in

[1952] devgan.in

[1953] en.wikipedia.org

representations will be punished with either type of imprisonment for a maximum of three years, a fine, or both[1954].

Key Differences: BNS 299: Updated version in the new Bharatiya Nyaya Sanhita, with specific provisions for different types of offenses.IPC 295A: Part of the older Indian Penal Code framework, now replaced by BNS 299.

BNS Section 300

Definition: Disturbing Religious Assembly[1955] Section 300 of the Bharatiya Nyaya Sanhita (BNS) 2023 addresses the offense of voluntarily causing disturbance to any assembly lawfully engaged in the performance of religious worship or religious ceremonies.

Illustration: If someone disrupts a church service by shouting or creating a commotion, they are committing an offense under BNS 300.

Example: Suppose an individual intentionally plays loud music near a temple during a religious ceremony, disturbing the worshippers. This act falls under BNS 300.

Comment: This section underlines the importance of maintaining respect for religious practices and the potential impact on public order and harmony.

Classification of Offence and Punishment Classification: This offense is classified as a criminal offense due to its potential to disrupt public order and religious harmony.

Punishment: The punishment for committing this offense under BNS 300 is imprisonment of either description for a term which may extend to one year, or a fine, or both.[1956]

Cognizable or Non-Cognizable, Bailable or Non-Bailable: This offense is cognizable, meaning the police can arrest the accused without a warrant.

[1954] odishapolicecidcb.gov.in

[1955] Ministry of Home Affairs. (2024). The Bharatiya Nyaya Sanhita, 2023. Retrieved from https://www.mha.gov.in/sites/default/files/250883_english_01042024.pdf

[1956] devgan.in

Bailable: This offense is bailable, indicating that the accused can secure bail and be released from custody until the trial is completed.

Comparison: Section 296 of the Indian Penal Code[1957] (IPC) also addresses the offense of disturbing a religious assembly: IPC Section 296: It declares that anyone who willfully disrupts a gathering that is legally performing religious worship or religious rites faces up to a year in prison of any kind, a fine, or both sanctions[1958].

Key Differences: BNS 300: Updated version in the new Bharatiya Nyaya Sanhita, with specific provisions for different types of offenses. IPC 296: Part of the older Indian Penal Code framework, now replaced by BNS 300.

BNS Section 301

Definition: Trespassing on Burial Places[1959], etc Section 301 of the Bharatiya Nyaya Sanhita (BNS) 2023 addresses the offense of trespassing on burial places, cremation grounds, or places set apart for the disposal of the dead with the intention of wounding the feelings of any person or insulting the religion of any person.

Illustration: If someone enters a cemetery and vandalizes a tombstone with the intent to insult the religion of the deceased's family, they are committing an offense under BNS 301.

Example: Suppose an individual deliberately disturbs a funeral procession by causing a commotion, knowing it will hurt the sentiments of the mourners. This act falls under BNS 301.

Comment: This section emphasizes the significance of respecting places dedicated to the deceased and the potential for emotional harm and disruption of religious practices when such sites are violated.

[1957] www.bareactslive.com

[1958] odishapolicecidcb.gov.in

[1959] Ministry of Home Affairs. (2024). The Bharatiya Nyaya Sanhita, 2023. Retrieved from https://www.mha.gov.in/sites/default/files/250883_english_01042024.pdf

Classification of Offence and Punishment Classification: This offense is classified as a criminal offense due to its potential to cause emotional distress and disrupt religious practices.

Punishment: The punishment for committing this offense under BNS 301 is imprisonment of either description for a term which may extend to one year, or a fine, or both.[1960]

Cognizable or Non-Cognizable, Bailable or Non-Bailable: This offense is cognizable, meaning the police can arrest the accused without a warrant.

Bailable: This offense is bailable, indicating that the accused can secure bail and be released from custody until the trial is completed.

Comparison: Section 297 of the Indian Penal Code[1961] (IPC) also addresses the offense of trespassing on burial places[1962], etc. However, IPC Section 297 has been replaced by BNS 301 with effect from July 1, 2024.

Key Differences: BNS 301: Updated version in the new Bharatiya Nyaya Sanhita, with specific provisions for different types of offenses. IPC 297: Part of the older Indian Penal Code framework, now replaced by BNS 301.

BNS Section 302

Definition: Uttering Words, etc., with Deliberate Intent to Wound Religious Feelings of Any erson[1963] Section 302 of the Bharatiya Nyaya Sanhita (BNS) 2023 addresses the offense of deliberately and maliciously acting to wound the religious feelings of any person by uttering words, making sounds, gestures, or placing objects in their sight with the intent to insult their religion or religious beliefs.

[1960] devgan.in

[1961] www.bareactslive.com

[1962] odishapolicecidcb.gov.in

[1963] Ministry of Home Affairs. (2024). The Bharatiya Nyaya Sanhita, 2023. Retrieved from https://www.mha.gov.in/sites/default/files/250883_english_01042024.pdf

Illustration: If someone shouts offensive remarks about a religious group's beliefs in a crowded place, intending to provoke and insult them, they are committing an offense under BNS 302.

Example: Suppose an individual distributes flyers with derogatory content about a particular religion, knowing it will hurt the followers' sentiments. This act falls under BNS 302.

Comment: This section underscores the importance of respecting religious sentiments and the severe impact that deliberate provocations can have on social harmony.

Classification of Offence and Punishment Classification: This offense is classified as a criminal offense due to its potential to incite religious disharmony and cause emotional distress to the affected community[1964].

Punishment: The punishment for committing this offense under BNS 302 is imprisonment of either description for a term which may extend to one year, or a fine, or both[1965].

Cognizable or Non-Cognizable, Bailable or Non-Bailable: This offense is cognizable, meaning the police can arrest the accused without a warrant.

Bailable: This offense is bailable, indicating that the accused can secure bail and be released from custody until the trial is completed.

Comparison: Section 298 of the Indian Penal Code[1966] (IPC) also addresses the offense of uttering words, etc., with deliberate intent to wound the religious feelings of any person: IPC Section 298: States that whoever, with the deliberate intention of wounding the religious feelings of any person, utters any word or makes any sound in the hearing of that person or makes any gesture in the sight of that person or places any object in the sight of that person, shall be punished with imprisonment of either

[1964] blog.ipleaders.in

[1965] blog.ipleaders.in

[1966] blog.ipleaders.in

description for a term which may extend to one year, or with a fine, or with both[1967].

Key Differences: BNS 302: Updated version in the new Bharatiya Nyaya Sanhita, with specific provisions for different types of offenses. IPC 298: Part of the older Indian Penal Code framework, now replaced by BNS 302.

[1967] www.indiacode.nic.in

CHAPTER-XVII; OF OFFENCES AGAINST PROPERTY

BNS Section 303 (1)

Definition: Theft Section 303 (1) of the Bharatiya Nyaya Sanhita (BNS) 2023 defines theft as the act of dishonestly taking movable[1968] property out of the possession of any person without their consent, with the intention[1969] of permanently depriving the person of that property.

Illustration: If someone takes a bicycle parked outside a store without the owner's permission, intending to keep it for themselves, they are committing theft under BNS 303.

Example: Suppose an individual secretly takes a wallet left on a table in a café, planning to use the money inside. This act falls under BNS 303.

Comment: This section emphasizes the severity of theft due to its impact on victims' financial well-being and the breach of trust it represents.

Classification of Offence and Punishment Classification: This offense is classified as a criminal offense due to its potential to cause financial loss and breach of trust.

Punishment: The punishment for committing this offense under BNS 303 is imprisonment of either description for a term which may extend to three years, or a fine which may extend to ten thousand rupees, or both[1970].

Cognizable or Non-Cognizable, Bailable or Non-Bailable: This offense is cognizable, meaning the police can arrest the accused without a warrant.

[1968] en.wikipedia.org

[1969] www.indiacode.nic.in

[1970] blog.ipleaders.in

Bailable: This offense is bailable, indicating that the accused can secure bail and be released from custody until the trial is completed.

Comparison: Section 378 of the Indian Penal Code (IPC) also addresses the offense of theft: IPC Section 378: States that whoever, intending to take dishonestly any movable property out of the possession of any person without that[1971] person's consent, moves that property in order to such[1972] taking, is said to commit theft[1973].

Key Differences: BNS 303: Updated version in the new Bharatiya Nyaya Sanhita, with specific provisions for different types of offenses. IPC 378: Part of the older Indian Penal Code framework, now replaced by BNS 303.

BNS Section 303 (2)

Definition: Punishment for Theft Section 303 (2) of the Bharatiya Nyaya Sanhita (BNS) 2023 outlines the punishment for the offense of theft.

Illustration: If an individual is caught stealing a mobile phone from someone's pocket, they are subject to punishment under BNS 303 (2).

Example: Suppose a person is found guilty of stealing a laptop from a coworker's desk. This act falls under BNS 303 (2).

Comment: This section highlights the necessity of stringent punishment to deter theft and ensure justice for the victims of such crimes, reinforcing the seriousness of theft as an offense.

Classification of Offence and Punishment Classification: This offense is classified as a criminal offense due to its potential to cause financial loss and breach of trust.

Punishment: The punishment for committing this offense under BNS 303 (2) is imprisonment [1974]of either description for a term which may extend

---

[1971] pdfcookie.com

[1972] en.wikipedia.org

[1973] www.icsi.edu

[1974] blog.ipleaders.in

to three years, or a fine which may extend to ten thousand rupees, or both[1975].

Cognizable or Non-Cognizable, Bailable or Non-Bailable: This offense is cognizable, meaning the police can arrest the accused without a warrant.

Bailable: This offense is bailable, indicating that the accused can secure bail and be released from custody until the trial is completed.

Comparison: Section 379 of the Indian Penal Code (IPC) also addresses the punishment for theft: IPC Section 379: States that whoever commits theft shall be punished with imprisonment of either description for a term which may extend to three years, or with a fine, or with both[1976].

Key Differences: BNS 303 (2): Updated version in the new Bharatiya Nyaya Sanhita, with a specific fine limit of ten thousand rupees. IPC 379: Part of the older legal framework, now replaced by BNS 303 (2).

BNS Section 304

Definition: Snatching Section 304 of the Bharatiya Nyaya Sanhita (BNS) 2023 defines snatching as a specific type of theft characterized by the sudden, quick, or forceful seizure of movable property from a person or their possession.

Illustration: If someone forcefully grabs a purse from a pedestrian's hand while riding a motorcycle, they are committing snatching under BNS 304.

Example: Suppose an individual suddenly snatches a necklace from someone's neck in a crowded market. This act falls under BNS 304.

Comment: This section highlights the importance of addressing snatching separately from general theft due to its violent nature and the immediate harm and distress it causes to victims.

[1975] www.indiacode.nic.in

[1976] www.icsi.edu

Classification of Offence and Punishment Classification: This offense is classified as a criminal offense due to its potential to cause immediate harm and distress to the victim.

Punishment: The punishment for committing this offense under BNS 304 is imprisonment of either description for a term which may extend to three years, or a fine, or both[1977].

Cognizable or Non-Cognizable, Bailable or Non-Bailable: This offense is cognizable, meaning the police can arrest the accused without a warrant.

Bailable: This offense is bailable, indicating that the accused can secure bail and be released from custody until the trial is completed.

Comparison: Section 378 of the Indian Penal Code (IPC) also addresses the offense of theft, but it does not specifically define snatching. The new addition in BNS 304 provides a more detailed and specific description of snatching as a form of theft.

Key Differences: BNS 304: Specifically defines snatching as a form of theft characterized by sudden, quick, or forceful seizure of property. IPC 378: Part of the older Indian Penal Code framework, addresses theft in a broader context without distinguishing snatching.

BNS Section 305

Definition: Theft in a Dwelling House, or Means of Transportation or Place of Worship, etc Section 305 of the Bharatiya Nyaya Sanhita (BNS) 2023 addresses the offense of committing theft in specific locations such as dwelling houses, means of transportation, places of worship, and government property.

Illustration: If someone breaks into a house and steals valuable items, they are committing theft under BNS 3053.

Example: Suppose an individual steals a bicycle from a garage or a valuable artifact from a temple. These acts fall under BNS 3054.

[1977] blog.ipleaders.in

Comment: This section underscores the gravity of theft in these protected environments due to the significant financial loss and breach of trust it can cause, highlighting the need for stringent measures to prevent such offenses.

Classification of Offence and Punishment Classification: This offense is classified as a criminal offense due to its potential to cause significant financial loss and breach of trust.

Punishment: The punishment for committing this offense under BNS 305 is imprisonment of either description for a term which may extend to seven years, or a fine, or both[1978].

Cognizable or Non-Cognizable, Bailable or Non-Bailable: This offense is cognizable, meaning the police can arrest the accused without a warrant.

Bailable: This offense is bailable, indicating that the accused can secure bail and be released from custody until the trial is completed.

Comparison: Section 380 of the Indian Penal Code (IPC) also addresses the offense of theft in a dwelling house, etc. However, IPC Section 380 has been replaced by BNS 305 with effect from July 1, 202410.

Key Differences: BNS 305: Updated version in the new Bharatiya Nyaya Sanhita, with specific provisions for theft in various contexts such as means of transportation and places of worship11.IPC 380: Part of the older Indian Penal Code framework, now replaced by BNS 30512.

BNS Section 306

Definition: Theft by Clerk or Servant of Property in Possession of Master[1979] Section 306 of the Bharatiya Nyaya Sanhita (BNS) 2023 addresses the offense of theft committed by a clerk or servant[1980] in

---

[1978] blog.ipleaders.in

[1979] Ministry of Home Affairs. (2024). The Bharatiya Nyaya Sanhita, 2023. Retrieved from https://www.mha.gov.in/sites/default/files/250883_english_01042024.pdf

[1980] www.indiacode.nic.in

respect of any property in the possession of their master or employer[1981].

Illustration: If a housekeeper takes jewelry from their employer's home without permission, they are committing theft under BNS 306.

Example: Suppose an office assistant secretly takes office supplies from their workplace to use at home. This act falls under BNS 306.

Comment: This section emphasizes the breach of trust involved when an employee steals from their employer, highlighting the need for strict penalties to maintain trust in employer-employee relationships.

Classification of Offence and Punishment Classification: This offense is classified as a criminal offense due to its breach of trust and potential financial loss to the employer.

Punishment: The punishment for committing this offense under BNS 306 is imprisonment of either description for a term which may extend to seven years, or a fine, or both[1982].

Cognizable or Non-Cognizable, Bailable or Non-Bailable: This offense is cognizable, meaning the police can arrest the accused without a warrant.

Bailable: This offense is bailable, indicating that the accused can secure bail and be released from custody until the trial is completed.

Comparison: Section 381 of the Indian Penal Code[1983] (IPC) also addresses the offense of theft by a clerk or servant of property in possession[1984] of their master: IPC Section 381: States that whoever, being a clerk or servant, or being employed in the capacity of a clerk or servant, commits theft in respect of any property in the possession of his master or employer, shall be punished with imprisonment of either description for a term which may extend to seven years, and shall also be liable to fine.

[1981] en.wikipedia.org

[1982] blog.ipleaders.in

[1983] www.indiacode.nic.in

[1984] en.wikipedia.org

Key Differences: BNS 306: Updated version in the new Bharatiya Nyaya Sanhita, with specific provisions for different types of offenses. IPC 381: Part of the older Indian Penal Code framework, now replaced by BNS 306.

BNS Section 307

Definition: Theft after Preparation for Causing Death, Hurt, or Restraint Section 307 of the Bharatiya Nyaya Sanhita (BNS) 2023 addresses the offense of committing theft after making preparations to cause death, hurt, or restraint to any person in order to facilitate the theft, effect an escape, or retain the stolen property.

Illustration: If someone breaks into a house with a loaded weapon, intending to use it if the homeowner resists, they are committing theft under BNS 307.

Example: Suppose an individual plans to steal a valuable item from a store and brings along a tool to incapacitate the security guard if necessary. This act falls under BNS 307.

Comment: This section underscores the increased severity of theft when it involves preparations to cause harm or use force, reflecting the serious nature of such offenses and the need for strict legal measures to prevent them.

Classification of Offence and Punishment Classification: This offense is classified as a criminal offense due to its potential to cause significant harm and breach of trust.

Punishment: The punishment for committing this offense under BNS 307 is rigorous imprisonment for a term which may extend to ten years, and the offender shall also be liable to a fine[1985].

Cognizable or Non-Cognizable, Bailable or Non-Bailable: This offense is cognizable, meaning the police can arrest the accused without a warrant.

Bailable: This offense is bailable, indicating that the accused can secure bail and be released from custody until the trial is completed.

[1985] en.wikipedia.org

Comparison: Section 382 of the Indian Penal Code[1986] (IPC) also addresses the offense of theft after preparation for causing death, hurt, or restraint: IPC Section 382: States that whoever commits theft, having made preparation for causing death, or hurt, or restraint, or fear of death, or of hurt, or of restraint, to any person, in order to the committing of such theft, or in order to the effecting of his escape after the committing of such theft, or in order to the retaining of property taken by such theft, shall be punished with rigorous imprisonment for a term which may extend to ten years, and shall also be liable to a fine[1987].

Key Differences: BNS 307: Updated version in the new Bharatiya Nyaya Sanhita, with specific provisions for different types of offenses. IPC 382: Part of the older Indian Penal Code framework, now replaced by BNS 307.

BNS Section 308 (1)

Definition: Extortion[1988] Section 308(1) of the Bharatiya Nyaya Sanhita (BNS) 2023 defines extortion as the act of intentionally putting any person in fear of injury to that person or another, and thereby dishonestly inducing the person so put in fear to deliver any property[1989], valuable security, or anything signed or sealed which may be converted into a valuable security[1990].

Illustration: If someone threatens to publish defamatory information about another person unless they pay money[1991], they are committing extortion under BNS 308 (1).

[1986] www.indiacode.nic.in

[1987] en.wikipedia.org

[1988] Ministry of Home Affairs. (2024). The Bharatiya Nyaya Sanhita, 2023. Retrieved from https://www.mha.gov.in/sites/default/files/250883_english_01042024.pdf

[1989] www.bareactslive.com

[1990] blog.ipleaders.in

[1991] moam.info

Example: Suppose an individual threatens to harm someone's child unless they sign a promissory note to pay a certain amount of money. This act falls under BNS 308 (1).

Comment: This section highlights the serious nature of extortion, acknowledging the profound psychological and emotional impact such threats can have on victims, alongside the financial consequences.

Classification of Offence and Punishment Classification: This offense is classified as a criminal offense due to its potential to cause significant harm and distress to the victim.

Punishment: The punishment for committing this offense under BNS 308 (1) is imprisonment of either description for a term which may extend to seven years, or a fine, or both[1992].

Cognizable or Non-Cognizable, Bailable or Non-Bailable: This offense is cognizable, meaning the police can arrest the accused without a warrant6.Bailable: This offense is bailable, indicating that the accused can secure bail and be released from custody until the trial is completed.

Comparison: Section 383 of the Indian Penal Code[1993] (IPC) also addresses the offense of extortion: IPC Section 383: States that whoever intentionally puts any person in fear of any injury to that person, or to any other, and thereby dishonestly induces the person so put in fear to deliver to any person any property[1994] or valuable security, or anything signed or sealed which may be converted into a valuable security, commits "extortion"[1995].

Key Differences: BNS 308 (1): Updated version in the new Bharatiya Nyaya Sanhita, with specific provisions for different types of offenses9.IPC 383: Part of the older Indian Penal Code framework, now replaced by BNS 308 (1)10.

[1992] blog.ipleaders.in

[1993] blog.ipleaders.in

[1994] www.icsi.edu

[1995] blog.ipleaders.in

BNS Section 308 (2)

Definition: Punishment for Extortion Section 308 (2) of the Bharatiya Nyaya Sanhita (BNS) 2023 outlines the punishment for the offense of extortion.

Illustration: If a person threatens to harm someone's reputation unless they hand over a valuable item, they are committing extortion and subject to punishment under BNS 308 (2).

Example: Suppose an individual demands money from a shopkeeper by threatening to damage their property if they do not comply. This act falls under BNS 308 (2).

Comment: This section emphasizes the need for strict penalties to deter extortion, reflecting its serious nature and the significant harm and distress it can cause to victims.

Classification of Offence and Punishment Classification: This offense is classified as a criminal offense due to its potential to cause significant harm and distress to the victim.

Punishment: The punishment for committing this offense under BNS 308 (2) is imprisonment of either description for a term which may extend to three years, or a fine, or both.[1996]

Cognizable or Non-Cognizable, Bailable or Non-Bailable: This offense is cognizable, meaning the police can arrest the accused without a warrant.

Bailable: This offense is bailable, indicating that the accused can secure bail and be released from custody until the trial is completed.

Comparison: Section 384 of the Indian Penal Code[1997] (IPC) also addresses the punishment for extortion: IPC Section 384: States that whoever commits extortion shall be punished with imprisonment of either

---

[1996] blog.ipleaders.in

[1997] blog.ipleaders.in

description for a term which may extend to three years, or with a fine, or with both[1998].

Key Differences: BNS 308 (2): Updated version in the new Bharatiya Nyaya Sanhita, with specific provisions for different types of offenses. IPC 384: Part of the older Indian Penal Code framework, now replaced by BNS 308 (2).

BNS Section 308 (3)

Definition: Putting Person in Fear of Injury in Order to Commit Extortion[1999] Section 308 (3) of the Bharatiya Nyaya Sanhita (BNS) 2023 defines the offense of putting any person in fear of injury to themselves or another person in order to commit extortion[2000].

Illustration: If someone threatens to injure a person unless they hand over their wallet, they are committing extortion under BNS 308 (3).

Example: Suppose an individual threatens to burn down a business unless the owner pays them a large sum of money. This act falls under BNS 308 (3).

Comment: This section emphasizes the seriousness of using threats of injury to coerce someone into delivering property, recognizing both the psychological and financial damage inflicted on victims.

Classification of Offence and Punishment Classification: This offense is classified as a criminal offense due to its potential to cause significant harm and distress to the victim.

Punishment: The punishment for committing this offense under BNS 308 (3) is imprisonment of either description for a term which may extend to two years, or a fine, or both[2001].

[1998] www.icsi.edu

[1999] Ministry of Home Affairs. (2024). The Bharatiya Nyaya Sanhita, 2023. Retrieved from https://www.mha.gov.in/sites/default/files/250883_english_01042024.pdf

[2000] www.bareactslive.com

[2001] blog.ipleaders.in

Cognizable or Non-Cognizable, Bailable or Non-Bailable: This offense is cognizable, meaning the police can arrest the accused without a warrant.

Bailable: This offense is bailable, indicating that the accused can secure bail and be released from custody until the trial is completed.

Comparison: Section 385 of the Indian Penal Code (IPC) also addresses the offense of putting a person in fear of injury in order to commit extortion[2002] : IPC Section 385: States that whoever, in order to the committing of extortion, puts any person in fear of any injury[2003] to that person or to any other, shall be punished with imprisonment of either description for a term which may extend to two years, or with a fine, or with both[2004].

Key Differences: BNS 308 (3): Updated version in the new Bharatiya Nyaya Sanhita, with specific provisions for different types of offenses. IPC 385: Part of the older Indian Penal Code framework, now replaced by BNS 308 (3).

BNS Section 308 (4)

Definition: Putting Person in Fear of Death or Grievous Hurt in Order to Commit Extortion[2005] Section 308 (4) of the Bharatiya Nyaya Sanhita (BNS) 2023 addresses the offense of putting any person in fear of death or of grievous hurt to themselves or another person, in order to commit extortion[2006].

Illustration: If someone threatens to kill a person's family member unless they hand over their valuables, they are committing extortion under BNS 308 (4).

[2002] www.icsi.edu

[2003] blog.ipleaders.in

[2004] www.bareactslive.com

[2005] Ministry of Home Affairs. (2024). The Bharatiya Nyaya Sanhita, 2023. Retrieved from https://www.mha.gov.in/sites/default/files/250883_english_01042024.pdf

[2006] www.bareactslive.com

Example: Suppose an individual threatens to cause serious bodily harm to a person's friend unless they pay a large sum of money. This act falls under BNS 308 (4).

Comment: This section reflects the seriousness of using extreme threats to extort, acknowledging the severe psychological trauma and danger such threats pose to victims and their families.

Classification of Offence and Punishment Classification: This offense is classified as a very serious criminal offense due to its potential to cause extreme fear and distress to the victim.

Punishment: The punishment for committing this offense under BNS 308 (4) is imprisonment[2007] of either description for a term which may extend to ten years, and the offender shall also be liable to a fine[2008].

Cognizable or Non-Cognizable, Bailable or Non-Bailable: This offense is cognizable, meaning the police can arrest the accused without a warrant.

Non-Bailable: This offense is non-bailable, indicating that the accused cannot secure bail and must remain in custody until the trial is completed.

Comparison: Section 387 of the Indian Penal Code[2009] (IPC) also addresses the offense of putting[2010] a person in fear of death or of grievous hurt in order to commit extortion: IPC Section 387: States that whoever, in order to the committing of extortion, puts or attempts to put any person in fear of death or of grievous hurt to that person or to any other, shall be punished with imprisonment of either description for a term which may extend to seven years, and shall also be liable to a fine[2011].

[2007] blog.ipleaders.in

[2008] en.wikipedia.org

[2009] blog.ipleaders.in

[2010] www.icsi.edu

[2011] www.bareactslive.com

Key Differences: BNS 308 (4): Provides for a more severe punishment with imprisonment up to ten years and a fine. IPC 387: Specifies imprisonment up to seven years[2012] and a fine.

BNS Section 308 (5)

Definition: Extortion by Putting a Person in Fear of Death or Grievous Hurt[2013] Section 308 (5) of the Bharatiya Nyaya Sanhita (BNS) 2023 addresses the offense of committing extortion by putting a person in fear of death or grievous hurt.

Illustration: If someone threatens to kill a person's spouse unless they hand over a valuable item, they are committing extortion under BNS 308 (5).

Example: Suppose an individual demands money from a business owner by threatening to inflict serious bodily harm on them if they do not comply. This act falls under BNS 308 (5).

Comment: This section acknowledges the extreme severity of extortion involving threats of death or grievous hurt, emphasizing the significant emotional and psychological toll on victims, in addition to potential physical harm.

Classification of Offence and Punishment Classification: This offense is classified as a very serious criminal offense due to its potential to cause extreme fear and distress to the victim.

Punishment: The punishment for committing this offense under BNS 308 (5) is imprisonment of either description for a term which may extend to ten years, and the offender shall also be liable to a fine[2014].

Cognizable or Non-Cognizable, Bailable or Non-Bailable: This offense is cognizable, meaning the police can arrest the accused without a warrant.

2012 forest.jharkhand.gov.in

2013 Ministry of Home Affairs. (2024). The Bharatiya Nyaya Sanhita, 2023. Retrieved from https://www.mha.gov.in/sites/default/files/250883_english_01042024.pdf

2014 en.wikipedia.org

Non-Bailable: This offense is non-bailable, indicating that the accused cannot secure bail and must remain in custody until the trial is completed.

Comparison: Section 386 of the Indian Penal Code[2015] (IPC) also addresses the offense of extortion by putting a person in fear of death or grievous[2016] hurt:IPC Section 386: States that whoever commits extortion[2017] by putting any person in fear of death or grievous hurt shall be punished with imprisonment of either description for a term which may extend to ten years, and shall also be liable to a fine[2018].

Key Differences: BNS 308 (5): Updated version in the new Bharatiya Nyaya Sanhita, with specific provisions for different types of offenses. IPC 386: Part of the older Indian Penal Code framework, now replaced by BNS 308 (5).

BNS Section 308 (6)

Definition: Extortion by Threat of Accusation of an Offence Punishable with Death or Imprisonment for Life[2019] Section 308 (6) of the Bharatiya Nyaya Sanhita (BNS) 2023 addresses the offense of committing extortion by putting a person in fear of an accusation of having committed an offense punishable with death, imprisonment for life, or imprisonment[2020] for a term which may extend to ten years[2021].

Illustration: If someone threatens to falsely accuse another person of a serious crime, such as murder, unless they hand over their property, they are committing extortion under BNS 308 (6).

2015 www.bareactslive.com

2016 forest.jharkhand.gov.in

2017 www.icsi.edu

2018 en.wikipedia.org

2019 Ministry of Home Affairs. (2024). The Bharatiya Nyaya Sanhita, 2023. Retrieved from https://www.mha.gov.in/sites/default/files/250883_english_01042024.pdf

2020 pdfcookie.com

2021 en.wikipedia.org

Example: Suppose an individual threatens to report someone for a major financial fraud unless they pay a large sum of money. This act falls under BNS 308 (6).

Comment: This section acknowledges the severe psychological impact and potential legal consequences for victims falsely accused of serious crimes, stressing the need for rigorous punishment to deter such extortion.

Classification of Offence and Punishment Classification: This offense is classified as a very serious criminal offense due to its potential to cause extreme fear and distress to the victim.

Punishment: The punishment for committing this offense under BNS 308 (6) is imprisonment of either description for a term which may extend to ten years, and the offender shall also be liable to a fine.

Cognizable or Non-Cognizable, Bailable or Non-Bailable: This offense is cognizable, meaning the police can arrest the accused without a warrant.

Non-Bailable: This offense is non-bailable, indicating that the accused cannot secure bail and must remain in custody until the trial is completed.

Comparison: Section 388 of the Indian Penal Code[2022] (IPC) also addresses the offense of extortion by threat of accusation of an offense punishable with death or imprisonment for life: IPC Section 388: States that whoever commits extortion by putting any person in fear of an accusation against that person or any other, of having committed or attempted to commit any[2023] offense punishable with death, or with imprisonment for life, or with imprisonment for a term which may extend to ten years, shall be punished with imprisonment of either description for a term which may extend to ten years, and shall also be liable to a fine[2024].

Key Differences: BNS 308 (6): Updated version in the new Bharatiya Nyaya Sanhita, with specific provisions for different types of offenses.

[2022] www.bareactslive.com

[2023] forest.jharkhand.gov.in

[2024] en.wikipedia.org

IPC 388: Part of the older Indian Penal Code framework, now replaced by BNS 308 (6).

BNS Section 308 (7)

Definition: Putting Person in Fear of Accusation of Offence in Order to Commit Extortion[2025] Section 308 (7) of the Bharatiya Nyaya Sanhita (BNS) 2023 addresses the offense of committing extortion by putting any person in fear of an accusation of having committed or attempted to commit an offense.

Illustration: If someone threatens to falsely accuse another person of a minor theft unless they hand over their property, they are committing extortion under BNS 308 (7).

Example: Suppose an individual threatens to report someone for a petty crime they did not commit unless they pay a sum of money. This act falls under BNS 308 (7).

Comment: This section highlights the manipulative nature of extortion through false accusations, emphasizing the psychological and emotional distress inflicted on victims, as well as the potential legal consequences.

Classification of Offence and Punishment Classification: This offense is classified as a very serious criminal offense due to its potential to cause extreme fear and distress to the victim.

Punishment: The punishment for committing this offense under BNS 308 (7) is imprisonment of either description for a term which may extend to ten years, and the offender shall also be liable to a fine[2026].

Cognizable or Non-Cognizable, Bailable or Non-Bailable: This offense is cognizable, meaning the police can arrest the accused without a warrant.

Non-Bailable: This offense is non-bailable, indicating that the accused cannot secure bail and must remain in custody until the trial is completed.

[2025] Ministry of Home Affairs. (2024). The Bharatiya Nyaya Sanhita, 2023. Retrieved from https://www.mha.gov.in/sites/default/files/250883_english_01042024.pdf

[2026] en.wikipedia.org

Comparison Section 389 of the Indian Penal Code[2027] (IPC) also addresses the offense of putting a person in fear of accusation of an offense in order to commit extortion : IPC Section 389: States that whoever, in order to the committing of extortion, puts or attempts to put any person in fear of an accusation against that person or any other, of having committed or attempted to commit any offense[2028] punishable with death or with imprisonment for life, or with imprisonment for a term which may extend to ten years, shall be punished with imprisonment of either description for a term which may extend to ten years, and shall also be liable to a fine[2029].

Key Differences: BNS 308 (7): Updated version in the new Bharatiya Nyaya Sanhita, with specific provisions for different types of offenses. IPC 389: Part of the older Indian Penal Code framework, now replaced by BNS 308 (7).

BNS Section 309 (1), (2), (3)

Definition: Robbery Section 309 of the Bharatiya Nyaya Sanhita (BNS) 2023 defines robbery and specifies when theft or extortion is considered robbery[2030].

(1) In all robbery, there is either theft or extortion.

Illustration: If someone forcibly takes another person's property, it is considered robbery because it involves theft.

Example: A person snatches a wallet from someone's hand and runs away. This act is considered robbery because it involves theft.

(2) Theft is "robbery" if, in order to the committing of the theft, or in committing the theft, or in carrying away or attempting to carry away property obtained by the theft, the offender, for that end, voluntarily causes

---

[2027] www.bareactslive.com

[2028] forest.jharkhand.gov.in

[2029] en.wikipedia.org

[2030] Ministry of Home Affairs. (2024). The Bharatiya Nyaya Sanhita, 2023. Retrieved from https://www.mha.gov.in/sites/default/files/250883_english_01042024.pdf

or attempts to cause to any person death or hurt or wrongful restraint, or fear of instant death or of instant hurt, or of instant wrongful restraint[2031].

Illustration: If someone breaks into a house and, in the process, injures the homeowner to steal valuables, it is considered robbery because it involves theft accompanied by violence.

Example: A thief threatens a shopkeeper with a knife to hand over money. This act is considered robbery because it involves theft with the threat of violence.

(3) Extortion is "robbery" if the offender, at the time of committing the extortion, is in the presence of the person put in fear, and commits the extortion by putting that person in fear of instant death, of instant hurt, or of instant wrongful restraint to that person or to some other person, and, by so putting in fear, induces the person so put in fear then and there to deliver up the thing extorted[2032].

Illustration: If someone threatens to harm a person unless they hand over their valuables, it is considered robbery because it involves extortion with the threat of immediate harm.

Example: An individual threatens to shoot someone unless they hand over their phone. This act is considered robbery because it involves extortion with the threat of immediate harm.

Comment: This section emphasizes the need to clearly define and classify robbery, taking into account the involvement of violence, threats, and the immediate presence of fear to ensure strict legal measures are in place to protect victims and maintain public safety.

Classification of Offence and Punishment Classification: This offense is classified as a very serious criminal offense due to its potential to cause significant harm and distress to the victim.

[2031] pdfcookie.com

[2032] forest.jharkhand.gov.in

Punishment: The punishment for committing this offense under BNS 309 is imprisonment of either description for a term which may extend to ten years, and the offender shall also be liable to a fine[2033].

Cognizable or Non-Cognizable, Bailable or Non-Bailable: This offense is cognizable, meaning the police can arrest the accused without a warrant.

Non-Bailable: This offense is non-bailable, indicating that the accused cannot secure bail and must remain in custody until the trial is completed.

Comparison: Section 390 of the Indian Penal Code[2034] (IPC) also addresses the offense of robbery: IPC Section 390: States that robbery involves either theft or extortion. Theft is considered robbery if it involves violence, threat, or injury to a person, and extortion is considered robbery if it involves the victim being put in fear of instant death, grievous hurt, or wrongful restraint.

Key Differences: BNS 309: Updated version in the new Bharatiya Nyaya Sanhita, with specific provisions for different types of offenses. IPC 390: Part of the older Indian Penal Code framework, now replaced by BNS 309.

BNS Section 309 (4)

Definition: Punishment for Robbery Section 309 (4) of the Bharatiya Nyaya Sanhita (BNS) 2023 specifies the punishment for the offense of robbery.

Illustration: If someone forcibly takes another person's handbag by threatening them with a weapon, they are committing robbery and are subject to punishment under[2035] BNS 309 (4).

Example: Suppose an individual robs a store by pointing a gun at the cashier and demanding money. This act falls under BNS 309 (4).

[2033] en.wikipedia.org

[2034] forest.jharkhand.gov.in

[2035] forest.jharkhand.gov.in

Comment: This section reflects the stringent measures imposed to deter robbery, underlining the severe consequences of using violence or threats to unlawfully acquire property and the resulting distress to victims.

Classification of Offence and Punishment Classification: This offense is classified as a very serious criminal offense due to its potential to cause significant harm and distress to the victim.

Punishment: The punishment for committing this offense under BNS 309 (4) is rigorous imprisonment for a term which may extend to fourteen years, and the offender shall also be liable to a fine[2036].

Cognizable or Non-Cognizable, Bailable or Non-Bailable: This offense is cognizable, meaning the police can arrest the accused without a warrant.

Non-Bailable: This offense is non-bailable, indicating that the accused cannot secure bail and must remain in custody until the trial is completed.

Comparison: Section 392 of the Indian Penal Code[2037] (IPC) also addresses the punishment for robbery: IPC Section 392: States that whoever commits robbery shall be punished with rigorous imprisonment for a term which may extend to ten years, and shall also be liable to a fine. If the robbery[2038] is committed on the highway between sunset and sunrise, the imprisonment may be extended to fourteen years[2039].

Key Differences: BNS 309 (4): Provides a maximum punishment of fourteen years for robbery without specifying the time or place of occurrence. IPC 392: Specifies that robbery on the highway between sunset and sunrise may result in extended imprisonment up to fourteen years, otherwise ten years.

[2036] en.wikipedia.org

[2037] www.bareactslive.com

[2038] www.icsi.edu

[2039] forest.jharkhand.gov.in

BNS Section 309 (5)

Definition: Attempt to Commit Robbery Section 309 (5) of the Bharatiya Nyaya Sanhita (BNS) 2023 addresses the offense of attempting to commit robbery.

Illustration: If someone is caught trying to break into a house with the intent to steal[2040] valuables, but they are apprehended before completing the theft, they are committing an attempt to robbery under BNS 309 (5).

Example: Suppose an individual attempts to rob a bank but is caught by the security guard before they can take any money. This act falls under BNS 309 (5).

Comment: This section emphasizes the seriousness of attempted robbery, recognizing the potential for significant harm and distress to victims, even when the theft is not completed.

Classification of Offence and Punishment Classification: This offense is classified as a very serious criminal offense due to its potential to cause significant harm and distress to the victim.

Punishment: The punishment for committing this offense under BNS 309 (5) is rigorous imprisonment for a term which may extend to seven years, and the offender shall also be liable to a fine[2041].

Cognizable or Non-Cognizable, Bailable or Non-Bailable: This offense is cognizable, meaning the police can arrest the accused without a warrant.

Non-Bailable: This offense is non-bailable, indicating that the accused cannot secure bail and must remain in custody until the trial is completed.

Comparison: Section 393 of the Indian Penal Code[2042] (IPC) also addresses the offense of attempting to commit robbery: IPC Section 393: States that whoever attempts to commit robbery shall be punished with

---

[2040] forest.jharkhand.gov.in

[2041] en.wikipedia.org

[2042] www.bareactslive.com

rigorous imprisonment for a term which may extend to seven years, and shall also be liable to a fine[2043].

Key Differences: BNS 309 (5): Updated version in the new Bharatiya Nyaya Sanhita, with specific provisions for different types of offenses. IPC 393: Part of the older Indian Penal Code framework, now replaced by BNS 309 (5).

BNS Section 309 (6)

Definition: Robbery - Voluntarily Causing Hurt in Committing Robbery[2044] Section 309 (6) of the Bharatiya Nyaya Sanhita (BNS) 2023 addresses the offense of voluntarily causing hurt to any person in the act of committing robbery.

Illustration: If someone forcibly takes another person's belongings and, in the process, injures them, they are committing robbery under BNS 309 (6).

Example: Suppose an individual robs a pedestrian and punches them to incapacitate them, causing physical harm. This act falls under BNS 309 (6).

Comment: This section underscores the increased severity and consequences of robbery when it involves causing physical harm to the victim, highlighting the need for strict penalties to deter such violent offenses and protect public safety.

Classification of Offence and Punishment Classification: This offense is classified as a very serious criminal offense due to its potential to cause significant harm and distress to the victim.

[2043] forest.jharkhand.gov.in

[2044] Ministry of Home Affairs. (2024). The Bharatiya Nyaya Sanhita, 2023. Retrieved from https://www.mha.gov.in/sites/default/files/250883_english_01042024.pdf

Punishment: The punishment for committing this offense under BNS 309 (6) is rigorous imprisonment for a term which may extend to ten years, and the offender shall also be liable to a fine[2045].

Cognizable or Non-Cognizable, Bailable or Non-Bailable: This offense is cognizable, meaning the police can arrest the accused without a warrant.

Non-Bailable: This offense is non-bailable, indicating that the accused cannot secure bail and must remain in custody until the trial is completed.

Comparison: Section 394 of the Indian Penal Code[2046] (IPC) also addresses the offense of voluntarily causing hurt in committing robbery: IPC Section 394: States that if any person, in committing or in attempting to commit robbery, voluntarily causes hurt, such person, and any other person jointly concerned in committing or attempting to commit such robbery, shall be punished with rigorous imprisonment for a term which may extend to ten years, and shall also be liable to a fine; and, if hurt is grievous, the imprisonment may be extended to fourteen years[2047].

Key Differences: BNS 309 (6): Specifies rigorous imprisonment up to ten years for voluntarily causing hurt in committing robbery, without differentiating if the hurt is grievous. IPC 394: Provides a maximum punishment of ten years for causing hurt, and fourteen years if the hurt is grievous.

BNS Section 310 (1)

Definition: Dacoity Definition Section 310 (1) of the Bharatiya Nyaya Sanhita (BNS) 2023 defines dacoity as an offense committed by five or more persons jointly in the act of robbery or aiding in the commission of robbery[2048].

2045 en.wikipedia.org

2046 www.bareactslive.com

2047 forest.jharkhand.gov.in

2048 pdfcookie.com

Illustration: If a group of five or more people collaborates to rob a bank, they are committing dacoity under BNS 310 (1).

Example: Suppose a gang of six individuals plans and executes a robbery at a jewellery store. This act falls under BNS 310 (1) as dacoity.

Comment: This section underscores the organized nature of dacoity, highlighting the severe consequences for victims and the societal threat posed by such coordinated criminal activities.

Classification of Offence and Punishment Classification: This offense is classified as a very serious criminal offense due to its potential to cause significant harm and distress to the victim.

Punishment: The punishment for committing dacoity under BNS 310 (1) is imprisonment for life, or rigorous imprisonment for a term which may extend to ten years, and the offender shall also be liable to a fine[2049].

Cognizable or Non-Cognizable, Bailable or Non-Bailable: This offense is cognizable, meaning the police can arrest the accused without a warrant.

Non-Bailable: This offense is non-bailable, indicating that the accused cannot secure bail and must remain in custody until the trial is completed.

Comparison: Section 391 of the Indian Penal Code (IPC) also addresses the offense of dacoity: IPC Section 391: explains that if five or more people commit or attempt to commit a robbery together, or if the total number of people committing or attempting to commit a robbery, including those present and assisting in the commission or attempt, equals five or more, then everyone involved is considered to have committed dacoity[2050].

Key Differences: BNS 310 (1): Updated version in the new Bharatiya Nyaya Sanhita, with specific provisions for different types of offenses. IPC 391: Part of the older Indian Penal Code framework, now replaced by BNS 310 (1).

[2049] en.wikipedia.org

[2050] forest.jharkhand.gov.in

BNS Section 310 (2)

Definition: Punishment for Dacoity Section 310 (2) of the Bharatiya Nyaya Sanhita (BNS) 2023 outlines the punishment for the offense[2051] of dacoity.

Illustration: If a group of five or more people robs a bank, they are committing dacoity and are subject to punishment under BNS 310 (2)[2052].

Example: Suppose a gang of seven individuals carries out a robbery at a jewellery store. This act falls under BNS 310 (2) as dacoity.

Comment: This section highlights the severe consequences of dacoity, reflecting the legal system's commitment to deterring such organized criminal activities and protecting victims from significant harm and distress.

Classification of Offence and Punishment Classification: This offense is classified as a very serious criminal offense due to its potential to cause significant harm and distress to the victims.

Punishment: The punishment for committing this offense under BNS 310 (2) is imprisonment[2053] for life, or rigorous imprisonment for a term which may extend to ten years, and the offender shall[2054] also be liable to a fine.

Cognizable or Non-Cognizable, Bailable or Non-Bailable: This offense is cognizable, meaning the police can arrest the accused without a warrant.

Non-Bailable: This offense is non-bailable, indicating that the accused cannot secure bail and must remain in custody until the trial is completed.

Comparison: Section 395 of the Indian Penal Code[2055] (IPC) also addresses the punishment for dacoity: IPC Section 395: States that

---

[2051] Ministry of Home Affairs. (2024). The Bharatiya Nyaya Sanhita, 2023. Retrieved from https://www.mha.gov.in/sites/default/files/250883_english_01042024.pdf

[2052] forest.jharkhand.gov.in

[2053] pdfcookie.com

[2054] en.wikipedia.org

[2055] www.bareactslive.com

whoever commits dacoity shall be punished with imprisonment for life[2056], or with rigorous imprisonment for a term which may extend to ten years, and shall also be liable to a fine.

Key Differences: BNS 310 (2): Provides a similar framework for punishment, ensuring rigorous imprisonment and fines for the offense of dacoity. IPC 395: Part of the older Indian Penal Code framework, now replaced by BNS 310 (2).

BNS Section 310 (3)

Definition: Dacoity with Murder Section 310 (3) of the Bharatiya Nyaya Sanhita (BNS) 2023 addresses the offense of committing dacoity where a murder is also committed in the course of the dacoity.

Illustration: If a gang of five or more individuals robs a house and, in the process, kills the homeowner, they are committing dacoity with murder under BNS 310 (3).

Example: Suppose a group of robbers targets a jewelry store, and during the robbery, they kill the store owner. This act falls under BNS 310 (3) as dacoity with murder[2057].

Comment: This section highlights the extreme gravity of committing dacoity coupled with murder, acknowledging the profound impact on victims and their families and underscoring the necessity for severe legal repercussions.

Classification of Offence and Punishment Classification: This offense is classified as a heinous criminal offense due to its potential to cause extreme harm and distress to the victims and their families.

[2056] forest.jharkhand.gov.in

[2057] pdfcookie.com

Punishment: The punishment for committing this offense under BNS 310 (3) is death, or imprisonment[2058] for life, and the offender shall also be liable to a fine[2059].

Cognizable or Non-Cognizable, Bailable or Non-Bailable: This offense is cognizable, meaning the police can arrest the accused without a warrant[2060].

Non-Bailable: This offense is non-bailable, indicating that the accused cannot secure bail and must remain in custody until the trial is completed.

Comparison: Section 396 of the Indian Penal Code[2061] (IPC) also addresses the offense of dacoity with murder : IPC Section 396: States that if any one of five or more persons who are conjointly committing dacoity commits murder in so committing dacoity, every one of those persons shall be punished with death, or imprisonment for life, or rigorous imprisonment for a term which may extend to ten years, and shall also be liable to a fine[2062].

Key Differences: BNS 310 (3): Updated version in the new Bharatiya Nyaya Sanhita, emphasizing severe punishment with death or life imprisonment. IPC 396: Specifies similar severe punishments for the offense of dacoity with murder.

BNS Section 310 (4)

Definition: Making Preparation to Commit Dacoity[2063] Section 310 (4) of the Bharatiya Nyaya Sanhita (BNS) 2023 addresses the offense of making preparations to commit dacoity.

2058 mnlumumbai.edu.in

2059 en.wikipedia.org

2060 mnlumumbai.edu.in

2061 www.bareactslive.com

2062 mnlumumbai.edu.in

2063 Ministry of Home Affairs. (2024). The Bharatiya Nyaya Sanhita, 2023. Retrieved from https://www.mha.gov.in/sites/default/files/250883_english_01042024.pdf

Illustration: If a gang is found planning a robbery with weapons and tools specifically intended for dacoity, they are committing an offense under BNS 310 (4).

Example: Suppose a group of individuals is caught with detailed plans, weapons, and other equipment necessary for a large-scale robbery at a bank. This act falls under BNS 310 (4).

Comment: This section stresses the importance of preventive measures in the legal framework, recognizing the potential danger posed by those preparing to commit large-scale robberies and aiming to deter such activities through stringent punishment.

Classification of Offence and Punishment Classification: This offense is classified as a serious criminal offense due to its potential to cause significant harm and distress to the victims.

Punishment: The punishment for committing this offense under BNS 310 (4) is rigorous imprisonment for a term which may extend to ten years, and the offender shall also be liable to a fine.[2064]

Cognizable or Non-Cognizable, Bailable or Non-Bailable: This offense is cognizable, meaning the police can arrest the accused without a warrant[2065].

Non-Bailable: This offense is non-bailable, indicating that the accused cannot secure bail and must remain in custody until the trial is completed.

Comparison: Section 399 of the Indian Penal Code [2066](IPC) also addresses the offense of making preparations to commit dacoity: IPC Section 399: States that whoever makes, any preparation for committing dacoity, shall be punished with rigorous imprisonment for a term which may extend to ten years, and shall also be liable to a fine[2067].

[2064] en.wikipedia.org

[2065] mnlumumbai.edu.in

[2066] www.bareactslive.com

[2067] pdfcookie.com

Key Differences: BNS 310 (4): Provides a similar framework for punishment, ensuring rigorous imprisonment and fines for making preparations to commit dacoity. IPC 399: Part of the older Indian Penal Code framework, now replaced by BNS 310 (4).

BNS Section 310 (5)

Definition: Assembling for the Purpose of Committing Dacoity[2068] Section 310 (5) of the Bharatiya Nyaya Sanhita (BNS) 2023 addresses the offense of assembling with the intent to commit dacoity.

Illustration: If a group of five or more individuals gathers with weapons, planning to rob a bank, they are committing an offense under BNS 310 (5).

Example: Suppose a gang of six people is found in a secluded location with tools and a plan to rob a jewellery store. This act falls under BNS 310 (5).

Comment: This section highlights the importance of pre-emptive legal measures to prevent large-scale robberies, recognizing the potential for significant harm and distress to victims when groups assemble with the intention of committing dacoity.

Classification of Offence and Punishment Classification: This offense is classified as a serious criminal offense due to its potential to cause significant harm and distress to the victims.

Punishment: The punishment for committing this offense under BNS 310 (5) is rigorous imprisonment for a term which may extend to seven years, and the offender shall also be liable to a fine[2069].

[2068] Ministry of Home Affairs. (2024). The Bharatiya Nyaya Sanhita, 2023. Retrieved from https://www.mha.gov.in/sites/default/files/250883_english_01042024.pdf

[2069] en.wikipedia.org

Cognizable or Non-Cognizable, Bailable or Non-Bailable: This offense is cognizable, meaning the police can arrest the accused without a warrant[2070].

Non-Bailable: This offense is non-bailable, indicating that the accused cannot secure bail and must remain in custody until the trial is completed.

Comparison: Section 402 of the Indian Penal Code (IPC) also addresses the offense of assembling for the purpose of committing dacoity: IPC Section 402: declares that anyone who is among five or more people gathered to conduct dacoity at any point after this Act's passage faces a harsh jail sentence of up to seven years in addition to a fine[2071].

Key Differences: BNS 310 (5): Provides a similar framework for punishment, ensuring rigorous imprisonment and fines for assembling with the intent to commit dacoity. IPC 402: Part of the older Indian Penal Code framework, now replaced by BNS 310 (5).

BNS Section 310 (6)

Definition: Punishment for Belonging to Gang of Dacoits[2072] Section 310 (6) of the Bharatiya Nyaya Sanhita (BNS) 2023 addresses the offense of belonging to a gang of dacoits[2073].

Illustration: If someone is found to be a member of a gang[2074] that regularly engages in dacoity, they are committing an offense under BNS 310 (6).

[2070] mnlumumbai.edu.in

[2071]mnlumumbai.edu.in

[2072] Ministry of Home Affairs. (2024). The Bharatiya Nyaya Sanhita, 2023. Retrieved from https://www.mha.gov.in/sites/default/files/250883_english_01042024.pdf

[2073] pdfcookie.com

[2074] pdfcoffee.com

Example: Suppose an individual is identified as part of a gang that has committed multiple robberies together. This act falls under BNS 310 (6) as belonging to a gang of dacoits[2075].

Comment: This section underscores the necessity of tackling organized crime by imposing stringent penalties on those who belong to gangs involved in habitual dacoity, thereby aiming to dismantle such criminal networks and protect society.

Classification of Offence and Punishment Classification: This offense is classified as a very serious criminal offense due to its potential to cause significant harm and distress to the victims and society at large.

Punishment: The punishment for committing this offense under BNS 310 (6) is imprisonment[2076] for life, or rigorous imprisonment for a term which may extend to ten years, and the offender shall also be liable to a fine[2077].

Cognizable or Non-Cognizable, Bailable or Non-Bailable: This offense is cognizable, meaning the police can arrest the accused without a warrant[2078].

Non-Bailable: This offense is non-bailable, indicating that the accused cannot secure bail and must remain in custody until the trial is completed.

Comparison: Section 400 of the Indian Penal Code[2079] (IPC) also addresses the offense of belonging to a gang of dacoits[2080]: IPC Section 400: States that whoever belongs to a gang of persons associated for the purpose of habitually committing dacoity shall be punished with

---

[2075] pdfcookie.com

[2076] mnlumumbai.edu.in

[2077] en.wikipedia.org

[2078] mnlumumbai.edu.in

[2079] www.bareactslive.com

[2080] pdfcookie.com

imprisonment[2081] for life, or with rigorous imprisonment for a term which may extend to ten years, and shall also be liable to a fine[2082].

Key Differences: BNS 310 (6): Provides a similar framework for punishment, ensuring rigorous imprisonment and fines for belonging to a gang of dacoits[2083]. IPC 400: Part of the older Indian Penal Code framework, now replaced by BNS 310 (6).

BNS Section 311

Definition: Robbery or Dacoity with Attempt to Cause Death or Grievous Hurt[2084] Section 311 of the Bharatiya Nyaya Sanhita (BNS) 2023 addresses the offense of committing robbery or dacoity with an attempt to cause death or grievous hurt.

Illustration: If someone robs a store and, in the process, attempts to stab the owner, they are committing an offense under BNS 311.

Example: Suppose a group of dacoits attacks a house, and one of them shoots at the homeowner, causing serious injury. This act falls under BNS 311 as robbery or dacoity with an attempt to cause death or grievous hurt[2085].

Comment: This section underscores the necessity of tackling organized crime by imposing stringent penalties on those who belong to gangs involved in habitual dacoity, thereby aiming to dismantle such criminal networks and protect society.

Classification of Offence and Punishment Classification: This offense is classified as a very serious criminal offense due to its potential to cause extreme harm and distress to the victims.

[2081] en.wikipedia.org

[2082] mnlumumbai.edu.in

[2083] pdfcookie.com

[2084] mnlumumbai.edu.in

[2085] mnlumumbai.edu.in

Punishment: The punishment for committing this offense under BNS 311 is rigorous imprisonment for a term which may extend to ten years, and the offender shall also be liable to a fine[2086].

Cognizable or Non-Cognizable, Bailable or Non-Bailable: This offense is cognizable, meaning the police can arrest the accused without a warrant.

Non-Bailable: This offense is non-bailable, indicating that the accused cannot secure bail and must remain in custody until the trial is completed.

Comparison: Section 397 of the Indian Penal Code[2087] (IPC) also addresses the offense of robbery or dacoity with an attempt to cause death or grievous hurt: IPC Section 397: States that if, at the time of committing robbery or dacoity, the offender uses any deadly weapon, or causes grievous hurt to any person, or attempts to cause death or grievous hurt to any person, the imprisonment with which such offender shall be punished shall not be less than seven years[2088].

Key Differences: BNS 311: Provides a similar framework for punishment, ensuring rigorous imprisonment and fines for committing robbery or dacoity with an attempt to cause death or grievous hurt[2089]. IPC 397: Part of the older Indian Penal Code framework, now replaced by BNS 311.

BNS Section 312

Definition: Attempt to Commit Robbery or Dacoity When Armed with Deadly Weapon[2090] Section 312 of the Bharatiya Nyaya Sanhita (BNS) 2023 addresses the offense of attempting to commit robbery or dacoity while being armed with a deadly weapon.

[2086] en.wikipedia.org

[2087] mnlumumbai.edu.in

[2088] www.drishtijudiciary.com

[2089] mnlumumbai.edu.in

[2090] Ministry of Home Affairs. (2024). The Bharatiya Nyaya Sanhita, 2023. Retrieved from https://www.mha.gov.in/sites/default/files/250883_english_01042024.pdf

Illustration: If an individual attempts to rob a store and is found carrying a loaded gun, they are committing an offense under BNS 312.

Example: Suppose a person tries to break into a house with a knife in hand, intending to steal valuables. This act falls under BNS 312 as an attempt to commit robbery[2091] or dacoity when armed with a deadly weapon.

Comment: This section emphasizes the increased danger posed by individuals attempting to commit robbery or dacoity while armed with deadly weapons[2092], highlighting the need for strict penalties to prevent such violent crimes and protect public safety.

Classification of Offence and Punishment Classification: This offense is classified as a serious criminal offense due to the increased threat and potential for harm when offenders are equipped with weapons.

Punishment: The punishment for committing this offense under BNS 312 is imprisonment for not less than seven years.

Cognizable or Non-Cognizable, Bailable or Non-Bailable: This offense is cognizable, meaning the police can arrest the accused without a warrant[2093].

Non-Bailable: This offense is non-bailable, indicating that the accused cannot secure bail and must remain in custody until the trial is completed.

Comparison: Section 398 of the Indian Penal Code[2094] (IPC) also addresses the offense of attempting to commit robbery or dacoity when armed with a deadly weapon: IPC Section 398: States[2095] that if, at the time of attempting to commit robbery or dacoity, the offender is armed with

[2091] student.manupatra.com

[2092] pdfcookie.com

[2093] mnlumumbai.edu.in

[2094] mnlumumbai.edu.in

[2095] www.drishtijudiciary.com

any deadly weapon, the imprisonment with which such offender shall be punished shall not be less than seven years[2096].

Key Differences: BNS 312: Provides a similar framework for punishment, ensuring imprisonment for not less than seven years for attempting robbery or dacoity while armed with a deadly weapon. IPC 398: Part of the older Indian Penal Code framework, now replaced by BNS 312[2097].

BNS Section 313

Definition: Punishment for Belonging to Gang of Robbers[2098] Section 313 of the Bharatiya Nyaya Sanhita (BNS) 2023 addresses the offense of belonging to a gang[2099] of robbers.

Illustration: If a person is found to be a member of a gang[2100] that habitually commits robberies, they are committing an offense under BNS 313.

Example: Suppose an individual is identified as part of a group that regularly engages in robbery. This act falls under BNS 313 as belonging to a gang of robbers[2101].

Comment: This section emphasizes the need to curb organized criminal activities by imposing stringent penalties on those who belong to gangs involved in habitual robberies, thus aiming to protect society and reduce crime rates.

2096 pdfcookie.com

2097 pdfcookie.com

2098 Ministry of Home Affairs. (2024). The Bharatiya Nyaya Sanhita, 2023. Retrieved from https://www.mha.gov.in/sites/default/files/250883_english_01042024.pdf

2099 pdfcookie.com

2100 pdfcoffee.com

2101 pdfcookie.com

Classification of Offence and Punishment Classification: This offense is classified as a very serious criminal offense due to its potential to cause significant harm and distress to the victims and society at large.

Punishment: The punishment for committing this offense under BNS 313 is rigorous imprisonment for a term which may extend to ten years, and the offender shall also be liable to a fine[2102].

Cognizable or Non-Cognizable, Bailable or Non-Bailable: This offense is cognizable, meaning the police can arrest the accused without a warrant[2103].

Non-Bailable: This offense is non-bailable, indicating that the accused cannot secure bail and must remain in custody until the trial is completed.

Comparison: Section 401 of the Indian Penal Code[2104] (IPC) also addresses the offense of belonging to a gang of robbers[2105]: IPC Section 401: It states that anyone who is a member of a traveling gang or other group of people who have come together to conduct theft or robbery on a regular basis and who is not a gang of dacoits faces a heavy prison sentence of up to seven years in prison and a fine[2106].

Key Differences: BNS 313: Provides for rigorous imprisonment up to ten years for belonging to a gang of robbers[2107], emphasizing the severity of the offense. IPC 401: Specifies imprisonment up to seven years for the same offense.

2102 en.wikipedia.org

2103 mnlumumbai.edu.in

2104 www.bareactslive.com

2105 pdfcookie.com

2106 mnlumumbai.edu.in

2107 pdfcookie.com

BNS Section 314

Definition: Dishonest Misappropriation of Property[2108] **Section 314** of the Bharatiya Nyaya Sanhita (BNS) 2023 addresses the offense of dishonest misappropriation of property[2109].

Illustration: If someone finds a lost wallet and decides to keep it for themselves instead of trying to return it to the owner, they are committing dishonest misappropriation of property under BNS 314.

Example: Suppose an employee takes company funds for personal use without permission. This act falls under BNS 314.

Comment: This section underscores the ethical and legal obligations to return lost property or use resources for their intended purpose, recognizing the breach of trust and financial impact on victims when these obligations are ignored.

Classification of Offence and Punishment Classification: This offense is classified as a criminal offense due to its potential to cause financial loss and breach of trust.

Punishment: The punishment for committing this offense under BNS 314 is imprisonment of either description for a term which may extend to two years, or a fine, or both[2110].

Cognizable or Non-Cognizable, Bailable or Non-Bailable: This offense is non-cognizable, meaning the police cannot arrest the accused without a warrant[2111].

Bailable: This offense is bailable, indicating that the accused[2112] can secure bail and be released from custody until the trial is completed.

[2108] Ministry of Home Affairs. (2024). The Bharatiya Nyaya Sanhita, 2023. Retrieved from https://www.mha.gov.in/sites/default/files/250883_english_01042024.pdf

[2109] pdfcookie.com

[2110] en.wikipedia.org

[2111] mnlumumbai.edu.in

[2112] pdfcookie.com

Comparison: Section 403 of the Indian Penal Code (IPC) also addresses the offense of dishonest misappropriation of property: IPC Section 403: States that whoever dishonestly misappropriates or converts to his own use any[2113] movable property, shall be punished with imprisonment of either description for a term which may extend to two years, or with a fine, or with both[2114].

Key Differences: BNS 314: Updated version in the new Bharatiya Nyaya Sanhita, with specific provisions for different types of offenses. IPC 403: Part of the older Indian Penal Code framework, now replaced by BNS 314.

BNS Section 315

Definition: Dishonest Misappropriation of Property Possessed by Deceased Person[2115] Section 315 of the Bharatiya Nyaya Sanhita (BNS) 2023 addresses the offense of dishonestly misappropriating property possessed by a deceased person at the time of their death.

Illustration: If a servant takes valuable items from the house of a deceased person before the legal heirs take possession, they are committing an offense under BNS 315.

Example: Suppose a housekeeper finds jewelry in the home of a deceased individual and decides to keep it for themselves instead of handing it over to the rightful heirs. This act falls under BNS 315.

Comment: This section underscores the ethical and legal duty to respect the property of deceased persons and ensure it reaches its rightful heirs, emphasizing the breach of trust and financial harm caused by dishonest misappropriation.

Classification of Offence and Punishment Classification: This offense is classified as a criminal offense due to its potential to cause financial loss and breach of trust.

2113 mnlumumbai.edu.in

2114 pdfcoffee.com

2115 mnlumumbai.edu.in

Punishment: The punishment for committing this offense under BNS 315 is imprisonment of either description for a term which may extend to three years[2116], and the offender shall also be liable to a fine. If the offender was employed by the deceased as a clerk or servant, the imprisonment may extend to seven years[2117].

Cognizable or Non-Cognizable, Bailable or Non-Bailable: This offense is non-cognizable, meaning the police cannot arrest the accused without a warrant3.Bailable: This offense is bailable, indicating that the accused can secure bail and be released from custody until the trial is completed.

Comparison: Section 404 of the Indian Penal Code[2118] (IPC) also addresses the offense of dishonest misappropriation of property[2119] possessed by a deceased person at the time of their death: IPC Section 404: States that[2120] whoever dishonestly misappropriates or converts to his own use any property, knowing that such property was in the possession of a deceased person at the time of that person's decease, and has not since been in the possession of any person legally entitled to such possession, shall be punished with imprisonment of either description for a term which may extend to three years, and shall also be liable to a fine[2121].

Key Differences: BNS 315: Updated version in the new Bharatiya Nyaya Sanhita, with specific provisions for different types of offenses6.IPC 404: Part of the older Indian Penal Code[2122] framework, now replaced by BNS 315.

2116 en.wikipedia.org

2117 mnlumumbai.edu.in

2118 www.bareactslive.com

2119 pdfcookie.com

2120 mnlumumbai.edu.in

2121 pdfcookie.com

2122 pdfcookie.com

BNS Section 316 (1)

Definition: Criminal Breach of Trust[2123] Section 316 (1) of the Bharatiya Nyaya Sanhita (BNS) 2023 addresses the offense of criminal breach of trust.

Illustration: If a bank employee misuses customer funds for personal expenses, they are committing an offense under BNS 316 (1).

Example: Suppose a trustee of a trust fund[2124] uses the money for personal investments instead of using it for the beneficiaries. This act falls under BNS 316 (1) as criminal breach of trust.

Comment: This section highlights the serious nature of breaching trust, especially when it involves fiduciary responsibilities, emphasizing the legal and ethical implications of such actions.

Classification of Offence and Punishment Classification: This offense is classified as a serious criminal offense due to the breach of trust and potential financial harm to the victim[2125].

Punishment: The punishment for committing this offense under BNS 316 (1) is imprisonment of either description for a term which may extend to five years, and the offender shall also be liable to a fine.[2126]

Cognizable or Non-Cognizable, Bailable or Non-Bailable: This offense is cognizable, meaning the police can arrest the accused without[2127] a warrant.

Bailable: This offense is bailable, indicating that the accused[2128] can secure bail and be released from custody until the trial is completed.

[2123] Ministry of Home Affairs. (2024). The Bharatiya Nyaya Sanhita, 2023. Retrieved from https://www.mha.gov.in/sites/default/files/250883_english_01042024.pdf

[2124] pdfcookie.com

[2125] en.wikipedia.org

[2126] en.wikipedia.org

[2127] mnlumumbai.edu.in

[2128] pdfcookie.com

Comparison: Section 405 of the Indian Penal Code (IPC) also addresses the offense of criminal breach of trust: IPC Section 405: States that whoever, being in any manner entrusted with property, or with any dominion over property, dishonestly[2129] misappropriates or converts to his own use that property, or dishonestly uses or disposes of that property in violation of any direction of law prescribing the mode in which such trust is to be discharged, or of any legal contract, express or implied, which he has made touching the discharge of such trust, or wilfully suffers any other person so to do, commits criminal breach of trust[2130].

Key Differences: BNS 316 (1): Provides a similar framework for punishment, ensuring imprisonment for up to five years for criminal breach of trust. IPC 405: Part of the older Indian Penal Code framework, now replaced by BNS 316 (1).

BNS Section 316 (2)

Definition: Punishment for Criminal Breach of Trust[2131] Section 316 (2) of the Bharatiya Nyaya Sanhita (BNS) 2023 addresses the punishment for criminal breach of trust.

Illustration: If financial advisor misuses client funds for personal gain, they are committing an offense under BNS 316 (2).

Example: Suppose a company manager uses business funds for personal expenses without authorization. This act falls under BNS 316 (2) as criminal breach of trust.

Comment: This section emphasizes the seriousness of breaching trust, particularly in fiduciary relationships, and underscores the legal consequences of such actions to ensure accountability and protect the interests of those who have entrusted their property to others.

[2129] pdfcookie.com

[2130] www.bareactslive.com

[2131] Ministry of Home Affairs. (2024). The Bharatiya Nyaya Sanhita, 2023. Retrieved from https://www.mha.gov.in/sites/default/files/250883_english_01042024.pdf

Classification of Offence and Punishment Classification: This offense is classified as a serious criminal offense due to the breach of trust and potential financial harm to the victim[2132].

Punishment: The punishment for committing this offense under BNS 316 (2) is imprisonment of either description for a term which may extend to five years, or a fine, or both[2133].

Cognizable or Non-Cognizable, Bailable or Non-Bailable: This offense is cognizable, meaning the police can arrest the accused without a warrant[2134].

Bailable: This offense is bailable, indicating that the accused can secure bail and be released from custody until the trial is completed.

Comparison: Section 406 of the Indian Penal Code[2135] (IPC) also addresses the punishment for criminal breach of trust: IPC Section 406: States that whoever commits criminal breach of trust shall be punished with imprisonment of either description for a term which may extend to three years, or with fine, or with both[2136].

Key Differences: BNS 316 (2): Provides a similar framework for punishment, ensuring imprisonment for up to five years for criminal breach of trust[2137]. IPC 406: Part of the older Indian Penal Code framework, now replaced by BNS 316 (2).

2132 en.wikipedia.org

2133 mnlumumbai.edu.in

2134 mnlumumbai.edu.in

2135 www.bareactslive.com

2136 pdfcookie.com

2137 www.bareactslive.com

BNS Section 316 (3)

Definition: Criminal Breach of Trust by Carrier[2138], etc. Section 316 (3) of the Bharatiya Nyaya Sanhita (BNS) 2023 addresses the offense of criminal breach of trust by a carrier, wharfinger, or warehouse-keeper.

Illustration: If a warehouse-keeper uses goods stored in the warehouse for personal use without the owner's permission, they are committing an offense under BNS 316 (3).

Example: Suppose a carrier transporting goods decides to sell some of the items for personal profit instead of delivering them to the intended recipient. This act falls under BNS 316 (3) as criminal breach of trust by a carrier.

Comment: This section stresses the importance of trust in commercial transactions and the serious legal consequences when individuals entrusted with goods for transport or storage breach this trust for personal gain.

Classification of Offence and Punishment Classification: This offense is classified as a serious criminal offense due to the breach of trust and potential financial harm to the victim.

Punishment: The punishment for committing this offense under BNS 316 (3) is imprisonment of either description for a term which may extend to seven years, and the offender shall also be liable to a fine[2139].

Cognizable or Non-Cognizable, Bailable or Non-Bailable: This offense is cognizable, meaning the police can arrest the accused without a warrant[2140].

[2138] Ministry of Home Affairs. (2024). The Bharatiya Nyaya Sanhita, 2023. Retrieved from https://www.mha.gov.in/sites/default/files/250883_english_01042024.pdf

[2139] blog.scconline.com

[2140] mnlumumbai.edu.in

Bailable: This offense is bailable, indicating that the accused can secure bail and be released from custody until the trial is completed.

Comparison: Section 407 of the Indian Penal Code[2141] (IPC) also addresses the offense of criminal breach of trust[2142] by a carrier, wharfinger, or ware house-keeper: IPC Section 407: It states that anyone who violates the law while acting as a carrier, wharfinger, or warehouse-keeper and is entrusted with property will be penalized with either type of imprisonment for a maximum of seven years, in addition to a fine[2143].

Key Differences: BNS 316 (3): Provides a similar framework for punishment, ensuring imprisonment for up to seven years for criminal breach of trust by a carrier, wharfinger, or warehouse-keeper. IPC 407: Part of the older Indian Penal Code framework[2144], now replaced by BNS 316 (3).

BNS Section 316 (4)

Definition: Criminal Breach of Trust by Clerk or Servant[2145] Section 316 (4) of the Bharatiya Nyaya Sanhita (BNS) 2023 addresses the offense of criminal breach[2146] of trust by a clerk or servant.

Illustration: If a clerk entrusted with the company's finances uses the funds for personal expenses, they are committing an offense under BNS 316 (4).

Example: Suppose an employee is responsible for depositing company money into the bank but instead takes the cash for personal use. This act falls under BNS 316 (4) as criminal breach of trust by a clerk or servant.

2141 www.bareactslive.com

2142 blog.scconline.com

2143 www.bareactslive.com

2144 pdfcoffee.com

2145 Ministry of Home Affairs. (2024). The Bharatiya Nyaya Sanhita, 2023. Retrieved from https://www.mha.gov.in/sites/default/files/250883_english_01042024.pdf

2146 blog.scconline.com

Comment: This section emphasizes the critical importance of trust in employer-employee relationships, highlighting the significant breach of trust and financial harm caused when clerks or servants misuse entrusted property for personal gain.

Classification of Offence and Punishment Classification: This offense is classified as a serious criminal offense due to the breach of trust and potential financial harm to the employer.

Punishment: The punishment for committing this offense under BNS 316 (4) is imprisonment of either description for a term which may extend to seven years, and the offender shall also be liable to a fine[2147].

Cognizable or Non-Cognizable, Bailable or Non-Bailable: This offense is cognizable, meaning the police can arrest the accused without a warrant[2148].

Bailable: This offense is bailable, indicating that the accused can secure bail and be released from custody until the trial is completed.

Comparison: Section 408 of the Indian Penal Code[2149] (IPC) also addresses the offense of criminal breach of trust[2150] by a clerk or servant: IPC Section 408: States that whoever, being a clerk or servant or employed as a clerk or servant, and being in any manner entrusted[2151] with property, or with any dominion over property, commits criminal breach of trust in respect of that property, shall be punished with imprisonment of either description for a term which may extend to seven years, and shall also be liable to a fine[2152].

Key Differences: BNS 316 (4): Provides a similar framework for punishment, ensuring imprisonment for up to seven years for criminal

---

[2147] blog.scconline.com

[2148] mnlumumbai.edu.in

[2149] www.bareactslive.com

[2150] blog.scconline.com

[2151] mnlumumbai.edu.in

[2152] blog.scconline.com

breach of trust by a clerk or servant. IPC 408: Part of the older Indian Penal Code[2153] framework, now replaced by BNS 316 (4).

BNS Section 316 (5)

Definition: Criminal Breach of Trust by Public Servant, or by Banker, Merchant or Agent[2154] Section 316 (5) of the Bharatiya Nyaya Sanhita (BNS) 2023 addresses the offense of criminal breach of trust by a public servant, banker, merchant, or agent.

Illustration: If a public servant uses government property for personal gain[2155], they are committing an offense under BNS 316 (5).

Example: Suppose a bank manager diverts customer funds into their personal account. This act falls under BNS 316 (5) as criminal breach[2156] of trust by a banker.

Comment: This section emphasizes the critical importance of trust in employer-employee relationships, highlighting the significant breach of trust and financial harm caused when clerks or servants misuse entrusted property for personal gain.

Classification of Offence and Punishment Classification: This offense is classified as a very serious criminal offense due to the breach of trust and potential significant financial harm to the victim.

Punishment: The punishment for committing this offense under BNS 316 (5) is imprisonment for life, or imprisonment of either description for a term which may extend to ten years[2157], and the offender shall also be liable to a fine[2158].

[2153] pdfcoffee.com

[2154] Ministry of Home Affairs. (2024). The Bharatiya Nyaya Sanhita, 2023. Retrieved from https://www.mha.gov.in/sites/default/files/250883_english_01042024.pdf

[2155] albertapolitics.ca

[2156] blog.scconline.com

[2157] pdfcookie.com

[2158] blog.scconline.com

Cognizable or Non-Cognizable, Bailable or Non-Bailable: This offense is cognizable, meaning the police can arrest the accused without[2159] a warrant.

Non-Bailable: This offense is non-bailable, indicating that the accused cannot secure bail and must remain in custody until the trial is completed.

Comparison: Section 409 of the Indian Penal Code[2160] (IPC) also addresses the offense of criminal breach of trust by a public servant, banker, merchant, or agent : IPC Section 409: It states that anyone who violates the law by committing a criminal breach of trust with regard to property that they have been entrusted with in any way, or who has dominion over property in their capacity as a public servant or in the course of their business as a banker, merchant, factor, broker, attorney, or agent, faces a life sentence in prison or a term of imprisonment of any kind that can last up to ten years, in addition to a fine[2161].

Key Differences: BNS 316 (5): Provides a similar framework for punishment, ensuring imprisonment for up to ten years for criminal breach of trust by a public servant, banker, merchant, or agent. IPC 409: Part of the older Indian Penal Code framework[2162], now replaced by BNS 316 (5).

BNS Section 317 (1)

Definition: Stolen Property Section 317 (1) of the Bharatiya Nyaya Sanhita (BNS) 2023 defines stolen property and its implications.

Illustration: If someone steals a valuable painting from a museum, the painting is considered stolen property under BNS 317 (1).

Example: Suppose an individual robs a jewellery store and takes away several pieces of jewellery. The jewellery is designated as stolen property under BNS 317 (1).

2159 mnlumumbai.edu.in

2160 www.bareactslive.com

2161 blog.scconline.com

2162 pdfcoffee.com

Comment: This section highlights the importance of categorizing stolen property to ensure proper legal handling and facilitate the process of returning the property to its rightful owner.

Classification of Offence and Punishment Classification: This offense is classified as a criminal offense due to the act of theft or misappropriation.

Punishment: The punishment for possessing or dealing with stolen property under BNS 317 (2) is imprisonment of either description for a term which may extend to three years, or a fine, or both[2163].

Cognizable or Non-Cognizable, Bailable or Non-Bailable: This offense is cognizable, meaning the police can arrest the accused without a warrant[2164].

Bailable: This offense is bailable, indicating that the accused[2165] can secure bail and be released from custody until the trial is completed.

Comparison: Section 410 of the Indian Penal Code (IPC) also addresses stolen property: IPC Section 410: Declares that property whose possession has been transferred through robbery, extortion, or theft, as well as property that has been criminally misappropriated or for which a criminal breach of trust has occurred, is considered stolen property, regardless of whether the transfer or the misappropriation or breach of trust occurred inside or outside of India[2166].

Key Differences: BNS 317 (1): Updated version in the new Bharatiya Nyaya Sanhita, with specific provisions for different types of offenses. IPC 410: Part of the older Indian Penal Code framework, now replaced by BNS 317 (1).

[2163] blog.scconline.com

[2164] mnlumumbai.edu.in

[2165] pdfcoffee.com

[2166] mnlumumbai.edu.in

BNS Section 317 (2)

Definition: Dishonestly Receiving Stolen Property Section 317 (2) of the Bharatiya Nyaya Sanhita (BNS) 2023 addresses the offense of dishonestly receiving stolen property.

Illustration: If someone knowingly buys a stolen laptop from a thief, they are committing an offense under BNS 317 (2).

Example: Suppose a person receives a stolen watch from a friend, knowing that it was stolen. This act falls under BNS 317 (2) as dishonestly receiving stolen property.

Comment: This section highlights the legal responsibility of individuals to avoid engaging in transactions involving stolen property, emphasizing the broader impact on public trust and the importance of due diligence in verifying the origins of purchased goods.

Classification of Offence and Punishment Classification: This offense is classified as a criminal offense due to the act of receiving stolen property.

Punishment: The punishment for committing this offense under BNS 317 (2) is imprisonment of either description for a term which may extend to three years, or a fine, or both[2167].

Cognizable or Non-Cognizable, Bailable or Non-Bailable: This offense is cognizable, meaning the police can arrest the accused without a warrant[2168].

Bailable: This offense is bailable, indicating that the accused can secure bail and be released from custody until the trial is completed.

Comparison: Section 411 of the Indian Penal Code[2169] (IPC) also addresses the offense of dishonestly receiving stolen property: IPC Section 411: stipulates that anybody who dishonestly accepts or keeps any stolen

---

[2167] blog.scconline.com

[2168] mnlumumbai.edu.in

[2169] www.bareactslive.com

item, knowing or having reason to believe it to be stolen property, faces a maximum sentence of three years in either type of jail, a fine, or both[2170].

Key Differences: BNS 317 (2): Updated version in the new Bharatiya Nyaya Sanhita, with specific provisions for different types of offenses. IPC 411: Part of the older Indian Penal Code framework, now replaced by BNS 317 (2).

BNS Section 317 (3)

Definition: Dishonestly Receiving Property Stolen in the Commission of a Dacoity[2171] Section 317 (3) of the Bharatiya Nyaya Sanhita (BNS) 2023 addresses the offense of dishonestly receiving property stolen in the commission of a dacoity.

Illustration: If someone knowingly buys a stolen artifact from a dacoity gang, they are committing an offense under BNS 317 (3).

Example: Suppose an individual receives a stolen car from a person they know is part of a dacoity gang. This act falls under BNS 317 (3) as dishonestly receiving property stolen in the commission of a dacoity[2172].

Comment: This section highlights the significant role that buyers of stolen goods play in perpetuating organized crime. By imposing severe penalties on those who deal in property stolen through dacoity, the law aims to dismantle the network that supports such criminal activities.

Classification of Offence and Punishment Classification: This offense is classified as a very serious criminal offense due to the involvement of organized crime and the potential significant financial harm to the victim.

[2170] mnlumumbai.edu.in

[2171] Ministry of Home Affairs. (2024). The Bharatiya Nyaya Sanhita, 2023. Retrieved from https://www.mha.gov.in/sites/default/files/250883_english_01042024.pdf

[2172] pdfcookie.com

Punishment: The punishment for committing this offense under BNS 317 (3) is imprisonment for life, or rigorous imprisonment for a term which may extend to ten years, and the offender shall also be liable to a fine[2173].

Cognizable or Non-Cognizable, Bailable or Non-Bailable: This offense is cognizable, meaning the police can arrest the accused without a warrant[2174].

Non-Bailable: This offense is non-bailable, indicating that the accused cannot secure bail and must remain in custody until the trial is completed.

Comparison: Section 412 of the Indian Penal Code[2175] (IPC) also addresses the offense of dishonestly receiving property stolen in the commission of a dacoity : IPC Section 412: States that whoever dishonestly receives or retains any stolen property[2176], the possession whereof he knows or has reason to believe to have been transferred by the commission of dacoity, or dishonestly receives from a person, whom he knows or has reason to believe to belong or to have belonged to a gang of dacoits, property which he knows or has reason to believe to have been stolen, shall be punished with imprisonment for life, or with rigorous imprisonment for a term which may extend to ten years, and shall also be liable to a fine[2177].

Key Differences: BNS 317 (3): Updated version in the new Bharatiya Nyaya Sanhita, with specific provisions for different types of offenses.IPC 412: Part of the older Indian Penal Code framework, now replaced by BNS 317 (3).

[2173] blog.scconline.com

[2174] mnlumumbai.edu.in

[2175] www.bareactslive.com

[2176] mnlumumbai.edu.in

[2177] pdfcookie.com

BNS Section 317 (4)

Definition: Habitually Dealing in Stolen Property Section 317 (4) of the Bharatiya Nyaya Sanhita (BNS) 2023 addresses the offense of habitually dealing in stolen property[2178].

Illustration: If someone regularly buys and sells stolen electronics, knowing they are stolen, they are committing an offense under BNS 317 (4).

Example: Suppose a person runs a pawn shop and frequently purchases stolen jewelry from thieves, knowing it is stolen. This act falls under BNS 317 (4) as habitually dealing in stolen property.

Comment: This section highlights the significant role that repeat offenders play in perpetuating criminal activities. By imposing severe penalties on those who habitually deal in stolen property, the law aims to disrupt the ongoing cycle of crime and ensure stricter accountability.

Classification of Offence and Punishment Classification: This offense is classified as a very serious criminal offense due to the habitual nature of the crime and its impact on victims.

Punishment: The punishment for committing this offense under BNS 317 (4) is imprisonment[2179] for life, or imprisonment of either description for a term which may extend to ten years, and the offender shall also be liable to a fine[2180].

Cognizable or Non-Cognizable, Bailable or Non-Bailable: This offense is cognizable, meaning the police can arrest the accused without a warrant[2181].

Non-Bailable: This offense is non-bailable, indicating that the accused cannot secure bail and must remain in custody until the trial is completed.

[2178] www.bareactslive.com

[2179] pdfcookie.com

[2180] blog.scconline.com

[2181] mnlumumbai.edu.in

Comparison: Section 413 of the Indian Penal Code[2182] (IPC) also addresses the offense of habitually dealing in stolen property: IPC Section 413: It stipulates that anyone who regularly receives or deals in property that they know or have reason to suspect is stolen faces a life sentence in jail or a period of imprisonment of any kind that can last up to 10 years, in addition to a fine[2183].

Key Differences: BNS 317 (4): Updated version in the new Bharatiya Nyaya Sanhita, with specific provisions for different types of offenses. IPC 413: Part of the older Indian Penal Code[2184] framework, now replaced by BNS 317 (4).

BNS 317 Section (5)

Definition: Assisting in Concealment of Stolen Property[2185] Section 317 (5) of the Bharatiya Nyaya Sanhita (BNS) 2023 addresses the offense of assisting in the concealment, disposal, or transmission of stolen property.

Illustration: If someone helps a thief hide stolen goods to prevent their discovery, they are committing an offense under BNS 317 (5).

Example: Suppose an individual provides storage space for stolen items, knowing they are stolen, to help the thief avoid detection. This act falls under BNS 317 (5) as assisting in the concealment of stolen property.

Comment: This section highlights the broader responsibility of individuals in not abetting theft indirectly. Ensuring harsh penalties aim to curb this supportive network of criminal activity by legally targeting those who assist in the concealment or disposal of stolen property.

[2182] www.bareactslive.com

[2183] pdfcookie.com

[2184] mnlumumbai.edu.in

[2185] Ministry of Home Affairs. (2024). The Bharatiya Nyaya Sanhita, 2023. Retrieved from https://www.mha.gov.in/sites/default/files/250883_english_01042024.pdf

Classification of Offence and Punishment Classification: This offense is classified as a criminal offense due to its involvement in supporting theft and the potential financial harm to the victim.

Punishment: The punishment for committing this offense under BNS 317 (5) is imprisonment[2186] of either description for a term which may extend to three years, or a fine, or both.

Cognizable or Non-Cognizable, Bailable or Non-Bailable: This offense is cognizable, meaning the police can arrest the accused without a warrant[2187].

Bailable: This offense is bailable, indicating that the accused can secure bail and be released from custody until the trial is completed.

Comparison: Section 414 of the Indian Penal Code[2188] (IPC) also addresses the offense of assisting in the concealment of stolen property: IPC Section 414: It stipulates that anyone who willingly aids in the concealment, disposal, or taking away of property while knowing or having reasonable suspicion that it is stolen faces a maximum sentence of three years in either type of jail, a fine, or both[2189].

Key Differences: BNS 317 (5): Updated version in the new Bharatiya Nyaya Sanhita, with specific provisions for different types of offenses. IPC 414: Part of the older Indian Penal Code framework, now replaced by BNS 317 (5).

BNS Section 318 (1)

Definition: Cheating Section 318 (1) of the Bharatiya Nyaya Sanhita (BNS) 2023 defines the offense of cheating.

[2186] blog.scconline.com

[2187] mnlumumbai.edu.in

[2188] www.bareactslive.com

[2189] mnlumumbai.edu.in

Illustration: If someone falsely claims to be a government official to obtain goods on credit without intending to pay, they are committing an offense under BNS 318 (1).

Example: Suppose A pretends to be a bank officer and convinces Z to lend money, promising to repay it, but A has no intention of doing so. This act falls under BNS 318 (1) as cheating.

Comment: This section highlights the importance of trust and honesty in financial transactions, emphasizing the severe consequences of deceptive practices that lead to financial harm for the victims.

Classification of Offence and Punishment Classification: This offense is classified as a criminal offense due to the act of deception and potential financial harm to the victim.

Punishment: The punishment for committing this offense under BNS 318 (1) is imprisonment of either description for a term which may extend to three years, or a fine[2190], or both.

Cognizable or Non-Cognizable, Bailable or Non-Bailable: This offense is cognizable, meaning the police can arrest the accused without a warrant[2191].

Bailable: This offense is bailable, indicating that the accused[2192] can secure bail and be released from custody until the trial is completed.

Comparison: Section 415 of the Indian Penal Code (IPC) also addresses the offense of cheating: IPC Section 415: It states that anyone who intentionally coerces someone into doing or not doing something that they would not do or not do if they were not deceived, or who fraudulently or dishonestly persuades someone to give up property to someone else or consent to someone keeping property, and whose actions or inactions

---

2190 blog.scconline.com

2191 mnlumumbai.edu.in

2192 pdfcoffee.com

cause or are likely to cause harm to that person's body, mind, reputation, or property, is considered to be cheating[2193].

Key Differences: BNS 318 (1): Updated version in the new Bharatiya Nyaya Sanhita, with specific provisions for different types of offenses8.IPC 415: Part of the older Indian Penal Code framework, now replaced by BNS 318 (1).

BNS Section 318 (2)

Definition: Punishment for Cheating[2194] Section 318 (2) of the Bharatiya Nyaya Sanhita (BNS) 2023 outlines the punishment for the offense of cheating.

Illustration: If an individual deceives another person by pretending to sell a valuable item, but delivers a worthless object instead, they are committing an offense under BNS 318 (2).

Example: Suppose a person convinces someone to invest in a fake business scheme, taking their money with no intention of delivering on the promised returns. This act falls under BNS 318 (2) as cheating.

Comment: This section highlights the importance of integrity in business and financial dealings, emphasizing the need for stringent penalties to deter deceptive practices and protect individuals from financial exploitation.

Classification of Offence and Punishment Classification: This offense is classified as a criminal offense due to the act of deception and potential financial harm to the victim.

Punishment: The punishment for committing this offense under BNS 318 (2) is imprisonment of either description for a term which may extend to three years, or a fine, or both[2195].

[2193] www.icsi.edu

[2194] Ministry of Home Affairs. (2024). The Bharatiya Nyaya Sanhita, 2023. Retrieved from https://www.mha.gov.in/sites/default/files/250883_english_01042024.pdf

[2195] blog.scconline.com

Cognizable or Non-Cognizable, Bailable or Non-Bailable: This offense is cognizable, meaning the police can arrest the accused without a warrant[2196].

Bailable: This offense is bailable, indicating that the accused can secure bail and be released from custody until the trial is completed.

Comparison: Section 417 of the Indian Penal Code[2197] (IPC) also addresses the punishment for cheating: IPC Section 417: States that whoever cheats shall be punished with imprisonment of either description for a term which may extend to one year, or with a fine, or with both[2198].

Key Differences: BNS 318 (2): Provides a maximum punishment of three years for cheating, reflecting a more severe penalty compared to IPC Section 417.IPC 417: Specifies imprisonment for a term which may[2199] extend to one year for cheating.

BNS Section 318 (3)

Definition: Cheating with Knowledge of Wrongful Loss[2200] Section 318 (3) of the Bharatiya Nyaya Sanhita (BNS) 2023 addresses the offense of cheating with the knowledge that wrongful loss may ensue to a person whose interest[2201] the offender is bound to protect.

Illustration: If a lawyer, knowing that their client will suffer a financial loss, deceives a third party to gain an advantage in a case, they are committing an offense under BNS 318 (3).

Example: Suppose a financial advisor, who is legally bound to protect their client's interests, misrepresents investment opportunities, knowing

---

2196 mnlumumbai.edu.in

2197 appforest.jharkhand.gov.in

2198 mnlumumbai.edu.in

2199 appforest.jharkhand.gov.in

2200 Ministry of Home Affairs. (2024). The Bharatiya Nyaya Sanhita, 2023. Retrieved from https://www.mha.gov.in/sites/default/files/250883_english_01042024.pdf

2201 appforest.jharkhand.gov.in

that the client will likely incur a loss. This act falls under BNS 318 (3) as cheating with knowledge of wrongful loss.

Comment: This section stresses the critical importance of fiduciary duty and the trust placed in professionals. The severe penalties reflect society's intolerance for those who exploit their positions of trust for personal gain.

Classification of Offence and Punishment Classification: This offense is classified as a criminal offense due to the act of deception and the betrayal of a fiduciary duty.

Punishment: The punishment for committing this offense under BNS 318 (3) is imprisonment of either description for a term which may extend to five years, or a fine, or both.[2202]

Cognizable or Non-Cognizable, Bailable or Non-Bailable: This offense is cognizable, meaning the police can arrest the accused without a warrant.

Bailable: This offense is bailable, indicating that the accused can secure bail and be released from custody until the trial is completed.

Comparison: Section 418 of the Indian Penal Code[2203] (IPC) also addresses the offense of cheating with knowledge that wrongful loss may ensue to a person whose interest the offender is bound to protect : IPC Section 418: States that whoever cheats with the knowledge that they are likely thereby to cause wrongful loss to a person whose interest in the transaction to which the cheating relates[2204], they were bound either by law, or by a legal contract, to protect, shall be punished with imprisonment of either description for a term which may extend to three years, or with a fine, or with both.

Key Differences: BNS 318 (3): Provides a more severe punishment of up to five years imprisonment compared to IPC Section 418, which has a maximum of three years.IPC 418: Part of the older Indian Penal Code framework, now replaced by BNS 318 (3).

[2202] appforest.jharkhand.gov.in

[2203] www.bareactslive.com

[2204] appforest.jharkhand.gov.in

BNS Section 318 (4)

Definition: Cheating and Dishonestly Inducing Delivery of Property[2205] Section 318 (4) of the Bharatiya Nyaya Sanhita (BNS) 2023 addresses the offense of cheating and dishonestly inducing the delivery of property.

Illustration: If an individual deceives another person by pretending to be a bank official and convinces them to hand over valuable securities, they are committing an offense under BNS 318 (4).

Example: Suppose a person falsely claims to be a real estate agent and convinces a property owner to transfer ownership documents, promising to handle the sale, but with no intention of doing so. This act falls under BNS 318 (4) as cheating and dishonestly inducing delivery of property.

Comment: This section underscores the severe implications of deceit and misrepresentation in business transactions, aiming to protect individuals from substantial financial losses and ensuring accountability for fraudulent actions.

Classification of Offence and Punishment Classification: This offense is classified as a criminal offense due to the act of deception and potential financial harm to the victim. **Punishment:** The punishment for committing this offense under BNS 318 (4) is imprisonment of either description for a term which may extend to seven years, or a fine, or both[2206].

Cognizable or Non-Cognizable, Bailable or Non-Bailable: This offense is cognizable, meaning the police can arrest the accused without a warrant.

Bailable: This offense is bailable, indicating that the accused can secure bail and be released from custody until the trial is completed.

[2205] Ministry of Home Affairs. (2024). The Bharatiya Nyaya Sanhita, 2023. Retrieved from https://www.mha.gov.in/sites/default/files/250883_english_01042024.pdf

[2206] appforest.jharkhand.gov.in

Comparison: Section 420 of the Indian Penal Code[2207] (IPC) also addresses the offense of cheating and dishonestly inducing delivery of property : According to IPC Section 420, anyone who deceives someone into delivering property to someone else, creating, altering, or destroying all or a portion of a valuable security, or anything that is signed or sealed and has the potential to be turned into a valuable security, faces up to seven years in prison of any kind in addition to a fine[2208].

Key Differences: BNS 318 (4): Updated version in the new Bharatiya Nyaya Sanhita, with specific provisions for different types of offenses. IPC 420: Part of the older Indian Penal Code framework, now replaced by BNS 318 (4).

BNS Section 319 (1)

Definition: Cheating by Personation[2209] Section 319 (1) of the Bharatiya Nyaya Sanhita[2210] (BNS) 2023 defines the offense of cheating by personation.

Illustration: If someone pretends to be a wealthy individual to gain access to a bank account, they are committing an offense under BNS 319 (1).

Example: Suppose A pretends to be a famous businessman and convinces a bank to grant a loan, knowing that they are not the actual person. This act falls under BNS 319 (1) as cheating by personation.

Comment: This section underscores the dangers of identity fraud and the significant impact it can have on victims and institutions. By penalizing personation strictly, the law aims to protect individuals and entities from deception-based financial harm.

[2207] www.bareactslive.com

[2208] appforest.jharkhand.gov.in

[2209] Ministry of Home Affairs. (2024). The Bharatiya Nyaya Sanhita, 2023. Retrieved from https://www.mha.gov.in/sites/default/files/250883_english_01042024.pdf

[2210] www.azbpartners.com

Classification of Offence and Punishment Classification: This offense is classified as a criminal offense due to the act of deception and potential financial harm to the victim.

Punishment: The punishment for committing this offense under BNS 319 (1) is imprisonment of either description for a term which may extend to three years, or a fine[2211], or both.

Cognizable or Non-Cognizable, Bailable or Non-Bailable: This offense is cognizable, meaning the police can arrest the accused without a warrant.

Bailable: This offense is bailable, indicating that the accused can secure bail and be released from custody until the trial is completed.

Comparison: Section 416 of the Indian Penal Code (IPC) also addresses the offense of cheating by personation: IPC Section 416: States that a person is said to cheat by personation if they pretend to be someone else, either real or imaginary, or if they knowingly substitute[2212] one person for another, or represent that they or any other person is someone else. This personation can occur in various contexts, including transactions and legal matters[2213].

Key Differences: BNS 319 (1): Updated version in the new Bharatiya Nyaya Sanhita, with specific provisions for different types of offenses. IPC 416: Part of the older Indian Penal Code framework, now replaced by BNS 319 (1).

BNS Section 319 (2)

Definition: Cheating by personation punishment[2214] Section 319 (2) of the Bharatiya Nyaya Sanhita (BNS) 2023 outlines the punishment for the offense of cheating by personation.

[2211] appforest.jharkhand.gov.in

[2212] slate.com

[2213] appforest.jharkhand.gov.in

[2214] Ministry of Home Affairs. (2024). The Bharatiya Nyaya Sanhita, 2023. Retrieved from https://www.mha.gov.in/sites/default/files/250883_english_01042024.pdf

Illustration: If an individual pretends to be a wealthy banker to gain access to someone's bank account, they are committing an offense under BNS 319 (2).

Example: Suppose A pretends to be a famous celebrity and convinces a bank to grant a loan, knowing that they are not the actual person. This act falls under BNS 319 (2) as cheating by personation.

Comment: This section highlights the significance of identity authenticity in financial dealings, ensuring severe repercussions for those who exploit personation to cause financial damage.

Classification of Offence and Punishment Classification: This offense is classified as a criminal offense due to the act of deception and potential financial harm to the victim.

Punishment: The punishment for committing this offense under BNS 319 (2) is imprisonment of either description for a term which may extend to five years, or a fine[2215], or both.

Cognizable or Non-Cognizable, Bailable or Non-Bailable: This offense is cognizable, meaning the police can arrest the accused without a warrant.

Bailable: This offense is bailable, indicating that the accused can secure bail and be released from custody until the trial is completed.

Comparison: Section 419 of the Indian Penal Code[2216] (IPC) also addresses the punishment for cheating by personation: IPC Section 419: States that whoever cheats by personation shall[2217] be punished with imprisonment of either description for a term which may extend to three years, or with a fine, or with both[2218].

Key Differences: BNS 319 (2): Provides a more severe punishment of up to five years imprisonment compared to IPC Section 419, which has a

---

[2215] appforest.jharkhand.gov.in

[2216] www.bareactslive.com

[2217] www.icsi.edu

[2218] appforest.jharkhand.gov.in

maximum of three years. IPC 419: Part of the older Indian Penal Code framework, now replaced by BNS 319 (2).

BNS Section 320

Definition: Dishonest or fraudulent removal or concealment of property to prevent distribution among creditors[2219]. Section 320 of the Bharatiya Nyaya Sanhita (BNS) 2023 addresses the offense of dishonest or fraudulent removal or concealment of property to prevent its distribution among creditors[2220].

Illustration: If a business owner, knowing they owe money to creditors, hides assets or transfers them to a friend without adequate consideration, they are committing an offense under BNS 320.

Example: Suppose a company director, facing bankruptcy, transfers company funds to a personal account to keep them away from creditors. This act falls under BNS 320 as dishonest or fraudulent removal or concealment of property.

Comment: This section emphasizes the importance of transparency and fairness in financial dealings, particularly during insolvency, to ensure creditors receive their due share and to prevent fraudulent asset concealment.

Classification of Offence and Punishment Classification: This offense is classified as a criminal offense due to the act of deception and potential financial harm to creditors.

Punishment: The punishment for committing this offense under BNS 320 is imprisonment of either description for a term which shall not be less than six months but which may extend to two years, or a fine, or both[2221].

[2219] Ministry of Home Affairs. (2024). The Bharatiya Nyaya Sanhita, 2023. Retrieved from https://www.mha.gov.in/sites/default/files/250883_english_01042024.pdf

[2220] appforest.jharkhand.gov.in

[2221] pdfcookie.com

Cognizable or Non-Cognizable, Bailable or Non-Bailable: This offense is cognizable, meaning the police can arrest the accused without a warrant.

Bailable: This offense is bailable, indicating that the accused can secure bail and be released from custody until the trial is completed.

Comparison: Section 421 of the Indian Penal Code[2222] (IPC) also addresses the offense of dishonest or fraudulent removal or concealment of property to prevent its distribution among creditors: IPC Section 421: States that whoever dishonestly or fraudulently removes, conceals or delivers to any person, or transfers or causes to be transferred to any person, without adequate consideration, any property, intending thereby to prevent, or knowing it to be likely that he will thereby prevent, the distribution of that property according to law among his creditors or the creditors[2223] of any other person, shall be punished with imprisonment of either description for a term which may extend to two years, or with a fine, or with both[2224].

Key Differences: BNS 320: Provides a minimum punishment of six months imprisonment[2225], whereas IPC Section 421 specifies imprisonment for up to two years. IPC 421: Part of the older Indian Penal Code framework, now replaced by BNS 320.

BNS Section 321

Definition: Dishonestly or Fraudulently Preventing Debt Being Available for Creditors[2226] Section 321 of the Bharatiya Nyaya Sanhita (BNS) 2023 addresses the offense of dishonestly or fraudulently preventing debt from being available for creditors.

[2222] appforest.jharkhand.gov.in

[2223] www.icsi.edu

[2224] appforest.jharkhand.gov.in

[2225] www.azbpartners.com

[2226] Ministry of Home Affairs. (2024). The Bharatiya Nyaya Sanhita, 2023. Retrieved from https://www.mha.gov.in/sites/default/files/250883_english_01042024.pdf

Illustration: If a debtor, knowing they owe money to creditors, hides assets or transfers them to a friend without adequate consideration, they are committing an offense under BNS 321.

Example: Suppose a business owner, facing bankruptcy, transfers company funds to a personal account to keep them away from creditors. This act falls under BNS 321 as dishonestly or fraudulently preventing debt being available for creditors.

Comment: This section emphasizes the importance of transparency and fairness in financial dealings, particularly during insolvency, to ensure creditors receive their due share and to prevent fraudulent asset concealment.

Classification of Offence and Punishment Classification: This offense is classified as a criminal offense due to the act of deception and potential financial harm to creditors.

Punishment: The punishment for committing this offense under BNS 321 is imprisonment of either description for a term which may extend to two years, or a fine, or both[2227].

Cognizable or Non-Cognizable, Bailable or Non-Bailable: This offense is non-cognizable, meaning the police cannot arrest the accused without a warrant.

Bailable: This offense is bailable, indicating that the accused can secure bail and be released from custody until the trial is completed.

Comparison: Section 422 of the Indian Penal Code (IPC) also addresses the offense of dishonestly or fraudulently preventing debt being available for creditors: IPC Section 422: It states that anyone who dishonestly or fraudulently keeps a debt or demand owed to him or to another person from being made available under the law for the payment of his or her debts or the debts of others will be punished with either type of imprisonment for a maximum of two years, a fine, or both[2228].

[2227] appforest.jharkhand.gov.in

[2228] appforest.jharkhand.gov.in

Key Differences: BNS 321: Updated version in the new Bharatiya Nyaya Sanhita, with specific provisions for different types of offenses. IPC 422: Part of the older Indian Penal Code framework, now replaced by BNS 321.

BNS Section 322

Definition Dishonest or Fraudulent Execution of Deed of Transfer[2229] Section 322 of the Bharatiya Nyaya Sanhita (BNS) 2023 addresses the offense of dishonestly or fraudulently executing a deed of transfer containing a false statement of consideration.

Illustration: If an individual signs a deed to transfer property, falsely stating the consideration amount to deceive creditors, they are committing an offense under BNS 322.

Example: Suppose a person sells a property and intentionally misrepresents the sale price in the deed to avoid paying the full amount to creditors. This act falls under BNS 322 as dishonest or fraudulent execution of a deed of transfer.

Comment: This section emphasizes the importance of honesty and transparency in property transactions, especially when creditors are involved, to prevent financial harm and ensure fair dealings.

Classification of Offence and Punishment Classification: This offense is classified as a criminal offense due to the act of deception and potential financial harm to creditors.

Punishment: The punishment for committing this offense under BNS 322 is imprisonment of either description for a term which may extend to three years, or a fine, or both.[2230]

Cognizable or Non-Cognizable, Bailable or Non-Bailable: This offense is cognizable, meaning the police can arrest the accused without a warrant.

[2229] Ministry of Home Affairs. (2024). The Bharatiya Nyaya Sanhita, 2023. Retrieved from https://www.mha.gov.in/sites/default/files/250883_english_01042024.pdf

[2230] appforest.jharkhand.gov.in

Bailable: This offense is bailable, indicating that the accused can secure bail and be released from custody until the trial is completed.

Comparison: Section 423 of the Indian Penal Code (IPC) also addresses the offense of dishonestly or fraudulently executing a deed of transfer containing a false statement of consideration: IPC Section 423: Declares that anyone who dishonestly or fraudulently signs, executes, or becomes a party to any document that purports to transfer or subject to a charge any property, or any interest therein, and that contains any false statements about the consideration for such a transfer or charge, or about the person or people for whose use or benefit it is actually intended to operate, faces a maximum sentence of two years in prison of any kind, a fine,[2231] or both.

Key Differences: BNS 322: Provides a more severe punishment of up to three years imprisonment compared to IPC Section 423, which has a maximum of two years. IPC 423: Part of the older Indian Penal Code framework, now replaced by BNS 322.

BNS Section 323

Definition: Dishonest or Fraudulent Removal or Concealment of Property[2232] Section 323 of the Bharatiya Nyaya Sanhita (BNS) 2023 addresses the offense of dishonestly or fraudulently removing or concealing property.

Illustration: If an individual hides asset or transfers them to a friend without adequate consideration to avoid paying creditors, they are committing an offense under BNS 323.

Example: Suppose a business owner, facing bankruptcy, transfers company funds to a personal account to keep them away from creditors. This act falls under BNS 323 as dishonest or fraudulent removal or concealment of property.

[2231] pdfcookie.com

[2232] Ministry of Home Affairs. (2024). The Bharatiya Nyaya Sanhita, 2023. Retrieved from https://www.mha.gov.in/sites/default/files/250883_english_01042024.pdf

Comment: This section emphasizes the critical importance of honesty and transparency, particularly when financial obligations are owed to creditors. The goal is to ensure that assets are available for rightful claims rather than being hidden or misappropriated.

Classification of Offence and Punishment Classification: This offense is classified as a criminal offense due to the act of deception and potential financial harm to creditors.

Punishment: The punishment for committing this offense under BNS 323 is imprisonment of either description for a term which may extend to three years, or a fine, or both.[2233]

Cognizable or Non-Cognizable, Bailable or Non-Bailable: This offense is cognizable, meaning the police can arrest the accused without a warrant.

Bailable: This offense is bailable, indicating that the accused can secure bail and be released from custody until the trial is completed.

Comparison: Section 424 of the Indian Penal Code[2234] (IPC) also addresses the offense of dishonestly or fraudulently removing or concealing property: IPC Section 424: It states that anyone who dishonestly or fraudulently removes or conceals property belonging to himself or another person, or who dishonestly or fraudulently aids in the removal or concealment of property, or who dishonestly releases any demand or claim to which he is entitled, faces a maximum sentence of two years in either type of jail, a fine, or both[2235].

Key Differences: BNS 323: Provides a more severe punishment of up to three years imprisonment compared to IPC Section 424, which has a maximum of two years. IPC 424: Part of the older Indian Penal Code[2236] framework, now replaced by BNS 323.

[2233] appforest.jharkhand.gov.in

[2234] www.icsi.edu

[2235] pdfcookie.com

[2236] ww.azbpartners.com

BNS Section 324 (1)

Definition: Mischief[2237] Section 324 (1) of the Bharatiya Nyaya Sanhita (BNS) 2023 defines the offense of mischief.

Illustration: If a person intentionally damages a public park bench, knowing it will cause loss or damage to the public, they are committing an offense under BNS 324 (1)[2238].

Example: Suppose someone deliberately breaks a streetlight, causing it to stop working and affecting public safety. This act falls under BNS 324 (1) as mischief.

Comment: This section underscores the significance of maintaining public property and the repercussions of damaging it, aiming to deter such actions and ensure community assets are preserved for everyone's benefit.

Classification of Offence and Punishment Classification: This offense is classified as a criminal offense due to the act of causing wrongful loss or damage.

Punishment: The punishment for committing this offense under BNS 324 (1) is imprisonment of either description for a term which may extend to three years, or a fine, or both[2239].

Cognizable or Non-Cognizable, Bailable or Non-Bailable: This offense is cognizable, meaning the police can arrest the accused without a warrant.

Bailable: This offense is bailable, indicating that the accused can secure bail and be released from custody until the trial is completed.

Comparison: Section 425 of the Indian Penal Code (IPC) also addresses the offense of mischief: IPC Section 425: According to this, mischief is committed by anyone who intentionally causes, or knows he is likely to cause, wrongful loss or damage to the public or to any individual, destroys

---

[2237] Ministry of Home Affairs. (2024). The Bharatiya Nyaya Sanhita, 2023. Retrieved from https://www.mha.gov.in/sites/default/files/250883_english_01042024.pdf

[2238] pdfcookie.com

[2239] appforest.jharkhand.gov.in

property, or alters property or its circumstances in a way that destroys or reduces its value or utility, or has an adverse effect on it[2240].

Key Differences: BNS 324 (1): Updated version in the new Bharatiya Nyaya Sanhita, with specific provisions for different types of offenses. IPC 425: Part of the older Indian Penal Code framework, now replaced by BNS 324 (1).

BNS Section 324 (2)

Definition: Punishment for Mischief[2241] Section 324 (2) of the Bharatiya Nyaya Sanhita (BNS) 2023 outlines the punishment for the offense of mischief.

Illustration: If a person intentionally damages a public park bench, knowing it will cause loss or damage to the public, they are committing an offense under BNS 324 (2).

Example: Suppose someone deliberately breaks a streetlight, causing it to stop working and affecting public safety. This act falls under BNS 324 (2) as mischief.

Comment: This section underlines the necessity of upholding public property, showing that damaging such property not only affects aesthetics but also impacts public welfare. The punishment is intended to deter such actions and maintain communal facilities.

Classification of Offence and Punishment Classification: This offense is classified as a criminal offense due to the act of causing wrongful loss or damage.

Punishment: The punishment for committing this offense under BNS 324 (2) is imprisonment of either description for a term which may extend to six months, or a fine, or both[2242].

[2240] pdfcookie.com

[2241] Ministry of Home Affairs. (2024). The Bharatiya Nyaya Sanhita, 2023. Retrieved from https://www.mha.gov.in/sites/default/files/250883_english_01042024.pdf

[2242] appforest.jharkhand.gov.in

Cognizable or Non-Cognizable, Bailable or Non-Bailable: This offense is cognizable, meaning the police can arrest the accused without a warrant.

Bailable: This offense is bailable, indicating that the accused can secure bail and be released from custody until the trial is completed.

Comparison: Section 426 of the Indian Penal Code[2243] (IPC) also addresses the punishment for mischief: IPC Section 426: States that whoever commits mischief shall be punished with imprisonment of either description for a term which may extend to three months, or with a fine, or with both[2244].

Key Differences: BNS 324 (2): Provides a more severe punishment of up to six months imprisonment compared to IPC Section 426, which has a maximum of three months. IPC 426: Part of the older Indian Penal Code framework, now replaced by BNS 324 (2).

BNS Section 324 (3)

Definition: Mischief - causes loss or damage to any property including the property of Government or Local Authority[2245] Section 324 (3) of the Bharatiya Nyaya Sanhita (BNS) 2023 addresses the offense of mischief causing loss or damage to any property, including the property of the Government or Local Authority[2246].

Illustration: If a person intentionally damages a public road sign, knowing it will cause inconvenience and potential harm, they are committing an offense under BNS 324 (3).

Example: Suppose someone deliberately breaks a window of a government office, causing damage and requiring repair. This act falls under BNS 324 (3) as mischief causing loss or damage to property.

[2243] www.lawfinderlive.com

[2244] advocatetanmoy.com

[2245] Ministry of Home Affairs. (2024). The Bharatiya Nyaya Sanhita, 2023. Retrieved from https://www.mha.gov.in/sites/default/files/250883_english_01042024.pdf

[2246] prsindia.org

Comment: This section emphasizes the responsibility of maintaining and respecting public and government property, aiming to deter actions that can disrupt public services and cause unnecessary harm and inconvenience.

Classification of Offence and Punishment Classification: This offense is classified as a criminal offense due to the act of causing wrongful loss or damage.

Punishment: The punishment for committing this offense under BNS 324 (3) is imprisonment of either description for a term which may extend to one year, or a fine, or both[2247].

Cognizable or Non-Cognizable, Bailable or Non-Bailable: This offense is cognizable, meaning the police can arrest the accused without a warrant.

Bailable: This offense is bailable, indicating that the accused can secure bail and be released from custody until the trial is completed.

Comparison: Section 426 of the Indian Penal Code[2248] (IPC) also addresses the offense of mischief causing loss or damage to property: IPC Section 426: States that whoever commits mischief and thereby causes loss or damage[2249] to any property, including the property of the Government or Local Authority, shall be punished with imprisonment of either description for a term which may extend to one year, or with a fine, or with both[2250].

Key Differences: BNS 324 (3): Updated version in the new Bharatiya Nyaya Sanhita, with specific provisions for different types of offenses. IPC 426: Part of the older Indian Penal Code framework, now replaced by BNS 324 (3).

[2247] advocatetanmoy.com

[2248] blog.ipleaders.in

[2249] bprd.nic.in

[2250] prsindia.org

BNS Section 324 (4)

Definition: Mischief causing damage to the amount of twenty thousand rupees and more but less than one lakh rupees[2251]. Section 324 (4) of the Bharatiya Nyaya Sanhita (BNS) 2023 addresses the offense of mischief causing damage to property amounting to twenty thousand rupees and more but less than one lakh rupees.

Illustration: If a person intentionally damages a storefront window, causing damage worth twenty thousand rupees, they are committing an offense under BNS 324 (4).

Example: Suppose someone deliberately damages a car, resulting in repair costs of fifty thousand rupees. This act falls under BNS 324 (4) as mischief causing damage to property.

Comment: This section underscores the serious consequences of causing significant property damage, aiming to deter such actions and ensure accountability for the resulting financial loss.

Classification of Offence and Punishment Classification: This offense is classified as a criminal offense due to the act of causing wrongful loss or damage.

Punishment: The punishment for committing this offense under BNS 324 (4) is imprisonment of either description for a term which may extend to two years, or a fine, or both.[2252]

Cognizable or Non-Cognizable, Bailable or Non-Bailable: This offense is cognizable, meaning the police can arrest the accused without a warrant.

Bailable: This offense is bailable, indicating that the accused can secure bail and be released from custody until the trial is completed.

[2251] Ministry of Home Affairs. (2024). The Bharatiya Nyaya Sanhita, 2023. Retrieved from https://www.mha.gov.in/sites/default/files/250883_english_01042024.pdf

[2252] advocatetanmoy.com

Comparison: Section 427 of the Indian Penal Code[2253] (IPC) also addresses the offense of mischief causing damage to property: IPC Section 427: States that whoever commits mischief and thereby[2254] causes loss or damage to the amount of fifty rupees or upwards, shall be punished with imprisonment of either description for a term which may extend to two years, or with a fine, or with both[2255].

Key Differences: BNS 324 (4): Updated version in the new Bharatiya Nyaya Sanhita, with specific provisions for different amounts of damage. IPC 427: Part of the older Indian Penal Code framework, now replaced by BNS 324 (4).

BNS Section 324 (5)

Definition: Mischief- cause loss or damage to amount of one lakh rupees onwards[2256] Section 324 (5) of the Bharatiya Nyaya Sanhita (BNS) 2023 addresses the offense of mischief causing damage to property amounting to one lakh rupees or more.

Illustration: If a person intentionally sets fire to a commercial building, causing damage worth one lakh rupees, they are committing an offense under BNS 324 (5).

Example: Suppose someone deliberately damages a factory, resulting in repair costs of one lakh rupees. This act falls under BNS 324 (5) as mischief causing damage to property.

Comment: This section underscores the significant financial impact of severe acts of mischief, reflecting the need for proportionate punishment to deter such actions and provide justice for substantial financial losses.

[2253] blog.ipleaders.in

[2254] bprd.nic.in

[2255] advocatetanmoy.com

[2256] Ministry of Home Affairs. (2024). The Bharatiya Nyaya Sanhita, 2023. Retrieved from https://www.mha.gov.in/sites/default/files/250883_english_01042024.pdf

Classification of Offence and Punishment Classification: This offense is classified as a criminal offense due to the act of causing significant financial loss or damage.

Punishment: The punishment for committing this offense under BNS 324 (5) is imprisonment of either description for a term which may extend to five years, or a fine, or both[2257].

Cognizable or Non-Cognizable, Bailable or Non-Bailable: This offense is cognizable, meaning the police can arrest the accused without a warrant.

Bailable: This offense is bailable, indicating that the accused can secure bail and be released from custody until the trial is completed.

Comparison: Section 427 of the Indian Penal Code [2258](IPC) also addresses the offense of mischief causing damage to property: IPC Section 427: States that whoever commits mischief and thereby causes loss or damage to the amount[2259] of fifty rupees or upwards, shall be punished with imprisonment of either description for a term which may extend to two years, or with a fine, or with both[2260].

Key Differences: BNS 324 (5): Provides a more severe punishment of up to five years imprisonment compared to IPC Section 427, which has a maximum of two years. IPC 427: Part of the older Indian Penal Code framework, now replaced by BNS 324 (5).

BNS Section 324 (6)

Definition: Mischief Committed After Preparation for Causing Death or Hurt[2261] Section 324 (6) of the Bharatiya Nyaya Sanhita (BNS) 2023

[2257] advocatetanmoy.com

[2258] blog.ipleaders.in

[2259] bprd.nic.in

[2260] advocatetanmoy.com

[2261] Ministry of Home Affairs. (2024). The Bharatiya Nyaya Sanhita, 2023. Retrieved from https://www.mha.gov.in/sites/default/files/250883_english_01042024.pdf

addresses the offense of committing mischief after making preparations to cause death, hurt, or wrongful restraint.

Illustration: If a person sets up a trap with the intent to cause serious injury to someone, they are committing an offense under BNS 324 (6).

Example: Suppose someone rigs a door with a spring-loaded mechanism designed to cause harm to anyone who opens it. This act falls under BNS 324 (6) as mischief committed after preparation for causing death or hurt.

Comment: This section emphasizes the heightened severity of mischief when accompanied by preparations to cause serious harm or death, reflecting the potential danger to individuals and the need for strict legal repercussions.

Classification of Offence and Punishment Classification: This offense is classified as a criminal offense due to the potential for causing serious harm or death.

Punishment: The punishment for committing this offense under BNS 324 (6) is imprisonment of either description for a term which may extend to five years, or a fine, or both[2262].

Cognizable or Non-Cognizable, Bailable or Non-Bailable: This offense is cognizable, meaning the police can arrest the accused without a warrant.

Bailable: This offense is bailable, indicating that the accused can secure bail and be released from custody until the trial is completed.

Comparison: Section 440 of the Indian Penal Code [2263](IPC) also addresses the offense of mischief committed after preparation for causing death or hurt[2264] : IPC Section 440: States that whoever commits mischief, having made preparation for causing to any person death, or hurt, or wrongful restraint, or fear of death, or of hurt, or of wrongful restraint,

---

[2262] advocatetanmoy.com

[2263] www.bareactslive.com

[2264] www.readbag.com

shall be punished with imprisonment of either description for a term which may extend to five years, or with a fine, or with both[2265].

Key Differences: BNS 324 (6): Updated version in the new Bharatiya Nyaya Sanhita, with specific provisions for different types of offenses. IPC 440: Part of the older Indian Penal Code framework, now replaced by BNS 324 (6).

BNS Definition 325

Definition: Mischief by Killing or Maiming Animal[2266] Section 325 of the Bharatiya Nyaya Sanhita (BNS) 2023 addresses the offense of mischief by killing, poisoning, maiming, or rendering useless any animal[2267].

Illustration: If a person intentionally poisons a neighbor's pet dog, causing its death, they are committing an offense under BNS 325.

Example: Suppose someone deliberately harms a farm animal, such as a cow, rendering it useless for agricultural work. This act falls under BNS 325 as mischief by killing or maiming an animal[2268].

Comment: This section underscores the importance of animal welfare and the severe consequences for those who cause harm to animals, reflecting society's commitment to protecting animals from cruelty[2269].

Classification of Offence and Punishment Classification: This offense is classified as a criminal offense due to the act of causing harm to animals.

[2265] advocatetanmoy.com

[2266] Ministry of Home Affairs. (2024). The Bharatiya Nyaya Sanhita, 2023. Retrieved from https://www.mha.gov.in/sites/default/files/250883_english_01042024.pdf

[2267] www.readbag.com

[2268] advocatetanmoy.com

[2269] files.eric.ed.gov

Punishment: The punishment for committing this offense under BNS 325 is imprisonment of either description for a term which may extend to five years, or a fine, or both[2270].

Cognizable or Non-Cognizable, Bailable or Non-Bailable: This offense is cognizable, meaning the police can arrest the accused without a warrant.

Bailable: This offense is bailable, indicating that the accused can secure bail and be released from custody until the trial is completed.

Comparison: Section 428 and 429 of the Indian Penal Code[2271] (IPC) also address the offense of mischief by killing or maiming animals: IPC Section 428: Declares that anyone who kills, poisons, maims, or renders unusable an animal worth fifty rupees or more is guilty of mischief and faces a maximum sentence of two years in prison of any kind, a fine, or both. Section 429 of the Indian Penal Code states that anyone who kills, poisons, maims, or renders useless any elephant, camel, horse, mule, buffalo, bull, cow, or ox, regardless of its value, or any other animal worth fifty rupees or more, will be punished with either type of imprisonment for a maximum of five years, a fine, or both[2272].

Key Differences: BNS 325: Consolidates and replaces IPC Sections 428 and 429, providing a uniform punishment of up to five years imprisonment for any animal, regardless of its value. IPC Sections 428 and 429: Provided different punishments based on the value of the animal and specific types of animals.

BNS Section 326 (a)

Definition: Mischief by Injury, Inundation, Fire or Explosive Substance, etc. Section 326 [2273](a) of the Bharatiya Nyaya Sanhita

---

[2270] files.eric.ed.gov

[2271] blog.ipleaders.in

[2272] advocatetanmoy.com

[2273] Ministry of Home Affairs. (2024). The Bharatiya Nyaya Sanhita, 2023. Retrieved from https://www.mha.gov.in/sites/default/files/250883_english_01042024.pdf

(BNS) 2023 addresses the offense of mischief by causing injury, inundation, fire, or using explosive substances.

Illustration: If a person intentionally sets fire to a public building, causing significant damage, they are committing an offense under BNS 326 (a).

Example: Suppose someone deliberately damages an irrigation canal, leading to the inundation of agricultural fields. This act falls under BNS 326 (a) as mischief by inundation.

Comment: This section reflects the critical importance of protecting public and private properties from acts that can cause severe harm[2274] or disruption, aiming to deter such actions through substantial penalties.

Classification of Offence and Punishment Classification: This offense is classified as a criminal offense due to the act of causing significant harm or damage.

Punishment: The punishment for committing this offense under BNS 326 (a) is imprisonment of either description for a term which may extend to five years, or a fine, or both[2275].

Cognizable or Non-Cognizable, Bailable or Non-Bailable: This offense is cognizable, meaning the police can arrest the accused without a warrant.

Bailable: This offense is bailable, indicating that the accused can secure bail and be released from custody until the trial is completed.

Comparison: Section 430 of the Indian Penal Code[2276] (IPC) also addresses the offense of mischief by injury, inundation, fire, or explosive substances: IPC Section 430It says that anyone who commits mischief by doing anything that reduces the amount of water available for agricultural use, for human or animal food and drink, for cleanliness, or for manufacturing, or for any other reason, will be punished with either type of imprisonment for a maximum of five years, a fine, or both[2277].

[2274] cda.psych.uiuc.edu

[2275] advocatetanmoy.com

[2276] www.bareactslive.com

[2277] advocatetanmoy.com

Key Differences: BNS 326 (a): Updated version in the new Bharatiya Nyaya Sanhita, with specific provisions for different types of mischief. IPC 430: Part of the older Indian Penal Code framework, now replaced by BNS 326 (a).

BNS Section 326 (b)

Definition: Mischief by Injury to Public Road, Bridge, River or Channel[2278] Section 326 (b) of the Bharatiya Nyaya Sanhita (BNS) 2023 addresses the offense of mischief by causing injury to public infrastructure such as roads, bridges, rivers, or channels.

Illustration: If a person intentionally damages a bridge, making it unsafe for public use, they are committing an offense under BNS 326 (b).

Example: Suppose someone deliberately blocks a river channel, causing flooding and damage to nearby properties. This act falls under BNS 326 (b) as mischief by injury to public infrastructure.

Comment: This section reflects the critical importance of protecting public infrastructure from intentional harm. The law aims to ensure safety and service continuity for the community by imposing strict penalties on those who jeopardize public facilities.

Classification of Offence and Punishment Classification: This offense is classified as a criminal offense due to the act of causing significant harm or damage to public infrastructure.

Punishment: The punishment for committing this offense under BNS 326 (b) is imprisonment of either description for a term which may extend to five years, or a fine, or both[2279].

Cognizable or Non-Cognizable, Bailable or Non-Bailable: This offense is cognizable, meaning the police can arrest the accused without a warrant.

[2278] Ministry of Home Affairs. (2024). The Bharatiya Nyaya Sanhita, 2023. Retrieved from https://www.mha.gov.in/sites/default/files/250883_english_01042024.pdf

[2279] advocatetanmoy.com

Bailable: This offense is bailable, indicating that the accused can secure bail and be released from custody until the trial is completed.

Comparison: Section 431 of the Indian Penal Code[2280] (IPC) also addresses the offense of mischief by injury to public roads, bridges, rivers, or channels: IPC Section 431: explains that anyone who commits mischief by doing anything that makes or is likely to make any public road, bridge, navigable river, or navigable channel—natural or man-made—impassable or less safe for travel or property conveyance will be punished with either type of imprisonment for a maximum of five years, a fine, or both[2281].

Key Differences: BNS 326 (b): Updated version in the new Bharatiya Nyaya Sanhita, with specific provisions for different types of public infrastructure. IPC 431: Part of the older Indian Penal Code framework, now replaced by BNS 326 (b).

BNS Section 326 (c)

Definition: Mischief by Causing Inundation or Obstruction to Public Drainage Attended with Damage[2282] Section 326 (c) of the Bharatiya Nyaya Sanhita (BNS) 2023 addresses the offense of mischief by causing inundation or obstruction to public drainage, which results in damage.

Illustration: If a person intentionally blocks a public drainage system, causing water to overflow and damage nearby properties, they are committing an offense under BNS 326 (c).

Example: Suppose someone deliberately dumps debris into a public sewer, leading to flooding and damage to residential areas. This act falls under BNS 326 (c) as mischief by causing inundation or obstruction to public drainage.

[2280] www.bareactslive.com

[2281] advocatetanmoy.com

[2282] Ministry of Home Affairs. (2024). The Bharatiya Nyaya Sanhita, 2023. Retrieved from https://www.mha.gov.in/sites/default/files/250883_english_01042024.pdf

Comment: This section underscores the crucial role of public drainage systems and the serious consequences of tampering with them. The intent is to deter acts that can lead to significant infrastructure damage and public inconvenience.

Classification of Offence and Punishment Classification: This offense is classified as a criminal offense due to the act of causing significant harm or damage to public infrastructure.

Punishment: The punishment for committing this offense under BNS 326 (c) is imprisonment of either description for a term which may extend to five years, or a fine, or both.[2283]

Cognizable or Non-Cognizable, Bailable or Non-Bailable: This offense is cognizable, meaning the police can arrest the accused without a warrant.

Bailable: This offense is bailable, indicating that the accused can secure bail and be released from custody until the trial is completed.

Comparison: Section 432 of the Indian Penal Code [2284](IPC) also addresses the offense of mischief by causing inundation or obstruction to public drainage attended with damage: IPC Section 432: It states that anyone who commits mischief by doing anything that causes or that he knows will cause an inundation or an obstruction to any public drainage system that results in harm or damage faces a maximum sentence of five years in prison of any kind, a fine, or both[2285].

Key Differences: BNS 326 (c): Updated version in the new Bharatiya Nyaya Sanhita, with specific provisions for different types of public infra structure. IPC 432: Part of the older Indian Penal Code framework[2286], now replaced by BNS 326 (c).

[2283] advocatetanmoy.com

[2284] www.bareactslive.com

[2285] advocatetanmoy.com

[2286] bprd.nic.in

BNS Section 326(d)

Mischief by Injury, Inundation, Fire or Explosive Substance[2287], etc. Section 326(d) of the Bharatiya Nyaya Sanhita (BNS) 2023 addresses the offense of committing mischief by causing injury, inundation, fire, or using explosive substances.

Illustration: If a person sets fire to a building, causing damage and injury to people inside, it constitutes an offense under BNS 326(d).

Example: Suppose someone places an explosive device in a public place, causing an explosion that injures people and damages property. This act falls under BNS 326(d) as it involves causing injury and damage through mischief.

Comment: This section aims to address acts of mischief that result in significant harm, injury, or damage to property. It emphasizes the seriousness of such actions and the need to hold individuals accountable for causing widespread harm.

Classification of Offence and Punishment Offence Classification: This offense is cognizable and non-bailable.

Punishment: The punishment for committing this offense under BNS 326(d) is imprisonment of either description for a term which may extend to seven years, and a fine[2288].

Cognizable or Non-Cognizable Cognizable: The police can arrest the accused without a warrant.

Bailable or Non-Bailable: Non-Bailable: Bail is not granted as a matter of right, and the accused can be released on bail only at the discretion of the court[2289].

[2287] Ministry of Home Affairs. (2024). The Bharatiya Nyaya Sanhita, 2023. Retrieved from https://www.mha.gov.in/sites/default/files/250883_english_01042024.pdf

[2288] advocatetanmoy.com

[2289] www.bareactslive.com

Comparison: Section 433 of the Indian Penal Code (IPC) also addresses the offense of mischief but focuses on specific acts such as destroying or moving a lighthouse or sea-mark, or rendering it less useful as a guide[2290] for navigators.

Key Differences: BNS 326(d): Broadly covers mischief causing injury, inundation, fire, or using explosive substances IPC Section 433: Specifically addresses mischief involving lighthouses, sea-marks, buoys, or other navigational aids

BNS Section 326 (e)

Definition: Mischief by Destroying or Moving a Land-Mark Fixed by Public Authority[2291] Section 326 (e) of the Bharatiya Nyaya Sanhita (BNS) 2023 addresses the offense of mischief by destroying or moving a land-mark fixed by public authority.

Illustration: If a person intentionally destroys a boundary stone placed by the government to mark property limits, they are committing an offense under BNS 326 (e).

Example: Suppose someone deliberately moves a milestone on a public road, causing confusion for travelers. This act falls under BNS 326 (e) as mischief by destroying or moving a land-mark[2292].

Comment: This section highlights the importance of maintaining public landmarks that serve essential navigational and property demarcation purposes. It aims to ensure that such intentional acts of mischief are deterred through appropriate legal consequences.

Classification of Offence and Punishment Classification: This offense is classified as a criminal offense due to the act of causing potential harm or confusion.

[2290] bprd.nic.in

[2291] Ministry of Home Affairs. (2024). The Bharatiya Nyaya Sanhita, 2023. Retrieved from https://www.mha.gov.in/sites/default/files/250883_english_01042024.pdf

[2292] advocatetanmoy.com

Punishment: The punishment for committing this offense under BNS 326 (e) is imprisonment of either description for a term which may extend to one year, or a fine, or both[2293].

Cognizable or Non-Cognizable, Bailable or Non-Bailable: This offense is cognizable, meaning the police can arrest the accused without a warrant.

Bailable: This offense is bailable, indicating that the accused can secure bail and be released from custody until the trial is completed.

Comparison: Section 434 of the Indian Penal Code [2294](IPC) also addresses the offense of mischief by destroying or moving a land-mark fixed by public authority: IPC Section 434Declares that anyone who commits mischief by destroying or moving a landmark that has been placed under the authority of a public servant, or by doing anything that makes the landmark less useful, faces up to a year in jail of any kind, a fine, or both[2295].

Key Differences: BNS 326 (e): Updated version in the new Bharatiya Nyaya Sanhita, with specific provisions for different types of mischief. IPC 434: Part of the older Indian Penal Code framework, now replaced by BNS 326 (e).

BNS Section 326 (f)

Definition: Mischief by Injury, Inundation, Fire or Explosive Substance, etc. Section 326 (f) of the Bharatiya Nyaya Sanhita (BNS) 2023 addresses the offense of mischief by causing injury, inundation, fire, or using explosive substances.

Illustration: If someone intentionally sets fire to a farmer's crops, causing significant damage, they are committing an offense under BNS 326 (f).

[2293] advocatetanmoy.com

[2294] blog.ipleaders.in

[2295] hyderabadpolice.gov.in

Example: Suppose an individual uses explosive to damage a dam, leading to flooding and property damage. This act falls under BNS 326 (f) as mischief by causing inundation or using explosive substances.

Comment: This section underscores the severe implications of using fire or explosives to cause significant harm or damage, reflecting the law's commitment to deterring such dangerous activities.

Classification of Offence and Punishment Classification: This offense is classified as a serious criminal offense due to the potential for causing significant harm or damage.

Punishment: The punishment for committing this offense under BNS 326 (f) is imprisonment of either description for a term which may extend to seven years, or a fine, or both[2296].

Cognizable or Non-Cognizable, Bailable or Non-Bailable: This offense is cognizable, meaning the police can arrest the accused without a warrant.

Non-Bailable: This offense is non-bailable, indicating that the accused cannot secure bail and must remain in custody until the trial is completed.

Comparison: Section 435 of the Indian Penal Code[2297] (IPC) also addresses the offense of mischief by causing injury, inundation, fire, or using explosive substances: IPC Section 435: It states that anyone who uses fire or any explosive material to cause mischief with the intent to cause, or knowing that it is likely that he will cause, damage to any property worth at least one hundred rupees will be punished with either type of imprisonment for a maximum of seven years, in addition to a fine[2298].

Key Differences: BNS 326 (f): Updated version in the new Bharatiya Nyaya Sanhita, with provisions for different types of mischief causing

---

[2296] doku.pub

[2297] www.bareactslive.com

[2298] hyderabadpolice.gov.in

significant harm or damage.IPC 435: Part of the older Indian Penal Code[2299] framework, now replaced by BNS 326 (f).

BNS Section 326 (g)

Definition: Mischief by Fire or Explosive Substance with Intent to Destroy House[2300], etc. Section 326 (g) of the Bharatiya Nyaya Sanhita (BNS) 2023 addresses the offense of mischief by using fire or explosive substances with the intent to destroy buildings used for worship, human habitation, or the custody of property.

Illustration: If a person sets fire to a church, mosque, or residential building, intending to destroy it, they are committing an offense under BNS 326 (g).

Example: Suppose someone plants explosives in a temple, aiming to cause its destruction. This act falls under BNS 326 (g) as mischief by fire or explosive substance with intent to destroy a place of worship[2301].

Comment: This section highlights the gravity of using fire or explosives to cause significant destruction, especially to places of worship and residences. It aims to protect these spaces by ensuring severe penalties for such dangerous acts.

Classification of Offence and Punishment Classification: This offense is classified as a serious criminal offense due to the potential for causing significant harm or damage.

Punishment: The punishment for committing this offense under BNS 326 (g) is imprisonment for life, or imprisonment of either description for a term which may extend to ten years[2302], and the offender shall also be liable to a fine.

2299 doku.pub

2300 Ministry of Home Affairs. (2024). The Bharatiya Nyaya Sanhita, 2023. Retrieved from https://www.mha.gov.in/sites/default/files/250883_english_01042024.pdf

2301 doku.pub

2302 hyderabadpolice.gov.in

Cognizable or Non-Cognizable, Bailable or Non-Bailable: This offense is cognizable, meaning the police can arrest the accused without a warrant.

Non-Bailable: This offense is non-bailable, indicating that the accused cannot secure bail and must remain in custody until the trial is completed.

Comparison: Section 436 of the Indian Penal Code[2303] (IPC) also addresses the offense of mischief by fire or explosive substances with intent to destroy buildings used for worship, human habitation, or the custody of property [2304]: IPC Section 436: It states that anyone who uses fire or any explosive material to cause mischief with the intent to destroy, or knowing that he will do so, any building that is typically used as a place of worship, a place for people to live, or a place to store property will be punished with life in prison or with imprisonment of any kind for a maximum of ten years, in addition to a fine[2305].

Key Differences: BNS 326 (g): Updated version in the new Bharatiya Nyaya Sanhita, with specific provisions for different types of mischief causing significant harm or damage. IPC 436: Part of the older Indian Penal Code framework[2306], now replaced by BNS 326 (g).

BNS Section 327 (1)

Definition: Mischief with Intent to Destroy or Make Unsafe a Rail, Aircraft, Decked Vessel, or One of Twenty Tons Burden[2307] Section 327 (1) of the Bharatiya Nyaya Sanhita (BNS) 2023 addresses the offense of mischief with the intent to destroy or make unsafe a rail, aircraft, decked vessel, or any vessel of twenty tons burden or more.

2303 www.bareactslive.com

2304 doku.pub

2305 hyderabadpolice.gov.in

2306 doku.pub

2307 Ministry of Home Affairs. (2024). The Bharatiya Nyaya Sanhita, 2023. Retrieved from https://www.mha.gov.in/sites/default/files/250883_english_01042024.pdf

Illustration: If a person intentionally damages railway tracks, causing a potential derailment, they are committing an offense under BNS 327 (1).

Example: Suppose someone plants explosives on an aircraft, aiming to destroy it. This act falls under BNS 327 (1) as mischief with intent to destroy or make unsafe an aircraft[2308].

Comment: This section underscores the serious threat posed by acts of mischief targeting critical transportation infrastructure and aims to ensure severe penalties to deter such dangerous activities.

Classification of Offence and Punishment Classification: This offense is classified as a serious criminal offense due to the potential for causing significant harm or damage.

Punishment: The punishment for committing this offense under BNS 327 (1) is imprisonment of either description for a term which may extend to ten years, or a fine, or both[2309].

Cognizable or Non-Cognizable, Bailable or Non-Bailable: This offense is cognizable, meaning the police can arrest the accused without a warrant.

Non-Bailable: This offense is non-bailable, indicating that the accused cannot secure bail and must remain in custody until the trial is completed.

Comparison: Section 437 of the Indian Penal Code[2310] (IPC) also addresses the offense of mischief with intent to destroy or make unsafe a rail, aircraft, decked vessel, or any vessel of twenty tons burden or more[2311]: IPC Section 437: It states that anyone who mistreats a rail, an airplane, a decked vessel, or a vessel carrying twenty tons or more with the intent to destroy or make unsafe, or who knows that he will do so, faces a maximum sentence of ten years in prison of any kind, a fine, or both[2312].

[2308] doku.pub

[2309] doku.pub

[2310] www.bareactslive.com

[2311] doku.pub

[2312] hyderabadpolice.gov.in

Key Differences: BNS 327 (1): Updated version in the new Bharatiya Nyaya Sanhita, with specific provisions for different types of mischief causing significant harm or damage. IPC 437: Part of the older Indian Penal Code framework[2313], now replaced by BNS 327 (1).

BNS Section 327 (2)

Definition: Punishment for Mischief by Fire or Explosive Substance[2314] Section 327 (2) of the Bharatiya Nyaya Sanhita (BNS) 2023 addresses the punishment for committing mischief by fire or explosive substances with the intent to destroy or make unsafe a rail, aircraft, decked vessel, or any vessel of twenty tons burden or more.

Illustration: If a person attempts to blow up a railway track using explosives, they are committing an offense under BNS 327 (2).

Example: Suppose someone sets fire to an aircraft with the intent to destroy it. This act falls under BNS 327 (2) as mischief by fire or explosive[2315] substance.

Comment: This section reflects the seriousness of using fire or explosives to cause significant harm, stressing the need for stringent punishment to deter such dangerous acts and protect public safety.

Classification of Offence and Punishment Classification: This offense is classified as a serious criminal offense due to the potential for causing significant harm or damage.

Punishment: The punishment for committing this offense under BNS 327 (2) is imprisonment[2316] for life, or imprisonment of either description for

---

[2313] doku.pub

[2314] Ministry of Home Affairs. (2024). The Bharatiya Nyaya Sanhita, 2023. Retrieved from https://www.mha.gov.in/sites/default/files/250883_english_01042024.pdf

[2315] doku.pub

[2316] hyderabadpolice.gov.in

a term which may extend to ten years, and the offender shall also be liable to a fine[2317].

Cognizable or Non-Cognizable, Bailable or Non-Bailable: This offense is cognizable, meaning the police can arrest the accused without a warrant.

Non-Bailable: This offense is non-bailable, indicating that the accused cannot secure bail and must remain in custody until the trial is completed.

Comparison: Section 438 of the Indian Penal Code[2318] (IPC) also addresses the punishment for mischief by fire or explosive substances: IPC Section 438: It stipulates that anyone who commits or attempts to commit the mischief listed in the last section (Section 437), using fire or any explosive material, faces a life sentence or a term of imprisonment of any kind that can last up to ten years, in addition to a fine[2319].

Key Differences: BNS 327 (2): Updated version in the new Bharatiya Nyaya Sanhita, with specific provisions for different types of mischief causing significant harm or damage. IPC 438: Part of the older Indian Penal Code framework[2320], now replaced by BNS 327 (2).

BNS Section 328

Definition: Punishment for Intentionally Running Vessel Aground or Ashore with Intent to Commit Theft[2321], etc. Section 328 of the Bharatiya Nyaya Sanhita (BNS) 2023 addresses the offense of intentionally running any vessel aground or ashore with the intent to commit theft or dishonest misappropriation of property.

Illustration: If a person intentionally runs a cargo ship aground to steal valuable goods on board, they are committing an offense under BNS

[2317] doku.pub

[2318] doku.pub

[2319] hyderabadpolice.gov.in

[2320] doku.pub

[2321] Ministry of Home Affairs. (2024). The Bharatiya Nyaya Sanhita, 2023. Retrieved from https://www.mha.gov.in/sites/default/files/250883_english_01042024.pdf

328.Example: Suppose someone deliberately runs a fishing boat ashore to steal the catch. This act falls under BNS 328 as mischief with intent to commit theft[2322].

Comment: This section highlights the serious nature of using vessels for committing theft, emphasizing the significant risk to property and public safety.

Classification of Offence and Punishment Classification: This offense is classified as a serious criminal offense due to the potential for significant harm or damage.

Punishment: The punishment for committing this offense under BNS 328 is imprisonment of either description for a term which may extend to ten years[2323], or a fine, or both.

Cognizable or Non-Cognizable, Bailable or Non-Bailable: This offense is cognizable, meaning the police can arrest the accused without a warrant.

Non-Bailable: This offense is non-bailable, indicating that the accused cannot secure bail and must remain in custody until the trial is completed.

Comparison: Section 439 of the Indian Penal Code[2324] (IPC) also addresses the offense of intentionally running a vessel aground or ashore with intent to commit theft or dishonest misappropriation of property[2325]: IPC Section 439: Declares that anyone who intentionally runs a vessel aground or ashore with the intent to steal or dishonestly misappropriate any property within, or with the knowledge that such theft or misappropriation of property may be committed, faces a maximum sentence of ten years in either type of jail, a fine, or both[2326].

Key Differences: BNS 328: Updated version in the new Bharatiya Nyaya Sanhita, with specific provisions for different types of mischief causing

[2322] hyderabadpolice.gov.in

[2323] doku.pub

[2324] www.bareactslive.com

[2325] doku.pub

[2326] hyderabadpolice.gov.in

significant harm or damage. IPC 439: Part of the older Indian Penal Code framework, now replaced by BNS 328.

BNS Section 329 (1)

Definition: Criminal Trespass and House-Trespass Section 329 (1) of the Bharatiya Nyaya Sanhita (BNS) 2023 addresses the offense of criminal trespass and house-trespass.

Illustration: If a person enters someone's property without permission with the intent to commit theft, they are committing an offense under BNS 329 (1).

Example: Suppose someone unlawfully enters a neighbor's house to steal valuables. This act falls under BNS 329 (1) as criminal trespass and house-trespass.

Comment: This section emphasizes the legal protections against unauthorized entry into private properties, aiming to safeguard individuals' rights to privacy and security

Classification of Offence and Punishment Classification: This offense is classified as a criminal offense due to the act of unlawfully entering or remaining on someone else's property.

Punishment: The punishment for committing this offense under BNS 329 (1) is imprisonment of either description for a term which may extend to three years, or a fine[2327], or both.

Cognizable or Non-Cognizable, Bailable or Non-Bailable: This offense is cognizable, meaning the police can arrest the accused without a warrant.

Bailable: This offense is bailable, indicating that the accused can secure bail and be released from custody until the trial is completed.

Comparison: Section 441 of the Indian Penal Code[2328] (IPC) also addresses the offense of criminal trespass: IPC Section 441: defines

---

[2327] doku.pub

[2328] doku.pub

criminal trespass as anyone who enters or is on someone else's property with the intent to commit an offense, to intimidate, insult, or annoy someone who is in possession of that property, or who, after entering or being on that property lawfully, unlawfully remains there with the intent to commit an offense or to intimidate, insult, or annoy someone who is in possession of that property[2329].

Key Differences: BNS 329 (1): Updated version in the new Bharatiya Nyaya Sanhita, with specific provisions for different types of trespassing offenses. IPC 441: Part of the older Indian Penal Code framework, now replaced by BNS 329 (1).

BNS Section 329 (2)

Definition: Criminal Trespass and House-Trespass Section 329 (2) of the Bharatiya Nyaya Sanhita (BNS) 2023 addresses the offense of house-trespass specifically.

Illustration: If a person unlawfully enters another person's house with the intent to commit theft or any other offense, they are committing an offense under BNS 329 (2)[2330].

Example: Suppose someone breaks into a house at night to steal valuables. This act falls under BNS 329 (2) as house-trespass.

Comment: This section underscores the sanctity and legal protection of one’s home, recognizing the serious nature of unlawful entry and its potential to cause distress and harm to residents.

Classification of Offence and Punishment Classification: This offense is classified as a criminal offense due to the act of unlawfully entering someone else's home[2331].

[2329] hyderabadpolice.gov.in

[2330] hyderabadpolice.gov.in

[2331] doku.pub

Punishment: The punishment for committing this offense under BNS 329 (2) is imprisonment of either description for a term which may extend to one year, or a fine, or both[2332].

Cognizable or Non-Cognizable, Bailable or Non-Bailable: This offense is cognizable, meaning the police can arrest the accused without a warrant.

Bailable: This offense is bailable, indicating that the accused can secure bail and be released from custody until the trial is completed.

Comparison: Section 442 of the Indian Penal Code[2333] (IPC) also addresses the offense of house-trespass: IPC Section 442: explains that entering or staying in a building, tent, or vessel intended for human habitation or a building used for property custody is considered house-trespass, which is a criminal trespass[2334].

Key Differences: BNS 329 (2): Updated version in the new Bharatiya Nyaya Sanhita, with specific provisions for house-trespassing offenses. IPC 442: Part of the older Indian Penal Code framework, now replaced by BNS 329 (2).

BNS Section 329 (3)

Definition: Criminal Trespass Punishment'[2335] Section 329 (3) of the Bharatiya Nyaya Sanhita (BNS) 2023 outlines the punishment for the offense of criminal trespass.

Illustration: If someone enters another person's property without permission, with the intent to commit a crime, they are committing criminal trespass under BNS 329 (3).

[2332] doku.pub

[2333] doku.pub

[2334] hyderabadpolice.gov.in

[2335] Ministry of Home Affairs. (2024). The Bharatiya Nyaya Sanhita, 2023. Retrieved from https://www.mha.gov.in/sites/default/files/250883_english_01042024.pdf

Example: Suppose an individual unlawfully enters a house with the intention of stealing valuables. This act falls under BNS 329 (3) as criminal trespass.

Comment: This section highlights the serious consequences of unlawful entry into private property, emphasizing the need for stringent penalties to deter such actions and protect individuals' rights to privacy and security.

Classification of Offence and Punishment Classification: This offense is classified as a criminal offense due to the act of unlawfully entering or remaining on someone else's property.

Punishment: The punishment for committing this offense under BNS 329 (3) is imprisonment of either description for a term which may extend to three years, or a fine, or both[2336].

Cognizable or Non-Cognizable, Bailable or Non-Bailable: This offense is cognizable, meaning the police can arrest the accused without a warrant.

Bailable: This offense is bailable, indicating that the accused can secure bail and be released from custody until the trial is completed.

Comparison: Section 447 of the Indian Penal Code[2337] (IPC) also addresses the punishment for criminal trespass: IPC Section 447: The law stipulates that anyone found guilty of illegal trespassing faces a maximum sentence of three months in prison of any kind, a maximum fine of five hundred rupees, or both[2338].

Key Differences: BNS 329 (3): Provides a more severe punishment of up to three years imprisonment compared to IPC Section 447, which has a maximum of three months. IPC 447: Part of the older Indian Penal Code framework, now replaced by BNS 329 (3).

[2336] doku.pub

[2337] www.bareactslive.com

[2338] hyderabadpolice.gov.in

BNS Section 329 (4)

Definition: Punishment for House-Trespass Section 329 (4) of the Bharatiya Nyaya Sanhita (BNS) 2023 outlines the punishment for the offense of house-trespass.

Illustration: If someone unlawfully enters a person's house with the intent to commit a theft, they are committing an offense under BNS 329 (4).

Example: Suppose an individual breaks into a home at night to steal valuables. This act falls under BNS 329 (4) as house-trespass.

Comment: This section emphasizes the importance of legal protection against unauthorized entry into homes, ensuring the safety and privacy of individuals and their properties.

Classification of Offence and Punishment Classification: This offense is classified as a criminal offense due to the act of unlawfully entering someone else's home.

Punishment: The punishment for committing this offense under BNS 329 (4) is imprisonment of either description for a term which may extend to one year, or a fine, or both[2339].

Cognizable or Non-Cognizable, Bailable or Non-Bailable: This offense is cognizable, meaning the police can arrest the accused without a warrant.

Bailable: This offense is bailable, indicating that the accused can secure bail and be released from custody until the trial is completed.

Comparison: Section 448 of the Indian Penal Code[2340] (IPC) also addresses the punishment for house-trespass: IPC Section 448: It stipulates that anyone found guilty of house trespassing faces a maximum sentence of one year in either type of jail, a fine, or both[2341].

Key Differences: BNS 329 (4): Updated version in the new Bharatiya Nyaya Sanhita, aligning closely with the provisions of IPC 448.IPC 448:

[2339] doku.pub

[2340] doku.pub

[2341] hyderabadpolice.gov.in

Part of the older Indian Penal Code framework, now replaced by BNS 329 (4).

BNS Section 330 (1)

Definition: Lurking House-Trespass Section 330 (1) of the Bharatiya Nyaya Sanhita (BNS) 2023 addresses the offense of lurking house-trespass.

Illustration: If a person enters someone's house without permission and takes steps to hide their presence from the owner, they are committing an offense under BNS 330 (1).

Example: Suppose someone sneaks into a house through a window and hides in a closet to avoid detection. This act falls under BNS 330 (1) as lurking house-trespass.

Comment: This section underscores the seriousness of unlawful entry into someone else's home while taking precautions to conceal one's presence, aiming to protect individuals' privacy and safety.

Classification of Offence and Punishment Classification: This offense is classified as a criminal offense due to the act of unlawfully entering someone else's home while concealing their presence.

Punishment: The punishment for committing this offense under BNS 330 (1) is imprisonment of either description for a term which may extend to three years, or a fine, or both[2342].

Cognizable or Non-Cognizable, Bailable or Non-Bailable: This offense is cognizable, meaning the police can arrest the accused without a warrant.

Bailable: This offense is bailable, indicating that the accused can secure bail and be released from custody until the trial is completed.

Comparison: Section 443 of the Indian Penal Code[2343] (IPC) also addresses the offense of lurking house-trespass: IPC Section 443: explains

---

[2342] doku.pub

[2343] doku.pub

that a person who trespasses into a structure, tent, or vessel while taking steps to hide their actions from someone who has the authority to bar them or evict them is guilty of lurking house-trespass[2344].

Key Differences: BNS 330 (1): Updated version in the new Bharatiya Nyaya Sanhita, with specific provisions for different types of house-trespassing offenses. IPC 443: Part of the older Indian Penal Code framework, now replaced by BNS 330 (1).

BNS Section 330 (2)

Definition: House-Breaking Section 330 (2) of the Bharatiya Nyaya Sanhita (BNS) 2023 addresses the offense of house-breaking.

Illustration: If a person breaks into a house by creating a new entry point, such as breaking a window or door, they are committing an offense under BNS 330 (2).

Example: Suppose someone uses a crowbar to force open a locked door to gain entry into a house. This act falls under BNS 330 (2) as house-breaking.

Comment: This section underscores the serious nature of unlawful entry into homes by force, reflecting the need for legal consequences to protect individuals and their properties from such intrusions.

Classification of Offence and Punishment Classification: This offense is classified as a criminal offense due to the act of unlawfully entering someone else's home by force.

Punishment: The punishment for committing this offense under BNS 330 (2) is imprisonment of either description for a term which may extend to three years[2345], or a fine, or both.

Cognizable or Non-Cognizable, Bailable or Non-Bailable: This offense is cognizable, meaning the police can arrest the accused without a warrant.

[2344] hyderabadpolice.gov.in

[2345] bprd.nic.in

Bailable: This offense is bailable, indicating that the accused can secure bail and be released from custody until the trial is completed.

Comparison: Section 445 of the Indian Penal Code[2346] (IPC) also addresses the offense of house-breaking: IPC Section 445: States that a person is said to commit house-breaking who commits house-trespass if he effects his entrance into the house or any part of it in any of the six ways[2347] described, such as by creating a new passage or using criminal force.

Key Differences: BNS 330 (2): Updated version in the new Bharatiya Nyaya Sanhita, with specific provisions for different types of house-breaking offenses. IPC 445: Part of the older Indian Penal Code framework, now replaced by BNS 330 (2).

BNS Section 331 (1)

Definition: Punishment for House-Trespass or House-Breaking Section 331 (1) of the Bharatiya Nyaya Sanhita (BNS) 2023 outlines the punishment for the offense of house-trespass or house-breaking.

Illustration: If a person unlawfully enters a house by breaking a window or door, they are committing an offense under BNS 331 (1).

Example: Suppose someone forcefully opens a locked door to enter a house and steal valuables. This act falls under BNS 331 (1) as house-trespass or house-breaking.

Comment: This section underscores the serious nature of unlawful entry into homes by force, reflecting the need for legal consequences to protect individuals and their properties from such intrusions.

Classification of Offence and Punishment Classification: This offense is classified as a criminal offense due to the act of unlawfully entering someone else's home by force.

[2346] eparlib.nic.in

[2347] bprd.nic.in

Punishment: The punishment for committing this offense under BNS 331 (1) is imprisonment of either description for a term which may extend to two years, or a fine, or both[2348].

Cognizable or Non-Cognizable, Bailable or Non-Bailable: This offense is cognizable, meaning the police can arrest the accused without a warrant.

Bailable: This offense is bailable, indicating that the accused can secure bail and be released from custody until the trial is completed.

Comparison Section 353 of the Indian Penal Code[2349] (IPC) addresses a different offense: IPC Section 353: It states that anyone who assaults or uses criminal force against a public servant while they are performing their duties as such, or with the intention of preventing or discouraging them from doing so, faces a maximum sentence of two years in prison of any kind, a fine, or both[2350].

Key Differences: BNS 331 (1): Focuses on the punishment for house-trespass or house-breaking. IPC 353: Focuses on the punishment for assaulting or using criminal force[2351] against a public servant.

BNS Section 331 (2)

Definition: Punishment for Lurking House-Trespass or House-Breaking by Night[2352] Section 331 (2) of the Bharatiya Nyaya Sanhita (BNS) 2023 outlines the punishment for the offense of lurking house-trespass or house-breaking by night.

2348 bprd.nic.in

2349 eparlib.nic.in

2350 legislative.gov.in

2351 pdfcookie.com

2352 Ministry of Home Affairs. (2024). The Bharatiya Nyaya Sanhita, 2023. Retrieved from https://www.mha.gov.in/sites/default/files/250883_english_01042024.pdf

Illustration: If a person sneaks into a house through a window at night and hides, intending to commit a crime[2353], they are committing an offense under BNS 331 (2).

Example: Suppose someone breaks into a home at night with the intention of stealing valuables and hides in a closet to avoid detection. This act falls under BNS 331 (2) as lurking house-trespass or house-breaking[2354] by night.

Comment: This section highlights the heightened severity of unlawful entries at night, reflecting the increased threat to personal safety and property during nighttime and aiming to deter such actions through strict legal consequences.

Classification of Offence and Punishment Classification: This offense is classified as a criminal offense due to the act of unlawfully entering someone else's home by night and concealing their presence.

Punishment: The punishment for committing this offense under BNS 331 (2) is imprisonment of either description for a term which may extend to three years, or a fine[2355], or both.

Cognizable or Non-Cognizable, Bailable or Non-Bailable: This offense is cognizable, meaning the police can arrest the accused without a warrant.

Bailable: This offense is bailable, indicating that the accused can secure bail and be released from custody until the trial is completed.

Comparison: Section 456 of the Indian Penal Code[2356] (IPC) also addresses the punishment for lurking house-trespass or house-breaking by night: IPC Section 456: specifies that anyone found guilty of either lurking house trespassing or house breaking at night faces a maximum sentence of three years in prison of any kind in addition to a fine[2357].

[2353] bprd.nic.in

[2354] pdfcookie.com

[2355] bprd.nic.in

[2356] www.bareactslive.com

[2357] pdfcookie.com

Key Differences: BNS 331 (2): Provides a similar framework for punishment, ensuring imprisonment for up to three years for lurking house-trespass or house-breaking by night. IPC 456: Part of the older Indian Penal Code framework, now replaced by BNS 331 (2).

BNS Definition 331 (3)

Definition: Lurking House-Trespass or House-Breaking in Order to Commit Offence Punishable with Imprisonment[2358] Section 331 (3) of the Bharatiya Nyaya Sanhita (BNS) 2023 addresses the offense of lurking house-trespass or house-breaking with the intent to commit an offense punishable with imprisonment.

Illustration: If a person breaks into a house at night with the intention of committing theft, they are committing an offense under BNS 331 (3).

Example: Suppose someone sneaks into a house through a window at night, hides, and then steals valuables. This act falls under BNS 331 (3) as lurking house-trespass or house-breaking in order to commit[2359] an offense punishable with imprisonment.

Comment: This section underscores the severity of committing house-trespass with the intent to commit a punishable offense, highlighting the legal system's effort to deter such crimes and protect the safety and property of individuals.

Classification of Offence and Punishment Classification: This offense is classified as a criminal offense due to the act of unlawfully entering someone else's home with the intent to commit a crime punishable with imprisonment.

[2358] Ministry of Home Affairs. (2024). The Bharatiya Nyaya Sanhita, 2023. Retrieved from https://www.mha.gov.in/sites/default/files/250883_english_01042024.pdf

[2359] pdfcookie.com

Punishment: The punishment for committing this offense under BNS 331 (3) is imprisonment of either description for a term which may extend to three years, or a fine[2360], or both.

Cognizable or Non-Cognizable, Bailable or Non-Bailable: This offense is cognizable, meaning the police can arrest the accused without a warrant.

Bailable: This offense is bailable, indicating that the accused can secure bail and be released from custody until the trial is completed.

Comparison: Section 454 of the Indian Penal Code[2361] (IPC) also addresses the offense of lurking house-trespass or house-breaking in order to commit an offense punishable with imprisonment: IPC Section 454: It stipulates that anyone who engages in housebreaking or lurking trespassing in order to commit any crime that carries a jail sentence will be punished with a term of imprisonment of any kind that can last up to three years, in addition to a fine. If the intended offense is theft, the sentence may be extended to ten years[2362].

Key Differences: BNS 331 (3): Updated version in the new Bharatiya Nyaya Sanhita, with specific provisions for lurking house-trespass or house-breaking in order to commit[2363] an offense punishable with imprisonment. IPC 454: Part of the older Indian Penal Code framework, now replaced by BNS 331 (3).

BNS Section 331 (4)

Definition: Lurking House-Trespass or House-Breaking by Night in Order to Commit Offence Punishable with Imprisonment[2364] Section 331 (4) of the Bharatiya Nyaya Sanhita (BNS) 2023 addresses the

---

[2360] bprd.nic.in

[2361] www.bareactslive.com

[2362] bprd.nic.in

[2363] pdfcookie.com

[2364] Ministry of Home Affairs. (2024). The Bharatiya Nyaya Sanhita, 2023. Retrieved from https://www.mha.gov.in/sites/default/files/250883_english_01042024.pdf

offense of lurking house-trespass or house-breaking by night with the intent to commit an offense punishable with imprisonment.

Illustration: If a person breaks into a house at night with the intention of committing theft, they are committing an offense under BNS 331 (4).

Example: Suppose someone sneaks into a house through a window at night, hides, and then steals valuables. This act falls under BNS 331 (4) as lurking house-trespass or house-breaking by night in order to commit an offense punishable with imprisonment[2365].

Comment: This section highlights the increased danger and potential harm of crimes committed under the cover of night, aiming to protect individuals from such violations by imposing strict penalties.

Classification of Offence and Punishment Classification: This offense is classified as a criminal offense due to the act of unlawfully entering someone else's home by night with the intent to commit a crime punishable with imprisonment.

Punishment: The punishment for committing this offense under BNS 331 (4) is imprisonment of either description for a term which may extend to five years, or a fine, or both[2366].

Cognizable or Non-Cognizable, Bailable or Non-Bailable: This offense is cognizable, meaning the police can arrest the accused without a warrant.

Bailable: This offense is bailable, indicating that the accused can secure bail and be released from custody until the trial is completed.

Comparison: Section 457 of the Indian Penal Code[2367] (IPC) also addresses the offense of lurking house-trespass or house-breaking[2368] by night in order to commit an offense punishable with imprisonment: IPC Section 457: States that whoever commits lurking house-trespass by night,

---

[2365] pdfcookie.com

[2366] bprd.nic.in

[2367] www.bareactslive.com

[2368] bprd.nic.in

or house-breaking by night, in order to the committing of any offense[2369] punishable with imprisonment, shall be punished with imprisonment of either description for a term which may extend to five years, and shall also be liable to fine; and, if the offense intended to be committed is theft, the term of the imprisonment may be extended to fourteen years[2370].

Key Differences: BNS 331 (4): Updated version in the new Bharatiya Nyaya Sanhita, with specific provisions for lurking house-trespass or house-breaking by night in order to commit an offense punishable with imprisonment[2371]. IPC 457: Part of the older Indian Penal Code framework, now replaced by BNS 331 (4).

BNS Section 331 (5)

Definition: Lurking House-Trespass or House Breaking After Preparation for Hurt, Assault, or Wrongful Restraint[2372] Section 331 (5) of the Bharatiya Nyaya Sanhita (BNS) 2023 addresses the offense of lurking house-trespass or house-breaking after making preparations to cause hurt, assault, or wrongful restraint[2373].

Illustration: If a person breaks into a house at night after arming themselves with a weapon to assault the occupants, they are committing an offense under BNS 331 (5).

Example: Suppose someone breaks into a house with a knife, intending to harm the residents. This act falls under BNS 331 (5) as lurking house-trespass or house-breaking after preparation for hurt, assault, or wrongful restraint[2374].

[2369] pdfcookie.com

[2370] bprd.nic.in

[2371] pdfcookie.com

[2372] Ministry of Home Affairs. (2024). The Bharatiya Nyaya Sanhita, 2023. Retrieved from https://www.mha.gov.in/sites/default/files/250883_english_01042024.pdf

[2373] eparlib.nic.in

[2374] eparlib.nic.in

Comment: This section underscores the gravity of unlawfully entering a home with the intention of causing physical harm, reflecting the need for severe legal consequences to protect residents from such threats.

Classification of Offence and Punishment Classification: This offense is classified as a criminal offense due to the act of unlawfully entering someone else's home with the intent to cause harm, assault, or wrongful restraint.

Punishment: The punishment for committing this offense under BNS 331 (5) is imprisonment of either description for a term which may extend to ten years, or a fine, or both[2375].

Cognizable or Non-Cognizable, Bailable or Non-Bailable: This offense is cognizable, meaning the police can arrest the accused without a warrant.

Non-Bailable: This offense is non-bailable, indicating that the accused cannot secure bail and must remain in custody until the trial is completed.

Comparison: Section 455 of the Indian Penal Code[2376] (IPC) also addresses the offense of lurking house-trespass or house-breaking after preparation for hurt, assault, or wrongful restraint : IPC Section 455: According to the law, anyone found guilty of lurking house trespass, house breaking, preparing to harm someone, assaulting someone, wrongfully restraining someone, or instilling fear of harm, assault, or wrongful restraint will be punished with either type of imprisonment for a maximum of ten years, in addition to a fine[2377].

Key Differences: BNS 331 (5): Updated version in the new Bharatiya Nyaya Sanhita, with specific provisions for lurking house-trespass or house-breaking after preparation for hurt, assault, or wrongful restraint[2378]. IPC 455: Part of the older Indian Penal Code framework, now replaced by BNS 331 (5).

2375 bprd.nic.in

2376 www.bareactslive.com

2377 bprd.nic.in

2378 pdfcookie.com

BNS Section 331 (6)

Definition: Lurking House-Trespass or House-Breaking by Night After Preparation for Hurt, Assault, or Wrongful Restraint[2379] Section 331 (6) of the Bharatiya Nyaya Sanhita (BNS) 2023 addresses the offense of lurking house-trespass or house-breaking by night after making preparations to cause hurt, assault, or wrongful restraint.

Illustration: If a person breaks into a house at night after arming themselves with a weapon to assault the occupants, they are committing an offense under BNS 331 (6).

Example: Suppose someone breaks into a house with a knife at night, intending to harm the residents. This act falls under BNS 331 (6) as lurking house-trespass or house-breaking by night after preparation for hurt, assault, or wrongful restraint[2380].

Comment: This section underscores the extreme danger and violation involved when an offender enters a home at night with the intent to cause physical harm. The law aims to provide stringent deterrence through severe punishment to protect individuals in their homes.

Classification of Offence and Punishment Classification: This offense is classified as a criminal offense due to the act of unlawfully entering someone else's home by night with the intent to cause harm, assault, or wrongful restraint[2381].

Punishment: The punishment for committing this offense under BNS 331 (6) is imprisonment of either description for a term which may extend to fourteen years, and the offender shall also be liable to a fine[2382].

Cognizable or Non-Cognizable, Bailable or Non-Bailable: This offense is cognizable, meaning the police can arrest the accused without a warrant.

[2379] Ministry of Home Affairs. (2024). The Bharatiya Nyaya Sanhita, 2023. Retrieved from https://www.mha.gov.in/sites/default/files/250883_english_01042024.pdf

[2380] pdfcookie.com

[2381] pdfcookie.com

[2382] bprd.nic.in

Non-Bailable: This offense is non-bailable, indicating that the accused cannot secure bail and must remain in custody until the trial is completed.

Comparison: Section 458 of the Indian Penal Code[2383] (IPC) also addresses the offense of lurking house-trespass or house-breaking by night after preparation for hurt, assault, or wrongful restraint: IPC Section 458: It states that anyone who engages in nighttime house trespassing or housebreaking while preparing to harm someone, assault someone, or wrongfully restrain someone, or who puts someone in fear of harm, assault, or wrongful restraint, faces a maximum sentence of fourteen years in prison of any kind, in addition to a fine[2384].

Key Differences: BNS 331 (6): Updated version in the new Bharatiya Nyaya Sanhita, with specific provisions for lurking house-trespass or house-breaking by night after preparation for hurt, assault, or wrongful restraint. IPC 458: Part of the older Indian Penal Code framework[2385], now replaced by BNS 331 (6).

BNS Section 331 (7)

Definition: Grievous Hurt Caused Whilst Committing Lurking House-Trespass or House-Breaking[2386] Section 331 (7) of the Bharatiya Nyaya Sanhita (BNS) 2023 addresses the offense of causing grievous hurt while committing lurking house-trespass or house-breaking.

Illustration: If a person breaks into a house at night and causes grievous hurt to a resident during the act, they are committing an offense under BNS 331 (7).

Example: Suppose someone sneaks into a house through a window at night and, when confronted by the homeowner, attacks them, causing

[2383] eparlib.nic.in

[2384] pdfcookie.com

[2385] eparlib.nic.in

[2386] Ministry of Home Affairs. (2024). The Bharatiya Nyaya Sanhita, 2023. Retrieved from https://www.mha.gov.in/sites/default/files/250883_english_01042024.pdf

serious injuries. This act falls under BNS 331 (7) as grievous hurt caused whilst committing lurking house-trespass or house-breaking[2387].

Comment: This section underscores the heinous nature of causing serious harm during a break-in, stressing the need for harsh penalties to protect individuals from such violent acts.

Classification of Offence and Punishment Classification: This offense is classified as a heinous criminal offense due to the act of causing serious harm while unlawfully entering someone else's home.

Punishment: The punishment for committing this offense under BNS 331 (7) is imprisonment for life, or rigorous imprisonment for a term which may extend to ten years, and the offender shall also be liable to a fine[2388].

Cognizable or Non-Cognizable, Bailable or Non-Bailable: This offense is cognizable, meaning the police can arrest the accused without a warrant.

Non-Bailable: This offense is non-bailable, indicating that the accused cannot secure bail and must remain in custody until the trial is completed.

Comparison: Section 459 of the Indian Penal Code[2389] (IPC) also addresses the offense of causing grievous hurt while committing lurking house-trespass or house- breaking: According to IPC Section 459, anyone who knowingly causes serious harm to another person while engaging in lurking house trespassing or house breaking faces a life sentence or a term of imprisonment of any kind that can last up to ten years, in addition to a fine[2390].

Key Differences: BNS 331 (7): Updated version in the new Bharatiya Nyaya Sanhita, with specific provisions for causing grievous hurt during lurking house-trespass or house-breaking. IPC 459: Part of the older Indian Penal Code framework, now replaced by BNS 331 (7).

[2387] eparlib.nic.in

[2388] pdfcookie.com

[2389] www.bareactslive.com

[2390] bprd.nic.in

BNS Section 331 (8)

Definition: All Persons Jointly Concerned in Lurking House-Trespass or House-Breaking by Night Punishable Where Death or Grievous Hurt Caused by One of Them[2391] Section 331 (8) of the Bharatiya Nyaya Sanhita (BNS) 2023 addresses the offense where all persons jointly concerned in lurking house-trespass or house-breaking by night are punishable when death or grievous hurt is caused by any one of them[2392].

Illustration: If a group of five individuals breaks into a house at night, and one of them causes death or grievous hurt to a resident, all five are punishable under BNS 331 (8)[2393].

Example: Suppose a gang of individuals breaks into a house at night, and one of them attacks the homeowner, causing serious injuries. All members of the gang are punishable under BNS 331 (8) for the grievous hurt caused by one of them.

Comment: This section ensures that all participants in a group crime are held accountable for the actions of any member, emphasizing the collective responsibility and the serious consequences of participating in such offenses.

Classification of Offence and Punishment Classification: This offense is classified as a heinous criminal offense due to the potential for causing serious harm or death.

Punishment: The punishment for committing this offense under BNS 331 (8) is imprisonment for life, or imprisonment of either description for a term which may extend to ten years, and the offenders shall also be liable to a fine[2394].

[2391] Ministry of Home Affairs. (2024). The Bharatiya Nyaya Sanhita, 2023. Retrieved from https://www.mha.gov.in/sites/default/files/250883_english_01042024.pdf

[2392] eparlib.nic.in

[2393] bprd.nic.in

[2394] bprd.nic.in

Cognizable or Non-Cognizable, Bailable or Non-Bailable: This offense is cognizable, meaning the police can arrest the accused without a warrant.

Non-Bailable: This offense is non-bailable, indicating that the accused cannot secure bail and must remain in custody until the trial is completed.

Comparison: Section 460 of the Indian Penal Code[2395] (IPC) also addresses the offense where all persons jointly concerned in lurking house-trespass or house-breaking by night are punishable when death or grievous hurt is caused by any one of them: IPC Section 460: States that all persons jointly concerned in committing[2396] lurking house-trespass by night, or house-breaking by night, and any one of them causes death or grievous hurt to any person, shall be punished with imprisonment for life, or with imprisonment of either description for a term which may extend to ten years, and shall also be liable to a fine[2397].

Key Differences: BNS 331 (8): Updated version in the new Bharatiya Nyaya Sanhita, with specific provisions for different types of house-trespassing offenses by night.IPC 460: Part of the older Indian Penal Code framework[2398], now replaced by BNS 331 (8).

BNS Section 332 (A):

Definition: House-Trespass in Order to Commit Offense Punishable with Death Section 332 (A) [2399]of the Bharatiya Nyaya Sanhita (BNS) 2023 addresses the offense of house-trespass with the intent to commit an offense punishable with death.

Illustration: If someone breaks into a house with the intention of committing murder, they are committing an offense under BNS 332 (A).

[2395] www.bareactslive.com

[2396] eparlib.nic.in

[2397] bprd.nic.in

[2398] bprd.nic.in

[2399] Ministry of Home Affairs. (2024). The Bharatiya Nyaya Sanhita, 2023. Retrieved from https://www.mha.gov.in/sites/default/files/250883_english_01042024.pdf

Example: Suppose an individual enters a home at night with the aim of killing the homeowner. This act falls under BNS 332 (A) as house-trespass in order to commit an offense punishable with death[2400].

Comment: This section emphasizes the serious nature of such offenses, highlighting the intent to commit a crime punishable by death, which demands strict legal consequences.

Classification of Offence and Punishment Classification: This offense is classified as a heinous criminal offense due to its severe nature and intent to commit a crime punishable by death.

Punishment: The punishment for committing this offense under BNS 332 (A) is imprisonment for life, or rigorous imprisonment for a term not exceeding ten years, and the offender shall also be liable to a fine[2401].

Cognizable or Non-Cognizable, Bailable or Non-Bailable: This offense is cognizable, meaning the police can arrest the accused without a warrant.

Non-Bailable: This offense is non-bailable, indicating that the accused cannot secure bail and must remain in custody until the trial is completed.

Comparison: Section 449 of the Indian Penal Code[2402] (IPC) also addresses the offense of house-trespass with the intent to commit an offense punishable with death: IPC Section 449: States that whoever commits house-trespass in order to the committing of any offense punishable with death, shall be punished with imprisonment for life, or with rigorous imprisonment for a term not exceeding ten years, and shall also be liable to a fine[2403].

Key Differences: BNS 332 (A): Reflects updated legal terminology and provisions in the new Bharatiya Nyaya Sanhita. IPC 449: Part of the older Indian Penal Code framework, now replaced by BNS 332 (A).

[2400] bprd.nic.in

[2401] pdfcookie.com

[2402] www.bareactslive.com

[2403] bprd.nic.in

BNS Section 332 (B)

Definition: House-Trespass in Order to Commit Offense Punishable with Imprisonment for Life[2404] Section 332 (B) of the Bharatiya Nyaya Sanhita (BNS) 2023 addresses the offense of house-trespass with the intent to commit an offense punishable with imprisonment for life.

Illustration: If a person breaks into a house with the intention of committing a crime that is punishable by imprisonment for life, they are committing an offense under BNS 332 (B).

Example: Suppose someone breaks into a house at night with the intent to kidnap someone, which is punishable by imprisonment for life. This act falls under BNS 332 (B) as house-trespass in order to commit an offense punishable with imprisonment for life[2405].

Comment: This section emphasizes the serious nature of such offenses, highlighting the intent to commit a crime punishable by life imprisonment, which necessitates strict legal consequences.

Classification of Offence and Punishment Classification: This offense is classified as a serious criminal offense due to the intent to commit a crime punishable by imprisonment for life.

Punishment: The punishment for committing this offense under BNS 332 (B) is imprisonment of either description for a term not exceeding ten years, and the offender shall also be liable to a fine[2406].

Cognizable or Non-Cognizable, Bailable or Non-Bailable: This offense is cognizable, meaning the police can arrest the accused without a warrant.

Non-Bailable: This offense is non-bailable, indicating that the accused cannot secure bail and must remain in custody until the trial is completed.

[2404] Ministry of Home Affairs. (2024). The Bharatiya Nyaya Sanhita, 2023. Retrieved from https://www.mha.gov.in/sites/default/files/250883_english_01042024.pdf

[2405] www.bareactslive.com

[2406] bprd.nic.in

Comparison: Section 450 of the Indian Penal Code[2407] (IPC) also addresses the offense of house-trespass with the intent to commit an offense punishable with imprisonment for life: According to IPC Section 450, anyone who trespasses into another person's home with the intent to commit a crime that carries a life sentence may be imprisoned for a maximum of ten years in either type of jail and will also be subject to a fine[2408].

Key Differences: BNS 332 (B): Updated version in the new Bharatiya Nyaya Sanhita, with specific provisions for house-trespass in order to commit an offense punishable with imprisonment for life.IPC 450: Part of the older Indian Penal Code framework, now replaced by BNS 332 (B)[2409].

BNS Section 332 (C)

Definition: House-Trespass in Order to Commit Offense Punishable with Imprisonment[2410] Section 332 (C) of the Bharatiya Nyaya Sanhita (BNS) 2023 addresses the offense of house-trespass with the intent to commit an offense punishable with imprisonment.

Illustration: If a person breaks into a house with the intention of committing theft, which is punishable by imprisonment, they are committing an offense under BNS 332 (C).

Example: Suppose someone sneaks into a house through an unlocked window with the intention of stealing electronics. This act falls under BNS 332 (C) as house-trespass in order to commit[2411] an offense punishable with imprisonment.

[2407] upslc.upsdc.gov.in

[2408] bprd.nic.in

[2409] bprd.nic.in

[2410] Ministry of Home Affairs. (2024). The Bharatiya Nyaya Sanhita, 2023. Retrieved from https://www.mha.gov.in/sites/default/files/250883_english_01042024.pdf

[2411] bprd.nic.in

Comment: This section emphasizes the severity of house-trespass combined with the intent to commit a punishable offense, highlighting the need for strict penalties to deter such actions.

Classification of Offence and Punishment Classification: This offense is classified as a criminal offense due to the intent to commit a crime punishable by imprisonment.

Punishment: The punishment for committing this offense under BNS 332 (C) is imprisonment of either description for a term which may extend to seven years, and the offender shall also be liable to a fine[2412].

Cognizable or Non-Cognizable, Bailable or Non-Bailable: This offense is cognizable, meaning the police can arrest the accused without a warrant.

Bailable: This offense is bailable, indicating that the accused can secure bail and be released from custody until the trial is completed.

Comparison: Section 451 of the Indian Penal Code [2413](IPC) also addresses the offense of house-trespass in order to commit an offense punishable with imprisonment: IPC Section 451It stipulates that anyone who trespasses into a house with the intent to commit an offense that carries a jail sentence will be punished with a term of imprisonment of any kind, up to two years, and will also be subject to a fine[2414].

Key Differences: BNS 332 (C): Provides a more severe punishment of up to seven years imprisonment compared to IPC Section 451, which has a maximum of two years. IPC 451: Part of the older Indian Penal Code framework, now replaced by BNS 332 (C).

[2412] bprd.nic.in

[2413] upslc.upsdc.gov.in

[2414] bprd.nic.in

BNS Section 333

Definition: House-Trespass After Preparation for Hurt, Assault, or Wrongful Restraint[2415] Section 333 of the Bharatiya Nyaya Sanhita (BNS) 2023 addresses the offense of house-trespass after making preparations to cause hurt, assault, or wrongful restraint.

Illustration: If a person breaks into a house with the intent to harm someone inside, they are committing an offense under BNS 333[2416].

Example: Suppose someone breaks into a house with a weapon, intending to assault the occupant. This act falls under BNS 333 as house-trespass after preparation for hurt, assault, or wrongful restraint[2417].

Comment: This section reflects the serious nature of such premeditated offenses, emphasizing the need for stringent legal consequences to deter individuals from planning and executing harmful actions during a trespass.

Classification of Offence and Punishment Classification: This offense is classified as a criminal offense due to the intent to commit a crime involving hurt, assault, or wrongful restraint[2418].

Punishment: The punishment for committing this offense under BNS 333 is imprisonment of either description for a term which may extend to seven years, and the offender shall also be liable to a fine[2419].

Cognizable or Non-Cognizable, Bailable or Non-Bailable: This offense is cognizable, meaning the police can arrest the accused without a warrant.

Non-Bailable: This offense is non-bailable, indicating that the accused cannot secure bail and must remain in custody until the trial is completed.

[2415] Ministry of Home Affairs. (2024). The Bharatiya Nyaya Sanhita, 2023. Retrieved from https://www.mha.gov.in/sites/default/files/250883_english_01042024.pdf

[2416] www.bareactslive.com

[2417] bprd.nic.in

[2418] www.bareactslive.com

[2419] bprd.nic.in

Comparison: Section 452 of the Indian Penal Code[2420] (IPC) also addresses the offense of house-trespass after preparation for hurt, assault, or wrongful restraint: IPC Section 452: It states that anyone who trespasses into a house with the intent to harm someone, assault someone, wrongfully restrain someone, or instill fear of harm, assault, or wrongful restraint will be punished with either type of imprisonment for a maximum of seven years, in addition to a fine[2421].

Key Differences: BNS 333: Updated version in the new Bharatiya Nyaya Sanhita, with specific provisions for house-trespass after preparation for hurt, assault, or wrongful restraint. IPC 452: Part of the older Indian Penal Code framework[2422], now replaced by BNS 333.

BNS Section 334 (1)

Definition: Dishonestly Breaking Open Receptacle Containing Propert[2423]y Section 334 (1) of the Bharatiya Nyaya Sanhita (BNS) 2023 addresses the offense of dishonestly breaking open a receptacle containing property.

Illustration: If a person breaks open a locked drawer believing it contains valuable items, they are committing an offense under BNS 334 (1).

Example: Suppose someone breaks into a locked cabinet in an office with the intent to steal documents. This act falls under BNS 334 (1) as dishonestly breaking open a receptacle containing property[2424].

Comment: This section highlights the serious nature of dishonest actions aimed at accessing property, emphasizing the need for strict legal repercussions to deter such behavior.

2420 www.bareactslive.com

2421 bprd.nic.in

2422 bprd.nic.in

2423 Ministry of Home Affairs. (2024). The Bharatiya Nyaya Sanhita, 2023. Retrieved from https://www.mha.gov.in/sites/default/files/250883_english_01042024.pdf

2424 bprd.nic.in

Classification of Offence and Punishment Classification: This offense is classified as a criminal offense due to the dishonest intent to access property.

Punishment: The punishment for committing this offense under BNS 334 (1) is imprisonment of either description for a term which may extend to two years, or with fine, or with both[2425].

Cognizable or Non-Cognizable, Bailable or Non-Bailable: This offense is cognizable, meaning the police can arrest the accused without a warrant.

Bailable: This offense is bailable, indicating that the accused can secure bail and be released from custody until the trial is completed.

Comparison: Section 461 of the Indian Penal Code[2426] (IPC) also addresses the offense of dishonestly breaking open a receptacle containing property: IPC Section 461: It states that anyone who willfully or dishonestly opens or unfastens a closed container that contains or that he believes contains property will be penalized with either type of imprisonment for a maximum of two years, a fine, or both[2427].

Key Differences: BNS 334 (1): Updated version in the new Bharatiya Nyaya Sanhita, with specific provisions for dishonestly breaking open a receptacle containing propert[2428]y. IPC 461: Part of the older Indian Penal Code framework, now replaced by BNS 334 (1).

BNS Section 334 (2)

Definition: Punishment for Same Offence When Committed by Person Entrusted with Custody[2429] Section 334 (2) of the Bharatiya Nyaya Sanhita (BNS) 2023 addresses the offense of house-trespass

---

[2425] bprd.nic.in

[2426] upslc.upsdc.gov.in

[2427] bprd.nic.in

[2428] upslc.upsdc.gov.in

[2429] Ministry of Home Affairs. (2024). The Bharatiya Nyaya Sanhita, 2023. Retrieved from https://www.mha.gov.in/sites/default/files/250883_english_01042024.pdf

committed by a person entrusted with custody of a closed receptacle containing property.

Illustration: If a housekeeper, who is entrusted with a locked safe containing valuable, breaks open the safe without permission, they are committing an offense under BNS 334 (2)[2430].

Example: Suppose a security guard, who has access to a locked storage room, opens it without authorization to steal items inside. This act falls under BNS 334 (2) as house-trespass by a person entrusted[2431] with custody.

Comment: This section reflects the severe breach of trust when someone entrusted with the custody of property acts dishonestly. It underscores the significant legal consequences to deter such actions.

Classification of Offence and Punishment Classification: This offense is classified as a criminal offense due to the breach of trust and dishonest intent.

Punishment: The punishment for committing this offense under BNS 334 (2) is imprisonment of either description for a term which may extend to three years, or with fine[2432], or with both.

Cognizable or Non-Cognizable, Bailable or Non-Bailable: This offense is cognizable, meaning the police can arrest the accused without a warrant.

Non-Bailable: This offense is non-bailable, indicating that the accused cannot secure bail and must remain in custody until the trial is completed.

Comparison: Section 462 of the Indian Penal Code[2433] (IPC) also addresses the offense of house-trespass committed by a person entrusted with custody of a closed receptacle containing property: IPC Section 462: It states that anyone who is entrusted with a closed container that contains or that he believes contains property and who opens it dishonestly, with

---

[2430] upslc.upsdc.gov.in

[2431] upslc.upsdc.gov.in

[2432] bprd.nic.in

[2433] www.bareactslive.com

the intent to cause trouble, or without the proper authority will be punished with either type of imprisonment for a maximum of three years, a fine, or both[2434].

Key Differences: BNS 334 (2): Updated version in the new Bharatiya Nyaya Sanhita, with specific provisions for house-trespass by a person entrusted with custody. IPC 462: Part of the older Indian Penal Code framework[2435], now replaced by BNS 334 (2).

[2434] bprd.nic.in

[2435] bprd.nic.in

CHAPTER-XVIII; OF OFFENCES RELATING TO DOCUMENTS AND TO PROPERTY MARKS

BNS Section 335

Definition: Making a False Document[2436] Section 335 of the Bharatiya Nyaya Sanhita (BNS) 2023 addresses the offense of making a false document or false electronic record.

Illustration: If a person creates a fake contract in someone else's name with the intent to deceive, they are committing an offense under BNS 335.

Example: Suppose someone forges a signature on a property deed to claim ownership falsely. This act falls under BNS 335 as making a false document.

Comment: This section reflects the serious consequences of creating false documents, emphasizing the need for legal repercussions to deter such deceitful actions.

Classification of Offence and Punishment Classification: This offense is classified as a criminal offense due to the dishonest intent to deceive.

Punishment: The punishment for committing this offense under BNS 335 is imprisonment of either description for a term which may extend to two years, or with fine, or with both[2437].

Cognizable or Non-Cognizable, Bailable or Non-Bailable: This offense is cognizable, meaning the police can arrest the accused without a warrant.

2436 Ministry of Home Affairs. (2024). The Bharatiya Nyaya Sanhita, 2023. Retrieved from https://www.mha.gov.in/sites/default/files/250883_english_01042024.pdf

2437 bprd.nic.in

Bailable: This offense is bailable, indicating that the accused can secure bail and be released from custody until the trial is completed.

Comparison: Section 464 of the Indian Penal Code[2438] (IPC) also addresses the offense of making a false document[2439] : IPC Section 464: explains that anyone who dishonestly or fraudulently creates, signs, seals, or executes a document or part of a document, or makes any mark indicating the execution of a document, with the intent of making it appear as though the document or part of it was created, signed, sealed, or executed by or by the authority of a person by whom or by whose authority he knows that it was not created, signed, sealed, or executed, faces a maximum sentence of two years in prison of any kind, a fine, or both[2440].

Key Differences: BNS 335: Updated version in the new Bharatiya Nyaya Sanhita, with specific provisions for making a false document or false electronic record. IPC 464: Part of the older Indian Penal Code[2441] framework, now replaced by BNS 335.

BNS Section 336 (1)

Definition: Forgery Section 336 (1) of the Bharatiya Nyaya Sanhita (BNS) 2023 addresses the offense of forgery.

Illustration: If a person creates a fake bank statement with the intent to deceive a financial institution, they are committing an offense under BNS 336 (1).

Example: Suppose someone alters a signature on a check to make it appear as if it was signed by the account holder. This act falls under BNS 336 (1) as forgery.

Comment: This section underscores the critical importance of integrity in financial and legal documents. Forgery undermines trust and can cause

---

[2438] upslc.upsdc.gov.in

[2439] forest.jharkhand.gov.in

[2440] bprd.nic.in

[2441] bprd.nic.in

significant harm to individuals and institutions, necessitating strong legal measures.

Classification of Offence and Punishment Classification: This offense is classified as a criminal offense due to the intent to deceive by creating false documents.

Punishment: The punishment for committing this offense under BNS 336 (1) is imprisonment of either description for a term which may extend to two years, or with fine, or with both[2442].

Cognizable or Non-Cognizable, Bailable or Non-Bailable: This offense is cognizable, meaning the police can arrest the accused without a warrant.

Bailable: This offense is bailable, indicating that the accused can secure bail and be released from custody until the trial is completed.

Comparison: Section 463 of the Indian Penal Code[2443] (IPC) also addresses the offense of forgery: IPC Section 463: Forgery is defined as the creation of any false document or electronic record, or a portion of a document or electronic record, with the intent to harm the public or any individual, to bolster a claim or title, to induce someone to give up property, to enter into an express or implied contract, or with the intent to commit fraud or the belief that fraud may be committed[2444].

Key Differences: BNS 336 (1): Updated version in the new Bharatiya Nyaya Sanhita, with specific provisions for forgery. IPC 463: Part of the older Indian Penal Code[2445] framework, now replaced by BNS 336 (1).

BNS Section 336 (2)

Definition: Punishment for Forgery Section 336 (2) of the Bharatiya Nyaya Sanhita (BNS) 2023 outlines the punishment for the offense of forgery.

[2442] bprd.nic.in

[2443] upslc.upsdc.gov.in

[2444] bprd.nic.in

[2445] bprd.nic.in

Illustration: If a person creates a fake document to claim ownership of property that doesn't belong to them, they are committing an offense under BNS 336 (2).

Example: Suppose someone alters a birth certificate to change their age and gain certain benefits. This act falls under BNS 336 (2) as forgery.

Comment: This section underscores the serious nature of forgery, which involves deceit and potential harm. The law aims to deter such acts by imposing strict penalties.

Classification of Offence and Punishment Classification: This offense is classified as a serious criminal offense due to the intent to deceive and cause harm through false documents.

Punishment: The punishment for committing this offense under BNS 336 (2) is imprisonment of either description for a term which may extend to two years, or with fine, or with both[2446].

Cognizable or Non-Cognizable, Bailable or Non-Bailable: This offense is cognizable, meaning the police can arrest the accused without a warrant.

Bailable: This offense is bailable, indicating that the accused can secure bail and be released from custody until the trial is completed.

Comparison: Section 465 of the Indian Penal Code[2447] (IPC) also addresses the punishment for forgery: IPC Section 465: States that whoever commits forgery shall be punished with imprisonment of either description for a term which may extend to two years, or with a fine, or with both[2448].

Key Differences: BNS 336 (2): Reflects updated legal provisions and terminology in the new Bharatiya Nyaya Sanhita for the offense of forgery. IPC 465: Part of the older Indian Penal Code[2449] framework, now replaced by BNS 336 (2).

[2446] bprd.nic.in

[2447] upslc.upsdc.gov.in

[2448] bprd.nic.in

[2449] bprd.nic.in

BNS Section 336 (3)

Definition: Forgery for Purpose of Cheating[2450] Section 336 (3) of the Bharatiya Nyaya Sanhita (BNS) 2023 addresses the offense of forgery with the intent to use the forged document or electronic record for the purpose of cheating.

Illustration: If a person creates a fake identification document to deceive a bank and withdraw money, they are committing an offense under BNS 336 (3).

Example: Suppose someone forges a property deed to sell a piece of land that they do not own. This act falls under BNS 336 (3) as forgery for the purpose of cheating[2451].

Comment: This section stresses the importance of authenticity in legal and financial transactions. Forgery undermines trust and can lead to significant losses, which is why the law imposes severe penalties to deter such acts.

Classification of Offence and Punishment Classification: This offense is classified as a serious criminal offense due to the intent to deceive[2452] and cause financial or personal harm.

Punishment: The punishment for committing this offense under BNS 336 (3) is imprisonment of either description for a term which may extend to seven years, and the offender shall also be liable to a fine[2453].

Cognizable or Non-Cognizable, Bailable or Non-Bailable: This offense is cognizable, meaning the police can arrest the accused without a warrant.

Non-Bailable: This offense is non-bailable, indicating that the accused cannot secure bail and must remain in custody until the trial is completed.

[2450] Ministry of Home Affairs. (2024). The Bharatiya Nyaya Sanhita, 2023. Retrieved from https://www.mha.gov.in/sites/default/files/250883_english_01042024.pdf

[2451] www.indiacode.nic.in

[2452] www.indiacode.nic.in

[2453] bprd.nic.in

Comparison: Section 468 of the Indian Penal Code[2454] (IPC) also addresses the offense of forgery for the purpose of cheating: IPC Section 468: It stipulates that anyone who forges a document or electronic record with the intent to use it for cheating faces up to seven years in prison of any kind and a fine[2455].

Key Differences: BNS 336 (3): Updated version in the new Bharatiya Nyaya Sanhita, with specific provisions for forgery for the purpose of cheating. IPC 468: Part of the older Indian Penal Code framework, now replaced by BNS 336 (3)[2456].

BNS Section 336 (4)

Definition: Forgery for Purpose of Harming Reputation[2457] Section 336 (4) of the Bharatiya Nyaya Sanhita (BNS) 2023 addresses the offense of forgery with the intent to harm the reputation of any party or knowing that it is likely to be used for that purpose.

Illustration: If a person creates a fake letter in someone's name to defame them, they are committing an offense under BNS 336 (4).

Example: Suppose someone forges a document that falsely accuses a public figure of misconduct, intending to damage their reputation. This act falls under BNS 336 (4) as forgery for the purpose of harming reputation[2458].

Comment: This section emphasizes the damaging impact that forged documents can have on a person's reputation. It aims to protect individuals from malicious actions that could unjustly tarnish their character.

[2454] www.bareactslive.com

[2455] bprd.nic.in

[2456] www.indiacode.nic.in

[2457] Ministry of Home Affairs. (2024). The Bharatiya Nyaya Sanhita, 2023. Retrieved from https://www.mha.gov.in/sites/default/files/250883_english_01042024.pdf

[2458] www.indiacode.nic.in

Classification of Offence and Punishment Classification: This offense is classified as a criminal offense due to the malicious intent to harm someone's reputation.

Punishment: The punishment for committing this offense under BNS 336 (4) is imprisonment of either description for a term which may extend to three years, and the offender shall also be liable to a fine[2459].

Cognizable or Non-Cognizable, Bailable or Non-Bailable: This offense is cognizable, meaning the police can arrest the accused without a warrant.

Bailable: This offense is bailable, indicating that the accused can secure bail and be released from custody until the trial is completed.

Comparison: Section 469 of the Indian Penal Code[2460] (IPC) also addresses the offense of forgery for the purpose of harming reputation: IPC Section 469: States that whoever commits forgery, intending that the document or electronic record forged shall harm the reputation of any party, or knowing that it is likely to be used for that purpose, shall be punished with imprisonment of either description for a term which may extend to three years, and shall also be liable to a fine[2461].

Key Differences: BNS 336 (4): Updated version in the new Bharatiya Nyaya Sanhita, with specific provisions for forgery for the purpose of harming reputation. IPC 469: Part of the older Indian Penal Code framework, now replaced by BNS 336 (4)[2462].

BNS Section 337

Definition: Forgery of Record of Court or of Public Register[2463], etc Section 337 of the Bharatiya Nyaya Sanhita (BNS) 2023 addresses the

---

2459 bprd.nic.in

2460 www.bareactslive.com

2461 devgan.in

2462 www.bareactslive.com

2463 Ministry of Home Affairs. (2024). The Bharatiya Nyaya Sanhita, 2023. Retrieved from https://www.mha.gov.in/sites/default/files/250883_english_01042024.pdf

offense of forging a document or electronic record purporting to be a record or proceeding of or in a Court, or a register of birth, marriage, or burial, or a certificate made by a public servant in their official capacity[2464].

Illustration: If a person creates a fake court judgment to claim ownership of property, they are committing an offense under BNS 337.

Example: Suppose someone forges a birth certificate to falsely claim citizenship. This act falls under BNS 337 as forgery of a public register.

Comment: This section underscores the critical importance of maintaining the integrity of official records. Forging such documents can have far-reaching consequences, undermining trust in legal and governmental institutions and necessitating strict legal penalties.

Classification of Offence and Punishment Classification: This offense is classified as a serious criminal offense due to the intent to deceive and misuse official documents.

Punishment: The punishment for committing this offense under BNS 337 is imprisonment of either description for a term which may extend to seven years, and the offender shall also be liable to a fine[2465].

Cognizable or Non-Cognizable, Bailable or Non-Bailable: This offense is cognizable, meaning the police can arrest the accused without a warrant.

Non-Bailable: This offense is non-bailable, indicating that the accused cannot secure bail and must remain in custody until the trial is completed.

Comparison: Section 466 of the Indian Penal Code[2466] (IPC) also addresses the offense of forgery of a record of Court or of a public register: IPC Section 466: Declares that anyone who forges a document or electronic record that appears to be a court of justice record or proceeding, a birth, baptism, marriage, or burial register, a register maintained by a public servant as such, a certificate or document that appears to have been

---

[2464] devgan.in

[2465] devgan.in

[2466] www.bareactslive.com

made by a public servant in his official capacity, or an authority to institute or defend a suit, to take any proceedings therein, to confess judgment, or a power of attorney, faces up to seven years in prison of any kind, in addition to a fine[2467].

Key Differences: BNS 337: Updated version in the new Bharatiya Nyaya Sanhita, with specific provisions for forgery of records of Court or public registers. IPC 466: Part of the older Indian Penal Code[2468] framework, now replaced by BNS 337.

BNS Section 338

Definition: Forgery of Valuable Security, Will, etc. Section 338 [2469]of the Bharatiya Nyaya Sanhita (BNS) 2023 addresses the offense of forging documents that purport to be valuable securities, wills, or other significant documents.

Illustration: If a person creates a fake will to claim someone's inheritance, they are committing an offense under BNS 338.

Example: Suppose someone forges a document that falsely represents a valuable security, such as a stock certificate, to deceive others. This act falls under BNS 338 as forgery of valuable security.

Comment: This section underscores the serious implications of forging critical documents like wills and securities. Such forgeries can lead to severe financial losses and disputes, necessitating stringent penalties to deter such actions.

Classification of Offence and Punishment Classification: This offense is classified as a serious criminal offense due to the intent to deceive and misuse important documents.

[2467] devgan.in

[2468] devgan.in

[2469] Ministry of Home Affairs. (2024). The Bharatiya Nyaya Sanhita, 2023. Retrieved from https://www.mha.gov.in/sites/default/files/250883_english_01042024.pdf

Punishment: The punishment for committing this offense under BNS 338 is imprisonment for life, or imprisonment of either description for a term which may extend to ten years, and the offender shall also be liable to a fine[2470].

Cognizable or Non-Cognizable, Bailable or Non-Bailable: This offense is cognizable, meaning the police can arrest the accused without a warrant.

Non-Bailable: This offense is non-bailable, indicating that the accused cannot secure bail and must remain in custody until the trial is completed.

Comparison: Section 467 of the Indian Penal Code[2471] (IPC) also addresses the offense of forgery of valuable security, will, etc.:IPC Section 467: It states that anyone who forges a document that looks like a will, a valuable security, an authority to adopt a son, or a document that gives someone the power to make or transfer a valuable security, to receive the principal, interest, or dividends thereon, or to receive or deliver any money, movable property, or valuable security, or that looks like an acquittance or receipt acknowledging the payment of money, or an acquittance or receipt for the delivery of any movable property or valuable security, faces life in prison, or imprisonment of any kind for a maximum of ten years, in addition to a fine[2472].

Key Differences: BNS 338: Updated version in the new Bharatiya Nyaya Sanhita, with specific provisions for forgery of valuable securities, wills, etc8.IPC 467: Part of the older Indian Penal Code framework[2473], now replaced by BNS 338.

BNS Section 339

Definition: Having possession of document described in Section 337 or Section 338, knowing it to be forged and intending to use it as

[2470] devgan.in

[2471] www.bareactslive.com

[2472] devgan.in

[2473] devgan.in

genuine[2474] Section 339 of the Bharatiya Nyaya Sanhita (BNS) 2023 addresses the offense of possessing a forged document described in Section 337 or Section 338, knowing it to be forged and intending to use it as genuine.

Illustration: If a person holds a forged will, knowing it's fake, and intends to present it as genuine to claim an inheritance, they are committing an offense under BNS 339.

Example: Suppose someone possesses a forged property deed, fully aware of its falsity, and plans to use it to secure a loan. This act falls under BNS 339 as possession of a forged document.

Comment: This section highlights the significant risk and malicious intent behind using forged documents. Such actions can lead to severe legal and financial consequences, which is why the law imposes stringent penalties to prevent these offenses.

Classification of Offence and Punishment Classification: This offense is classified as a serious criminal offense due to the intent to use a forged document deceitfully.

Punishment: The punishment for committing this offense under BNS 339 is imprisonment of either description for a term which may extend to seven years, and the offender shall also be liable to a fine[2475].

Cognizable or Non-Cognizable, Bailable or Non-Bailable: This offense is cognizable, meaning the police can arrest the accused without a warrant.

Non-Bailable: This offense is non-bailable, indicating that the accused cannot secure bail and must remain in custody until the trial is completed.

Comparison: Section 474 of the Indian Penal Code[2476] (IPC) also addresses the offense of possession of a document, knowing it to be forged, and intending to use it as genuine: IPC Section 474: Declares that

---

[2474] Ministry of Home Affairs. (2024). The Bharatiya Nyaya Sanhita, 2023. Retrieved from https://www.mha.gov.in/sites/default/files/250883_english_01042024.pdf

[2475] devgan.in

[2476] www.bareactslive.com

anyone in possession of a document or electronic record that they know is a fake and that they intend to use as authentic in a dishonest or fraudulent manner faces up to seven years in prison of any kind and a fine. The maximum sentence is ten years in prison if the document fits any of the descriptions listed in sections 466 or 467[2477].

Key Differences: BNS 339: Reflects updated legal terminology and provisions in the new Bharatiya Nyaya Sanhita. IPC 474: Part of the older Indian Penal Code[2478] framework, now replaced by BNS 339.

BNS Section 340 (1)

Definition: Forged Document or Electronic Record and Using it as Genuine[2479] Section 340 (1) of the Bharatiya Nyaya Sanhita (BNS) 2023 addresses the offense of using a forged document or electronic record as if it were genuine[2480].

Illustration: If a person presents a forged contract in a business deal, claiming it to be genuine, they are committing an offense under BNS 340 (1).

Example: Suppose someone uses a falsified driver's license to gain employment. This act falls under BNS 340 (1) as using a forged document as genuine.

Comment: This section underscores the serious consequences of using forged documents with the intent to deceive. Such acts undermine trust and can cause significant harm, which is why the law imposes strict penalties.

[2477] devgan.in

[2478] devgan.in

[2479] Ministry of Home Affairs. (2024). The Bharatiya Nyaya Sanhita, 2023. Retrieved from https://www.mha.gov.in/sites/default/files/250883_english_01042024.pdf

[2480] devgan.in

Classification of Offence and Punishment Classification: This offense is classified as a criminal offense due to the intent to deceive by using forged documents.

Punishment: The punishment for committing this offense under BNS 340 (1) is imprisonment of either description for a term which may extend to seven years, and the offender shall also be liable to a fine[2481].

Cognizable or Non-Cognizable, Bailable or Non-Bailable: This offense is cognizable, meaning the police can arrest the accused without a warrant.

Non-Bailable: This offense is non-bailable, indicating that the accused cannot secure bail and must remain in custody until the trial is completed.

Comparison: 470 of the Indian Penal Code[2482] (IPC) also addresses the offense of using a forged document or electronic record as genuine: IPC Section 470: States that a forged document or electronic record is one that is made falsely with intent to commit fraud or to support any false claim[2483].

Key Differences: BNS 340 (1): Reflects updated legal terminology and provisions in the new Bharatiya Nyaya Sanhita.IPC 470: Part of the older Indian Penal Code[2484] framework, now replaced by BNS 340 (1).

BNS Section 340 (2)

Definition: Using as Genuine a Forged Document or Electronic Record[2485] Section 340 (2) of the Bharatiya Nyaya Sanhita (BNS) 2023 addresses the offense of using a forged document or electronic record, knowing it to be forged, as if it were genuine.

2481 devgan.in

2482 jhpolice.gov.in

2483 devgan.in

2484 devgan.in

2485 Ministry of Home Affairs. (2024). The Bharatiya Nyaya Sanhita, 2023. Retrieved from https://www.mha.gov.in/sites/default/files/250883_english_01042024.pdf

Illustration: If a person presents a fake identification card to gain entry into a restricted area, knowing it is forged, they are committing an offense under BNS 340 (2).

Example: Suppose someone uses a falsified diploma to secure a job, knowing that the document is not genuine. This act falls under BNS 340 (2) as using a forged document as genuine.

Comment: This section highlights the significant risks and ethical breaches associated with using forged documents. Such actions undermine trust and can lead to serious legal consequences, making it imperative to deter such offenses through stringent penalties.

Classification of Offence and Punishment Classification: This offense is classified as a criminal offense due to the intent to deceive by using forged documents.

Punishment: The punishment for committing this offense under BNS 340 (2) is imprisonment of either description for a term which may extend to seven years, and the offender shall also be liable to a fine[2486].

Cognizable or Non-Cognizable, Bailable or Non-Bailable: This offense is cognizable, meaning the police can arrest the accused without a warrant.

Non-Bailable: This offense is non-bailable, indicating that the accused cannot secure bail and must remain in custody until the trial is completed.

Comparison: Section 471 of the Indian Penal Code[2487] (IPC) also addresses the offense of using a forged document or electronic record as genuine: IPC Section 471: States that whoever fraudulently or dishonestly uses as genuine any document or electronic record which he knows or has reason to believe to be a forged document or electronic record, shall be punished in the same manner as if he had forged such document or electronic record[2488].

[2486] devgan.in

[2487] www.bareactslive.com

[2488] devgan.in

Key Differences: BNS 340 (2): Reflects updated legal terminology and provisions in the new Bharatiya Nyaya Sanhita. IPC 471: Part of the older Indian Penal Code[2489] framework, now replaced by BNS 340 (2).

BNS Section 341 (1)

Definition: Making or Possessing Counterfeit Seal[2490], etc. Section 341 (1) of the Bharatiya Nyaya Sanhita (BNS) 2023 addresses the offense of making or possessing a counterfeit seal, plate, or other instrument for making an impression, with the intent to use it for committing forgery punishable under Section 338.

Illustration: If a person creates a fake company seal to forge official documents, they are committing an offense under BNS 341 (1).

Example: Suppose someone possesses a counterfeit stamp used for forging property deeds, knowing its purpose, they are committing an offense under BNS 341 (1).

Comment: This section highlights the gravity of making or possessing counterfeit seals or instruments used for forgery. The intent to deceive using such tools undermines the integrity of official documents, leading to significant legal consequences.

Classification of Offence and Punishment Classification: This offense is classified as a serious criminal offense due to the intent to commit forgery.

Punishment: The punishment[2491] for committing this offense under BNS 341 (1) is imprisonment for life, or imprisonment of either description for a term which may extend to seven years, and the offender shall also be liable to a fine[2492].

[2489] devgan.in

[2490] Ministry of Home Affairs. (2024). The Bharatiya Nyaya Sanhita, 2023. Retrieved from https://www.mha.gov.in/sites/default/files/250883_english_01042024.pdf

[2491] www.bareactslive.com

[2492] devgan.in

Cognizable or Non-Cognizable, Bailable or Non-Bailable: This offense is cognizable, meaning the police can arrest the accused without a warrant.

Non-Bailable: This offense is non-bailable, indicating that the accused cannot secure bail and must remain in custody until the trial is completed.

Comparison: Section 472 of the Indian Penal Code[2493] (IPC) also addresses the offense of making or possessing counterfeit seals, etc., with intent to commit forgery punishable under Section 467:IPC Section 472: It states that anyone who creates or forges a seal, plate, or other impression-making tool with the intent that it be used to commit a forgery that would be punishable under section 467 of this Code, or who knowingly possesses such a seal, plate, or other tool knowing it is a fake, faces life in prison or imprisonment of any kind for a maximum of seven years, in addition to a fine[2494].

Key Differences: BNS 341 (1): Reflects updated legal terminology and provisions in the new Bharatiya Nyaya Sanhita. IPC 472: Part of the older Indian Penal[2495] Code framework, now replaced by BNS 341 (1).

BNS Section 341 (2)

Definition: Making or Possessing Counterfeit Seal[2496], etc. Section 341 (2) of the Bharatiya Nyaya Sanhita (BNS) 2023 addresses the offense of making or possessing a counterfeit seal, plate, or other instrument for making an impression, with the intent to use it for committing forgery punishable under any section of this Chapter other than Section 338 punishable otherwise.

Illustration: If a person creates a fake company seal to forge official documents, they are committing an offense under BNS 341 (2).

2493 www.bareactslive.com

2494 devgan.in

2495 devgan.in

2496 Ministry of Home Affairs. (2024). The Bharatiya Nyaya Sanhita, 2023. Retrieved from https://www.mha.gov.in/sites/default/files/250883_english_01042024.pdf

Example: Suppose someone possesses a counterfeit stamp used for forging property deeds, knowing its purpose, they are committing an offense under BNS 341 (2).

Comment: This section stresses the severity of creating or possessing counterfeit instruments for forgery, highlighting the need for robust legal measures to deter such malicious activities.

Classification of Offence and Punishment Classification: This offense is classified as a serious criminal offense due to the intent to commit forgery.

Punishment: The punishment for committing this offense under BNS 341 (2) is imprisonment of either description for a term which may extend to seven years, and the offender shall also be liable to a fine[2497].

Cognizable or Non-Cognizable, Bailable or Non-Bailable: This offense is cognizable, meaning the police can arrest the accused without a warrant.

Bailable: This offense is bailable, indicating that the accused can secure bail and be released from custody until the trial is completed.

Comparison: Section 473 of the Indian Penal Code[2498] (IPC) also addresses the offense of making or possessing counterfeit seals, etc., with intent to commit forgery punishable otherwise: IPC Section 473: The law stipulates that anyone who creates or forges a seal, plate, or other impression-making tool with the intent that it be used to commit any forgery that would be punishable under any section of this chapter other than section 467, or who knowingly possesses such a seal, plate, or other tool knowing it is a fake, faces up to seven years in prison of any kind and a fine[2499].

[2497] devgan.in

[2498] jhpolice.gov.in

[2499] devgan.in

Key Differences: BNS 341 (2): Reflects updated legal terminology and provisions in the new Bharatiya Nyaya Sanhita. IPC 473: Part of the older Indian Penal Code[2500] framework, now replaced by BNS 341 (2).

BNS Section 341 (3)

Definition: Possession of Counterfeit Seal[2501], etc. Section 341 (3) of the Bharatiya Nyaya Sanhita (BNS) 2023 addresses the offense of possessing any seal, plate, or other instrument knowing the same to be counterfeit[2502].

Illustration: If a person knowingly holds a fake company seal, they are committing an offense under BNS 341 (3).

Example: Suppose someone has a counterfeit stamp used for forging documents, fully aware that it is not genuine. This act falls under BNS 341 (3) as possession of a counterfeit instrument.

Comment: This section underscores the serious implications of holding counterfeit instruments, highlighting the potential for deceit and misuse. It aims to deter such actions through strict legal repercussions.

Classification of Offence and Punishment Classification: This offense is classified as a criminal offense due to the intent to deceive or misuse the counterfeit instrument.

Punishment: The punishment for committing this offense under BNS 341 (3) is imprisonment of either description for a term which may extend to three years, and the offender shall also be liable to a fine[2503].

Cognizable or Non-Cognizable, Bailable or Non-Bailable: This offense is cognizable, meaning the police can arrest the accused without a warrant.

[2500] devgan.in

[2501] Ministry of Home Affairs. (2024). The Bharatiya Nyaya Sanhita, 2023. Retrieved from https://www.mha.gov.in/sites/default/files/250883_english_01042024.pdf

[2502] prsindia.org

[2503] devgan.in

Bailable: This offense is bailable, indicating that the accused can secure bail and be released from custody until the trial is completed.

Comparison: Section 474 of the Indian Penal Code[2504] (IPC) also addresses the offense of possession of a document, knowing it to be forged, and intending to use it as genuine: IPC Section 474: specifies that anyone found in possession of a document or electronic record that they know to be a fake and plan to use it dishonestly or fraudulently as authentic faces up to seven years in prison of any kind in addition to a fine[2505].

Key Differences: BNS 341 (3): Reflects updated legal terminology and provisions in the new Bharatiya Nyaya Sanhita. IPC 474: Part of the older Indian Penal Code[2506] framework, now replaced by BNS 341 (3).

BNS Section 341 (4)

Definition: Fraudulently or Dishonestly Uses as Genuine Any Seal, Plate, or Other Instrument Knowing it to be Counterfeit[2507] Section 341 (4) of the Bharatiya Nyaya Sanhita (BNS) 2023 addresses the offense of fraudulently or dishonestly using as genuine any seal, plate, or other instrument, knowing or having reason to believe it to be counterfeit.

Illustration: If a person uses a counterfeit official seal to authenticate documents, they are committing an offense under BNS 341 (4).

Example: Suppose someone uses a fake government stamp to validate forged property documents. This act falls under BNS 341 (4) as using a counterfeit instrument as genuine.

Comment: This section highlights the critical issue of using counterfeit instruments to deceive. The law aims to protect the integrity of official

---

[2504] www.bareactslive.com

[2505] devgan.in

[2506] devgan.in

[2507] Ministry of Home Affairs. (2024). The Bharatiya Nyaya Sanhita, 2023. Retrieved from https://www.mha.gov.in/sites/default/files/250883_english_01042024.pdf

documents and deter individuals from exploiting counterfeit seals, stamps, and other instruments through stringent penalties.

Classification of Offence and Punishment Classification: This offense is classified as a serious criminal offense due to the intent to deceive by using counterfeit instruments.

Punishment: The punishment for committing this offense under BNS 341 (4) is imprisonment of either description for a term which may extend to seven years, and the offender shall also be liable to a fine[2508].

Cognizable or Non-Cognizable, Bailable or Non-Bailable: This offense is cognizable, meaning the police can arrest the accused without a warrant.

Bailable: This offense is bailable, indicating that the accused can secure bail and be released from custody until the trial is completed.

BNS Section 342 (1)

Definition: Counterfeiting Device or Mark Used for Authenticating Documents[2509] Section 342 (1) of the Bharatiya Nyaya Sanhita (BNS) 2023 addresses the offense of counterfeiting a device or mark used for authenticating documents described in Section 338, or possessing counterfeit marked material[2510].

Illustration: If a person creates a fake official seal to authenticate a valuable security, they are committing an offense under BNS 342 (1).

Example: Suppose someone possesses counterfeit certificates marked with a forged government seal, knowing their fraudulent nature. This act falls under BNS 342 (1) as possessing counterfeit marked material.

Comment: This section underscores the severe implications of counterfeiting authentication devices. Such actions can severely

---

[2508] devgan.in

[2509] Ministry of Home Affairs. (2024). The Bharatiya Nyaya Sanhita, 2023. Retrieved from https://www.mha.gov.in/sites/default/files/250883_english_01042024.pdf

[2510] prsindia.org

undermine the credibility of critical documents and have far-reaching consequences, necessitating strict legal measures.

Classification of Offence and Punishment Classification: This offense is classified as a serious criminal offense due to the intent to deceive by counterfeiting authentication devices or marks.

Punishment: The punishment for committing this offense under BNS 342 (1) is imprisonment of either description for a term which may extend to seven years, and the offender shall also be liable to a fine[2511].

Cognizable or Non-Cognizable, Bailable or Non-Bailable: This offense is cognizable, meaning the police can arrest the accused without a warrant.

Bailable: This offense is bailable, indicating that the accused can secure bail and be released from custody until the trial is completed.

Comparison: Section 475 of the Indian Penal Code[2512] (IPC) also addresses the offense of counterfeiting devices or marks used for authenticating documents: IPC Section 475: It states that anyone who falsifies the impression of a seal, mark, or signature on, or in the substance of, any material used for document authentication, the signature of any person who is legally permitted to place or affix such a seal, mark, or signature, or who possesses any such material, faces up to seven years in prison of any kind in addition to a fine[2513].

Key Differences: BNS 342 (1): Reflects updated legal terminology and provisions in the new Bharatiya Nyaya Sanhita. IPC 475: Part of the older Indian Penal Code framework[2514], now replaced by BNS 342 (1).

[2511] copyright.gov.in

[2512] www.bareactslive.com

[2513] bprd.nic.in

[2514] bprd.nic.in

BNS Section 342 (2)

Definition: Counterfeiting Device or Mark Used for Authenticating Documents[2515] Section 342 (2) of the Bharatiya Nyaya Sanhita (BNS) 2023 addresses the offense of counterfeiting a device or mark used for authenticating documents described in Section 338, or possessing counterfeit marked material.

Illustration: If a person creates a fake official seal to authenticate a valuable security, they are committing an offense under BNS 342 (2).

Example: Suppose someone possesses counterfeit certificates marked with a forged government seal, knowing their fraudulent nature. This act falls under BNS 342 (2) as possessing counterfeit marked material.

Comment: This section emphasizes the severe consequences of counterfeiting authentication devices. Such activities can significantly erode trust in official documents and lead to considerable harm, which is why the law imposes strict penalties.

Classification of Offence and Punishment Classification: This offense is classified as a serious criminal offense due to the intent to deceive by counterfeiting authentication devices or marks.

Punishment: The punishment for committing this offense under BNS 342 (2) is imprisonment[2516] of either description for a term which may extend to seven years, and the offender shall also be liable to a fine[2517].

Cognizable or Non-Cognizable, Bailable or Non-Bailable: This offense is cognizable, meaning the police can arrest the accused without a warrant.

Bailable: This offense is bailable, indicating that the accused can secure bail and be released from custody until the trial is completed.

[2515] Ministry of Home Affairs. (2024). The Bharatiya Nyaya Sanhita, 2023. Retrieved from https://www.mha.gov.in/sites/default/files/250883_english_01042024.pdf

[2516] copyright.gov.in

[2517] bprd.nic.in

Comparison: With IPC Section 476Section 476 of the Indian Penal Code[2518] (IPC) also addresses the offense of counterfeiting devices or marks used for authenticating documents: IPC Section 476: It states that anyone who falsifies the impression of a seal, mark, or signature on, or in the substance of, any material used for document authentication, the signature of any person who is legally permitted to place or affix such a seal, mark, or signature, or who possesses any such material, faces up to seven years in prison of any kind in addition to a fine[2519].

Key Differences: BNS 342 (2): Reflects updated legal terminology and provisions in the new Bharatiya Nyaya Sanhita.IPC 476: Part of the older Indian Penal Code[2520] framework, now replaced by BNS 342 (2).

BNS Section 343

Definition: Fraudulent Cancellation, Destruction[2521], etc., of Will, Authority to Adopt, or Valuable Security Section 343 of the Bharatiya Nyaya Sanhita (BNS) 2023 addresses the offense of fraudulently or dishonestly canceling, destroying, defacing, or attempting to cancel, destroy, deface, or secrete any document which is or purports to be a will, an authority to adopt a son, or any valuable security.

Illustration: If a person intentionally destroys a will to alter the inheritance, they are committing an offense under BNS 343.

Example: Suppose someone defaces a valuable security document to prevent its use, knowing it will cause financial harm to the rightful owner. This act falls under BNS 343 as fraudulent destruction of a valuable security.

[2518] www.bareactslive.com

[2519] bprd.nic.in

[2520] bprd.nic.in

[2521] Ministry of Home Affairs. (2024). The Bharatiya Nyaya Sanhita, 2023. Retrieved from https://www.mha.gov.in/sites/default/files/250883_english_01042024.pdf

Comment: This section stresses the gravity of tampering with significant legal documents. Such acts can cause substantial harm, and the law ensures strict penalties to protect the integrity of these documents.

Classification of Offence and Punishment Classification: This offense is classified as a serious criminal offense due to the intent to deceive or cause harm.

Punishment: The punishment for committing this offense under BNS 343 is imprisonment for life, or imprisonment of either description for a term which may extend to seven years, and the offender shall also be liable to a fine[2522].

Cognizable or Non-Cognizable, Bailable or Non-Bailable: This offense is cognizable, meaning the police can arrest the accused without a warrant.

Bailable: This offense is bailable, indicating that the accused can secure bail and be released from custody until the trial is completed.

Comparison: Section 477 of the Indian Penal Code[2523] (IPC) also addresses the offense of fraudulent cancellation, destruction, etc., of will, authority to adopt, or valuable security: IPC Section 477: States that whoever fraudulently or dishonestly, or with intent to cause damage or injury to the public or to any person, cancels, destroys or defaces, or attempts to cancel, destroy or deface, or secretes or attempts to secrete any document which is or purports to be a will, or an authority to adopt a son, or any valuable security, or commits mischief in respect of such document, shall be punished with imprisonment for life, or with imprisonment of either description for a term which may extend to seven years, and shall also be liable to a fine[2524].

Key Differences: BNS 343: Reflects updated legal terminology and provisions in the new Bharatiya Nyaya Sanhita. IPC 477: Part of the older Indian Penal Code framework, now replaced by BNS 343.

[2522] bprd.nic.in

[2523] www.bareactslive.com

[2524] bprd.nic.in

BNS Section 344

Definition: Falsification of Accounts[2525] **Section 344** of the Bharatiya Nyaya Sanhita (BNS) 2023 addresses the offense of falsification of accounts by a clerk, officer, or servant, or anyone acting in such a capacity, with the intent to defraud.

Illustration: If an employee deliberately alters financial records to hide losses, they are committing an offense under BNS 344.

Example: Suppose a company accountant knowingly makes false entries in the company's financial books to misrepresent profits. This act falls under BNS 344 as falsification of accounts.

Comment: This section highlights the severity of tampering with financial records. Such acts can lead to significant financial harm and undermine trust in financial systems, emphasizing the need for strict penalties to deter such fraudulent activities.

Classification of Offence and Punishment Classification: This offense is classified as a serious criminal offense due to the intent to defraud and the potential financial harm it can cause.

Punishment: The punishment for committing this offense under BNS 344 is imprisonment[2526] of either description for a term which may extend to seven years, and the offender shall also be liable to a fine[2527].

Cognizable or Non-Cognizable, Bailable or Non-Bailable: This offense is cognizable, meaning the police can arrest the accused without a warrant.

Bailable: This offense is bailable, indicating that the accused can secure bail and be released from custody until the trial is completed.

[2525] Ministry of Home Affairs. (2024). The Bharatiya Nyaya Sanhita, 2023. Retrieved from https://www.mha.gov.in/sites/default/files/250883_english_01042024.pdf

[2526] copyright.gov.in

[2527] bprd.nic.in

Comparison: Section 477A of the Indian Penal Code[2528] (IPC) also addresses the offense of falsification of accounts: IPC Section 477A: States that whoever, being a clerk, officer or servant, or employed or acting in the capacity of a clerk, officer or servant, willfully, and with intent to defraud, destroys, alters, mutilates or falsifies any book, electronic record, paper, writing, valuable security or account which belongs to or is in the possession of his employer, or has been received by him for or on behalf of his employer, or willfully, and with intent to defraud, makes or abets the making of any false entry in, or omits or alters or abets the omission or alteration of any material particular from or in any such book, electronic record, paper, writing, valuable security or account, shall be punished with imprisonment of either description for a term which may extend to seven years, and shall also be liable to a fine.[2529]

Key Differences: BNS 344: Reflects updated legal terminology and provisions in the new Bharatiya Nyaya Sanhita. IPC 477A: Part of the older Indian Penal Code[2530] framework, now replaced by BNS 344.

BNS Section 345 (1)

Definition: Property Mark[2531] Section 345 (1) of the Bharatiya Nyaya Sanhita (BNS) 2023 defines a property mark as a mark used for denoting that movable property belongs to a particular person.

Illustration: If a person marks their initials on their bicycle to indicate ownership, they are using a property mark.

Example: Suppose someone paints their name on a suitcase to show it belongs to them. This act falls under BNS 345 (1) as using a property mark.

Comment: This section establishes the concept of property marks to denote ownership and prevent disputes. Although marking property for

---

[2528] www.livelaw.in

[2529] devgan.in

[2530]

[2531] Ministry of Home Affairs. (2024). The Bharatiya Nyaya Sanhita, 2023. Retrieved from https://www.mha.gov.in/sites/default/files/250883_english_01042024.pdf

identification seems minor, it maintains ownership rights and prevents potential theft or confusion.

Classification of Offence and Punishment Classification: This offense is classified as a minor criminal offense due to its nature of marking property to denote ownership.

Punishment: The punishment for committing this offense under BNS 345 (1) is imprisonment[2532] of either description for a term which may extend to one year, and the offender shall also be liable to a fine[2533].

Cognizable or Non-Cognizable, Bailable or Non-Bailable: This offense is cognizable, meaning the police can arrest the accused without a warrant.

Bailable: This offense is bailable, indicating that the accused can secure bail and be released from custody until the trial is completed.

Comparison: Section 479 of the Indian Penal Code[2534] (IPC) also addresses the offense of property mark: IPC Section 479: States that a mark used for denoting that movable property belongs to a particular person is called a property mark[2535].

Key Differences: BNS 345 (1): Reflects updated legal terminology and provisions in the new Bharatiya Nyaya Sanhita. IPC 479: Part of the older Indian Penal Code framework[2536], now replaced by BNS 345 (1).

BNS Section 345 (2)

Definition: Using a False Property Mark[2537] Section 345 (2) of the Bharatiya Nyaya Sanhita (BNS) 2023 addresses the offense of using a false property mark. This involves marking any movable property,

---

[2532] copyright.gov.in

[2533] bprd.nic.in

[2534] copyright.gov.in

[2535] bprd.nic.in

[2536] bprd.nic.in

[2537] Ministry of Home Affairs. (2024). The Bharatiya Nyaya Sanhita, 2023. Retrieved from https://www.mha.gov.in/sites/default/files/250883_english_01042024.pdf

goods, or any case, package, or other receptacle containing movable property or goods in a manner that reasonably causes it to be believed that the property or goods belong to a person to whom they do not belong[2538].

Illustration: If a person marks a suitcase with a false name to make it appear as if it belongs to someone else, they are committing an offense under BNS 345 (2).

Example: Suppose someone labels a package with a fake company logo to deceive others into thinking it belongs to a particular business. This act falls under BNS 345 (2) as using a false property mark[2539].

Comment: This section emphasizes the serious consequences of using false property marks. Such acts can lead to confusion, potential theft, and misrepresentation of ownership, underlining the need for legal measures to prevent and penalize such deceptive practices.

Classification of Offence and Punishment Classification: This offense is classified as a criminal offense due to the intent to deceive or misrepresent ownership[2540].

Punishment: The punishment for committing this offense under BNS 345 (2) is imprisonment of either description for a term which may extend to one year, and the offender shall also be liable to a fine[2541].

Cognizable or Non-Cognizable, Bailable or Non-Bailable: This offense is cognizable, meaning the police can arrest the accused without a warrant.

Bailable: This offense is bailable, indicating that the accused can secure bail and be released from custody until the trial is completed.

Comparison: Section 481 of the Indian Penal Code[2542] (IPC) also addresses the offense of using a false property mark: IPC Section 481:

[2538] bprd.nic.in

[2539] www.bareactslive.com

[2540] copyright.gov.in

[2541] bprd.nic.in

[2542] copyright.gov.in

States that whoever marks any movable property or goods or any case[2543], package, or other receptacle containing movable property or goods, or uses any case, package, or other receptacle having any mark thereon, in a manner reasonably calculated to cause it to be believed that the property or goods so marked, or any property or goods contained in any such receptacle so marked, belong to a person to whom they do not belong, is said to use a false property mark[2544].

Key Differences: BNS 345 (2): Reflects updated legal terminology and provisions in the new Bharatiya Nyaya Sanhita.IPC 481: Part of the older Indian Penal Code[2545] framework, now replaced by BNS 345 (2).

BNS Section 345 (3)

Definition: Punishment for Using a False Property Mark[2546] Section 345 (3) of the Bharatiya Nyaya Sanhita (BNS) 2023 outlines the punishment for the offense of using a false property mark.

Illustration: If a person uses a counterfeit brand label on a product to deceive customers, they are committing an offense under BNS 345 (3).

Example: Suppose someone marks fake designer logos on ordinary handbags to sell them as high-end products. This act falls under BNS 345 (3) as using a false property mark[2547].

Comment: This section underscores the severity of using false property marks to deceive consumers. Misrepresenting products with counterfeit labels can lead to consumer fraud and significant financial losses, highlighting the importance of legal deterrents.

2543 www.icsi.edu

2544 bprd.nic.in

2545 bprd.nic.in

2546 Ministry of Home Affairs. (2024). The Bharatiya Nyaya Sanhita, 2023. Retrieved from https://www.mha.gov.in/sites/default/files/250883_english_01042024.pdf

2547 www.bareactslive.com

Classification of Offence and Punishment Classification: This offense is classified as a criminal offense due to the intent to deceive or misrepresent ownership[2548].

Punishment: The punishment for committing this offense under BNS 345 (3) is imprisonment[2549] of either description for a term which may extend to one year, and the offender shall also be liable to a fine[2550].

Cognizable or Non-Cognizable, Bailable or Non-Bailable: This offense is non-cognizable, meaning the police cannot arrest the accused without a warrant.

Bailable: This offense is bailable, indicating that the accused can secure bail and be released from custody until the trial is completed.

Comparison: Section 482 of the Indian Penal Code[2551] (IPC) also addresses the punishment for using a false property mark: IPC Section 482: States that whoever uses any false property mark shall be punished with imprisonment of either description for a term which may extend to one year, or with a fine, or with both[2552].

Key Differences: BNS 345 (3): Reflects updated legal terminology and provisions in the new Bharatiya Nyaya Sanhita. IPC 482: Part of the older Indian Penal Code[2553] framework, now replaced by BNS 345 (3).

BNS Section 346

Definition: Tampering with Property Mark with Intent to Cause Injury[2554] Section 346 of the Bharatiya Nyaya Sanhita (BNS) 2023

2548 copyright.gov.in

2549 copyright.gov.in

2550 bprd.nic.in

2551 copyright.gov.in

2552 bprd.nic.in

2553 bprd.nic.in

2554 Ministry of Home Affairs. (2024). The Bharatiya Nyaya Sanhita, 2023. Retrieved from https://www.mha.gov.in/sites/default/files/250883_english_01042024.pdf

addresses the offense of tampering with a property mark with the intent to cause injury.

Illustration: If a person removes or defaces a property mark on a bicycle to make it appear as if it belongs to someone else, they are committing an offense under BNS 346.

Example: Suppose someone scratches off the owner's initials from a car to sell it fraudulently. This act falls under BNS 346 as tampering with a property mark with intent to cause injury.

Comment: This section emphasizes the importance of maintaining the integrity of property marks. Tampering with property marks can lead to ownership disputes, fraud, and significant harm to the rightful owner, making it essential to have strict legal consequences.

Classification of Offence and Punishment Classification: This offense is classified as a criminal offense due to the intent to deceive or cause harm.

Punishment: The punishment for committing this offense under BNS 346 is imprisonment[2555] of either description for a term which may extend to one year, and the offender shall also be liable to a fine[2556].

Cognizable or Non-Cognizable, Bailable or Non-Bailable: This offense is non-cognizable, meaning the police cannot arrest the accused without a warrant.

Bailable: This offense is bailable, indicating that the accused can secure bail and be released from custody until the trial is completed.

Comparison: Section 489 of the Indian Penal Code[2557] (IPC) also addresses the offense of tampering with a property mark with intent to cause injury: IPC Section 489: It states that anybody who removes, destroys, defaces, or adds to a property mark with the intent or knowledge

---

[2555] copyright.gov.in

[2556] bprd.nic.in

[2557] copyright.gov.in

that doing so will injure someone would be penalized with either type of imprisonment for a maximum of one year, a fine, or both[2558].

Key Differences: BNS 346: Reflects updated legal terminology and provisions in the new Bharatiya Nyaya Sanhita. IPC 489: Part of the older Indian Penal Code framework[2559], now replaced by BNS 346.

BNS Section 347 (1)

Definition: Counterfeiting a Property Mark[2560] Section 347 (1) of the Bharatiya Nyaya Sanhita (BNS) 2023 addresses the offense of counterfeiting a property mark used by another person.

Illustration: If a person creates a fake logo to mark someone else's property as their own, they are committing an offense under BNS 347 (1).

Example: Suppose someone forges a company's trademark on products to sell them as if they were produced by that company. This act falls under BNS 347 (1) as counterfeiting a property mark.

Comment: This section stresses the severe implications of counterfeiting property marks, which can lead to significant financial and reputational damage. It aims to uphold the integrity of genuine marks and protect against misrepresentation.

Classification of Offence and Punishment Classification: This offense is classified as a criminal offense due to the intent to deceive or misrepresent ownership.

Punishment: The punishment for committing this offense under BNS 347 (1) is imprisonment[2561] of either description for a term which may extend to two years, and the offender shall also be liable to a fine[2562].

[2558] bprd.nic.in

[2559] bprd.nic.in

[2560] Ministry of Home Affairs. (2024). The Bharatiya Nyaya Sanhita, 2023. Retrieved from https://www.mha.gov.in/sites/default/files/250883_english_01042024.pdf

[2561] copyright.gov.in

[2562] bprd.nic.in

Cognizable or Non-Cognizable, Bailable or Non-Bailable: This offense is non-cognizable, meaning the police cannot arrest the accused without a warrant.

Bailable: This offense is bailable, indicating that the accused can secure bail and be released from custody until the trial is completed.

Comparison: Section 483 of the Indian Penal Code[2563] (IPC) also addresses the offense of counterfeiting a property mark used by another person: IPC Section 483: States that whoever counterfeits any property mark used by any other person shall be punished with imprisonment of either description for a term which may extend to two years, or with a fine, or with both[2564].

Key Differences: BNS 347 (1): Reflects updated legal terminology and provisions in the new Bharatiya Nyaya Sanhita. IPC 483: Part of the older Indian Penal Code[2565] framework, now replaced by BNS 347 (1).

BNS Section 347 (2)

Definition: Counterfeiting a Mark Used by a Public Servant[2566] Section 347 (2) of the Bharatiya Nyaya Sanhita (BNS) 2023 addresses the offense of counterfeiting a mark used by a public servant.

Illustration: If a person creates a fake stamp used by a government official to certify documents, they are committing an offense under BNS 347 (2).

Example: Suppose someone forges a mark indicating that a product has passed a quality inspection by a public servant. This act falls under BNS 347 (2) as counterfeiting a mark used by a public servant[2567].

[2563] copyright.gov.in

[2564] bprd.nic.in

[2565] bprd.nic.in

[2566] Ministry of Home Affairs. (2024). The Bharatiya Nyaya Sanhita, 2023. Retrieved from https://www.mha.gov.in/sites/default/files/250883_english_01042024.pdf

[2567] copyright.gov.in

Comment: This section emphasizes the serious consequences of counterfeiting marks used by public servants. Such actions undermine trust in official processes and can lead to significant harm, necessitating stringent legal measures to prevent and penalize such deceit.

Classification of Offence and Punishment Classification: This offense is classified as a criminal offense due to the intent to deceive or misrepresent official approval.

Punishment: The punishment for committing this offense under BNS 347 (2) is imprisonment[2568] of either description for a term which may extend to three years, and the offender shall also be liable to a fine[2569].

Cognizable or Non-Cognizable, Bailable or Non-Bailable: This offense is non-cognizable, meaning the police cannot arrest the accused without a warrant.

Bailable: This offense is bailable, indicating that the accused can secure bail and be released from custody until the trial is completed.

Comparison: Section 484 of the Indian Penal Code[2570] (IPC) also addresses the offense of counterfeiting a mark used by a public servant[2571] : IPC Section 484: The law stipulates that anyone who forges a property mark used by a public servant, or any mark used by a public servant to indicate that a piece of property was manufactured by a specific individual, at a specific time or location, or that the property is of a certain quality, has been approved by a specific office, or is eligible for any exemption, or passes off any such mark as authentic while knowing it is a fake, faces up to three years in prison of any kind and a fine[2572].

[2568] copyright.gov.in

[2569] bprd.nic.in

[2570] www.bareactslive.com

[2571] copyright.gov.in

[2572] bprd.nic.in

Key Differences: BNS 347 (2): Reflects updated legal terminology and provisions in the new Bharatiya Nyaya Sanhita. IPC 484: Part of the older Indian Penal Code framework[2573], now replaced by BNS 347 (2).

BNS Section 348

Definition: Making or Possession of Any Instrument for Counterfeiting a Property Mark[2574] Section 348 of the Bharatiya Nyaya Sanhita (BNS) 2023 addresses the offense of making or possessing any instrument for counterfeiting a property mark.

Illustration: If a person creates a fake stamp used by a government official to certify documents, they are committing an offense under BNS 348.

Example: Suppose someone forges a mark indicating that a product has passed a quality inspection by a public servant. This act falls under BNS 348 as making or possessing an instrument for counterfeiting a property mark.

Comment: This section underscores the seriousness of making or possessing counterfeit instruments. Such actions can lead to significant deceit and fraud, impacting individuals and institutions, hence requiring stringent legal repercussions.

Classification of Offence and Punishment Classification: This offense is classified as a criminal offense due to the intent to deceive or misrepresent official approval.

Punishment: The punishment for committing this offense under BNS 348 is imprisonment[2575] of either description for a term which may extend to three years, and the offender shall also be liable to a fine[2576].

[2573] bprd.nic.in

[2574] Ministry of Home Affairs. (2024). The Bharatiya Nyaya Sanhita, 2023. Retrieved from https://www.mha.gov.in/sites/default/files/250883_english_01042024.pdf

[2575] copyright.gov.in

[2576] bprd.companydemo.in

Cognizable or Non-Cognizable, Bailable or Non-Bailable: This offense is non-cognizable, meaning the police cannot arrest the accused without a warrant.

Bailable: This offense is bailable, indicating that the accused can secure bail and be released from custody until the trial is completed.

Comparison: Section 485 of the Indian Penal Code[2577] (IPC) also addresses the offense of making or possessing any instrument for counterfeiting a property mark: IPC Section 485: States that whoever makes or has in his possession any die, plate or other instrument for the purpose of counterfeiting a property mark, or has in his possession a property mark for the purpose of denoting that any goods belong to a person to whom they do not belong, shall be punished with imprisonment of either description for a term which may extend to three years, or with a fine, or with both[2578].

Key Differences: BNS 348: Reflects updated legal terminology and provisions[2579] in the new Bharatiya Nyaya Sanhita. IPC 485: Part of the older Indian Penal Code framework, now replaced by BNS 348.

BNS Section 349

Definition: Selling Goods Marked with a Counterfeit Property Mark[2580] Section 349 of the Bharatiya Nyaya Sanhita (BNS) 2023 addresses the offense of selling goods marked with a counterfeit property mark.

Illustration: If a person sells handbags with a fake designer logo, they are committing an offense under BNS 349.

[2577] www.bareactslive.com

[2578] bprd.nic.in

[2579] bprd.companydemo.in

[2580] Ministry of Home Affairs. (2024). The Bharatiya Nyaya Sanhita, 2023. Retrieved from https://www.mha.gov.in/sites/default/files/250883_english_01042024.pdf

Example: Suppose someone sells electronics labeled with a counterfeit brand name to make them appear as high-end products. This act falls under BNS 349 as selling goods marked with a counterfeit property mark[2581].

Comment: This section brings to light the deceptive practice of using counterfeit property marks to mislead consumers. Such actions erode consumer trust and distort fair trade practices, making it essential to enforce legal penalties.

Classification of Offence and Punishment Classification: This offense is classified as a criminal offense due to the intent to deceive consumers and misrepresent the origin of the goods.

Punishment: The punishment for committing this offense under BNS 349 is imprisonment[2582] of either description for a term which may extend to one year, and the offender shall also be liable to a fine[2583].

Cognizable or Non-Cognizable, Bailable or Non-Bailable: This offense is cognizable, meaning the police can arrest the accused without a warrant.

Bailable: This offense is bailable, indicating that the accused can secure bail and be released from custody until the trial is completed.

Comparison: Section 486 of the Indian Penal Code[2584] (IPC) also addresses the offense of selling goods marked with a counterfeit property mark : IPC Section 486: States that whoever sells, or exposes, or has in possession for sale, any goods or things with a counterfeit property mark affixed to or impressed upon the same or to or upon any case, package or other receptacle in which such goods are contained, shall, unless he proves that, having taken all reasonable precautions against committing an offense against this section, he had at the time of the commission of the alleged offense no reason to suspect the genuineness[2585] of the mark, and that, on demand made by or on behalf of the prosecutor, he gave all the

---

[2581] bprd.nic.in

[2582] copyright.gov.in

[2583] bprd.companydemo.in

[2584] bprd.companydemo.in

[2585] bprd.nic.in

information in his power with respect to the persons from whom he obtained such goods or things, or that otherwise he had acted innocently, be punished with imprisonment of either description for a term which may extend to one year, or with a fine, or with both[2586].

Key Differences: BNS 349: Reflects updated legal terminology and provisions in the new Bharatiya Nyaya Sanhita. IPC 486: Part of the older Indian Penal Code framework[2587], now replaced by BNS 349.

BNS Section 350 (1)

Definition: Making a False Mark upon Any Receptacle Containing Goods[2588] Section 350 (1) of the Bharatiya Nyaya Sanhita (BNS) 2023 addresses the offense of making a false mark upon any receptacle containing goods.

Illustration: If a person marks a package with a false label indicating it contains high-quality electronics when it actually contains low-quality items, they are committing an offense under BNS 350 (1).

Example: Suppose someone labels a box of cheap imitation jewelry as containing genuine gold items. This act falls under BNS 350 (1) as making a false mark upon any receptacle containing goods[2589].

Comment: This section highlights the serious implications of misrepresenting the contents of goods. Such actions can deceive consumers, lead to financial losses, and undermine trust, making it essential to have stringent penalties to deter such deceptive practices.

Classification of Offence and Punishment Classification: This offense is classified as a criminal offense due to the intent to deceive or misrepresent the contents of the receptacle.

[2586] devgan.in

[2587] devgan.in

[2588] Ministry of Home Affairs. (2024). The Bharatiya Nyaya Sanhita, 2023. Retrieved from https://www.mha.gov.in/sites/default/files/250883_english_01042024.pdf

[2589] bprd.nic.in

Punishment: The punishment for committing this offense under BNS 350 (1) is imprisonment[2590] of either description for a term which may extend to three years, and the offender shall also be liable to a fine[2591].

Cognizable or Non-Cognizable, Bailable or Non-Bailable: This offense is non-cognizable, meaning the police cannot arrest the accused without a warrant.

Bailable: This offense is bailable, indicating that the accused can secure bail and be released from custody until the trial is completed.

Comparison: Section 487 of the Indian Penal Code [2592](IPC) also addresses the offense of making a false mark upon any receptacle containing goods: IPC Section 487: It states that unless he can demonstrate that he did not intend to defraud, anyone who places a false mark on a case, package, or other container containing goods in a way that is reasonably calculated to lead a public servant or other individual to believe that the container contains goods that it does not contain, that it does not contain goods that it does contain, or that the goods contained in the container are of a nature or quality different from the real nature or quality of them will be punished with either type of imprisonment for a maximum of three years, a fine, or both.[2593]

Key Differences: BNS 350 (1): Reflects updated legal terminology and provisions in the new Bharatiya Nyaya Sanhita. IPC 487: Part of the older Indian Penal Code framework[2594], now replaced by BNS 350 (1).

[2590] copyright.gov.in

[2591] bprd.companydemo.in

[2592] www.bareactslive.com

[2593] bprd.nic.in

[2594] bprd.nic.in

BNS Section 350 (2)

Definition: Punishment for Making Use of Any Such False Mark[2595] Section 350 (2) of the Bharatiya Nyaya Sanhita (BNS) 2023 addresses the punishment for making use of any false mark in a manner prohibited under sub-section (1).

Illustration: If a person uses a package marked with a false label to deceive customers into believing the contents are of higher quality, they are committing an offense under BNS 350 (2).

Example: Suppose someone sells a product in a box labeled as containing premium items, but the actual contents are of inferior quality. This act falls under BNS 350 (2) as making use of a false mark.

Comment: This section emphasizes the consequences of misusing false marks on goods. Misleading consumers with false labels can lead to distrust and financial harm, highlighting the necessity of legal repercussions to deter such fraudulent activities.

Classification of Offence and Punishment Classification: This offense is classified as a criminal offense due to the intent to deceive or misrepresent the contents of the receptacle[2596].

Punishment: The punishment for committing this offense under BNS 350 (2) is imprisonment of either description for a term which may extend to three years, and the offender shall also be liable to a fine[2597].

Cognizable or Non-Cognizable, Bailable or Non-Bailable: This offense is non-cognizable, meaning the police cannot arrest the accused without a warrant.

Bailable: This offense is bailable, indicating that the accused can secure bail and be released from custody until the trial is completed.

[2595] Ministry of Home Affairs. (2024). The Bharatiya Nyaya Sanhita, 2023. Retrieved from https://www.mha.gov.in/sites/default/files/250883_english_01042024.pdf

[2596] copyright.gov.in

[2597] bprd.companydemo.in

Comparison: Section 488 of the Indian Penal Code[2598] (IPC) also addresses the punishment for making use of any such false mark: IPC Section 488: States that whoever makes use of any such false mark in any manner prohibited by the last foregoing section shall, unless he proves that he acted without intent to defraud, be punished as if he had committed an offense against that section[2599].

Key Differences: BNS 350 (2): Reflects updated legal terminology and provisions in the new Bharatiya Nyaya Sanhita. IPC 488: Part of the older Indian Penal Code framework[2600], now replaced by BNS 350 (2).

[2598] www.bareactslive.com

[2599] copyright.gov.in

[2600] copyright.gov.in

CHAPTER-XIX; OF CRIMINAL INTIMIDATION, INSULT, ANNOYANCE, DEFAMATION, ETC

BNS Section 351 (1)

Definition: Criminal Intimidation[2601] Section 351 (1) of the Bharatiya Nyaya Sanhita (BNS) 2023 addresses the offense of criminal intimidation.

Illustration: If a person threatens to harm another's reputation or property to compel them to act against their will, they are committing an offense under BNS 351 (1).

Example: Suppose someone threatens to burn down another person's house unless they drop a civil lawsuit. This act falls under BNS 351 (1) as criminal intimidation.

Comment: This section highlights the seriousness of criminal intimidation, where the intent is to cause alarm or compel someone to act against their will. Legal provisions aim to protect individuals from such threats and ensure a sense of safety and security.

Classification of Offence and Punishment Classification: This offense is classified as a criminal offense due to the intent to cause alarm or compel someone to act against their will[2602].

[2601] Ministry of Home Affairs. (2024). The Bharatiya Nyaya Sanhita, 2023. Retrieved from https://www.mha.gov.in/sites/default/files/250883_english_01042024.pdf

[2602] copyright.gov.in

Punishment: The punishment for committing this offense under BNS 351 (1) is imprisonment of either description for a term which may extend to two years, and the offender shall also be liable to a fine[2603].

Cognizable or Non-Cognizable, Bailable or Non-Bailable Cognizable: This offense is cognizable, meaning the police can arrest the accused without a warrant.

Bailable: This offense is bailable, indicating that the accused can secure bail and be released from custody until the trial is completed.

Comparison: Section 503 of the Indian Penal Code[2604] (IPC) also addresses the offense of criminal intimidation: IPC Section 503: According to the law, criminal intimidation occurs when someone threatens to harm another person's person, reputation, or property, or the person or reputation of someone in whom that person has an interest, with the intention of alarming that person, making them do something they are not legally required to do, or causing them to refrain from doing something they are legally entitled to do in order to avoid carrying out that threat[2605].

Key Differences: BNS 351 (1): Reflects updated legal terminology and provisions in the new Bharatiya Nyaya Sanhita. IPC 503: Part of the older Indian Penal Code framework, now replaced by BNS 351 (1).

BNS Section 351 (2) and (3)

Definition: Criminal Intimidation Punishment Section 351 (2) and (3) [2606]of the Bharatiya Nyaya Sanhita (BNS) 2023 address the punishment for criminal intimidation.

[2603] bprd.companydemo.in

[2604] www.hrw.org

[2605] bprd.companydemo.in

[2606] Ministry of Home Affairs. (2024). The Bharatiya Nyaya Sanhita, 2023. Retrieved from https://www.mha.gov.in/sites/default/files/250883_english_01042024.pdf

Illustration: If a person threatens to cause death or grievous hurt, or to destroy property by fire, they are committing an offense under BNS 351 (3).

Example: Suppose someone threatens to burn down another person's house unless they drop a civil lawsuit. This act falls under BNS 351 (3) as criminal intimidation.

Comment: This section underscores the gravity of criminal intimidation, especially when threats involve severe harm or property destruction. The increased penalties for such threats reflect the need to protect individuals from extreme coercion and fear.

Classification of Offence and Punishment Classification: This offense is classified as a criminal offense due to the intent to cause alarm or compel someone to act against their will[2607].

Punishment: The punishment for committing this offense under BNS 351 (2) is imprisonment [2608]of either description for a term which may extend to two years, and the offender shall also be liable to a fine. Under BNS 351 (3), the punishment is imprisonment of either description for a term which may extend to seven years, and the offender shall also be liable to a fine[2609].

Cognizable or Non-Cognizable, Bailable or Non-Bailable Cognizable: This offense is cognizable, meaning the police can arrest the accused without a warrant.

Bailable: This offense is bailable, indicating that the accused can secure bail and be released from custody until the trial is completed.

Comparison: Section 506 of the Indian Penal Code[2610] (IPC) also addresses the punishment for criminal intimidation: IPC Section 506: Declares that anyone found guilty of criminal intimidation faces a maximum sentence of two years in prison of any kind, a fine, or both. If

---

[2607] copyright.gov.in

[2608] copyright.gov.in

[2609] bprd.companydemo.in

[2610] www.hrw.org

the threat is to cause death or serious injury, to destroy property by fire, to commit an offense that carries a life sentence or a maximum sentence of seven years in prison, or to impute unchastity to a woman, the punishment will be either type of imprisonment for a maximum sentence of seven years with a fine, or both[2611].

Key Differences: BNS 351 (2): Reflects updated legal terminology and provisions in the new Bharatiya Nyaya Sanhita. IPC 506: Part of the older Indian Penal Code framework, now replaced by BNS 351 (2) and (3).

BNS Section 351 (4)

Definition: Criminal Intimidation by an Anonymous Communication[2612] Section 351 (4) of the Bharatiya Nyaya Sanhita (BNS) 2023 addresses the offense of criminal intimidation by an anonymous communication.

Illustration: If a person sends an anonymous letter threatening to harm someone unless they drop a lawsuit, they are committing an offense under BNS 351 (4).

Example: Suppose someone sends an anonymous email threatening to burn down another person's house unless they stop pursuing a legal matter. This act falls under BNS 351 (4) as criminal intimidation by an anonymous communication.

Comment: This section highlights the gravity of criminal intimidation when anonymity is used to conceal identity, adding an element of psychological distress to the threat. The law seeks to address the enhanced fear and alarm caused by anonymous threats, ensuring that perpetrators face additional penalties.

[2611] bprd.companydemo.in

[2612] Ministry of Home Affairs. (2024). The Bharatiya Nyaya Sanhita, 2023. Retrieved from https://www.mha.gov.in/sites/default/files/250883_english_01042024.pdf

Classification of Offence and Punishment Classification: This offense is classified as a criminal offense due to the intent to cause alarm or compel someone to act against their will[2613].

Punishment: The punishment for committing this offense under BNS 351 (4) is imprisonment of either description for a term which may extend to two years, in addition to the punishment provided for the offense under sub-section (1)[2614].

Cognizable or Non-Cognizable, Bailable or Non-Bailable Cognizable: This offense is non-cognizable, meaning the police cannot arrest the accused without a warrant.

Bailable: This offense is bailable, indicating that the accused can secure bail and be released from custody until the trial is completed.

Comparison: Section 507 of the Indian Penal Code[2615] (IPC) also addresses the offense of criminal intimidation by an anonymous communication: IPC Section 507: States that whoever commits the offense of criminal intimidation by an anonymous communication, or having taken precaution to conceal the name or abode of the person from whom the threat comes, shall be punished with imprisonment of either description for a term which may extend to two years, in addition to the punishment provided for the offense by the last preceding section[2616].

Key Differences: BNS 351 (4): Reflects updated legal terminology and provisions in the new Bharatiya Nyaya Sanhita. IPC 507: Part of the older Indian Penal Code framework, now replaced by BNS 351 (4).

[2613] copyright.gov.in

[2614] bprd.companydemo.in

[2615] www.hrw.org

[2616] bprd.companydemo.in

BNS Section 352

Definition: Intentional Insult with Intent to Provoke Breach of the Peace[2617] Section 352 of the Bharatiya Nyaya Sanhita (BNS) 2023 addresses the offense of intentional insult with the intent to provoke a breach of the peace.

Illustration: If a person intentionally insults another in a manner that provokes them to cause a disturbance or fight, they are committing an offense under BNS 352.

Example: Suppose someone publicly insults another person, knowing that it is likely to provoke them to retaliate violently. This act falls under BNS 352 as intentional insult with intent to provoke breach of the peace[2618].

Comment: This section highlights the importance of maintaining public peace and preventing intentional provocations that can lead to disturbances or violence. Legal provisions aim to deter individuals from engaging in behavior that could incite breaches of the peace, ensuring a more harmonious society.

Classification of Offence and Punishment Classification: This offense is classified as a criminal offense due to the intent to cause alarm or provoke a breach of the peace.

Punishment: The punishment for committing this offense under BNS 352 is imprisonment[2619] of either description for a term which may extend to two years, and the offender shall also be liable to a fine[2620].

Cognizable or Non-Cognizable, Bailable or Non-Bailable Cognizable: This offense is non-cognizable, meaning the police cannot arrest the accused without a warrant.

[2617] Ministry of Home Affairs. (2024). The Bharatiya Nyaya Sanhita, 2023. Retrieved from https://www.mha.gov.in/sites/default/files/250883_english_01042024.pdf

[2618] bprd.nic.in

[2619] copyright.gov.in

[2620] bprd.companydemo.in

Bailable: This offense is bailable, indicating that the accused can secure bail and be released from custody until the trial is completed.

Comparison: Section 504 of the Indian Penal Code[2621] (IPC) also addresses the offense of intentional insult with intent to provoke breach of the peace: IPC Section 504: States that whoever intentionally insults, and thereby gives provocation to any person, intending or knowing it to be [2622]likely that such provocation will cause him to break the public peace, or to commit any other offense, shall be punished with imprisonment of either description for a term which may extend to two years, or with a fine, or with both[2623].

Key Differences: BNS 352: Reflects updated legal terminology and provisions in the new Bharatiya Nyaya Sanhita. IPC 504: Part of the older Indian Penal Code framework, now replaced by BNS 352.

BNS Section 353

Definition: Statements Conducing to Public Mischief[2624] Section 353 of the Bharatiya Nyaya Sanhita (BNS) 2023 addresses the offense of making, publishing, or circulating any statement, false information, rumor, or report, including through electronic means, with the intent to cause public mischief.

Illustration: If a person spreads a false rumor about a food shortage in a community to create panic, they are committing an offense under BNS 353.

Example: Suppose someone circulates a fake news article claiming that a particular community is planning to overthrow the government. This act

[2621] bprd.nic.in

[2622] odishapolicecidcb.gov.in

[2623] bprd.companydemo.in

[2624] Ministry of Home Affairs. (2024). The Bharatiya Nyaya Sanhita, 2023. Retrieved from https://www.mha.gov.in/sites/default/files/250883_english_01042024.pdf

falls under BNS 353 as it is likely to cause fear or alarm to the public and may induce people to commit offenses against public tranquility[2625].

Comment: This section underscores the importance of preventing the spread of false information that can incite public fear, panic, or disorder. By penalizing such actions, the law aims to maintain public order and protect the community from the disruptive effects of misinformation.

Classification of Offence and Punishment Classification: This offense is classified as a criminal offense due to the intent to cause public mischief and disrupt public order.

Punishment: The punishment for committing this offense under BNS 353 is imprisonment[2626] of either description for a term which may extend to three years, and the offender shall also be liable to a fine[2627].

Cognizable or Non-Cognizable, Bailable or Non-Bailable Cognizable: This offense is cognizable, meaning the police can arrest the accused without a warrant.

Bailable: This offense is bailable, indicating that the accused can secure bail and be released from custody until the trial is completed.

Comparison: Section 505 of the Indian Penal Code[2628] (IPC) also addresses the offense of statements conducing to public mischief : IPC Section 505: States that whoever makes, publishes, or circulates any statement, rumour, or report with intent to cause, or which is likely to cause, any officer, soldier, sailor, or airman in the Army, Navy, or Air Force of India to mutiny or otherwise disregard or fail in his duty as such; or with intent to cause, or which is likely to cause, fear or alarm to the public, or to any section of the public whereby any person may be induced to commit an offense against the State or against public tranquility; or with intent to incite, or which is likely to incite, any class or community of persons to commit any offense against any other class or community, shall

---

[2625] www.bareactslive.com

[2626] copyright.gov.in

[2627] bprd.companydemo.in

[2628] www.bareactslive.com

be punished with imprisonment of either description for a term which may extend to three years, or with a fine, or with both. [2629]

Key Differences: BNS 353: Reflects updated legal terminology and provisions in the new Bharatiya Nyaya Sanhita. IPC 505: Part of the older Indian Penal Code framework, now replaced by BNS 353.

BNS Section 354

Definition: Act Caused by Inducing Person to Believe that He Will Be Rendered an Object of the Divine Displeasure[2630] Section 354 of the Bharatiya Nyaya Sanhita (BNS) 2023 addresses the offense of causing someone to act or omit to act by inducing them to believe that they or someone they care about will be rendered an object of Divine displeasure[2631].

Illustration: If a person threatens another by saying that they will be cursed by God if they do not comply with a demand, they are committing an offense under BNS 354.

Example: Suppose someone tells another person that they will be struck by lightning if they do not hand over their property. This act falls under BNS 354 as it involves inducing fear of Divine displeasure.

Comment: This section highlights the seriousness of exploiting people's religious beliefs to coerce them into actions against their will. It protects individuals from manipulative threats that leverage the fear of divine retribution.

Classification of Offence and Punishment Classification: This offense is classified as a criminal offense due to the intent to cause fear or compel someone to act against their will. **Punishment:** The punishment for committing this offense under BNS 354 is imprisonment of either

---

[2629] bprd.nic.in

[2630] Ministry of Home Affairs. (2024). The Bharatiya Nyaya Sanhita, 2023. Retrieved from https://www.mha.gov.in/sites/default/files/250883_english_01042024.pdf

[2631] pdfcookie.com

description for a term which may extend to one year, and the offender shall also be liable to a fine[2632].

Cognizable or Non-Cognizable, Bailable or Non-Bailable Cognizable: This offense is cognizable, meaning the police can arrest the accused without a warrant.

Bailable: This offense is bailable, indicating that the accused can secure bail and be released from custody until the trial is completed.

Comparison: Section 508 of the Indian Penal Code[2633] (IPC) also addresses the offense of causing someone to act or omit to act by inducing them to believe that they or someone they care about will be rendered an object of Divine displeasure: IPC Section 508: States that whoever voluntarily causes or attempts to cause any person to do anything which that person is not legally bound to do, or to omit to do anything which he is legally entitled to do, by inducing or attempting to induce that person to believe that he or any person in whom he is interested will become or will be rendered by some act of the offender an object of Divine displeasure if he does not do the thing which it is the object of the offender to cause him to do, or if he does the thing which it is the object of the offender to cause him to omit, shall be punished with imprisonment of either description for a term which may extend to one year, or with a fine, or with both.[2634]

Key Differences: BNS 354: Reflects updated legal terminology and provisions in the new Bharatiya Nyaya Sanhita.IPC 508: Part of the older Indian Penal Code framework, now replaced by BNS 354.

[2632] old.nmu.ac.in

[2633] blog.ipleaders.in

[2634] pdfcookie.com

BNS Section 355

Definition: Misconduct in Public by a Drunken Person[2635] Section 355 of the Bharatiya Nyaya Sanhita (BNS) 2023 addresses the offense of misconduct in public by a drunken person.

Illustration: If a person, while intoxicated, loudly argues and causes a disturbance in a public park, they are committing an offense under BNS 355.

Example: Suppose someone, after consuming alcohol, starts shouting and behaving aggressively in a crowded market, causing annoyance to others. This act falls under BNS 355 as misconduct in public by a drunken person[2636].

Comment: This section underscores the importance of maintaining public order and decency. Drunken behavior that causes disturbances can be highly disruptive and offensive, highlighting the need for legal measures to ensure such conduct is appropriately penalized. The inclusion of community service as a penalty reflects an approach that aims to rehabilitate and contribute positively to society.

Classification of Offence and Punishment Classification: This offense is classified as a criminal offense due to the intent to cause public disturbance.

Punishment: The punishment for committing this offense under BNS 355 is simple imprisonment[2637] for a term which may extend to twenty-four hours, or with a fine which may extend to one thousand rupees, or with both, or with community service[2638].

[2635] Ministry of Home Affairs. (2024). The Bharatiya Nyaya Sanhita, 2023. Retrieved from https://www.mha.gov.in/sites/default/files/250883_english_01042024.pdf

[2636] pdfcookie.com

[2637] old.nmu.ac.in

[2638] pdfcookie.com

Cognizable or Non-Cognizable, Bailable or Non-Bailable Cognizable: This offense is non-cognizable, meaning the police cannot arrest the accused without a warrant.

Bailable: This offense is bailable, indicating that the accused can secure bail and be released from custody until the trial is completed.

Comparison: Section 510 of the Indian Penal Code[2639] (IPC) also addresses the offense of misconduct in public by a drunken person: IPC Section 510: Declares that anyone who shows up in a public place while intoxicated or in a place that is inappropriate for him to enter and behaves in a way that annoys others will be punished with simple imprisonment for up to 24 hours, a fine of up to 10 rupees, or both[2640].

Key Differences: BNS 355: Reflects updated legal terminology and provisions in the new Bharatiya Nyaya Sanhita, with a higher fine and the option of community service. IPC 510: Part of the older Indian Penal Code framework, now replaced by BNS 355.

BNS Section 356 (1)

Definition: Defamation[2641] Section 356 (1) of the Bharatiya Nyaya Sanhita (BNS) 2023 addresses the offense of defamation.

Illustration: If a person spreads false rumors about another individual, claiming they have committed a crime, they are committing an offense under BNS 356 (1).

Example: Suppose someone publishes a blog post falsely accusing a colleague of embezzlement. This act falls under BNS 356 (1) as defamation, as it harms the reputation of the accused person.

Comment: This section underscores the importance of protecting individuals' reputations from false and harmful statements. Defamation

---

[2639] blog.ipleaders.in

[2640] pdfcookie.com

[2641] Ministry of Home Affairs. (2024). The Bharatiya Nyaya Sanhita, 2023. Retrieved from https://www.mha.gov.in/sites/default/files/250883_english_01042024.pdf

can severely impact a person's life, career, and social standing, making it crucial to have legal provisions to deter and address such actions.

Classification of Offence and Punishment Classification: This offense is classified as a criminal offense due to the intent to harm someone's reputation.

Punishment: The punishment for committing this offense under BNS 356 (1) is imprisonment of either description for a term which may extend to two years, and the offender shall also be liable to a fine[2642].

Cognizable or Non-Cognizable, Bailable or Non-Bailable Cognizable: This offense is cognizable, meaning the police can arrest the accused without a warrant.

Bailable: This offense is bailable, indicating that the accused can secure bail and be released from custody until the trial is completed.

Comparison: Section 499 of the Indian Penal Code[2643] (IPC) also addresses the offense of defamation: IPC Section 499: States that whoever, by words either spoken or intended to be read, or by signs[2644] or by visible representations, makes or publishes any imputation concerning any person intending to harm, or knowing or having reason to believe that such imputation will harm, the reputation of such person, is said, except in the cases hereinafter excepted, to defame that person[2645].

Key Differences: BNS 356 (1): Reflects updated legal terminology and provisions in the new Bharatiya Nyaya Sanhita. IPC 499: Part of the older Indian Penal Code framework[2646], now replaced by BNS 356 (1).

[2642] old.nmu.ac.in

[2643] en.wikipedia.org

[2644] www.deccanherald.com

[2645] en.wikipedia.org

[2646] blog.ipleaders.in

BNS 356 (2)

Definition: Defamation Punishment[2647] Section 356 (2) of the Bharatiya Nyaya Sanhita (BNS) 2023 addresses the punishment for defamation.

Illustration: If a person is found guilty of spreading false information about another[2648] individual, they will be subject to the punishment outlined in BNS 356 (2).

Example: Suppose someone falsely accuses a colleague of theft in a public forum, causing harm to the colleague's reputation. If found guilty, the defamer will face the punishment specified in BNS 356 (2).

Comment: This section emphasizes the importance of safeguarding individuals' reputations from false accusations. It not only seeks to penalize defamers but also aims to rehabilitate them through community service. By incorporating updated legal terminology and provisions, BNS 356 (2) aims to reflect contemporary societal values and protect against defamation effectively.

Classification of Offence and Punishment Classification: This offense is classified as a criminal offense due to the intent to harm someone's reputation.

Punishment: The punishment for committing this offense under BNS 356 (2) is simple[2649] imprisonment for a term which may extend to two years, or with a fine, or with community service, or with both[2650].

Cognizable or Non-Cognizable, Bailable or Non-Bailable Cognizable: This offense is cognizable, meaning the police can arrest the accused without a warrant.

[2647] Ministry of Home Affairs. (2024). The Bharatiya Nyaya Sanhita, 2023. Retrieved from https://www.mha.gov.in/sites/default/files/250883_english_01042024.pdf

[2648] blog.ipleaders.in

[2649] old.nmu.ac.in

[2650] www.bareactslive.com

Bailable: This offense is bailable, indicating that the accused can secure bail and be released from custody until the trial is completed.

Comparison: With IPC Section 500Section 500 of the Indian Penal Code[2651] (IPC) also addresses the punishment for defamation: IPC Section 500: States that whoever defames another shall be punished with simple imprisonment for a term which may extend to two years, or with a fine, or with both[2652].

Key Differences: BNS 356 (2): Reflects updated legal terminology and provisions in the new Bharatiya Nyaya Sanhita, with the addition of community service as a possible punishment. IPC 500: Part of the older Indian Penal Code framework[2653], now replaced by BNS 356 (2).

BNS Section 356 (3)

Definition: Printing or Engraving Matter Known to be Defamatory[2654] Section 356 (3) of the Bharatiya Nyaya Sanhita (BNS) 2023 addresses the offense of printing or engraving matter known to be defamatory.

Illustration and Examples Illustration: If a person prints a pamphlet containing false accusations about someone, knowing that it will harm the person's reputation, they are committing an offense under BNS 356 (3).

Example: Suppose someone publishes a book that falsely claims a public figure has committed a crime, knowing that this information is untrue and will damage the figure's reputation. This act falls under BNS 356 (3) as printing or engraving defamatory matter.

Comment: This section highlights the significance of protecting individuals from defamation through printed or engraved materials. The emphasis is on preventing the spread of false and damaging information

---

[2651] old.nmu.ac.in

[2652] pdfcookie.com

[2653] old.nmu.ac.in

[2654] Ministry of Home Affairs. (2024). The Bharatiya Nyaya Sanhita, 2023. Retrieved from https://www.mha.gov.in/sites/default/files/250883_english_01042024.pdf

that can harm a person's reputation and integrity. Legal measures are necessary to hold individuals accountable for such actions.

Classification of Offence and Punishment Classification: This offense is classified as a criminal offense due to the intent to harm someone's reputation[2655].

Punishment: The punishment for committing this offense under BNS 356 (3) is simple imprisonment for a term which may extend to two years, or with a fine, or with both[2656].

Cognizable or Non-Cognizable, Bailable or Non-Bailable Cognizable: This offense is cognizable, meaning the police can arrest the accused without a warrant.

Bailable: This offense is bailable, indicating that the accused can secure bail and be released from custody until the trial is completed.

Comparison: Section 501 of the Indian Penal Code[2657] (IPC) also addresses the offense of printing or engraving matter known to be defamatory: IPC Section 501: States that whoever prints or engraves any matter, knowing or having good reason to believe that such matter is defamatory of any person, shall be punished with simple imprisonment for a term which may extend to two years, or with a fine, or with both[2658].

Key Differences: BNS 356 (3): Reflects updated legal terminology and provisions in the new Bharatiya Nyaya Sanhita. IPC 501: Part of the older Indian Penal Code framework, now replaced by BNS 356 (3).

[2655] old.nmu.ac.in

[2656] www.bareactslive.com

[2657] www.bareactslive.com

[2658] pdfcookie.com

BNS Section 356 (4)

Definition: Sale of Printed or Engraved Substance Containing Defamatory Matter[2659] Section 356 (4) of the Bharatiya Nyaya Sanhita (BNS) 2023 addresses the offense of selling or offering for sale any printed or engraved substance containing defamatory matter.

Illustration: If a bookstore owner knowingly sells a book that contains false and defamatory statements about an individual, they are committing an offense under BNS 356 (4).

Example: Suppose a vendor sells pamphlets that falsely accuse a public figure of criminal activities, knowing that the content is defamatory. This act falls under BNS 356 (4) as it involves selling defamatory material.

Comment: This section highlights the importance of preventing the distribution of defamatory content, which can significantly harm an individual's reputation. The provisions aim to ensure that sellers are held accountable for knowingly distributing false and damaging information.

Classification of Offence and Punishment Classification: This offense is classified as a criminal offense due to the intent to harm someone's reputation by distributing defamatory content[2660].

Punishment: The punishment for committing this offense under BNS 356 (4) is simple imprisonment for a term which may extend to two years, or with a fine, or with both[2661].

Cognizable or Non-Cognizable, Bailable or Non-Bailable Cognizable: This offense is cognizable, meaning the police can arrest the accused without a warrant.

Bailable: This offense is bailable, indicating that the accused can secure bail and be released from custody until the trial is completed.

[2659] Ministry of Home Affairs. (2024). The Bharatiya Nyaya Sanhita, 2023. Retrieved from https://www.mha.gov.in/sites/default/files/250883_english_01042024.pdf

[2660]old.nmu.ac.in

[2661] www.bareactslive.com

Comparison: Section 502 of the Indian Penal Code[2662] (IPC) also addresses the offense of selling or offering for sale any printed or engraved substance containing defamatory matter: IPC Section 502: Declares that anybody who sells or offers for sale any printed or engraved material that contains defamatory content knowing that it does so faces a maximum sentence of two years in simple imprisonment, a fine, or both[2663].

Key Differences: BNS 356 (4): Reflects updated legal terminology and provisions in the new Bharatiya Nyaya Sanhita. IPC 502: Part of the older Indian Penal Code framework, now replaced by BNS 356 (4).

BNS Section 357

Definition: Breach of Contract to Attend on and Supply Wants of Helpless Person[2664] Section 357 of the Bharatiya Nyaya Sanhita (BNS) 2023 addresses the offense of breaching a contract to attend on and supply the needs of a helpless person.

Illustration: If a caregiver, bound by a lawful contract, fails to provide necessary care and support to an elderly person who cannot fend for themselves, they are[2665] committing an offense under BNS 357.

Example: Suppose a nurse hired to look after an elderly patient with dementia neglects their duties, leaving the patient without food, medication, or assistance. This act falls under BNS 357 as it breaches the contract to attend to and supply the needs of a helpless person.

Comment: This section emphasizes the critical importance of fulfilling contracts involving the care of vulnerable individuals. Neglecting such responsibilities can have severe consequences for those who are unable to care for themselves, underscoring the need for stringent legal measures to ensure proper care and support.

[2662] www.bareactslive.com

[2663] pdfcookie.com

[2664] Ministry of Home Affairs. (2024). The Bharatiya Nyaya Sanhita, 2023. Retrieved from https://www.mha.gov.in/sites/default/files/250883_english_01042024.pdf

[2665] devgan.in

Classification of Offence and Punishment Classification: This offense is classified as a criminal offense due to the neglect of duty towards a vulnerable individual.

Punishment: The punishment for committing this offense under BNS 357 is imprisonment[2666] of either description for a term which may extend to three months, or with a fine which may extend to five thousand rupees, or with both[2667].

Cognizable or Non-Cognizable, Bailable or Non-Bailable Cognizable: This offense is cognizable, meaning the police can arrest the accused without a warrant.

Bailable: This offense is bailable, indicating that the accused can secure bail and be released from custody until the trial is completed.

Comparison: Section 491 of the Indian Penal Code[2668] (IPC) also addresses the offense of breaching a contract to attend on and supply the wants of a helpless person: IPC Section 491: It states that if someone who is legally obligated to provide for or meet the needs of someone who is unable to do so voluntarily due to a disease, physical weakness, youth, or mental illness faces imprisonment of any kind for up to three months, a fine of up to two hundred rupees, or both, they will be punished[2669].

Key Differences: BNS 357: Reflects updated legal terminology and provisions in the new Bharatiya Nyaya Sanhita, with a higher fine. IPC 491: Part of the older Indian Penal Code framework, now replaced by BNS 357.

[2666] old.nmu.ac.in

[2667] pdfcookie.com

[2668] www.bareactslive.com

[2669] pdfcookie.com

Chapter-XX; Repeal and Saving

BNS Section 358

Definition: Repeal and Savings[2670] Section 358 of the Bharatiya Nyaya Sanhita (BNS) 2023 addresses the repeal of the Indian Penal Code (IPC) and the savings provisions related to it.[2671]

Illustration: When the BNS was enacted, it repealed the IPC. However, actions taken under the IPC before its repeal remain valid and enforceable.

Example: If a person was convicted under the IPC before its repeal, their conviction and any ongoing legal proceedings related to it continue to be valid under the BNS.

Comment: This section ensures a smooth transition from the IPC to the BNS, providing legal continuity and preserving the validity of actions and proceedings initiated under the IPC. It reflects an organized approach to updating the legal framework while maintaining the integrity of ongoing legal matters.

Classification of Offence and Punishment Classification: This section is not classified as an offense but rather as a legal provision ensuring continuity and transition.

Punishment: There is no specific punishment associated with this section as it deals with legal procedures and not criminal conduct.

Cognizable or Non-Cognizable, Bailable or Non-Bailable Cognizable: Not applicable as this section does not pertain to a criminal offense.

[2670] Ministry of Home Affairs. (2024). The Bharatiya Nyaya Sanhita, 2023. Retrieved from https://www.mha.gov.in/sites/default/files/250883_english_01042024.pdf

[2671] blog.ipleaders.in

Bailable: Not applicable as this section does not pertain to a criminal offense.

Comparison: Section 484 of the Indian Penal Code[2672] (IPC) also addresses the repeal and savings provisions: IPC Section 484: States that previous laws related to criminal procedure are repealed with the introduction of the Code of Criminal Procedure, 1973[2673], but certain actions taken under those repealed laws remain valid.

Key Differences: BNS 358: Reflects updated legal terminology and provisions in the new Bharatiya Nyaya Sanhita, ensuring continuity of actions taken under the IPC.IPC 484: Part of the older Indian Penal Code[2674] framework, now replaced by BNS 358.

"A COMPARATIVE OVERVIEW: BHARATIYA NYAYA SANHITA, 2023 (BNS) AND INDIAN PENAL CODE, 1860 (IPC)"

BNS Sections/ Subsections	Subject	IPC Sections	Summary of comparison
1(1)	Short title, commencement and application.	1	This subject is covered by six subsections of Section 1 of BNS, corresponding to five separate sections of IPC, sans separate headings thereof. In IPC, the extent of code operation is also given, which is absent in BNS.

2672 www.bareactslive.com

2673 www.nmu.ac.in

2674 www.nmu.ac.in

1(2)	Commencement.	New	By subsection 1(2) of the BNS, the power to appoint the date of commencement is delegated to the Central Government, which was absent in the IPC.
1(3)	Punishment of offences committed within India.	2	No change except "Code" is replaced with "Sanhita". Wherever the word "Code" is used in IPC, the word "Sanhita" is used in BNS; therefore, this fact will not be specifically mentioned in this table hereinafter.
1(4)	Punishment of offences committed beyond, which by law may be tried within, India.	3	Section is included as a subsection in BNS sans heading. "Indian laws" is replaced with "law" and "for the time being in force in India" is inserted.
1(5)	Short title, commencement and application- Extension of Code to extra-territorial offences.	4	Section is included as a subsection in BNS sans heading. In the illustration, "Uganda" has been replaced with "any place outside India."

1(6)	Short title, commencement and application- "Certain laws not to be affected by this Act".	5	IPC section is included as a subsection in BNS sans heading.
2	Definitions.		In the IPC, definitions are not consolidated in a single section; instead, they are given in independent sections from Section 8 to Section 52A in Chapter II, "General Explanations". These have been conveniently organised and consolidated in a single section, i.e., Section-2, in alphabetical order as sub sections with Arabic numerals to facilitate easier reference.
2(1)	"act".	33	In the IPC, Section 33 addressed both "Act" and "Omission" collectively. However, in the BNS, "act" and "omission" are separately defined in sub-sections 2(1) and 2(25) respectively.

2(2)	"animal".	47	No change.
2(3)	"child".	New	Definition of 'child' in section 2(3) of BNS (child- any person below the age of eighteen years.) This is a new addition.
2(4)	"Counterfeit".	28	No change.
2(5)	"Court".	20	Section 2(5) of BNS excludes the illustration and uses the word "Court" in place of the words "Court of Justice".
2(6)	"Death".	46	No change.
2(7)	"Dishonestly".	24	Words "whoever does" and "is said to do that thing dishonestly" are excluded.
2(8)	"Document".	29 and 29A	Words "and includes electronic and digital record" are added. BNS Section 2(8) incorporates both the sections 29 and 29A of IPC and adds digital records.
2(9)	Fraudulently.	25	Phraseology changed but essence is same.

2(10)	Gender.	8	Word "transgender" is added apart from genders of "male" and "female".
2(11)	Good faith.	52	No change.
2(12)	Government.	17	Words "Government of a State" are replaced by "State Government".
2(13)	Harbour.	52A	Words "Except in section 157 and in section 130, in the case in which the harbour is given by the wife or husband of the person harboured, the word" have been excluded.
2(14)	Injury.	44	Word "denotes" is replaced with "means".
2(15)	Illegal and legally bound to do.	43	No change.
2(16)	Judge.	19	Simplified the definition of Judge, paragraphs are given numbers (i) and (ii). Out of four illustrations, only (b) is kept, while (a), (c), and (d) are excluded.

2(17)	Life.	45	Word "denotes" is replaced with "means".
2(18)	Local law.	42	No change.
2(19)	Man.	10	The word "denotes" is replaced with "means" Unlike in IPC Section 10, "man" and "woman" are bifurcated into two subsections, 2(19) and 2(35) in BNS.
2(20)	Month and year.	49	"British calendar" is replaced by "Gregorian calendar".
2(21)	Movable property.	22	By removing word "corporeal" the scope is expanded.
2(22)	Number.	9	No change.
2(23)	Oath.	51	'Court of Justice' is changed to 'Court'.
2(24)	Offence.	40	Word "denotes" is replaced by "means".
2(25)	Omission.	33	Words "Act" and "Omission" are bifurcated into two subsections 2(1) and 2(25) respectively.
2(26)	Person.	11	No change.

2(27)	Public.	12	No change.
2(28)	Public servant.	21	"Military, Naval" are replaced by "Army, and Navy" respectively. "Juryman" is excluded.
2(29)	Reason to believe.	26	No change.
2(30)	Special law.	41	The word 'is' is replaced by 'means'.
2(31)	Valuable security.	30	Word "denotes" replaced by "means".
2(32)	Vessel.	48	Word "denotes" replaced by "means".
2(33)	Voluntarily.	39	No change.
2(34)	Will.	31	"A will" is replaced by "Will".
2(35)	Woman.	10	The corresponding section of the IPC contains definitions of man and woman both whereas the BNS deals with them in separate provisions 2(19) and 2(35), respectively.
2(36)	Wrongful gain.	23 Clause-1	Word "is" is replaced by "means".
2(37)	Wrongful loss.	23 Clause-2	Ditto.
2(38)	Gaining wrongfully, losing wrongfully.	23 Clause-3	No change.

2(39)	Words and expressions used but not defined.	29A	The scope of Section 29A IPC is broadened. For words and expressions used in BNS but not defined in BNS but defined in IT Act, 2000 and Bharatiya Nagarik Suraksha Sanhita, 2023 (BNSS), they shall have the meanings respectively assigned to them in that Act and Sanhita.
3(1)	General explanations.	6	Section is included as sub-section in BNS sans heading.
3(2)	General explanations- Sense of expression once explained.	7	Ditto.
3(3)	General explanations- Property in possession of wife, clerk or servant.	27	Section is included as a sub-section in BNS sans heading. “Wife” is replaced by “Spouse”.
3(4)	General explanations- "Words referring to acts include illegal omissions".	32	Section is included as sub-section in BNS sans heading.
3(5)	General explanations- Acts done by several persons in furtherance of common intention.	34	Section is included as sub-section in BNS sans heading. No other change.
3(6)	General explanations- When such an act is criminal by reason of	35	Ditto.

	its being done with a criminal knowledge or intention.		
3(7)	General explanations-Effect caused partly by act and partly by omission.	36	Ditto.
3(8)	General explanations-Co-operation by doing one of several acts constituting an offence.	37	Ditto.
3(9)	General explanations-Persons concerned in Criminal act may be guilty of different offences.	38	Ditto.
4	Punishments.	53	'Community service' is added to punishments. The definition of community service is not given in BNS, but the explanation in Section 23 of the BNSS defines it as the "work which the court may order a convert to perform as a form of punishment that benefits the community, for which he shall not be entitled to any remuneration".
5	Commutation of sentence.	54 & 55	In this section, a cross reference to BNSS has

			been made, whereas IPC does not refer to CrPC in this context.
Explanation to section 5	Commutation of sentence.	55A	The heading is dropped as the IPC section is given as an explanation in BNS. The expression "for the purposes of this" is added.
6	Fractions of terms of punishment.	57	Words "unless otherwise provided" are added
7	Sentence may be (in certain cases of imprisonment) wholly or partly rigorous or simple.	60	No change.
8(1)	Amount of fine, liability in default of payment of fine, etc.	63	IPC section is included as subsection in BNS with addition of words 'liability in default of payment of fine, etc.' in heading.
8(2)	Sentence of imprisonment for non- payment of fine.	64	IPC section is included as sub-section in BNS sans heading.
8(3)	Limit to imprisonment for non- payment of fine, when imprisonment and fine awardable.	65	Ditto.

8(4)	Description of imprisonment for non- payment of fine.	66	The IPC section is included as a sub-section in BNS, sans heading. "or in default of community service" is added..
8(5)	Imprisonment for non-payment of fine, when offence punishable with fine only.	67	IPC section is included as sub-section in BNS, sans heading. Words "or in default of community service" are added. Imprisonment and fine are increased.
8(6)	Imprisonment to terminate on payment of fine. Termination of imprisonment on payment of proportional part of fine.	68 & 69	Heading is dropped as two sections of IPC are merged in this one sub-section of BNS.
8(7)	Fine leviable within six years, or during imprisonment. Death not to discharge property from liability.	70	Section is included as sub-section in BNS, sans heading.
9	Limit of punishment of offence made up of several offences.	71	No change.
10	Punishment of person guilty of one of several offences, the judgment stating that	72	No change.

	it is doubtful of which.		
11	Solitary confinement.	73	Word "that is to say" is replaced with "namely".
12	Limit of solitary confinement.	74	No Change
13	Enhanced punishment for certain offences after previous conviction.	75	No changes were made except for the corresponding chapter numbers mentioned in heading are dropped in BNS.
14	Act done by a person bound, or by mistake of fact believing himself bound, by law.	76	No change.
15	Act of Judge when acting judicially.	77	No change.
16	Act done pursuant to the judgment or order of Court.	78	Words 'Court of Justice' is replaced by "Court".
17	Act done by a person justified, or by mistake of fact believing himself justified, by law.	79	No change.
18	Accident in doing a lawful act.	80	No change.

19	Act likely to cause harm, but done without criminal intent, and to prevent other harm.	81	Word "steam" is excluded in illustration.
20	Act of a child under seven years of age.	82	No change.
21	Act of a child above seven and under twelve of immature understanding.	83	No change.
22	Act of a person of unsound mind.	84	No change.
23	Act of a person incapable of judgment by reason of intoxication caused against his will.	85	No change.
24	Offence requiring a particular intent or knowledge committed by one who is intoxicated.	86	No change.
25	Act not intended and not known to be likely to cause death or grievous hurt, done by consent.	87	No change.
26	Act not intended to cause death, done by	88	No change.

	consent in good faith for person's benefit.		
27	Act done in good faith for benefit of child or person, by or by consent of guardian.	89	Words "insane person" are replaced with "person of unsound mind".
28	Consent known to be given under fear or misconception.	90	No change.
29	Exclusion of acts which are offences independently of harm caused.	91	No change.
30	Act done in good faith for benefit of a person without consent.	92	No change.
31	Communication made in good faith.	93	No change.
32	Act to which a person is compelled by threats.	94	No change.
33	Act causing slight harm.	95	No change.
34	Things done in private defence.	96	No change.
35	Right of private defence of body and of property.	97	Paragraphs are rephrased as clauses (a), (b), (c).

36	Right of private defence against the act of a person of unsound mind, etc.	98	In Illustrations, words "under the influence of madness" are replaced by "a person of unsound mind".
37	Act against which there is no right to private defence Extent to which the right may be exercised.	99	The IPC section is reframed into two subsections, and the first paragraph is reframed as sub-section 1 with clauses (a), (b), and (c). The second paragraph is reproduced as subsection (2) sans heading.
38	When the right of private defence of property extends to causing death.	100	First, secondly, thirdly, fourthly, fifthly, sixthly, seventhly are replaced with (a),(b),(c),(d),(e),(f),(g).
39	When such right extends to causing any harm other than death.	101	No change.
40	Commencement and continuance of the right of private defence of the body.	102	No change.
41	When the right of private defence of property extends to causing death.	103	Words "by night" are replaced by "after sunset and before sunrise" and "Mischief by fire", replaced by "Mischief by fire or any explosive substance".
42	When such right extends to causing	104	No change.

	any harm other than death.		
43	Commencement and continuance of the right of private defence of property.	105	Words "by night" are replaced by "after sunset and before sunrise".
44	Right of private defence against deadly assault when there is risk of harm to innocent person.	106	No change.
45	Abetment of a thing.	107	Words "Court of justice" are replaced with "Court".
46	Abettor.	108	Word "lunatic" is replaced by words "a person of unsound mind".
47	Abetment in India of offences outside India.	108A	Word "Goa" is replaced by "country X" in illustration.
48	Abetment outside India for offence in India.	-	"A person abets an offence within the meaning of this Sanhita who, without and beyond India, abets the commission of any act in India which would constitute an offence if committed in India".
49	Punishment of abetment if act abetted is committed in consequence and where no express	109	No change.

	provision is made for its punishment.		
50	Punishment of abetment if person abetted does act with different intention from that of abettor.	110	No change.
51	Liability of abettor when one act abetted and different act done.	111	No change.
52	Abettor when liable to cumulative punishment for act abetted and for act done.	112	Words "the last preceding section" is replaced by "section 51".
53	Liability of abettor for an effect caused by the act abetted different from that intended by the abettor.	113	No change.
54	Abettor present when offence committed.	114	No change.
55	Abetment of offence punishable with death or imprisonment for life.	115	No change.

56	Abetment of offence punishable with imprisonment.	116	The words "if offence be not committed" are excluded from the heading. The heading of paragraph 2, "If abettor or person abetted be a public servant whose duty it is to prevent offence" is excluded. The word "by" is replaced by "under"
57	Abetting commission of offence by the public or by more than ten persons.	117	Imprisonment is increased from three years to seven years.
58	Concealing design to commit offence punishable with death or imprisonment for life.	118	Words "in either case" are excluded from clause (b).
59	Public servant concealing design to commit offence which it is his duty to prevent.	119	No change.
60	Concealing design to commit offence punishable with imprisonment.	120	No change.
61(1)	Criminal conspiracy definition.	120A	IPC section is included as sub-section in BNS.

61(2)	Criminal conspiracy punishment.	120B	IPC section is included as sub-section in BNS, sans heading.
62	Punishment for attempting to commit offences punishable with imprisonment for life or other imprisonment.	511	No change.
63	Rape definition.	375	Age of Consent: 15 years is replaced by 18 years in BNS. Exception 2 of Section 63 states that "sexual intercourse or acts by a man with his wife, the wife not being under 18 years of age, is not rape".
64	Punishment for rape.	376(1) & 376(2)	Word "military" is replaced with "army".
65(1)	Punishment for rape in certain cases- rape on a woman under sixteen years.	376(3)	No change.
65(2)	Punishment for rape in certain cases- rape on a woman under twelve years.	376AB	Section is included as sub-section in BNS sans heading.
66	Punishment for causing death or resulting in persistent vegetative state of victim.	376A	No change.

67	Sexual intercourse by husband upon his wife during separation.	376B	No change.
68	Sexual intercourse by a person in authority.	376C	No change.
69	Sexual intercourse by employing deceitful means etc.	-	"Whoever, by deceitful means or by making promise to marry to a woman without any intention of fulfilling the same, has sexual intercourse with her, such sexual intercourse not amounting to the offence of rape, shall be punished with imprisonment of either description for a term which may extend to ten years and shall also be liable to fine. Explanation. — "deceitful means" shall include inducement for, or false promise of employment or promotion, or marrying by suppressing identity."
70(1)	Gang rape.	376D	No Change except IPC section is included as subsection in BNS.

70(2)	Gang rape on women under the age of eighteen.	376DB	In 376DB IPC, the age of the victim is 12 years, and punishment is the death penalty. In 70(2) BNS, the age of the victim is under 18 years, and punishment is the death penalty. Section is included as a sub-section in BNS, sans heading.
71	Punishment for repeat offenders.	376E	No change.
72	Disclosure of identity of victim of certain offences etc.	228A (1)/(2)	Word "minor' is replaced by 'child'.
73	Printing or publishing any matter relating to court proceedings without permission.	228A (3)	Sub-section of IPC is treated as individual section in BNS with heading.
74	Assault or use of criminal force to woman with intent to outrage her modesty.	354	No change.
75	Sexual harassment.	354A	No change.
76	Assault or use of criminal force to woman with intent disrobe.	354B	Words "Any man who" is replaced by "Whoever".
77	Voyeurism.	354C	Ditto.
78	Stalking.	354D	No change.

79	Word, gesture or act intended to insult the modesty of a woman.	509	No change.
80	Dowry death.	304B	No change.
81	Cohabitation caused by man deceitfully inducing belief of lawful marriage.	493	No change.
82(1)	Marrying again during lifetime of husband or wife.	494	IPC section is included as a sub-section.
82(2)	Marrying again during lifetime of husband or wife with concealment of former marriage from person with whom subsequent marriage is contracted.	495	IPC section is included as sub-section in BNS sans heading. Words "defined in last preceding section" are excluded.
83	Marriage ceremony fraudulently gone through without lawful marriage.	496	No change.
84	Enticing or taking away or detaining with criminal intent a married Woman.	498	The words "from that man or from any person having the care of her on behalf of that man" are excluded.

85	Husband or relative of husband of a woman subjecting her to cruelty.	498A	No change.
86	Cruelty defined.	498A Explanation	IPC Section 498A has been bifurcated into Sections 85 and 86. The IPC explanation part has been provided in Section 86 BNS under the heading Cruelty defined.
87	Kidnapping or abducting in order to murder or for ransom, etc.	366	No change.
88	Causing miscarriage.	312	No change.
89	Causing miscarriage without woman's consent.	313	In place of words "defined in last preceding section" previous section number is mentioned in BNS.
90	Death caused by act done with intent to cause miscarriage.	314	Heading of para-2 "if act done without woman's consent" is excluded. The words "Where the act referred to in sub-section (1)" are added.

91	Act done with intent to prevent child being born alive or to cause it to die after birth.	315	No change.
92	Causing death of quick unborn child by act amounting to culpable homicide.	316	No change.
93	Exposure and abandonment of child under twelve years, by parent or person having care of it.	317	No change.
94	Concealment of birth by secret disposal of dead body.	318	No change.
95	Hiring, employing or engaging a child to commit an offence.	-	"Whoever hires, employs or engages any child to commit an offence shall be punished with imprisonment of either description which shall not be less than three years but which may extend to ten years, and with fine; and if the offence be committed shall also be punished with the punishment provided for that offence as if the offence has been committed by such person himself.

			Explanation. —Hiring, employing, engaging or using a child for sexual exploitation or pornography is covered within the meaning of this section".
96	Procuration of child.	366A	Words "minor girl under the age of eighteen years" are replaced by word "child" and made gender neutral.
97	Kidnapping or abducting child under ten years with intent to steal from its person.	369	No change.
98	Selling minor for purposes of prostitution, etc.	372	"minor" is replaced by "child" in heading and words "any person under the age of eighteen years" are replaced by the word "child'.
99	Buying minor for purposes of prostitution, etc.	373	Minimum mandatory punishment is introduced as seven years, and the upper limit of imprisonment is extended up to fourteen

			years in BNS, in place of ten years in IPC. Words “any person under the age of eighteen years” are replaced by the word "child'.
100	Culpable homicide.	299	No change.
101	Murder.	300	Formal changes, but essence is the same, Secondly, thirdly, and fourthly, are replaced by clauses (a), (b), (c), and (d). The word “it” is replaced by the words "the act by which death is caused".
102	Culpable homicide by causing death of person other than person whose death was intended.	301	No change.
103 (1)	Punishment for murder.	302	No Change, except IPC section is included as subsection in BNS.
103 (2)	Punishment for murder.	-	“When a group of five or more persons acting in concert commits murder on the ground of race, caste or community, sex, place of birth, language, personal belief or any other similar ground each member of such group shall be punished with death or with
104	Punishment for murder by life-convict.	303	

			imprisonment for life, and shall also be liable to fine”.
			BNS gives an alternate punishment for the life-convict murderer as death 'or with imprisonment for life, which shall mean the remainder of that person’s natural life', whereas in IPC, only punishment is a death sentence for murder by a life convict.
105	Punishment for culpable homicide not amounting to murder.	304	Minimum imprisonment for five years is added and fine is made mandatory.
106 (1)	Causing death by negligence.	304A	IPC section is included as subsection in BNS. Imprisonment is increased and offence by registered medical practitioner and its explanation are added.
106 (2)	Causing death by negligence.	-	This is a new addition, but it will not come into force from 1st July 2024 with other new laws, it is kept on hold.
107	Abetment of suicide of child or person of unsound mind.	305	Formal changes but essence is same- 'insane person' is replaced by 'person of unsound mind'.

108	Abetment of suicide.	306	No change.
109	Attempt to murder.	307	Under IPC, Section 307 Clause 2 prescribes the death penalty only for an attempt to murder by a life-convict, but alternate punishment is given in Section 109(2) of the BNS, which states that "be punished with death or with imprisonment for life, which shall mean the remainder of that person's natural life".
110	Attempt to commit culpable homicide.	308	No change.years, and shall also be liable to fine".

111	Organized crime.	-	Newly added section. "Any continuing unlawful activity including kidnapping, robbery, vehicle theft, extortion, land grabbing, contract killing, economic offence, cyber- crimes, trafficking of persons, drugs, weapons or illicit goods or services, human trafficking for prostitution or ransom, by any person or a group of persons acting in concert, singly or jointly, either as a member of an organized crime syndicate or on behalf of such syndicate, by use of violence, threat of violence, intimidation, coercion, or by any other unlawful means to obtain direct or indirect material benefit including a financial benefit, shall constitute organised crime".
112	Petty organized crime.	-	Newly added section. "Whoever, being a member of a group or gang, either singly or jointly, commits any act of theft, snatching, cheating, unauthorised selling of tickets,

			unauthorised betting or gambling, selling of public examination question papers or any other similar criminal act, is said to commit petty organised crime".
113	Terrorist act.	-	Newly added section.
114	Hurt.	319	No change.
115 (1)	Voluntarily causing hurt.	321	No Change except IPC section is included as subsection in BNS.
115 (2)	Punishment for voluntarily causing hurt.	323	Section is included as sub-section in BNS sans heading. Fine is increased (which may extend to ten thousand rupees).
116	Grievous hurt definition.	320	Suffering threshold period for grievous hurt is reduced from twenty days to fifteen days.
117 (1)	Voluntarily causing grievous hurt punishment.	322	No change.

117 (2)	Punishment for voluntarily causing grievous hurt.	325	Formal changes but essence is same.
117 (3)	Voluntarily causing grievous hurt.	-	New addition. "Whoever commits an offence under sub-section (*1*) and in the course of such commission causes any hurt to a person which causes that person to be in permanent disability or in persistent vegetative state, shall be punished with rigorous imprisonment for a term which shall not be less than ten years but which may extend to imprisonment for life, which shall mean imprisonment for the remainder of that person's natural life".
117 (4)	Voluntarily causing grievous hurt.	-	New addition. "When a group of five or more persons acting in concert, causes grievous hurt to a person on the ground of his race, caste or community, sex, place of birth, language, personal belief or any other similar ground, each member of such group shall be guilty of the offence of causing grievous

			hurt, and shall be punished with imprisonment of either description for a term which may extend to seven
118 (1)	Voluntarily causing hurt or grievous hurt by dangerous weapons or means.	324	IPC section is included as a sub-section in BNS. Fine is increased which may extend to twenty thousand rupees and words "'grievous hurt" are added in heading.
118 (2)	Voluntarily causing hurt or grievous hurt by dangerous weapons or means.	326	IPC section is included as a sub-section in BNS sans heading. Mandatory minimum imprisonment for one year is added.
119 (1)	Voluntarily causing hurt or grievous hurt to extort property, or to constrain to an illegal act.	327	No change except that the IPC section is included as a sub-section in BNS.
119 (2)	Voluntarily causing hurt or grievous hurt to extort property, or to constrain to an illegal act.	329	IPC section is included as a sub-section in BNS sans heading. The words "any purpose referred to in sub-section (1)" is added.
120 (1)	Voluntarily causing hurt or grievous hurt to extort confession or to compel	330	IPC section is included as a sub-section in BNS.

	restoration of property.		
120 (2)	Voluntarily causing grievous hurt to extort confession, or to compel restoration of property.	331	IPC section is included as a sub-section in BNS sans heading. Words "any purpose referred to in sub-section (1)" are added.
121 (1)	Voluntarily causing hurt to deter public servant from his duty.	332	IPC section is included as a subsection in BNS. Imprisonment is increased from three to five years.
121 (2)	Voluntarily causing grievous hurt to deter public servant from his duty.	333	IPC section is included as a sub-section in BNS sans heading. Mandatory minimum imprisonment of one year is added.
122 (1)	Voluntarily causing provocation hurt on.	334	IPC section is included as a subsection in BNS. Fine is increased from five hundred to five thousand rupees
122 (2)	Voluntarily causing grievous hurt on provocation.	335	IPC section is included as a sub-section in BNS sans heading. Imprisonment is increased from four to five years and fine is increased from two thousand to ten thousand rupees.
123	Causing harm by means of poison etc with intent to commit an offence.	328	No change.

124 (1)	Voluntarily causing grievous hurt by use of acid etc.	326A	The IPC section is included as a subsection in BNS. Words "causes a person to be in a permanent vegetative state" are added in Section 124(1) of the BNS.
124 (2)	Voluntarily causing grievous hurt by throwing or attempting to throw acid.	326B	IPC section is included as a sub-section in BNS, sans heading. Words "permanent vegetative state" are added
125	Act endangering life or personal safety of others.	336	Fine is increased from rupees two hundred and fifty to two thousand five hundred.
125 (a)	Where hurt is caused.	337	Fine is increased from five hundred to five thousand rupees.
125 (b)	Where grievous hurt is caused.	338	Imprisonment is increased from two years to three years and fine is increased from one thousand to ten thousand rupees.
126 (1)	Wrongful restraint.	339	IPC section is included as a subsection in BNS.
126 (2)	Punishment for Wrongful restraint.	341	IPC section is included as a sub-section in BNS, sans heading. Fine is increased from five hundred rupees to five thousand rupees.

127 (1)	Wrongful confinement.	340	IPC section is included as a subsection in BNS.
127 (2)	Punishment for Wrongful confinement.	342	IPC section is included as a sub-section in BNS sans heading. Fine is increased from one thousand to five thousand rupees.
127 (3)	Wrongful confinement for three or more days.	343	The IPC section is included as a sub-section in the BNS sans heading. Imprisonment is increased from two years to three years, and the fine is extended up to ten thousand rupees.
127 (4)	Wrongful confinement for ten or more days.	344	The IPC section is included as a sub-section in the BNS sans heading. Imprisonment is increased from three to five years, and a minimum fine of ten thousand rupees is stipulated.
127 (5)	Wrongful confinement of person for whose liberation writ has been issued.	345	IPC section is included as a sub-section in BNS sans heading. Fine is added.
127 (6)	Wrongful confinement in secret.	346	IPC section is included as a sub-section in BNS sans heading. Imprisonment is increased from two to three years and fine is added

127 (7)	Wrongful confinement to extort property, or constrain to illegal act.	347	No Change except that IPC section is included as a sub-section in BNS.
127 (8)	Wrongful confinement to extort confession, or compel restoration of property.	348	IPC section is included as a sub-section in BNS sans heading. No other change.
128	Force.	349	There is a change in phraseology; also, first, secondly, and thirdly have been replaced with (a), (b), and (c).
129	Criminal force.	350	No change.
130	Assault.	351	No change.
131	Punishment for assault or criminal force otherwise than on grave provocation.	352	Fine is increased from five hundred to one thousand rupees.
132	Assault or criminal force to deter public servant from discharge of his duty.	353	No change.
133	Assault or criminal force with intent to dishonour person, otherwise than on grave provocation.	355	No change.

134	Assault or criminal force in attempt to commit theft of property carried by a person.	356	No change.
135	Assault or criminal force in attempt to wrongfully confine a person.	357	Fine is increased from one thousand to five thousand rupees.
136	Assault or criminal force on grave provocation.	358	Fine is increased from two hundred to one thousand rupees.
137 (1)	Kidnapping.	359	IPC section is included as a sub-section in BNS.
137 (1) (a)	Kidnapping from India.	360	Ditto.
137 (1) (b)	Kidnapping from lawful guardianship.	361	The IPC section is included as a clause in the BNS. Words "minor under the age of sixteen years of male or under eighteen years of age if a female" are replaced by "child" thus making it gender neutral.

137 (2)	Punishment for kidnapping.	363	IPC section is included as a sub-section in BNS sans heading.
138	Abduction.	362	No change.
139	Kidnapping or maiming a child for purposes of begging.	363A,	The word "minor" is replaced by "child". The word "rigorous" is added. Imprisonment is extended up to life, i.e., imprisonment for the remainder of that person's natural life. The clause (b) of sub-section (4) definition is excluded.
140 (1)	Kidnapping or abducting in order to murder, etc.	364	No Change except that IPC section is included as a sub-section in BNS.
140 (2)	Kidnapping for ransom, etc.	364A	Section is included as a sub-section in BNS sans heading.
140 (3)	Kidnapping or abducting with intent secretly and wrongfully to confine person.	365	Ditto.
140 (4)	Kidnapping or abducting in order to subject person to	367	Ditto.

	grievous hurt, slavery, etc.		
141	Importation of girl or boy from foreign country.	366B	Words "any boy under the age of eighteen years" added and "she" is replaced by "girl or boy".
142	Wrongfully concealing or keeping in confinement, kidnapped or abducted person.	368	No change.
143	Trafficking of person.	370	Word "minor" is replaced by "child".
144	Exploitation of a trafficked person.	370A	The upper limit of imprisonment is increased from seven years to ten years, and for sub- section (2), from five years to seven years. "minor" is replaced by "child".
145	Habitual dealing in slaves.	371	No change.
146	Unlawful compulsory labour.	374	No change.

147	Waging, or attempting to wage war. or abetting waging of war, against the Government of India.	121	No change.
148	Conspiracy to commit offences punishable by Section 147.	121A	"and beyond" is added.
149	Collecting arms, etc., with intention of waging war against the Government of India.	122	No change.
150	Concealing with intent to facilitate design to wage war.	123	No change.
151	Assaulting President, Governor, etc., with intent to compel or restrain the exercise of any lawful power.	124	No change.

152	Act endangering sovereignty, unity and integrity of India.	-	Newly added section. "Whoever, purposely or knowingly, by words, either spoken or written, or by signs, or by visible representation, or by electronic communication or by use of financial mean, or otherwise, excites or attempts to excite, secession or armed rebellion or subversive activities, or encourages feelings of separatist activities or endangers sovereignty or unity and integrity of India; or indulges in or commits any such act shall be punished with imprisonment for life or With imprisonment which may extend to seven years, and shall also be liable to fine."
153	Waging war against Government of any Foreign State at peace with Government of India.	125	Words "any Asiatic power in alliance" are replaced by "Government of any foreign State at peace".
154	Committing depredation on territories of Foreign State at peace with Government of India.	126	Words "any power in alliance" are replaced by "any foreign State".

155	Receiving property taken by war or depredation mentioned in Sections 153 and 154.	127	No change.
156	Public servant voluntarily allowing prisoner of State or war to escape.	128	No change.
157	Public servant negligently suffering such prisoner to escape.	129	No change.
158	Aiding escape of, rescuing or harbouring such prisoner.	130	No change.
159	Abetting mutiny, attempting to seduce a soldier, sailor or airman from his duty.	131	No change.
160	Abetment of mutiny, if mutiny is committed in consequence thereof.	132	Upper limit of imprisonment is increased from three years to ten years.
161	Abetment of assault by soldier, sailor or airman on his superior officer, when in execution of his office.	133	No change.

162	Abetment of such assault, if the assault is committed.	134	No change.
163	Abetment of desertion of soldier, sailor or airman.	135	No change.
164	Harbouring deserter.	136	Word "wife" is replaced by "spouse" in the exception of this section thereby made gender nuetral.
165	Deserter concealed on board, of master merchant vessel through negligence.	137	Upper limit of fine is increased from five hundred to three thousand rupees.
166	Abetment of act of insubordination by soldier, sailor or airman.	138	Upper limit of imprisonment is increased from six months to two years.
167	Persons subject to certain Acts.	139	No change.
168	Wearing garb or carrying token used by soldier, sailor or airman.	140	"Military" is replaced by "Army." The upper limit of the fine has been increased from five hundred to two thousand rupees.
169	Candidate, electoral right defined.	171A	No change.
170	Bribery.	171B	No change.

171	Undue influence at elections.	171C	No change.
172	Personation at elections.	171D	No change.
173	Punishment for bribery.	171E	No change.
174	Punishment for undue influence or personation at an election.	171F	No change.
175	False statement in connection with an election.	171G	No change.
176	Illegal payment in connection with an election.	171H	Upper limit of fine is increased from five hundred to ten thousand rupees.
177	Failure to keep election accounts.	171-I	Upper limit of fine is increased from five hundred to five thousand rupees.
178	Counterfeiting coin, Government stamps, currency- notes or bank- notes.	230 to 232, 246 to 249, 255, 489A	Nine sections of IPC have been covered in this single section of BNS. Thus, in a single stroke, the number of sections and offences

			Has been reduced by eight. Illustrations given u/s 230 IPC are excluded.
179	Using as genuine, forged or counterfeit coin, Government stamp, currency-notes or bank-notes.	237 to 241, 250, 251, 254, 258, 260, 489B	Eleven sections of IPC have been covered in this single section of BNS. Thus, in a single stroke, the number of section and offences has been reduced by ten.
180	Possession of forged or counterfeit coin, Government stamp, currency- notes or bank-notes.	242, 243, 252, 253, 259, 489C	Six sections of IPC have been covered in this single section of BNS. Thus, in a single stroke, the number of sections and offences has been reduced by five. and 'not constitute an offence' is added.
181	Making or possessing instruments or materials for forging or counterfeiting coin, govt stamps, currency notes or bank notes.	233 / 234 / 235 / 256 / 257 / 489D	Six sections of IPC have been covered in this single section of BNS. Thus, in a single stroke, the number of sections and offences has been reduced by five, and 'any coin, stamp issued by Government for the purpose of revenue' is added.
182	Making or using documents	489E	Upper limit of fine is increased from one hundred to three hundred rupees and

	resembling currency-notes or bank- notes.		two hundred to six hundred rupees.
183	Effacing, writing from substance bearing Government stamp, removing from document a stamp used for it, with intent to cause loss to Government.	261	No change.
184	Using Government stamp known to have been before used.	262	No change.
185	Erasure of mark denoting that stamp has been used.	263	No change.
186	Prohibition of fictitious stamps.	263A	Words "'and also in any part of Her Majesty's dominions" are excluded.
187	Person employed in mint causing coin to be of different weight or composition from that fixed by law.	244	No change.
188	Unlawfully taking coining instrument from mint.	245	No change.

189 (1)	Unlawful assembly.	141	First, second, third, fourth, fifth, have been replaced by (a),(b),(c), (d) and(e).
189 (2)	Unlawful assembly-Being member of unlawful assembly.	142	Section is included as a sub-section in BNS sans heading. No other Changes.
189 (3)	Unlawful assembly-Joining or continuing in unlawful assembly, knowing it has been commanded to disperse.	145	Ditto.
189 (4)	Unlawful assembly-Joining unlawful assembly armed with deadly weapon. —	144	Ditto.
189 (5)	Unlawful assembly-Knowingly joining or continuing in assembly of five or more persons after it has been commanded to disperse. —	151	Ditto.
189 (6)	Unlawful assembly-Hiring, or conniving at hiring, of persons to join unlawful assembly.	150	Ditto.

189 (7)	Unlawful assembly-Harbouring persons hired for an unlawful assembly.	157	Ditto.
189 (8)/ (9)	Unlawful assembly-Being hired to take part in an unlawful assembly or riot. Or to go armed.	158	IPC Section 158 both paragraphs, are reproduced in two different sub-sections (8) and (9) of 189 BNS sans heading.
190	Every member of unlawful assembly guilty of offence committed in prosecution of common object.	149	No change.
191 (1)	Rioting-Offence defined.	146	This IPC section defines the offence which is included in BNS as a sub-section.
191 (2)	Rioting- Punishment for rioting.	147	IPC section is included as a sub-section in BNS, sans heading.
191 (3)	Rioting- Being armed with deadly weapon. —	148	IPC section is included as a sub-section in BNS, sans heading. Upper limit ofimprisonment is increased from three years to five years.

192	Wantonly giving provocation with intent to cause riot if rioting be committed if not committed.	153	No change.
193 (1)	Liability of owner, occupier, etc., of land on which an unlawful assembly or riot takes place.	154	Section is included as a sub-section in BNS. Words "Liability of" and "or riot" are added in the heading.
193 (2)	Liability of person for whose benefit riot is committed.	155	Section is included as a sub-section in BNS sans heading.
193 (3)	Liability of agent of owner or occupier for whose benefit riot is committed.	156	Ditto.
194 (1)	Affray- defined.	159	IPC section is included as a subsection in BNS.
194 (2)	Punishment for Affray.	160	Section is included as a sub-section in BNS sans heading. Upper limit of fine is increased from one hundred to one thousand rupees.

195 (1)	Assaulting or obstructing public servant when suppressing riot, etc.	152	The Section 152 in the IPC regarding 'assaulting or obstructing public servants when suppressing riots, etc.' has been divided into two parts and included in Section 195 of the new law (BNS): one for the offence of assaulted in the section of public servants and the other for threatening to assault or attempt to obstruct, having different punishments and fines. The minimum threshold for a fine is twenty-five thousand rupees, and ‘or uses criminal force on any public servant' is added.
195 (2)	Assaulting or obstructing public servant when suppressing riot, etc.	152	In cases where the offender threatens to assault or attempts to obstruct a public servant or threatens or attempts to use criminal force on a public servant in the described situations, the punishment includes imprisonment of a term that may extend to one year. A fine may also be imposed under this sub-section. This is a rare case of a reduction in punishment.

196	Promoting enmity between different groups on grounds of religion, race, place of birth, residence, language, etc., and doing acts prejudicial to maintenance of harmony.	153A	The word "or through electronic communication" is added as one of the modes of spreading disharmony, etc.
197	Imputations, assertions prejudicial to national integration.	153B	Words "or through electronic communication" as the mode of spreading specified activities are added.
197 (1)d	Makes or publishes false or misleading information, jeopardising the sovereignty, unity and integrity or security of India.	New	New Clause 197(1) (d) "makes or publishes false or misleading information, jeopardising the sovereignty, unity and integrity or security of India".
198	Public servant disobeying law, with intent to cause injury to any person.	166	No change.
199	Public servant disobeying direction under law.	166A	No change.

200	Punishment for non-treatment of victim.	166B	No change.
201	Public servant framing an incorrect document with intent to cause injury.	167	No change.
202	Public servant unlawfully engaging in trade.	168	New punishment of "community service" is added.
203	Public servant unlawfully buying or bidding for property.	169	No change.
204	Personating a public servant.	170	Mandatory minimum imprisonment is introduced as six months and upper limit is increased from two years to three years.
205	Wearing garb or carrying token used by public servant with fraudulent intent.	171	Upper limit of fine is increased from rupees two hundred to five thousand.
206	Absconding to avoid service of summons or other proceeding.	172	The upper limit of the fine is increased from five hundred to five thousand rupees and one

			thousand to ten thousand rupees; 'Court of justice' is replaced by 'Court' etc.
207	Preventing service of summons or other proceeding, or preventing publication thereof.	173	Ditto.
208	Non-attendance in obedience to an order from public servant.	174	Ditto.
209	Non-appearance in response to a proclamation under section 84 of Bharatiya Nagarik Suraksha Sanhita, 2023.	174A	New punishment of "as with community service" is added in regard to proclamation under section 84 (1) BNSS [82(1) CrPC].
210	Omission to produce document or electronic record to public servant by person, legally bound to produce it.	175	The upper limit of the fine has been increased from five hundred to five thousand rupees and from one thousand to ten thousand rupees. "Or if" is replaced by "where" 'Court of Justice' is replaced by 'Court'.

211	Omission to give notice or information to public servant by person legally bound to give it.	176	Upper limit of fine are increased from five hundred to five thousand rupees and one thousand to ten thousand rupees.
212	Furnishing false information.	177	The upper limit of the fine has been increased from one thousand to five thousand rupees. "Bound under clause 5, section VII, Regulation III, 1821,of the Bengal Code" is replaced by "legally bound" in the illustration (b).
213	Refusing oath or affirmation when duly required by public servant to make it.	178	Upper limit of fine is increased from one thousand to five thousand rupees.
214	Refusing to answer public servant authorised to question.	179	Ditto.
215	Refusing to sign statement.	180	Upper limit of fine is increased from five hundred to three thousand rupees.
216	False statement on oath or affirmation to public servant or person authorised to	181	No change.

	administer an oath or affirmation.		
217	False information, with intent to cause public servant to use his lawful power to the injury of another person.	182	The upper limit of imprisonment increased from six months to one year, and the fine increased from one thousand to ten thousand rupees.
218	Resistance to the taking of property by the lawful authority of a public servant.	183	Upper limit of fine has been increased from one thousand to ten thousand rupees.
219	Obstructing sale of property offered by authority of public servant for sale.	184	Upper limit of fine has been increased from five hundred to five thousand rupees.
220	Illegal purchase or bid for property offered for sale by authority of public servant.	185	No change.
221	Obstructing public servant in discharge of public functions.	186	Upper limit of fine is increased from five hundred to two thousand and five hundred rupees.

222	Omission to assist public servant when bound by law to give assistance.	187	Section is reorganised in the form of clauses (a) and (b) without changing the essence, and the upper limit of the fine is increased from two hundred to two thousand and five hundred rupees and five hundred to five thousand rupees.
223	Disobedience to order duly promulgated by public servant.	188	The section is reorganised in the form of clauses (a) and (b). In clause (a), the upper limit of imprisonment is increased from one month to six months, and the fine is increased from two hundred to two thousand and five hundred rupees. In clause (b), the limit of imprisonment is increased from six months to one year, and the fine from one thousand rupees to five thousand rupees.
224	Threat of injury to public servant.	189	No change.
225	Threat of injury to induce person to	190	No change.

	refrain from applying for protection.		
226	Attempt to commit suicide to compel or restrain from applying or restrain of lawful power.	new	"Whoever attempts to commit suicide with the intent to compel or restrain any public servant from discharging his official duty shall be punished with simple imprisonment for a term which may extend to one year, or with fine, or with both, or with community service".
227	Giving false evidence.	191	No change.
228	Fabricating false evidence.	192	No change.
229	Punishment for false evidence.	193	Fine is defined in sub-section (1) as up to ten thousand rupees and in sub-section (2) as up to five thousand rupees.
230	Giving or fabricating false evidence with intent to procure conviction of capital offence.	194	Fine defined in this section as up to fifty thousand rupees.

231	Giving or fabricating false evidence with intent to procure conviction of offence punishable with imprisonment for life or imprisonment.	195	No change.
232	Threatening any person to give false evidence.	195A	Reorganized in form of sub-section (1) and (2) without changing a word.
233	Using evidence known to be false.	196	No change.
234	Issuing or signing false certificate.	197	No change.
235	Using as true a certificate known to be false.	198	No change.
236	False statement made in declaration which is by law receivable as evidence.	199	Words “Court of Justice” is replaced by “Court”.
237	Using as true such declaration knowing it to be false.	200	“This section” is used instead of "200" (section) in the explanation of IPC u/s 200 IPC.

238	Causing disappearance of evidence, or giving false information to screen offender.	201	Clauses named as (a), (b), (c) sans heading.
239	Intentional omission to give information of offence by person bound to inform.	202	Fine defined in this section is five thousand rupees, whereas in IPC fine is not defined.
240	Giving false information respecting an offence committed.	203	No change.
241	Destruction of document or electronic record to prevent its production as evidence.	204	The upper limit is imprisonment from two years to three years, and the fine is defined as up to five thousand rupees.
242	False personation for purpose of act or proceeding in suit or prosecution.	205	No change.
243	Fraudulent removal or concealment of property to prevent its seizure as forfeited or in execution.	206	The upper limit of imprisonment increased from two years to three years, and the fine is defined as up to five thousand rupees. "Court of

			Justice" is replaced by "Court".
244	Fraudulent claim to property to prevent its seizure as forfeited or in execution.	207	"Court of Justice" is replaced by "Court".
245	Fraudulently suffering decree for sum not due.	208	No change.
246	Dishonestly making false claim in Court.	209	"'Court of Justice" is replaced by 'Court'.
247	Fraudulently obtaining decree for sum not due.	210	IPC section is reorganized in form of clauses (a), (b) in BNS.
248	False charge of offence made with intent to injure.	211	The upper limit of imprisonment is increased from two years to five years and from seven years to ten years, and the fine is defined as up to two lakh rupees.
249	Harbouring offender.	212	Section is reorganized in form of clauses (a), (b) and (c) and sub-headings are dropped.

			'husband or wife' is replaced by 'spouse'.
250	Taking gift, etc., to screen an offender from punishment.	213	Formal change but essence is same. Section is reorganized in form of clauses (a), (b) and (c) and sub-headings are dropped.
251	Offering gift or restoration of property in consideration of screening offender.	214	Ditto.
252	Taking gift to help to recover stolen property, etc.	215	No change.
253	Harbouring offender who has escaped from custody or whose apprehension has been ordered.	216	Section is reorganized in form of clauses (a), (b) And (c) and sub-headings are dropped. "Husband or wife" is replaced by "spouse".
254	Penalty for harbouring robbers or dacoits.	216A	Formal changes but essence is same- "husband or wife" is replaced by "spouse".
255	Public servant disobeying direction of law with intent to	217	No change.

	save person from punishment or property from forfeiture.		
256	Public servant framing incorrect record or writing with intent to save person from punishment or property from forfeiture.	218	No change.
257	Public servant in judicial proceeding corruptly making report, etc. contrary to law.	219	No change.
258	Commitment for trial or confinement by person having authority who knows that he is acting contrary to law.	220	No change.
259	Intentional omission to apprehend on part of public servant bound to apprehend.	221	Section is reorganized in form of clauses (a), (b) and (c).
260	Intentional omission to apprehend on part of public servant	222	Ditto.

	bound to apprehend person under sentence or lawfully committed.		
261	Escape from confinement or custody negligently suffered by public servant.	223	No change.
262	Resistance or obstruction by a person to his lawful apprehension.	224	No change.
263	Resistance or obstruction to lawful apprehension of another person.	225	Section is reorganized in form of clauses (a), (b) and (c).
264	Omission to apprehend, or sufferance of escape, on part of public servant, in cases not otherwise provided for.	225A	No change.
265	Resistance or obstruction to lawful apprehension or escape or rescue in	225B	No change.

	cases not otherwise provided for.		
266	Violation of condition of remission of punishment.	227	No change.
267	Intentional insult or interruption to public servant sitting in judicial proceeding.	228	Upper limit of fine is increased from one thousand to five thousand rupees.
268	Personation of assessor.	229	In heading "Personation of assessor" is used in place of "juror or assessor" and word "juryman" is excluded.
269	Failure by person released on bail or bond to appear in Court.	229A	No change.
270	Public nuisance.	268	Two paragraphs were merged together with the help of the coordinating conjunction "but".
271	Negligent act likely to spread infection of	269	No change.

	disease dangerous to life.		
272	Malignant act likely to spread infection of disease dangerous to life.	270	No change.
273	Disobedience to quarantine rule.	271	Word "vessel" is replaced by the phrase “mode of transport etc.”
274	Adulteration of food or drink intended for sale.	272	Upper limit of fine is increased from one thousand to five thousand rupees.
275	Sale of noxious food or drink.	273	Upper limit of fine is increased from one thousand to five thousand rupees.
276	Adulteration of drugs.	274	Upper limit of imprisonment is increased from six months to one years and fine is increased from one thousand to five thousand rupees.
277	Sale of adulterated drugs.	275	Upper limit of fine is increased from one thousand to five thousand rupees.

278	Sale of drug as a different drug or preparation.	276	The upper limit of fine is increased from one thousand to five thousand rupees.
279	Fouling water of public spring or reservoir.	277	The upper limit of the imprisonment is increased from three months to six months and fine is increased from five hundred to five thousand rupees.
280	Making atmosphere noxious to health.	278	The upper limit of the fine is increased from five hundred to one thousand rupees.
281	Rash driving or riding on a public way.	279	No change.
282	Rash navigation of vessel.	280	The upper limit of the fine has been increased from one thousand to ten thousand rupees. .
283	Exhibition of false light, mark or buoy.	281	Fine is added as punishment in addition to imprisonment rupees ten thousand is fixed as lower limit of fine. Word "and" has replaced "or".

284	Conveying person by water for hire in unsafe or overloaded vessel.	282	The upper limit of the fine is increased from one thousand to five thousand rupees.
285	Danger or obstruction in public way or line of navigation.	283	The upper limit of the fine is increased from two hundred to five thousand rupees.
286	Negligent conduct with respect to poisonous substance.	284	The upper limit of the fine is increased from one thousand to five thousand rupees.
287	Negligent conduct with respect to fire or combustible matter.	285	The upper limit of the fine is increased from one thousand to two thousand rupees.
288	Negligent conduct with respect to explosive substance.	286	The upper limit of the fine is increased from one thousand to five thousand rupees.
289	Negligent conduct with respect to machinery.	287	Upper limit of the fine is increased from one thousand to five thousand rupees.
290	Negligent conduct with respect to pulling down,	288	BNS added "or constructing".

	repairing or constructing buildings, etc.		The upper limit of the fine is increased from one thousand to five thousand rupees. "Measures" replaces "order".
291	Negligent conduct with respect to animal.	289	Word "measure" replaces "order" The upper limit of the fine is increased from one thousand to five thousand rupees.
292	Punishment for public nuisance in cases not otherwise provided for.	290	The upper limit of the fine is increased from two hundred to one thousand rupees.
293	Continuance of nuisance after injunction to discontinue.	291	Fine is defined as up to five thousand rupees.
294	Sale, etc., of obscene books, etc.	292	The fine is increased from two thousand to five thousand rupees and from five thousand to ten thousand rupees on subsequent conviction. "Including display of any content in electronic form'" is added. "In whatever manner" is also added.

295	Sale, etc., of obscene objects to young person.	293	"Person under the age of twenty years" is replaced by "child", thereby curtailing the scope of this provision.
296	Obscene acts and songs.	294	Fine is defined as up to one thousand rupees.
297	Keeping lottery office.	294A	The upper limit of the fine is increased from one thousand to five thousand rupees.
298	Injuring or defiling place of worship with intent to insult the religion of any class.	295	No change.
299	Deliberate and malicious acts intended to outrage religious feelings of any class, by insulting its religion or religious beliefs.	295A	Words "or through electronic means" are added.
300	Disturbing religious assembly.	296	No change.
301	Trespassing on burial places, etc.	297	No change.

302	Uttering words, etc., with deliberate intent to wound the religious feelings of any person.	298	No change.
303 (1)	Theft.	378	IPC section is included as sub section. "Definition" is replaced by "Section" in explanation 5.
303 (2)	Punishment for theft.	379	Punishment for subsequent convictions is added.
304	Snatching.	-	New addition.
305	Theft in a dwelling house, or means of transportation or place of worship, etc.	380	The definition enlarged "means of transportation or place of worship,' is added in the heading is reframed containing various sub-sections wherein sub-sections (b), (c), (d), (e) Are new additions.
306	Theft by clerk or servant of property in possession of master.	381	No change.
307	Theft after preparation made for causing death, hurt or	382	No change.

	restraint in order to committing of theft.		
308 (1)	Extortion.	383	Clause (e) is newly added in the illustrations.
308 (2)	Extortion punishment.	384	IPC section is included as a sub-section in BNS sans heading. The upper limit of the imprisonment is increased from three years to seven years.
308 (3)	Putting person in fear of injury in order to commit extortion.	385	IPC section is included as a sub-section in BNS sans heading. No other change.
308 (4)	Putting person in fear of death or of grievous hurt, in order to commit extortion.	387	Ditto.
308 (5)	Extortion by putting a person in fear of death or grievous hurt.	386	Ditto.
308 (6)	Extortion by threat of accusation of an offence punishable with death or imprisonment for life, etc.	388	IPC section is included as a sub-section in BNS sans heading. Words "and, if the offence by punishable under section 377 of this Code, may be punished with imprisonment for life" are

			removed as the section 377 IPC has been excluded altogether.
308 (7)	Putting person in fear or accusation of offence, in order to commit extortion.	389	Ditto.
309 (1), (2), (3)	Robbery- When theft is robbery When extortion is robbery.	390	Formal changes reorganized in form of clauses (1), (2), and (3) and sub-heading is dropped.
309 (4)	Robbery- Punishment for robbery.	392	IPC Section is included as sub-section in BNS sans heading. No other change.
309 (5)	Robbery- Attempt to commit robbery.	393	Ditto.
309 (6)	Robbery- Voluntarily causing hurt in committing robbery.	394	Ditto.
310 (1)	Dacoity definition.	391	Ditto.
310 (2)	Dacoity punishment.	395	Ditto.

310 (3)	Dacoity with murder.	396	IPC section is included as sub-section in BNS sans heading. Minimum mandatory punishment of imprisonment is "shall not be less than ten years".
310 (4)	Making preparation to commit dacoity.	399	IPC section is included as sub-section in BNS sans heading. No other change.
310 (5)	Assembling for purpose of committing dacoity.	402	The IPC section is included as sub-section in BNS, sans heading. Words "at any time after the passing of this Act, shall" is removed.
310 (6)	Punishment for belonging to gang of dacoits.	400	Ditto.
311	Robbery or dacoity, with attempt to cause death or grievous hurt.	397	No change.
312	Attempt to commit robbery or dacoity when armed with deadly weapon.	398	No change.

313	Punishment for belonging to gang of robbers, etc.	401	The word 'thieves' is replaced by "robbers" in the heading. The words "at any time after the passing of this Act, shall" "at wandering or other"and "for the purpose of" are excluded.
314	Dishonest misappropriation of property.	403	Minimum mandatory imprisonment of six months and with fine added.
315	Dishonest misappropriation of property possessed by deceased person at the time of his death.	404	No change.
316 (1)	Criminal breach of trust.	405	Definition presented in BNS as a sub-section.
316 (2)	Punishment for criminal breach of trust.	406	IPC Section is included as sub-section in BNS sans heading. The upper limit of the imprisonment is increased from three years to five years.
316 (3)	Criminal breach of trust by carrier, etc.	407	Section is included as sub-section in BNS sans heading.

316 (4)	Criminal breach of trust by clerk or servant.	408	Ditto.
316 (5)	Criminal breach of trust by public servant, or by banker, merchant or agent.	409	Ditto.
317 (1)	Stolen property.	410	Word "cheating" is added.
317 (2)	Dishonestly receiving stolen property.	411	IPC Section is included as sub-section in BNS sans heading.
317 (3)	Dishonestly receiving property stolen in the commission of a dacoity.	412	Ditto.
317 (4)	Habitually dealing in stolen property.	413	Ditto.
317 (5)	Assisting in concealment of stolen property.	414	Ditto.
318 (1)	Cheating.	415	IPC section defining cheating is presented in BNS as a sub-section.

318 (2)	Cheating punishment.	417	The IPC section is included as a sub-section in the BNS sans heading. The upper limit of imprisonment is increased from one year to three years.
318 (3)	Cheating with knowledge that wrongful loss may ensue to person whose interest offender is bound to protect.	418	IPC section is included as a sub-section in BNS sans heading. The upper limit of imprisonment is increased from three years to five years.
318 (4)	Cheating and dishonestly inducing delivery of property.	420	IPC section is included as a sub-section in BNS sans heading.
319 (1)	Cheating by personation.	416	Formal change. This is a definition section which is presented as a sub-section in BNS without any change.
319 (2)	Cheating by personation punishment.	419	IPC section is included as a sub-section in BNS sans heading. Upper limit of imprisonment is increased from three years to five years.
320	Dishonest or fraudulent removal or concealment of	421	Minimum mandatory punishment for

	property to prevent distribution among creditors.		imprisonment of six months has been introduced.
321	Dishonestly or fraudulently preventing debt being available for creditors.	422	No change.
322	Dishonest or fraudulent execution of deed of transfer containing false statement of consideration.	423	Upper limit of imprisonment is increased from two years to three years.
323	Dishonest or fraudulent removal or concealment of property.	424	Ditto.
324 (1)	Mischief.	425	No change.
324 (2)	Mischief punishment.	426	The upper limit of imprisonment is increased from three months to six months.
324 (3)	Mischief - causes loss or damage to any property including the property of	New	This is a new addition.

	Government or Local Authority.		
324 (4)	Mischief causing damage to the amount of twenty thousand rupees and more but less than one lakh rupees.	427	Newly added
324 (5)	Mischief- cause loss or damage to amount of one lakh rupees onwards.	New	Value of damaged property amount threshold increased from fifty rupees to one lakh rupees. Punishment increased from two years to five years.
324 (6)	Mischief committed after preparation made for causing death or hurt.	440	No change.
325	Mischief by killing or maiming animal.	428/ 429	The upper limit of imprisonment is increased from two years to five years. Scope is expanded greatly by amending it to "any animal".
326 (a)	Mischief by injury, inundation, fire or explosive substance, etc.	430	IPC section is included as a sub-section sans heading.

326 (b)	Mischief by injury to public road, bridge, river or channel.	431	Words “whoever commits mischief” is excluded. Section is included as a sub-section sans heading.
326 (c)	Mischief by causing inundation or obstruction to public drainage attended with damage.	432	IPC section is included as a sub-section sans heading.
326 (d)	Mischief by injury, inundation, fire or explosive substance, etc.	433	Words “light house or other light used as sea marks or any sea mark or buoy” are replaced by “any sign or signal used for navigation of rail, aircraft, or ship,” thus the scope is widened immensely.
326 (e)	Mischief by destroying or moving, etc., a land-mark fixed by public authority.	434	IPC section is included as a sub-section sans heading.
326 (f)	Mischief by injury, inundation, fire or explosive substance, etc.	435	Words "including agricultural produce" added.
326 (g)	Mischief by fire or explosive substance	436	IPC section is included as a sub-section sans heading.

	with intent to destroy house, etc.		
327 (1)	Mischief with intent to destroy or make unsafe a rail, aircraft, decked vessel or one of twenty tons burden.	437	Formal changes, but essence is same-“rail, aircraft" are added in the heading.
327 (2)	Punishment for above offence.	438	IPC section is included as a sub-section sans heading.
328	Punishment for intentionally running vessel aground or ashore with intent to commit theft, etc.	439	No change.
329 (1)	Criminal trespass and house- trespass.	441	IPC section is included as a sub-section.
329 (2)	Criminal trespass and house- trespass.	442	Ditto.
329 (3)	Criminal trespass punishment.	447	The IPC section is included as a sub-section in the BNS sans heading. The fine increased from five hundred rupees to five thousand rupees.

329 (4)	Punishment for house- trespass.	448	The IPC section is included as a sub-section in the BNS sans heading. The upper limit of the fine has been increased from one thousand to five thousand rupees.
330 (1)	Lurking house trespass.	443	IPC section is included as a sub-section.
330 (2)	House breaking.	445	The IPC section is included as a sub-section in the BNS sans heading. Words "any of such six ways" are replaced with "in any of the following ways".
331 (1)	Punishment for house- trespass or house-breaking.	453	IPC section is included as a sub-section. "Lurking" is dropped from heading.
331 (2)	Punishment for lurking house-trespass or house-breaking by night.	456	IPC section is included as a sub-section in BNS sans heading. "by night' is replaced by after "sunset and before sunrise".
331 (3)	Lurking house-trespass or house-breaking in order to commit offence	454	IPC section is included as a sub-section in BNS sans heading.

	punishable with imprisonment.		
331 (4)	Lurking house-trespass or house-breaking by night in order to commit offence punishable with imprisonment.	457	The words “by night” are replaced by “after sunset and before sunrise”.
331 (5)	Lurking house-trespass or house-breaking after preparation for hurt, assault or wrongful restraint.	455	Section is included as a sub-section in BNS sans heading.
331 (6)	Lurking house-trespass or house-breaking by night after preparation for hurt, assault, or wrongful restraint.	458	IPC section is included as a sub-section in BNS sans heading. “by night” is replaced by “after sunset and before sunrise”.
331 (7)	Grievous hurt caused whilst committing lurking house-trespass or house-breaking.	459	IPC section is included as a sub-section in BNS sans heading.
331 (8)	All persons jointly concerned in lurking house-trespass or house- breaking by	460	IPC section is included as a sub-section in BNS sans heading. “By night” is

	night punishable where death or grievous hurt caused by one of them.		replaced by "after sunset and before sunrise".
332 (a)	House-trespass in order to commit offence punishable with death.	449	IPC section is included as a sub-section in BNS.
332 (b)	House-trespass in order to commit offence punishable with imprisonment for life.	450	IPC section is included as a sub-section sans heading.
332 (c)	House-trespass in order to commit offence punishable with imprisonment.	451	IPC section is included as a sub-section sans heading.
333	House-trespass after preparation for hurt, assault or wrongful restraint.	452	No change.
334 (1)	Dishonestly breaking open receptacle containing property.	461	IPC section is included as a sub-section in BNS.
334 (2)	Punishment for same offence when committed by person	462	IPC section is included as a sub-section in BNS sans heading.

	entrusted with custody.		
335	Making a false document.	464	Heading changed and first, secondly, thirdly replaced with (A), (B), (C).
336 (1)	Forgery.	463	Section is included as a sub-section in BNS. No other change.
336 (2)	Forgery punishment.	465	Section is included as a sub-section in BNS sans heading. No other Change.
336 (3)	Forgery for purpose of cheating.	468	Ditto.
336 (4)	Forgery for purpose of harming reputation.	469	Ditto.
337	Forgery of record of Court or of public register, etc.	466	"Court or an identity document issued by the government, including a voter identity card or Aadhaar card," is added, and "baptism" is excluded.
338	Forgery of valuable security, will, etc.	467	No change.

339	Having possession of document described in Section 337 or Section 338, knowing it to be forged and intending to use it as genuine.	474	No change.
340 (1)	Forged document or electronic record. And using it as genuine.	470	IPC section is included as a sub-section in BNS. "Using it as genuine" is added in the heading.
340 (2)	Using as genuine a forged document or electronic record.	471	IPC section is included as a sub-section in BNS sans heading.
341 (1)	Making or possessing counterfeit seal, etc., with intent to commit forgery, punishable under section 338.	472	IPC section is included as a sub-section in BNS.
341 (2)	Making or possessing counterfeit seal, etc., with intent to commit forgery punishable otherwise.	473	IPC section is included as a sub-section in BNS sans heading.

341 (3)	Possesses any seal, plate or other instrument knowing the same to be counterfeit.	New sub-section	"Whoever possesses any seal, plate or other instrument knowing the same to be counterfeit, shall be punished with imprisonment of either description for a term which may extend to three years, and shall also be liable to fine".
341 (4)	Fraudulently or dishonestly uses as genuine any seal, plate or other instrument knowing or having reason to believe the same to be counterfeit.	New sub-section	"Whoever fraudulently or dishonestly uses as genuine any seal, plate or other instrument knowing or having reason to believe the same to be counterfeit, shall be punished in the same manner as if he had made or counterfeited such seal, plate or other instrument".
342 (1)	Counterfeiting device or mark used for authenticating documents described in section 338, or possessing counterfeit marked material.	475	IPC section is included as a sub-section in BNS.

342 (2)	Counterfeiting device or mark used for authenticating documents described in section 338, or possessing counterfeit marked material.	476	IPC section is included as a sub-section in BNS sans heading.
343	Fraudulent cancellation, destruction, etc. of will, authority to adopt, or valuable security.	477	No change.
344	Falsification of accounts.	477A	No change.
345 (1)	Property mark.	479	IPC section is included as a sub-section in BNS.
345 (2)	Using a false property mark.	481	IPC section is included as a sub-section in BNS sans heading.
345 (3)	Punishment for using a false property mark.	482	Ditto.
346	Tampering with property mark with intent to cause injury.	489	No change.

347 (1)	Counterfeiting a property mark.	483	IPC section is included as a sub-section in BNS.
347 (2)	Counterfeiting a mark used by a public servant.	484	IPC Section is included as a sub-section in BNS sans heading.
348	Making or possession of any instrument for counterfeiting a property mark.	485	No change.
349	Selling goods marked with counterfeit property mark.	486	No change.
350 (1)	Making a false mark upon any receptacle containing goods.	487	IPC section is included as a sub-section in BNS.
350 (2)	Punishment for making use of any such false mark.	488	IPC section is included as a sub-section in BNS sans heading.
351 (1)	Criminal intimidation.	503	IPC section is included as a sub-section in BNS. "By any means" is added.
351 (2)/ (3)	Criminal intimidation punishment.	506	IPC Section is included as a sub-section in BNS sans heading.

351 (4)	Criminal intimidation by an anonymous communication.	507	Ditto.
352	Intentional insult with intent to provoke breach of the peace.	504	Words "in any manner" are added.
353	Statements conducing to public mischief.	505	"False information" and "including through electronic means" are added.
354	Act caused by inducing person to believe that he will be rendered an object of the Divine displeasure.	508	No change.
355	Misconduct in public by a drunken person.	510	Fine is increased from ten rupees to one thousand, or with community service is added.
356 (1)	Defamation.	499	IPC Section is included as a sub section.
356 (2)	Defamation punishment.	500	IPC section is included as a sub-section in BNS sans heading. "or with community service" is

			added as an alternate punishment.
356 (3)	Printing or engraving matter known to be defamatory.	501	IPC Section is included as a sub-section in BNS sans heading.
356 (4)	Sale of printed or engraved substance containing defamatory matter.	502	Ditto.
357	Breach of contract to attend on and supply wants of helpless person.	491	Fine increased from two hundred rupees to five thousand rupees.
358	Repeal and Savings.	-	This section is a new addition. The Indian Penal Code, 1860, was enacted by the British Colonisers de novo; therefore, the Repeal and Savings Section was not required at all. Vide sub-section (1) and subsequent Government of India notifications, the IPC will be repealed on 1st July 2024. However, sub-sections (2) to (4) Stipulate savings related to the repealed code.

Bibliography

B

1. Bharatiya Nyaya Sanhita (BNS), 2024. Ministry of Law and Justice, Gazette of India.
2. Bharatiya Nyaya Sanhita Bill (2023). Ministry of Home Affairs, Government of India.
3. BNS Section 358 (2024). Repeal and Savings: Bharatiya Nyaya Sanhita.

C

4. Charter Act of 1833. (1834). First Law Commission of India. T. B. Macaulay, Chairman.
5. Code of Conduct for Public Servants (Various Years). Revisions made in the BNS for penalizing misconduct by public servants.
6. Code of Criminal Procedure (CrPC) (1973). Legislation accompanying procedural aspects of the IPC.
7. Comparative Studies on Penal Laws (2024). Analysis of BNS and IPC: Historical and Legal Perspectives.
8. Comparative Review of Legal Codes: IPC vs. BNS (2024). Indian Law Institute.
9. Constitution of India (1950). Government of India.
10. Constitutional Law Amendments (Various Years). Addressing changes to sections on sovereignty and national integrity under the BNS.
11. Cybercrime Legislation Amendments (2023). Added provisions under the BNS to address cyber offenses.

F

12. Fraud and Forgery Laws (Various Years). Sections related to cybercrime and corporate fraud under BNS.

G

13. Gender-Specific Legislation Amendments (Various Years). Analyzed under IPC and BNS reforms.

I

14. Indian Law Institute (2024). Comparative Review of Legal Codes: IPC vs. BNS.

15. Indian Penal Code (1860). Act No. 45 of 1860. Passed by the Governor-General of India in Council.

16. 16. Indian Penal Code, Post-Independence Amendments (Various Years). Relevant societal and legal reforms.

17. Indian Penal Code, Sections 230 to 232 (Various Years). Related to offenses such as counterfeiting and forgery.

L

18. Law Commission of India (2013). Report on Cyber Offenses under IPC.

19. Law Commission Reports (2023). Comparative studies on modernizing penal law systems in India.

20. Lok Sabha Proceedings (2023, December 20). Debates on Bharatiya Nyaya Sanhita Bill.

21. Lok Sabha Secretariat (2023). The Bharatiya Nyaya Sanhita Bill - Second Reading.

22. Landmark Judgements of Supreme Court (2024). Analysis of key cases affecting criminal law and penal reforms.

M

23. Macaulay, T. B. (1834). Draft Penal Code of India. First Law Commission of India.

24. Ministry of Home Affairs, Government of India (2023). Introduction of Bharatiya Nyaya Sanhita (BNS) and its key reforms.

O

25. Organized Crime Legislation (2024). Provisions related to tackling organized crime under BNS.

P

26. Penal Laws Amendment Act (1949). Post-Independence changes to colonial penal laws.

27. President of India (2023, December 25). Assent to Bharatiya Nyaya Sanhita Bill.

28. Public Interest Litigation Studies (2024). Impact of BNS on Public Interest Cases in India.

29. Procedural Changes in Criminal Law (2023). Amendments made to ensure a streamlined judicial process under BNS.

R

30. Rajya Sabha Proceedings (2023, December 21). Debates on Bharatiya Nyaya Sanhita Bill.

31. Rajya Sabha Secretariat (2023). Legislative Procedure for the Passing of BNS.

32. Reforms in Sentencing Laws (2024). Sentencing reforms in BNS, including community service for minor offenses.

S

33. Supreme Court of India Judgements (Various Years). Landmark Judgements under IPC and BNS.

34. Supreme Court of India (2024). Key Decisions on Criminal Justice Reform.

35. Statutory Amendments on Cybercrime (2024). BNS reforms regarding online crime.

36. Streamlined Judicial Processes (2023). Changes introduced in the BNS to fast-track justice delivery.

T

37. The Criminal Law (Amendment) Act (2013). Legislation concerning gender-based violence and crimes against women.

38. Terrorism and National Security Laws (2024). Updated sections related to terrorism under BNS.

39. Tribal Rights and BNS (2023). New provisions for safeguarding indigenous and tribal rights under the Bharatiya Nyaya Sanhita.

U

40. Uniform Civil Code and BNS (2024). Amendments and provisions concerning personal laws under the BNS.

41. Updated Criminal Procedure Reforms (2023). Streamlining procedures for criminal trials under BNS.

V

42. Victim Compensation Schemes (2023). Provisions under the BNS for compensation to victims of crime.

W

43. White Collar Crime Legislation (2024). Provisions under BNS targeting financial fraud and corruption.

44. Women's Rights Amendments (2023). New laws introduced in BNS to protect women's rights.

Y

45. Youth Offenders Legislation (2023). Updated reforms in juvenile justice under the BNS.

Z

46. Zero Tolerance Policies (2024). Provisions in BNS for zero tolerance towards crimes like terrorism, trafficking, and child exploitation.

47. Zonal Policing Regulations (2023). Regional changes in policing laws under BNS, focusing on federal cooperation.

48. Zoological Crime Legislation (2023). New provisions under the BNS to address crimes involving wildlife and environmental protection.

www.ingramcontent.com/pod-product-compliance
Lightning Source LLC
Chambersburg PA
CBHW041258210926
51847CB00009B/59
* 9 7 8 9 3 6 5 5 4 5 8 4 5 *